Data Warehouse Development Tools

Covering Informatica, Cognos, Business Objects and DataStage with Case Studies

Dr. K.V. K.K. Prasad

Published by:

dreamtech PRESS

Reprint Edition: 2011

Printed at: **Himal Impressions, New Delhi**

Preface

Information is Power. In this age of cut-throat competition, every organization must make effective use of information to reduce manufacturing costs, operational costs and to increase employee productivity—the bottom line is to increase profits. This objective cannot be achieved unless the management gets the right information at the right time.

Since 1980's, the corporate data is being organized systematically using Relational Database Management Systems. Using back-end database engines such as Oracle, Sybase, DB2, Informix, MS SQL, etc., and sophisticated front-end tools such as VB, VC++ and Java, Database Management Systems (DBMS) are being developed to provide easy access to corporate data. Management Information Systems (MIS) and Enterprise Resource Planning (ERP) systems are sophisticated applications developed over DBMS to help the management in taking right operational decisions.

Nowadays, the management needs much more than just processed data. They want the information that helps them in making strategic decisions; in other words, they need "decision support systems". They want to get replies for complex queries from the database and these replies should provide the necessary "business intelligence". This objective is achieved through data warehouses.

We are witnessing major changes in the corporate world. Organizations are becoming global—with offices at multiple locations in multiple countries, diverse products, highly demanding customers and so on. Such organizations must use data warehouses to provide effective and efficient management. So, for large organizations to survive, data warehouses are a must. Even medium and small organizations are now using data warehouses to maintain edge over their competitors by effectively using the business intelligence.

Hence, in future, every organization, large or small, must use data warehouses to survive and grow. Realizing this, all over the world, data warehouses are being implemented. So, naturally during the last few years, the demand for data warehouse specialists has increased exponentially and there is an acute shortage of skilled human resources. For young software professionals with a background in databases, it is a good career move to jump on the bandwagon of data warehouses.

This book has been written keeping in view the requirements of the industry for professionals with expertise in data warehouse development tools. The most popular data warehousing tools are covered with case studies so that the reader can get a good hands-on experience in working on the tools and at the same time developing a data warehouse while understanding the underlying concepts.

Though a large number of excellent textbooks are available on data warehouses, all these books cover only theory and do not deal with any of the tools. This book covers the concepts, technology and tools in detail so that by the time you complete reading this book, you are ready and hungry to take up a bright career in data warehousing.

Who should read this book

This book is addressed to fresh graduates who would like to learn data warehousing technology and tools. A basic knowledge of RDBMS is all that is assumed.

If you are a software professional with work experience either in database management or ERP packages, and if you want to enhance your skill set and increase your market value, data warehousing is the best bet and this book will give you all the ammunition—theoretical and practical knowledge—of developing data marts and data warehouses. This is the only book that explains how to use all the popular commercial data warehouse development tools.

If you are a project manager and your new assignment is to manage a data warehouse project, then also this book is of immense use to you as it provides a detailed description of the data warehouse concepts and development process.

Data warehouse development is a very challenging task as it provides a good aid to the management and the management talks in its own jargon, which is different from the software professionals' jargon! Data warehouse professionals need to learn a bit of this management jargon, which is introduced wherever required.

Burning desire, tons of enthusiasm and ability to put in hard work to become a data warehouse professional is enough to get started.

Organization of the Book

Chapter 1 explains the data warehouse concepts. The fundamental concepts of data warehousing—multidimensional data modeling, data warehouse architecture, data extraction, transformation and loading are discussed. A good conceptual understanding will make it easy to learn the tools very fast.

Chapter 2 gives the data warehouse development process. The various stages in data warehouse software development are discussed along with important management processes.

Chapter 3 gives an overview of the data warehouse development tools. The features of different categories of tools are briefly discussed along with the capabilities of the various popular commercial tools.

Chapter 4 deals with the tool "Informatica". Using case studies, the various steps involved in data Extraction, Transformation and Loading (ETL) are explained in detail. As ETL is the most important task in data warehouse development, a good understanding of the ETL process is very crucial.

Chapter 5 explains how to create a target database from an existing database through a case study using Informatica.

Chapter 6 focuses on the tool "Cognos". Using a number of case studies and the target database developed in Chapter 5, how to generate reports is described.

Chapter 7 is about "Business Objects". Again, using the database developed in Chapter 5 and a number of case studies, how to generate business intelligence reports is explained.

Chapter 8 focuses on "DataStage". How to use this tool for the entire ETL life cycle is explained with practical examples.

Appendix A gives a list of acronyms and abbreviations.

Appendix B gives a glossary of important terms and phrases used in data warehousing technology. It also explains the business terminology used in data warehouses.

Appendix C gives the list of Internet resources and reference books on data warehousing and related technologies.

Appendix D gives a list of review questions, the most frequently asked questions in job interviews. It is not enough if you gain expertise in using the tools, it is equally important that you should be able to answer these questions with abundant confidence to come out with flying colors in the interviews. Good luck!

And, here we go, on our exciting journey into the world of data warehouses!

Credits

The author thanks Mr. A. Veerraju for his immense contribution to the development of the case studies. The figures are the handiwork on Mr. Vipul Pawaskar.

Contents

1 Data Warehousing Concepts

Chapter Objectives

- A quick review of Database Management Systems (DBMS) and Enterprise Resource Planning systems
- Problems with Relational Database Management System (RDBMS) implementation
- Data mart and data warehouse—definitions and advantages
- OLTP versus OLAP
- Multi-dimensional modeling of data
- Architecture of data warehouse

This chapter lays the foundation for data warehousing with a quick overview of the data warehousing. As you keep working on the development tools discussed in the later chapters, you will gain a deeper understanding of the concepts presented here. Nevertheless, having a basic understanding is a must before you start using the tools.

1.1 Database Management Systems

To survive and grow in this highly competitive business world, the management of every organization has to meet the following goals:

- Respond quickly to the customer demands
- React fast to the market opportunities and threats
- Increase productivity of the employees
- Decrease infrastructure costs
- Decrease production and maintenance costs

It is extremely difficult to even attempt to achieve these goals if the management relies on data that is available in paper files stacked in racks and on tables. If the organization is spread over a large geographical area, say in different offices in different countries, getting the information from multiple locations becomes much more complex. The only solution to this problem is to automate the entire information storage and retrieval.

Ever since the computerization started in 1960's, organizations have been using computers effectively for efficient storage and retrieval. In 1980's, the Relational Database Management Systems (RDBMS) became popular and many large, medium and small organizations started automating their information processing activities.

For implementation of RDBMS, the data is converted into Entity-Relationship model represented as an E-R Diagram (ERD). An entity represents a person or an item. Relationship is defined between two entities. E-R model is a logical data model. This logical model is converted into physical model. In RDBMS, the physical model consists of tables with each table containing a number of attributes (or fields). In a table, each row is uniquely identified by a field (or a combination of fields) that is known as *Primary Key.* A table can have Foreign Keys, a foreign key being a field in another table. The RDBMS ensures that the data is consistent, that the integrity of data is maintained and it also removes redundancy to a great extent.

Fig. 1.1 shows an E-R diagram of the sample database "Northwind" that comes with the MS SQL RDBMS. It contains a number of tables such as Employees, Products, Suppliers, Categories and Orders.

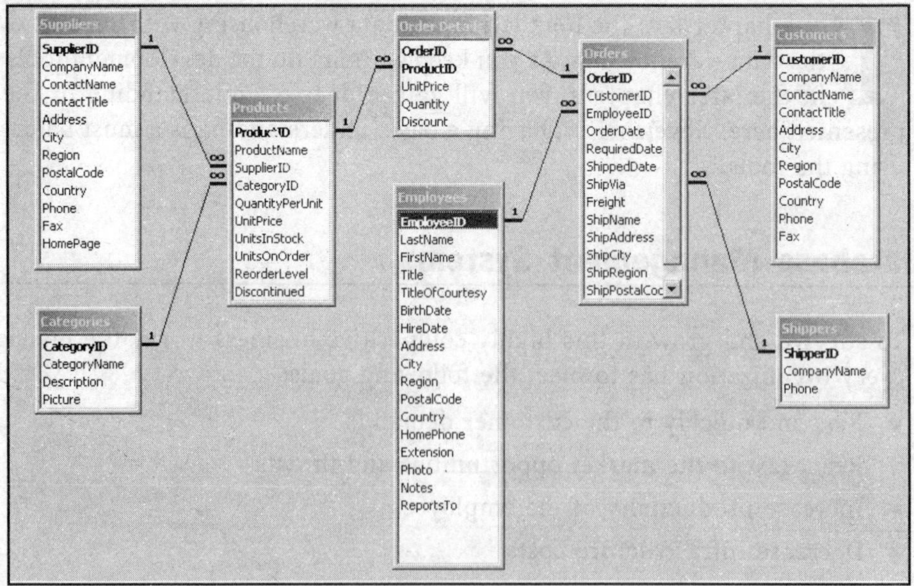

Fig. 1.1: E-R Diagram of Northwind Database

The RDBMS are being used by operational people to record, retrieve and analyze the transactional data, where as the GUI to update, delete and modify the records as well as to generate the reports is developed using popular front-end tools such as VB, VC++ and Java.

The phrase "Management Information System (MIS)" became very popular in those days. MIS is basically a system that provides the necessary reports to the top management to take day-to-day decisions at the right time.

In Brief...

Relational Database Management Systems (RDBMS) are used for providing operational information to the management. These are based on Entity-Relationship model of the data. The processing done on the RDBMS is On-Line Transaction Processing (OLTP).

Note...

E-R model is a logical data model. The E-R model is converted into physical model—the physical model consists of tables and fields.

1.2 Enterprise Resource Planning

The RDBMS paved way for "Enterprise Resource Planning (ERP)". ERP systems facilitate better utilization of the organization's resources. Fig. 1.2 shows the various modules covered by an ERP package.

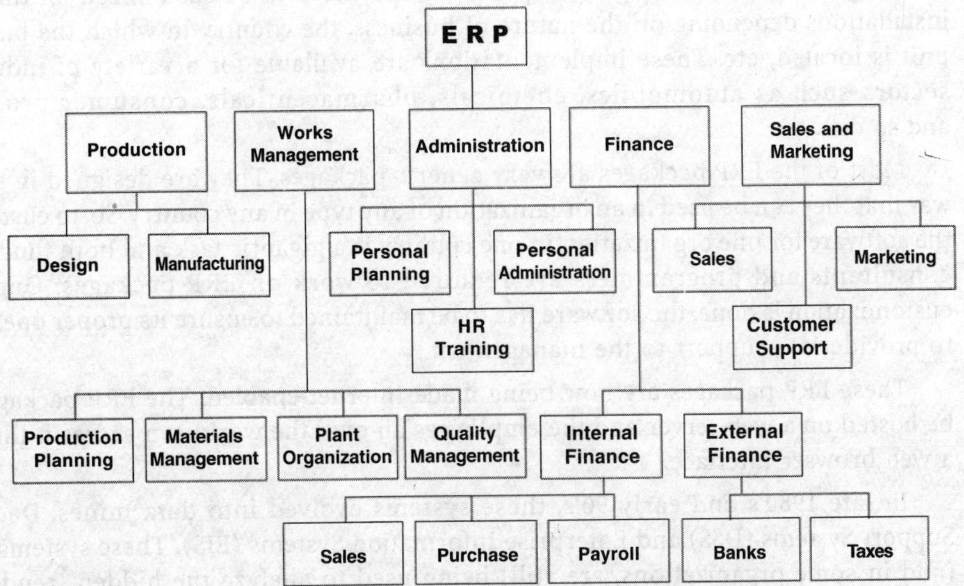

Fig. 1.2 Modules Covered by an ERP Package

In many organizations, for an effective planning of the resources (money, material and manpower), Enterprise Resource Planning (ERP) packages are used extensively. The ERPs are specialized application software packages. To work on development using these packages, both functional skills such as material management, financial management, human resource management, production management etc. and programming skills are required.

For an effective planning and management of resources in an organization, a unified package is required and the ERP packages fit the bill. As the ERP packages are based on RDBMS with a GUI front-end, basic knowledge of RDBMS and front-end tools is a must before you start learning the domain-specific tools. Some of the popular ERP packages available commercially are:

- SAP (Systems, Applications and Products in data processing)
- BaaN
- PeopleSoft
- JD Edwards
- Oracle Financials

Each module shown in Fig. 1.2 covers all the aspects related to a particular area—for example, the finance module handles external finance (such as bank loans, dealings with other financial institutions, sales tax, duties, etc.) and internal finance such as salaries, purchases, sales receipts, etc. Any company with 50 employees or 50,000 employees can use this software for their ERP activities. As they are very generic packages, they need to be customized for different installations depending on the nature of business, the country in which the business unit is located, etc. These implementations are available for a variety of industrial sectors such as automobiles, chemicals, pharmaceuticals, consumer products, and so on.

Most of the ERP packages are very generic packages. They are designed in such a way that they can be used in an organization of any type in any country. So, to customize the software for one organization in one country is a gigantic task and both functional consultants and programmers are required to work on ERP packages. Once the customization is done, the software has to be maintained to ensure its proper operation to provide MIS support to the management.

These ERP packages are now being made Internet-enabled. The ERP package can be hosted on a web server and the employees all over the world can access it through a web browser interface.

In late 1980's and early 90's, these systems evolved into data mines, Decision Support Systems (DSS) and Enterprise Information Systems (EIS). These systems were (and in some organizations, are still) being used to analyze the hidden trends and patterns in the enterprise data which help in making better decisions by the management.

In Brief...

Enterprise Resource Planning (ERP) systems provide a packaged solution for automation of the various departments of the organization and also inter-communication among the offices paving way for an efficient 'paperless' office.

Note...

ERP packages are now evolving into data marts and data warehouses. Many ERP solution providers are also providing data warehousing tools.

1.3 Problems with the Present DBMS

Almost every organization—big or small—is using DBMS for its day-to-day operations. However, database systems have many major problems to be addressed—out of these problems, some problems are due to the RDBMS technology itself, but most problems are due to improper implementation. Here is a list of some problems/issues:

- If an organization has multiple offices, each office will develop its own DBMS. If the development is not centrally controlled and no coding guidelines are followed across the different branches of the organization, it is difficult to integrate the databases to obtain consolidated information. Note that for databases to be integrated, the table names and even the field names have to be the same. For example, in different databases, the employee name can be represented as:

  Employee_name

  Emp_name

  EN

  Though all these variable names refer to the same attribute, integration of the databases becomes cumbersome. Hence, retrieving the data from the database becomes proprietary for each location.
- The same object (say, customer table) may have different fields. In one database, the table may contain

  Customer name, address1, address2, address3, customer id

  Another database may contain different number of fields for the same object:

  Customer name, address1, address2, city, state, country, customer id
- Another problem arises due to the interpretation of the fields. For example, price may include tax or exclude tax. One database may use the first definition and the second database, the second definition.

- Another problem is due to units of measure. The units may be dollars, but the database in USA will indicate US dollars whereas the database in Singapore will indicate Singapore dollars. While accessing the data and consolidating the information from these two databases, the values cannot be directly added.
- Some fields in the database may remain the same (e.g., the date of birth of an employee), but some fields may change over a period of time (e.g., address, marital status, etc.) In such a case, normally, the old values in the database are overwritten by the new values. Sometimes, it may be necessary to preserve the old data. For example, if you want to answer the query "how many employees got married in the last one year?", you can answer it only if you know in how many records, the marital status field has changed from "single" to "married", and also when the change was made.
- As RDBMS is for operational data, historical data is not preserved (for the last 5 years, for example). It is generally kept only for archival purposes in a backup media.
- Above all, the E-R modeling becomes very complicated for large databases. Even to study and understand the E-R Diagram (ERD) is extremely difficult.

In Brief...

Some of the problems with the DBMS are: lack of consistency in the naming of database tables and fields, lack of proper quality assurance of the data to ensure that the fields in different tables and fields in different databases are consistent and reliable. Also, generally the historical data is not preserved.

Note...

It is important to differentiate the terms data, information and knowledge. ***Data*** *is unprocessed/raw facts collected during a business transaction.* ***Information*** *is processed data that provides the analysis of the Collected data.* ***Knowledge*** *is processed information that is used for decision-making and creativity.*

1.4 Data Mart and Data Warehouse

Warehouse, as Oxford dictionary defines it, is a "building in which goods are stored or displayed for sale". So, **data warehouse** is simply a place in which the data is stored or made available for analysis. However, today's data warehouses do much more than that.

In today's competitive business environment, information is power. To get the right information at the right time, for by the decision makers, is the key to success. To obtain routine management information, RDBMS are extensively used by all the organizations but to make strategic decisions, information using complex queries is required. For instance, consider a TV manufacturer. The database may contain a lot of information about the profile of the purchasers, time of purchase, model purchased, etc. The management may like to know the answer to a complex query such as "what is the fastest selling model of the TVs, what is the period in which the highest number of sets of this model have been sold, and what is the profile of the customers who are buying this model?" The information is important to plan the production schedule and also to change the marketing strategy so that the marketing team can focus on a particular market segment during a particular period of time in a year. Such ad hoc complex information that needs to be obtained from the historical data stored in the database, after necessary analytical processing, is called business "intelligence". The systems that provide this business intelligence are now being known as 'data warehouses'.

In 1980, Bill Inmon coined the phrase 'data warehouse'. His definition for data warehouse is as follows: "*A data warehouse is a subject-oriented, integrated, time-variant and non-volatile collection of data in support of management's decision-making process*".

In this definition, it is very important to understand the catch phrases: subject-oriented, integrated, time-variant and non-volatile. "Subject-oriented" means that the data addresses a specific subject such as sales, inventory, etc. "Integrated" means that the data is obtained from a variety of sources. "Time-variant" implies that the data is stored in such a way that when some data is changed, when that the data has been changed is also stored. "Non-volatile" implies that data is never removed, i.e., historical data is also kept. So, whenever a change takes place in any of the field values of a table, the previous values also need to be kept in addition to the present values.

Another definition that captures the essence of data warehouse functionality is: "*A data warehouse is a database management system that facilitates on-line analytical processing by allowing the data to be viewed in different dimensions or perspectives, to provide business intelligence.*"

In this definition, note that we use the term "analytical processing"—in a data warehouse, the data is analyzed to obtain useful information, as against transaction processing done in RDBMS. Also, note that, we view the data in different dimensions or different perspectives. For example, we can view the data from 'time dimension'—when a particular TV model sales were the highest. We can view the data from 'location' dimension—in which location (say city), the sales were the highest.

Note that the important requirement of a data warehouse is that it is an on-line query analysis based on historical data for decision support rather than on-line transaction processing of operational data. Hence, On-Line Transaction Processing (OLTP) refers to operational data whereas On-Line Analytical Processing (OLAP) refers to warehousing data which contains historical data that is derived from transaction data.

In Brief...

A data warehouse can be defined as follows: "A data warehouse is a database management system that facilitates on-line analytical processing by allowing the data to be viewed in different dimensions or perspectives to provide business intelligence."

An organization has different departments such as manufacturing department, accounts department, HR department, sales department, marketing department, etc. In stead of developing a data warehouse that addresses all the activities of all the departments, *a scaled down version can be developed for only one department, say, sales. In other words, the management wants business intelligence only for the sales data. Such a scaled-down version of the data warehouse that addresses only one subject is called a* ***"data mart".***

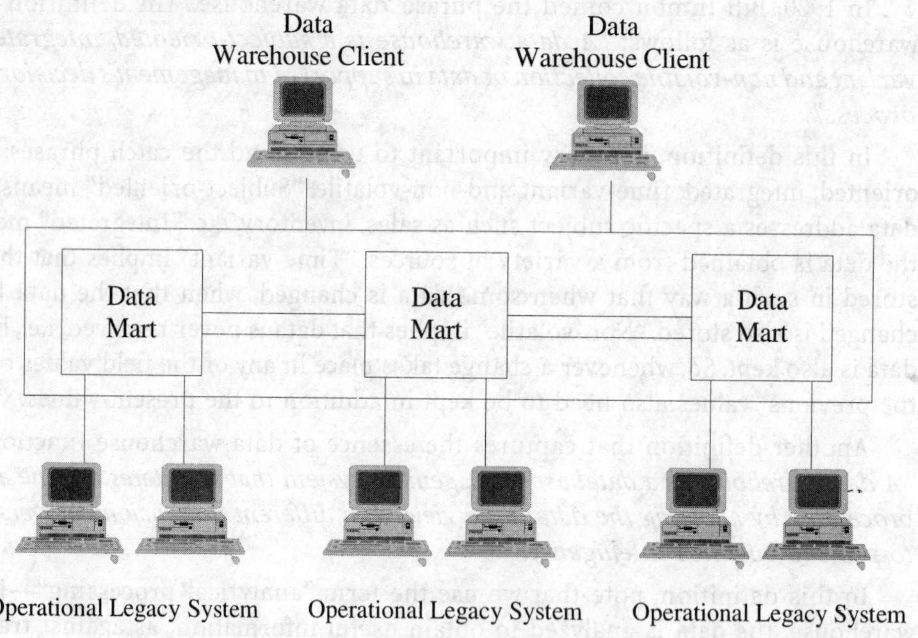

Fig 1.3: Data Mart & Data Warehouse

As shown in Fig. 1.3, a data warehouse is a collection of data marts. Data marts are well-suited for medium and small business enterprises as well as for different departments of large organizations. Data marts can be combined together to form a data warehouse.

Use of data marts and data warehouses is catching up. Nowadays, organizations are very keen on carrying out profitability analysis, analysis of customer feedback, analysis of market research/surveys, production planning, etc. Data marts and data warehouses will bring in the next revolution in the field of IT, just as RDBMS brought in a revolution in the IT field in the 1980's.

1.4.1 Types of Data Warehouses

Depending on the functionality, there are different nomenclatures for data warehouses/ data marts.

Stand-alone Data Marts: Data marts that do not interact with other data marts are called stand-alone data marts. On the other hand, data marts can be integrated to create a data warehouse.

Multi-source Data Mart: A data mart for which the input data is obtained from multiple sources is called a multi-source data mart.

Personal Data Mart: A data mart for use by individuals such as Chief Executive Officer (CEO), Chief Technology Officer (CTO) or Chief Financial Officer (CFO) is called Personal Data Mart.

Operational Data Store: ODS is a database system that obtains data from different sources, consolidates it and keeps it at a single location. However, it does not have the sophistication of a data mart or a data warehouse for analytical processing. ODS is generally developed as a pre-cursor for ERP systems.

1.4.2 Data Mining Versus Data Warehousing

In data mining, the operational data is analyzed using statistical techniques and clustering techniques to find the hidden patterns and trends. So, the data mines do some kind of summarization of the data and can be used by data warehouses for faster analytical processing for business intelligence.

Data warehouse may make use of a data mine for analytical processing of the data in a faster way.

1.5 OLTP Versus OLAP

The traditional RDBMS technology and the data warehouse technology differ in terms of the type of processing. The database applications are tuned for On Line Transaction Processing (OLTP) whereas the data warehouses are tuned for On Line Analytical Processing (OLAP).

The main differences between OLTP and OLAP are:

- OLTP systems are for doing clerical/operational processing of data whereas OLAP systems are for carrying out analytical processing of the data.
- OLTP systems look at data in one dimension; whereas in OLAP systems, data can be viewed in different dimensions and hence interesting business intelligence can be extracted from the data.

- Operational personnel of an organization use the OLTP systems whereas management uses OLAP systems, though operational personnel may also use portions of OLAP system.
- OLTP systems contain the current data as well as the details of the transactions. OLAP systems contain historical data, and also data in summarized form.
- OLTP database size is smaller as compared to OLAP systems. If the OLTP database occupies Gigabytes (GB) of storage space, OLAP database occupies Terabytes (TB) of storage space.

1.6 Dimensional Modeling

REGION	PRODUCT	SALES IN QUARTER-I	SALES IN THE YEAR	SALES IN QUARTER-II	SALES IN THE YEAR
Region I	Product I (TV)	20	20	25	45
Region I	Product II (Washing machine)	30	30	35	65
Region 2	Product I (TV)	70	70	60	130
Region 2	Product II(Washing machine)	60	60	50	110

Table 1.1: Sales Data of a Trading Organization

With reference to Table 1.1, consider a trading organization which has two offices to cater to two regions. In each of these regions, the trader sells two products. At each of the regional offices, the DBMS stores each transaction (sale of a product). The database contains the product sold, model number of the product, date of sale, price of product sold and the customer details such as name, address, average monthly salary, etc. Based on this data, you can derive the information given in Table 1.1 which gives the sales volume (quantity of the product sold) in a month and cumulative sales volume in a year. This is a summary of the transaction data and the management can derive much more information than that can be obtained by generating the report for monthly sales transaction. This summary indicates the data from the sales volume perspective. The transaction data can be processed and viewed from a customer point of view to find out which model of a product is popular among the middle class population of each region. This business intelligence can be used by the management to discontinue a particular model or to open a new regional office.

So, we can look at the data in different dimensions or perspectives. It is achieved through dimensional modeling.

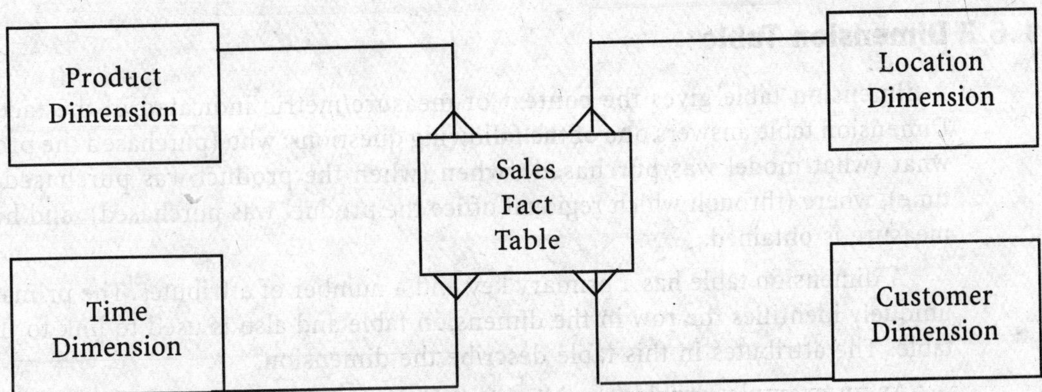

Fig 1.4: Dimensional Modeling: Star Schema

Dimensional modeling is a logical data modeling technique. As shown in Fig. 1.4, in this model, there will be two types of tables:

- Fact table
- Dimension table

The fact table is central to this model and all the dimension tables are linked to this fact table. Hence, this model can be represented as a star, and hence this model is also referred to as *star schema.*

1.6.1 Fact Table

A fact table is the central table that contains the measures or facts of a business process. For example, in the sales fact table, a measure can be the sales quantity indicated in Table 1.1. A fact table contains two types of fields—facts or measures and foreign keys from dimension tables.

A data mart can contain one fact table to address one subject. In such a case, when a number of data marts are integrated to create a data warehouse, it is important that the facts in each table mean the same thing. Such facts (i.e., measures or metrics) that have the same meaning in different data marts are called *conformed facts.*

Grain: Granularity of data is a very important factor in the design of fact table. In a fact table, we can represent data at different atomic levels, called grains. In the above example of sales data, if the transaction data does not record the model number of the product sold to each customer, then the sales volume represents the quantity of the product, not each model. So, some useful data is lost and we cannot get business intelligence related to models of the products. In the fact table, what detail has to be stored (i.e., what granularity is required) is decided based on the business intelligence reports to be generated.

1.6.2 Dimension Table

A dimension table gives the context of measure/metric indicated in the fact table. Dimension table answers one of the following questions: who (purchased the product), what (what model was purchased), when (when the product was purchased, date/time), where (through which regional office the product was purchased) and how the measure is obtained.

A dimension table has a primary key and a number of attributes. The primary key uniquely identifies the row in the dimension table and also is used to link to the fact table. The attributes in this table describe the dimension.

As an example, consider a data mart that analyzes the sales data. As shown in Fig. 1.3, in multidimensional model, we need to create a fact table and different dimension tables such as product dimension, time dimension, location dimension and customer dimension. Conceptually, this is very useful because we can analyze sales data from different views or different dimensions. For example, we can analyze the sales patterns of different brands/models, sales in different regions based on sales to different customers, sales at different periods in a year. So, from the dimension tables, you can get the information such as:

- Persons of what average monthly income purchased a particular model?
- When a particular model's sales were the highest?

As another example, in a data warehouse for ATMs, the fact table contains the attributes: transaction amount as the fact and also account number, transaction number, and a number of foreign keys. The dimension tables are: transaction dimension, time dimension, location dimension and account dimension.

The time dimension is a dimension you will come across in many data marts and data warehouses. The time dimension can contain the following attributes:

Time_ID (an integer)
CalendarMonth (small integer)
CalendarQuarter (small integer)
CalendarYear (small integer)
FiscalMonth (small integer)
FiscalQuarter (small integer)
FiscalYear (small integer)

If the calendar year and the fiscal year are the same, then there is no need for separate attributes for calendar year and fiscal year.

The concept of surrogate key is important in data warehouse. Surrogate means 'deputy' or 'substitute'. Surrogate key is a small integer (say, 4 byte integer) that can uniquely identify a record in a dimension table. However, it has no meaning. Some data warehouse experts suggest that the production keys used in the databases should not be used in dimension tables as primary keys. Instead, in their place, surrogate keys have to be used which are generated automatically.

Note...

In data warehouse design, the storage space requirement needs to be estimated to plan the hardware configuration of the servers. For database size estimation, the inputs are: size of the fact table records, the size of the dimension table records, the number of years for which data has to be stored and the data type of each attribute.

1.6.3 Slowly Changing Dimension

In a dimension table, the values of some attributes (fields) do not change at all. For example, the date of birth of an employee in the employee table does not change at all. On the other hand, the values of some attributes are likely to change over a period of time, but not very frequently. For example, educational qualification, address and marital status of the employee (single, married, divorced) are the attributes whose values may change for some employees over a period of time.

If the values of attributes in a dimension table change over a period of time, then these dimensions are called *slowly changing dimensions (SCDs).* Slowly changing dimensions can be represented in three forms which are:

Type 1 SCD: In the dimension table, the new data replaces the old data. In other words, the historical data is not preserved.

Type 2 SCD: New records are added to the dimension table. The old record containing the old data is retained and the new record contains the new data.

Type 3 SCD: New fields are added to the dimension table so that the table can hold both old values and new values in the same record.

Snowflaking: In some dimension tables, there may be a need to take out some data, to keep that data in a separate table and link that table to the original dimension table. This is called snowflaking. For example, in the product dimension, the attributes related to the model (model number, model name, etc.) can be separated out and this can be linked to the product dimension. However, note that snowflaking will increase the query processing time and should be used with caution.

Junk dimension: Sometimes, while designing the fact table and the dimension tables from the operational databases, you may find that some attributes in the original database cannot be discarded, but they do not fit into the fact table and the dimension tables. In such a case, the options are (i) to discard them which may result in the loss of information, (ii) to put them in different dimension tables which unnecessarily increases the number of dimensions or, (iii) to use junk dimensions wherein a junk dimension table is created with the 'junk' attributes.

Similar to conformed facts, conformed dimension is also important in data warehouses. A dimension that carries the same meaning across the different fact tables is called conformed dimension. Conformed dimensions are a must to put a number of data marts together to create the enterprise data warehouse.

1.7 Architecture of Data Warehouse

The architecture of a data warehouse is shown in Fig. 1.5. We will describe each of these components in the following sections:

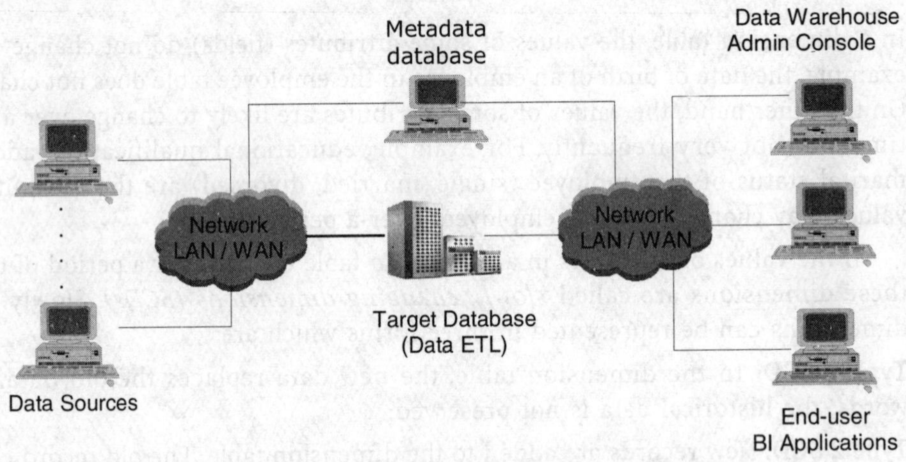

Fig. 1.5: Data Warehouse Architecture

The architecture of a data warehouse is shown in Fig. 1.5. Data warehouse obtains the data from a number of operational database systems which can be based on RDBMS or ERP packages, etc. These are called data sources. The data from these sources are converted into a form suitable for data warehouse. This process is called *Extraction, Transformation and Loading (ETL)* of data into the target database. In addition to target database, there will be another database to store the metadata, called metadata repository or metadata database. This database contains data about data—description of source data, target data and how the source data has been modified into target data. The client software will be used to generate the business intelligence reports. The user interface can be based on a custom-built GUI or it can be a browser interface. An administration console is used to carry out data warehouse administration including the periodic ETL process to update the data into the data warehouse from the data sources.

1.7.1 Data Sources

An organization interested in developing a data warehouse has to first study where the existing information is located. These are the data sources. It is likely that most of the data is residing in RDBMS. However, there is no guarantee. Some organizations are using databases developed decades ago, some organizations use advanced systems such as ERP, Customer Relations Management (CRM) and Supply Chain Management (SCM) packages. So, various data sources can be as:

- Flat files, which contain the data with one record per line in a proprietary format.
- Relational databases based on Oracle, MS SQL, Sybase, Informix, IBM DB2, etc. with ODBC connectivity.
- ERP and CRM applications such as Oracle Applications, JDEdwards, PeopleSoft, SAP, etc.
- Mainframe databases such as DB2, VSAM

If an organization has offices located at different places (perhaps in different countries), it is likely that the database systems were also developed without any standardization of the field names and their attributes. Data warehouse developers need to keep in mind the following differences in various data sources:

- The character representation may be different (most computers use ASCII code, the mainframes use EBCDIC format).
- The table names may be different (customer details table can be customer_details in one database and Cust_details in another database)
- The field names may be different (emp_name and Employee_name both mean the same thing for us but for computers, they are different).
- The date may be stored in different formats in different databases (16 Sept 05 or 16/9/05 or 9/16/2005, etc.)
- Units of measure may be different (liters or gallons)
- Currency values may be different (price field may contain dollars but in one database, US dollars and in another database, Singapore dollars).
- In some databases, the fields may be NULL.
- The data warehouse specialists need to study the minute details of these data sources before starting the development of the warehouse.

In Brief...

The data sources can be flat files, relational databases with ODBC connectively, ERP or CRM or SCM applications. The data from these heterogeneous sources has to be extracted for development of the data warehouse. The differences in the data tables and fields need to be kept in mind.

Note...

The quality of the business intelligence you provide to the top management is mainly dependent on the quality of the source data.

1.7.2 Data Staging

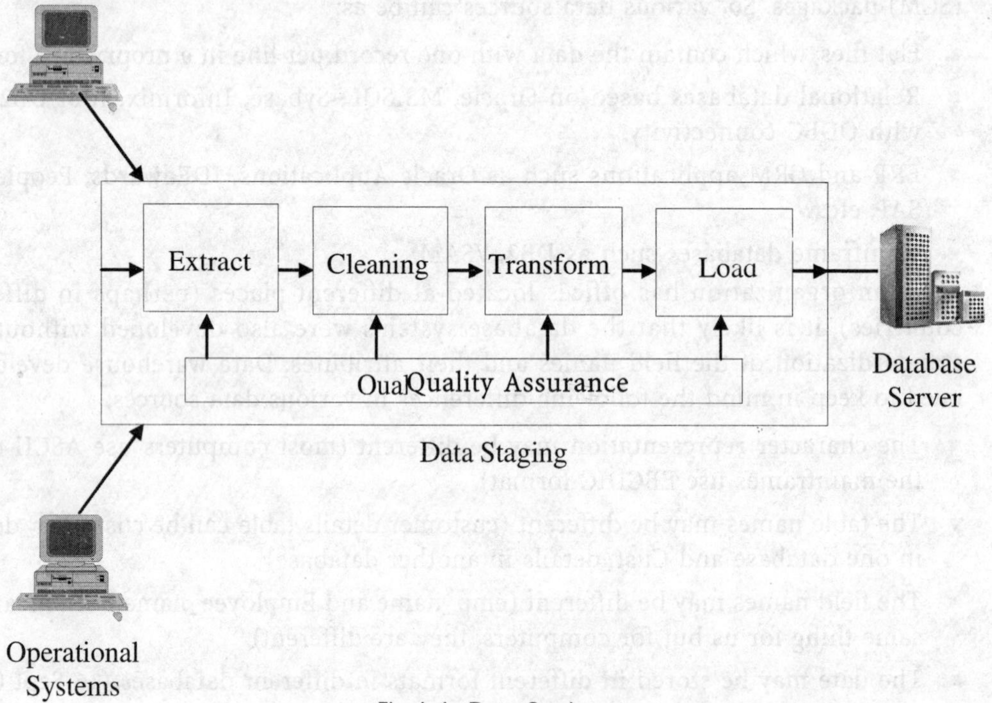

Fig 1.6: Data Staging

As shown in Fig. 1.6, data staging is the process of transferring the data from the data sources (operational systems) into the target database of the data warehouse. The ETL process can be divided into the following stages:

- Extraction of data from various data sources
- Cleansing of data which includes trying to ensure that important data is not missing, field names are changed appropriately for good readability, etc.
- Transformation of the source data in a form suitable for data warehouse. (see below for various transformations)
- Loading of data into the target database
- Quality Assurance of data which is done at every stage of ETL to ensure that the data that is going into the data warehouse is accurate, consistent and reliable. This is also known as data scrubbing.

Transformation of the data from the source databases involves a number of modifications to be done on the data to make it suitable for data warehouse. The various transforms that can be carried out include:

- Joining of two or more tables
- Dimensionalization of data, i.e. converting E-R model into multi-dimensional model
- Normalization of data
- Sorting of the records
- Ranking of the records
- Aggregation or summarization of the data
- Changing data types

In Brief...

Data staging is the process of data extraction from the source database, carrying out the necessary transformations and loading into the target database as well as carrying out the data quality assurance before a formal release of the data warehouse.

Note...

The ETL jobs can be run either in batch mode or in real-time mode. In batch mode, the ETL jobs are bundled together and executed at a scheduled time (e.g., night time) whereas in real-time mode, the ETL process is executed in real time.

Aggregates: Data stored in summarized form is called aggregate and the process of summarizing is aggregation. In DBMS, the transaction data is stored which is the source data for a data warehouse. On line analysis of large transaction data takes lots of time and hence the queries cannot be processed fast. Hence, some important data is stored in summarized or aggregated form so that on line analytical processing is fast. These aggregates have another advantage that the storage space can also be reduced considerably.

As an example, OLTP systems may store each and every transaction of an ATM. An aggregate can store the total transactions made by each individual in a month in a summarized form. Alternatively, an aggregate may store only the total transaction amount on a daily basis without keeping individual information. How much aggregation is required and what data has to be aggregated are design decisions made keeping in view the business intelligence requirements.

Consider the example of sales of a trader mentioned earlier. Assume that for each product, there are there are three models. At each of the show rooms, separate databases are maintained to track the daily transactions and take the necessary reports at the end of the day and end of the month. Now the trader wants to develop a data mart. He wants to discontinue a particular brand and introduce a new brand in each of the three products. Now, he wants information periodically so that he can take the right decision at the right time. A simple mechanism for this purpose is to use aggregates from which month-wise sales of each product can be taken and summarized.

However, note that the manager's requirements cannot be predicted. To start with, he may ask for summarized data, and then he may go in for detail. To change the view of the data to analyze the data to a greater detail is called "drill-down". To change the view of the data to view only the aggregates or summaries is called "drill-up".

1.7.3 Metadata

Metadata is defined as the data about data. Metadata describes the entity and attribute description. The description of the source data, target data and the transformations carried out is stored in a separate database (or repository) called metadata repository.

1.7.4 Front-end

The entire ETL process is generally carried out though a GUI. The GUI facilitates:

- Selection of data sources (flat files, RDBMS, ERP, etc.)
- Carrying out the necessary transformations
- Loading the data on target database
- Creation of metadata repository
- Administration of ETL process, monitoring the ETL process, scheduling the ETL jobs, user management when the ETL tools are used in a multi-user environment
- Provision to either clean the data (such as range checks, alerting on the missing data, etc.) or provision to integrate third party tools for data QA
- Provision to rollback in case major errors are encountered in the ETL process
- Debugging capability
- Error logging

Business Intelligence report generation is also done using a GUI. The OLAP and query analysis tools provide this facility. Some of the important features of GUI are:

- Analyze data from different dimensions
- Ad hoc queries generation
- Data mining
- Drill-down and drill-up
- What-if analysis
- Standard report generation and presenting it in graphical and tabular forms.
- Setting of alerts to give indications to the managers on occurrence of important events (e.g., the sales target for the month has been achieved, time to celebrate!).

Note...

Drill across is a process of creating a report from two or more fact tables. Drill through is accessing data from ODS. To browse the data in the multidimensional model (also called cube/hyper-cube) is called "slice and dice". Slicing is viewing the data of a particular dimension by cutting (slicing) the cube. Dicing is rotating the cube to view the data in a different dimension.

1.7.5 MOLAP Architecture

Fig 1.7: MOLAP Architecture

The architecture of MOLAP system is shown in Fig. 1.7. The system consists of:

- OLAP client that provides the front-end GUI for giving the queries and obtaining the reports.
- OLAP server, also known as Multi-Dimensional Database Management System (MDBMS) server. This is a proprietary database management system which stores the multidimensional data in 'multidimensional cubes' and contains the data in summarized form, based on the type of reports required.
- A machine that carries out the data staging, i.e. that converts the data from RDBMS format to MDBMS and sends the 'multidimensional cube' data to OLAP server.

The main **advantages** of MOLAP are:

- It provides excellent performance in terms of response time to queries as the data is already stored in summarized form.
- Only the results are sent to the client machine and hence the network bandwidth requirements are low.
- Drill-down is very fast.

The **disadvantages** of MOLAP are:

- MDBMS are proprietary to the vendor, who sells the data warehouse development tools.
- The cubes require high storage.
- Data cubes have to be updated periodically as the summaries keep changing.

- MOLAP tools are costlier as compared to ROLAP tools.
- MOLAP lacks flexibility because the data cubes in the server have to be predefined keeping in view the requirements analysis. Hence, drill-up is very difficult.

Hence, multidimensional OLAP is used when the database size is small, say less than 100 GB and the data is available in summarized form.

1.7.6 ROLAP Architecture

Relational OLAP is the preferred technology when the database size is large, i.e. greater than 100 GB. Here, the data will not be in summarized form. Its response time is poor, minutes to hours, depending on the query type.

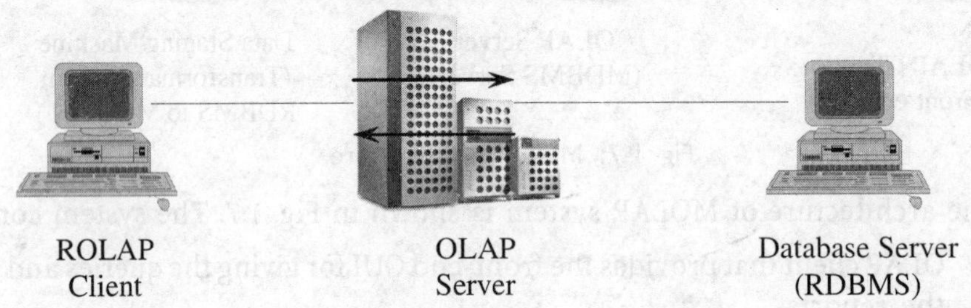

Fig 1.8: ROLAP Architecture

The ROLAP architecture is shown in Fig. 1.8. As the name implies, the ROLAP systems are based on relational data model. There will be ROLAP clients and a database server which is based on RDBMS. The OLAP server sends the request to the database server and obtains the request.

In this architecture, user interacts with the database more often. The query is processed by OLAP server and/or database server.

The **advantages** of this architecture are as follows:

- It provides a lot of flexibility because ad hoc queries can be given. Also, there is no limit on the number of dimensions.
- The tools are less expensive.
- RDBMS requires less storage.
- The network bandwidth requirements will be low because only the results are sent to the client over the network.

However, the disadvantages are:

- Response time is poor.
- Iterative analysis and drill-down are very slow.

1.7.7 Web-based Data Warehouse

The architecture of web-based data warehouse is shown in Fig. 1.9. The client software will be based on a web browser. The query will be sent to the web server. The web server passes the query to the target (data warehouse) database. The result obtained will be passed on to the client via the web server. The main advantage of this architecture is that the user interface is a very familiar interface to all the users and hence minimal training is required. Another advantage is that the data warehouse can be Intranet-enabled or even Internet-enabled. However, in such a case, security will be an issue to be addressed.

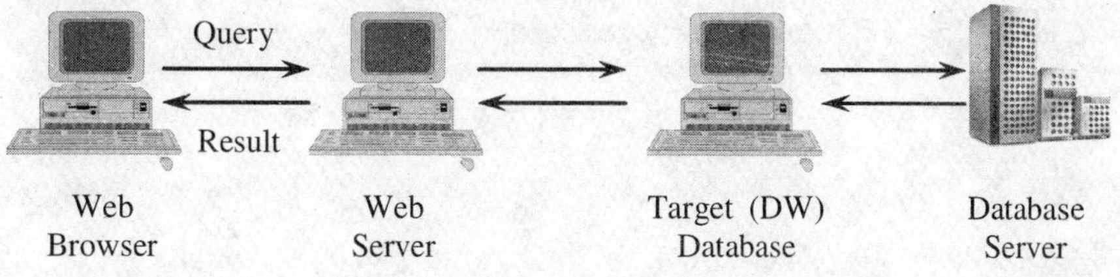

Fig 1.9: ROLAP Architecture

Summary

- Bill Inmon coined the phrase **'data warehouse'** in 1990. According to him, "a data warehouse is a subject-oriented, integrated, time-variant and non-volatile collection of data in support of management's decision-making process."
- **Data warehouse** is a system that provides business intelligence based on historical data with a provision to view the data in different dimensions.
- Data warehouses are built using multi-dimensional data model. In contrast, the RDBMS are built using Entity-Relationship Model (ER Model).
- Data staging involves extraction of data from the data sources, cleansing the data, transforming the data and then loading the data into the target database. Quality assurance of the data has to be carried out at every stage.
- **Aggregates** store the data in summarized form. Aggregates improve the performance of the business intelligence tools and also reduce the storage space.
- In slowly changing dimensions, the attributes of a dimension table change with respect to time. Slowly Changing Dimensions (SCDs) are of three types: in *Type 1 SCD,* the data is overwritten in the dimension table in *Type 2 SCD,* new records are added to the dimension table which contains the new data, in *Type 3 SCD,* new fields are added to the dimension table and the new dimension table contains the old and new attribute values.
- The data warehouse can be based on either Client/Server architecture or web-based architecture.
- The **OLAP systems** can be based on Relational model or Multidimensional model. Accordingly, the systems can be broadly divided into *ROLAP systems* and *MOLAP systems.*
- **Hybrid OLAP systems** provide a solution which has the advantages of both ROLAP and MOLAP systems.

2 Data Warehousing Development Process

CHAPTER OBJECTIVES

- Various stages in software development and waterfall model
- Specific aspects of data warehouse development process
- Importance of data warehouse development tools
- Overview of various project management issues to be considered in data warehouse development

Development of a data warehouse is like development of any software product or execution of a turnkey software project. However, data warehouse development poses certain challenges because the software has to be developed for managers to provide business intelligence and hence the development process needs special discussion, which is the topic of this chapter. The chapter provides a brief review of the waterfall model and then describes the various stages of data warehouse development. We will also discuss the importance of using commercially available development tools for fast development of the data warehouse. The chapter also cover some important project management issues.

2.1 The Software Development Process

Data warehouse development project is like any other software development project with many more challenges than the regular commercial software development projects. This is due to the fact that the data warehouse should meet the needs of the topmost management people in the organization, and satisfying them by meeting all their demands or needs is not an easy task. Many of them understand more of business and less of technology. So, the data warehouse project manager and developers need to follow a systematic approach to the development. You can refer to the excellent textbooks by Sommerville and Pressman for a complete coverage of software engineering, the discipline that deals with systematic approach to software development.

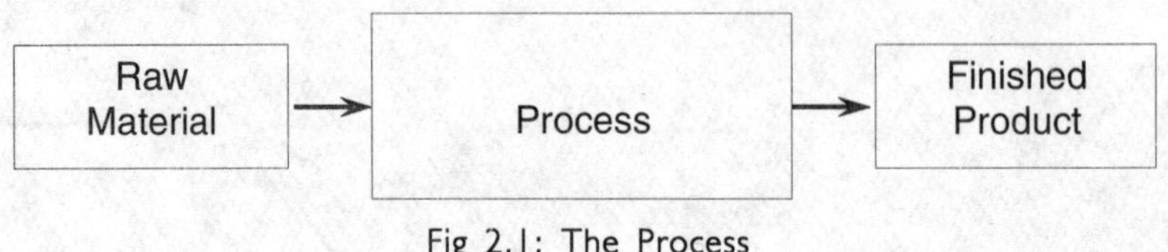

Fig 2.1: The Process

A process can be defined as a "step-by-step procedure". For instance, as shown in Fig. 2.1, the "process" takes raw material as input and produces the finished product as output. For example, the process to manufacture a car is the step-by-step procedure to assemble various parts and finally do a test drive of the car. In the case of software development, there is no 'raw material' and hence we define the software development process as shown in Fig. 2.2 Sotware process takes user requirements as input and produces a working software product as an output as per the user requirements.

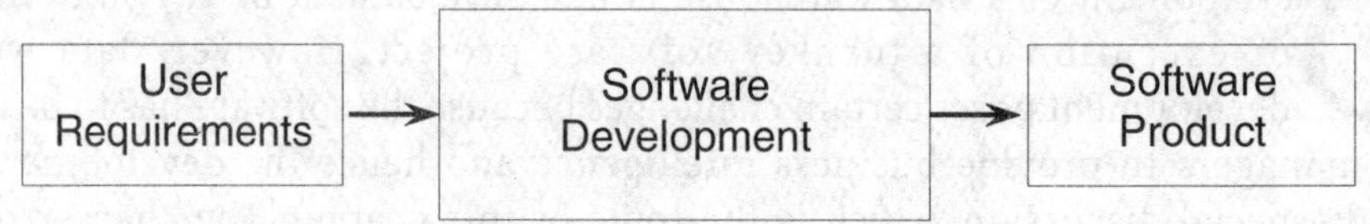

Fig 2.2: Software Development Process

In commercial software projects, the most widely used process model is the waterfall model, which is explained in the next section.

In Brief...

A process is defined as the step-by-step procedure to convert raw material into finished product. In software development process, a vague problem definition is converted into a working product using a systematic procedure.

2.1.1 Waterfall Model

The waterfall model is the most widely used model in software development process. The diagram below shows different stages Fig. 2.3.

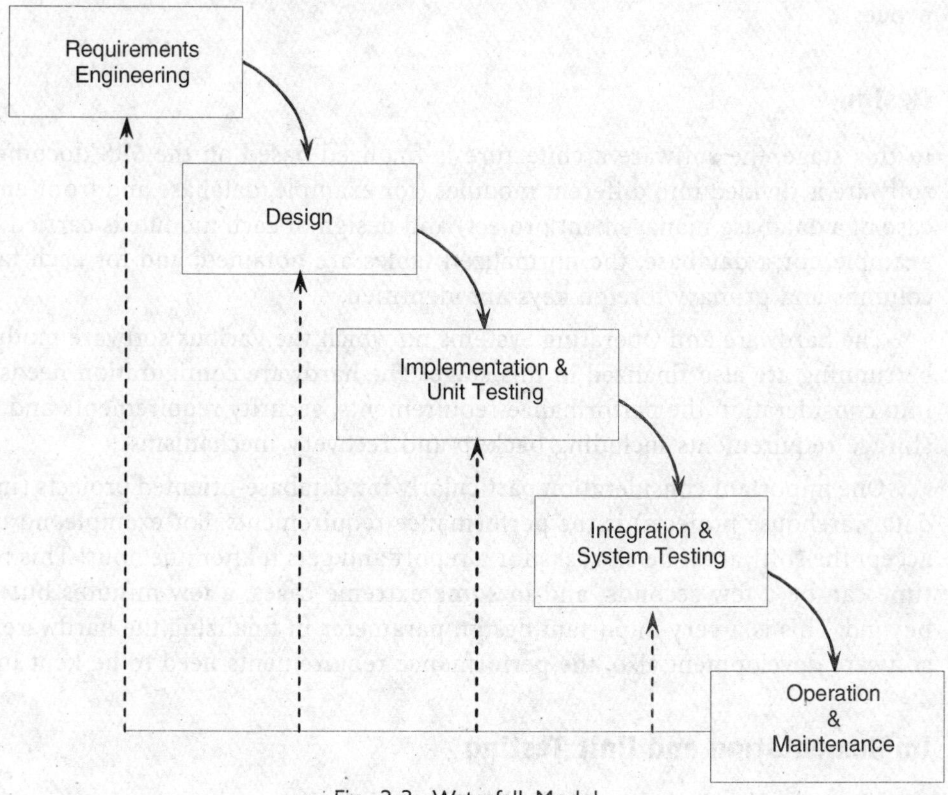

Fig. 2.3: Waterfall Model

In the waterfall model shown in Fig. 2.3. the software development process is divided into 5 stages viz.,

- Requirements engineering
- Design
- Implementation and unit testing
- Integration and system testing
- Operation and maintenance

Requirements Engineering

In this stage, the development team interacts with the users and finds out what they want. This is the most difficult and time consuming stage as different users have different requirements, sometimes contradicting one another. The development team has to consolidate all the important requirements and prepare a document called "Software Requirements Specifications (SRS)" document and then submit it to the users and get the approval. The SRS is an important document throughout the software development process.

Design

In this stage, the software architecture is finalized based on the SRS document. The software is divided into different modules (for example, database and front-end in the case of a database management project) and design of each module is carried out. For example, for a database, the normalized tables are obtained; and for each table, the columns and primary/foreign keys are identified.

The hardware and Operating Systems on which the various software modules will be running are also finalized in this stage. The hardware configuration needs to take into consideration the performance requirements, security requirements and also the storage requirements including backup and recovery mechanisms.

One important consideration particularly for database-oriented projects (including data warehouse projects) is the performance requirements. For example, no user will accept the software if he/she asks for a report and gets it after one hour! This response time can be a few seconds, and in some extreme cases, a few minutes but nothing beyond. This is a very important design parameter in finalizing the hardware. During software development also, the performance requirements need to be kept in mind.

Implementation and Unit Testing

In this stage, the design is converted into code using a programming language or a development tool such as database management engine. While carrying out the coding the individual units are also tested and bugs are removed.

A "unit" is defined as the smallest piece of software that can be coded and tested independently. For instance, small SQL programs or procedures are developed and tested independently by the developers individually.

Integration and System Testing

In this stage, the various modules are integrated together and the testing of the complete software is carried out. If the software has many modules, it is not advisable to integrate all the modules in one shot—"incremental building" is done wherein two modules are integrated and tested, and then the third module is integrated and so on. Using this approach, testing the software becomes easy.

For example, to test a DBMS, to start with, the database can be tested using SQL statements. Then, the database can be integrated with the front-end GUI and the testing can be done.

In this stage, a number of tests are carried out on the system to ensure that the software meets all the requirements, it is highly reliable, it caters to the needs of the required number of users, it has no security flaws, etc. For details of software testing and the software testing tools refer to the book [Prasad 2005].

Operation and Maintenance

In this stage, the software is installed at the user premises and handed over for regular use. In case the user encounters any problem or finds any bugs, then the software is modified to remove the bug. This is a continuous process till the software warranty is over or the product retires.

The waterfall model is generally followed for most of the commercial software development projects. It can also be followed for data warehouse development projects. However, initially, the development team should not be too ambitious; but develop a small prototype (based on scaled down version of the SRS by taking only some important user requirements into consideration). This approach is known as prototyping model.

In the next section, we will give a more detailed process for data warehouse development.

2.2 Data Warehouse Development Process

Many data warehouse projects do not succeed due to various reasons. For a data warehouse project to be successful, following points must be considered:

- The organization should feel the importance of information. If information is not considered as power, particularly by the top management, then 'Business Intelligence' does not carry any meaning. Then, it is not worth implementing a data warehouse. Hence, for the data warehouse project to be successful, the management should be strongly committed to the project.
- The organization should be IT-savvy and already a good amount of computerization—at least for departments such as finance, human resources, administration, stores etc.—should have been done.
- Required budget and human resources must be allocated for the project.

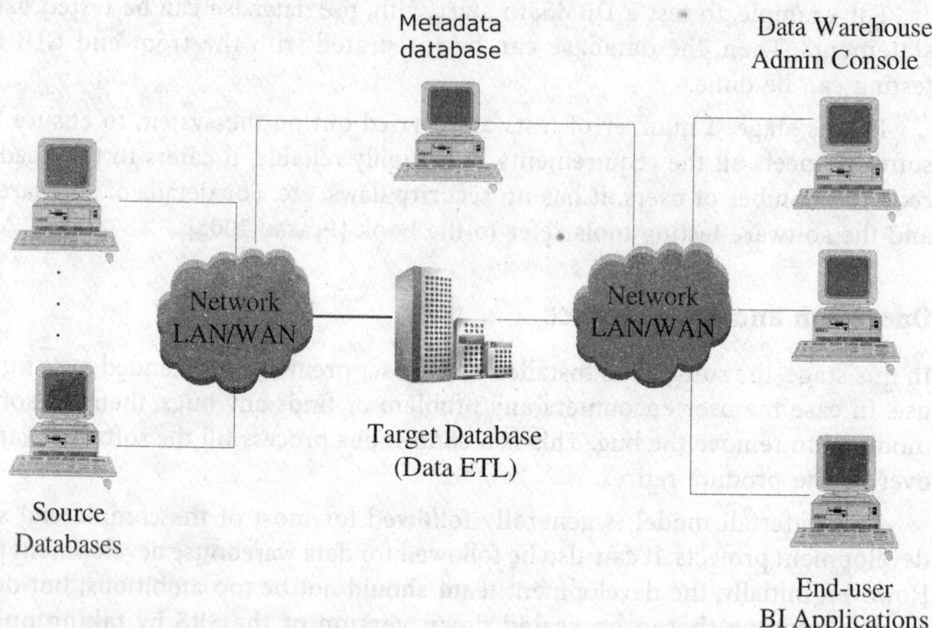

Fig. 2.4: Data Warehouse Architecture

The architecture diagram of a data warehouse is given in Fig. 2.4. The data presently available in various data sources (flat files, RDBMS or ERP applications) is put into the target database through the data Extraction, Transformation and Loading (ETL) process. During this process, the metadata is also created. Using front-end tools, the end-users access the data warehouse for obtaining the business intelligence. Administration tools are required for carrying out the regular admin activities on the data warehouse.

Based on this architecture, the data warehouse development process can be obtained. This process is shown in Fig. 2.5.

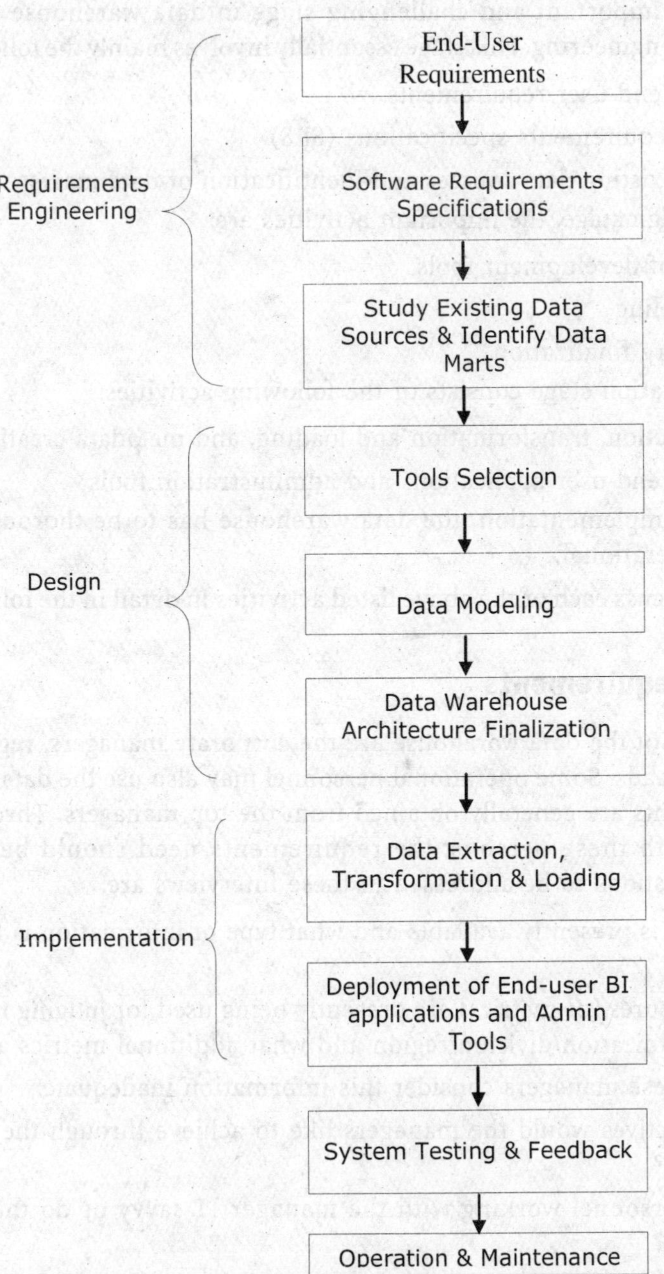

Fig. 2.5: Data Warehouse Development Process

The most important and challenging stage in data warehouse development is requirements engineering. This stage essentially involves mainly the following activities:

- Obtaining end-user requirements
- Software requirements specifications (SRS)
- Studying existing data sources and identification of data marts

In the design stage, the important activities are:

- Selection of development tools
- Data modeling
- Architecture finalization

Implementation stage consists of the following activities:

- Data extraction, transformation and loading, and metadata creation
- Deploying end-user applications and administration tools

After the implementation, the data warehouse has to be thoroughly tested and then made operational.

We will discuss each of the above listed activities in detail in the following sections.

2.2.1 End-user Requirements

The end-users of the data warehouse are the corporate managers, regional managers and division heads. Some operational personnel may also use the data warehouse, but the requirements are generally obtained from the top managers. Through a series of interviews with these persons, the requirements need should be obtained. The important questions to be addressed in these interviews are:

- What data is presently available and what type of information is being generated at present?
- What measures (or metrics) are presently being used for judging the performance of the organization/division/region and what additional metrics are required?
- Why do these managers consider this information inadequate?
- What objectives would the managers like to achieve through the data mart/data warehouse?
- Are the personnel working with the manager IT-savvy or do they dislike using computers?
- What are the immediate expectations from the data warehouse and what are the long-term expectations?
- Whether historical data (for the last how many years) is available and in what form it is available (paper form, flat files, databases, etc.)

Suppose you are interviewing a university registrar for the university data warehouse development. The university registrar certainly must be using RDBMS/ERP systems to obtain information about the admissions, faculty, etc. However, the present operational systems may not analyze the historical data and hence, if the registrar is interested in getting answers to queries such as:

(a) During the last five years, what is the trend of admissions for Indian students versus Chinese students in MS in Computer Science?

(b) During the last 4 years, who fared better in GRE scores—Indians or Chinese?

Similarly, if the manager of a production organization is interviewed, he will be able to tell you what are his broad objectives: whether it is reduction of the inventory of the inward goods in the stores, or whether it is reduction of wastage in the production process, etc. depending on his past 'intuitive' experience. Based on these qualitative inputs, you need to find the appropriate quantitative metrics to measure these values and monitor them in your data warehouse.

Note...

Managers are interested in business processes rather than technology. Hence, while obtaining the user requirements, the data warehouse specialists need to focus only on the business requirements rather than on technology and tools.

2.2.2 Software Requirements Specifications

After finishing the first round of interviews, you will realize that different users give different inputs. Some requirements are common to everyone, some requirements are unique to a manager, and some requirements given by two users may be contradictory to one another. You need to study all the inputs and prepare a consolidated list of user requirements and prepare a document "Software Requirements Specifications (SRS)". This SRS document should reflect all the important user requirements. If necessary, assign priority levels to these requirements. If there are too many requirements, you may like to implement some high priority requirements only to start with. The SRS document also should address issues such as security of data, how the data warehouse administration has to be carried out, etc.

After writing the SRS document, you need to circulate this document to all the users and ensure that the document captures all the important specifications. This is known as validation of the document. This is a very important step because even the end-users will be very clear as to what to expect from the data warehouse, once the validation of the document is done.

2.2.3 Study of Existing Data Sources

As the organization would have already implemented some RDBMS solutions or ERP solution, it is important to study these existing data sources and obtain the complete details from the database administrators and programmers. The information to be obtained includes:

- What are the data sources from which the data has to be extracted (flat files, database management systems, ERP applications, etc.)
- The physical location of the data sources and the communication links used to access this information by users.
- For each data source, the computer's hardware configuration and operating system.
- For RDBMS applications, the database engine that is being used (Oracle, Sybase, Informix, DB2, etc.) and the front-end tools used for developing the GUI (VB, VC++, Java, etc.)
- The size of the database size and the operational reports that are being generated.
- The table structure and the details of each and every field for RDBMS and ERP applications.
- The person responsible for database administration and the persons authorized to give permissions for accessing the data for use in data warehouse.
- The measures taken by the information security officer of the organization to provide data security.

Once you get this information from all the available databases/ERP packages, you will realize that there may not be any standardization in even naming the tables and fields. As a result, data extraction, transformation and loading into the target database becomes very challenging.

As a data warehouse is a combination of a number of data marts, the first step is to identify the data marts. Each data mart can be that of a functional area (sales, inventory, marketing, etc.) or that of a branch/sales office.

It is always good to start on a small scale with a single source data mart and then move on to multiple-source data mart.

Consider a bank that wants to develop a data warehouse for all its operations. It can have data marts for each of the important functional areas such as (a) ATMs (b) credit cards (c) bank accounts (d) loans etc. The data warehouse will integrate all these data marts to provide corporate business intelligence.

2.2.4 Selection of Development Tools

A detailed technical overview of the various data warehouse development tools is given in the next chapter. In this section, we will discuss the various issues related to selection of the tools.

A fundamental question: Is it necessary to buy commercial data warehouse development tools at all? Strictly, no! Well, certainly you can build a data warehouse for your organization, or for your client, if you have a world-class team of SQL programmers and domain experts. But then, the entire development calls for many, many people to work on the project, the development time will take many months and sometimes years, and then the software may not be highly reliable. If the team members leave in between, the whole project gets into more and more trouble (and, show me one project in which all the team members worked from the beginning to the end unless it is a project of a few hours duration!).

Hence, it is always a good idea to make use of the commercially available data warehouse development tools. Using commercially available tools has the following advantages:

- It makes the data warehouse development very fast. The management will feel that the investment on the tools is worth it, though initially the feeling may be that the tools are costly.
- Since the development is completed fast, the project cost will be very low.
- The productivity of the team members will be very high because the tools provide very powerful mechanisms to do the development and maintenance.
- As the tools provide the necessary software to access the data from various data sources, there is no need for writing lot of code in SQL or any programming language.
- Administration of the data warehouse will be very easy as tools are readily available for this activity as well.

So, it is always a good idea to invest on the tools. Certainly, the management has to allocate the necessary budget to procure the software tools and get the development team trained on these tools.

A number of tools are available commercially. These tools are broadly divided into two categories:

- Tools integrated with other development tools. Organizations such as Microsoft, Oracle, IBM, SAP, etc. supply these tools. These tools are integrated with database management systems, ERP applications, server software, etc. Hence, you can have a single-stop solution from these vendors.
- Specialized tools focusing only on business intelligence. Some popular tools that are now extensively used by various organizations for developing the data marts/ data warehouses are:
    - Informatica
    - Cognos
    - Business Objects
    - DataStage
    - Microstrategy

In this book, we will study the second category of tools.

As a prospective data warehouse specialist, you have to learn all the tools, but when you start working on a commercial development project, you may have to focus only on two tools since it would be very rare to work on more than two tools. Which two tools? It depends on the organization! If your job is to assess the various tools and select one or two tools for your development project, then you need to do the selection based on the following criteria:

- What type of architecture does the tool support? You may like to buy a tool that supports both C/S architecture as well as web-based architecture.
- What type of OLAP does the tool support? Some tools support only ROLAP and some tools support MOLAP. You may like to buy a tool that has HOLAP.
- What hardware platforms/Operating Systems/Databases do the tools require? Do you have that infrastructure or do you have to buy new hardware/software? Naturally, you prefer a tool that can run on your existing infrastructure.
- What are the features of the tool and does it meet all my requirements such as
  - Extraction of data from the data sources of your organization.
  - User interface that provides readily some important reports and facility to generate ad hoc queries and carry out the analysis.
  - Tools for administration.
- How good are the security mechanisms provided by the tool? As data warehouse contains highly sensitive data, it is very important to protect this data and the tools should not have any loopholes for leaking the data.
- Is it possible to mix-and-match? You may like to buy the front-end tools from one vendor and backend tools from another vendor.
- How good is the customer support? Customer support in your locality (country or state) is important, as you need to interact with the vendor to solve some of your operational problems. Though the vendor provides initial training on the tools, do not assume that it would be enough.
- What is the cost of software upgrades? Every vendor keeps updating the software with new features and also removes a few bugs. You need to check whether the upgrades are provided free of cost and for how long.
- What is the cost? Certainly the cost is an important factor. But it should not be the only factor (as in the case of some government procurement procedures). A tool may be costlier by a few hundred dollars, but it provides some additional features, perhaps that additional cost is worth it. Look at the cost keeping in view the return on investment rather than just the absolute dollar value of the software.

For evaluating the different tools to check whether they meet your needs, you need to study the technical features as well, and we will discuss these technical features in the next chapter.

2.2.5 Data Modeling

As the data warehouses are built based on multi-dimensional model, data modeling is an important step. Data modeling involves identification of fact tables, dimension tables for each data mart and the enterprise-wide data warehouse. During this process, you also need to work on the conformed dimensions and conformed facts to ensure that the meaning of the dimensions and facts is the same across the different databases of divisions/regional offices.

During this stage, the slowly changing dimensions have to be identified and what type of SCD implementation is required (Type 1, 2 or 3) has to be decided.

A number of tools are now becoming available that help in data modeling (ERwin being a popular tool). These tools are capable of converting the E-R model into a multidimensional model and also vice versa. Certainly, using these tools would be of great help; but they are yet to become very popular and many data warehouse designers prefer to do the data modeling manually.

2.2.6 Architecture Finalization

Finalization of the architecture is closely linked to the selection of the development tools. A decision on architecture should be taken based on the technical requirements as well as the tools.

There are mainly two types of architecture from an end-user point of view:

- Web-based architecture
- Client/Server architecture

Organizations, which are concerned about the security of the data, still prefer C/S architecture because web-based architecture (particularly when the data warehouse is Internet-enabled) poses many security challenges. Note that majority of the present tools provide you an option to use C/S architecture now and migrate to web-based architecture at a later point of time.

Another choice to be made is whether you need to take a tool that supports ROLAP or MOLAP or HOLAP. Certainly, HOLAP is the best choice as it gives the best of both worlds. If cost is an important consideration for you, then you need to study your data warehouse size requirements and then take a decision. If the size is likely to be less than about 100 GB, then MOLAP tools give good performance whereas for very large warehouses, ROLAP is better.

Data warehouse sizing is another important issue. You need to consider the data storage requirements keeping in view how much of historical data you need to keep. You need to list all the dimension tables, all the fact tables and the attributes for each table. And then, you need to estimate the number of rows in each table for a year and then calculate the database size. The estimate should take into consideration the future requirements (say for the next 10 years) because the data warehouse has to keep the historical data.

2.2.7 Data Extraction, Transformation and Loading & Metadata Creation

Extraction of the data from source databases, carrying out the necessary transformation and loading the data into the target database—in short, the ETL process, is the most time consuming process in the data warehouse development work.

Using commercially available tools will make the ETL process comparatively easy and fast. These tools provide a GUI to carry out all the ETL operations—defining the data sources, carrying out various transformations and then loading the data to the target database. These administration tools provide the facility to schedule the ETL jobs either in real-time mode or in batch mode, at specific times (say, during night time). These tools also provide the facility to monitor the complete process of ETL and check whether the data loaded into the target database is correct.

2.2.8 Deployment of End-user Applications and Administration Tools

Since you would have already taken the decision to use a commercial tool for developing the data warehouse, the next step is to deploy the end user applications and administration tools and also creating the necessary user required applications as well as configuring/customizing these tools for your requirements.

2.2.9 Data Warehouse Testing

After the individual modules are integrated, a thorough system testing has to be carried out. Initially, the data warehouse has to undergo a field trial—deploying the warehouse to a selected group of users who will have the patience to tolerate a few problems and give a positive feedback without complaining about your software. During the testing, certainly your focus will be mainly on meeting the functional requirements. In addition, you need to test the system for performance, reliability, usability and security requirements as well.

2.2.10 Operation and Maintenance

The operational phase involves ensuring that the data warehouse is functioning as per the user requirements. The operational data has to be regularly updated into the target database. As the user demands will keep increasing, particularly to add new features, the software needs will be upgraded continually by adding new reports, etc.

If a user informs of any bugs in the data warehouse, the data warehouse specialists need to carry out the necessary modifications using the configuration management process described in a later section.

2.3 Project Management

Managing a data warehouse development project is a very challenging task. In this section, we will touch upon a few issues.

2.3.1 Human Resources

Fig. 2.6: The Players in Data Warehouse Development

Like any other software project, data warehouse development involves a number of players as shown in Fig. 2.6. In addition, the data warehouse team may need to take the services of security specialists and infrastructure managers to take care of issues related to security and the overall infrastructure required for deploying the data warehouse. Data warehouse specialists need to coordinate with all the teams and hence, in addition to sound technical knowledge, good communication skills are also a must. The technical experts also need to appreciate the fact that the business people focus on business, not technology. So, they may not be interested in the database engines you are using or the tools you are using—their interest is only in getting the business intelligence to carry out their jobs more efficiently. So, the data warehouse specialists need to talk to managers in management jargon and not in technical jargon.

2.3.2 Infrastructure

The infrastructure requirements may be divided into two categories:

- Computing infrastructure
- Communication infrastructure

Computing Infrastructure

The data warehouse team may have to use the existing infrastructure or install new infrastructure for the computing facilities. Keeping in view the development tools being used, storage requirements, backup and recovery mechanisms, etc. the computing infrastructure needs to be identified. To keep the data secure and available, **RAID** (Redundant Array of Inexpensive Disks) technology can be used. RAID facilitates mirroring of the complete data.

Archive and Retrieval: As the data warehouse is likely to grow rapidly, the users may demand more features, more complex analysis and also they want to keep the historical data as active data for a long time. It is likely that the managers may ask for at least the past five years of data to be kept active. Hence, the data warehouse size is likely to grow up, even perhaps exponentially. To meet such user needs, an archive and retrieval process has to be worked out by the data warehouse administrators.

It is advisable to keep a separate **data center** at a location other than the location where the data warehouse is installed. This data center contains a mirror image of the data warehouse and it is updated periodically depending on the need. The advantage of such a data center at a different location is that if the primary data warehouse location is in an area of disaster (cyclone, typhoon, earthquake, terrorist attack, etc.), even then, the data warehouse is not affected.

Communication Infrastructure

The data sources of the organization may be spread over a large geographical area—they may be located at different parts of the country or in different countries. The communication infrastructure that interconnects these data sources (a Wide Area Network) has to be efficient, reliable and secure for data transfer. Similarly, the end users may be situated at different locations and hence they also may be accessing the data warehouse through a LAN or/and a WAN. Hence the communication infrastructure that meets the data warehouse requirements needs to be identified. Also, to provide data security, the necessary firewalls have to be provided and configured properly.

2.3.3 Documentation

In every software development project, documentation is an extremely important activity. Unfortunately, the engineers give the least important priority to it. During the course of development, a number of documents have to be generated. These documents, known as work products, include the following:

- Software Requirements Specifications Document
- Design Document
- Detailed Design Document
- Test Procedure and Acceptance Test Procedure
- Test Results
- Source Code
- Project Plan Document
- User Manual

All these documents should be kept under configuration management.

2.3.4 Configuration Management

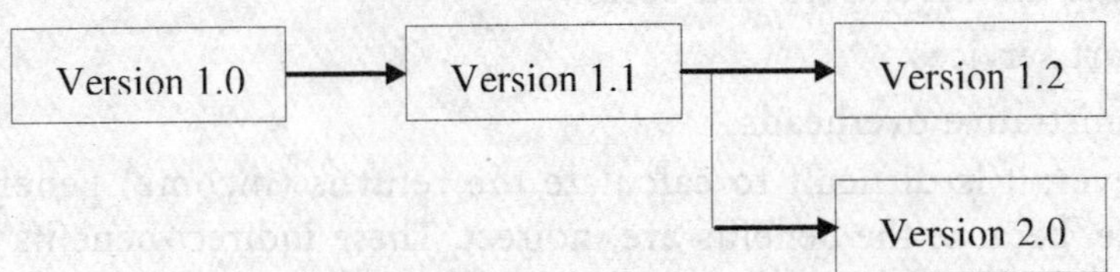

Fig 2.7: Versions/Releases of Software/Documentation

During the course of development of data warehouse, a number of 'work products' are prepared, as discussed in the previous section. To start with, the SRS document is prepared and then the design is started. During the design, the designers may conclude that a particular feature indicated in the SRS document cannot be implemented. In such a case, the SRS document has to be modified. Similarly, all other documents may undergo changes during the development as well as during maintenance. Whenever a document or the source code has to be modified, the modification has to be done using a systematic procedure. This procedure involves:

- Giving a written request on the proposed modification.
- A formal discussion on the impact of the modification on user requirements, time frame, budget, etc.
- A decision as to whether the proposed modification can be done or not.
- Issuing a written note on the accepted modification.
- Modification to the work product.

The whole process looks cumbersome, but it is very important. If the user asks for a "small" change, and if you innocently accept it, it may turn out to be a big problem later on. Nothing is small, unless you analyze the proposed change.

As shown in Fig. 2.7, whenever you make many changes to a work product, you need to change the version of the work product (version 1.0, 1.1, 1.2, etc.). If major modifications are done, you need to change the release of the product (version 2.0, 2.1, etc.).

As building a data warehouse is a continuous and iterative process, a good configuration management process should be in place.

2.3.5 Return on Investment

Expenditure for building a data warehouse is easy to measure. The various components are:

- Hardware and software
- Manpower for development and maintenance
- Training the developers and users
- Support services
- Administrative overheads

However, it is difficult to calculate the returns (income) generated by a data warehouse, because the benefits are indirect. These indirect benefits are reflected in such things as:

- Increased productivity of the employees
- More satisfied customers who bring in more business
- Less maintenance costs
- Less production costs for a manufacturing company due to less inventory, better quality control, etc.

However, for all these benefits, someone else may take the credit without giving any importance to the information source!

The top management has to give importance to the data warehouse project keeping in view the indirect benefits. Otherwise, everyone will think that the data warehouse specialists are spending/making, lot of money without doing anything productive!

Summary

- **The waterfall model** is the most widely used software development life cycle model for commercial projects. In this model, software development is divided into 5 stages—requirements engineering, design, implementation and unit testing, integration and system testing, and operation and maintenance.
- For **data warehouse development**, during requirements engineering stage, the business intelligence reports that need to be generated for different management domains have to be identified and the presently available data on different systems needs to be studied for the content and format.
- In **design stage,** the data warehouse architecture has to be finalized keeping in view the requirements of security, availability, storage requirements, etc. and the development tools need to be selected.
- The data warehouse development tools need to be selected keeping in view the following factors: hardware and software environment, features, training/support provided by the vendor, cost, etc.
- The data warehouse implementation will be extremely fast if the commercially available development tools are used.
- The data warehouse has to be tested thoroughly—not only for functionality, but also for its reliability, security features, user friendliness, etc.
- Once the data warehouse becomes operational and the users start appreciating its power, the traffic will increase and also the new requirements.
- All the work products generated during the development of the data warehouse have to be kept under configuration management.

3 Overview of Data Warehousing Tools

CHAPTER OBJECTIVES

- Appreciate the importance of using data warehouse development tools
- Learn the taxonomy of the tools
- Get an overview of the various commercially available tools
- Understand the various criteria used for selection of a particular tool for development of a data warehouse for your organization.

As a prospective data warehouse specialist, you need to make your data warehouse up and running in just a few months. You can achieve this goal only if you are highly productive and do a very fast job. Using commercially available software packages will improve your productivity tremendously. This chapter gives an overview of the features of these tools and also lists the various criteria based on which you need to select a particular tool for your organization.

Whether you are a developer or a manager, you need to have an understanding of the various tools available in the market.

3.1 The Importance of Tools

Some database specialists say that if you have a good team of people who have expertise in a front-end tool such as (VB.NET or Java) and SQL, you can develop a data warehouse without buying any data warehouse development tools. Well, strictly it is true. However, you need to appreciate that the development using this approach is very time consuming. It may take at least one year to develop the first version of your data warehouse. On the other hand, if you use the commercially available development tools, then you can do the development at lightning speed and the first version of your data warehouse will be ready in just a few months.

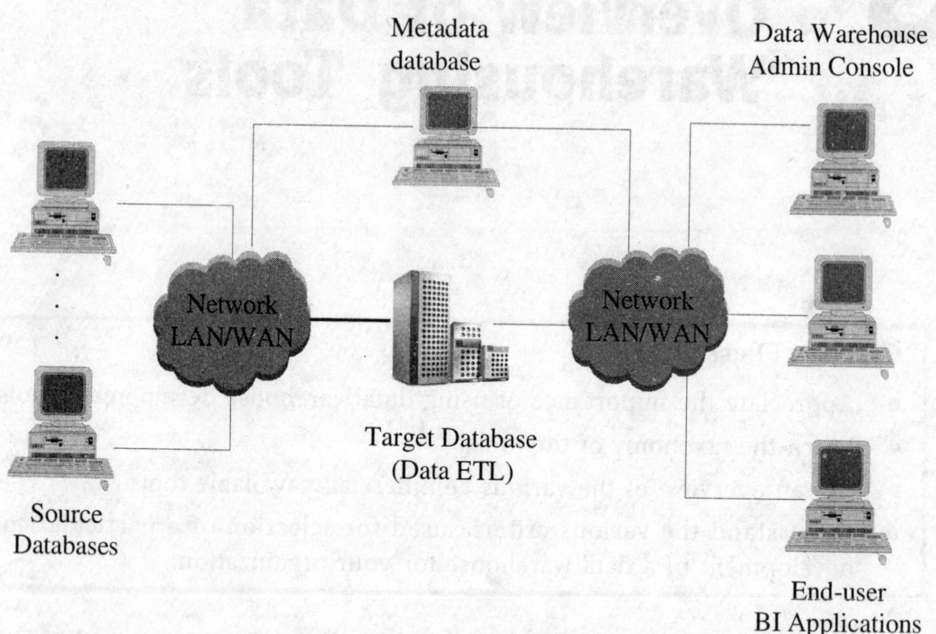

Fig. 3.1: Data Warehouse Architecture

From the data warehouse architecture shown in Fig. 3.1, we can make out that development of a data warehouse involves development of software for the following:

- Data extraction, transformation and loading into the target database and metadata generation.
- Data analysis and report generation.
- Administration of data warehouse.

Commercially available software packages address all these stages and tools are available for data ETL, on-line data analysis, standard report generation, ad hoc query processing as well as for administration of the data warehouse. The advantages of these tools are:

- The tools increase the productivity tremendously and the data warehouse can be built within a few months, not years.
- The total project cost will reduce considerably and the investment on the tools is worth it.
- The monotonous job involved in the development such as in the data staging is removed as tools handle this job more efficiently.
- The tools provide many features for report generation, which perhaps, we did not even imagine.

Hence, it is worth investing in the development tools. However, as a project manager, you need to appreciate that:

- The data warehouse development tools are certainly costly and you need to invest on the software.
- You need to spend considerable time and effort in evaluating the tools and decide which tool meets your requirement. As most of the tools have the same or similar features, you need to make a decision based on the following:
  - Operating environment needed for the tool (hardware and operating systems) and its availability in your organization.
  - The features of the tools
  - Cost of the tools
  - Training provided by the vendor
  - After-sales support provided by the vendor
- You need to train people on these tools or hire people with expertise.

3.2 Taxonomy of Tools

The data warehouse development tools can be broadly divided into two categories:

(a) Tools integrated with the generic software such as server OS, RDBMS, ERP packages etc. The tools supplied by Microsoft (along with Windows 2003 Server), Oracle (with Oracle Database), IBM with IBM servers and SAP (with the ERP package) belong to this category.

(b) Specialized tool for developing data marts/warehouses. Tools supplied by vendors such as Informatica, Cognos, Business Objects etc. belong to this category. Tools under this category can be classified as:

a. Data Modeling tools
b. ETL and Metadata creation tools with GUI and administration of ETL jobs.
c. Front-end tools (for OLAP, standard report generation and ad-hoc query analysis).

3.2.1 Data Modeling Tools

The data modeling tools come in handy to convert the existing E-R model to multi-dimensional model required for data warehousing. Some of the popular data modeling tools are:

- ERwin of Computer Associates

- Rational Rose of IBM Corporation
- Power Designer of Sybase Corporation
- Oracle Designer of Oracle Corporation

In spite of the availability of these tools, many engineers do not use these tools but prefer to do the modeling manually.

3.2.2 ETL and Metadata Creation Tools

These tools are also known as back-end tools as these tools are used by developers and administrators only; not end users. However, note that they provide the GUI to carry out the functions using a user-friendly interface. These tools extract the data from different data sources (such as flat files, legacy databases, RDBMS, ERP, CRM and SCM applications packages, etc.) The functionality of these tools includes:

- Carry out the necessary transformations such as joining of tables, sorting, applying various filters, etc.
- Create the metadata—data about the source data, target data and the transformation logic.
- Provide the GUI for carrying out the ETL operations.
- Provide the necessary administration tools to manage multiple users to access the tool simultaneously, start and stop the ETL jobs in real-time mode or batch mode, and monitor the ETL process through workflow monitoring.

Note...

ETL tools need to support legacy (old) databases as data sources. But then, what is "old" is difficult to decide—some consider 5 year old packages as legacy systems and some consider 30 year old packages as legacy systems. In Bangalore, for 20-year old IT professionals, 30 year old IT professionals are 'uncles' and 'aunties'—eh, in the world of IT, "old" has a different connotation.

Selection of a specific ETL tool must be based on the following criteria:

- The source databases from which the tool can extract the data. The tool should support flat files and all the RDBMS, ERP, CRM and SCM application packages which your organization is using presently.
- The target databases onto which the tool has to load the data. A tool that is capable of loading data simultaneously to multiple targets would be a good choice.
- User-friendly GUI with good capability for debugging.
- Multi-user support so that multiple users can use the tool simultaneously. If two or more users use the same table, then table-locking facility should be provided. Each user should have access control mechanisms and hence the necessity for admin tools for user management.

- Reliability of the software
- Speed of processing the data
- Rollback capability, i.e. in case there are major errors in the ETL process, the original state of the data sources and target database should be preserved.
- Storage of metadata repository and its format (flat file, RDBMS)
- Security of metadata
- Data cleansing tools integrated with the ETL tool itself or provision to integrate third party tools
- Error logging
- Runtime information regarding the records loaded into the target database
- Support for data QA
- The transformation logic supported and whether it meets your requirements. Some important transformations to be supported are:
  - Filters (and filter, or filter etc.)
  - Join
  - Translate
  - Lookup
  - Checking whether a field is within a particular range
  - Math functions
  - Aggregation
  - Merging records
  - Ranking and sorting
  - Custom transforms

A good number of such tools are available from a large number of vendors. In this book, we will study in detail how to make use of the ETL tools—Informatica tools in Chapters 4 and 5; and DataStage tools in Chapter 8.

3.2.3 Data Analysis and Report Generation Tools

These tools are also referred to as 'front-end' tools as they provide the end user applications. Essentially, these are On-Line Analytical Processing (OLAP) tools. These tools provide the following functionality:

- Analyze the data from multiple dimensions
- Generate standard reports for business intelligence
- Provide the capability to generate ad-hoc queries

- Present the data in graphical/tabular form and also provide a good number of statistical analysis features

Selection of data analysis and report generation tools should be based on the following criteria:

- What type of OLAP tool it is—ROLAP, MOLAP or HOLAP
- Hardware and software configuration of the computers on which these tools have to be installed. If the available infrastructure is enough for the tool, it would be an advantage because there will be no need to spend money on additional infrastructure.
- *Interoperability with other tools.* You may like to buy ETL software from one vendor and front-end tool from another vendor.
- *Information extraction and query formulation capabilities*—provision to give complex queries should be available.
- *Analysis capabilities.* It should be possible to carry out complex analysis. In addition to regular analysis such as aggregates, filters and graphics capabilities, the following are important features: applying new filter to an existing analysis, statistical capabilities, what-if analysis, etc.
- Standard reporting capabilities.
- Export of results to popular spread sheet-packages such as Microsoft Excel; and export to simple ASCII text files.
- APIs to build your own applications.
- Provision to transfer the results files to email.
- *Reliability of the software.* You should not keep on pressing (CTRL+ALT+DEL) on your Windows system, while using the tool.
- *Performance.* A good response time is very important. However, this depends on many factors such as the hardware configuration, RAM size, whether it is ROLAP tool or MOLAP tool and the size of the data warehouse.
- *Ease of use.* A good GUI is compulsory because the data warehouse is used by CEOs and top-level management (and we all know their computer skills!).

In this book, we will study how to generate reports using Cognos in Chapter 5 and Business Objects in Chapter 6.

Note...

It is very common for organizations to use ETL tools and data analysis & report generation tools from different vendors for the data warehouse project—for example, Informatica for ETL and Business Objects for OLAP. So, the OLAP tool must be capable of working with other popular ETL tools.

3.3 Commercial Tools

Following four tools are the commercial tools used in data warehouse development process. We will discuss them in details in the following chapters. Here only a brief review of their important features is being given. The tools are:

- Informatica
- Cognos
- Business Objects
- DataStage

We will briefly review their important features in the following sections.

3.3.1 Informatica

Informatica (www.informatica.com) suite provides the complete business intelligence solutions—from server components to the front-end tools. The important tools are:

1. Repository Server Administrator Console
2. Repository Manager
3. Designer
4. Workflow Manager
5. Workflow Monitor

Using these five tools, in conjunction with Informatica Server and Informatica Repository server, we can do the complete data staging or ETL. (Extraction, Transformation and Loading).

Repository Server Administrator Console: This tool is used to connect/ disconnect to the Repository Server.

Repository Manager: This tool is to create/organize/manage the repository (relational database managed by the Repository Server that stores information, or metadata, used by Informatica Server and Client tools). Using Repository Manager, we can handle the administrations tasks like creation of repository, creation and organization of folders and configuring permissions and privileges for users and groups.

Designer: Designer is used to create mappings that contain transformation instructions for the Informatica Server. Before you can create mappings, you must add source and target definitions to the repository. It contains Source Analyzer, Warehouse Designer and Mapping Designer.

Workflow Manager: This tool is used to create and run workflows and tasks.

Workflow Monitor: As the name implies, this tool is used to monitor scheduled and running workflows for each Informatica Server.

3.3.2 Cognos

Cognos (www.cognos.com) is a rich set of tools for development of data mines, data marts and data warehouses. Some of the tools in this suite are:

Cognos DecisionStream: A tool carrying out the ETL process and metadata creation.

Cognos Impromptu: A tool for generation of business intelligence reports.

Cognos Scenario: A tool suitable for data mining applications, i.e., to find the hidden trends and patterns in data.

Cognos Query: A tool for data navigation to process ad hoc queries.

Cognos PowerPlay: A tool for multi-dimensional on-line analysis of data.

3.3.3 Business Objects

Business Objects (www.businessobjects.com) provides a rich set of tools for business intelligence. The various tools of this suite are:

Data Integration Tools: These tools extract, transform and load the data from the source databases to the target database. There are two tools in this category: *Data Integrator* and *Rapid Marts.* Data Integrator is an ETL tool with a GUI. Rapid Marts is a packaged ETL with pre-built data models for reporting and query analysis that makes initial prototype development easy and fast for ERP applications. It provides pre-built reports also.

Data Integrator has 4 components:

- **Graphical designer:** GUI to build and test ETL jobs for data cleansing, validation and auditing.
- **Data integration server:** It integrates data from different source databases.
- **Metadata repository:** Metadata repository keeps source and target metadata as well as transformation rules.
- **Administrator:** It is a web-based tool that can be used to start, stop, schedule and monitor ETL jobs. The ETL jobs can be in batch mode or real-time mode. As multiple users can use the integrator, user management is also done by the administrator module.

The data integrator designer client runs on Windows platform. The Data Integrator server can be based on Windows, HP-UX, Solaris or Linux platform.

BI Platform: This platform provides a set of common services to deploy, use and manage the tools and applications. These services are: security, broadcasting, collaboration, metadata and developer services.

Reporting Tools and Query & Analysis Tools: These tools provide the facility for standard reports generation, ad hoc queries and data analysis.

Performance Management Tools: These tools help in managing the performance of a business by analyzing and tracking key metrics and goals. Using dashboards, scorecards and alerting features, these tools are of immense use to the top management.

3.3.4 DataStage

DataStage (www.ascential.com) provides a set of powerful tools for developing a data warehouse. It has a number of client and server components.

The server components consist of DataStage Repository, DataStage Server and DataStage Package Installer. The repository contains all the required data to build a data warehouse. DataStage Server runs the server jobs (A job is a process that carries out ETL). DataStage Package installer provides the GUI to install packaged server jobs and plug-ins.

The DataStage client components consist of DataStage Manager, DataStage Designer, DataStage Director and DataStage Administrator.

DataStage Manager: It provides the user interface to view and contents of the data repository.

DataStage Designer: This tool is used to create the DataStage jobs. Using this tool, the data sources, transformations required and the destination database are specified. These jobs are compiled and executable files are created. These executable files can be scheduled by the DataStage Director and run by the Server.

DataStage Director: This tool provides the user interface to schedule, run and monitor the server jobs.

DataStage Administrator: It is used to perform administration tasks such as administration of the users, creation of projects, etc.

Summary

- The use of data warehouse development tools increases the employee productivity tremendously, reduces development and maintenance cost and development time and results in reliable data warehouse.
- The management has to allocate the necessary funds for evaluation of different tools for their suitability, purchasing the tools and training the project team on the advanced features of these tools.
- The tools can be divided into (i) data modeling tools (ii) ETL and metadata creation tools (iii) data analysis and report generation tools and (iv) data warehouse administration tools.
- Data modeling tools are used to create the logical and physical data models and also to convert the E-R model into multidimensional model.
- Some popular data modeling tools are: Erwin of Computer Associates, Rational Rose of IBM, PowerDesigner of Sybase and OracleDesigner of Oracle.
- ETL and Metadata creation tools extract the data form the data sources, carry out the necessary transformations, and load the data into the target database as well as create metadata—data about the source and target data and transformation logic. They provide the user interface/GUI for ETL process and administration of ETL jobs and users.
- Data analysis and report generation tools can be based on ROLAP, MOLAP or HOLAP architectures. These tools provide the capability to generate standard reports, ad hoc query generation and data analysis and present the data in tabular and graphical form, and also export the results to other application programs such as spread sheets.

4 Informatica

CHAPTER OBJECTIVES

- Overview of Informatica tools
- Extraction, Transformation and Loading of data using Informatica tools
- Transformations using Informatica: aggregate, rank and router
- Implementation of slowly changing dimensions

Informatica suite is a powerful data warehouse development suite. In this chapter, we will demonstrate the complete process of extraction of data from data sources, carrying out transformations and then loading the data into target database using Informatica tools. As data Extraction, Transformation and Loading (ETL) is the most challenging task in the data warehouse development, a good understanding of the use of the tool presented in this chapter is very important for data warehouse specialists.

4.1 Overview of Informatica

Informatica suite contains five tools:

1. Repository Server Administrator Console
2. Repository Manager
3. Designer
4. Workflow Manager
5. Workflow Monitor

Using these five tools, we can do the complete data staging or ETL. (Extraction, Transformation and Loading).

Repository Server Administrator Console is used to connect/disconnect to the Repository Server.

Repository Manager is used to create/organize/manage the Repository (relational database managed by the Repository Server that stores information, or metadata, used by the Informatica Server and Client tools). Using Repository manager, we can handle the administrations tasks like creation of repository, creation and organization of folders and configuring permissions and privileges for users and groups.

Designer is used to create mappings that contain transformation instructions for the Informatica Server. Before you can create mappings, you must add source and target definitions to the repository. It contains Source Analyzer, Warehouse Designer and Mapping Designer.

Workflow Manager is used to create and run workflows and tasks.

Workflow Monitor is used to monitor scheduled and running workflows for each Informatica Server.

4.2 Development Environment

For the various examples presented in this chapter, the following development environment is used.

- Oracle database running on Windows 2003 server. The source and target database for the examples presented in this chapter are in Oracle.
- Informatica tools installed on Windows 2003 server.
- EMP, DEPT, SALGRADE and BONUS tables—the default Oracle database ("scott") tables available with Oracle installation. The table structure is described in the next section.

4.2.1 Basic Table Structure

For demonstration of ETL process and basic transformations, we will make use of the EMP, DEPT, SALGRADE and BONUS tables. These are default tables of the sample Oracle database "scott" and the default user name is scott and default password is tiger. If these default values are changed by your system administrator, you need to get them and login. The structures of tables are given below.

SQL> desc emp;

Name	Null?	Type	
EMPNO	NOT NULL	NUMBER(4)	Primary Key
ENAME		VARCHAR2(10)	
JOB		VARCHAR2(9)	
MGR		NUMBER(4)	
HIREDATE		DATE	
SAL		NUMBER(7, 2)	

COMM		NUMBER(7, 2)	
DEPTNO		NUMBER (2)	Foreign Key

SQL> desc dept;

Name	Null?	Type	
DEPTNO	NOT NULL	NUMBER(2)	Primary Key
DNAME		VARCHAR2(14)	
LOC		VARCHAR2(13)	

SQL> desc salgrade;

Name	Null?	Type	
GRADE		NUMBER	Primary Key
LOSAL		NUMBER	
HISAL		NUMBER	

SQL> desc bonus;

Name	Null?	Type
ENAME		VARCHAR2(10)
JOB		VARCHAR2(9)
SAL		NUMBER
COMM		NUMBER

Default data available in these tables is shown below:

SQL> select * from emp;

EMPNO	ENAME	JOB	MGR	HIREDATE	SAL	COMM	DEPTNO
7369	SMITH	CLERK	7902	17-DEC-80	800		20
7499	ALLEN	SALESMAN	7698	20-FEB-81	1600	300	30
7521	WARD	SALESMAN	7698	22-FEB-81	1250	500	30
7566	JONES	MANAGER	7839	02-APR-81	2975		20
7654	MARTIN	SALESMAN	7698	28-SEP-81	1250	1400	30
7698	BLAKE	MANAGER	7839	01-MAY-81	2850		30
7782	CLARK	MANAGER	7839	09-JUN-81	2450		10
7788	SCOTT	ANALYST	7566	19-APR-87	3000		20
7839	KING	PRESIDENT		17-NOV-81	5000		10

```
7844    TURNER  SALESMAN   7698   08-SEP-81  1500     0    30
7876    ADAMS   CLERK      7788   23-MAY-87  1100          20
7900    JAMES   CLERK      7698   03-DEC-81   950          30
7902    FORD    ANALYST    7566   03-DEC-81  3000          20
7934    MILLER  CLERK      7782   23-JAN-82  1300          10
14 rows selected.
SQL> select * from dept;
   DEPTNO DNAME              LOC
     10 ACCOUNTING           NEW YORK
    20 RESEARCH              DALLAS
    30 SALES                 CHICAGO
    40 OPERATIONS            BOSTON
4 rows selected.
SQL> select * from salgrade;
GRADE        LOSAL        HISAL
1            700          1200
2            1201         1400
3            1401         2000
4            2001         3000
5            3001         9999
5 rows selected.
SQL> select * from bonus;
no row is selected
```

4.3 ETL Life Cycle

For data extraction, transformation and loading (ETL), we need to carry out a number of steps in sequence. We will discuss these steps, in detail, in this section. Here are the steps:

- How to create a Repository
- How to create folders
- Design of transformations (mappings) between source and target
- How to create workflows and tasks

- How to execute tasks and monitor the workflows.

To illustrate the ETL process, we will use 'join' transformation between EMP and DEPT tables.

4.3.1 Creating a Repository User

Before working with Informatica, the administrator should create *Repository* user in Oracle database.

1. To create the repository user, the procedure is as follows:
   i) Login into SQL*PLUS as super user:
   SQL syntax: *CONN[ECT]* sys@<conn_string> *as sysdba;*
   E.g. SQL> connect sys as sysdba;
   You will be prompted for the password, press Enter, as there is no password for this user.
   ii) Create the repository user by using following SQL statement:
   SQL syntax: *create user <user name> identified by <password> default tablespace users;*
   E.g. SQL> create user scottrep identified by scottrep default tablespace users;
   iii) Grant permissions to the user using following SQL statement:
   SQL syntax: *grant <previlege1>, <previlege2> to <user name>;*
   e.g. SQL> grant connect, resource to scottrep;
   Check whether the repository user is created or not:
   e.g. SQL> connect scottrep/scottrep;
   Connected.
   SQL> select * from tab;
   No row is selected.

After extraction and transformation of data, we need to load the data into data warehouse (target database). So, we require a target database user.

4.3.2 Creating a Target Database User

To create the Target Database, the procedure is as follows:

i) Login into SQL*PLUS as super user:
SQL syntax: *CONN[ECT]* sys@<conn_string> *as sysdba;*
E.g. SQL> connect sys as sysdba;

ii) Create the Target Database user using following SQL statement:

SQL syntax: *create user <user name> identified by <password> default tablespace users;*

e.g. SQL> create user scottolap identified by scottolap default tablespace users;

iii) Grant permissions to the user with the following SQL statement:

SQL syntax: *grant <previlege1>, <previlege2> to <user name>;*

e.g. SQL> grant connect, resource to scottolap;

iv) Check whether the Target Database user is created or not:

e.g. SQL> connect scottolap/scottolap;
Connected.

SQL> select * from tab;

No row is selected.

4.3.3 Creating a Repository

To create a repository, the procedure is given below.

1. Check whether the *Informatica Repository Server* has been started or not from the services. If not, open services: ***Start → Administrator Tools → Services.*** Services window will open. Go to ***Informatica Repository Server*** Service, right click on it and select ***Start*** from the pop up menu. Informatica repository server service gets started.
2. To create repository, start ***Repository Server Administration Console:***
   i) ***Start → Programs → Informatica Power center 6.1 OEM for i2 → Repository Server Administration Console (Fig. 4.1).***

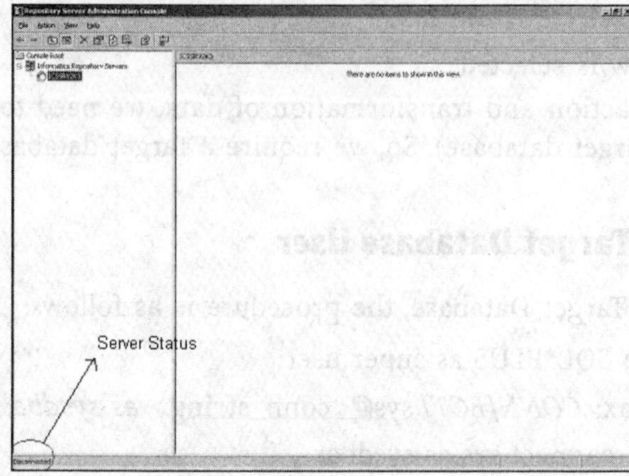

Fig. 4.1

ii) Explore Informatica repository servers and select the server name where the repository server is running.

iii) Right click on that server, and select **connect** option from the pop up menu and enter port Number, and Administrative password, as in Fig. 4.2.

E.g. Port Number=5001(default port number)

Administrator Password=password

Connecting to Repository Server ICSSRV2K3

Connection Information

Repository Server: ICSSRV2K3

Port Number: 5001

Administrator password: ********

OK

Cancel

Help

Fig. 4.2

iv) Explore Repositories folder (Fig. 4.3).

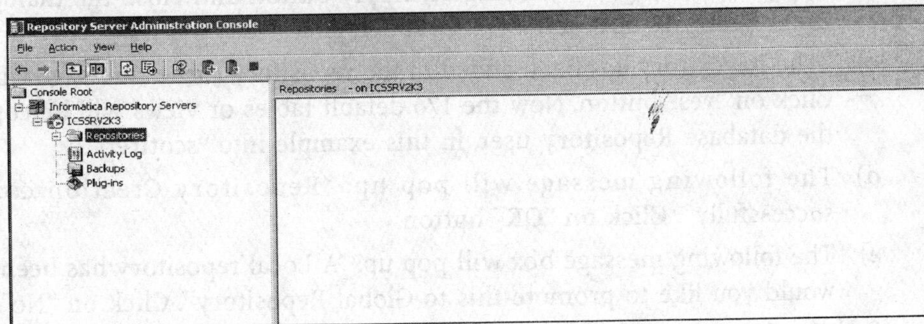

Fig. 4.3

v) Right click on Repositories folder and select *Add Repository* from the pop up menu.

a) As shown in Fig. 4.4, In "Add Repository dialog" go to Repository Tab and enter Repository Name, Connect String, Database user and Database Password:

e.g. Repository Name	:	scottrep
Connect String	:	oemrep(it is the database name)
Database User	:	scottrep
Database Password	:	scottrep

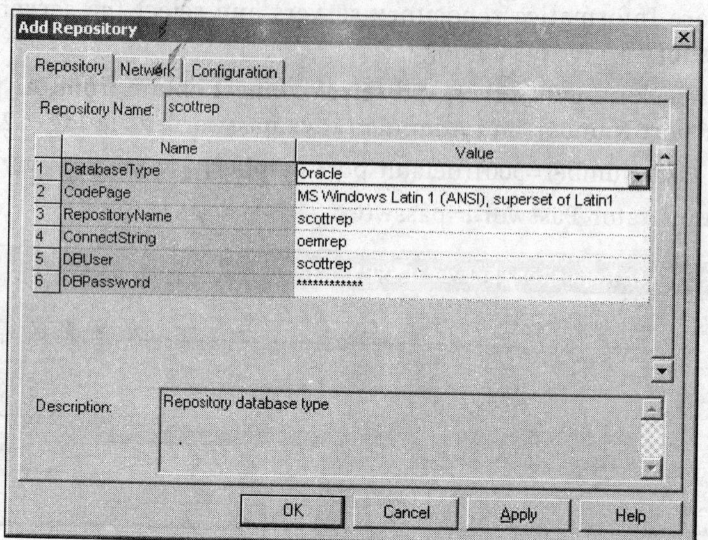

Fig. 4.4

b) Apply the settings by clicking on **Apply** button and close the dialog box by clicking on **OK** button.

c) "The Repository has been added to the repository cache" message will popup. Click on "yes" button. Now the 176 default tables or views will be copied into the database Repository user, in this example into "scottrep".

d) The following message will pop up: "Repository Creation completed successfully". Click on "OK" button.

e) The following message box will pop up: "A Local repository has been created, would you like to promote this to Global Repository". Click on "No" button.

f) The following message will pop up: "Repository scottrep startup completed successfully". Click on "OK" button.

g) Now our repository is created successfully.

vi) You can check whether the repository is created or not with the following SQL statements:

SQL> connect scottrep/scottrep

SQL> select count(*) from tab; 176.

4.3.4 Creating Folders in the Repository

To start a project and to save the project, we must have a folder in Repository. To create the folder we must start the "Repository Manager". Use the following steps to create a folder using the Repository Manager.

1. Open the Repository manager:

   Start → Programs → Informatica Power center 6.1 OEM for i2 → Repository Manager.

2. Informatica Repository Manager window shown in Fig. 4.5 is displayed.

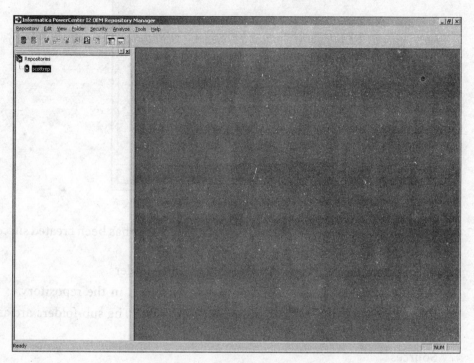

Fig. 4.5

3. Explore Repositories and select the created repository ("scottrep"), right click on it and select "connect" button from the pop up menu.
4. Create a new folder in the selected Repository by selecting the menu item: **Create → Folder.**
5. Enter the name of the folder from the popped up dialog box and click on "OK" button as shown in Fig. 4.6.

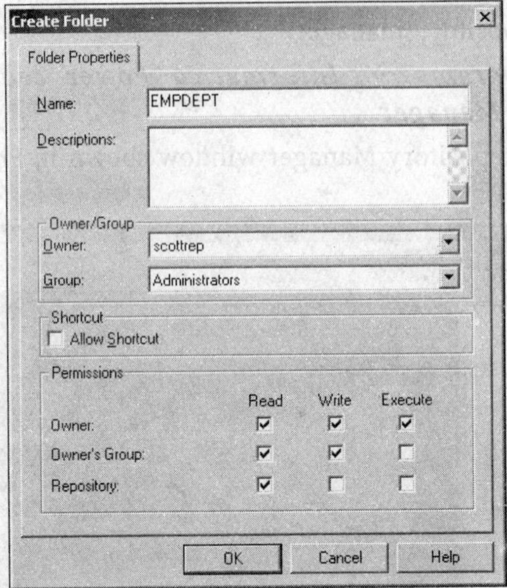

Fig. 4.6

6. The following message will be displayed: "The folder has been created successfully", click on "OK" button.
7. Repeat the process from step 4 to create more folders.
8. Now a folder has been created to save our projects in the repository.
9. By default, 8 sub-folders are created for this folder. The sub-folders are as follows:
   Business Components
   Sources
   Targets
   Cubes
   Dimensions
   Transformations
   Mapplets
   Mappings

4.3.5 Designer Tool

The Designer tool is used to select source and target databases and to map the flow of data from source to target with the applied transformations. Some of the transformations available in Informatica are: Source Qualifier, Joiner, Aggregator, Expression, Filter, Sequence Generator, Lookup, Update strategy. We will demonstrate some of these transformations in the following sections.

The sequences of operations performed in Designer tool are: Source Analyzer, Warehouse Designer, and Mapping Designer.

1. Open the Designer tool:

   Start → Programs → Informatica Power center 6.1 OEM for i2 → Designer. The screen shown in Fig. 4.7 is displayed.

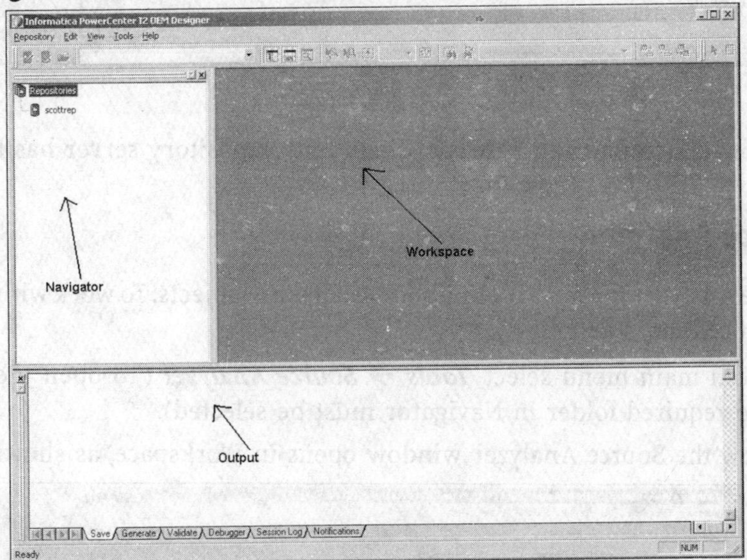

Fig. 4.7

2. As shown in this figure, the screen is divided into three parts. They are: **Navigator, Output** and **Workspace.**

   Navigator: We can navigate through different folders and sub folders of Repository. In short, we can navigate through different objects of your Repository.

   Output: We can see the output of different activities we perform.

   Workspace: This is the area where we define a work with different objects (Source objects, Target objects, Transformations, Mappings and Mapplets).

3. Whenever you want to work with Informatica, you need to connect to Repository first. Let us see how to connect to our created Repository (scottrep).

4. In the Navigator, select the Repository "scottrep", right click on it and select the "connect" from the pop up menu.

5. **Connect to Repository** window opens. Enter Repository name, Username and Password of Repository and click on "Connect" button as shown in Fig. 4.8.

   E.g. Repository name : scottrep(default)
   User name : scottrep
   Password : scottrep

Fig. 4.8

Now the connection between Client and Repository server has been established.

4.3.6 Source Analyzer

Source Analyzer is used to define source database objects. To work with Source Analyzer, the procedure is as follows:

1. From main menu select ***Tools → Source Analyzer*** (To open the source analyzer the required folder in Navigator must be selected).
2. Now the Source Analyzer window opens in Workspace, as shown in Fig. 4.9.

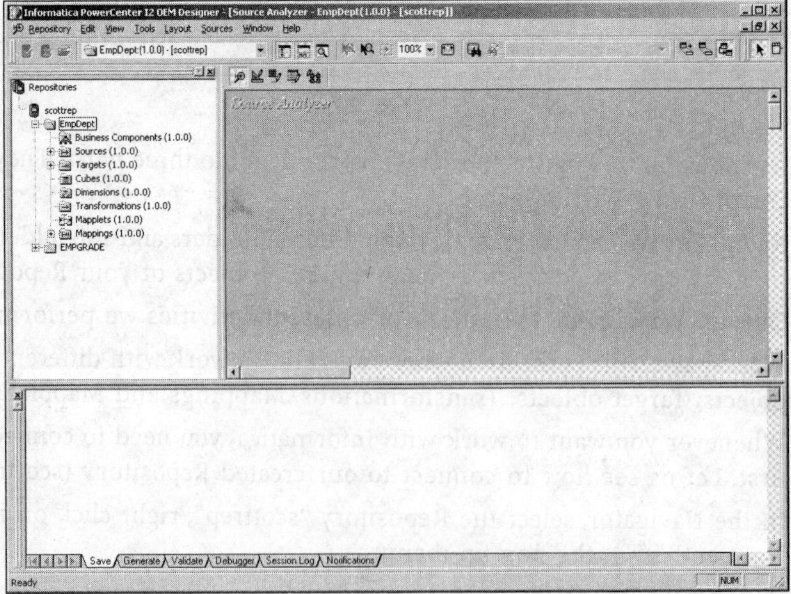

Fig. 4.9

3. The source objects can be created or imported from the required Database. Here we will show how to import the source Database object.
4. To import a source Database object, select the menu item from main menu ***Sources***

→ ***Import from Database.***

5. Now the "Import Table" window opens.
6. Select the ODBC Data source name, Username, Owner name, Password for the Database tables, which are to be imported as source, Database objects and click on "connect" button (Fig. 4.10).

e.g. ODBC data source name	:	scott (oracle in ora home 90)
Username	:	scott
Owner name	:	SCOTT (when you enter the user name then this will be automatically displayed).
Password	:	tiger

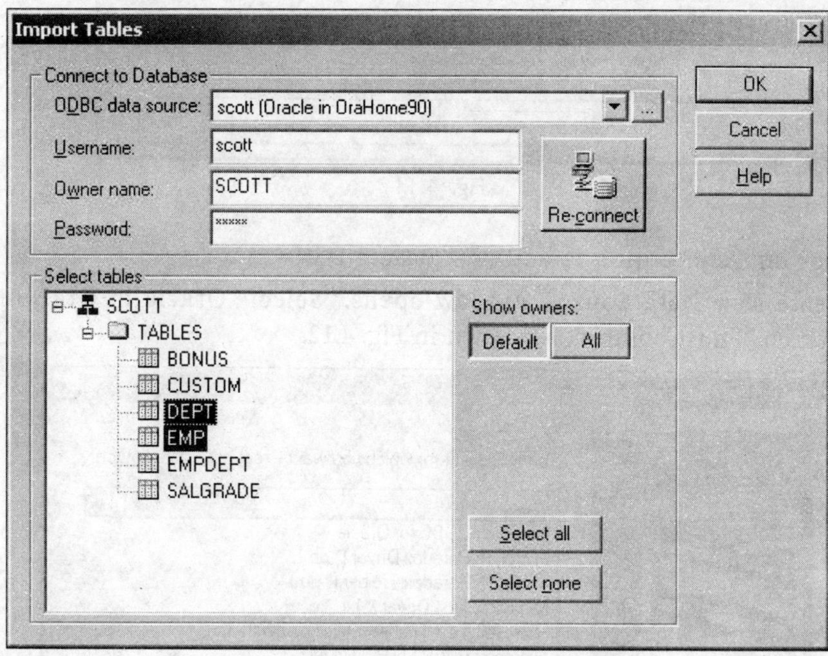

Fig. 4.10

7. If the ODBC data source is not created previously, then click on the button with three dots, which is there on the right side.
8. **ODBC Data Source Administrator** window opens. Go to "System DSN" tab. Then the screen looks as in Fig. 4.11.

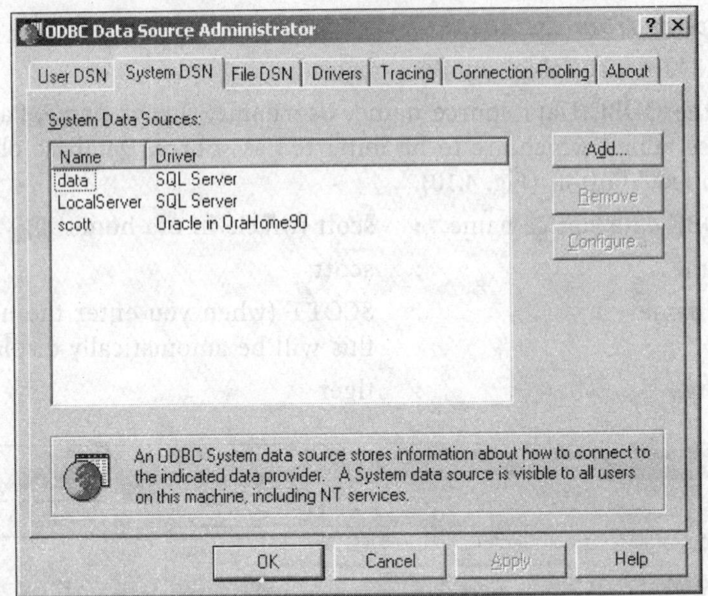

Fig. 4.11

9. Click on "Add" button to add new System DSN.
10. **Create New Data Source** window opens. Select "Oracle in OraHome90" and click on "Finish" button, as shown in Fig. 4.12.

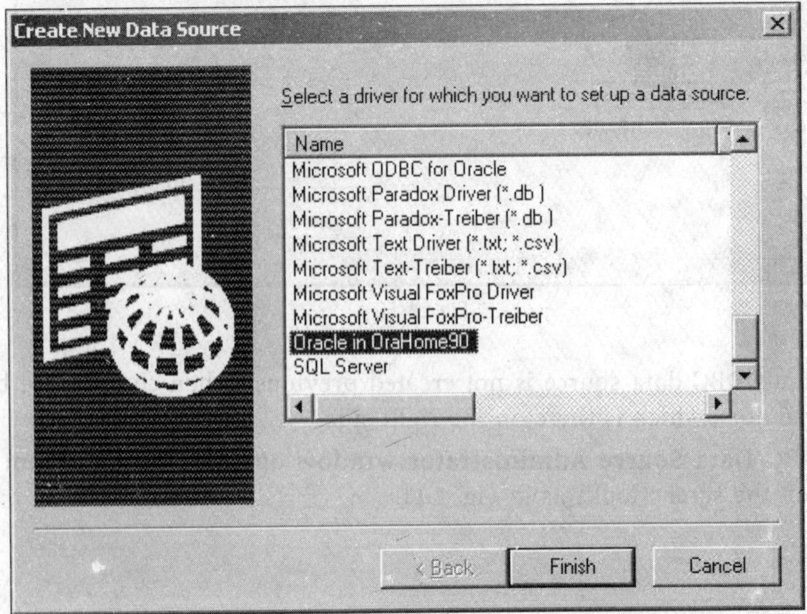

Fig. 4.12

11. **Oracle ODBC Driver Configuration** window opens. Enter the following details. Now the screen looks as shown in Fig. 4.13.

Data Source Name : scott
TNS Service Name : OEMREP (you need to change it, contact your Oracle administrator).
User ID : scott

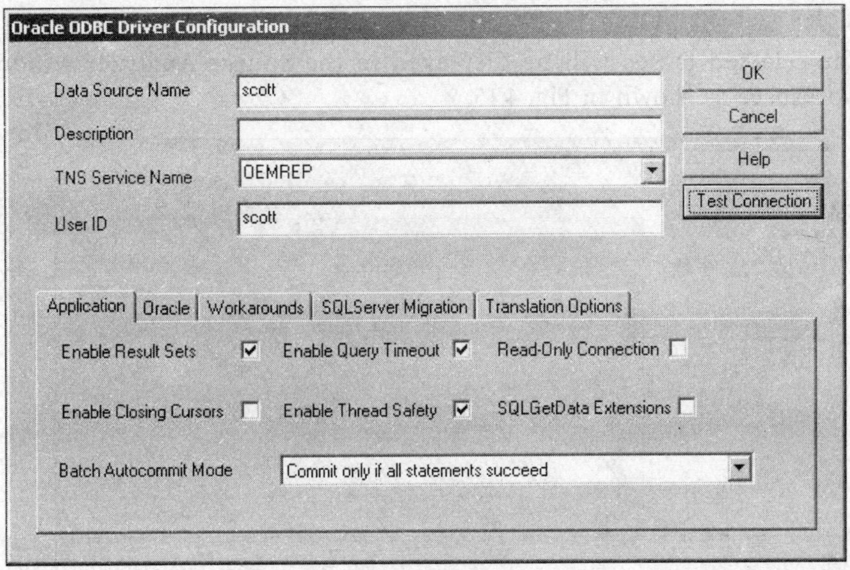

Fig. 4.13

12. Click on **Test Connection** button to test the connection. The **Oracle ODBC Driver Connect** window opens (Fig. 4.14). In that window, we will get the "Service Name" and "Username" by default. You need to enter the "Password" as shown in Fig. 4.14. Password: tiger.

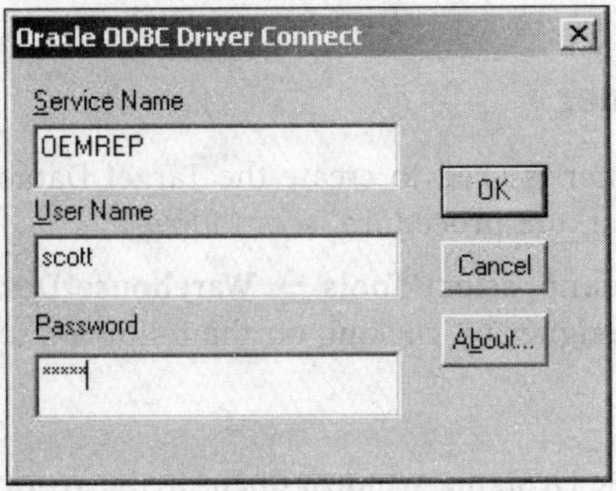

Fig. 4.14

13. Click on "OK" button to test the connection. "Connection success" message will be displayed, just "OK" that message.
14. Click on "OK" button of "Oracle ODBC Driver Configuration" window. Now the System DSN is created successfully. Click on "OK" button of "ODBC Data Source Administration".
15. After connecting, select the required tables from select tables list and click on "OK" button. For this example, select EMP, DEPT tables as shown in "Import Tables" screen shot.
16. The selected tables will be displayed in the Source Analyzer window of the Workspace as shown in Fig. 4.15.

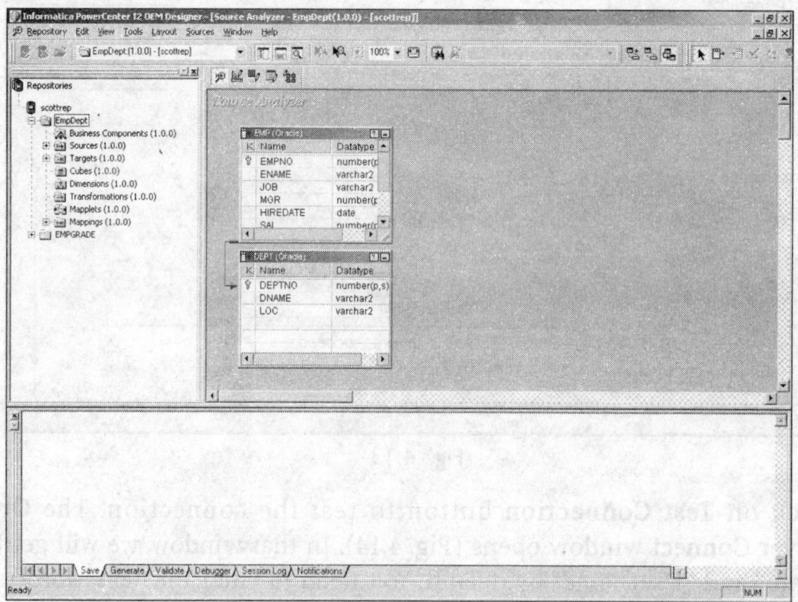

Fig. 4.15

4.3.7 Warehouse Designer

The warehouse designer is used to create the Target Database objects. To create the Target Database object, the procedure is as follows:

1. From the main menu, select **Tools → Warehouse Designer.** You can also open the Warehouse Designer by clicking on the following icon.

2. Now the Warehouse Designer window opens in the Workspace (Fig.4.16).

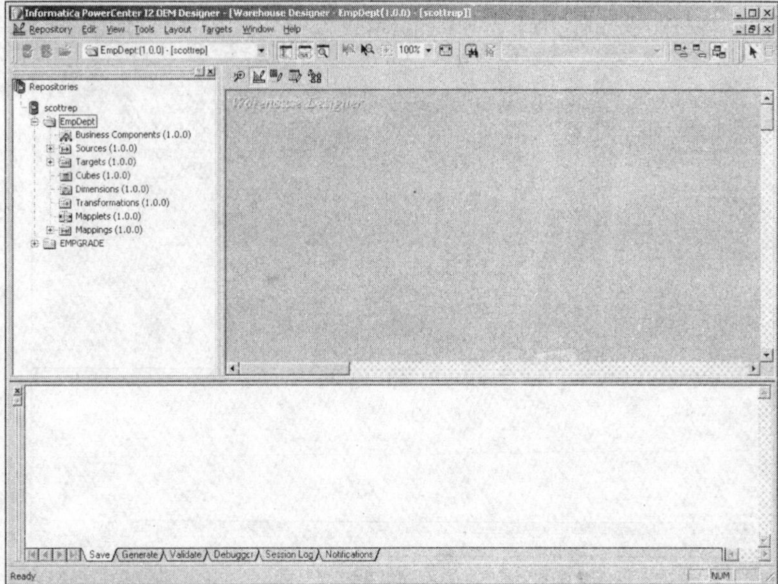

Fig. 4.16

3. To create the Target table, select the **Targets→Create** from the main menu
4. **Create Target Table** window opens. Enter the Target Table name and select the Database type for Target table, as shown in Fig. 4.17. e.g.

   Target Table Name : empdepttarget

   Database type : Oracle

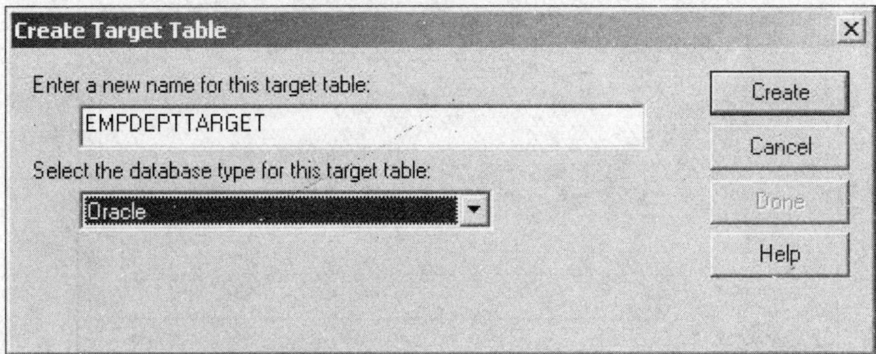

Fig. 4.17

5. After entering the details, click on **Create** button, then on **Done** button.
6. Now you can see the target table in the Warehouse Designer Workspace without any fields, as shown in Fig. 4.18.

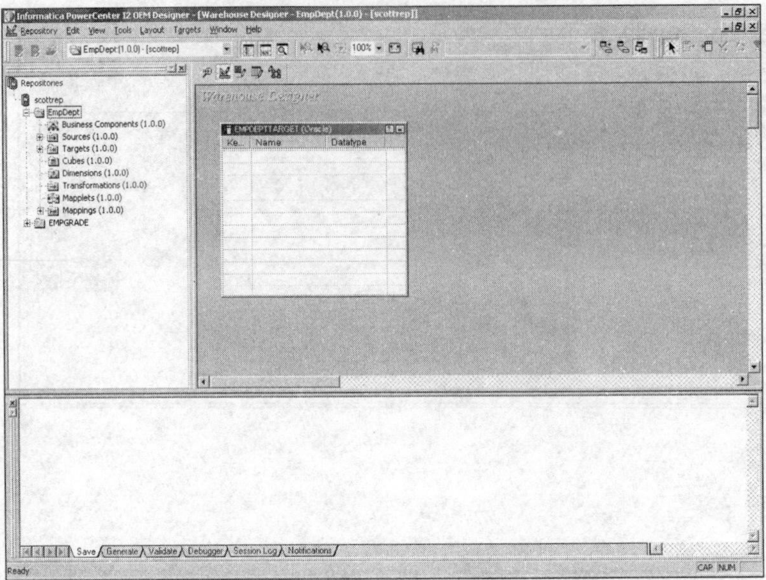

Fig. 4.18

7. To enter the fields of the target table double-click on it.
8. Now **"Edit Table"** window opens. Go to **"Columns"** tab.
9. To enter the New Fields, click on the icon shown in Fig. 4.19.

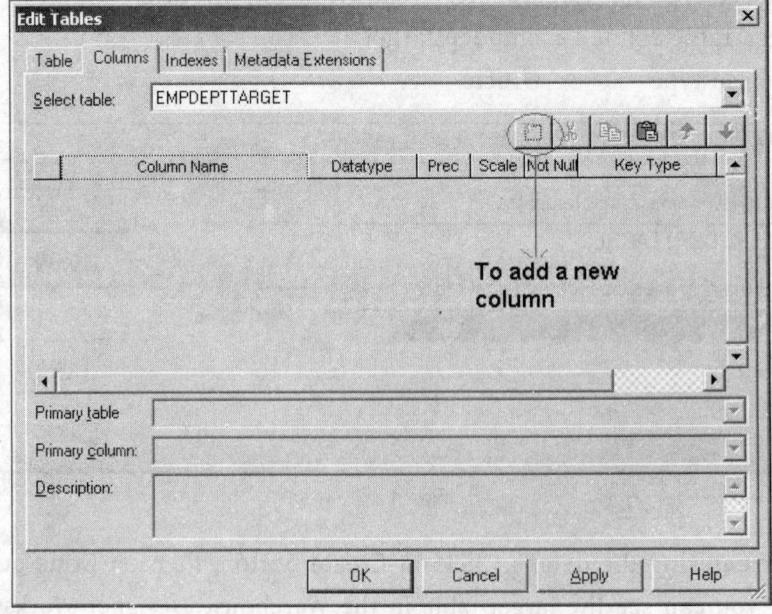

Fig. 4.19

6. Now the empty row will be displayed in the Columns tab. Enter the Column details as follows (See Fig. 4.20).

Column name	Data type	Precision	Scale	NULL not	Key type	Business name
EMPNO	Number	15	0	Yes	Primary Key	
DEPTNO	Number	15	0	No	Not a Key	
ENAME	Varchar2	25	0	No	Not a Key	
DNAME	Varchar2	25	0	No	Not a Key	
JOB	Varchar2	25	0	No	Not a Key	
MGR	Number	15	0	No	Not a Key	
HIREDATE	Date	19	0	No	Not a Key	
SAL	Number	15	0	No	Not a Key	
COMM	Number	15	0	No	Not a Key	
LOC	Varchar2	30	0	No	Not a Key	

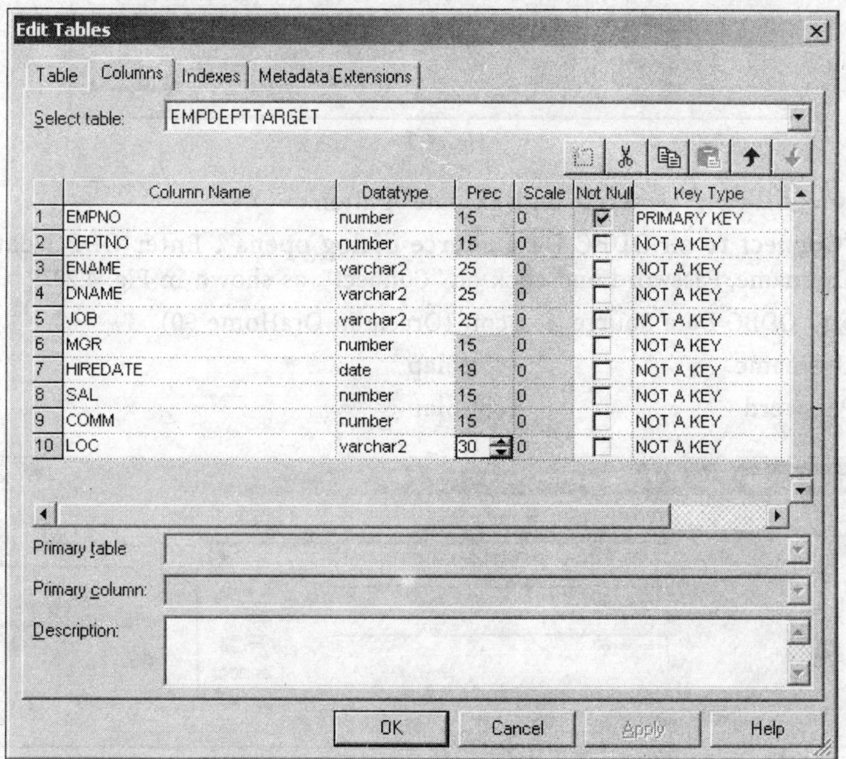

Fig. 4.20

11. Click on "Apply", then on "OK", after entering all the target Database fields.
12. Now the template for the target table is designed. To create the Target table in the Target Database, select the menu item **"Targets→Generate/Execute SQL"** from the main menu.
13. Now the **"Database Object Generation"** window opens.
14. In **"Generation objects"** group, check Create table and Primary key check boxes as shown in Fig. 4.21.

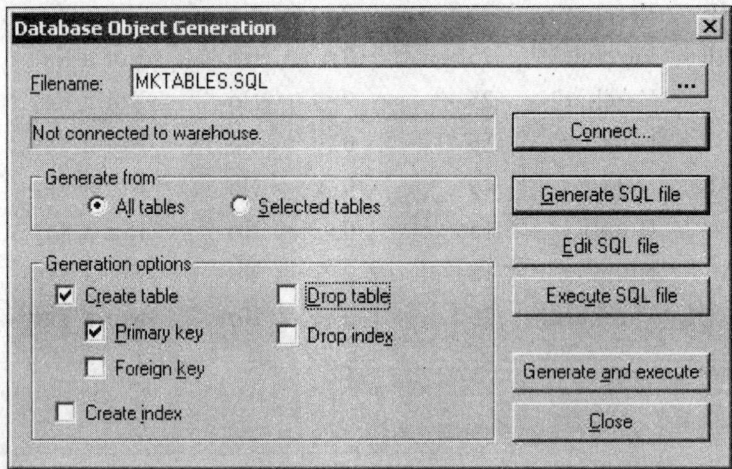

Fig. 4.21

15. Now click on "Generate and Execute" button.
16. **"Connect to an ODBC Data source dialog opens".** Enter ODBC data source, Username, Password and click on "Connect", as shown in Fig. 4.22.

e.g. ODBC Data Source : scott (Oracle in OraHome 90)

Username : scottolap

Password : scottolap

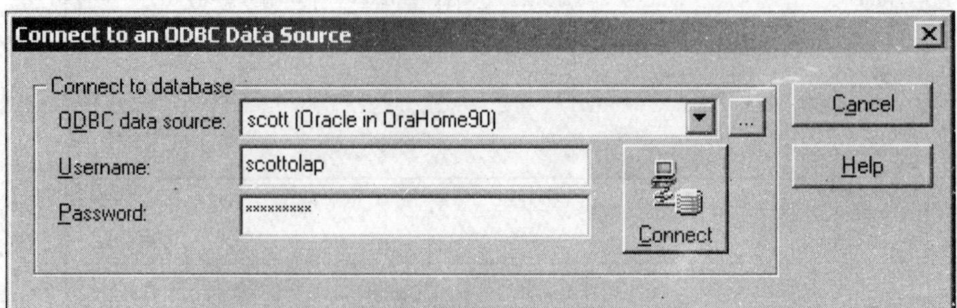

Fig. 4.22

17. A message box will pop up, with the message: "File MKTABLES.SQL already exists Do you want to overwrite the contents of this file?" Click on "OK" button.
18. Now, the Target table is created on the Target Data.

4.3.8 Mapping Designer

The Mapping Designer is used to map the flow of data from Source to Target. Here is the procedure to map our data from source to target.

1. Open the Mapping Designer by selecting **"Tools → Mapping Designer"** from the main menu. You can also open the Mapping Designer by clicking on the following icon.

Now the Mapping Designer window will open in the Workspace (Fig. 4.23).

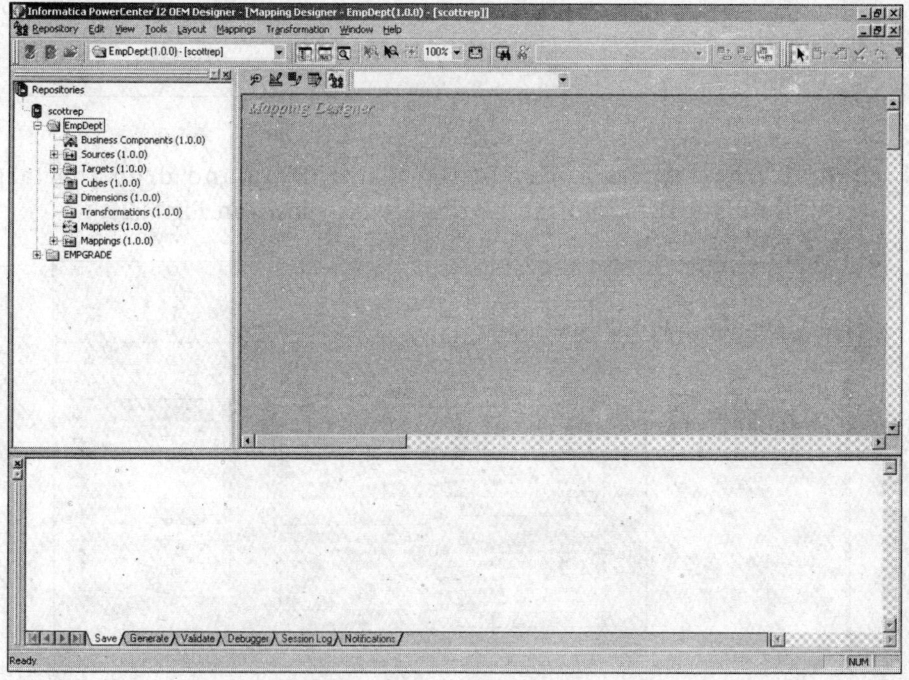

Fig. 4.23

2. From the Navigator window, explore the Source folder, drag and drop the EMP table to workspace and also drag and drop the DEPT table to workspace.
3. By default two source qualifiers are created for both EMP and DEPT table as shown in Fig. 4.24.

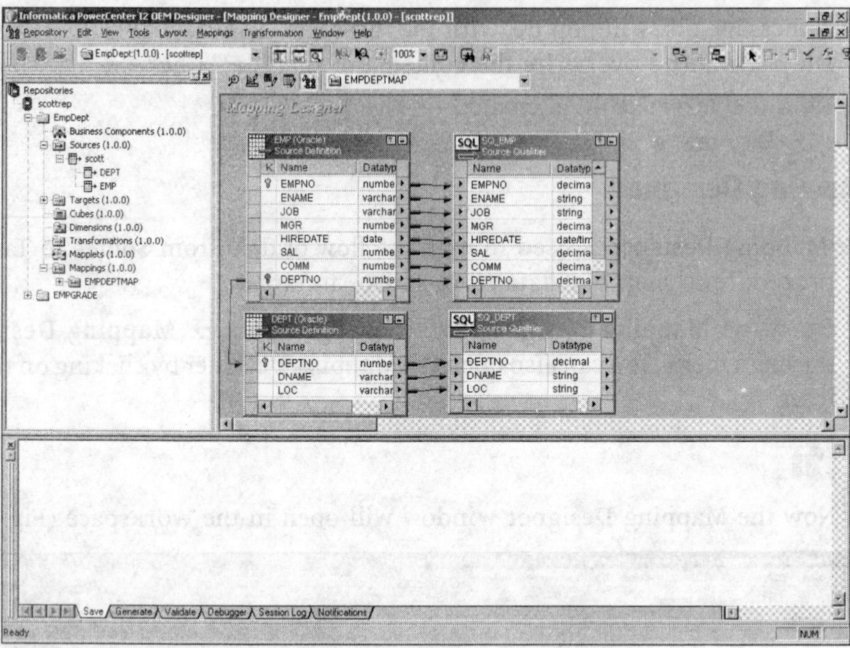

Fig. 4.24

4. Explore the Targets folder in Navigator, Drag and drop the target table (EMPDEPTTARGET) into the Workspace, as shown in Fig. 4.25.

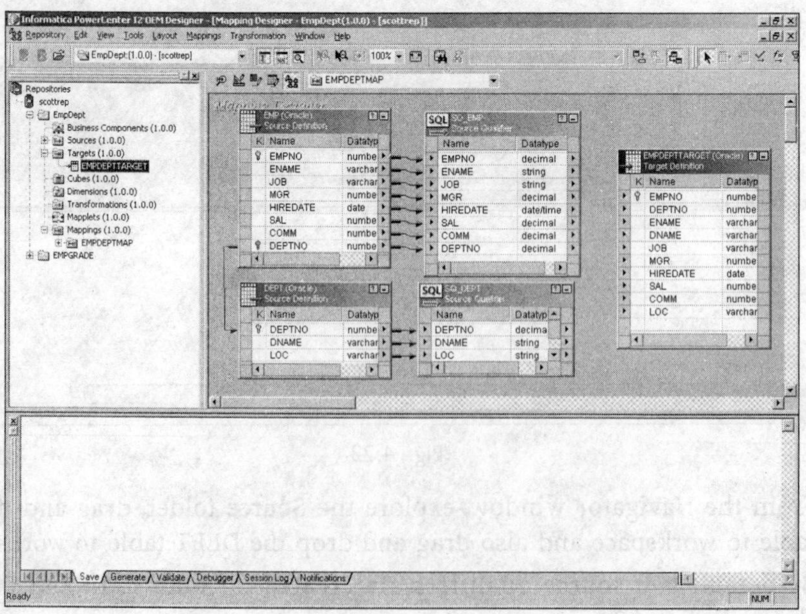

Fig. 4.25

5. Now we have to join both EMP and DEPT tables by using the join condition EMP.DEPTNO=DEPT.DEPTNO. The Source Qualifier can also be used as a joiner to join the data. Now as we are having two separate Source Qualifiers for both EMP and DEPT tables, we have to remove the DEPT Source Qualifier from the Mapping Designer.

   Select the DEPT Source Qualifier, and press the Delete button from the keyboard. "All selected Transformations will be deleted. Continue?" message will be displayed in the warning message box and click "OK" for this. Now drag each column of the DEPT source table in the Mapping Designer Workspace into the Source Qualifier of the EMP table.

6. Drag and drop each column of the source qualifier to respective columns of the target definition, as shown in Fig. 4.26.

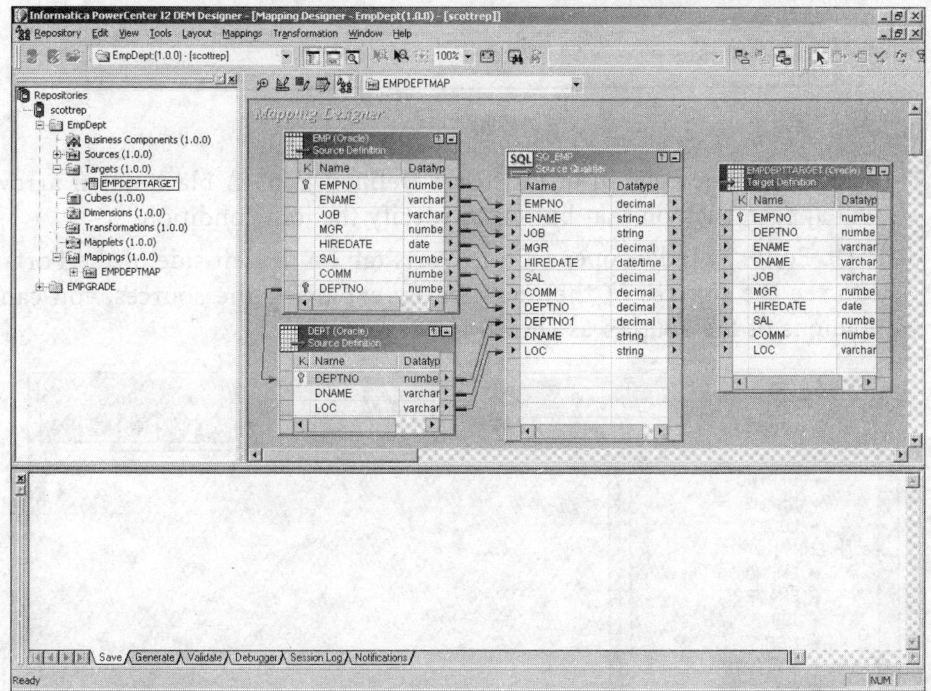

Fig. 4.26

7. Double click on the SQ_EMP source qualifier to go to Edit Transformations.
8. **"Edit Transformations"** window opens. Go to properties tab to add a join condition, as shown in Fig. 4.27.

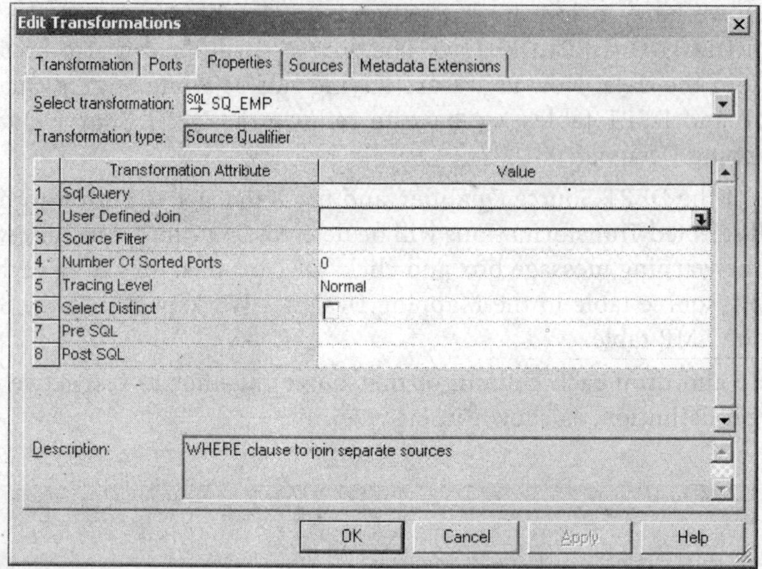

Fig. 4.27

9. Select the value column of the **"User Defined Join"**. A black down arrow button will appear, click on that button to specify the join condition.
10. "SQL Editor" window opens. Go to Ports tab on the left side of the Ports tab, you can see the sources of the qualifier. By exploring the sources, you can see the columns of the sources as shown in Fig.4.28.

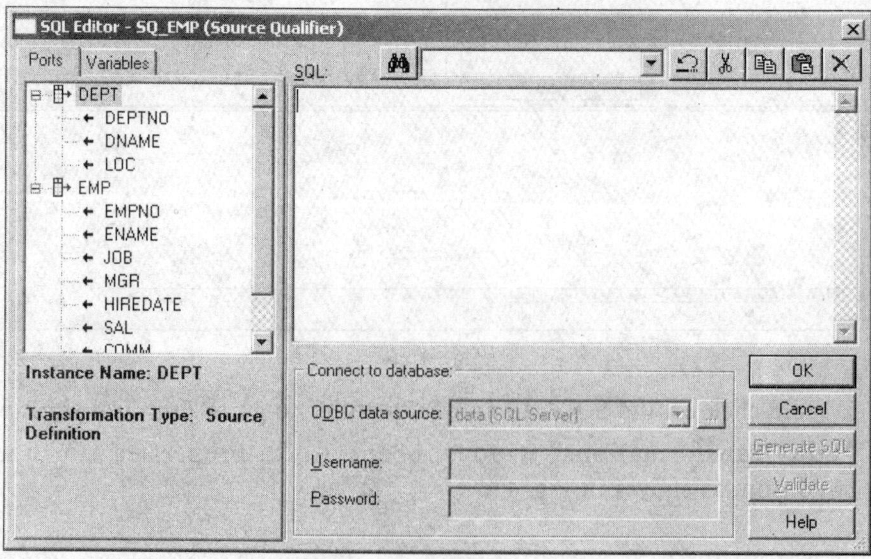

Fig. 4.28

11. Double click on the **DEPTNO** column of EMP table. EMP.DEPTNO will appear in the edit box provided on the right side. Place an **"="** symbol in the edit box and double click on the DEPTNO column of DEPT table. Now the complete join condition will appear as shown in Fig. 4.29.

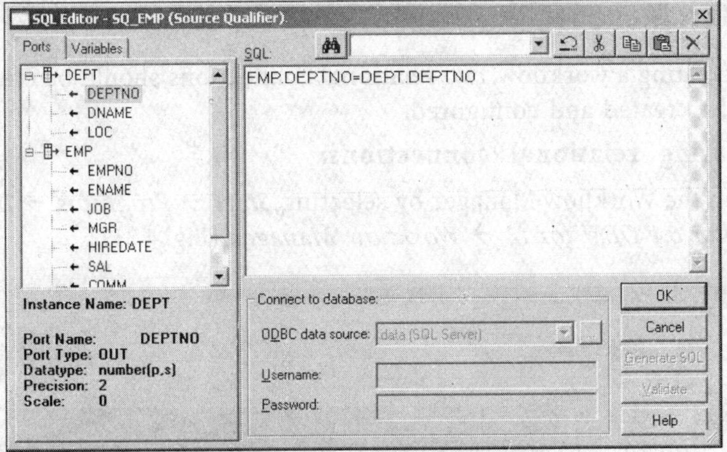

Fig. 4.29

12. Click on "OK" button to close the SQL Editor.
13. Click on "apply" then on "OK" button.
14. Now map the required columns from Source Qualifier to Target table as shown in Fig. 4.30.

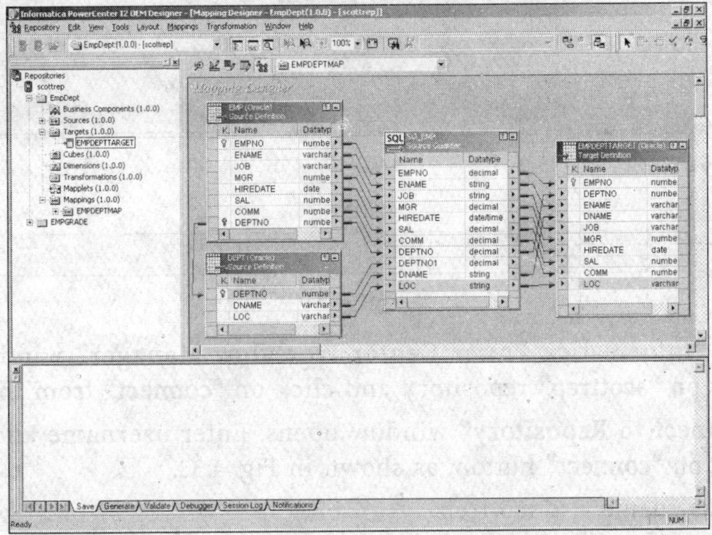

Fig. 4.30

15. Now the Mappings must be validated. To validate the Mappings, go to **"Mappings → Validate"** of the main menu.
16. After validating the Mappings, save the mappings: *RepositoryàSave.*

4.3.9 Workflow Manager

Before creating a workflow, two relational connections should be created and a server should be created and configured.

(I) Creating relational connections:

1. Open the Workflow Manager by selecting *Start → Programs → Informatica Power Center 6.1 OEM for i2 → Workflow Manager.* (Fig. 4.31).

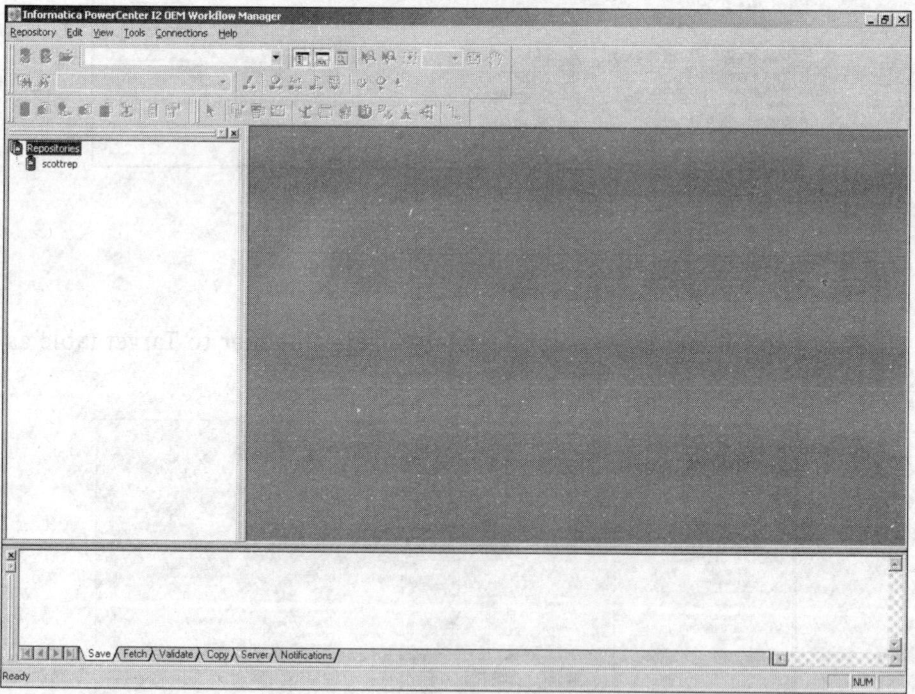

Fig. 4.31

2. The **"Informatica Power Center Workflow Manager"** window opens, right click on **"scottrep"** repository and click on **"connect"** from the popup menu.
3. **"Connect to Repository"** window opens. Enter username and password and click on **"connect"** button, as shown in Fig. 4.32.

   E.g. username : scottrep

   Password : scottrep

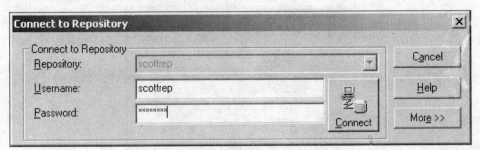

Fig. 4.32

4. Select the menu item **"Connections → Relational"**, **"Relational Connection Browser"** window, shown in Fig. 4.33, opens.

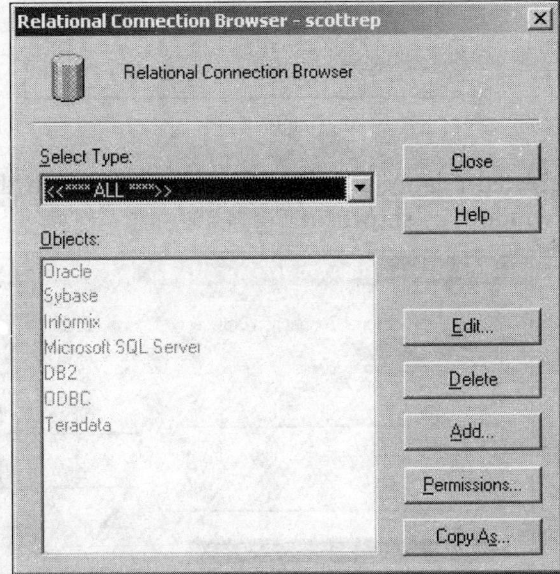

Fig. 4.33

5. Click on **"Add"** button to add a new connection. **"Select Subtype"** dialog opens. In this dialog, select the type as **"Oracle"** and click on **"OK"** button.
6. **"Connection Object Definition"** window opens. Enter the name, Username, Password and Connect String and click on **"OK"** button, as shown in Fig. 4.34.

   Name : scottsource
   Username : scott
   Password : tiger
   Connect String : oemrep

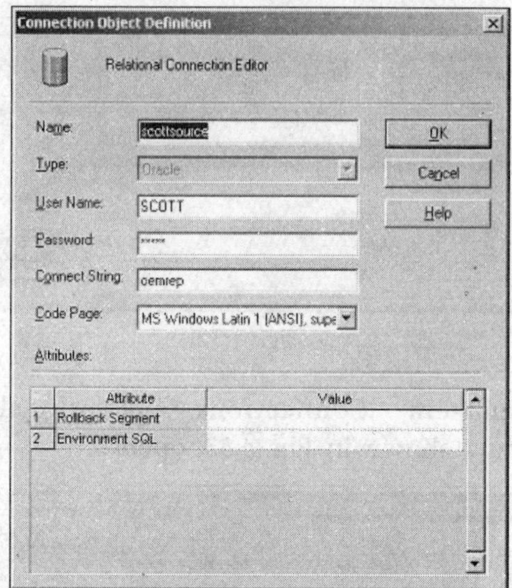

Fig. 4.34

7. Now the created relational connection is displayed in the "Relational Connection Browser" window, as shown in Fig. 4.35.

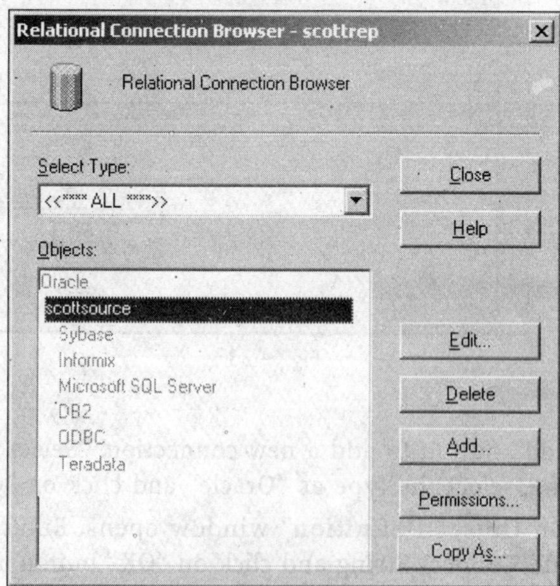

Fig. 4.35

8. Repeat the process from step (5) to create the relational target connection, as shown in Fig. 4.36.

The Target connection details are as follows:

Name : scotttarget

Username : scottolap

Password : scottolap

Connect String : oemrep

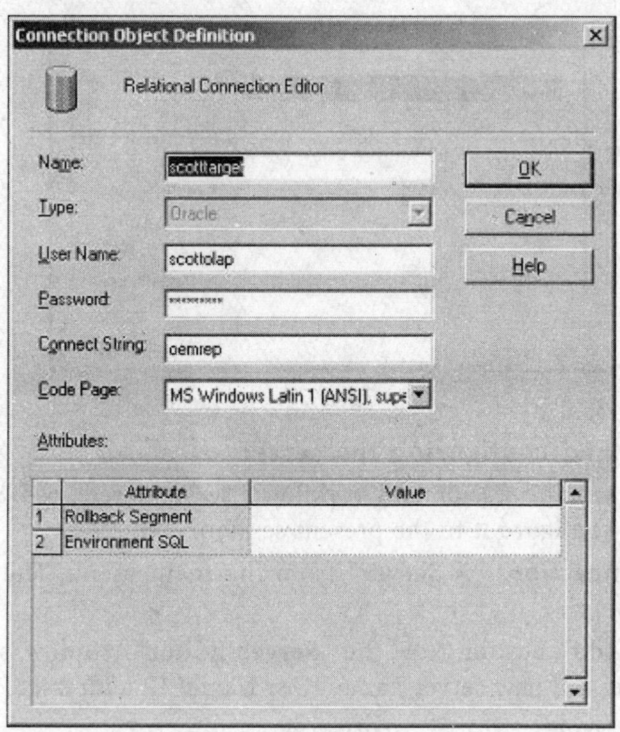

Fig. 4.36

9. Click on **"Close"** button of **"Relational Connection Browser"** after creating the source and target relational connections, as shown in Fig. 4.37.

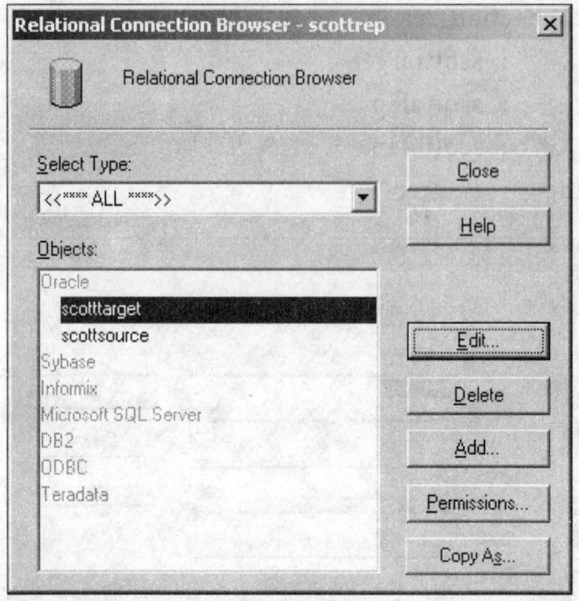

Fig. 4.37

(II) Creating and configuring the server:

1. In order to run the session and workflow a server is required. So we must create a server and configure it to the present session.
2. Select **"Connections → Server"** from the main menu. The **"Server Browser"** window opens.
3. Click on **"Add"** button. Now the **"Server Editor"** window, shown in Fig. 4.38, opens. Enter the new server name, Host Name/ IP address, $PMRootDir values.

E.g. Server Name	:	scottserver
Host Name/IP Address	:	icssrv2k3
$PMRootDir	:	"C:\Program Files\Informatica\Informatica PowerCenter 6.1 OEM for i2 - Server"

4. Now click on **"Resolve Server"** button to resolve the server.
5. Click on **"OK"** button.

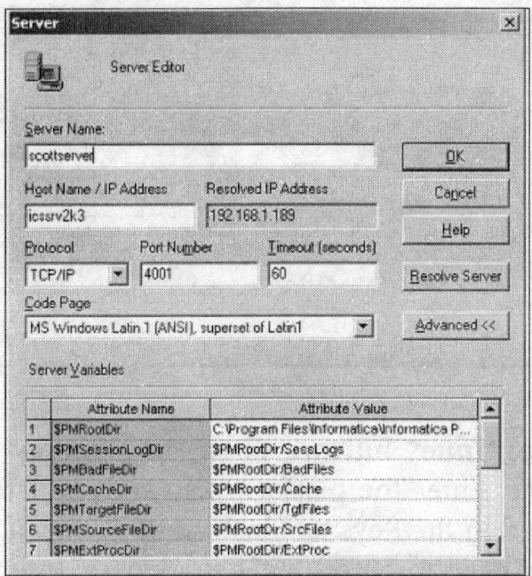

Fig. 4.38

6. The newly created server will be added to the **"Server Browser"** window, as shown in Fig. 4.39.
7. Click on **"Close"** button.

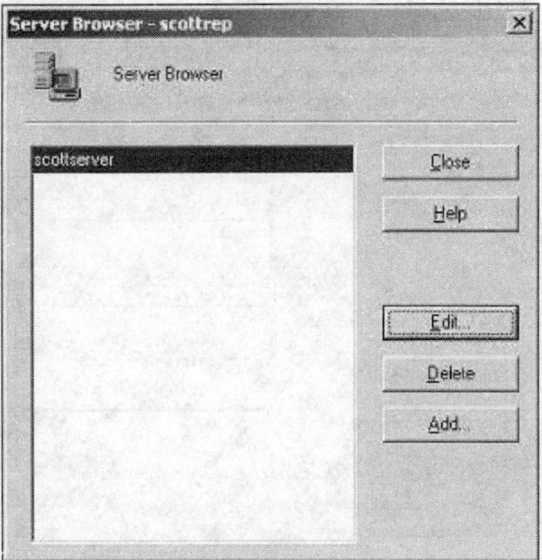

Fig. 4.39

8. The created server will be added to your repository and will be displayed in the repository navigator.
9. To configure the server, the steps are as follows:
   a) Select ***"Start→ Programs→ Informatica Server→ Informatica Server Setup"*** to open the server setup. Now the **"Informatica Server Setup Application – Options"** window will be displayed (Fig.4.40):

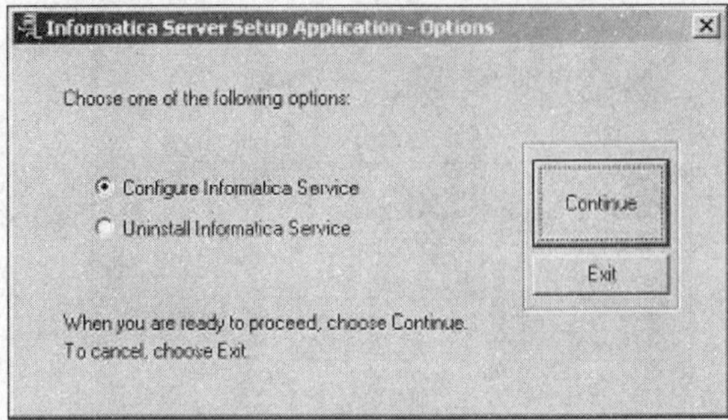

Fig. 4.40

b) Click on **"Continue"** button. Then the window **"Configure Informatica Service"** opens. Enter the platform key and the Oracle key in the text entry boxes provided in the Keys tab. Instead of Oracle, if you are using some other database, you need to enter that Key (Sybase, Informix, Microsoft SQL, DB2, ODBC or Teradata).

c) Go to server tab in the same window (shown in Fig. 4.41) and enter the Server Name,TCP/IP Host Address e.g.

Server Name : scottserver

TCP/IP Host Address : icssrv2k3.

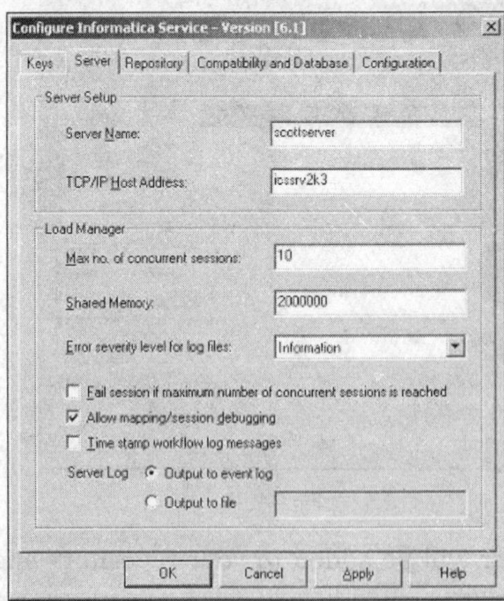

Fig. 4.41

d) Go to Repository tab (Fig. 4.42) and enter the Repository Name, Repository User, Repository Password, Repository Server Host Name and Repository Port Number. Click on **"Apply"** button and then on **"OK"** button.

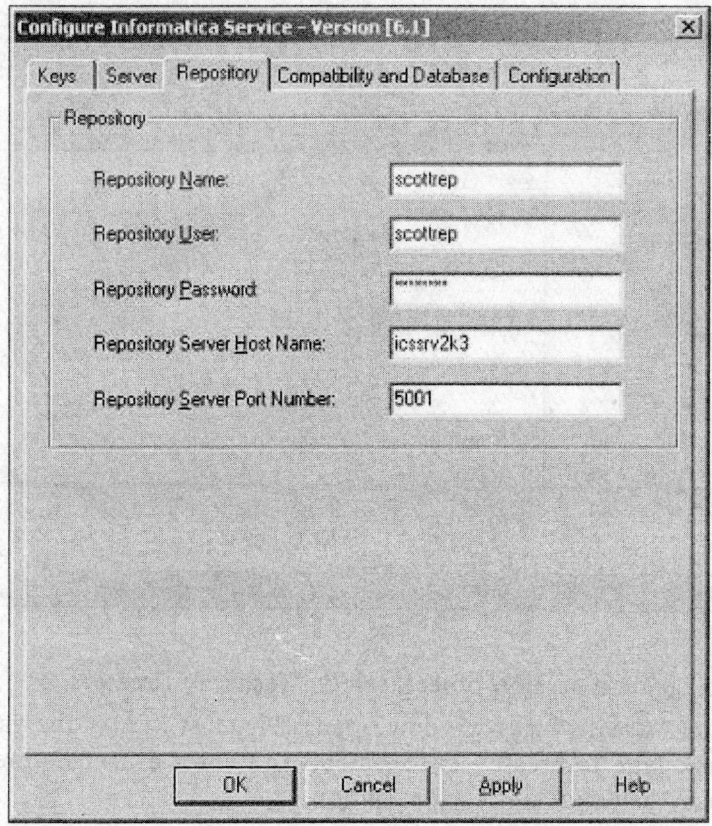

Fig. 4.42

e) **"Informatica Server Setup Application - Options"** window will open, click on **"Exit"** button.

f) Now the server is configured successfully.

10. After this, start the Informatica service from the "Services" window. To start the service, select **"Star → Administrator Tools → Services"**. In this **"Services"** window select **"Informatica"** service, right click on it and select **"Start"** from the popup menu.

(III) Defining Tasks:

1. To define the task, a session object must be created. Before creating a session, select the folder **"EMPDEPT"** and click on **"Tools → Task Developer"**.
2. **"Task Developer"** window opens in the workspace, as shown in Fig. 4.43.

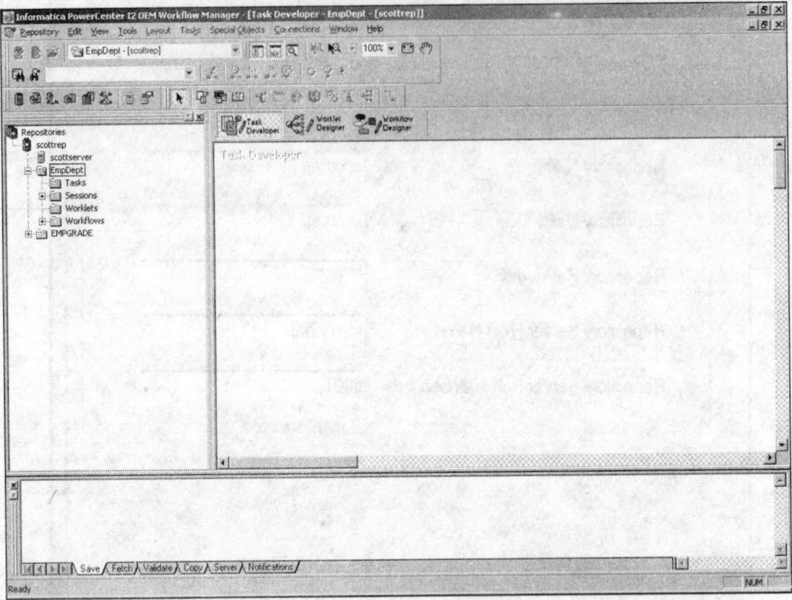

Fig. 4.43

3. To create a session object, select **"Tasks → Create"**.
4. Now **"Create Task"** window opens (Fig. 4.44). Enter the values **"Select the task type to create"** as **"Session"** and enter a user-defined name for the task, then click on "Create" button e.g.

   Select the task type to create : Session

   Enter a new name for this task : EMPDEPTSESSION.

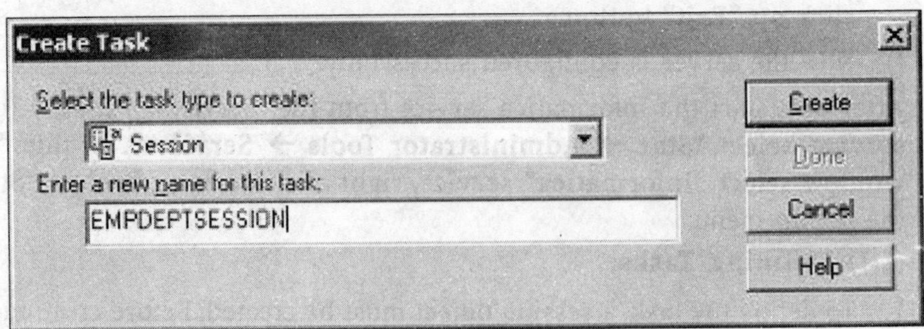

Fig. 4.44

5. The "Mappings" window opens (Fig. 4.45). You need to select the mapping which was created in "Designer" tool.

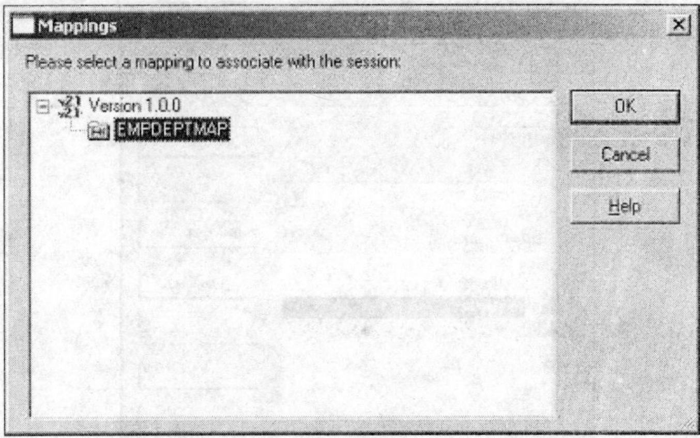

Fig. 4.45

6. Click on **"OK"** button, and on **"Done"** button of **"Create Task"** dialog.
7. Double click on the created session (EMPDEPTSESSION).
8. **"Edit Tasks"** window opens (Fig. 4.46), go to sources tab.
9. In the **"Value"** column, click on the Down Arrow button.

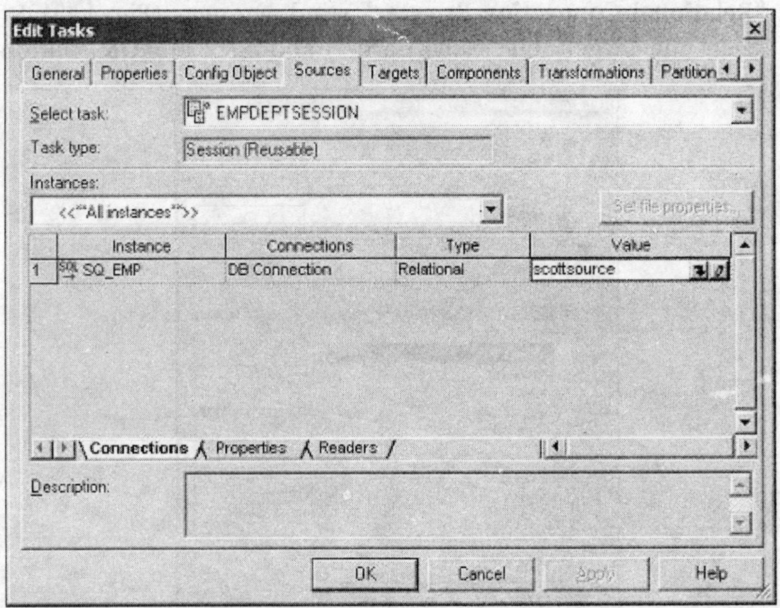

Fig. 4.46

10. **"Relational Connection Browser"** window, shown in Fig. 4.47, opens. Select the source relational connection. In our example, select the **"scottsource"** and click on **"OK"** button.

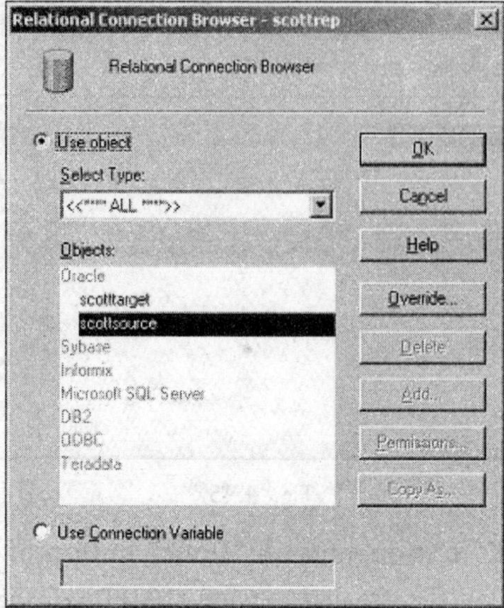

Fig. 4.47

11. Go to Targets tab and again select the Down arrow button of Values column.
12. **"Relational Connection Browser"** window opens (Fig. 4.48). In this window, select the Target object (scotttarget) and click on **"OK"** button.

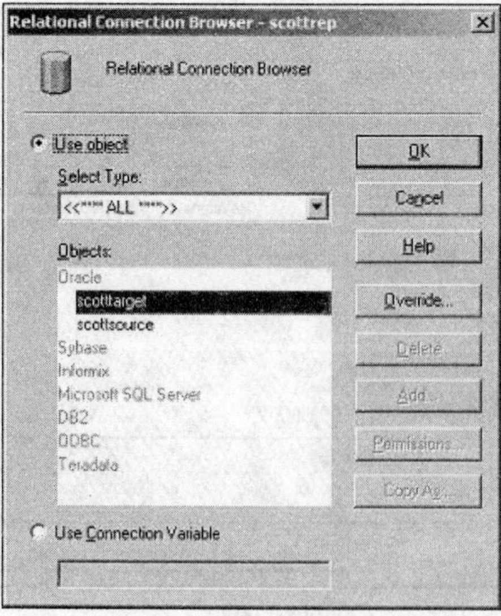

Fig. 4.48

13. In the Target tab, select the **"Properties"** tab located at the bottom.
14. Change the value of the **"Target Load Type"** as **"Normal"**. See Fig. 4.49.

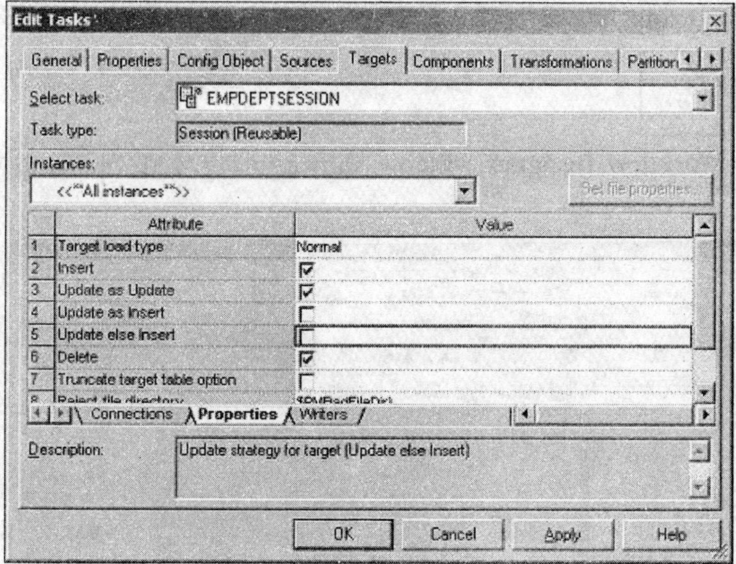

Fig. 4.49

15. Click on **"Apply"**, and on **"OK"** button. Then the task developer workspace appears as shown in Fig. 4.50.
16. Save the task by selecting **"Repository → Save"**.

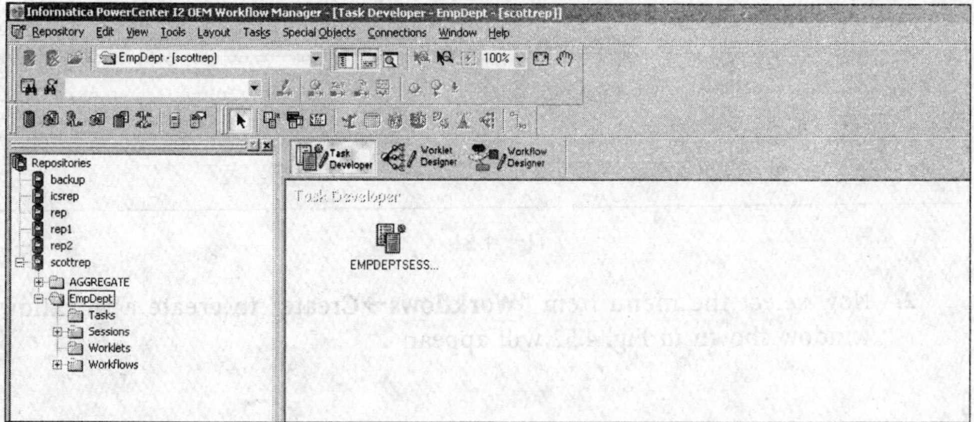

Fig. 4.50

17. To validate the session, select the task which is created and select the menu item **"Tasks→ Validate"**.

(IV) Creating a Workflow

1. Select the menu item **"Tools→Workflow Designer"**. You can also select the

following icon to open Workflow workspace.

Now the **Workflow Designer** window, shown in Fig. 4.51, opens in Workspace.

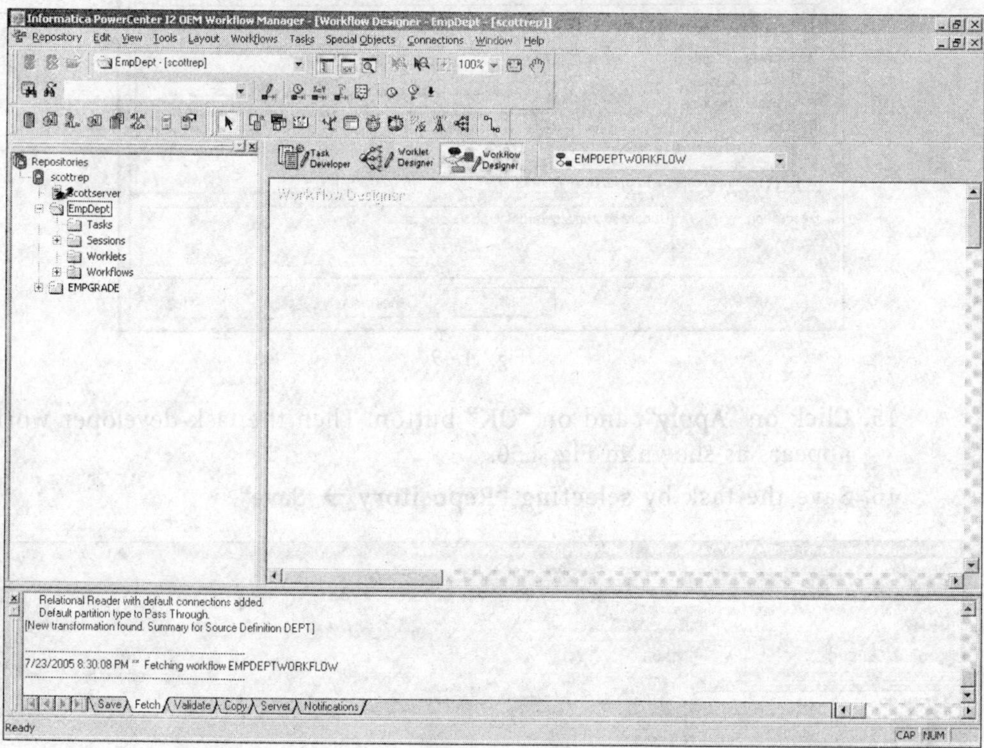

Fig. 4.51

2. Now select the menu item **"Workflows→Create"** to create a workflow. The window shown in Fig. 4.52 will appear.

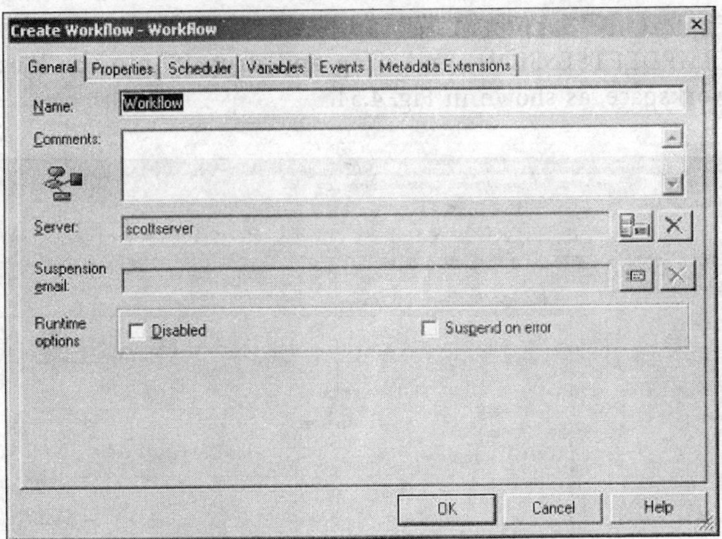

Fig. 4.52

3. In General tab, enter the name of workflow.

   e.g. Name: EMPDEPTWORKFLOW.

4. Click on **"OK"** button. Before clicking on **"OK"** button, check whether the server name is there in the server edit box or not. If not, configure the server and then start the server. In this example, the Server name is automatically assigned because we configured and started the server in previous steps. The screen will be as shown in Fig. 4.53.

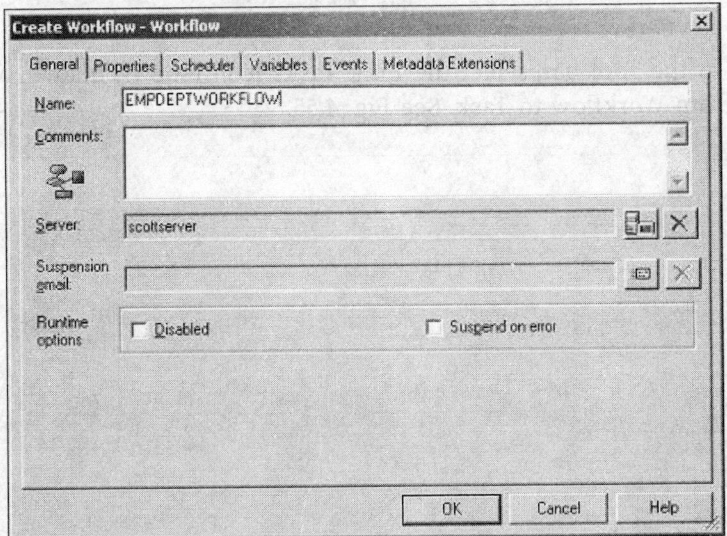

Fig. 4.53

5. Explore the Sessions folder from the Navigator, select the created session (EMPDEPTSESSION) and drag and drop it into the Workflow Designer workspace, as shown in Fig. 4.54.

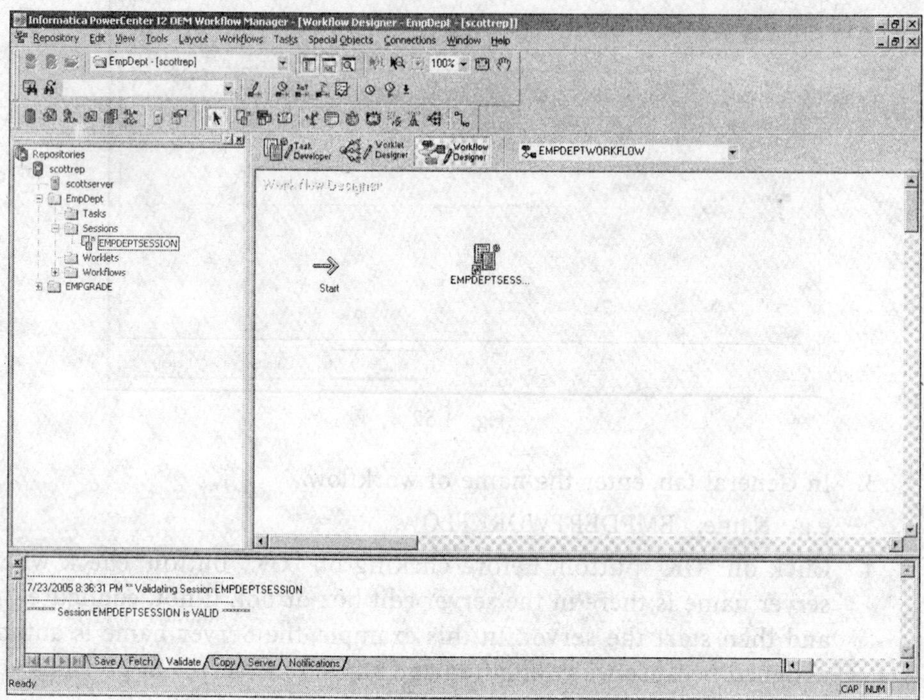

Fig. 4.54

6. In the Tool bar, select the Link Tasks icon (shown below), and drag the link from Workflow to Task. See Fig. 4.55.

Fig. 4.55

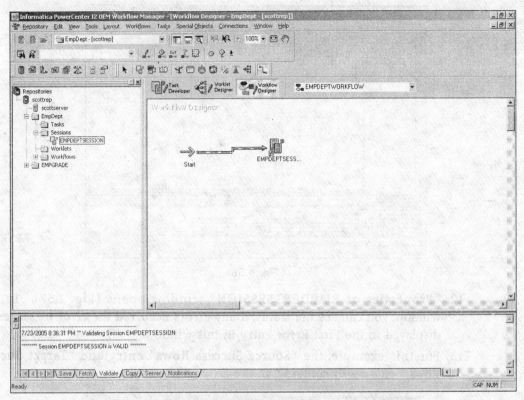

7. Save the workflow by selecting **"Repository→Save".**
8. To start workflow, select the menu item **"Workflow → Start Workflow".**
9. **"Work flow Monitor"** icon will appear on the System Tray.

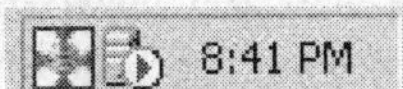

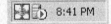

10 Open the **"Workflow Monitor"** by double clicking on it.

11. Now you can see the status of our workflow. If the Workflow is successful, **"EMPDEPTSESSION"** and **"EMPDEPTWORKFLOW"** are shown in the Succeeded part. To view how many rows got transferred from source to target, double click on the **"EMPDEPTSESSION"** (Fig. 4.56).

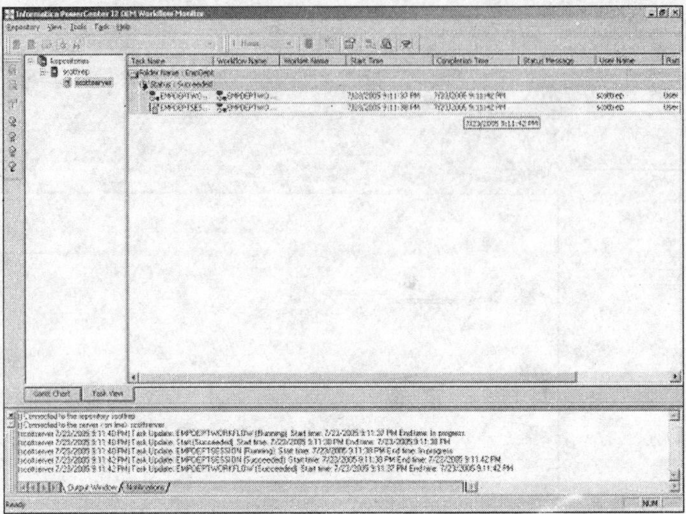

Fig. 4.56

12. **"Properties of EMPDEPTSESSION"** window opens (Fig. 4.57). In this window, you can see the status, if any errors occurred the error messages are displayed in the First Error entry in this window.
13. For this example, the **"Source Success Rows"** entry and **"Target Success Rows."** entry will contain 14.

Properties of EMPDEPTSESSION

Properties | Transformation Statistics

Attribute Name	Attribute Value
Instance Name	EMPDEPTSESSION
Task Name	Session
Task Type	Session
Start Time	7/23/2005 9:11:38 PM
End Time	7/23/2005 9:11:42 PM
Status	Succeeded
Status Message	
Deleted	No
********************	********************
Mapping Name	EMPDEPTMAP
Log File Name	C:\Program Files\Informatica\Informat...
Source Success Rows	14
Source Failed Rows	0
Target Success Rows	14
Target Failed Rows	0
Total Transformation Err...	0
First Error Code	0
First Error	No errors encountered.

OK Help

Fig. 4.57

We have successfully completed the workflow of transferring the sources rows from EMP and DEPT table by joining the two tables and moving the successful rows to the target table **"scottolap"**.

4.3.10 Checking the Output

To see whether the target rows have been dumped into the target table, connect to the target table in the target database using the following SQL statements.

SQL syntax: *connect <username>/<password>*
e.g. SQL> connect scottolap/scottolap; Connected.

To see the rows of the target table, use the following SQL statement.

SQL syntax: select * from <table name>;
e.g. SQL> select count(*) from empdepttarget; 14

4.4 Aggregator Transformation

Aggregator transformation givees summary reports. We will now study an aggregator transformation, SUM. This transformation is used to obtain the total monthly expenditure, department-wise, based on the individual salaries and the departments to which the employees belong.

To start with, create a separate folder for this task in Repository Manager tool.

Creating a Folder

1. Open the Repository Manager.

   Start→ Programs→ Informatica Power center 6.1 OEM for i2→ Repository Manager

   Informatica Repository Manager window, shown in Fig. 4.58, gets displayed.

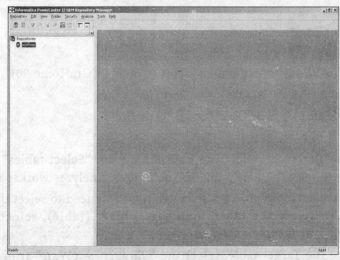

Fig. 4.58

2. Explore Repositories and select the repository, **"scottrep"**, right click on it and select **"Connect"** from the pop up menu.
3. Create a new folder in the selected Repository by selecting the menu item: ***"Create → Folder"***.
4. Enter the name for the folder from the popped up dialog box and click on **"OK"** button.

   e.g.: Folder name: AGGREGATE
5. The folder is created. Now we have to work on Designer tool to create mapping.

Designer Tool

In the Designer Tool, select the source database object and target database object and select the transformation as Aggregator. The source database object can be selected using the Source Analyzer and the target database object can be selected using the Warehouse Designer.

Procedure to select the source database object is as follows:

1. To work with the Source Analyzer, first we need to open the Informatica Designer Tool. Open the Designer tool:

   Start→ Programs→ Informatica Power center 6.1 OEM for i2 → Designer.
2. Connect to the repository (scottrep) by entering the username and password.
3. Now, select the folder "AGGREGATE" and select the menu item ***"Tools → Source Analyzer"***.
4. To import the source table, select the menu item ***"Sources → Import from database"***.
5. **"Import tables"** window opens. Enter the ODBC data source, username, owner name and password.

   e.g. : ODBC Data source name: scott (Oracle in OraHome 90)

   User name : scott

   Owner name : SCOTT

   Password : tiger
6. Click on **"Connect"**, select the EMP table from **"Select tables"** list and click on **"OK"** to import the EMP table to the Source Analyzer workspace.
7. The source database object is selected. Now you need to select the target database object. To select the target database object (table), select the menu item ***"Tools→ Warehouse Designer"***.
8. To create the Target table, select the ***"Targets → Create"*** from the main menu.

9. **"Create Target Table"** window opens. Enter the Target Table name and select the Database type for Target table.

   e.g.: Target Table Name: AGGREGATETARGET

   Database type: Oracle
10. After entering these details, click on **"Create"** and then click on **"Done"**.
11. You can now see the target table in the Warehouse Designer Workspace without any Fields.
12. To enter the fields of the target table, double-click on it.
13. **"Edit Table"** window opens. In Edit Tables window, go to **"Columns"** tab.
14. To enter the New Fields, click on the following icon:

15. The empty row will be displayed in the Columns tab. Now enter the Column details as shown in Fig. 4.59.

Column name	Data Type	Precision Name	Scale	NULL Not	Key Type	Business
deptno	number	15	0	No	Not a Key	
salaries	number(p,s)	10	2	No	Not a Key	

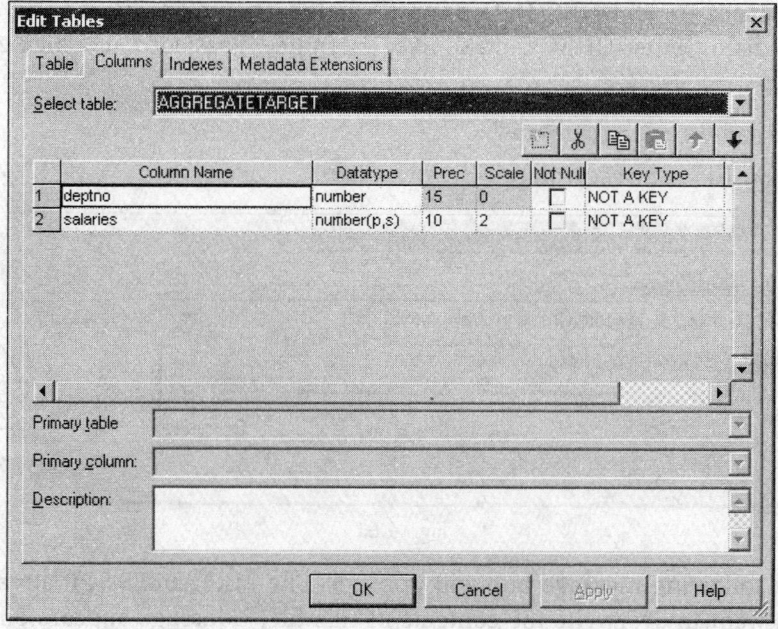

Fig. 4.59

16. Click on **"Apply"**, then on **"OK"**, after entering the target table fields.
17. The template for the target table is designed. To create the Target table in the Target Database, select the menu item "***Targets → Generate/Execute SQL***" from the main menu.
18. The **"Database Object Generation"** window opens. In **"Generation option"** group select the "***Create table***" check box as shown in Fig. 4.60

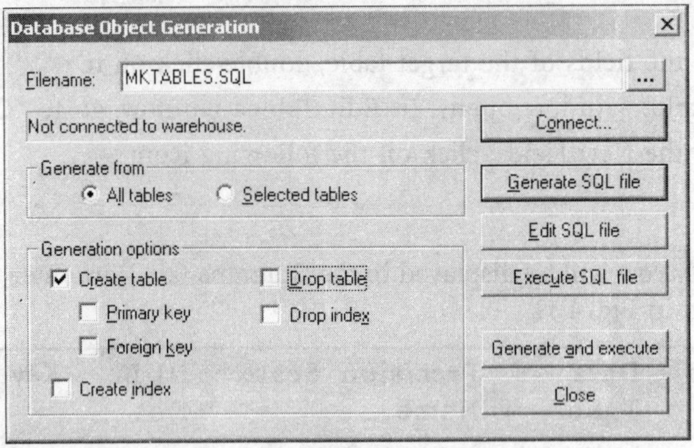

Fig. 4.60

19. Now click on **"Generate and execute"** button.
20. **"Connect to an ODBC Data source"** dialog shown in Fig. 4.61 is displayed. In this dialog, enter ODBC Data source, Username, Password and click on "***Connect***".

    e.g.: ODBC Data Source: scott

    Username : scottolap

    Password : scottolap

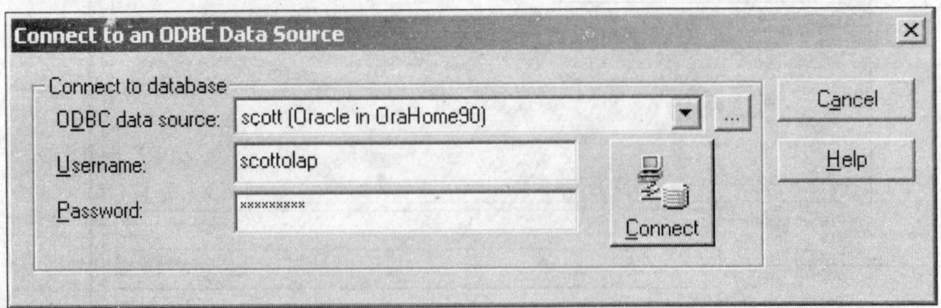

Fig. 4.61

21. The following message box will pop up: "File MKTABLES.SQL already exists, Do you want to overwrite the contents of this file?" Massage appears on screen. Click on **"OK"**.

22. The Target table is now created in the Target Database.

Mapping Designer

The Mapping Designer is used to map the flow of data from Source to Target. Here is the procedure to map our data from source to target.

1. Open the Mapping Designer by selecting "***Tools → Mapping Designer***" from the main menu. "Mapping Name" window opens. Enter a name for the new mapping.

   e.g.: New Mapping Name: AGGREGATORMAP
2. The **Mapping Designer** window will open in the workspace.
3. From the Navigator window, explore the Source folder, drag and drop the EMP table to workspace. By default a source qualifier is also created for the EMP table as shown in Fig. 4.62.

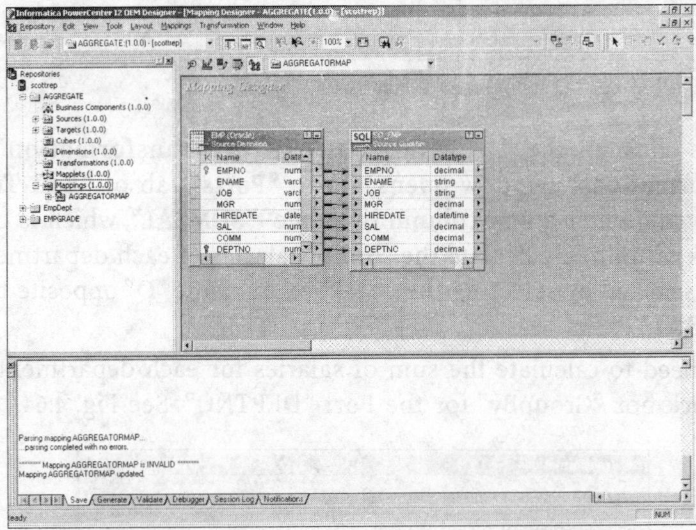

Fig. 4.62

4. Drag and drop the target table **"AGGREGATETARGET"** from the Navigator to Mapping Designer Workspace.
5. Select the Transformation of type "Aggregator" by selecting the menu item "***Transformation → Create***" to create the new transformation.
6. **"Create Transformation"** window opens. Select the "Type of transformation to create" as Aggregator and the name of transformation to create as **"AGGREGATORTRANS"**.
7. Click on **"Create"**, then on **"Done"**.
8. Drag and drop the DEPTNO, SAL columns of EMP Source Qualifier to

AGGREGATORTRANS. After dragging the respective columns, the workspace appears as shown in Fig. 4.63.

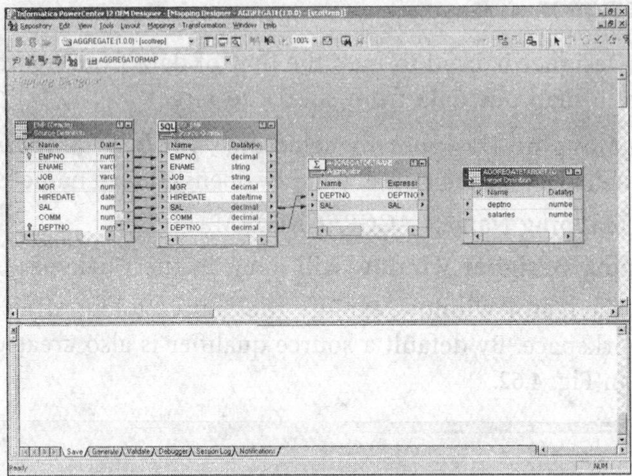

Fig. 4.63

9. Double click on the **"AGGREGATORTRANS"** transformation, then the **"Edit Transformations"** window opens. Go to **"Ports"** tab of **"Edit Transformations"** window and enter a new column by name **"SUMSAL"**, which is only out port, we use this column to calculate the sum of salaries of each department. The out port can be selected by selecting the checkbox by name "O" opposite to the Port Name **"SUMSAL"**.
10. As we need to calculate the sum of salaries for each department, we must select the check box "GroupBy" for the Port "DEPTNO". See Fig. 4.64.

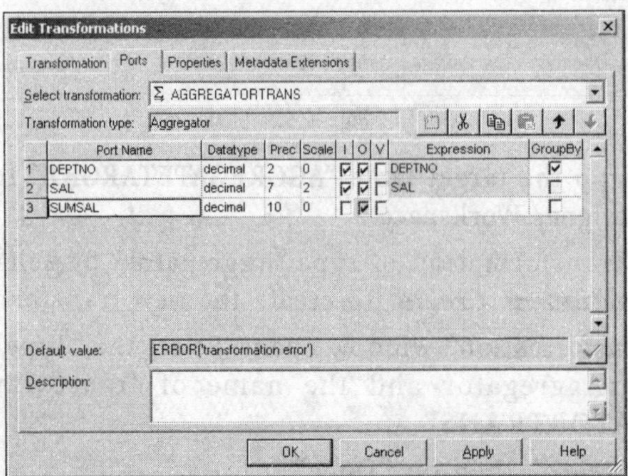

Fig. 4.64

11. To calculate the sum of the salaries, we need to add an expression to **"SUMSAL"** Port.
12. To write the expression, click on the **"Expression"** column opposite to the Port **"SUMSAL"**. Now a black down arrow button appears in the Expression column, click on that.
13. **"Expression Editor"** window opens, go to **"Functions"** tab and explore "Aggregate" folder (where all the aggregator functions are located)
14. Double click on the **"SUM"** function, then the screen looks as shown in Fig. 4.65.

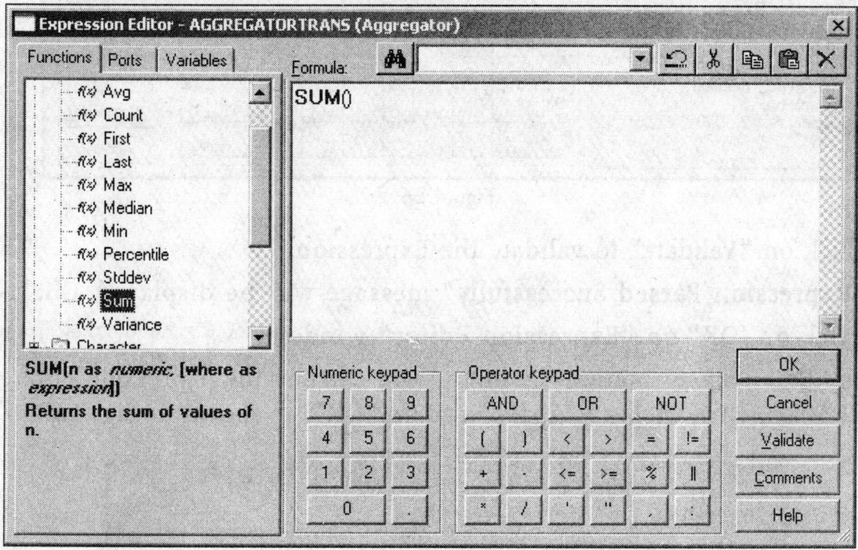

Fig. 4.65

15. Place the cursor between the two brackets of the SUM function and go to **"Ports"** tab.
16. Explore the AGGREGATORTRANS, so that we can see the IN Ports of Aggregator Transformation.
17. Double click on the **"SAL"** sub item (port), and then the screen will be as shown in **Fig. 4.66.**

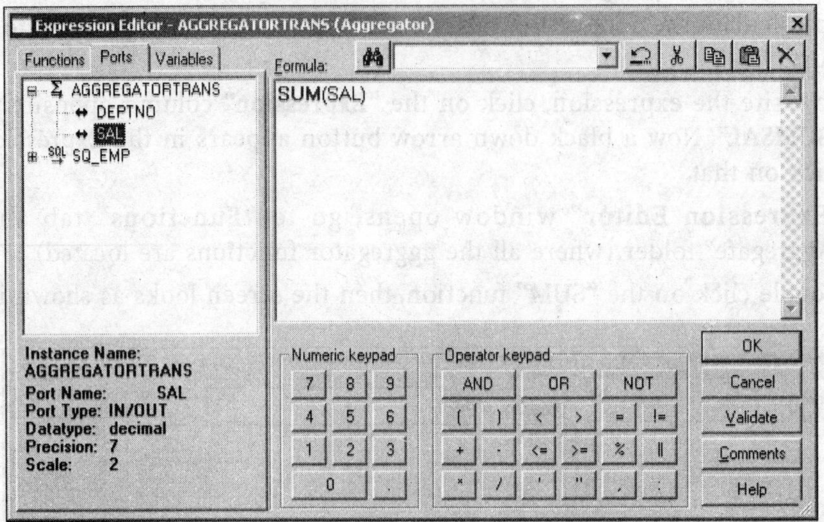

Fig. 4.66

18. Click on **"Validate"** to validate the Expression.
19. **"Expression Parsed Successfully"** message will be displayed. Click on **"OK"**.
20. Click on **'OK"** on **"Expression Editor"** window.
21. In **"Edit Transformations"** window, you can see the expression entered for the SUMSAL Port, click on **"Apply"** and on **"OK"**, as shown in Fig. 4.67.

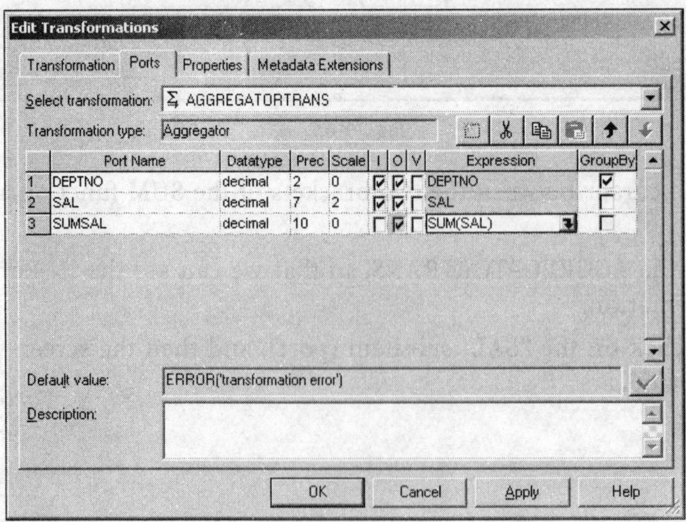

Fig. 4.67

22. In Mapping Designer Workspace, drag and drop the DEPTNO, SUMSAL columns to target table, then the complete mapping appears as shown in Fig. 4.68.

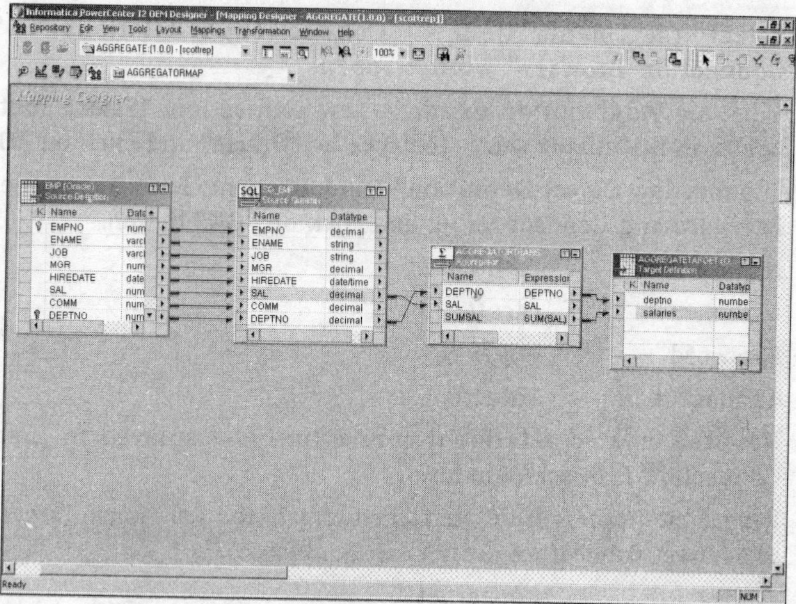

Fig. 4.68

23. Validate the Mapping by selecting the menu item "***Mappings→Validate***".
24. If the Mapping is valid, save the Mapping to Repository: Repository→Save.

Workflow Manager

Before creating a workflow, two relational connections should be created and a server should be configured and executed.

1. Creating relational connections

1. Open the Workflow Manager by selecting: **Start→ Programs→ Informatica Power center 6.1 OEM for i2→ Workflow Manager.**
2. **"Informatica Power Center Workflow Manager"** window opens, right click on **"scottrep"** repository and click on **"Connect"** from the popup menu.
3. **"Connect to Repository"** window opens, in this window enter username and password and click on **"Connect"** button.

   e.g.: Username : scottrep

   Password : scottrep

4. Select the menu item **"Connections→ Relational"**, **"Relational Connection Browser"** window opens.
5. Click on **"Add"** button to add a new connection. **"Select Subtype"** dialog opens, in this dialog select the type as **"Oracle"** and click on **"OK"** button.
6. **"Connection Object Definition"** window opens. Enter the name, Username, Password and Connect String and click on **"OK"** button.

   Name : scottsource

   User name : scott

   Password : tiger

   Connect String : oemrep
7. Now the created relational connection is displayed in the "Relational Connection Browser" window.
8. Repeat the process from step (5) to create the Relational Target connection. The Target connection details are as follows:

   Name : scotttarget

   Username : scottolap

   Password : scottolap

   Connect String : oemrep
9. Click on **"Close"** button of **"Relational Connection Browser"** after creating the source and target relational connections.

(II) Configuring the server

To configure the server, the procedure is as follows:

1. Select **"Start → Programs → Informatica Server → Informatica Server Setup"** to open the server setup. **"Informatica Server Setup Application – Options"** window will be displayed.
2. Click on **"Continue"** button. **"Configure Informatica Service"** window opens in which you have to input the license keys: Platform key, Oracle database key, MS SQL key and ODBC key. You can obtain these keys from your system administrator.
3. Go to Server tab on the "Configure Informatica Service" window and enter the Server Name, TCP/IP Host Address.

   e.g.: Server Name: scottserver

   TCP/IP Host Address: icssrv2k3.
4. Go to Repository tab and enter the Repository Name, Repository User, Repository Password, Repository Server Host Name and Repository Port

Number. Click on **"Apply"** and on **"OK"** as shown in Fig. 4.69.

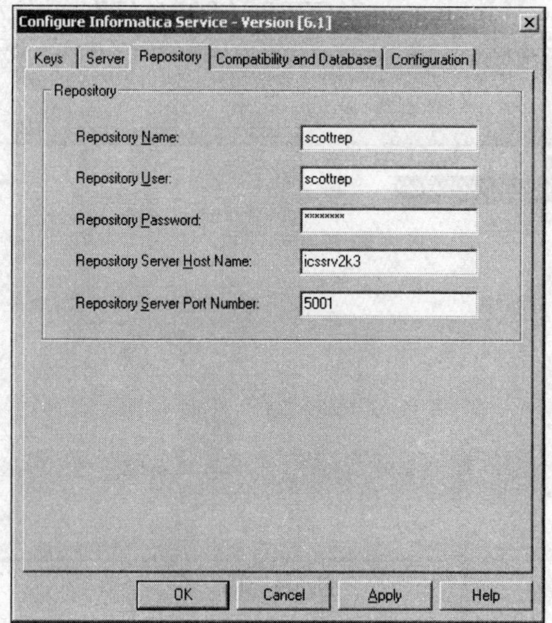

Fig. 4.69

5. "Informatica Server Setup Application – Options" window will open, click on **"Exit"**.
6. Now the server is configured successfully.
7. After this, start the Informatica service from the "Services" window. To start the service, select ***"Start → Administrator Tools → Services"***. **"Services"** window, select **"Informatica"** service and right click on it and select **"start"** from the popup menu.

(III) Defining Tasks

1. To define the task, a session object must be created. Before creating a session, select the folder **"AGGREAGATE"** and click on ***"Tools → Task Developer"***.
2. **"Task Developer"** window opens in the workspace.
3. To create a session object, select ***"Tasks → Create"***.
4. Now **"Create Task"** window opens. Enter the values **"Select the task type to create"** as **"Session"** and enter a user-defined name for the task, then click on ***"Create"***.

   e.g.: Select the task type to create: Session

   Enter a new name for this task: AGGREGATORSESSION

5. Now Mappings window, shown in Fig. 4.70 is displayed. In this dialog box, select the Mapping as **"AGGREGATORMAP"**.

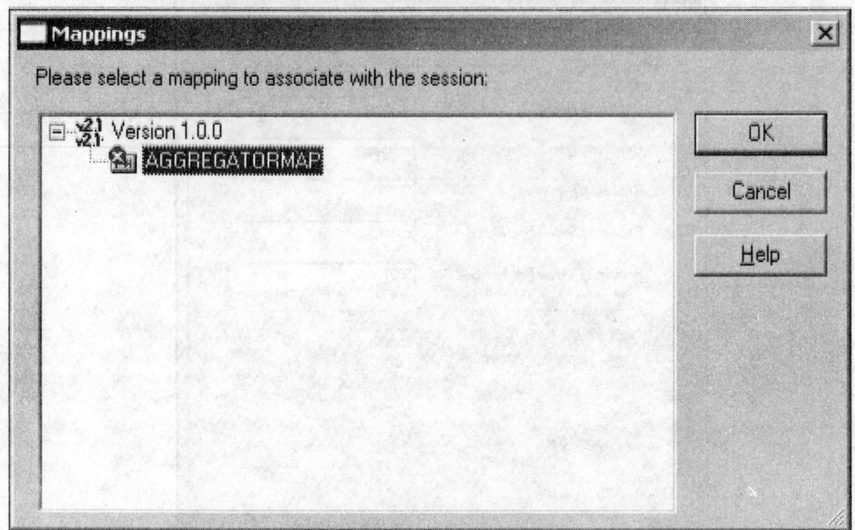

Fig. 4.70

6. Click on **"OK"**, and on **"Done"** of "Create Task" dialog box.
7. Double click on the created session (AGGREGATORSESSION).
8. **"Edit Tasks"** window opens, go to sources tab.
9. In the "Value" column, click on the down arrow button.
10. "Relational Connection Browser" window opens. Select the Source relational connection. In our example select the **"scottsource"** and click on **"OK"**.
11. Go to Targets tab and again select the down arrow button of Values column.
12. **"Relational Connection Browser"** window opens. Select the Target object (scotttarget) and click on **"OK"**.
13. In Target tab, select the **"Properties"** tab located at the bottom. Change the value of the **"Target Load Type"** as **"Normal"**.
14. Click on **"Apply"**, and on "OK".
15. To validate the session, select the task that is created and select the menu item "***Tasks → Validate***".

(IV) Creating a Workflow

1. Select the menu item "***Tools → Workflow Designer***". The Workflow Designer window opens in Workspace.
2. Select the menu item "***Workflows → Create***" to create a workflow. "Create Workflow" window opens.

3. In General tab, enter the name of workflow.

   e g: Name: AGGREGATORWORKFLOW.

4. Click on **"OK"**. Before clicking on **"OK"**, check whether the server name is there in the server edit box or not. If not, configure the server, then start the server and select that server here. Now Click on **"OK"**.

5. Explore the Sessions folder from the Navigator and select the created session (AGGREGATORSESSION) and drag and drop it into the Workflow Designer workspace.

6. From the Tool bar, select the **"Link Tasks"** icon, and drag the link from Workflow to Task. The **"Link Tasks"** icon is shown below:

7. Save the workflow by selecting ***"Repository → Save"***.

8. To start workflow, select the menu item ***" Workflow → Start Workflow"***.

   "Work flow Monitor" icon will appear on the System Tray.

9. Open the **"Workflow Monitor"** by double clicking on it.

10. Now we can see the status of our workflow. If the Workflow is successful, then the "AGGREGATORSESSION" and "AGGREGATORWORKFLOW" are shown in the Succeeded part. To view how many rows got transferred from source to target, double click on the "AGGREGATORSESSION".

11. "Properties of AGGREGATORSESSION" window opens. In this window, you can see the status, if any errors occurred the error messages are displayed in the First Error entry in this window. For this example, the "Source Success Rows" entry will contain 14 and the "Target Success Rows" will contain 3.

Thus we have successfully completed the workflow of transferring the sources rows from EMP table to AGGREGATETARGET table in "scottolap" by applying the "Aggregator" transformation to calculate the sum of salaries department-wise.

Checking the Output

To see whether the target rows have been dumped into the target table, connect to the target table in the target database using the following SQL statements.

SQL syntax: connect <username>/<password>

e.g.: SQL> connect scottolap/scottolap;

Connected.

To see the rows of the target table, use the following SQL statement.

SQL syntax: select * from <table name>;

e.g.: SQL> select * from aggregatetarget;

DEPTNO	SALARIES
10	8750
20	10875
30	9400

3 rows selected.

4.5 Filter Transformation

Using filter transformation, we can filter some information from the total data available in a table. We will demonstrate how to create the target table that contains records of employees working in department no. 10.

To work with Filter Transformation, create a separate folder for this project.

Creating a Folder using Repository Manager

1. Open the Repository manager:
   Start→ Programs → Informatica Power center 6.1 OEM for i2 → Repository Manager
   Informatica Repository Manager window opens.
2. Explore Repositories and select the repository **"scottrep"**, right click on it and select **"Connect"** from the pop up menu.
3. Create a new folder in the selected Repository by selecting the menu item: "*Create → Folder*".
4) Enter the name of the folder in the popped up dialog box and click on **"OK"**.
   e.g. Folder name: FILTER folder is created.
   Now we have to work on Designer tool to create the mapping.

Designer Tool

In the Designer Tool, select the source database object, target database object and select the transformation as "Filter". The source database object can be selected using the Source Analyzer and the target database object can be selected using the Warehouse Designer.

(I) Selecting the source database object

1. To work with the Source Analyzer, first open the Informatica Designer Tool. The

Steps are:

Start→ Programs→ Informatica Power center 6.1 OEM for i2 → Designer

2. Connect to the repository (scottrep) by entering the username and password.
3. Now select the folder "FILTER" and select the menu item "***Tools→ Source Analyzer***".
4. Select the menu item "***Sources→ Import from database***".
5. "Import tables" window opens. In this window, enter the ODBC data source, username, owner name, and password entries for example:

   e.g. ODBC Data source name : scott
   Username : scott
   Owner name : SCOTT .
   Password : tiger
6. Click on **"Connect"**, select the EMP table from **"Select tables"** list and click on "OK" to import the EMP table to the Source Analyzer workspace.
7. The source database object is selected.

   Now we have to select/create the target database object.

(II) Creating the target database object

1. To create the target database object, select the menu item "***Tools→ Warehouse Designer***".
2. Then select "***Targets→Create***" from the main and click on it. Edit table window opens.
3. **"Create Target Table"** window opens. Enter the Target Table name and select the Database type for Target table. For example:

   Target Table Name : FILTERTARGET
   Database type : Oracle
4. After entering these details, click on **"Create"**, and then click on **"Done"**.
5. Now, you can see the target table in the Warehouse Designer Workspace without any Fields.
6. To enter the fields of the target table, double-click on it.
7. In Edit Tables window go to **"Columns"** tab.
8. To enter the New Fields click on the following icon:

9. The empty row will be displayed in the Columns tab. Enter the Column details as shown in Fig. 4.71.

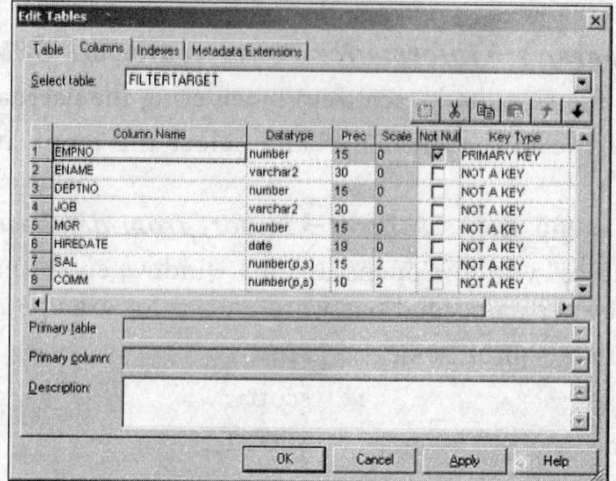

Fig. 4.71

10. Click on **"Apply"**, then on **"OK"**, after entering target Database fields. See Fig. 4.72.

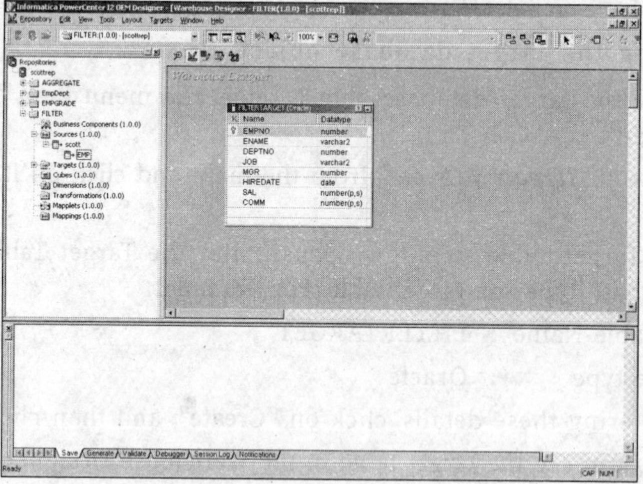

Fig. 4.72

11. Now the template for the target table is designed. To create the Target table in the Target Database, select the menu item **"Targets→Generate/Execute SQL"** from the main menu.
12. Now the **"Database Object Generation"** window opens.
13. In **"Generation objects"** group, click ok "Create table" check box.
14. Now click on **"Generate and Execute"**.
15. **"Connect to an ODBC Data source"** dialog box opens. In this dialog box,

enter ODBC Data source, Username, Password and click on **"Connect"** for example:

e.g. ODBC Data Source : scott
User name : scottolap
Password : scottolap

16. The following message box will pop up: "File MKTABLES.SQL already exists Do you want to overwrite the contents of this file?" Click on "OK" button.

Now the Target table is created in the target database, scottolap.

Mapping Designer

The Mapping Designer is used to map the data flow from Source to Target. The procedure for mapping the data from source to target is as follows:

1. Open the Mapping Designer by selecting **"Tools→Mapping Designer"** from the main menu."Mapping Name" window opens.
2. Enter the "New Mapping Name". e.g.

   New Mapping Name : FILTERMAP
3. Now the Mapping Designer window will open in the Workspace.
4. From the Navigator window, explore the Source folder, drag and drop the EMP table to Workspace. By default a source qualifier is also created for the EMP table.
5. Drag and drop the target table "FILTERTARGET" from the Navigator to Mapping Designer Workspace, as shown in Fig. 4.73.

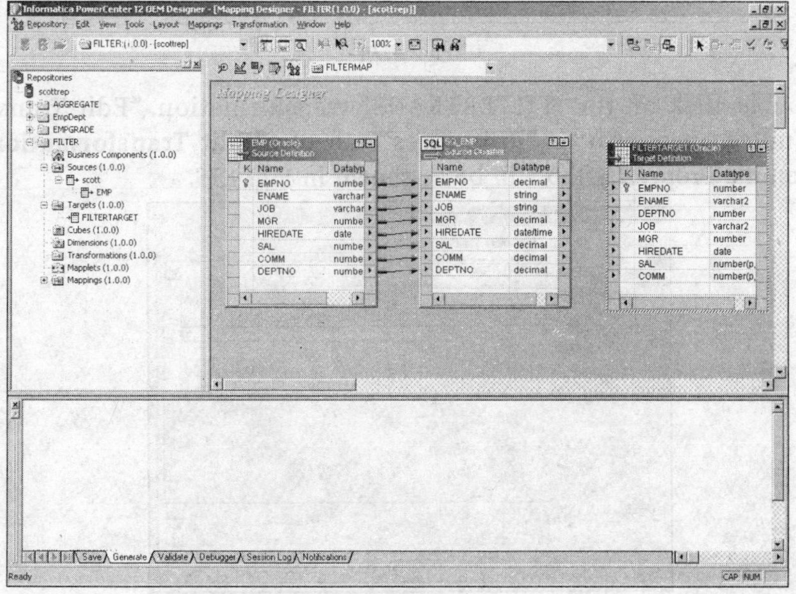

Fig. 4.73

6. Select the Transformation of type Filter by selecting the menu item "***Transformation→Create***" to create the new transformation.
7. "Create Transformation" window opens, select **"Type of transformation to create"** as Filter and the name of transformation to create as "FILTERTRANS".
8. Click on **"Create"** button, then on **"Done"** button.
9. Drag and drop the EMPNO, ENAME, DEPTNO, JOB, MGR, HIREDATE, SAL, COM columns of EMP Source Qualifier to FILTERTRANS. After dragging the respective columns, the workspace appears as shown in Fig. 4.74.

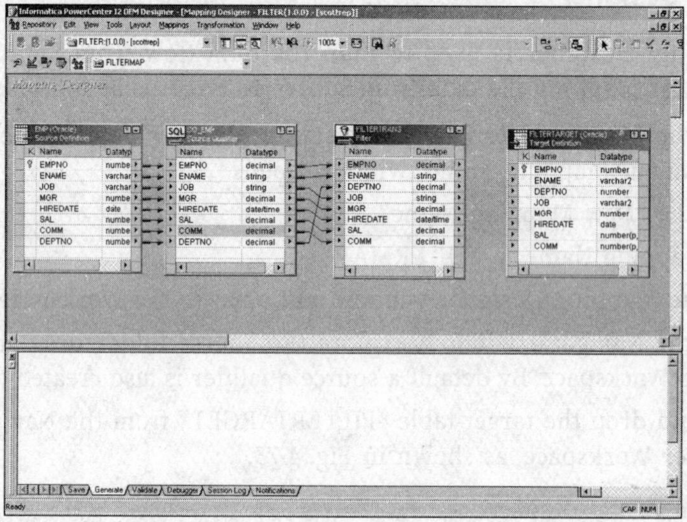

Fig. 4.74

10. Double click on the "FILTERTRANS" transformation. "Edit Transformations" window opens. Go to **"Properties"** tab of **"Edit Transformations"** window, then the Properties tab will be as shown in Fig. 4.75.

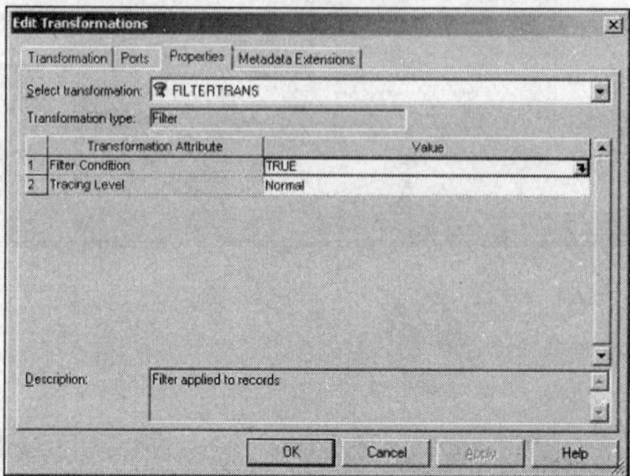

Fig. 4.75

In the properties tab, click on the down arrow button of value column of Filter Condition row.

11. The **"Expression Editor"** Dialog box will open. On the Formula side the value will be "TRUE". Remove that value from the Formula editor.
12. Go to Ports tab of **"Expression Editor"** window, explore the "FILTERTRANS" object and select the column on which to apply the filter condition. In this example, select the column DEPTNO and double click on it.
13. From the **"Operator Key Pad"** click on the **"="** symbol. In Formula editor, enter the number "10". After entering the details, the "Expression Editor" window appears as shown in Fig. 4.76.

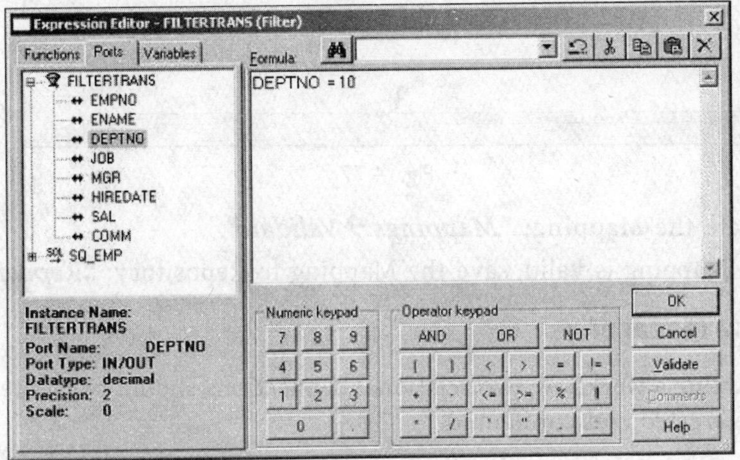

Fig. 4.76

14. Click on **"Validate"** button to validate the expression. "Expression parsed successfully" message will be displayed, click on **"OK"**.
15. Click on **"OK"** of "Expression Editor".
16. Apply the settings by clicking on **"Apply"** of "Edit Transformations" window, and on **"OK"**.
17. Drag the following columns EMPNO, ENAME, DEPTNO, JOB, MGR, HIREDATE, SAL, COMM of "FILTERTRANS" to Target table (FILTERTARGET). Now the Mapping designer workspace will appear as shown in Fig. 4.77.

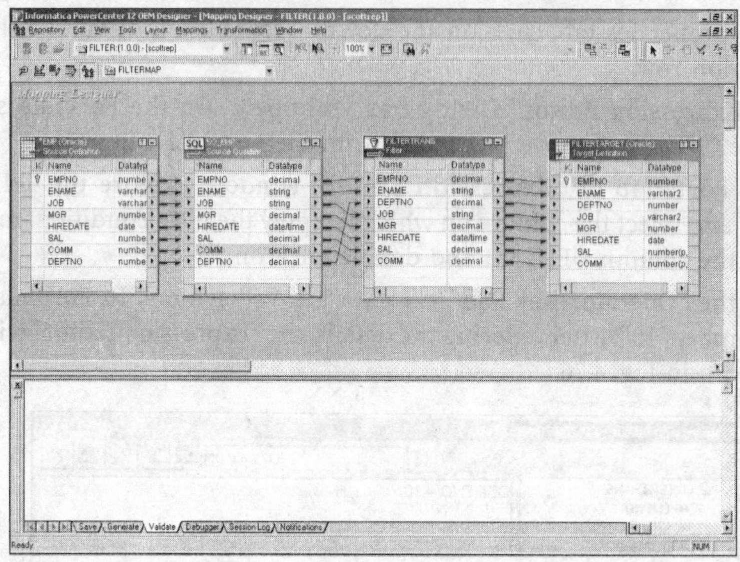

Fig. 4.77

18. Validate the Mapping: "***Mappings→ Validate***".
19. If the Mapping is valid, save the Mapping to Repository: "**R*epository → Save***".

Workflow Manager

Before creating a workflow, two relational connections should be created and a server should be created and configured.

1. If the relational connections are already created, then just ignore step2. If the server is already configured, then ignore the step3
2. **Creating relational connections**
   i) Open the Workflow Manager:
   Start→ Programs→ Informatica Power center 6.1 OEM for i2 → Workflow Manager.
   ii) The **"Informatica Power Center Workflow Manager"** window opens. Right click on "scottrep" repository and click on **"connect"** from the popup menu.
   iii) **"Connect to Repository"** window opens. In this window, enter username and password and click on **"connect"** button.
   e.g. Username : scottrep
   Password : scottrep
   iv) Select the menu item "***Connections → Relational***", "Relational Connection Browser" window opens.

v) Click on **"Add"** button to add a new connection. **"Select Subtype"** dialog box opens, in this dialog box select the type as **"Oracle"** and click on **"OK"** button.

vi) **"Connection Object Definition"** window opens. In this window enter the name, Username, Password and Connect String and click on **"OK"** button.

Name : scottsource

User name : scott

Password : tiger

Connect String : oemrep

Now the created relational connection gets displayed in the "Relational Connection Browser" window.

vii) Repeat the process from step (v) to create the relational target connection. The Target connection details are as follows:

Name : scotttarget

User name : scottolap

Password : scottolap

Connect String : oemrep

viii) Click on **"Close"** of **"Relational Connection Browser"** after creating the source and target relational connections.

3. **Configuring the server**

To configure the server, the procedure is as follows:

i) Select ***"Start→ Programs→ Informatica Server→ Informatica Server Setup"*** to open the server setup. Now the "Informatica Server Setup Application – Options" window will be displayed:

ii) Click on **"Continue"**. Enter the keys corresponding to the databases.

(a) Go to server tab and enter the Server Name, TCP/IP Host Address for example

e.g. Server Name: scottserver

TCP/IP Host Address: icssrv2k3.

(b) Go to Repository tab and enter the Repository Name, Repository User, Repository Password, Repository Server Host Name, and Repository Port Number. Click on **"Apply"** and on **"OK"**. See Fig. 4.78.

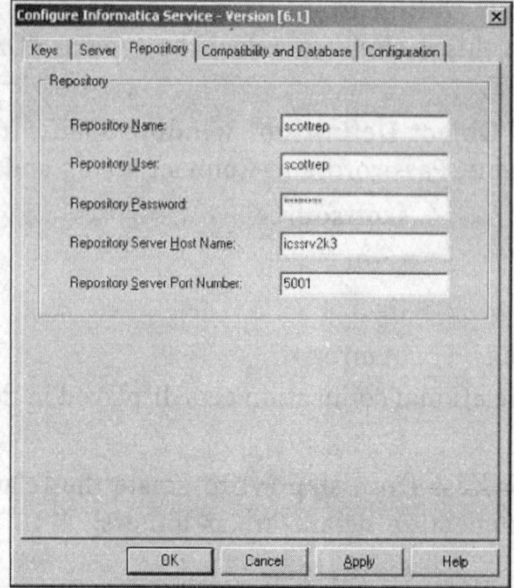

Fig. 4.78

c. "Informatica Server Setup Application – Options" window will open. Click on **"Exit"**.

d. Now the server is configured successfully.

e. After this, start the Informatica service from the **"Services"** window. To start the service, select ***"Start → Administrator Tools → Services"***. In this "Services" window, select **"Informatica"** service and right click on it and select "Start" from the popup menu.

4. **Defining Tasks**

i) To define the task, a session object must be created. Before creating a session, select the folder "FILTER" and click on ***"Tools → Task Developer"***.

ii) **"Task Developer"** window opens in the workspace.

iii) To create a session object, select "Tasks→ Create".

iv) Now **"Create Task"** window opens. Enter the values "Select the task type to create" as "Session" and enter a name for the task, then click on **"Create"** button.

e.g. Select the task type to create : Session

Enter a new name for this task : FILTERSESSION

v) Now Mappings dialog box opens. Select the Mapping as "FILTERMAP", as shown in Fig. 4.79.

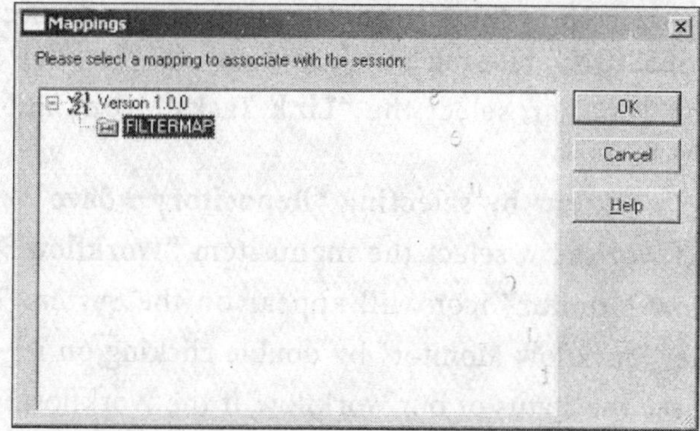

Fig. 4.79

vi) Click on **"OK"**, and on **"Done"** in the **"Create Task"** dialog box.

vii) Double click on the created session (FILTERSESSION).

viii) **"Edit Tasks"** window opens, go to sources tab.

ix) In the "Value" column, click on the down arrow button.

x) "Relational Connection Browser" window opens. Select the Source relational connection.

xi) In our example, select the **"scottsource"** and click on **"OK"**. Go to Targets tab and again select the down arrow button of Values column. **"Relational Connection Browser"** window opens. In this window, select the Target object (scotttarget) and click on **"OK"**.

xii) In the Target tab, select the **"Properties"** tab located at the bottom. Change the value of the "Target Load Type" as **"Normal"**.

xiii) Click on **"Apply"**, and on **"OK"** button.

xiv) To validate the session, select the task which is created and select the menu item **"Tasks→ Validate"**.

5. **Creating a Work flow**

i) Select the menu item "**Tools→ Workflow Designer**". Now the Workflow Designer window opens in Workspace.

ii) Now select the menu item "Workflows→Create" to create a workflow. **"Create Workflow"** window opens.

iii) In General tab enter the name of workflow.

e.g. Name: FILTERWORKFLOW

iv) Click on **"OK"** button. Before clicking on **"OK"**, check whether the server name is there in the server edit box or not. If not configure the server, then start the server and select that server here.

v) Explore the Sessions folder from the Navigator and select the created session (FILTERSESSION) and drag and drop it into the Workflow Designer workspace.

vi) From the Tool bar, select the **"Link Tasks"** icon, and drag the link from Workflow to Task.

vii) Save the workflow by selecting **"Repository→Save"**.

viii) To start workflow, select the menu item **"Workflow→Start Workflow"**.

"Workflow Monitor" icon will appear on the System Tray.

ix) Open the "Workflow Monitor" by double clicking on it.

x) You can see the status of our workflow. If the Workflow is successful, then the "FILTERSESSION" and "FILTERWORKFLOW" are shown in the Succeeded part. To view how many Rows got transferred from source to target double click on the "FILTERSESSION".

xi) "Properties of FILTERSESSION" window opens. In this window, you can see the status. If any errors occurred, the error messages are displayed in the First Error entry in this window.

xii) For this example the "Source Success Rows" entry will contain 14 and the "Target Success Rows" will contain 3.

Thus, we have successfully completed the workflow of transferring the sources rows from EMP table to FILTERTARGET table in "scottolap" by applying the "Filter" transformation to get the employees who belong to DEPTNO 10.

Checking the Output

To see whether the target rows have been dumped into the target table, connect to the target table in the target database using the following SQL statements.

SQL syntax: connect <username>/<password>

e.g. SQL> connect scottolap/scottolap; Connected.

To see the rows of the target table, use the following SQL statement:

SQL syntax: select * from <table name>;

e.g. SQL> select * from filtertarget;

EMPNO	ENAME	JOB	MGR	HIREDATE	SAL	COMM	DEPTNO
7782	CLARK	MANAGER	7839	09-JUN-81	2450		10
7839	KING	PRESIDENT		17-NOV-81	5000		10
7934	MILLER	CLERK	7782	23-JAN-82	1300		10

3 rows selected.

That completes filter transformation.

4.6 Rank Transformation

The Rank Transformation can be used to obtain the lowest three earners in the employees from the EMP table.

To start with, create a separate folder for this task in Repository Manager.

Creating a Folder

1. Open the Repository manager:

   Start → Programs → Informatica Power center 6.1 OEM for i2 → Repository Manager **Informatica Repository** Manager window opens.
2. Explore Repositories and select the repository "scottrep", right click on it and select "Connect" from the pop up menu.
3. Create a new folder in the selected Repository by selecting the menu item: "*create→Folder*".
4. Enter the name of the folder from the popped up dialog box and click on "OK" button. E.g. Folder name: RANK
5. The folder is now ready. Now, you need to work on Designer Tool to create mapping.

Designer Tool

In the Designer Tool, select the source database object, target database object and select the transformation as "Rank". The source database object can be selected using the Source Analyzer, the target database object can be selected using the Warehouse Designer and Mapping can be done using Mapping Designer.

Selecting the source database object:

1. To work with the Source Analyzer first open the Informatica Designer Tool.

   Start→Programs→Informatica Power center 6.1 OEM for i2 →Designer
2. Connect to the repository (scottrep) by entering the username and password.
3. Now select the folder **"RANK"** and select the menu item "***Tools→Source Analyzer***".
4. To import the source database object, select the menu item "***Sources → Import from database***".
5. "Import tables" window opens. Enter the ODBC data source, username, owner name, and password entries e.g.

   ODBC Data source name : scott
   User name : scott
   Owner name : SCOTT
   Password : tiger

6. Click on **"Connect"**, select the EMP table from "Select tables" list and click on "OK" button to import the EMP table to the Source Analyzer workspace.

   The source database object is now selected.

   Creating the target database object

1. Select the menu item ***"Tools → Warehouse Designer"***.
2. To create the Target table, select the ***"Targets→Create"*** from the main menu.
3. **"Create Target Table"** window opens. Enter the Target Table name and select the Database type for Target table e.g.

   Target Table Name: RANKTARGET

   Database type: Oracle
4. After entering the details, click on **"Create"**, and then click on **"Done"**.
5. You can see the target table, without any fields, in the Warehouse Designer Workspace.
6. To enter the fields of the target table, double-click on it.
7. Now **"Edit Table"** window opens. In Edit Tables window go to **"Columns"** tab.
8. To enter the New Fields, click on the following icon:

9. The empty row will be displayed in the Columns tab. Enter the Column details as shown in Fig. 4.80.

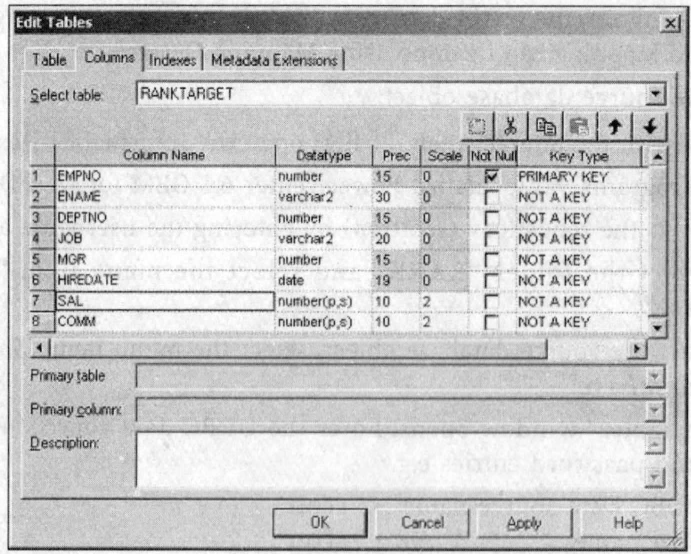

Edit Tables

Table | Columns | Indexes | Metadata Extensions

Select table: RANKTARGET

	Column Name	Datatype	Prec	Scale	Not Null	Key Type
1	EMPNO	number	15	0	☑	PRIMARY KEY
2	ENAME	varchar2	30	0	☐	NOT A KEY
3	DEPTNO	number	15	0	☐	NOT A KEY
4	JOB	varchar2	20	0	☐	NOT A KEY
5	MGR	number	15	0	☐	NOT A KEY
6	HIREDATE	date	19	0	☐	NOT A KEY
7	SAL	number(p,s)	10	2	☐	NOT A KEY
8	COMM	number(p,s)	10	2	☐	NOT A KEY

Primary table:

Primary column:

Description:

OK | Cancel | Apply | Help

Fig. 4.80

10. Click on **"Apply"** then on **"OK"**. (Fig. 4.81).

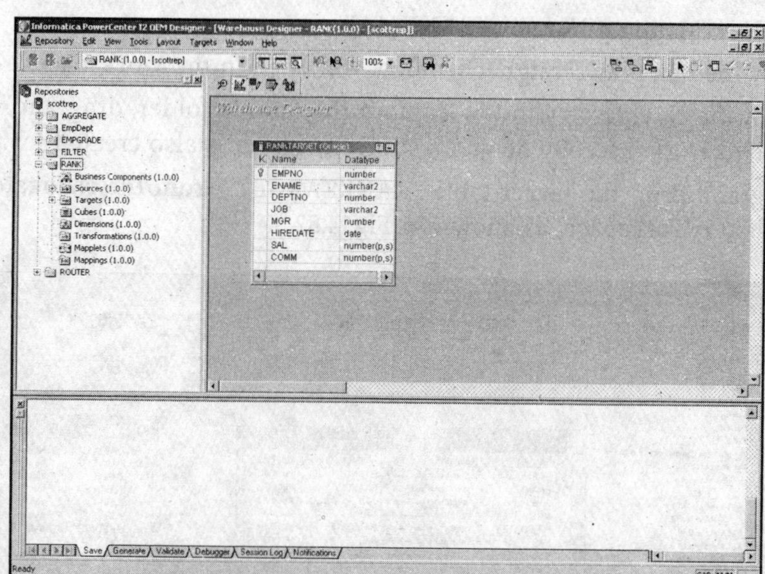

Fig. 4.81

11. Now the template for the target table is designed. To create the Target table in the Target Database, select the menu item **"Targets→ Generate/Execute SQL"** from the main menu. **"Database Object Generation"** window opens.
12. In "Generation objects" group, check Create table check box.
13. Now click on **"Generate** and **Execute"**.
14. "Connect to an ODBC Data source" dialog opens. Enter ODBC data source, user name, Password and click on "connect" button e.g.

    ODBC Data Source : scott
    User name : scottolap
    Password : scottolap

15. The following message box will pop up: "Files MKTABLES.SQL already exists Do you want to overwrite the contents of this file?" Click on **"OK"**.

Now the Target table is created in the Target Database.

Mapping Designer

The Mapping Designer is used to map the flow of data from Source to Target. The procedure to map the data from source to target is as follows:

1. Open the Mapping Designer by selecting **"Tools→ Mapping Designer"** from the main menu.

2. "Mapping Name" window opens. Enter the "New Mapping Name".

   e.g. New Mapping Name : RANKMAP

   Now the Mapping Designer window will open in the Workspace.

3. From the Navigator window explore the Source folder, drag and drop the EMP table to Workspace. By default a source qualifier is also created for the EMP table.

4. Drag and drop the target table "RANKTARGET" from the Navigator to Mapping Designer Workspace, as shown in Fig. 4.82.

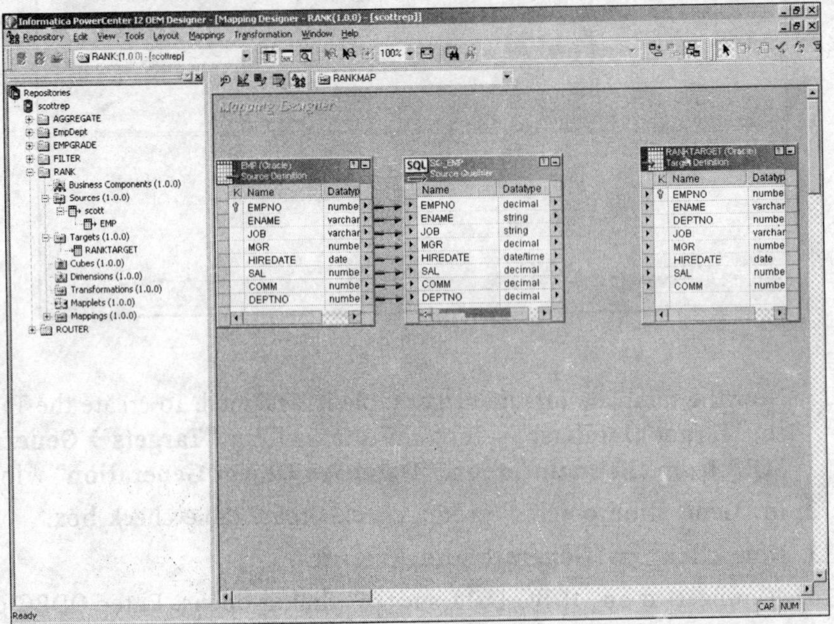

Fig. 4.82

5. Select the Transformation of type Rank by selecting the menu iter **"Transformation→Create"** to create the new transformation.

6. "Create Transformation" window opens. Select Type of transformation to creat as Rank and the name of transformation to create as "RANKTRANS".

7. Click on **"Create"** button , then on **"Done"** button.

8. Drag and drop the EMPNO, ENAME, DEPTNO, JOB, MGR, HIREDATE, SAL, CO columns of EMP Source Qualifier to RANKTRANS, after dragging the respectiv columns the workspace appears as shown in Fig. 4.83.

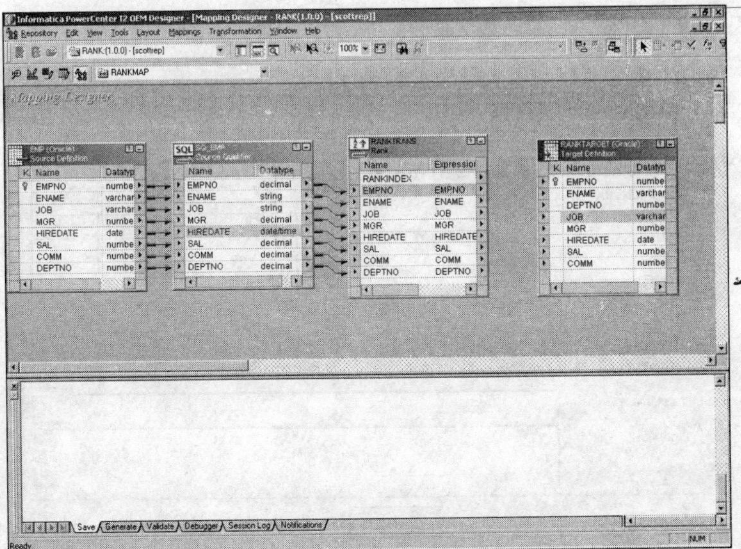

Fig. 4.83

9. Double click on the "RANKTRANS" transformation. The "Edit Transformations" window opens. Go to "Ports" tab of "Edit Transformations" window, then the Ports tab will be as shown in Fig. 4.84.

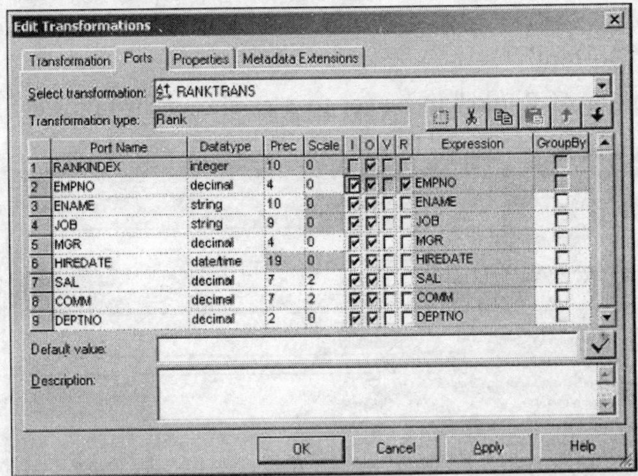

Fig. 4.84

10. In Fig. 4.84, the column "R" indicates the field for which the rank should be calculated. By default the Rank was assigned to EMPNO field, we can change the rank field. Now, we want to find the lowest salary earners of the EMP table. We will find the rank for the SAL column, so check the SAL field for Rank as shown in Fig. 4.85.

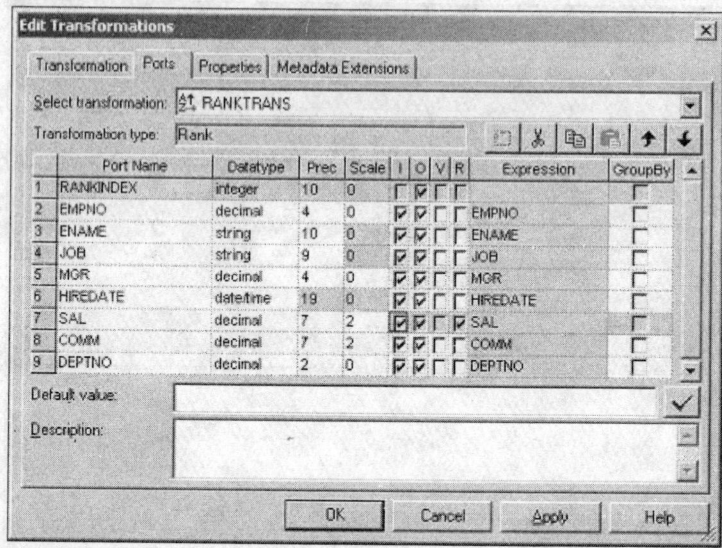

Fig. 4.85

11. Go to *Properties tab* of "Edit Transformations" window.
12. The Top/Bottom value indicates whether the Rank has to be calculated from Top to Bottom or from Bottom to Top. In this example, we want to find the details of the three employees who earn the lowest salaries. So change the "Top/Bottom" value to "Bottom".
13. The "Number of Ranks" to be set to 3 as shown in Fig. 4.86.

Edit Transformations

Transformation | Ports | Properties | Metadata Extensions

Select transformation: RANKTRANS

Transformation type: Rank

	Transformation Attribute	Value
1	Cache Directory	$PMCacheDir
2	Top/Bottom	Bottom
3	Number of Ranks	3
4	Case Sensitive String Comparison	☑
5	Tracing Level	Normal
6	Rank Data Cache Size	2000000
7	Rank Index Cache Size	1000000

Description: Number of records in each rank

OK Cancel Apply Help

Fig. 4.86

14. Now apply the settings, by clicking on **"Apply"** and on **"OK"**.
15. Now drag the following columns EMPNO, ENAME, DEPTNO, JOB, MGR, HIREDATE, SAL, COMM of "RANKTRANS" to Target table (RANKTARGET). Now the Mapping designer workspace will appear as shown in Fig. 4.87.

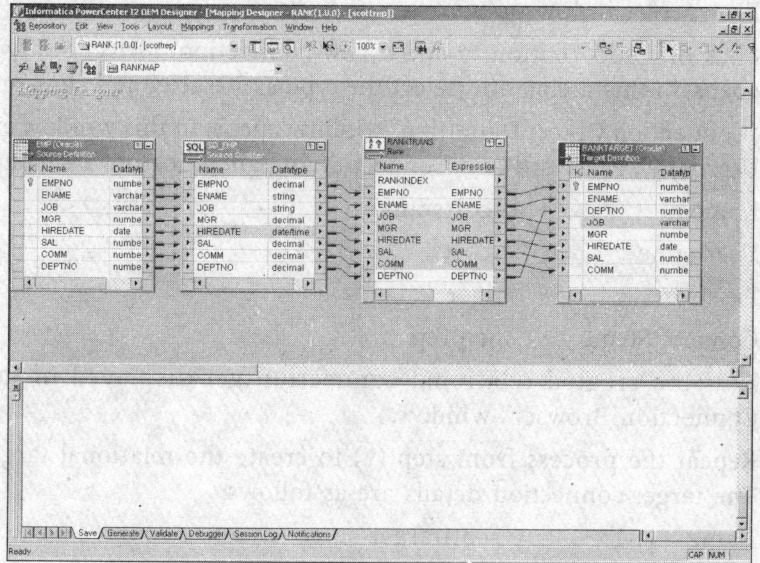

Fig. 4.87

16. Validate the Mapping: **"Mappings→Validate"**.
17. If the Mapping is valid, save the Mapping to Repository by selecting the menu item "Repositoryàsave" from the main menu.

Workflow Manager

Before creating a workflow, two relational connections should be created and a server should be created and configured.

1. If the relational connections are already created, then ignore step 2. If the server is already configured, then ignore step 3.
2. **Creating relational connections**
   i) Open the Workflow Manager by selecting:

      Start → Programs → Informatica Power center 6.1 OEM for i2 → Workflow Manager.

   ii) Informatica Power Center Workflow Manager" window opens, right click on **"scottrep"** repository and click on **"connect"** from the popup menu.

   iii) "Connect to Repository" window opens; in this window enter username and password and click on **"Connect"** button.

e.g. username : scottrep

Password : scottrep

iv) Select the menu item **"Connections→Relational"**, **"Relational Connection Browser"** window opens.

v) Click on **"Add"** button to add a new connection. "Select Subtype" dialog box opens, in this dialog box, select the type as "Oracle" and click on **"OK"** button.

vi) "Connection Object Definition" window opens. In this window enter the name, Username, Password and Connect String and click on "OK" button.

Name : scottsource

Username : scott

Password : tiger

Connect String : oemrep

v) Now the created relational connection get displayed in the "Relational Connection Browser" window.

vi) Repeat the process from step (v) to create the relational target connection. The target connection details are as follows:

Name : scotttarget

User name : scottolap

Password : scottolap

Connect String : oemrep

vii) Click on **"Close"** button of **"Relational Connection Browser"** after creating the source and target relational connections.

3. **Configuring the server**

To configure the server, the procedure is as follows:

i) Select **"Start → Programs → Informatica Server→ Informatica Server Setup"** to open the server setup. Now the "Informatica Server Setup Application – Options" window will be displayed.

ii) Click on **"Continue"** button. "Configure Informatica Service" window opens. In this you need to type the Platform Key, Oracle Key (or the key for the database you are using). These keys will be provided to you by your system administrator or the vendor.

iii) In the same window, select the server tab and enter the Server Name and TCP/IP Host Address.

e.g. Server Name: scottserver

TCP/IP Host Address: icssrv2k3.

iv) Go to Repository tab and enter the Repository Name, Repository User, Repository Password, Repository Server Host Name and Repository Port Number as shown in Fig. 4.88. Click on **"Apply"** button and on **"OK"** button.

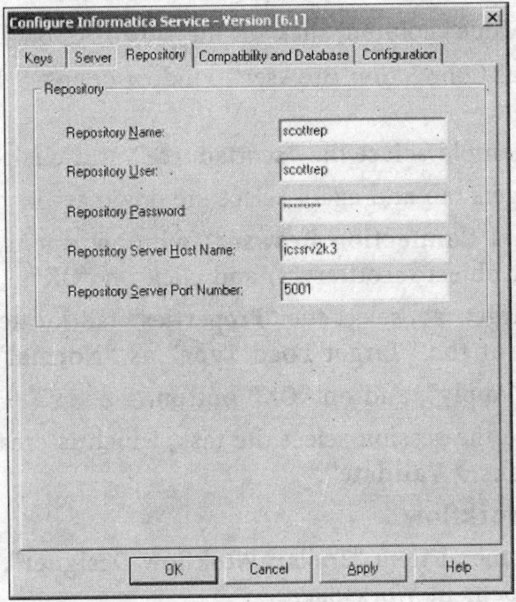

Fig. 4.88

v) "Informatica Server Setup Application – Options" window will open, click on **"Exit"**. Now, the server is configured successfully.

vi) After this, start the Informatica service from the "Services" window. To start the service, select **"Start→ Administrator Tools→ Services"**. In this "Services" window, select "Informatica" service and right click on it and select **"start"** from the popup menu.

4. **Defining Tasks**

i) To define the task, a session object must be created. Before creating a session select the folder **"RANK"** and click on **"Tools→ Task Developer"**. "Task Developer" window opens in the workspace.

ii) To create a session object. Select "Tasks→Create".

iii) Now **"Create Task"** window opens. Enter the values "Select the task type to create" as **"Session"** and enter a user-defined name for the task, then click on **"Create"**.

e.g. Select the task type to create: Session

iv) Enter a new name for this task: RANKSESSION.

v) Now Mappings window opens. Select the Mapping as "RANKMAP". Click on

"OK", and on **"Done"** of "Create Task" dialog box.

vi) Double click on the created session (RANKSESSION).

vii) **"Edit Tasks"** window opens, go to sources tab.

viii) In the **"Value"** column, click on the Down Arrow button.

ix) "Relational Connection Browser" window opens. Select the Source relational connection.

x) In our example select the **"scottsource"** and click on **"OK"**.

xi) Go to Targets tab and again select the down arrow button of Values column.

xii) **"Relational Connection Browser"** window opens. In this window, select the Target object (scotttarget) and click on **"OK"**.

xiii) In the Target tab, select the **"Properties"** tab located at the bottom. Change the value of the **"Target Load Type"** as **"Normal"**.

xiv) Click on **"Apply"**, and on **"OK"** button.

xv) To validate the session select the task, which is created and select the menu item **"Tasks→ Validate"**.

5. **Creating a workflow**

i) Select the menu item **"Tools→Workflow Designer"**. The Workflow Designer window opens in Workspace.

ii) Select the menu item **"Workflows→Create"** to create a workflow. **"Create Workflow"** window opens.

iii) In General tab, enter the name of workflow.

e.g. Name: RANKWORKFLOW

iv) Click on **"OK"** button. Before clicking on "OK" button check whether the server name is there in the server edit box or not. If not, configure the server and then start the server and select that server here.

v) Explore the Sessions folder from the Navigator and select the created session (RANKSESSION) and drag and drop it into the Workflow Designer workspace.

vi) From the Tool bar, select the **"Link Tasks"** icon, and drag the link from Workflow to Task.

vii) Save the workflow by selecting **"Repository→Save"**.

viii) To start workflow, select the menu item **"Workflow→Start Workflow"**.

ix) **"Work flow Monitor"** icon will appear on the System Tray.

x) Open the **"Workflow Monitor"** by double clicking on it.

xi) Now you can see the status of our workflow. If the workflow is successful, then the "RANKSESSION" and "RANKWORKFLOW" are shown in the Succeeded part.

xii) To view how many rows got transferred from source to target, double click on the "RANKSESSION".

xiii) "Properties of RANKSESSION" window opens. In this window, you can see the status. If any errors occurred, the error messages are displayed in the First Error entry in this window.

xiv) For this example, the "Source Success Rows" entry will contain 14 and the "Target Success Rows" will contain 3.

Thus we have successfully completed the workflow of transferring the sources rows from EMP table to RANKTARGET table in "scottolap" by applying the "Rank" transformation to get the three employees who earn the lowest salary.

Checking the Output

To see whether the target rows have been dumped into the target table, connect to the target table in the target database using the following SQL statements.

SQL syntax: connect <username>/<password>

e.g. SQL> connect scottolap/scottolap;

Connected.

To see the rows of the target table, use the following SQL statement.

SQL syntax: select * from <table name>;

E.g. SQL>select * from ranktarget;

EMPNO	ENAME	DEPTNO	JOB	MGR	HIREDATE	SAL	COMM
7369	SMITH	20	CLERK	7902	17-DEC-80	800	
7900	JAMES	30	CLERK	7698	03-DEC-81	950	
7876	ADAMS	20	CLERK	7788	23-MAY-87	1100	

3 rows selected.

4.7 Router Transformation

Using Router Transformation, we will study how to route the employee information from EMP table to different target tables, department-wise. DEPT10 table will be updated with all the employees belonging to department number 10, DEPT20 table will be updated with all the employees belonging to department number 20 and DEPTMS table will be updated all the employees belonging to department numbers other than 10 and 20.

To work with Router transformation, create a separate folder for this task in Repository Manager.

Creating a Folder

1. Open the Repository manager:
   Start→ Programs → Informatica Power center 6.1 OEM for i2 → Repository Manager
   Informatica Repository Manager window opens.
2. Explore Repository and select the repository **"scottrep"**, right click on it and select **"Connect"** from the pop up menu.
3. Create a new folder in the selected Repository by selecting the menu item: ***"Create→ Folder"***.
4. Enter the name of the folder in the popped up dialog box and click on **"OK"**.
   e.g.: Folder name: ROUTER
5. The folder is created. Now we need to work on Designer tool to create mapping.

Designer Tool

In the Designer Tool, select the source database object and target database object and select the transformation as "Router". The source database object can be selected using the Source Analyzer and the target database object can be selected using the Warehouse Designer. In Router transformation there is one INPUT group and any number of OUTPUT groups. In this example, we are taking three OUTPUT groups, out of these three OUTPUT groups, one is the DEFAULT OUTPUT group.

Selecting the Source Database Object:

1. To work with the Source Analyzer, first open the Informatica Designer Tool.
   "Start → Programs → Informatica Power center 6.1 OEM for i2 → Designer".
2. Connect to the repository (scottrep) by entering the username and password.
3. Select the folder **"ROUTER"** and select the menu item ***"Tools→Source Analyzer"***.
4. To import source tables, select the menu item ***"Sources→Import from database"***.
5. "Import tables" window opens. Enter the ODBC data source, username, owner name, and password.

   e.g : ODBC Data source name : scott
   Username : scott
   Owner name : SCOTT
   Password : tiger

6. Click on **"Connect"**, select the EMP table from "Select tables" list and click on **"OK"** to import the EMP table to the Source Analyzer workspace.
7. The source database object is selected and now we have to select the target database object.

Creating the Target Database Object:

1. To select the target database object, select the menu item ***"Tools→Warehouse Designer"***. For this example, we need three Target tables. To create the Target table, select the ***"Targets→Create"*** from the main menu.
2. "Create Target Table" window opens. In it enter the Target Table name and select the Database type for Target table.

   e.g. : Target Table Name : DEPT10

   Database type : Oracle
3. After entering the details click on **"create"** button, then on **"Done"** button.
4. Now you can see the target table in the Warehouse Designer Workspace without any Fields.
5. Similarly, create three target tables.

   e.g.: Target Table Name : DEPT20

   Database type : Oracle

   Target Table Name : DEPTMS

   Database type : Oracle
6. To enter the fields of the target table double-click on "DEPT10" target table.
7. Now "Edit Table" window opens. In Edit Tables window go to "Columns" tab.
8. To enter the New Fields, click on the following icon:

9. The empty row will be displayed in the Columns tab.
10. Now enter the Column details as shown in Fig. 4.89.

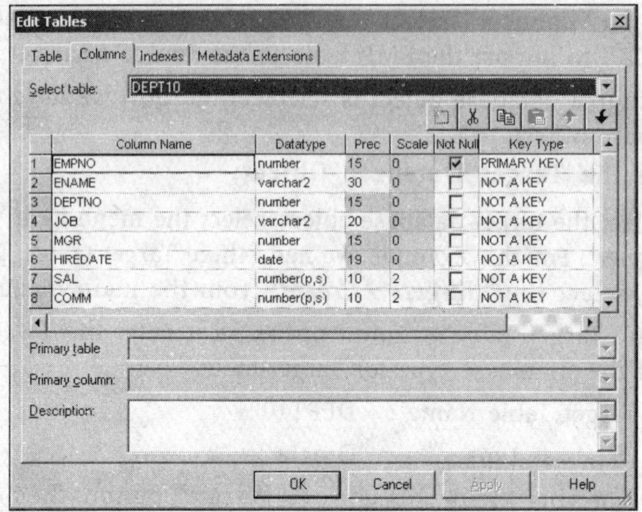

Fig. 4.89

11. To enter the fields of the target table double-click on "DEPT20" target table.
12. Now **"Edit Table"** window opens. In Edit Tables window go to **"Columns"** tab.
13. To enter the New Fields, click on the following icon:

14. The empty row will be displayed in the Columns tab. Enter the Column details as shown in Fig. 4.90.

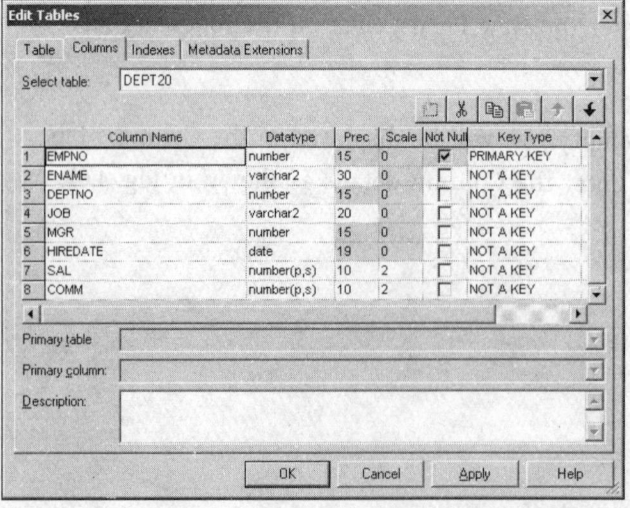

Fig. 4.90

15. Click on **"Apply"** then click **"OK"**.
16. To enter the fields of the target table, double-click on **"DEPTMS"** target table.
17. Now "Edit Table" window opens. In Edit Tables window go to "Columns" tab.
18. To enter the New Fields click on the following icon:

19. The empty row will be displayed in the Columns tab. Now enter the Column details as shown in Fig. 4.91.

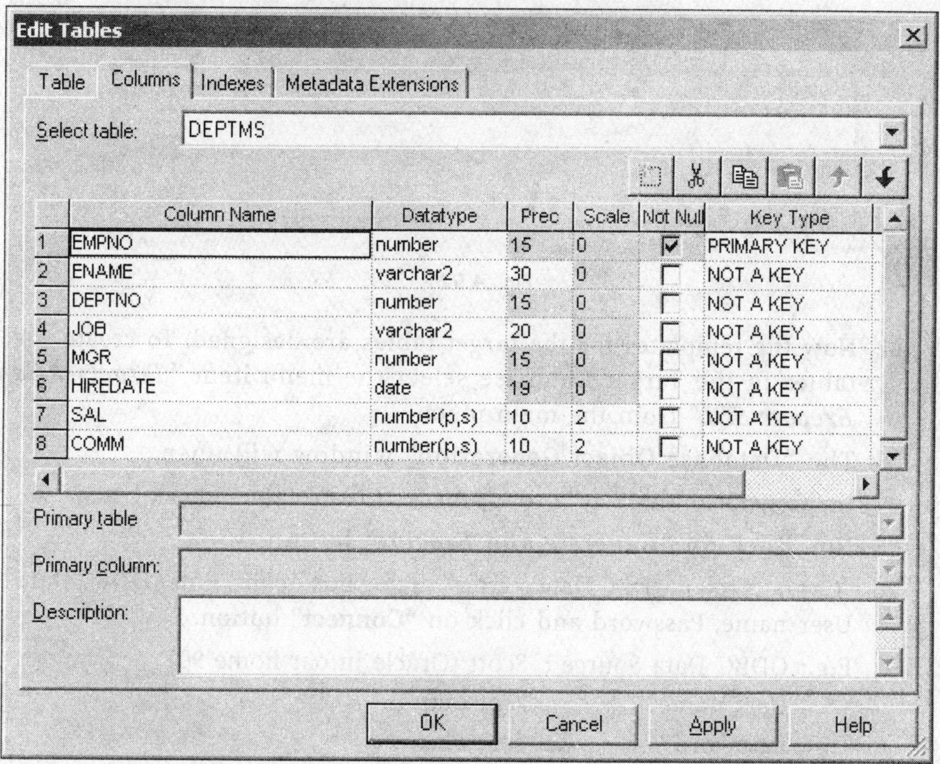

Fig. 4.91

20. Click on **"Apply"**, then on **"OK"**.
21. Now the Warehouse Designer workspace will be as shown in Fig. 4.92.

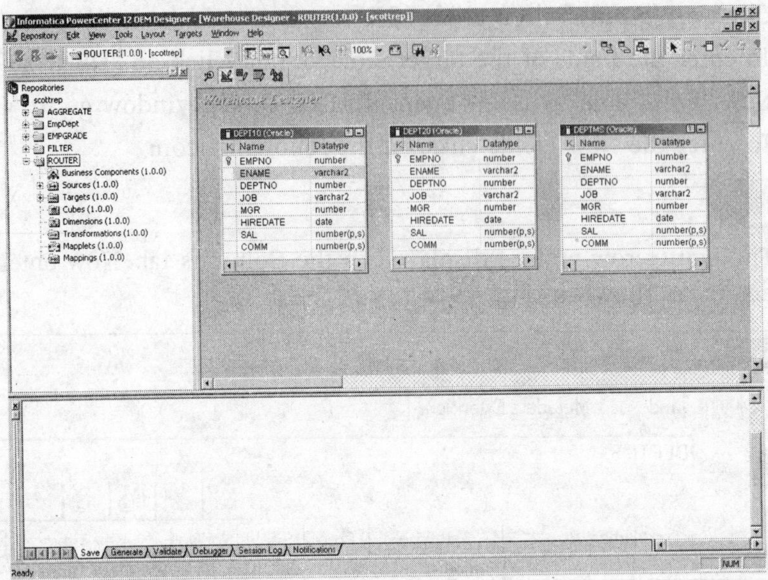

Fig. 4.92

22. Now the templates for the target tables are designed. To create the Target tables in the Target Database select the menu item ***"Targets→Generate/ Execute SQL"*** from the main menu.
23. The **"Database Object Generation"** window will open.
24. In "Generation objects" group, check "Create table" check box.
25. Now click on ***"Generate and Execute"*** button.
26. "Connect to an ODBC Data source" dialog box opens. Enter ODBC Data Source, User name, Password and click on **"Connect"** button.

    E.g.: ODBC Data Source : Scott (Oracle in oar home 90)
    User name : scottolap
    Password : scottolap
27. A message box will pop up with the message: "File MKTABLES.SQL already exists. Do you want to overwrite the contents of this file?" Click on **"OK"**.
28. Now the Target tables is created on the Target Database.

Mapping Designer

The Mapping Designer is used to map the flow of data from Source to Target. The procedure to map our data from source to target is as follows.

1. Open the Mapping Designer by selecting ***"Tools→Mapping Designer"*** from the main menu. "Mapping Name" window opens. Enter the name for the new mapping.

e.g.: New Mapping Name: ROUTERMAP

2. The Mapping Designer window will open in the Workspace.
3. From the Navigator window, explore the Source folder, drag and drop the EMP table to Workspace. By default a source qualifier is also created for the EMP table.
4. Drag and drop the target tables "DEPT10","DEPT20", DEPTMS from the Navigator to Mapping Designer Workspace. Now the Mapping Designer workspace will be as shown in Fig. 4.93.

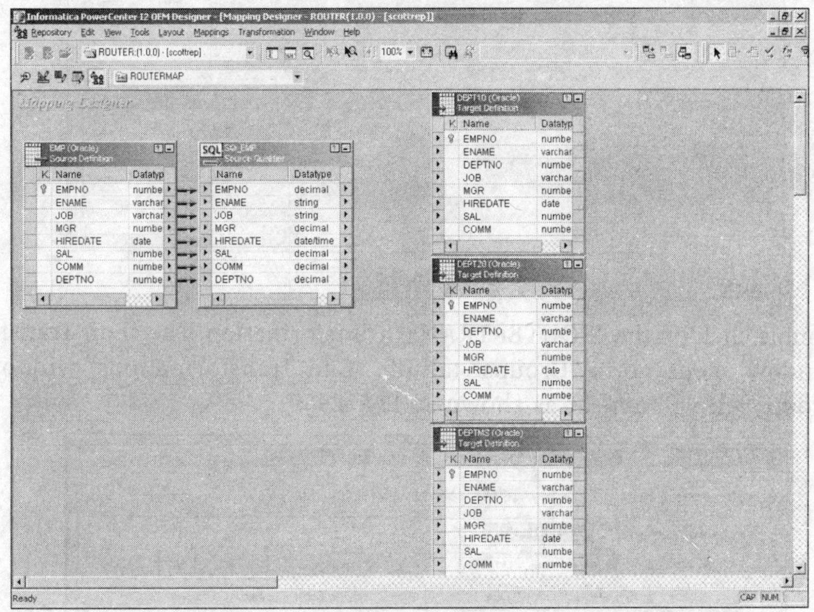

Fig. 4.93

5. Select the Transformation of type Router by selecting the menu item "***Transformation→Create***" to create the new transformation.
6. "Create Transformation" window opens. Select the "Type of transformation to create" as Router and the name of transformation to create as "ROUTERTRANS".
7. Click on **"Create"** and then on **"Done"**.
8. Drag and drop the EMPNO, ENAME, DEPTNO, JOB, MGR, HIREDATE, SAL, COM columns of EMP Source Qualifier to ROUTERTRANS, after dragging the respective columns, the workspace will be as shown in Fig. 4.94.

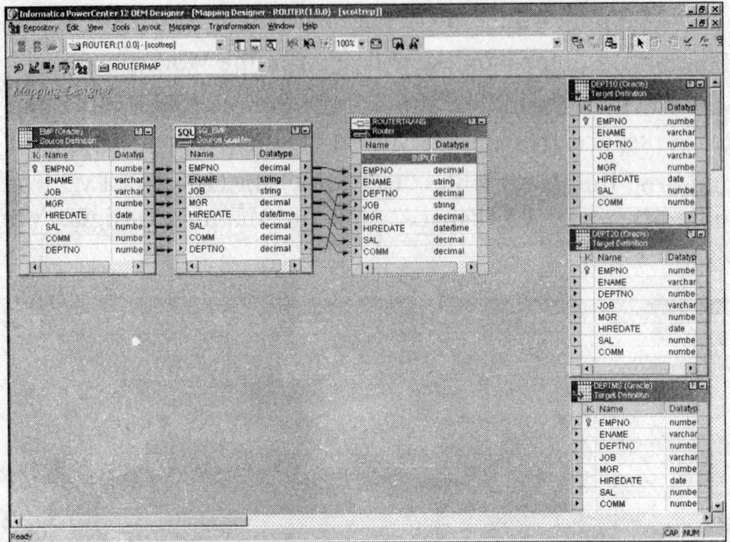

Fig. 4.94

9. Double click on the "ROUTERTRANS" transformation. The "Edit Transformations" window opens, go to "Groups" tab of "Edit Transformations" window, then the Groups tab will appear as shown in Fig. 4.95.

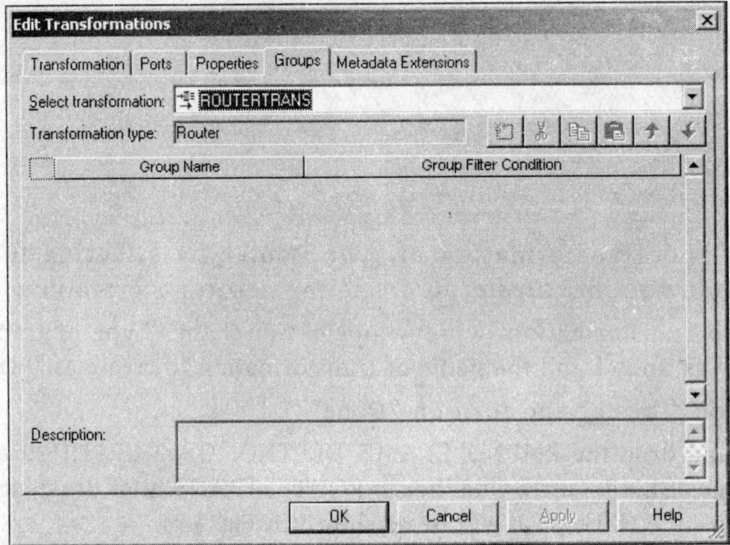

Fig. 4.95

10. In the Groups tab, click on the button as shown below:

11. Enter the Group Name and Group Filter Condition.

    e.g. Group Name: DEPT10.

12. To write the filter condition, click on the down arrow button to write the Group Filter Condition.

13. **"Expression Editor"** window opens. Remove the string (TRUE) from Formula editor.

14. Go to Ports tab and double click on "DEPTNO". Click on **"="** button from the Operator Key pad. Enter the value "10" in Formula editor. Now the complete expression appears as shown in Fig. 4.96.

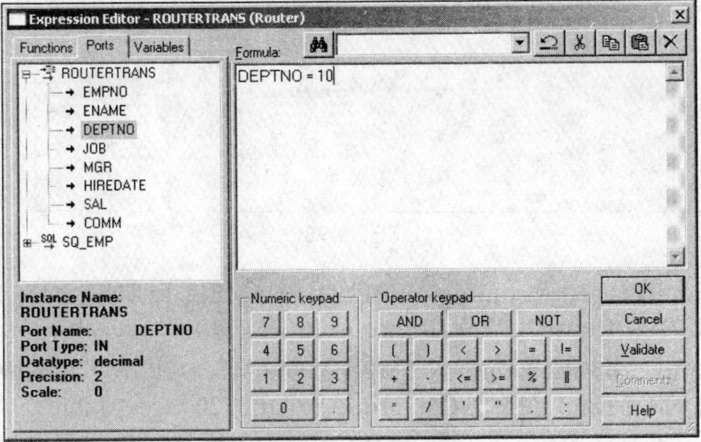

Fig. 4.96

15. Click on **"Validate"** to validate the expression.

16. Repeat the above steps to write second OUTPUT group expressions as shown in Fig. 4.97

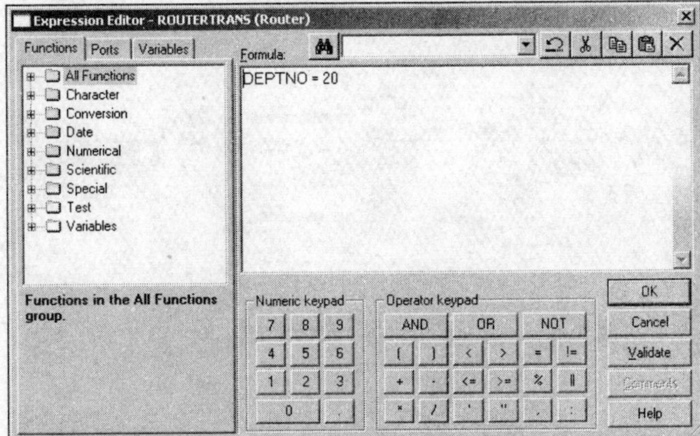

Fig. 4.97

17. Click on "Apply" and on "OK" in "Edit Transformations" window.
18. Now the Mapping Designer workspace will be as shown in Fig. 4.98.

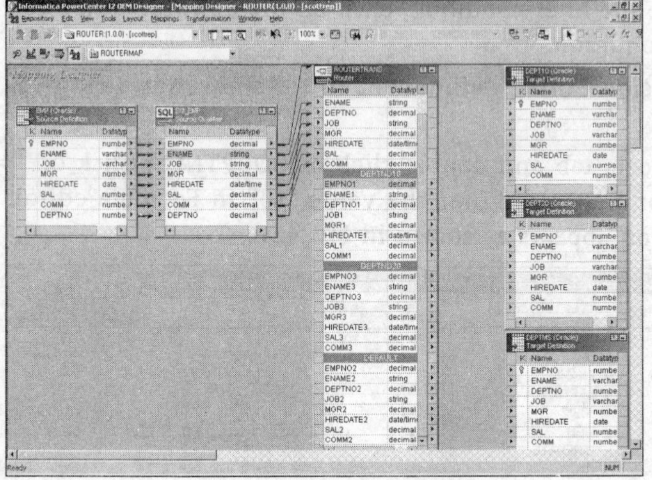

Fig. 4.98

19. Drag and drop the columns EMPNO, ENAME, DEPTNO, JOB, MGR, HIREDATE, SAL, COMM from DEPTNO10 group to DEPT10 target table.
20. Drag and drop the columns EMPNO, ENAME, DEPTNO, JOB, MGR, HIRE DATE, SAL, COMM from DEPTNO20 group to DEPT20 target table.
21. Drag and drop the columns EMPNO, ENAME, DEPTNO, JOB, MGR, HIREDATE, SAL, COMM from DEEFAULT group to DEPTMS target table.
22. Now the Mapping will be as shown in Fig. 4.99.

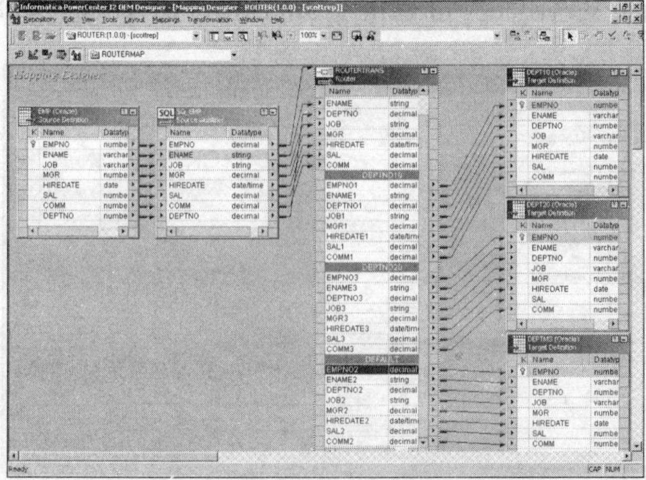

Fig. 4.99

23. Validate the Mapping: "***Mappings→ Validate***".
24. If the Mapping is valid, save the Mapping: "*Repository→save*".

Workflow Manager

Before creating a workflow, two relational connections should be created and a server should be created and configured. If the relational connections are already created, then just ignore step 2. If the server is already configured, then ignore the step 3.

1. Creating relational connections

i) Open the Workflow Manager by selecting:
Start→ Programs→ Informatica Power center 6.1 OEM for i2 → Workflow Manager.

ii) The **"Informatica Power Center Workflow Manager"** window opens, right click on **"scottrep"** repository and select **"Connect"** from the popup menu.

iii) "Connect to Repository" window opens, in this window enter username and password and click on **"Connect"** button.

e.g. Username : scottrep
Password : scottrep

iv) Select the menu item "***Connections→Relational***", "Relational Connection Browser" window opens.

v) Click on **"Add"** button to add a new connection. **"Select Subtype"** dialog opens. Select the type as **"Oracle"** and click on **"OK"** button.

vi) **"Connection Object Definition"** window opens. In this window, enter the name, Username, Password and Connect String and click on **"OK"** button.

Name : scottsource
Username : scott
Password : tiger
Connect String : oemrep

vii) Now the created relational connection is displayed in the "Relational Connection Browser" window.

viii) Repeat the process from step (v) to create the Relational target connection. The Target connection details are as follows:

Name : scotttarget
User name : scottolap
Password : scottolap
Connect String : oemrep

ix) Click on "Close" button of "Relational Connection Browser" after creating the source and target relational connections.

2. **Configuring the Server**

To configure the server, the procedure is:

i. Select ***"Start → Programs → Informatica Server → Informatica Server Setup"*** to open the server setup. Now the "Informatica Server Setup Application – Options" window will be displayed:

ii. Click on **"Continue"** button. Then **"Configure Informatica Service"** window opens. In this window, you need to enter the license keys such as the platform key, Oracle key (or whichever data base key you are using) and the ODBC key. These keys you can obtain from the system administrator or the vendor.

iii. In the same window, go to server tab and enter the Server Name, TCP/IP Host Address.

e.g. : Server Name : scottserver

TCP/IP Host Address : icssrv2k3.

iv. Go to Repository tab and enter the Repository Name, Repository User, Repository Password, Repository Server Host Name, Repository Port Number. Click on **"Apply"** and on **"OK"** button. See Fig. 4.100.

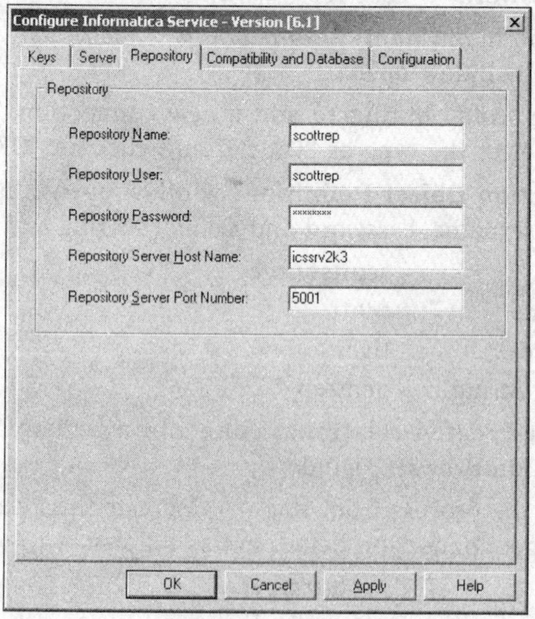

Fig. 4.100

e) "Informatica Server Setup Application – Options" window will open, click on **"Exit"**. Now the server is configured successfully.

f) After this, start the Informatica service from the "Services" window: select ***"Start → Administrator Tools → Services"***. In this "Services" window select "Informatica" service and right click on it and select "Start" from the popup menu.

3. **Defining Tasks**

i) To define the task, a session object must be created. Before creating a session select the folder "ROUTER" and click on ***"Tools→Task Developer"***. "Task Developer" window opens in the workspace.

ii) To create a session object. Select "*Tasks → Create*".

iii) Now **"Create Task"** window opens. Enter the values "Select the task type to create" as "Session" and enter a user-defined name for the task, then click on "Create".

E.g.: Select the task type to create : Session

Enter a new name for this task : ROUTERSESSION

iv) Now Mappings window opens, in this dialog box select the Mapping as "ROUTERMAP".

v) Click on **"ok"** button, and on **"Done"** button of "Create Task" dialog box.

vi) Double click on the created session (ROUTERSESSION).

vii) "Edit Tasks" window opens, in it go to sources tab.

viii) In the "Value" column click on the Down Arrow button. "Relational Connection Browser" window opens. Select the Source relational connection. In our example select the "scottsource" and click on **"OK"** button. Go to Targets tab and again select the Down arrow button of Values column. "Relational Connection Browser" window opens. In this window, select the Target object (scotttarget) for all the three target tables and click on **"OK"** button.

ix) In the Target tab, select the **"Properties"** tab located at the bottom. Change the value of the "Target Load Type" as "Normal" for all the three target tables.

x) Click on **"Apply"**, and on **"OK"** button.

xi) To validate the session, select the task, which was created, and select ***"Tasks→ Validate"***.

4. **Creating a Work flow**

i) Select the menu item ***"Tools → Workflow Designer"***. The Workflow Designer window opens in Workspace.

ii) Select the menu item ***"Workflows → Create"*** to create a workflow. "Create Workflow" window opens.

iii) In General tab, enter the name of workflow.
 e.g: Name: ROUTERWORKFLOW

iv) Click on **"OK"**. Before clicking on **"OK"**, check whether the server name is there in the server edit box or not. If not configure the server, then start the server and select that server here.

v) Explore the Sessions folder from the Navigator and select the created session (ROUTERSESSION) and drag and drop it into the Workflow Designer workspace.

vi) From the Tool bar, select the **"Link Tasks"** icon, and drag the link from "Workflow" to **"Task"**.

vii) Save the workflow by selecting ***"Repository→Save"***.

viii) To start workflow, select the menu item **"Workflow→Start Workflow"**. "Work flow Monitor" icon will appear on the System Tray.

ix) Open the "Workflow Monitor" by double clicking on it.

x) You can see the status of workflow. If the Workflow is successful, then the "ROUTERSESSION" and "ROUTERWORKFLOW" are shown in the succeeded part. To view how many Rows got transferred from source to target double click on the "ROUTERSESSION".

xi) "Properties of ROUTERSESSION" window opens. In this window, you can see the status. Error messages, in any, are displayed in the "First Error entry" in this window.

xii) For this example the "Source Success Rows" entry will contain 14 and the "Target Success Rows" will be 3, 5 and 6 for the three departments.

Thus we have successfully completed the workflow of transferring the sources rows from EMP table to DEPT10, DEPT20, DEPTMS tables in "scottolap" by applying the "Router" transformation to get the employees who belong to department number 10 to DEPT10 table, employees belong to department number 20 to DEPT20 table and remaining employee information to DEPTMS table.

Checking the Output

To see whether the target rows have been dumped into the target table, connect to the target table in the target database by using the following SQL statements.

SQL syntax: connect <username>/<password>

e.g. : SQL> connect scottolap/scottolap; Connected.

To see the rows of the target table, use the following SQL statement:

SQL syntax: select * from <table name>;

e. g: SQL>select * from dept10; 3 rows selected.
SQL> select * from dept20; 5 rows selected.
SQL> select * from deptms; 6 rows selected.

4.8 Sorter and Sequence Generator Transformations

Using Sorter Transformation, we can sort on employee salary column and using Sequence Generator Transformation, assign a sequence number for each employee in the same mapping.

To work with Sorter and Sequence Generator Transformations, create a folder for this project.

Creating a Folder

1. Open the Repository manager:
   Start→Programs→Informatica Power center 6.1 OEM for i2→Repository Manager.
   Informatica Repository manager window opens.
2. Explore Repository and select the Repository "scottrep", right click on it and select the **"Connect"** from the pop up menu.
3. Create a new folder in the selected Repository by selecting the menu item "*Folder→Create*".
4. Enter the name of the folder in the popped up dialog box and click on **"OK"**.
   e.g. Folder name : SORTER_SEQUENCE.
5. The folder is now created. Now we have to work on Designer tool to create mapping.

Designer Tool

In the Designer Tool, select the source Database object and Target Database object and select the Transformations of type Sorter and Sequence Generator. The source Database objects can be selected using the Source Analyzer and the target Database object can be selected using the Warehouse Designer. The *Sorter Transformation* is used to sort the data either in ascending or in descending order. The *Sequence Generator* is used to generate sequence of values.

Selecting the Source Database Object

1. To work with the Source Analyzer first open the Designer tool. Open the Designer Tool: ***"Start→Programs→ Informatica Power center 6.1 OEM for i2→ Designer"***.
2. Connect to the Repository (scottrep) by entering the user name and password.
3. Select the folder "SORTER_SEQUENCE" and select the menu item "*Tools→Source Analyzer*".
4. Select the menu item ***"Sources→Import from Database"***.
5. "Import Tables" window opens, in it enter the ODBC data source, username, owner name and password.

e.g. ODBC Data source name : scott
Username : scott
Owner name : SCOTT
Password : tiger

6. Click on **"Connect"** and select the "EMP" table from "Select Tables" list and click on **"OK"** to import the EMP table to the Source Analyzer workspace.
7. The Source Database object is selected and is ready to use.

Selecting/Creating Target Database object

1. To select the Target Database object, select the menu item ***"Tools→Warehouse Designer"***.
2. **"Create Target Table"** window opens. In it enter the Target table name and select the Database type for Target table.

   e.g. Target Table name : SORTSEQUENCETARGET
   Database type : Oracle
3. After entering the details click on **"Create"** then click on "Done".
4. To create the fields of the target table double click on "SORTSEQUENCETARGET".
5. Now **"Edit Table"** window opens, in Edit Tables window go to **"Columns"** tab.
6. To enter the new fields, click on the icon :
7. The empty row will be displayed in the Columns tab. Enter the column details as follows by doing repeatedly for all columns, as shown in Fig. 4.101

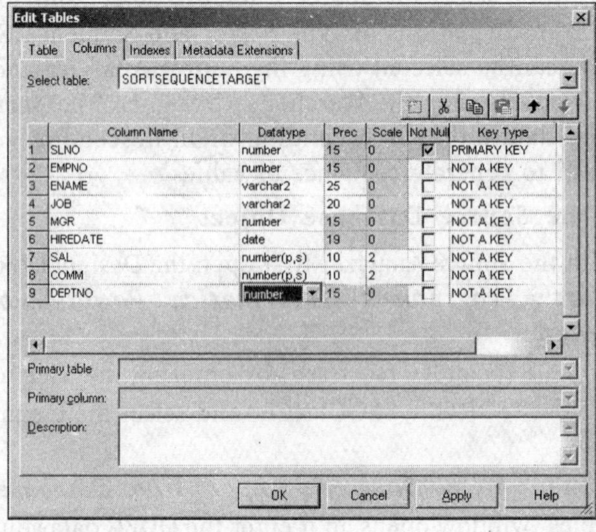

	Column Name	Datatype	Prec	Scale	Not Null	Key Type
1	SLNO	number	15	0	☑	PRIMARY KEY
2	EMPNO	number	15	0	☐	NOT A KEY
3	ENAME	varchar2	25	0	☐	NOT A KEY
4	JOB	varchar2	20	0	☐	NOT A KEY
5	MGR	number	15	0	☐	NOT A KEY
6	HIREDATE	date	19	0	☐	NOT A KEY
7	SAL	number(p,s)	10	2	☐	NOT A KEY
8	COMM	number(p,s)	10	2	☐	NOT A KEY
9	DEPTNO	number	15	0	☐	NOT A KEY

Fig.4.101

8. Click on **"Apply"** and on **"OK"**.
9. Now the Warehouse Designer workspace looks as in Fig. 4.102

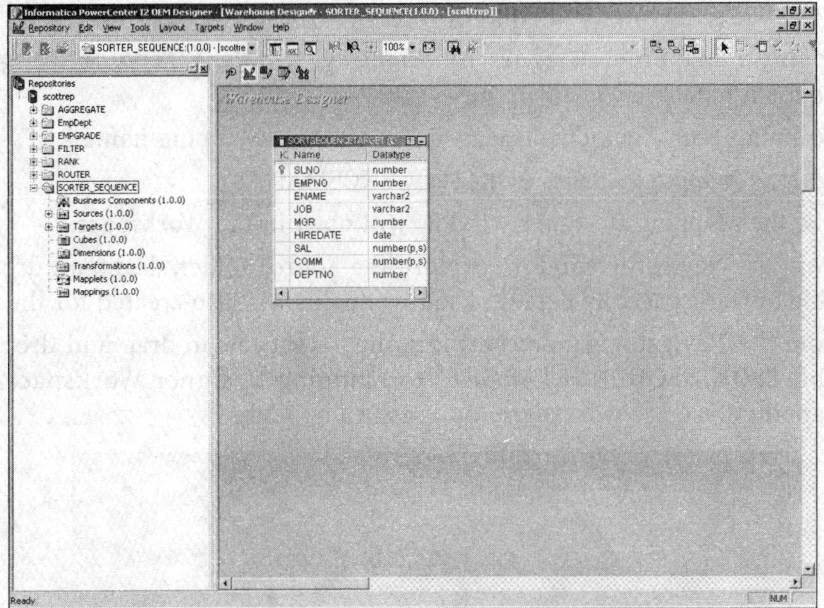

Fig. 4.102

10. The template for the target table is ready and we need to create the target table in the target Database. To create the table in the target database, select the menu item "Targets→Generate/Execute SQL" from the main menu.
11. Now the **"Database Object Generation"** window opens.
12. In "Generation Objects" group, check Create table check box and click on **"Generate** and **Execute"**.
13. *"Connect to an ODBC Data source"* dialog opens. In this dialog enter ODBC Data source, Username, Password and click on "Connect".

    e.g. ODBC Data source : scott (Oracle in oar home 90)

    Username : scottolap

    Password : scottolap
14. A message box will pop up with the following message "Files MKTABLES.SQL already exists. Do you want to overwrite the contents of this file?" click on **"OK"**.
15. The Target table got created on the Target Database.

Mapping Designer

The Mapping Designer is used to map the flow of data from Source to Target. Here is the procedure to create the mapping to transfer the data from source to target.

1. Open the Mapping Designer by selecting: "***Tools→Mapping Designer***" from the main menu.
2. "Mapping Name" window opens. Enter the New Mapping name.
   e.g. New Mapping Name: SORTSEQUENCEMAP.
3. Now the Mapping Designer window will open in the Workspace.
4. From the Navigator window, explore the Source folder, drag and drop the EMP table to workspace. By default a source qualifier is also created for the EMP table.
5. From the Navigator window, explore the Target folder, drag and drop the target table "SORTSEQUENCETARGET" to Mapping Designer Workspace. Now the Mapping Designer workspace looks as in Fig. 4.103.

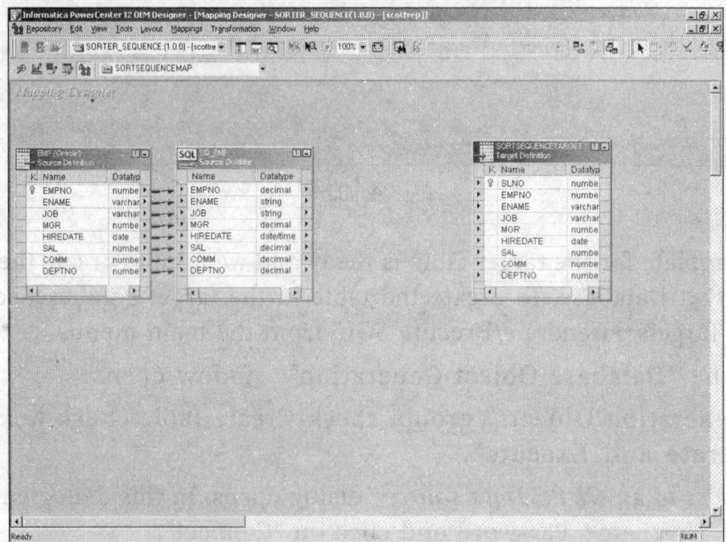

Fig. 4.103

6. Select the Transformation of type Router by selecting the menu "***Transformation→Create***" to create the new transformation.
7. **"Create Transformation"** window opens, select the **"Type of transformation"** as "Sorter" and enter name of transformation as **"SORTER"**.
8. Click on **"Create"**, then on **"Done"**.
9. Drag and drop the EMPNO, ENAME, DEPTNO, JOB, MGR, HIREDATE, SAL, COMM, DEPTNO columns of EMP Source Qualifier to "SORTER", after dragging the

respective columns in the workspace looks as in Fig. 4.104.

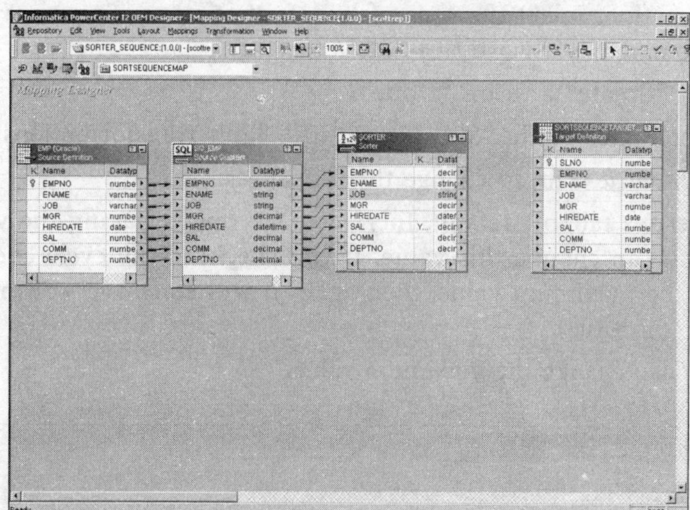

Fig. 4.104

10. Double click on the "SORTER" transformation. The "Edit Transformations" window opens; go to "Ports" tab of "Edit Transformations" window and then the Ports tab looks as in Fig. 4.105.

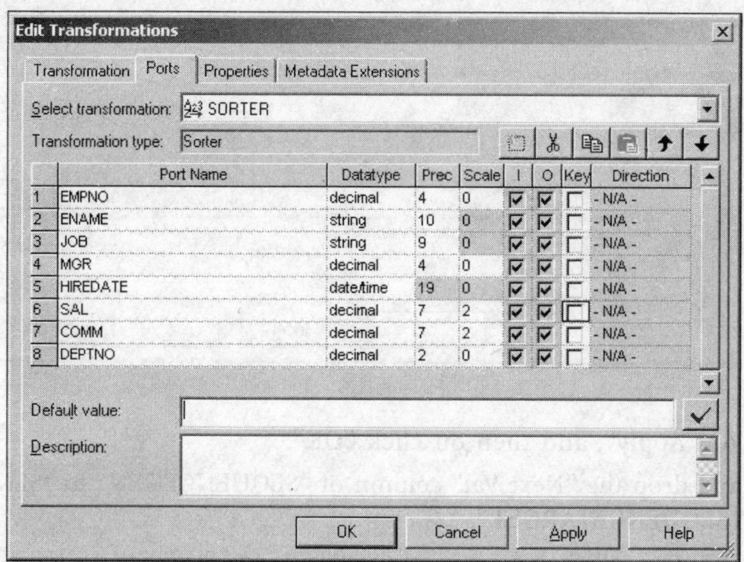

Fig. 4.105

11. Check on the key column of SAL Port name and on Direction column of SAL Port name select the "Ascending" value. Click on **"Apply"** and on **"OK"**.

12. Select the menu item "***Transformations→ Create***" to create a new transformation. Select the type of transformation as "Sequence Generator" and enter the name as "SEQUENCEGEN".
13. Click on **"Create"** and on **"Done"**.
14. Now double click on the "SEQUENCEGEN", "Edit Transformations" window opens.
15. Go to *Properties* tab, to change the properties.
16. In Properties tab, by default, Increment by row is having the value "1", if you want, you can change this value. If you check on the cycle check box, once it reaches the maximum value, then again it will start overwriting from the first number (Fig.4.106).
17. You can also change the maximum value.

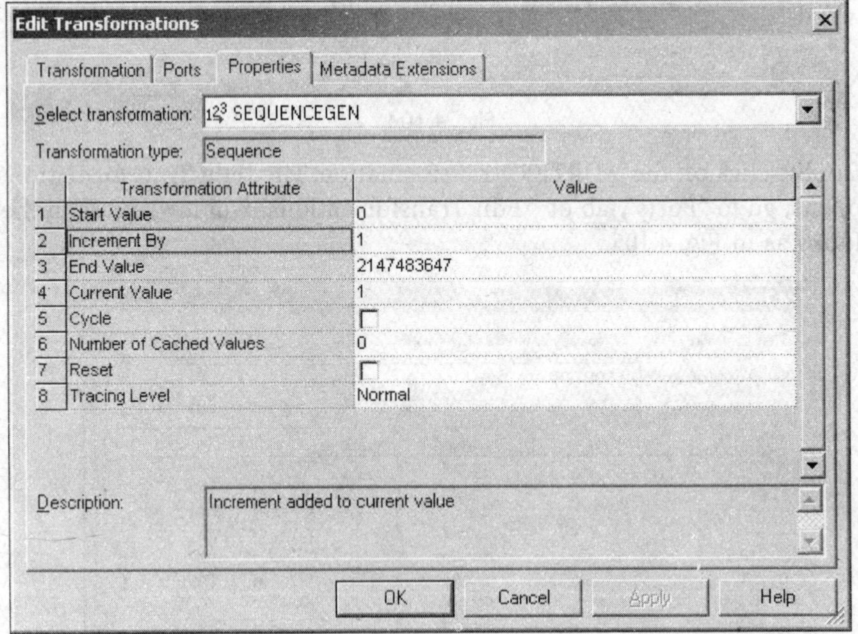

Fig. 4.106

18. Click on **"Apply"**, and then on click **"OK"**.
19. Drag and drop the "Next Val" column of "SEQUENCEGEN" to "SLNO" column of "SORTSEQUENCETARGET".
20. Drag and drop all the columns of "SORTER" to "SORTSEQUENCETARGET". Now the Mapping designer workspace looks as in Fig. 4.107.

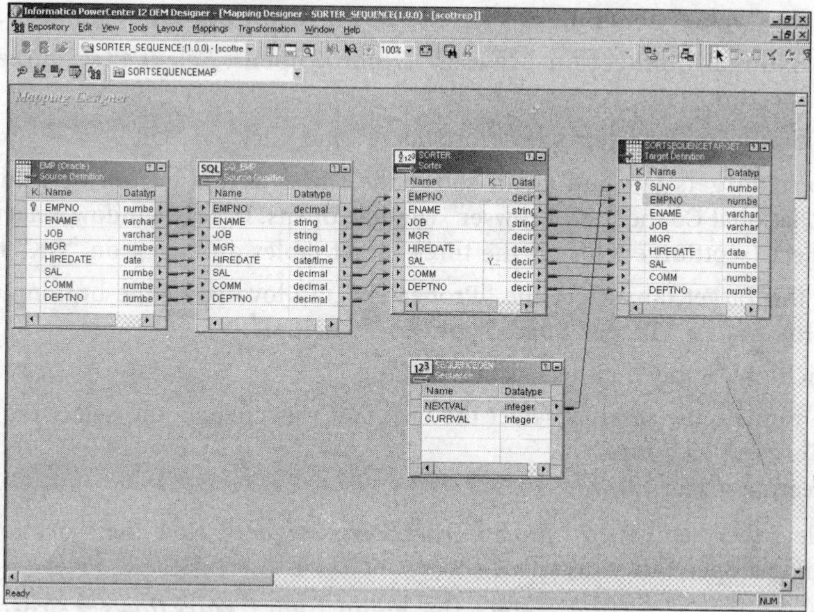

Fig. 4.107

21. Validate the mapping by selecting the menu item ***"Mappings→ Validate"***.
22. If the mapping is valid, save the mapping to Repository by selecting the menu item ***"Repository→Save"*** from the main menu.

Workflow Manager

Defining Tasks

1. To define the task, create a session object. Select the folder "SORTER_SEQUENCE" " and click on "*Tools→Task*".
2. **"Task Developer"** window opens in the workspace.
3. To create a session object, select "*Tasks→Create*".
4. **"Create Task"** window opens. Enter the values "Select the task type to create" as "Session" and enter a user-defined name for this task, then click on "Create".

   e.g. Select the task type to create : Session
   Enter a new name for this task : SORTSEQUENCESESS.
5. Mappings window opens, select the Mapping as "SORTSEQUENCEMAP".
6. Click on **"OK"** and on **"Done"** of **"Create Task"** dialog.
7. Double click on the created session (SORTSEQUENCESESS).
8. **"Edit Tasks"** window opens, go to *"Sources"* tab.

9. In the **"Value"** column, click on the Down Arrow button.
10. "Relational Connection Browser" window opens. Select the Source relational connection.
11. In our example, select the "scottsource" and click on **"OK"**.
12. Go to Targets tab and again select the Down arrow button of Values column. "Relational Connection Browser" window opens. In this window, select the Target object (scotttarget) for all the three target tables and click on **"OK"** button.
13. In the Target tab, select the **"Properties"** tab located at the bottom. Change the value of the **"Target Load Type"** as **"Normal"**.
14. Click on **"Apply"**, and click on **"OK"**.
15. To validate the session, select the task that was created and select the menu item "***Tasks→ Validate***".
    Creating a Workflow:

1. Select the menu item "***Tools→Workflow Designer***". Now the Workflow Designer window opens in Workspace.
2. To create a workflow, select the menu item "***Workflows→ Create***". "Create Workflow" window opens.
3. In General tab, enter the name of workflow.
   e.g. Name: SORTSEQUENCEWORKFLOW
4. Click on **"OK"**. (Before clicking on **"OK"**, check whether the server name is there in the server edit box or not. If not, configure the server (Informatica Server), then start the server and select that server here.
5. Explore the Sessions folder from the Navigator and select the created session (SORTSEQUENCESESS) and drag and drop it into the Workflow Designer workspace.
6. From the Tool bar, select the "Link Tasks", and drag the link from "Workflow" to Task.
7. Save the workflow by selecting "***Repository→Save***".
8. To start workflow, select the menu item "*Workflow→Start Workflow*".
   "Work flow Monitor" icon will appear on the System Tray.
9. Open the "Workflow Monitor" by double clicking on it.
10. Now you can see the status of our workflow. If the Workflow is successful, then the "SORTSEQUENCESESS" and "SORTSEQUENCEWORKFLOW" are shown in the succeeded part. To view how many Rows got transferred from source to target, double click on the "SORTSEQUENCESESS".
11. "Properties of SORTSEQUENCESESS" window opens. In this window, you can see the status, if any errors occurred, the error messages are displayed in the "First Error entry" in this window.

12. For this example, the "Source Success Rows" entry will contain 14 and the "Target Success Rows" will also contain 14.
13. Thus we have successfully completed the workflow of transferring the source rows from EMP table to SORTSEQUENCETARGET table in "scottolap" by applying the "Sorter" and "Sequence Generator" transformations to get the employees list in ascending order according to their salaries.

Checking the Output

To see whether the target rows have been dumped into the target table, connect to the target table in the target database using the following SQL statements.

SQL syntax: connect <username>/<password>

e.g : SQL> connect scottolap/scottolap;

Connected

To see the rows of the target table, use the following SQL statement.

SQL syntax: select * from <table name>;

e.g.: SQL>select * from sortsequencetarget;

SLNO	EMPNO	ENAME	JOB	MGR	HIREDATE	SAL	COMM	DEPTNO
1	7369	SMITH	CLERK	7902	17-DEC-80	800		20
2	7900	JAMES	CLERK	7698	03-DEC-81	950		30
3	7876	ADAMS	CLERK	7788	23-MAY-87	1100		20
4	7521	WARD	SALESMAN	7698	22-FEB-81	1250	500	30
5	7654	MARTIN	SALESMAN	7698	28-SEP-81	1250	1400	30
6	7934	MILLER	CLERK	7782	23-JAN-82	1300		10
7	7844	TURNER	SALESMAN	7698	08-SEP-81	1500	0	30
8	7499	ALLEN	SALESMAN	7698	20-FEB-81	1600	300	30
9	7782	CLARK	MANAGER	7839	09-JUN-81	2450		10
10	7698	BLAKE	MANAGER	7839	01-MAY-81	2850		30
11	7566	JONES	MANAGER	7839	02-APR-81	2975		20
12	7788	SCOTT	ANALYST	7566	19-APR-87	3000		20
13	7902	FORD	ANALYST	7566	03-DEC-81	3000		20
14	7839	KING	PRESIDENT		17-NOV-81	5000		10

14 rows selected.

4.9 Type 1 Slowly Changing Dimensions

In this section, we will discuss how to implement Type 1 slowly changing dimensions. In this type, the old attributes will be overwritten with the new fields. So, in the dimension table also, we will update the latest data available in the source tables. In other words, we will not maintain any previous data. To illustrate this, we will use the DEPT table in the "scott" database.

Create a separate folder for this task using Repository Manager tool.

Creating a Folder

1. Open the Repository Manager:

   Start → Programs → Informatica Power center 6.1 OEM for i2 → Repository Manager

   Informatica Repository Manager window, shown in Fig. 4.108 opens.

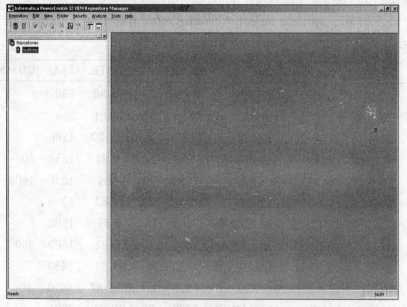

Fig. 4.108

2. Explore Repositories and select the repository **"scottrep"**, right click on it and select **"Connect"** from the pop up menu.
3. Create a new folder in the selected Repository by selecting the menu item: "***Create→ Folder***".
4. Enter the name for the folder in the popped up dialog box and click on **"OK"**.

   e.g.: Folder name: TYPE1

5. Now we have to work on Designer tool to create mapping.

Designer Tool

In the Designer Tool, select the source database object and target database object and select the transformation as Aggregator. The source database object can be selected using the Source Analyzer and the target database object can be selected using the Warehouse Designer.

Selecting the Source Database Object:

1. To work with the Source Analyzer, first we need to open the Informatica Designer Tool:

   Start→ Programs→ Informatica Power center 6.1 OEM for i2→ Designer
2. Connect to the repository (scottrep) by entering the username and password.
3. Now, select the folder "TYPE1" and select the menu item ***"Tools→Source Analyzer"***.
4. To import the source table, select the menu item "*Sources→Import from database*".
5. "Import tables" window opens. Enter the ODBC data source, username, owner name and password.

   e.g. : ODBC Data source name : scott (oracle in ora home 90)
   Username : scott
   Owner name : SCOTT
   Password : tiger
6. Click on "Connect", select the DEPT table from "Select tables" list and click on "OK" to import the DEPT table to the Source Analyzer workspace.
7. The source database object is selected and now we need to select the target database object.

Selecting/Creating the Target database object

1. Select the menu item ***"Tools→ Warehouse Designer"***.
2. To create the Target table, select the "*Targets → Create*" from the main menu.
3. "Create Target Table" window opens. Enter the Target Table name and select the Database type for Target table.

   e.g.: Target Table Name : TYPE1TARGET
   Database type : Oracle
4. After entering these details, click on **"Create"** and then click on **"Done"**.
5. Now, you can see the target table in the Warehouse Designer Workspace without any Fields.

6. To enter the fields of the target table double-click on it.
7. "Edit Table" window opens. In Edit Tables window, go to "Columns" tab.
8. To enter the New Fields, click on the following icon:

9. The empty row will be displayed in the Columns tab. Now enter the Column details and repeat the same procedure to add remaining fields of the table (Fig. 4.109).

Column name	Data Type	Precision	Scale	NULL Not	Key Type	Business Name
deptno	number	15	0	YES	Primary Key	
dname	Varchar2	25	0	No	Not a Key	
loc	Varchar2	25	0	No	Not a Key	

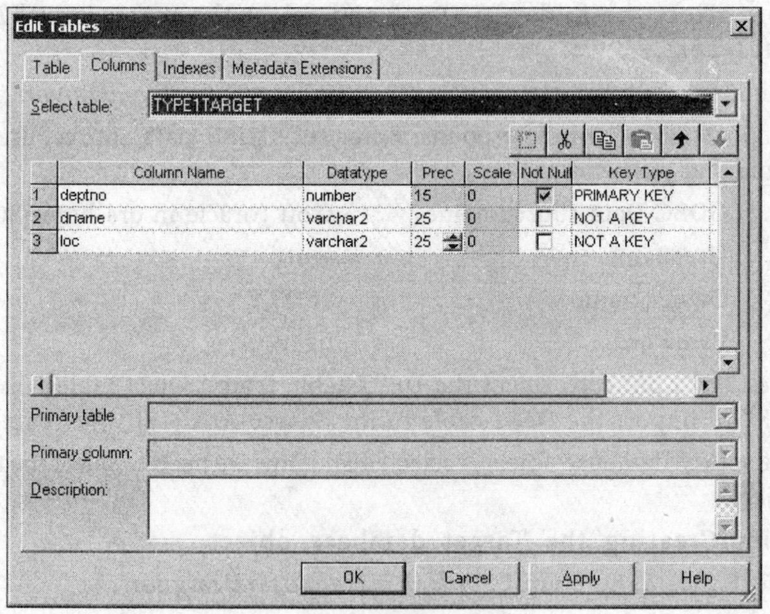

Fig. 4.109

10. Click on **"Apply"**, then on **"OK"**, after entering the target table fields.
11. The template for the target table is designed. To create the Target table in the Target Database, select the menu item **"*Targets → Generate/Execute SQL*"** from the main menu.
12. Now, the **"Database Object Generation"** window opens, in **"Generation objects"** group select the **"*Create table*"** check box and click on **"Generate and execute"** as shown in Fig. 4.110.

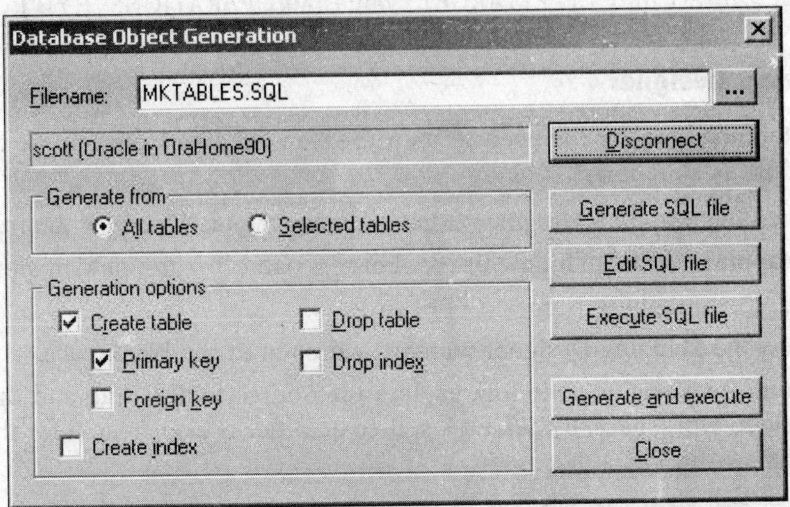

Fig. 4.110

13. "Connect to an ODBC Data Source" dialog opens. Enter ODBC Data source, Username, Password and click on "*Connect*", as shown in Fig. 4.111.

    e.g.: ODBC Data Source : scott (Oracle in ora home 90)
    Username : scottolap
    Password : scottolap

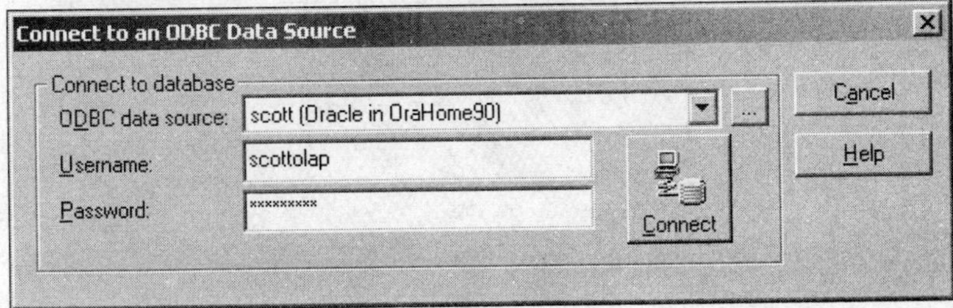

Fig. 4.111

14. A message box with the message: "Files MKTABLES.SQL already exists. Do you want to overwrite the contents of this file?" will appear; click on **"OK"**.
15. Now, the Target table got created in the Target Database.
16. After creating the Target table, insert four samples rows into target table by executing following SQL statements:

    SQL> insert into TYPE1TARGET values(10,'ACCOUNTING','NEWYORK');

    SQL> insert into TYPE1TARGET values(20,'RESEARCH','DALLAS');

    SQL> insert into TYPE1TARGET values(30,'SALES','CHICAGO');

SQL> insert into TYPE1TARGET values(40,'OPERATIONS','HYD');

Mapping Designer

The Mapping Designer is used to map the flow of data from Source to Target. The procedure is as follows:

1. Open the Mapping Designer from the main menu: **"*Tools → Mapping Designer*"**
2. **"Mapping Name"** window opens. Enter a name for the new mapping.
   e.g.: New Mapping Name: TYPE1MAP
   Now the Mapping Designer window will open in the Workspace.
3. From the Navigator window, explore the Source folder, drag and drop the DEPT table to Workspace. By default a source qualifier is also created for the DEPT table as shown in Fig. 4.112.

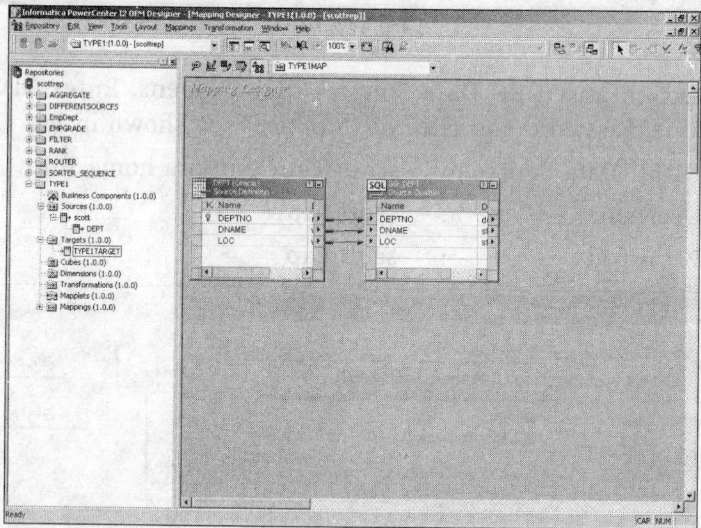

Fig. 4.112

4. Drag and drop the target table "TYPE1TARGET" from the Navigator to Mapping Designer Workspace.
5. To create the new transformation, select the Transformation of type "Look Up" by selecting the menu item **"*Transformation → Create*"**.
6. **"Create Transformation"** window opens. Select the "Type of transformation to create" as "Look Up" and the name of transformation to create as "LOOKUP" Click on **"Create"**, then on "Done".
7. **"Select Look** Up **Table for Look Up Transformation"** window opens. Select

the Location of Lookup table as "TARGET". Select the Lookup table you want this transformation to use as "TYPE1TARGET" and click on "OK", as shown in Fig. 4.113.

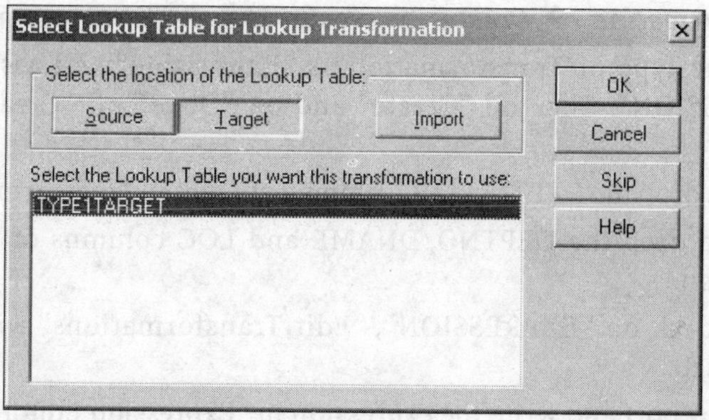

Fig. 4.113

8. In "Create Transformations" window, click on "Done".
9. Drag and drop the DEPTNO column of Source Qualifier to Lookup.
10. Double click on "LOOKUP" and go to "Conditions" tab to write the Lookup condition.
11. Select the "Add a new condition" icon and write the condition as shown in Fig. 4.114.

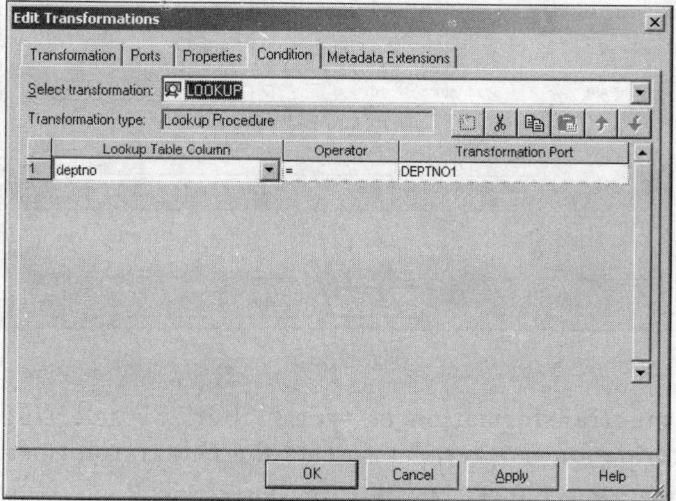

Fig. 4.114

12. Go to **"Properties"** tab. In the "Value" column of "Location Information", click on the down arrow button. **"Select Database"** window opens, select the Database

connection as "scotttarget" and click on **"OK"**.

13. Click on **"Apply"** and on **"OK"** of "Edit Transformations" window.
14. Select the Transformation of type "Expression" by selecting the menu item "***Transformation → Create***" to create the new transformation.
15. Select the type of Transformation as "Expression" and assign it the name as "EXPRESSION". Click on **"Create"** and on **"Done"** of "Create Transformation" window.
16. Drag and drop the DEPTNO, LOC columns of Lookup Transformation to Expression.
17. Drag and drop the DEPTNO, DNAME and LOC columns of Source Qualifier to Expression.
18. Double click on "EXPRESSION", "Edit Transformations" window opens, go to "Ports" tab.
19. Add a new port and write the expression in "Expression Editor" as specified below.

    e.g.: IFF (DEPTNO = DEPTNO1 AND LOC1 != LOC,TRUE,FALSE)
20. Validate the expression and apply the settings, as shown in Fig. 4.115.

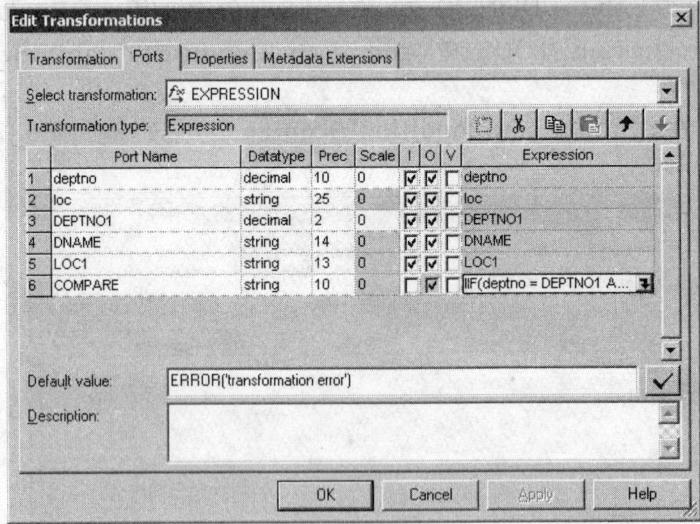

Fig. 4.115

21. Select the Transformation of type "Filter" by selecting the menu item "***Transformation → Create***" to create the new transformation.
22. Assign the name "FILTER" for this transformation.
23. Drag and drop the following columns from "EXPRESSION", DEPTNO, DNAME, LOC, we mapped from Source Qualifier of DEPT to "EXPRESSION", and also map COMPARE column from "EXPRESSION " to "FILTER".

24. Double click on "FILTER" to write the filter condition, just put the "COMPARE" column in the "Formula Editor" of "Expression Editor". Validate the condition and apply the settings.
25. Select the Transformation of type "Update Strategy" by selecting the menu item "*Transformation → Create*" to create the new transformation and name it as "UPDATESTRATEGY".
26. Drag and drop DEPTNO, DNAME, LOC columns of FILTER to UPDATESTRATEGY.
27. Double click on UPDATESTRATEGY. "Edit Transformations" window opens. Go to "Properties" tab and click on the down arrow button of "Update Strategy Expression".
28. In "Formula Editor", enter the following text.
    DD_UPDATE.
29. Validate the expression and apply the settings.
30. Drag and drop the DEPTNO, DNAME, LOC columns of UPDATESTRATEGY to target table (TYPE1TARGET).
31. The final mapping looks as shown in Fig. 4.116.

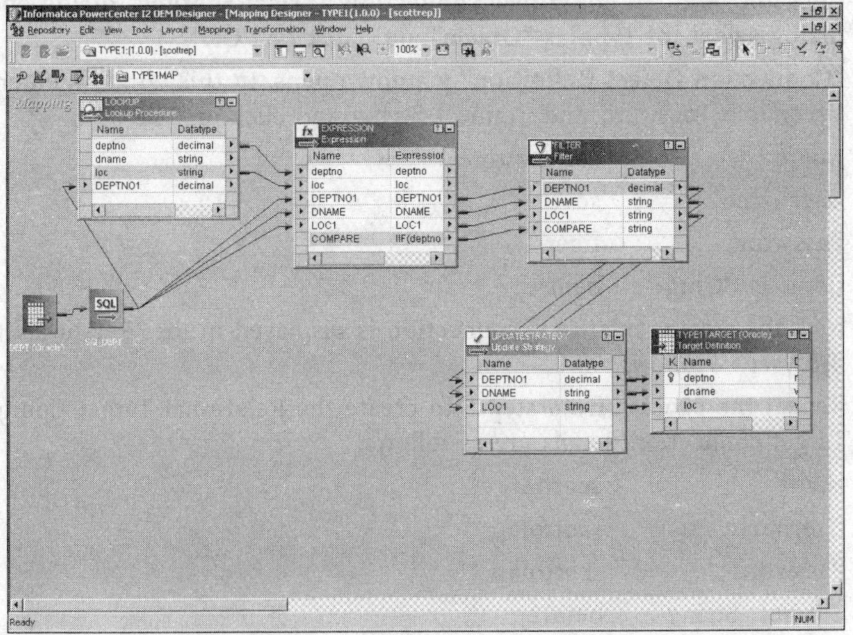

Fig. 4.116

32. Validate the Mapping: "***Mappings→ Validate***".
33. If the Mapping is valid, save the Mapping: "***Repository→Save***".

Workflow Manager

Before creating a workflow, two relational connections should be created and a server should be configured and executed.

Creating Relational Connections:

1. Open the Workflow Manager by selecting:
   Start→ Programs→ Informatica Power center 6.1 OEM for i2 → Workflow Manager
2. The "Informatica Power Center Workflow Manager" window opens, right click on **"scottrep"** repository and click on **"connect"** from the popup menu.
3. **"Connect to Repository"** window opens, in this window enter username and password and click on "Connect".

   e.g.: Username : scottrep
   Password : scottrep
4. Select the menu item "***Connections→ Relational***", **"Relational Connection Browser"** window opens.
5. Click on **"Add"** to add a new connection. **"Select Subtype"** dialog opens, in this dialog select the type as **"Oracle"** and click on **"OK"**.
6. **"Connection Object Definition"** window opens. In this window, enter the name, Username, Password and Connect String and click on **"OK"**.

   Name : scottsource
   Username : scott
   Password : tiger
   Connect String : oemrep
7. Now the created relational connection is displayed in the "Relational Connection Browser" window.
8. Repeat the process from step 5 to create the Relational Target Connection. The Target connection details are as follows:

   Name : scotttarget
   Username : scottolap
   Password : scottolap
   Connect String : oemrep
9. Click on **"Close"** button of "Relational Connection Browser" after creating the source and target relational connections.

Configuring the Server:

To configure the server, the procedure is as follows:

1. Select ***"Start → Programs → Informatica Server → Informatica Server Setup"*** to open the server setup. Now the "Informatica Server Setup Application– Options" window will be displayed.
2. Click on **"Continue"**, a window opens in which you need to enter the platform key and the keys for the database you are using.
3. Go to server tab in the same window and enter the Server Name, TCP/IP Host Address.

   e.g.: Server Name : scottserver

   TCP/IP Host Address : icssrv2k3.
4. Go to Repository tab and enter the Repository Name, Repository User, Repository Password, Repository Server Host Name and Repository Port Number. Click on **"Apply"** and on **"OK"**, as shown in Fig. 4.117.

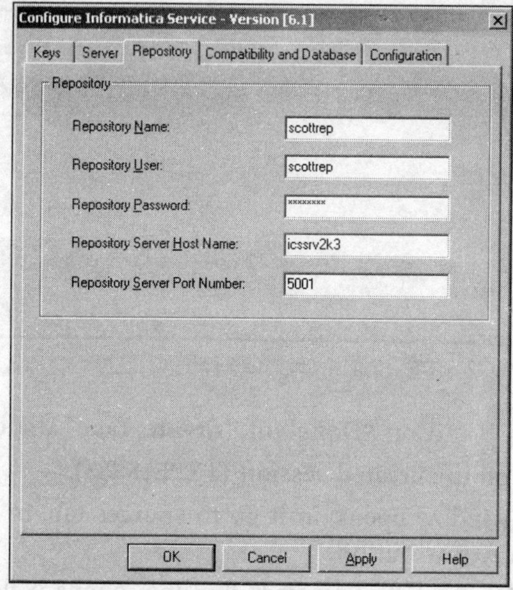

Fig. 4.117

5. **"Informatica Server Setup Application – Options"** window will open, click on "Exit".

Now the server is configured successfully. After this, start the Informatica service from the "Services" window. To start the service, select ***"Start → Administrator Tools → Services"***. In **"Services"** window, select **"Informatica"** service and right click on it and select ***"Start"*** from the popup menu.

Defining Tasks

1. To define the task, a session object must be created. Before creating a session, select the folder "TYPE1" and click on ***"Tools → Task Developer"***.
2. **"Task Developer"** window opens in the workspace.
3. To create a session object, select ***"Tasks → Create"***. Now **"Create Task"** window opens. Enter the values "Select the task type to create" as "Session" and enter a user-defined name for the task, then click on ***"Create"***.

   e.g.: Select the task type to create : Session

   Enter a new name for this task : TYPE1SESS
4. Now Mappings window opens, in this dialog box, select the Mapping as "TYPE1MAP", as shown in Fig. 4.118.

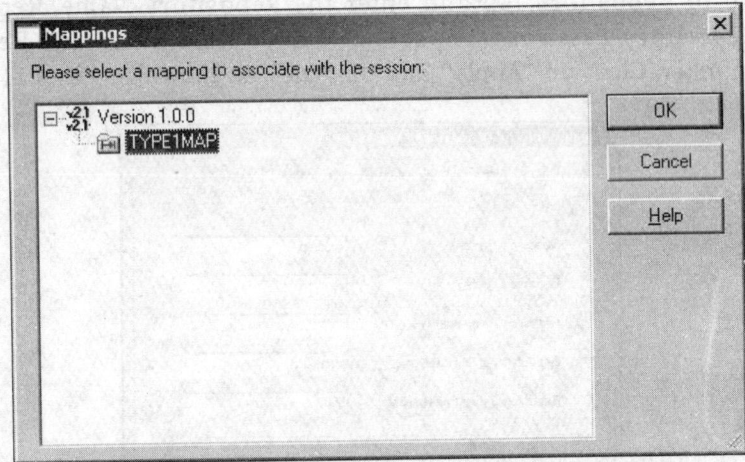

Fig. 4.118

5. Click on **"OK"**, and on **"Done"** of **"Create Task"** dialog.
6. Double click on the created session (TYPE1SESS).
7. **"Edit Tasks"** window opens, in it go to sources tab. In the **"Value"** column, click on the Down Arrow button.
8. **"Relational Connection Browser"** window opens. Select the Source relational connection. In our example, select the "scottsource" and click on **"OK"**.
9. Go to *Targets* tab and again, select the down arrow button of *Values* column.
10. **"Relational Connection Browser"** window opens. In this window, select the Target object (scotttarget) and click on **"OK"**.
11. In the Target tab select the **"Properties"** tab located at the bottom. Change the value of the "Target Load Type" as "Normal". Click on **"Apply"** and then on **"OK"**.

12. Select the task, which is created and select the menu item "*Tasks → Validate*".

Creating a Work flow:

1. Select the menu item ***"Tools → Workflow Designer"***. Now the Workflow Designer window opens in Workspace.
2. Now select the menu item ***"Workflows → Create"*** to create a workflow. **"Create Workflow"** window opens.
3. In General tab, enter the name of workflow.

   e.g.: Name: TYPE1WORKFLOW.
4. Click on **"OK"**. Before clicking on "OK", check whether the server name is there in the server edit box or not. If not, configure the server, then start the server and select that server here.
5. Explore the Sessions folder from the Navigator and select the created session (TYPE1SESS) and drag and drop it into the Workflow Designer workspace.
6. From the Tool bar select the "Link Tasks" icon, and drag the link from Workflow to Task. The "Link Tasks" icon shown below:

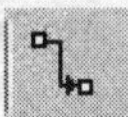

7. Save the workflow by selecting ***"Repository → Save"***.
8. To start workflow, select the menu item "*Workflow → Start Workflow*".

   "Workflow Monitor" icon will appear on the System Tray.
9. Open the **"Workflow Monitor"** by double clicking on it.
10. Now you can see the status of our workflow. If the Workflow is successful, "TYPE1SESS" and "TYPE1WORKFLOW" are shown in the Succeeded part. To view that how many Rows got transferred from source to target double click on the "TYPE1SESS".
11. "Properties of TYPE1SESS" window opens. In this window, you can see the status, if any errors occurred the error messages are displayed in the First Error entry in this window.
12. For this example, the "Source Success Rows" entry will contain 4 and the "Target Success Rows" will contain 1.

Thus we have successfully updated the LOC column of target table by using slowly changing dimension of type 1.

Checking the Output

To see whether the target rows have been dumped into the target table, connect to the target table in the target database using the following SQL statements.

SQL syntax: connect <username>/<password>

e.g.: SQL> connect scottolap/scottolap;

Connected.

To see the rows of the target table, use the following SQL statement.

SQL syntax: select * from <table name>;

e.g.: SQL> select * from TYPE1TARGET;

DEPTNO	DNAME	LOC
10	ACCOUNTING	NEWYORK
20	RESEARCH	DALLAS
30	SALES	CHICAGO
40	OPERATIONS	BOSTON

4 rows selected.

4.10 Type 2 Slowly Changing Dimensions

In this section, we will study the implementation of Type 2 slowly changing dimensions. In Type 2, historical data is maintained in the dimension tables and there are different ways of maintaining the historical data. We will discuss how to maintain historical data using flags.

In "scott" database, the location of a department may change. We will show how we can maintain the old data as well as the new data in the DEPT table.

In this example, we used two new columns. They are PMKEY (surrogate key) and FLAG. The PMKEY is a primary key. We are using this primary key to make the target accept duplicate rows and we make the DEPTNO not a key. For the above output, the recent record is assigned the flag value 1. If the record is duplicated, then the recent record flag value will be assigned 1 and the old record flag value will be assigned 0. In the above example, the DEPTNO=40, LOC is updated from HYDERABAD to BOSTON, so the old record flag value is set to 0 and the recent record flag value is set to 1.

To illustrate the Type 2 SCD, create a separate folder for this task in Repository Manager tool.

Creating a Folder

1. Open the Repository Manager:

   Start → Programs → Informatica Power center 6.1 OEM for i2 → Repository Manager

Informatica Repository Manager window, shown in Fig. 4.119 opens.

Fig. 4.119

2. Explore repositories and select the repository, "scottrep", right click on it and select **"Connect"** from the pop up menu.
3. Create a new folder in the selected repository by selecting the menu item: ***"Create → Folder"***.
4. Enter the name for the folder from the popped up dialog box and click on **"OK"**.

   e.g.: Folder name: TYPE2
5. The folder is created. Now we have to work on Designer tool to create mapping.

Designer Tool

To open the Informatica Designer Tool, open the Designer tool. The steps are:

Start→ Programs→ Informatica Power center 6.1 OEM for i2 → Designer.

Selecting the source database object

1. Connect to the repository (scottrep) by entering the username and password.
2. Now, select the folder "TYPE2" and select the menu item "*Tools à Source Analyzer*".
3. To import the source table, select the menu item "*Sources à Import from database*".
4. **"Import tables"** window opens. Enter the ODBC data source, username, owner name and password.

   e.g. : ODBC Data source name : scott
   Username : scott
   Owner name : SCOTT
   Password : tiger

5. Click on **"Connect"**, select the DEPT table from "Select tables" list and click on **"OK"** to import the DEPT table to the Source Analyzer workspace.
6. The source database object is selected. Now we need to select the target database object.

Selecting/Creating the Target Database Object

1. To select the target database object (table), select the menu item "***Tools→ Warehouse Designer***".
2. Open SQLPLUS and connect to SQLPLUS with username: "scottrep" and password: "scottrep". Enter the following SQL statements to create and insert the rows into target table.

   e.g.: SQL> create table TYPE2TARGET (PMKEY NUMBER, DEPTNO NUMBER, DNAME VARCHAR2(30), LOC VARCHAR2(20), FLAG NUMBER, CONSTRAINT PKCONSTRAINT PRIMARY KEY(PMKEY));

   Table Created.

   SQL> insert into type2target values(1, 10, 'ACCOUNTING', 'NEWYORK', 1);

   1 Row Inserted.

   SQL> insert into type2target values(2, 20, 'RESEARCH', 'DALLAS', 1);

   1 Row Inserted.

   SQL> insert into type2target values(3, 30, 'SALES', 'CHICAGO', 1);

   1 Row Inserted.

   SQL> insert into type2target values(4, 40, 'OPERATIONS', 'HYDERABAD', 1);

   1 Row Inserted.
3. To import the Target table, select the "***Targets → Import from Database***" from the main menu.
4. **"Import Tables"** window opens. Select ODBC Data Source, enter Username, Owner name and Password.

e.g.:	ODBC Data source name	:	scott
	Username	:	scottolap
	Owner name	:	SCOTTOLAP .
	Password	:	scottolap
5. Click on **"Connect"** and select the TYPE2TARGET table and click on **"OK"**.

Mapping Designer

The Mapping Designer is used to map the flow of data from Source to Target. The procedure to map our data from source to target is as follows:

1. Open the Mapping Designer by selecting "***Tools → Mapping Designer***" from the main menu. **"Mapping Name"** window opens. Enter a name for the new mapping.

   e.g.: New Mapping Name: TYPE2MAP

2. Now the Mapping Designer window will open in the Workspace. From the Navigator window, explore the Source folder, drag and drop the DEPT table to Workspace. By default a source qualifier is also created for the DEPT table.

3. Drag and drop the target table "TYPE2TARGET" twice from the Navigator to Mapping Designer Workspace. The screen looks as shown in Fig. 4.120.

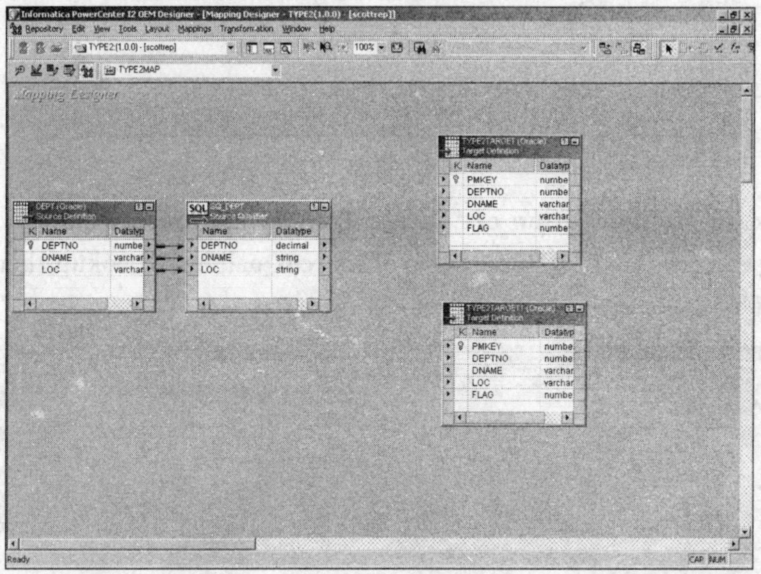

Fig. 4.120

4. In the above figure (Fig. 4.120), we are using the same target twice, because in TYPE2, if LOC column is modified in the source, that record will be inserted as a new record with FLAG value as 1, after inserting, the old FLAG value will be changed to 0. That is how we can maintain the previous values of attributes in Type 2 SCD.

5. Select the Transformation of type "Lookup" by selecting the menu item "***Transformation → Create***" to create the new transformation.

6. **"Create Transformation"** window opens, from it select the "Type of transformation to create" as Lookup and the name of transformation to create as "LOOKUP".

7. Click on **"Create"**, then on **"Done"**.

8. **"Select Lookup Table for Look Up Transformation"** window opens. Select

the Location of Lookup table as "TARGET". Select the Lookup table you want this transformation to use as "TYPE2TARGET" and click on **"OK"** button, as shown in Fig. 4.121.

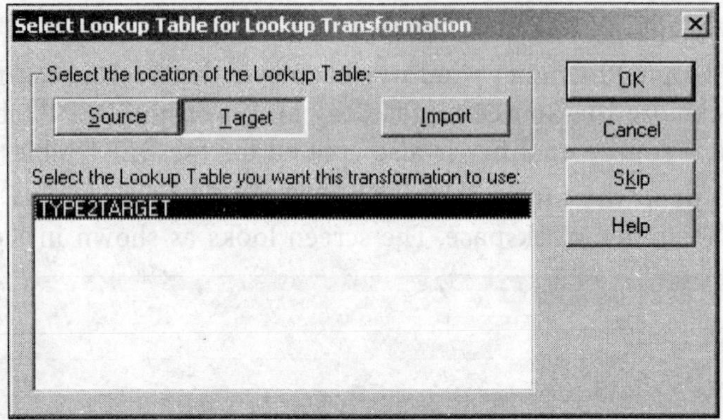

Fig. 4.121

9. Click on **"Done"** button of **"Create Transformations"** window.
10. Drag and drop the DEPTNO column of Source Qualifier to Lookup, then the Mapping Designer will appear as shown in Fig. 4.122.

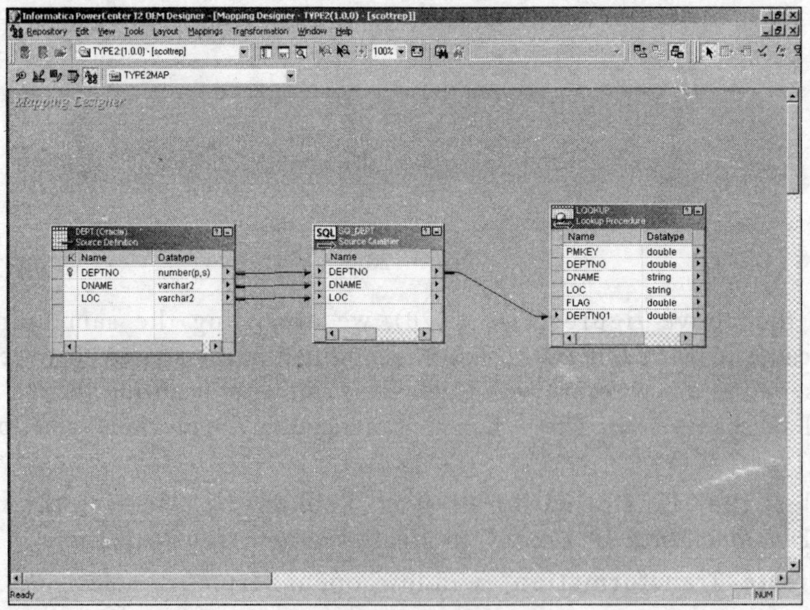

Fig. 4.122

11. Double click on "LOOKUP" and go to *"Conditions"* tab to write the Lookup condition.

12. Select the *"Add a new condition"* icon and write the condition as shown in Fig. 4.123.

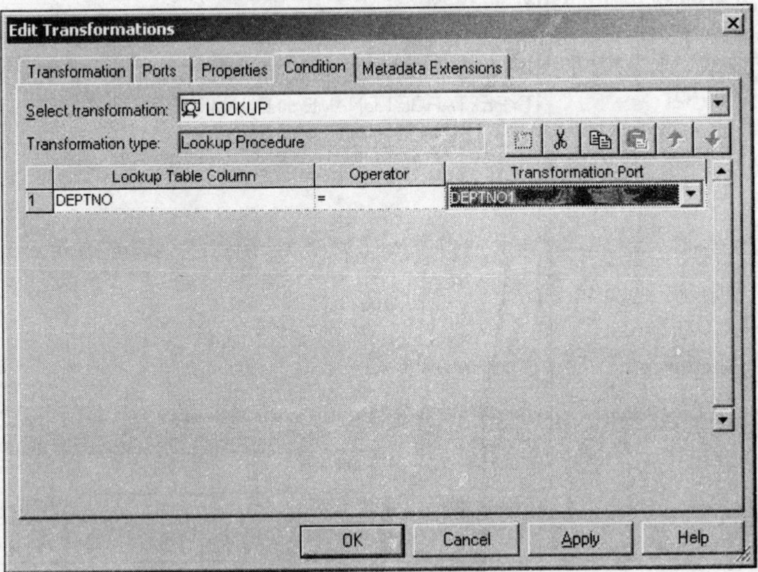

Fig. 4.123

13. Go to *"Properties"* tab. In *"Properties"* tab, in "Value" column of "Location Information", click on down arrow button. **"Select Database"** window opens, select the Database connection as "scotttarget".
14. Go to values column of "Lookup SQL override". "SQL Editor" window opens. Click on "Generate SQL" button, now the SQL query is generated. See Fig. 4.124.

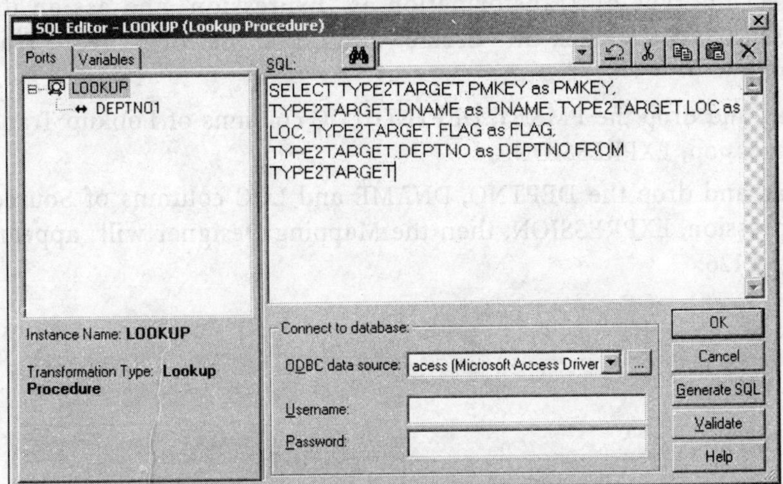

Fig. 4.124

15. Edit the SQL query as shown in Fig. 4.125 by connecting to database as scottolap.

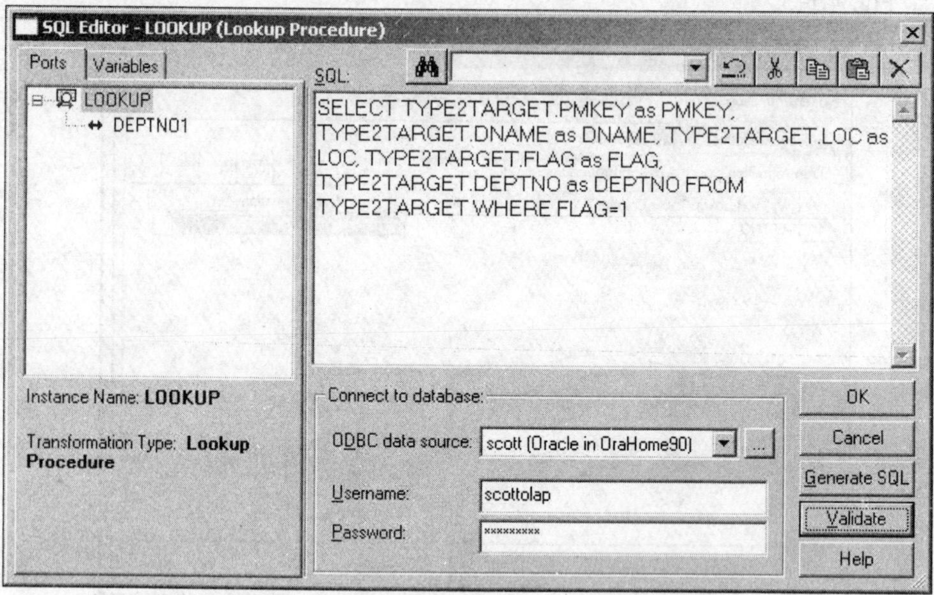

Fig. 4.125

16. Click on **"Validate"** and on **"OK"**.
17. Apply the settings in **"Edit Transformations"** window and click on **"OK"**. Select the Transformation of type "Expression" by selecting the menu item "***Transformation → Create***" to create the new transformation.
18. Select the type of Transformation as "Expression" and assign it the name as "EXPRESSION". Click on **"Create"** and on "Done" of "Create Transformation" window.
19. Drag and drop the PMKEY, DEPTNO, LOC columns of Lookup Transformation to Expression, EXPRESSION.
20. Drag and drop the DEPTNO, DNAME and LOC columns of Source Qualifier to Expression, EXPRESSION, then the Mapping Designer will appear as shown in Fig. 4.126.

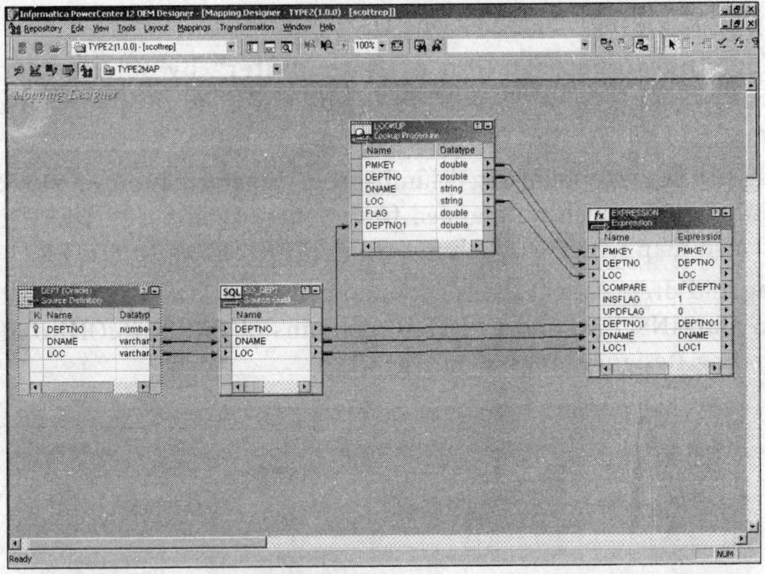

Fig. 4.126

21. Double click on "EXPRESSION", "Edit Transformations" window opens, go to "Ports" tab. Add a new port and write the expression in "Expression Editor" as specified below.

    e.g.: IIF (DEPTNO = DEPTNO1 AND LOC1! = LOC, TRUE, FALSE)

22. Add two more new ports and write the expression as shown in Fig. 4.127.

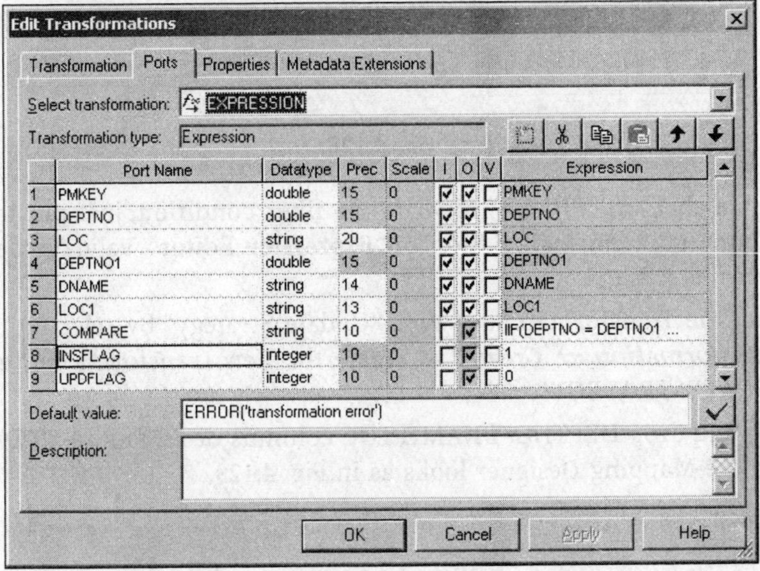

Fig. 4.127

23. Apply the settings and click on **"OK"**.
24. Select the Transformation of type **"Filter"** by selecting the menu item ***"Transformation → Create"*** to create the new transformation. Assign the name "FILTER" for this Transformation.
25. Drag and drop the following columns from transformation: EXPRESSION; DEPTNO, DNAME, LOC which we mapped from Source Qualifier of DEPT to EXPRESSION, and also map COMPARE column from EXPRESSION to FILTER.
26. Drag and drop PMKEY, which we mapped from LOOKUP to "EXPRESSION", and also map INSFLAG and UPDFLAG columns of EXPRESSION to FILTER, then the Mapping Designer looks as in Fig. 4.128.

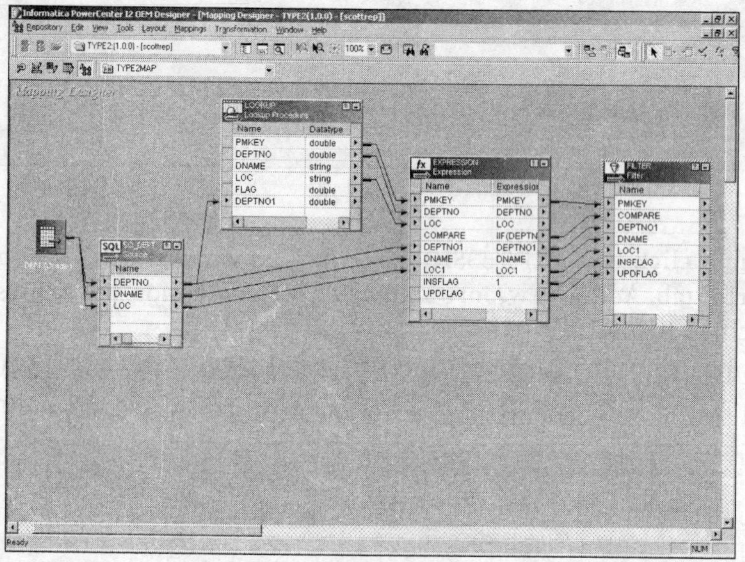

Fig. 4.128

27. Double click on "FILTER" to write the filter condition, just put the "COMPARE" column in the "Formula Editor" of "Expression Editor". Validate the condition and apply the settings.
28. Select the Transformation of type "Update Strategy" by selecting the menu item ***"Transformation → Create"*** to create the new transformation and name it as "UPDATESTRATEGY".
29. Drag and drop DEPTNO, DNAME, LOC columns of FILTER to UPDATESTRATEGY, then the Mapping Designer looks as in Fig. 4.129.

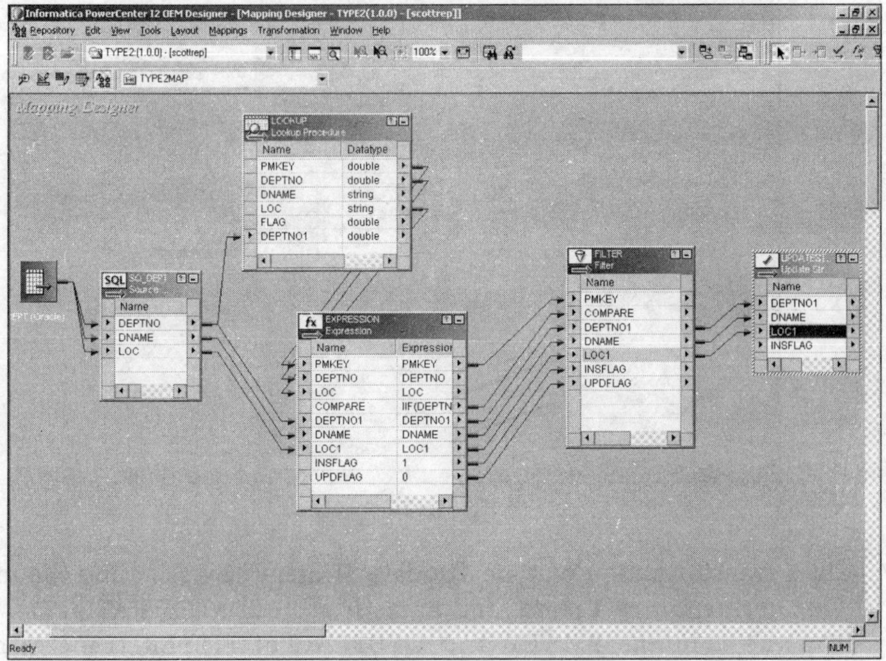
Fig. 4.129

30. Double click on UPDATESTRATEGY. "Edit Transformations" window opens. Go to "Properties" tab and click on the down arrow button of "Update Strategy Expression". In "Formula Editor", enter the following text: DD_INSERT.
31. Validate the expression and apply the settings.
32. Add one more transformation, "Sequence Generator" by selecting the menu item "***Transformation → Create***" and name it as "SEQGENERATOR".
33. Double click on "SEQGENERATOR" and go to properties tab.
34. Change the value of "Start value" to 5 and also the "Current value" to 5.
35. Apply the settings and click on **"OK"**.
36. Drag and drop the NEXTVAL column of "SEQGENERATOR" to PMKEY column of "TYPE2TARGET" table. Drag and drop the columns DEPTNO, DNAME, LOC, INSFLAG from FILTER to TYPE2TARGET, then the Mapping Designer looks as in Fig. 4.130.

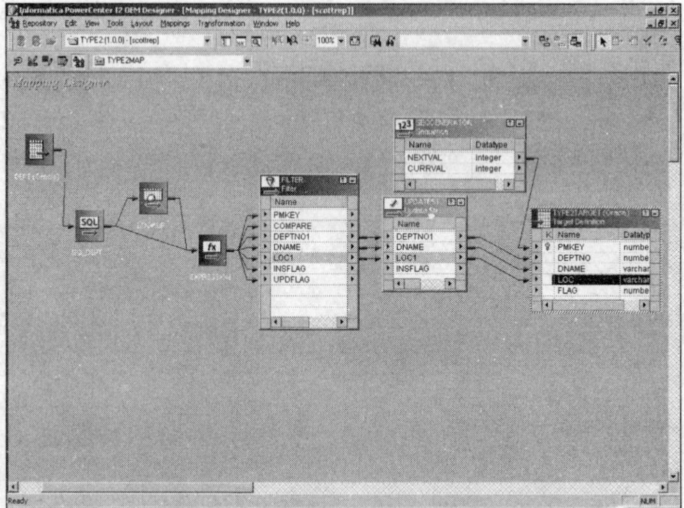

Fig. 4.130

37. Add a transformation of type **"Update Strategy"** by selecting the menu item "***Transformation → Create***" and name it as "UPDATESTRATEGY1". Drag and drop the columns PMKEY and UPDFLAG of FILTER transformation to UPDATESTRATEGY1, then the Mapping Designer will be as in Fig. 4.131.

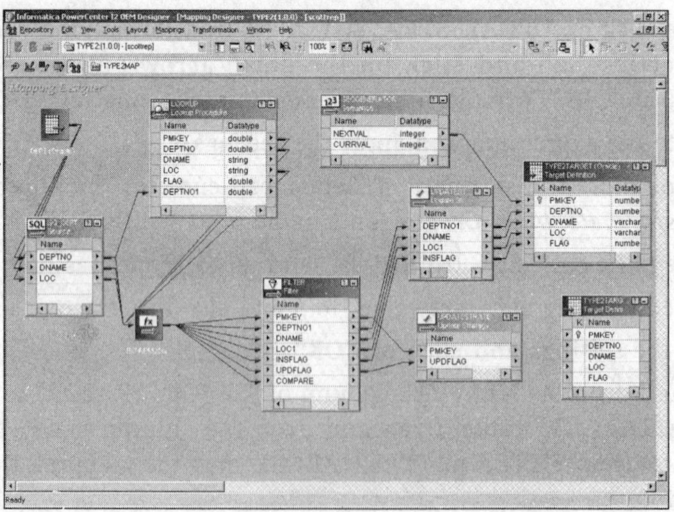

Fig. 4.131

38. Double click on UPDATESTRATEGY1. "Edit Transformations" window opens. Go to "Properties" tab and click on the down arrow button of "Update Strategy Expression". In "Formula Editor" enter the following text: DD_UPDATE. Validate the expression and apply the settings.

39. Drag and drop the columns PMKEY and UPDFLAG of UPDATESTRATEGY1 to second target table columns PMKEY and FLAG, then the Mapping Designer will be as shown in Fig. 4.132.

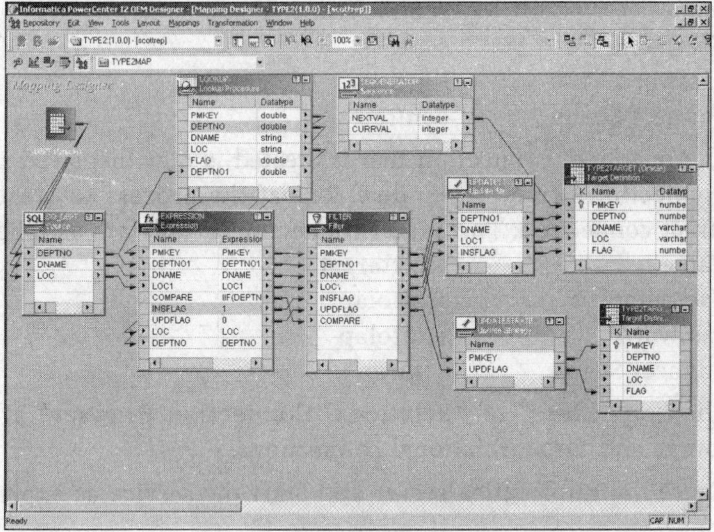

Fig. 4.132

40. Validate the Mapping: "***Mappings→ Validate***".
41. If the Mapping is valid, save the Mapping to Repository: "***Repository→Save***".

Workflow Manager

Before creating a workflow, two relational connections should be created and a server should be configured and executed.

1. **Creating Relational Connections**
   i. Open the Workflow Manager by selecting:
   Start→ Programs→ Informatica Power center 6.1 OEM for i2 → Workflow Manager
   ii. The "Informatica Power Center Workflow Manager" window opens, right click on **"scottrep"** repository and click on **"Connect"** from the popup menu.
   iii. **"Connect to Repository"** window opens, in this window enter username and password and click on **"Connect"**.
   e.g.: Username : scottrep
   Password : scottrep
   iv. Select the menu item *Connections→Relational*, "Relational Connection Browser" window opens. Click on "Add" to add a new connection. "Select

Subtype" dialog opens. Select the type as **"Oracle"** and click on **"OK"**.

v. "Connection Object Definition" window opens. Enter the name, Username, Password and Connect String and click on **"OK"**.

Name	:	scottsource
Username	:	scott
Password	:	tiger
Connect String	:	oemrep

vi. The relational connection that is created is now displayed in the "Relational Connection Browser" window. Repeat the process to create the Relational target connection. The Target connection details are as follows:

Name	:	scotttarget
Username	:	scottolap
Password	:	scottolap
Connect String	:	oemrep

vii. Click on **"Close"** of **"Relational Connection Browser"** after creating the source and target relational connections.

2. Configure the Informatica server and Start the service as explained in previous section.

3. **Defining Tasks**

i. To define the task, a session object must be created. Select the folder "TYPE2" and click on ***"Tools → Task Developer"***. "Task Developer" window opens in the workspace.

ii. To create a session object, select ***"Tasks → Create"***. Now "Create Task" window opens. Enter the values "Select the task type to create" as "Session" and enter a user-defined name for the task, then click on ***"Create"***.

E.g.: Select the task type to create: Session

Enter a new name for this task: TYPE2SESS

iii. Now Mappings window shown in Fig. 4.133 opens, in this dialog box select the Mapping as **"TYPE2MAP"**.

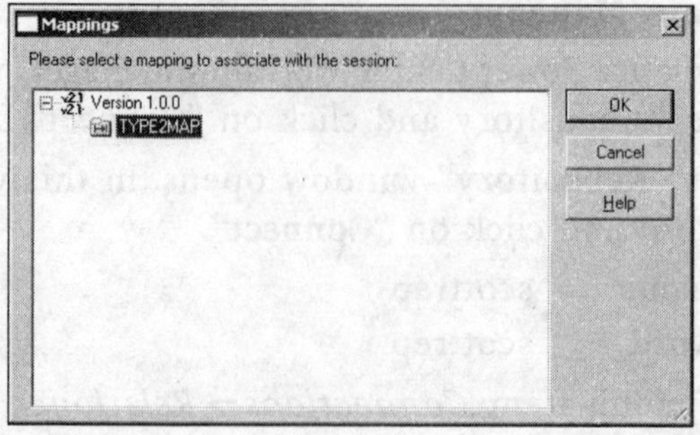

Fig. 4.133

iv. Click on **"OK"**, and on **"Done"** of "Create Task" dialog box.

v. Double click on the created session (TYPE2SESS). "Edit Tasks" window opens, in it go to sources tab. In the **"Value"** column, click on the down arrow button.

vi. **"Relational Connection Browser"** window opens. Select the Source relational connection. In our example, select the "scottsource" and click on **"OK"**

vii. Go to Targets tab and again select the Down arrow button of Values column. **"Relational Connection Browser"** window opens. Select the Target object (scotttarget) for both targets and click on **"OK"**.

viii. In the Target tab select the "Properties" tab located at the bottom. Change the value of the "Target Load Type" as "Normal" for both targets. Click on **"Apply"**, and on **"OK"**.

ix. To validate the session, select the task that which is created, select the menu item **"*Tasks → Validate*"**.

4. **Creating a Work flow**

i) Select the menu item **"*Tools → Workflow Designer*"**. Now the Workflow Designer window opens in workspace.

ii) Now select the menu item **"*Workflows → Create*"** to create a workflow. "Create Workflow" window opens.

iii) In General tab, enter the name of workflow, click on **"OK"**.

e.g.: Name: TYPE2WORKFLOW.

iv) Before clicking on **"OK"**, check whether the server name is there in the server edit box or not. If not, configure the server, then start the server and select that server here.

v) Explore the Sessions folder from the Navigator and select the created session (TYPE2SESS) and drag and drop it into the Workflow Designer workspace.

vi) From the Tool bar select the "Link Tasks" icon, and drag the link from Workflow to Task. The "Link Tasks" icon is shown below:

vii) Save the workflow: **"*Repository → Save*"**.

viii) Start the workflow: **"*Workflow → Start Workflow*"**.

"Work flow Monitor" icon will appear on the System Tray.

ix) Open the "Workflow Monitor" by double clicking on it.

x) Now you can see the status of our workflow. If the Workflow is successful, "TYPE2SESS" and "TYPE2WORKFLOW" are shown in the Succeeded part. To view how many rows got transferred from source to target, double click on the "TYPE2SESS".

xi) "Properties of TYPE2SESS" window opens. In this window, you can see the status, if any errors occurred the error messages are displayed in the First Error entry in this window.

xii) For this example, the "Source Success Rows" entry will contain 4 and the "Target Success Rows" will contain 2.

Thus, we have successfully updated the LOC column of target table using slowly changing dimension of type 2 by maintaining historical data with the help of a flag.

Checking the Output

To see whether the target rows have been dumped into the target table, connect to the target table in the target database using the following SQL statements.

SQL syntax: connect <username>/<password>

e.g.: SQL> connect scottolap/scottolap;
Connected.

To see the rows of the target table, use the following SQL statement.

SQL syntax: select * from <table name>;

e.g.: SQL> select * from TYPE2TARGET;

PMKEY	DEPTNO	DNAME	LOC	FLAG
1	10	ACCOUNTING	NEWYORK	1
2	20	RESEARCH	DALLAS	1
3	30	SALES	CHICAGO	1
4	40	OPERATIONS	HYDERABAD	0
5	40	OPERATIONS	BOSTON	1

5 rows selected.

4.11 Type 3 Slowly Changing Dimensions

In **Type 3 Slowly Changing Dimensions**, the previous (old data) and current (new data) data will be maintained in a single record itself by adding a duplicate column for the required field (the column, which is required to maintain duplicate data).

To illustrate the Type 3 SCD, create a separate folder for this task in Repository Manager tool.

Creating a Folder

1. Open the Repository Manager:

   Start → Programs → Informatica Power center 6.1 OEM for i2 → Repository Manager

2. Informatica Repository Manager window shown in Fig. 4.134 opens.

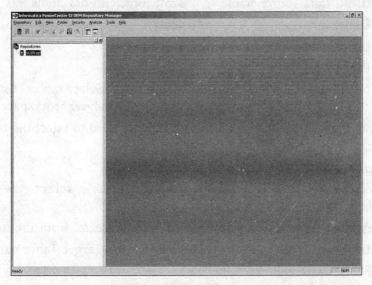

Fig. 4.134

3. Explore Repositories and select the repository, **"scottrep"**, right click on it and select **"Connect"** from the pop up menu.
4. Create a new folder in the selected Repository by selecting the menu item: ***"Create → Folder"***.
5. Enter the name for the folder in the popped up dialog box and click on **"OK"**.

   E.g.: Folder name: TYPE3

6. Now we have to work on Designer tool to create mapping.

Designer Tool

Open Informatica Designer Tool:

Start→ Programs→ Informatica Power center 6.1 OEM for i2 → Designer.

Selecting the source database object

1. Connect to the repository (scottrep) by entering the username and password.

2. Now, select the folder "TYPE3" and select the menu item "***Tools → Source Analyzer***".
3. To import the source table, select the menu item "***Sources → Import from database***".
4. "Import tables" window opens, in it enter the ODBC data source, username, owner name and password.

   e.g.: ODBC Data source name : scott (oracle in ora home 90)

   Username : scott

   Owner name : SCOTT

   Password : tiger
5. **Click on "Connect"**, select the DEPT table from "Select tables" list and click on **"OK"** to import the DEPT table to the Source Analyzer workspace.
6. The source database object is selected. Now we need to select the target database object.

Selecting/Creating the target database object

1. To select the target database object (table), select the menu item "***Tools→ Warehouse Designer***".
2. To create the Target table, select the "*Targets→Create*" from the main menu.
3. **"Create Target Table"** window opens. Enter the Target Table name and select the Database type for target table.

   e.g. Target Table Name : TYPE3TARGET

   Database type : Oracle
4. After entering the details, click on **"Create"** and then click on **"Done"**.
5. Now you can see the target table in the Warehouse Designer Workspace without any Fields.
6. To enter the fields of the target table double-click on it.
7. **"Edit Table"** window opens. In Edit Tables window go to *"Columns"* tab.
8. To enter the New Fields, click on the following icon.

9. The empty row will be displayed in the Columns tab. Now enter the Column details as shown in Fig. 4.135.

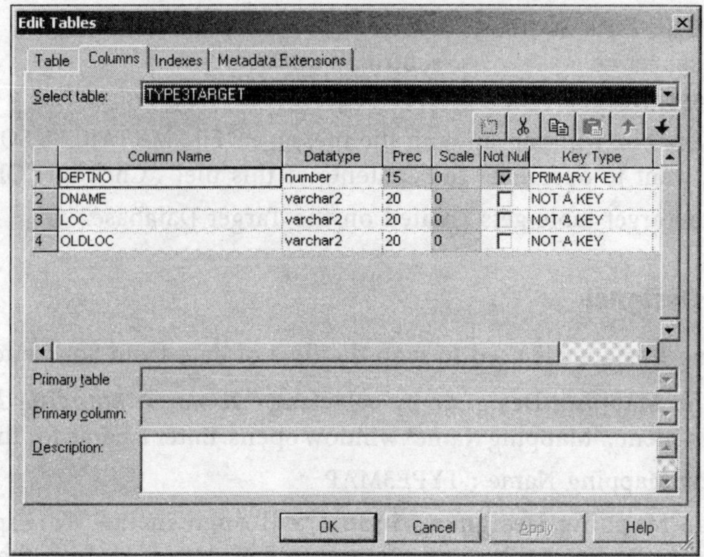

Fig. 4.135

10. Click on **"Apply"** and then on **"OK"**, after entering all fields of target table.
11. Now the template for the target table is designed. To create the Target table in the Target Database, select the menu item "***Targets → Generate/Execute SQL***" from the main menu. Now the "Database Object Generation" window opens.

    In "Generation objects" group, check "***Create table***" check box as shown in Fig. 4.136.

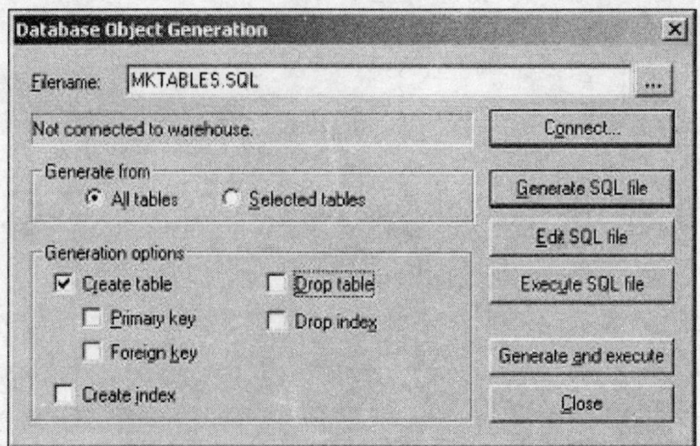

Fig. 4.136

12. Now click on "***Generate and Execute***".
13. "Connect to an ODBC Data source dialog opens". Enter ODBC Data Source, Username, Password and Click on **"Connect"**.

e.g.: ODBC Data Source : scott
User name : scottolap
Password : scottolap

14. A message box will pop up with the message: "File MKTABLES.SQL already exists Do you want to overwrite the contents of this file?". Click on **"OK"**.
15. Now the Target table gets created on the Target Database.

Mapping Designer

The Mapping Designer is used to map the flow of data from Source to Target.

1. Open the Mapping Designer by selecting **"*Tools → Mapping Designer*"** from the main menu. "Mapping Name" window opens. Enter a name for the new mapping.

   e.g.: New Mapping Name : TYPE3MAP
2. Now the **Mapping Designer** window will open in the Workspace. From the Navigator window explore the Source folder, drag and drop the DEPT table to Workspace. By default a source qualifier is also created for the DEPT table.
3. Drag and drop the target table "TYPE3TARGET" twice from the Navigator to Mapping Designer Workspace. Now the screen looks like as shown in Fig. 4.137.

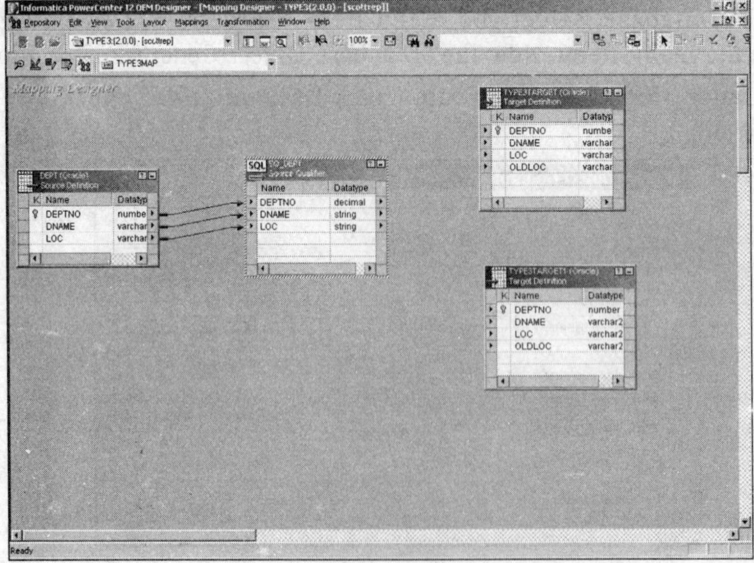

Fig. 4.137

4. In Fig. 4.137, we are using the same target twice, because in TYPE3, if the record is new, then that record is inserted into Target table. If the record is already there in the target table and LOC is changed, then the contents of Target LOC is shifted to OLDLOC and LOC is updated with new LOC.

5. Select the Transformation of type "Lookup" by selecting the menu item "***Transformation → Create***" to create the new transformation. "Create Transformation" window opens, select the "Type of transformation to create" as Lookup and the name of transformation to create as "LOOKUP". Click on **"Create"**, then on **"Done"**.

6. "Select Lookup Table for Lookup Transformation" window opens. Select the Location of Lookup table as "TARGET" and select the Lookup table you want this transformation to use as "TYPE3TARGET" and click on **"OK"** as shown in Fig. 4.138.

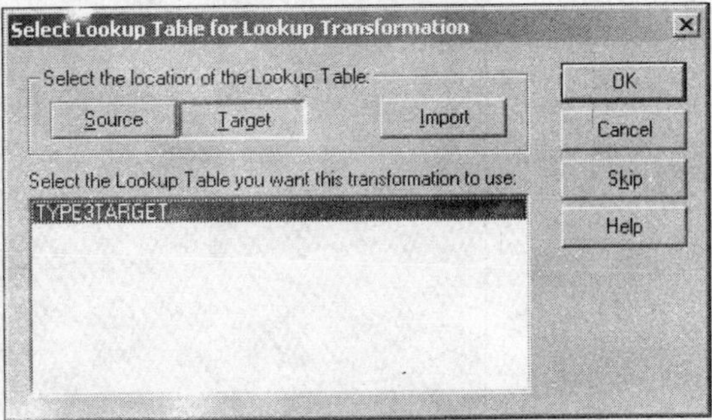

Fig. 4.138

7. Click on **"Done"** button of **"Create Transformations"** window. Drag and drop the DEPTNO column of Source Qualifier to Lookup, as shown in Fig. 4.139.

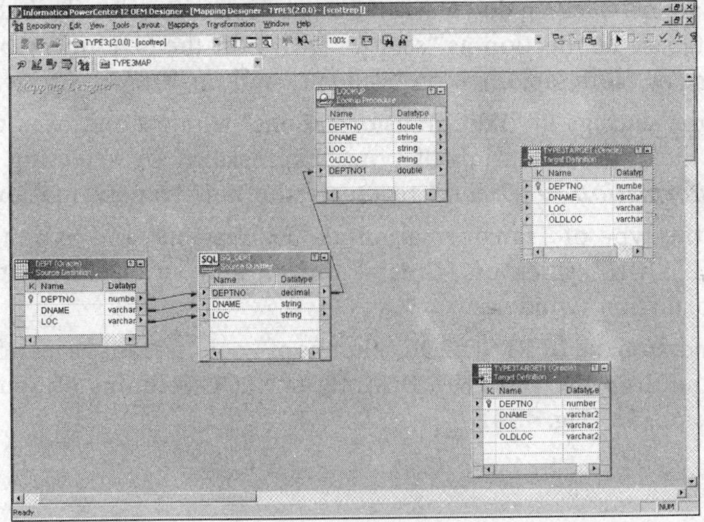

Fig. 4.139

8. Double click on "LOOKUP" and go to **"Conditions"** tab to write the Lookup condition. Select the "Add a new condition" icon and write the condition as shown in Fig. 4.140.

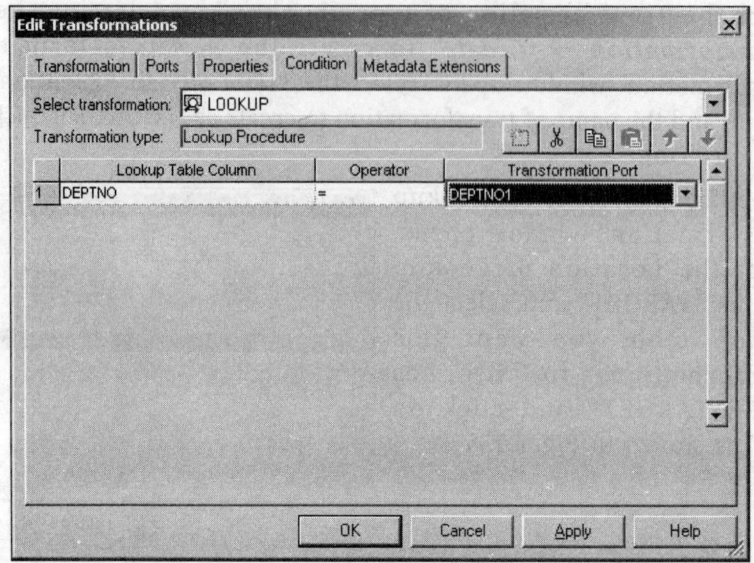

Fig. 4.140

8. Go to **"Properties"** tab. In "Properties" tab, in "Value" column of "Location Information". Click on down arrow button. "Select Database" window opens, select the Database connection as "scotttarget" . Edit the SQL query by connecting to database as scottolap. Click on "Validate" and on "OK".
9. Apply the settings in **"Edit Transformations"** window and click on **"OK"** button. Select the Transformation of type **"Expression"** by selecting the menu item "***Transformation → Create***" to create the new transformation.
10. Select the type of Transformation as **"Expression"** and assign it the name as **"EXPRESSION"**. Click on **"Create"** button and on **"Done"** button of "Create Transformation" window.
11. Drag and drop the DEPTNO, LOC columns of Lookup Transformation to Expression. Drag and drop the DEPTNO, DNAME and LOC columns of Source Qualifier to Expression. See Fig. 4.141.

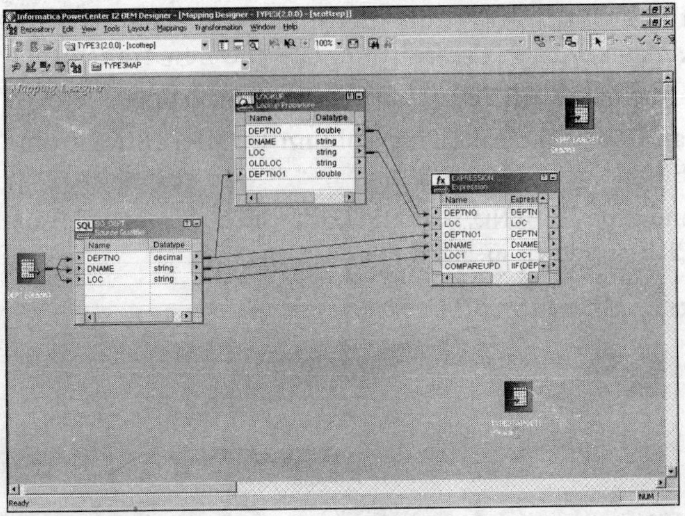

Fig. 4.141

12. Double click on "EXPRESSION", **"Edit Transformations"** window opens, go to "Ports" tab. Add a new OUT port by name "COMPAREUPD" and write the expression in "Expression Editor" as specified below.

    E.g.: IIF(DEPTNO = DEPTNO1 AND LOC1 != LOC,TRUE,FALSE)

13. Add one more OUT port by name "COMPAREINS" and write the expression in "Expression Editor" as specified below.

    e.g.: IIF(ISNULL(DEPTNO), TRUE,FALSE)

    Apply the settings and click on **"OK"**. (See Fig. 4.142)

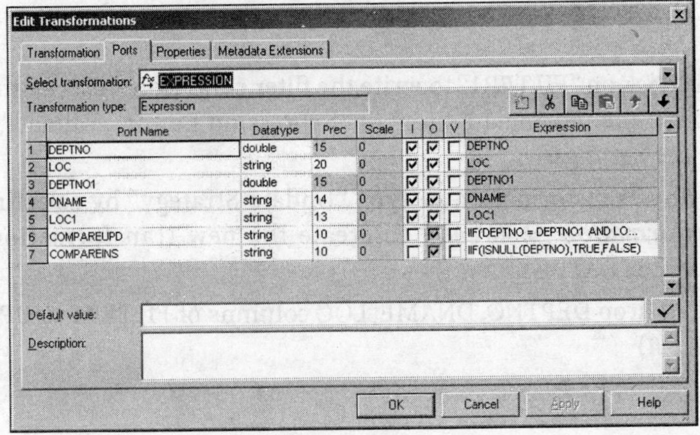

Fig. 4.142

14. Select the Transformation of type "Filter" by selecting the menu item "***Transformation → Create***" to create the new transformation.
15. Assign the name "FILTER1" for this Transformation.
16. Drag and drop the following column COMPAREINS from "EXPRESSION" to "FILTER1".
17. Drag and drop DEPTNO, DNAME, LOC; which we mapped from Source Qualifier to 4FILTER1, as shown in Fig. 4.143.

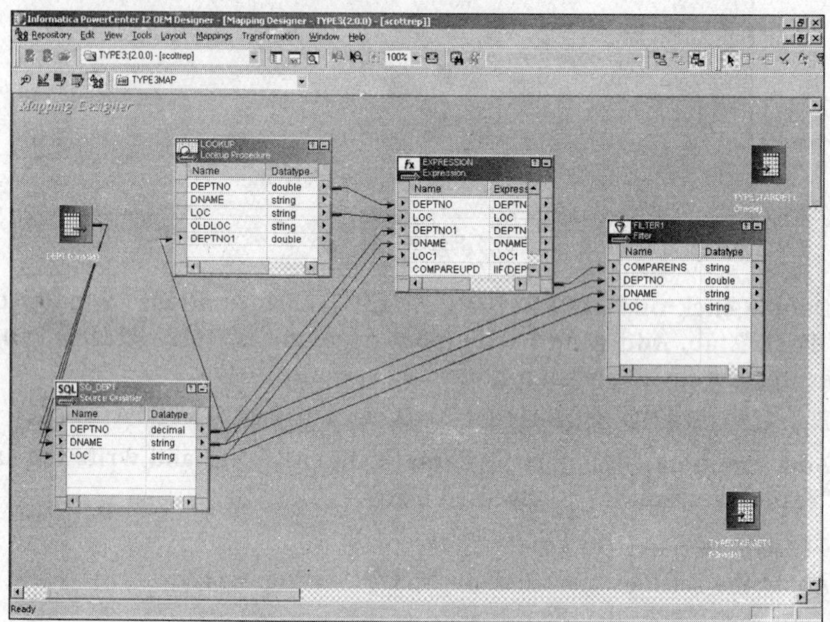

Fig. 4.143

18 Double click on "FILTER1" to write the filter condition, just put the "COMPAREINS" column in the "Formula Editor" of "Expression Editor". Validate the condition and apply the settings.
19 Select the Transformation of type "Update Strategy" by selecting the menu item "***Transformation → Create***" to create the new transformation and name it as "UPDATESTRATEGY1".
20. Drag and drop DEPTNO, DNAME, LOC columns of FILTER1 to UPDATESTRATEGY1 (Fig. 4.144)

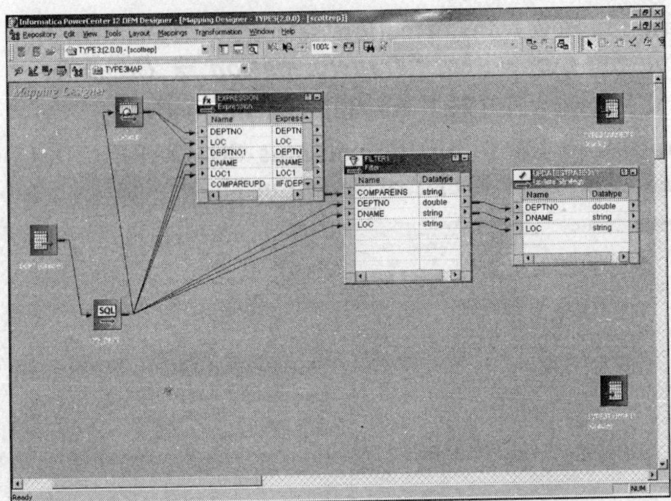

Fig. 4.144

21. Double click on UPDATESTRATEGY1. "Edit Transformations" window opens. Go to "Properties" tab and click on the down arrow button of **"Update Strategy Expression"**.
22. In **"Formula Editor"**, enter the text: DD_INSERT.
23. Validate the expression and apply the settings.
24. Drag and drop the columns DEPTNO, DNAME, LOC from UPDATESTRATEGY1 to TYPE3TARGET. See Fig. 4.145.

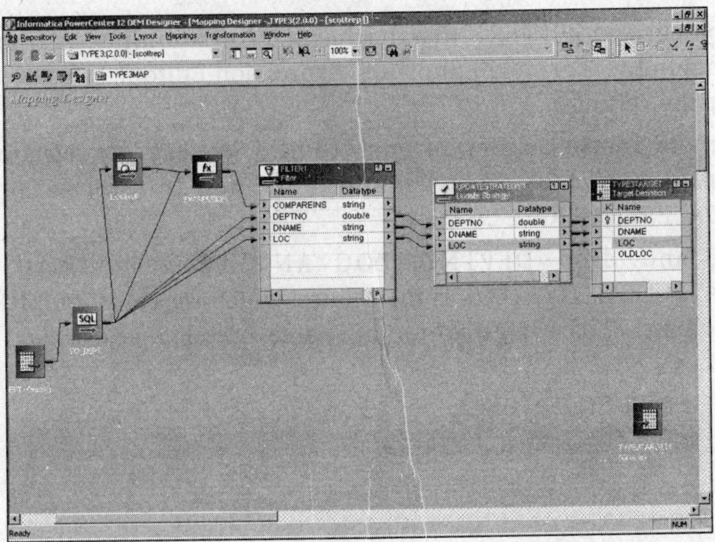

Fig. 4.145

25. To create the new transformation, select the Transformation of type "Filter" by selecting the menu item "***Transformation → Create***".
26. Assign the name "FILTER2" for this Transformation.
27. Drag and drop the following columns COMPAREUPD, LOC and LOC1 from "EXPRESSION" to "FILTER2, as shown in Fig. 4.146.

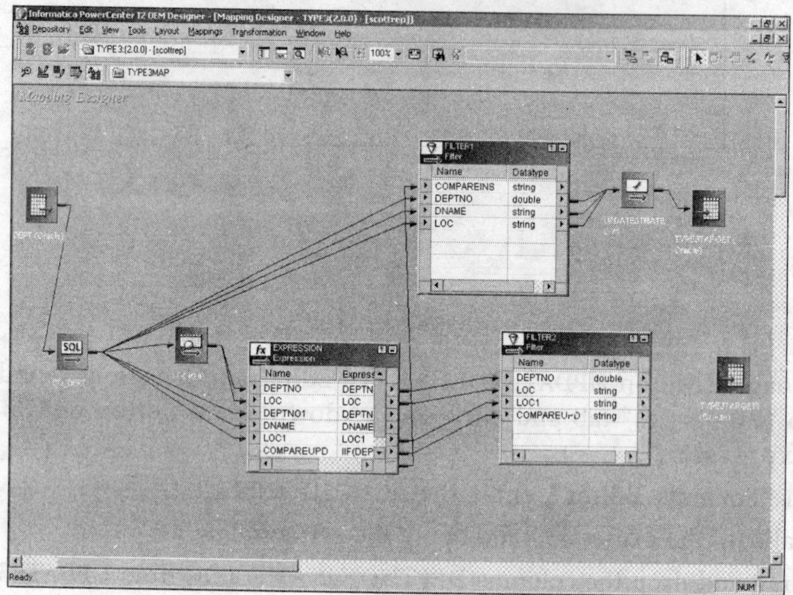

Fig. 4.146

28. Double click on "FILTER2" to write the filter condition, just put the "COMPAREUPD" column in the "Formula Editor" of "Expression Editor". Validate the condition and apply the settings.
29. Select the Transformation of type "Update Strategy" by selecting the menu item "***Transformation → Create***" to create the new transformation and name it as "UPDATESTRATEGY2".
30. Drag and drop DEPTNO, LOC AND LOC1 columns of FILTER2 to UPDATESTRATEGY2 (LOC is the column which we get from LOOKUP and LOC1 is the column which we get from the Source). See Fig. 4.147.

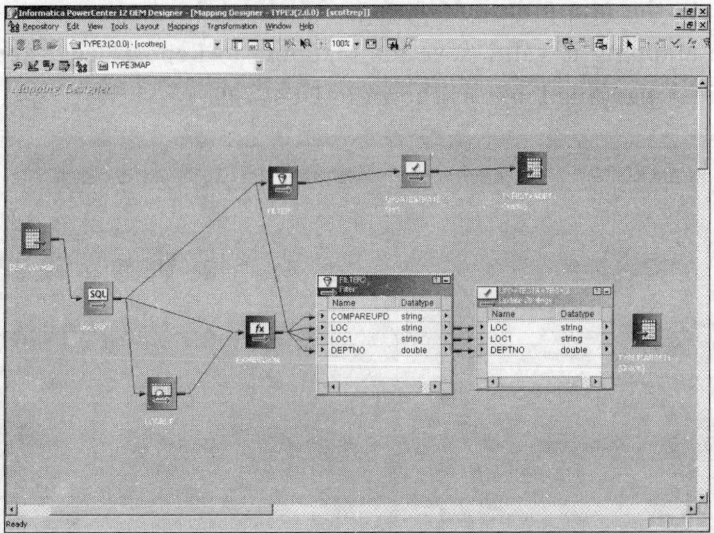

Fig. 4.147

31. Double click on UPDATESTRATEGY2. **"Edit Transformations"** window opens. Go to **"Properties"** tab and click on the down arrow button of **"Update Strategy Expression"**.
32. In **"Formula Editor"**, enter the text: DD_UPDATE.
33. Validate the expression, click on apply and click on OK.
34. Drag and drop the column DEPTNO to DEPTNO of target, LOC to OLDLOC and LOC1 to LOC. The screen looks as shown in Fig. 4.148.

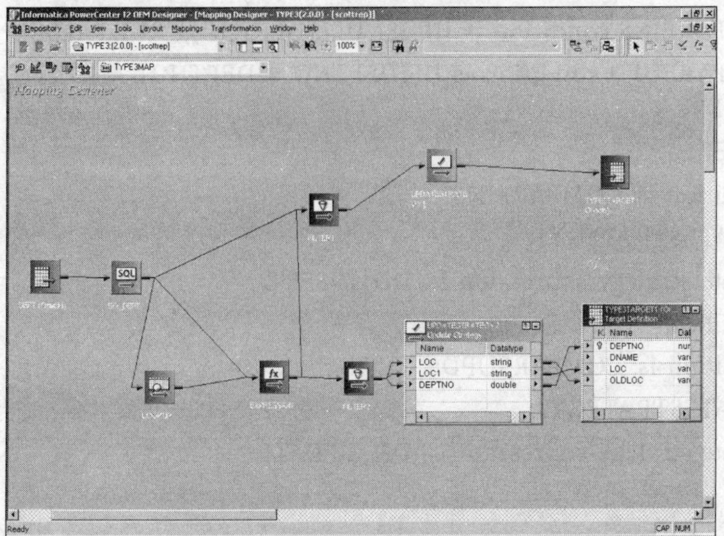

Fig. 4.148

35. Validate the Mapping: "***Mappings→ Validate***"
36. If the Mapping is valid, save the Mapping to Repository: "***Repository→Save***".
37. The final mapping looks as shown in Fig. 4.149.

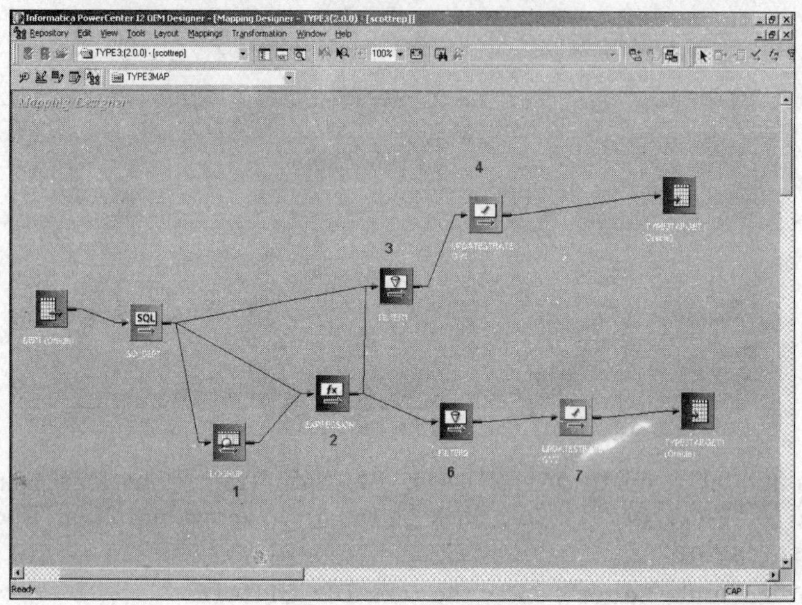

Fig. 4.149

1. LOOKUP TRANSFORMATION: condition is DEPTNO=DEPTNO1.
2. EXPRESSION:

   COMPAREINS condition is IIF(ISNULL(DEPTNO),TRUE,FALSE).

   COMPAREUPD condition is IIF(DEPTNO = DEPTNO1 AND LOC != LOC1, TRUE, FALSE).
3. FILTER1:

   Condition is: COMPAREINS.
4. UPDATESTRATEGY1:

   Update strategy expression is: DD_INSERT.
5. FILTER2:

   Condition is: COMPAREUPD.
6. UPDATESTRATEGY2:

   Update strategy expression is: DD_UPDATE.

Workflow Manager

Before creating a workflow, two relational connections should be created and a server should be configured and executed.

1. **Creating relational connections**

   i. Open the Workflow Manager by selecting:
   Start→ Programs→ Informatica Power center 6.1 OEM for i2→ Workflow Manager

   ii. The **"Informatica Power Center Workflow Manager"** window opens, right click on "scottrep" repository and click on **"Connect"** from the popup menu.

   iii. **"Connect to Repository"** window opens. Enter username and password and click on **"Connect"** button.

   e.g.: Username : scottrep
   Password : scottrep

   iv. Select the menu item ***"Connections→Relational"***, "Relational Connection Browser" window opens.

   v. Click on **"Add"** button to add a new connection. **"Select Subtype"** dialog box opens, select the type as **"Oracle"** and click on **"OK"** button.

   vi. **"Connection Object Definition"** window opens. Enter the name, Username, Password and Connect String and click on **"OK"** button.

   Name : scottsource
   Username : scott
   Password : tiger
   Connect String : oemrep

   vii. Now the created relational connection is displayed in the "Relational Connection Browser" window.

   viii. Repeat the process to create the Relational Target Connection. The Target connection details are as follows:

   Name : scotttarget
   Username : scottolap
   Password : scottolap
   Connect String : oemrep

   ix. Click on **"Close"** button of "Relational Connection Browser" after creating the source and target relational connections.

2. **Configure the server**

   Start → Programs → Informatica Server → Informatica Server Setup

   Start the Informatica server from Services: *Start → Administrator Tools → Services*

3. **Defining Tasks**

   i. To define the task, a session object must be created. Before creating a session, select the folder "TYPE3" from the navigator and click on ***"Tools → Task Developer"***, then "Task Developer" window opens in the workspace.

   ii. To create a session object, select ***"Tasks → Create"***. Now **"Create Task"** window opens. Enter the values "Select the task type to create" as "Session" and enter a user-defined name for the task, then click on ***"Create"***.

   e.g.: Select the task type to create : Session
   Enter a new name for this task : TYPE3SESS

   iii. Now Mappings window opens, select the Mapping as "TYPE3MAP", as shown in Fig. 4.150.

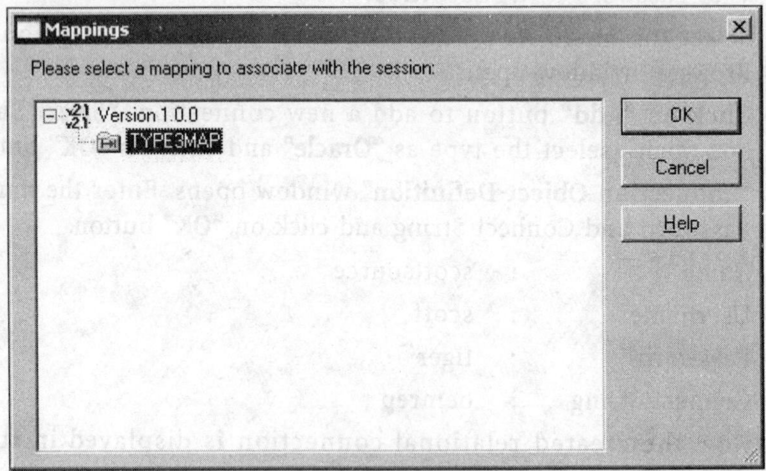

Fig. 4.150

   iv. Click on **"OK"**, and on **"Done"** of **"Create Task"** dialog. Double click on the created session (TYPE3SESS).

   v. **"Edit Tasks"** window opens, go to sources tab. In the "Value" column click on the down arrow button. **"Relational Connection Browser"** window opens. Select the Source relational connection. In our example, select the "scottsource" and click on **"OK"**.

   vi. Go to Targets tab and again select the Down arrow button of Values column. **"Relational Connection Browser"** window opens. In this window, select the Target object (scotttarget) for both targets and click on **"OK"**.

vii. In the Target tab, select the **"Properties"** tab located at the bottom. Change the value of the **"Target Load Type"** as "Normal" for both targets. Click on **"Apply"**, and on **"OK"**.

viii. To validate the session, select the task which is created and select the menu item ***"Tasks → Validate"***.

4. **Creating a Work flow**

i. Select the menu item ***"Tools → Workflow Designer"***. Now the Workflow Designer window opens in Workspace.

ii. Select the menu item ***"Workflows → Create"*** to create a workflow, then **"Create Workflow"** window opens.

iii. In General tab, enter the name of workflow.

E g: Name: TYPE3WORKFLOW.

iv. Click on **"OK"**. Check whether the server name is there in the server edit box or not. If not, configure the server, then start the server and select that server.

v. Explore the Sessions folder from the Navigator and select the created session (TYPE3SESS) and drag and drop it into the Workflow Designer workspace.

vi. From the Tool bar, select the **"Link Tasks"** icon, and drag the link from Workflow to Task.

vii. Save the workflow: ***"Repository → Save"***.

viii. Start the workflow: ***"Workflow → Start Workflow"***.

"Work flow Monitor" icon will appear on the System Tray.

ix. Open the "Workflow Monitor" by double clicking on it.

x. Now you can see the status of our workflow. If the Workflow is successful, then the "TYPE3SESS" and "TYPE3WORKFLOW" are shown in the Succeeded part. To view how many rows got transferred from source to target, double click on the "TYPE3SESS".

xi. "Properties of TYPE3SESS" window opens. In this window, you can see the status, if any errors occurred the error messages are displayed in the First Error entry in this window. For this example the "Source Success Rows" entry will contain 4 and the "Target Success Rows" will contain 4.

xii. To check the type3 working just update one record of source dept table using the following SQL statements.

SQL> connect scott/tiger;

Connected.

SQL> update dept set loc='HYDERABAD' where deptno=40;

1 row updated.

SQL> commit;

Commit complete.

xiii) Start the workflow again and see the result in workflow monitor.

xiv) Now, "Source Success Rows" entry will contain 4 and the "Target Success Rows" will contain 1.

This example demonstrates the slowly changing dimension of type 3.

Checking the Output

To see whether the target rows have been dumped into the target table, connect to the target table in the target database using the following SQL statements.

SQL syntax: connect <username>/<password>

e.g.: SQL> connect scottolap/scottolap;

Connected.

To see the output when the session is run for the first time, use the following SQL statement.

SQL syntax: select * from <table name>;

e.g.: SQL> select * from TYPE3TARGET;

DEPTNO	DNAME	LOC	OLDLOC
10	ACCOUNTING	NEWYORK	
20	RESEARCH	DALLAS	
30	SALES	CHICAGO	
40	OPERATIONS	BOSTON	

4 rows selected.

To see the output when the session is run for the second time, use the following SQL statement.

SQL syntax: select * from <table name>;

e.g.: SQL> select * from TYPE3TARGET;

DEPTNO	DNAME	LOC	OLDLOC
10	ACCOUNTING	NEWYORK	
20	RESEARCH	DALLAS	
30	SALES	CHICAGO	
40	OPERATIONS	HYDERABAD	BOSTON

4 rows selected

In this example, we used a new column, OLDLOC. If the record is inserted for the first time, then as there is no history for that record, so the value for OLDLOC will be NULL. If there is a change in the value of LOC, move the LOC value of target to OLDLOC of target; and LOC value of source to LOC of target. Thus the history is maintained by maintaining the current and previous values without maintaining duplicate rows.

Summary

- Using five tools of Informatica, the entire ETL process is carried out. These tools are: repository server administrator console, repository manager, designer, workflow manager and workflow monitor.
- **Repository Server Administrator Console** is used to connect/disconnect to the Repository Server.
- **Repository Manager** is used to create/organize/manage the Repository (relational database managed by the Repository Server) that stores information, or metadata, used by the Informatica Server and Client tools).
- **Designer is** used to create mappings that contain transformation instructions for the Informatica Server. Before you can create mappings, you must add source and target definitions to the repository. Designer contains Source Analyzer, Warehouse Designer and Mapping Designer.
- **Workflow Manager** is used to create and run workflows and tasks.
- **Workflow Monitor** is used to monitor scheduled and running workflows for each Informatica Server.
- The **process of ETL is**: creation of repository, creation of folders, design of transformations, creation of workflow and tasks, and execution of tasks and monitoring the workflow.
- In **Type 1 slowly changing dimension**, the attribute value will be overwritten with the new value.
- In **Type 2 slowly changing dimension**, the historical data is preserved by keeping the old values of the attributes in addition to the new values. One mechanism of achieving this is to use duplicate rows and whether the value has changed or not is checked using a flag.
- In **Type 3 slowly changing dimension**, the historical data is preserved in a single record by adding duplicate columns.

5 Creating Target Database: A Case Study

Chapter Objectives

- Creation of dimension tables and fact table from an existing database
- Incorporating Type 1 and Type 2 slowly changing dimensions
- Conversion of a database based on E-R model into a target database for data warehouse
- Use of the various features of Informatica in the ETL process

In this chapter, we will discuss a case study based on the ETL concepts and implementation details we learned in the previous chapter. We will take a source database in MS SQL and create a target database for the data warehouse in Oracle. We will study how to create four dimension tables and one fact table. We will also discuss how to incorporate Type 1 and Type 2 slowly changing dimensions.

5.1 Development Environment

The case study presented in this chapter has been tested in the following development environment:

- Source database MS SQL running on Windows 2003 server.
- Target database Oracle running on Windows 2003 server.
- Informatica server and Client running on Windows 2003 server.
- Informatica repository and repository client running on Windows 2003 server.

MS SQL database engine comes with a sample database "Northwind". The E-R diagram of Northwind is shown in Fig. 5.1.

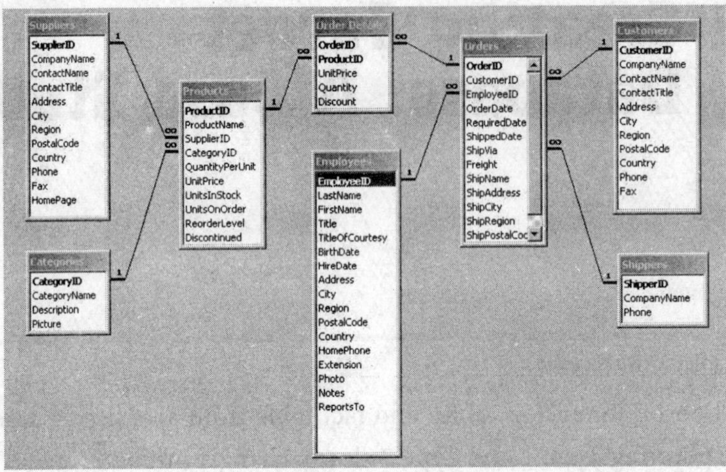

Fig. 5.1

From the above relational database, we will create four dimension tables: CUSTOMERDIM, PRODUCTDIMENSION, EMPLOYEEDIMENSION and TIMEDIMENSION, and one fact table SALESFACT.

We have taken some of the fields from the source database tables, which are required for this case study only. The structures of our dimension and fact tables are as follows:

Customerdim

Name	Null?	Type
CUSTOMERID	(PMKey) NOT NULL	NCHAR(5)
COMPANYNAME	NOT NULL	NVARCHAR2(40)
CONTACTNAME		NVARCHAR2(30)
CONTACTTITLE		NVARCHAR2(30)
ADDRESS		NVARCHAR2(60)
CITY		NVARCHAR2(15)
REGION		NVARCHAR2(15)
POSTALCODE		NVARCHAR2(10)
COUNTRY		NVARCHAR2(15)
PHONE		NVARCHAR2(24)
FAX		NVARCHAR2(24)

Productdimension

Name	Null?	Type
PRODUCTID	(PMKey) NOT NULL	NUMBER
PRODUCTNAME		VARCHAR2(40)
CATEGORYNAME		VARCHAR2(15)
SUPPLIERCOMPANYNAME		VARCHAR2(40)
SUPPLIERCONTACTNAME		VARCHAR2(30)
SUPPLIERCONTACTTITLE		VARCHAR2(30)
SUPPLIERADDRESS		VARCHAR2(60)
SUPPLIERCITY		VARCHAR2(15)
QUANTITYPERUNIT		NUMBER
UNITPRICE		NUMBER(19,4)
DISCONTINUED		VARCHAR2(15)

Employeedimension

Name		Null?	Type
EMPNO	(PMKey)	NOT NULL	NUMBER
EMPLOYEEID		NOT NULL	NUMBER(10)
EMPLOYEENAME		NOT NULL	NVARCHAR2(30)
TITLE			NVARCHAR2(30)
TITLEOFCOURTESY			NVARCHAR2(25)
BIRTHDATE			DATE
HIREDATE			DATE
ADDRESS			NVARCHAR2(60)
CITY			NVARCHAR2(15)
REGION			NVARCHAR2(15)
POSTALCODE			NVARCHAR2(10)
COUNTRY			NVARCHAR2(15)
HOMEPHONE			NVARCHAR2(24)
EXTENSION			NVARCHAR2(4)
REPORTSTO			NUMBER(10)
FLAG			NUMBER

Timedimension

Name		Null?	Type
SALEDATE	(PMKey)	NOT NULL	DATE
YEAR			NUMBER
MONTH			NUMBER
DAY			NUMBER
QUARTER			NUMBER
WEEKDAY			NUMBER

Salesfact

Name	Null?	Type
ORDERID		NUMBER
PRODUCTID		NUMBER
CUSTOMERID		NCHAR(5)
EMPNO		NUMBER
SALEDATE		DATE
QUANTITYSOLD		NUMBER
AMOUNTSOLD		NUMBER(15,2)

5.2 ETL Life Cycle Implementation

Using Informatica, we will demonstrate the entire ETL life cycle. This involves creation of a repository, creation of folders, design of transformation (mappings) between source and target, creation of workflows and tasks, execution of tasks and monitoring the workflows.

Before starting work on Informatica tool, the administrator should create ***Repository*** user in database. The procedure for creating a Repository user in Oracle database is as follows:

5.2.1 Creating a Repository User

To create the repository user, execute the following SQL statements:

i) Login into SQL*PLUS as super user:

SQL syntax: CONN[ECT] sys@<conn_string> as sysdba;

e.g. SQL> connect sys as sysdba;

You will be prompted for password. Press Enter, since there is no password for this user.

ii) Create the Repository user by using the SQL statement:

SQL syntax: ***create user <user name> identified by <password> default tablespace users;***

e.g. SQL> create user nwuser identified by nwpwd default tablespace users;

iii) Grant permissions to the user using the SQL statement:

SQL syntax: ***grant <previlege1>, <previlege2> to <user name>;***

e.g. SQL> grant connect, resource to nwuser;

iv) Check whether the Repository user is created or not:

e.g. SQL> connect nwuser/nwuser;
Connected.
SQL> select * from tab;
No rows selected.

After extraction and transformation of data, we need to load the data into data warehouse and so we require a target database user.

5.2.2 Creating a Target Database User in Oracle

To create the Target Database, execute the following SQL statements:

i) Login into SQL*PLUS as super user:

SQL syntax: CONN[ECT] sys@<conn_string> as sysdba;

e.g. SQL> connect sys as sysdba;

ii) Create the Target Database user with the following SQL statement:

SQL syntax: ***create user <user name> identified by <password> default tablespace users;***

e.g. SQL> create user nwdwh identified by nwdwh default tablespace users;

iii) Grant permissions to the user with the following SQL statement:

SQL syntax: grant <previlege1>, <previlege2> to <user name>;

e.g. SQL> grant connect, resource to nwdwh;

iv) Check whether the target database user is created or not.

e.g. SQL> connect nwdwh/nwdwh;
Connected.
SQL> select * from tab;
No row is selected.

5.2.3 Creating a Repository

The procedure for creating a Repository is as follows:

1. Check whether the *Informatica Repository Server* has started or not in the services. If not, start *Informatica Repository Server.* The procedure is:
   Open services by selecting:
   Start → Administrator Tools → Services.
   Services window will open. Go to "*Informatica Repository Server*" Service. Right click on it and select *Start* from the pop up menu.
   Now the *Informatica Repository Server* service has started.
2. To create repository, start *Repository Server Administration Console:*
   i) ***Start → Programs → Informatica Power center 6.1 OEM for i2 → Repository Server Administration Console.***
   ii) Explore Informatica repository servers and select the server name, where the repository server is running:
   iii) Right click on that server, and select connect option from the pop up menu and enter Port number, and Administrative password.
   E.g. Port Number = 5001 (default port number)
   Administrator Password = password (Administrator password)
   iv) Explore repositories folder.
   v) Right click on Repositories folder and select ***Add Repository*** from the pop up menu.
   vi) In **"Add Repository dialog"**, go to *Repository* Tab and enter Repository Name, Connect String, Database User and Database Password:
   e.g. Repository Name : nwrep
   Connect String : oemrep (it is the database name)
   Database User : nwuser
   Database Password : nwpwd
   vii) Apply the settings by clicking on **"Apply"** and close the dialog by clicking on **"OK"**.
   viii) A message box will be popup with the message: "The Repository has been added to the repository cache". Click on **"Yes"** button. Now 176 default tables or views will be created into the database Repository user, in this example in the **"nwuser"**.
   ix) A message box will be popup with the message: "Repository Creation completed successfully". Click on **"OK"**.

x) Another message box will be pop up with the message: "A Local repository has been created, would you like to promote this to Global Repository", choose the option **"No"**.

xi) Another message box will pop up with the message: "Repository nwrep startup completed successfully". Click on **"OK"**; the repository is created successfully.

xii) You can check whether the repository is created or not with the following SQL statements:

SQL> connect nwuser/nwpwd;

SQL> select count(*) from tab;

176.

5.2.4 Creating Folders in the Repository

To work on a project, you need to create a folder in Repository, using the following procedure:

1. Open the Repository manager by selecting the following:

   Start→ Programs→ Informatica Power center 6.1 OEM for i2 → Repository Manager.

   Informatica Repository Manager window opens.

2. Explore Repositories and select the created repository (created repository is **"nwrep"**), right click on it and select **"Connect"** from the pop up menu.
3. Create a new folder in the selected Repository by selecting the menu item: "***Create → Folder***".
4. Enter the name of the folder from the popped up dialog box and click on **"OK"**.

   e.g.: Folder name: NWFOLDER

5. A message box will pop up with the message, "The folder has been created successfully". Click on **"OK"**.
6. Repeat the process from step 3 to step 6, to create more folders.
7. Now a folder has been created to save our projects in the repository.
8. By default, 8 sub-folders are created in the created folder. The sub-folders are:

   i. Business Components

   ii. Sources

   iii. Targets

   iv. Cubes

   v. Dimensions

   vi. Transformations

vi. Mapplets

vii. Mappings

5.2.5 Designer Tool

The Designer tool is used to select source and target databases and to map the flow of data from source to target with the applied transformations. Some of the transformations available in Informatica are: Source Qualifier, Joiner, Aggregator, Expression, Filter, Sequence Generator, Lookup, Update strategy. The sequence of operations performed in Designer tool are: Source Analyzer, Warehouse Designer, and Mapping Designer.

1. Open the Designer tool:

   Start → Programs → Informatica Power center 6.1 OEM for i2→ Designer

   The designer tool will be opened.

2. In Designer tool, the screen is divided into three parts: Navigator, Output and Workspace.

   i. Navigator: We can navigate through different folders and sub-folders of Repository i.e., we can navigate through different objects of your Repository.

   ii. Output: We can see the output of different activities we perform.

   iii. Workspace: This is the area where we define a work with different objects (Source Objects, Target objects, Transformations, Mappings and Mapplets).

3. Whenever you want to work with Informatica, you need to connect to Repository first. This is done using the following procedure:

   i. In the Navigator select the Repository **"scottrep"**, right click on it and select the **"Connect"** from the pop up menu.

   ii. **"Connect to Repository"** window opens. Enter Repository name, Username and Password of Repository and click on **"Connect"** button.

   e.g. Repository name : nwrep(default)
   Username : nwuser
   Password : nwpwd

   Now the connection between client and Repository server is established.

5.2.6 Creation of Customer Dimension Mapping

Source Analyzer

Source Analyzer is used to define source Database objects. Here is the step-by step procedure:

1. From main menu select ***Tools → Source Analyzer*** (To open the source analyzer the required folder in Navigator must be selected).
2. Now the **Source Analyzer** window will open in workspace.
3. The source objects can be created or they can be imported from the required database. Here we will import the source database object.
4. To import a source database object, select the menu item from main menu "***Sources → Import from Database***".
5. Now the **"Import Table"** window opens.
6. Select the ODBC Data Source name, Username, Owner name, Password for the database tables, which are to be imported as source database objects and click on **"Connect"**.

   e.g. ODBC Data source name : nwdsn(SQL Server) (create DSN before connecting)

   User name : nwuser

   Owner name : nwuser (when you enter the username, then this will be automatically displayed).

   Password : nwuser
7. After connecting, select the required tables from select tables list. And click on **"OK"**. For this example, select Customers table.
8. The selected tables will be displayed in the Source Analyzer window of the Workspace.

Warehouse Designer

The warehouse designer is used to create the Target Database objects. To create the Target Database, the procedure is as follows:

1. From the main menu, select "***Tools → Warehouse Designer***". You can also open the Warehouse Designer by clicking on the following icon.

2. Now the **Warehouse Designer** window opens in the Workspace.
3. As our source and target table columns are one and the same, explore the Sources folder, drag and drop the customers table from Navigator to Warehouse Designer workspace.
4. Double click on the target table in the Warehouse designer workspace.
5. Go to **"Table"** tab and click on **"Rename"** button to rename the target table.
6. Enter the target table name as: **"customerdim"**.

7. Click on **"Apply"** and then on **"OK"** buttons of **"Edit tables"** window.
8. Now the template for the target table is designed. To create the Target table in the Target Database select the menu item ***"Targets → Generate/Execute SQL"*** from the main menu.
9. Now the **"Database Object Generation"** window opens.
10. In **"Generation objects"** group, check Create table and Primary key check boxes.
11. Now click on ***"Generate and Execute"***.
12. **"Connect to an ODBC Data Source"** dialog box opens. Enter ODBC Data Source, Username, Password and click on **"Connect"**.

    e.g. ODBC Data Source : scott (Oracle in ora home 90)

    Username : nwdwh

    Password : nwpwd
13. The following message box will pop up: "File MKTABLES.SQL already exists. Do you want to overwrite the contents of this file?" Click on **"OK"**.
14. Now the Target table is created on the Target Database.

Mapping Designer

The Mapping Designer is used to map the flow of data from Source to Target. The procedure to map our data from source to target is given below:

1. Open the Mapping Designer by selecting ***"Tools → Mapping Designer"*** from the main menu. Or, open the Mapping Designer by clicking on the following icon.

   Now the **Mapping Designer** window will open in the Workspace.
2. From the Navigator window, explore the Source folder, drag and drop the Customers table to workspace.
3. By default, a source qualifier is also created for Customers table.
4. Explore the Targets folder in Navigator, Drag and drop the target table (CUSTOMERDIM) into the workspace.
5. Drag and drop each column of the source qualifier to respective column of the target definition, then the Mapping Designer will be as shown in Fig. 5.2.

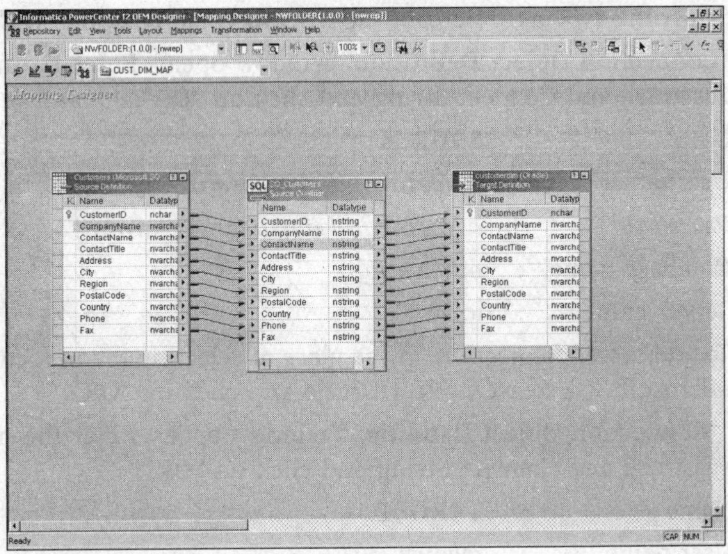

Fig. 5.2

6. Now the Mappings must be validated. To validate the Mappings, go to **"Mappings→ Validate"** of the main menu.
7. After validating the Mappings, save the mappings. To save the Mappings go to ***Repository→ Save.***

Workflow Manager

Before creating a workflow, two relational connections should be created and a server should be configured and executed.

1. **Creating relational connections**
   i) **Open the Workflow Manager: *Start → Programs → Informatica Power Center 6.1 OEM for i2 → Workflow Manager.***
   ii) "Informatica Power Center Workflow Manager" window opens, right click on **"nwrep"** repository and click on **"connect"** from the popup menu.
   iii) **"Connect to Repository"** window opens, enter username and password and click on **"Connect"** button.

      e.g. username : nwuser

      Password : nwpwd
   iv) Select the menu item **"Connections → Relational"**, "Relational Connection Browser" window opens.
   v) Click on **"Add"** button to add a new connection. "Select Subtype" dialog opens.

Select the type as "Microsoft SQL Server" and click on **"OK"**.

vi) **"Connection Object Definition"** window opens. Enter the name, Username, Password and Connect String and click on **"OK"**.

Name	:	SOURCE
Username	:	*<Northwind database username>*
Password	:	*<Northwind database password>*
Database name	:	northwind
Server name	:	icssrv2k3

vii) To add target connection, in the place of selecting the new connection type as Microsoft SQL Server, select Oracle and click on **"OK"**.

viii) **"Connection Object Definition"** window opens. Enter the name, Username, Password and Connect String and click on **"OK"**.

Name	:	TARGET
User name	:	nwdwh
Password	:	nwpwd
Connect String	:	oemrep

ix) Now the created relational connection is displayed in the **"Relational Connection Browser"** window.

x) Click on "Close" button of "Relational Connection Browser" after creating the source and target relational connections.

2. **Creating and configuring the server**

i) In order to run the session and workflow, a server is required. So we must create a server and configure it to the present session.

ii) Select **"*Connections → Server*"** from the main menu. The **"Server Browser"** window opens.

iii) Click on **"Add"** button. Now the **"Server Editor"** window opens. Enter the new server name, Host Name/ IP address, $PMRootDir values.

e.g. Server Name : nwserver
Host Name/IP Address : icssrv2k3
$PMRootDir : "C:\Program Files\Informatica\Informatica PowerCenter 6.1 OEM for i2 - Server"

iv) Now click on **"Resolve Server"** button to resolve the server.

v) Click on **"OK"**.

vi) The newly created server will be added to the **"Server Browser"** window.

vii) Click on **"Close"**.

viii) The created server will be added to your repository and will be displayed in the repository navigator.

ix) To configure the server, the procedure is as follows:

a) Select ***"Start→ Programs→ Informatica Server→ Informatica Server Setup"*** to open the server setup. Now the "Informatica Server Setup Application – Options" window will be displayed:

b) Click on **"Continue"**.

c) Go to server tab and enter the Server Name, TCP/IP Host Address.

e.g. Server Name : nwserver

TCP/IP Host Address : icssrv2k3.

d) Go to Repository tab and enter the Repository Name, Repository User, Repository Password, Repository Server Host Name, and Repository Port Number. Click on **"Apply"** button and on **"OK"**.

e) **"Informatica Server Setup Application – Options"** window opens, click on **"Exit"**.

f) Now the server is configured successfully.

x) After this, start the Informatica service from the "Services" window. To start the service, select ***"Star → Administrator Tools → Services"***. In this "Services" window select "Informatica" service and right click on it and select "Start" from the popup menu.

3. **Defining Tasks**:

i) To define the task, a session object must be created. To create a task, select the folder "NWFOLDER" and click on ***"Tools → Task Developer"***.

ii) "Task Developer" window opens in the workspace.

iii) To create a session object, select ***"Tasks → Create"***.

iv) Now **"Create Task"** window opens. Enter the values "Select the task type to create" as "Session" and enter a user-defined name for the task, then click on **"Create"** button.

e.g. Select the task type to create : Session

Enter a new name for this task : CUSTOMERDIMSESS.

v) The **"Mappings"** window opens. Now we have to select the mapping which was created in "Designer" tool. In this example, select CUST_DIM_MAP.

vi) Click on **"OK"** button, and click on **"Done"** of **"Create Task"** dialog box.

vii) Double click on the created session (CUSTOMERDIMSESS).

viii) **"Edit Tasks"** window opens. Go to Sources tab.

ix) In the **"Value"** column, click on the down arrow button.

x) **"Relational Connection Browser"** window opens. Select the Source relational connection. In our example, select the "SOURCE" and click on "OK".

xi) Go to Targets tab and again select the down arrow button of Values column.

xii) **"Relational Connection Browser"** window opens. Select the Target object (TARGET) and click on **"OK"**.

xiii) In the *Target* tab, select the **"Properties"** tab located at the bottom.

xiv) Change the value of the *"Target Load Type"* as *"Normal"*.

xv) Click on **"Apply"**, and on **"OK"**.

xvi) Save the task by selecting **"*Repository → Save*"**.

xvii) To validate the session, select the task which is created and select the menu item **"*Tasks→ Validate*"**.

4. **Creating a Work flow**

i) Select the menu item **"*Tools→ Workflow Designer*"**. Or, you can select the following icon to open Workflow workspace.

Now the **Workflow Designer** window opens in workspace.

ii) Now select the menu item **"*Workflows→ Create*"** to create a workflow. Workflow window will open.

iii) In *General* tab, enter the name of workflow.

e.g. Name: CUSTOMERDIMWF.

iv) Click on **"OK"** button. Before clicking on **"OK"**, check whether the server name is there in the server edit box or not. If not, configure the server and then start the server. In this example, the Server name is automatically assigned, because we configured and started the server in previous steps.

v) Explore the Sessions folder from the Navigator and select the created session (CUSTOMERDIMSESS); drag and drop it into the Workflow Designer workspace.

vi) From the Tool bar, select the Link Tasks icon (shown below) and drag the link from Workflow to Task.

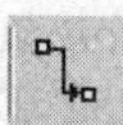

vii) Save the workflow by selecting **"*Repository → Save*"**.

viii) To start workflow select the menu item **"*Workflow → Start Workflow*"**.

ix) **"Workflow Monitor"** icon will appear on the System Tray.

x) Open the **"Workflow Monitor"** by double clicking on it.

xi) Now you can see the status of our workflow. If the workflow is successful, then the "CUSTOMERDIMSESS" and "CUSTOMERDIMWF" will be shown in the Succeeded part. To view how many rows got transferred from source to target, double click on the "CUSTOMERDIMSESS".

xii) "Properties of CUSTOMERDIMSESS" window opens. In this window, you can see the status; if any errors occurred, the error messages are displayed in the First Error entry in this window.

xiii) For this example, the "Source Success Rows" entry will contain 91 and the "Target Success Rows" will also contain 91.

Thus we have successfully completed the workflow of transferring the sources rows from Customers table and moving the successful rows to the target table "nwdwh".

Checking the Output

To see whether the target rows have been dumped into the target table, connect to the target table in the target database by using the following SQL statements.

SQL syntax: connect <username>/<password>

e.g. SQL> connect nwdwh/nwpwd;

Connected.

To see the rows of the target table use the following SQL statement.

SQL syntax: select * from <table name>;

e.g. SQL> select count(*) from customerdim; 91.

5.2.7 Creation of Product Dimension Mapping

Source Analyzer

Now we have to define source Database object for Product Dimension.

1. From Designer tool main menu, select ***"Tools → Source Analyzer"*** (To open the source analyzer, the required folder in Navigator must be selected). Now the Source Analyzer window opens in Workspace.
2. The source objects can be created or can be imported from the required Database.
3. To import a source Database object, select the menu item from main menu ***"Sources → Import from Database"***. The "Import Table" window opens.

4. Select the ODBC Data source name, Username, Owner name, Password for the Database tables, which are to be imported as source, Database objects and click on "Connect".

   e.g. ODBC Data source name : nwdsn(SQL Server)
   User name : nwuser
   Owner name : nwuser
   Password : nwuser
5. After connecting, select the required tables from select tables list and click on "OK". For this example, select Products table, Suppliers, Categories and Order Details.
6. The selected tables will be displayed in the Source Analyzer window of the Workspace along with the Customers table, which is used in CustomersDimension.

Warehouse Designer

The warehouse designer is used to create the Target Database objects. The procedure is as follows:

1. From the main menu, select "*Tools → Warehouse Designer*". Or, use the icon.

   The Warehouse Designer window opens in the Workspace.
2. Create a new target table (PRODUCTDIMENSION) with the columns as shown in Fig. 5.3.

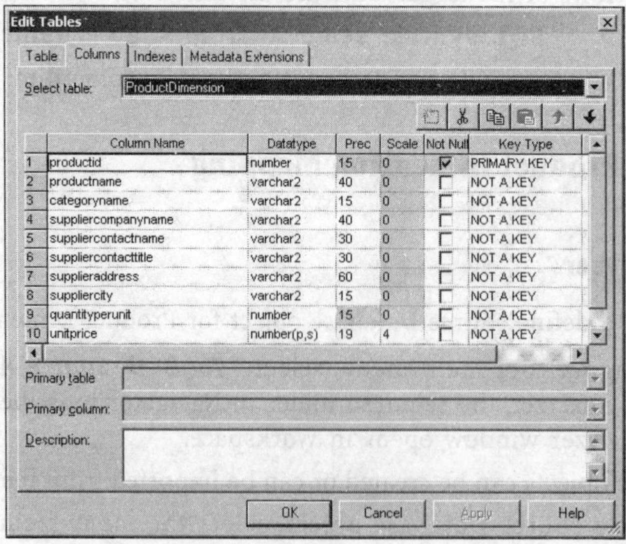

	Column Name	Datatype	Prec	Scale	Not Null	Key Type
1	productid	number	15	0	☑	PRIMARY KEY
2	productname	varchar2	40	0	☐	NOT A KEY
3	categoryname	varchar2	15	0	☐	NOT A KEY
4	suppliercompanyname	varchar2	40	0	☐	NOT A KEY
5	suppliercontactname	varchar2	30	0	☐	NOT A KEY
6	suppliercontacttitle	varchar2	30	0	☐	NOT A KEY
7	supplieraddress	varchar2	60	0	☐	NOT A KEY
8	suppliercity	varchar2	15	0	☐	NOT A KEY
9	quantityperunit	number	15	0	☐	NOT A KEY
10	unitprice	number(p,s)	19	4	☐	NOT A KEY

Fig. 5.3

3. The template for the target table is designed. To create the Target table in the Target Database, select the menu item "*Targets → Generate/Execute SQL*" from the main menu.
4. The "Database Object Generation" window opens.
5. In "Generation objects" group, check Create table and Primary key check boxes and from "Generate From" group, select the radio button "Selected tables".
6. Click on "*Generate and Execute*".
7. "Connect to an ODBC Data source dialog opens". Enter ODBC Data Source, Username, Password and click on "*Connect*".

   e.g. ODBC Data Source : scott (Oracle in ora home 90)

   Username : nwdwh

   Password : nwpwd
8. A message box will pop up with message, "File MKTABLES.SQL already exists Do you want to overwrite the contents of this file?" and click on "OK".
9. Now the Target table got created on the Target Database.

Mapping Designer

To map the flow of data from Source to Target, use the Mapping Designer, as per the following procedure:

1. Open the Mapping Designer by selecting "*Tools → Mapping Designer*" from the main menu; or by clicking on the following icon.

   The Mapping Designer window will open in the Workspace.
2. Select the menu item "*Mappings→Create*" to create a new mapping with the name PRODUCT_DIM_MAP.
3. From the Navigator window, explore the Source folder, drag and drop the Products, Suppliers, Categories, and Order_Details tables to workspace.
4. By default, a source qualifier will be created for each table.
5 Explore the Targets folder in Navigator, drag and drop the Target table (PRODUCTDIMENSION) into the workspace.
6. In this example, we use the "Joiner" transformation to join tables. A joiner can be used to join only two tables.
7. For this reason, we will use three joiners to get the final data from four tables.
8. Join Products and Order_details in first joiner.
9. Join the Suppliers table with the output of the first joiner.
10. Finally, join Categories with the output of the second joiner.

11. Drag and drop respective columns of the joiner3 to the target definition (PRODUCTDIMENSION). See Fig. 5.4.

    The join conditions are as follows:

    JOINER1 condition: ProductID=ProductID1

    JOINER2 condition: SupplierID=SupplierID1

    JOINER3 condition: CategoryID=CategoryID1.

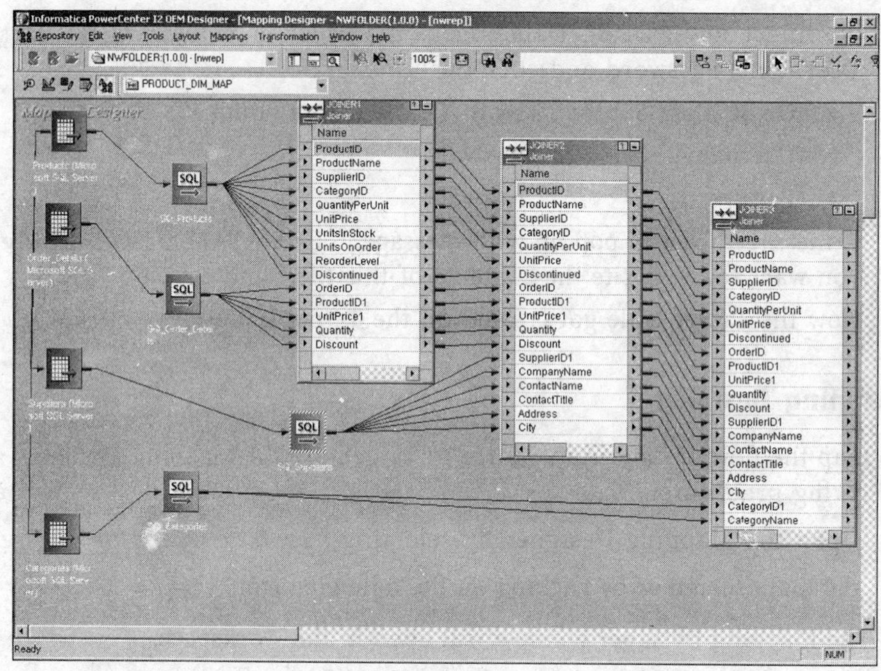

Fig. 5.4

12. Create a Transformation of type "Expression" and assign it the name "EXPRESSION". This transformation is used to change the values of the column "Discontinued" of table "Products" into meaningful values. Here we are going to change the 'T' value to "Discontinued" and 'F' value to "Continue".
13. Drag and drop 'Discontinued' column of JOINER3 to EXPRESSION.
14. Go to "Ports" tab of "Edit Transformations" window and create a new port and write the expression as follows. (See Fig.5.5)

    IIF(Discontinued = 'T','DISCONTINUED','CONTINUE')

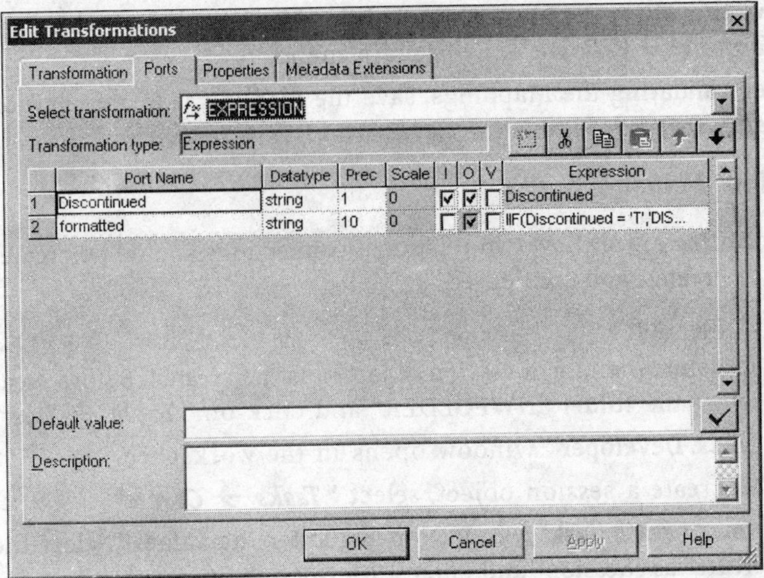

Fig. 5.5

15. Validate the expression and apply the settings.
16. Drag and drop the 'formatted' column of 'EXPRESSION' to 'Discontinued' column of target table.
17. Now the mapping will be as shown in Fig. 5.6.

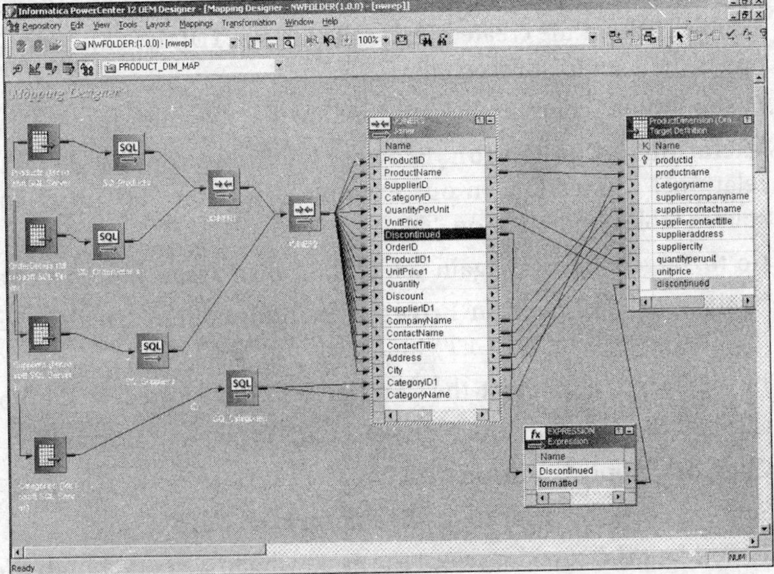

Fig. 5.6

18. Now the Mappings must be validated. To validate the Mappings go to "***Mappings→ Validate***" of the main menu.
19. After validating the Mappings, save the mappings. To save the Mappings go to "***Repository→ Save***".

Workflow Manager

Before creating a workflow two relational connections should be created and a server should be created and configured.

1. **Defining Tasks:**
   - i. To define the task, a session object must be created. Before creating a session, select the folder "NWFOLDER" and click on "***Tools → Task Developer***".
   - ii. **"Task Developer"** window opens in the workspace.
   - iii. To create a session object, select "***Tasks → Create***".
   - iv. Now **"Create Task"** window opens. Enter the values "Select the task type to create" as "Session" and enter a user-defined name for the task, then click on **"Create"** button.

     e.g.: Select the task type to create : Session

     Enter a new name for this task : PRODUCTDIMSESS.
   - v. The "Mappings" window opens. Now we have to select the mapping which was created in "Designer" tool (in this example, select PRODUCT_DIM_MAP).
   - vi. Click on **"OK"** button, and on **"Done"** of **"Create Task"** dialog box.
   - vii. Double click on the created session (PRODUCTDIMSESS). "Edit Tasks" window opens, in it go to sources tab.
   - viii. In the "Value" column click on the down arrow button.
   - ix. **"Relational Connection Browser"** window opens. Select the Source relational connection. In our example, select the "SOURCE" for all the four source tables and click on "OK".
   - x. Go to Targets tab and again select the Down arrow button of Values column.
   - xi **"Relational Connection Browser"** window opens. In this window, select the Target object (TARGET) and click on **"OK"**.
   - xii. In the Target tab, select the **"Properties"** tab located at the bottom.
   - xiii. Change the value of the **"Target Load Type"** as **"Normal"**.
   - xiv. Click on **"Apply"**, and on **"OK"**.
   - xv. Save the task by selecting "***Repository → Save***".
   - xvi. To validate the session, select the task, which is created and select the menu item "***Tasks→ Validate***".

2. **Creating a Workflow**

   i Select the menu item "*Tools → Workflow Designer*" or click on the icon .

   Now the Workflow Designer window opens in Workspace.

   ii Now select the menu item "*Workflows → Create*" to create a workflow.

   iii In General tab enter the name of workflow.

   e.g.: Name: PRODUCTDIMWF.

   iv Click on "OK". Before clicking on "OK", check whether the server name is there in the server edit box or not. If not, configure the server and then start the server.

   v Explore the Sessions folder from the Navigator and select the created session (PRODUCTDIMSESS) and drag and drop it into the Workflow Designer workspace.

   vi From the Tool bar, select the Link Tasks icon (shown below), and drag the link from Workflow to Task.

   vii Save the workflow by selecting **"Repository→Save"**.

   viii To start workflow select the menu item **"Workflow → Start Workflow"**.

   ix "Workflow Monitor" icon will appear on the System Tray.

   x Open the "Workflow Monitor" by double clicking on it.

   xi Now you can see the status of our workflow. If the Workflow is successful, then the "PRODUCTDIMSESS" and "PRODUCTDIMWF" are shown in the Succeeded part. To view how many Rows got transferred from source to target double click on the "PRODUCTDIMSESS".

   xii "Properties of PRODUCTDIMSESS" window opens. In this window, you can see the status. For this example the "Source Success Rows" entry will contain 77 and the "Target Success Rows" will also contain 77.

Thus we have successfully completed the workflow of transferring the sources rows and moving the successful rows to the target table "nwdwh".

Checking the Output

To see whether the target rows have been dumped into the target table, connect to the target table in the target database using the following SQL statements.

SQL syntax: connect <username>/<password>

e.g. SQL> connect nwdwh/nwpwd;

Connected.

To see the rows of the target table, use the following SQL statement.

SQL syntax: select * from <table name>;

e.g. SQL> select count(*) from productdimension; 91

5.2.8 Creation of Employee Dimension Mapping

Source Analyzer

Now we will define source Database object for Employee Dimension. To define the source for Employee Dimension through Source Analyzer, the procedure is as follows:

1. From Designer Tool main menu, select ***Tools → Source Analyzer*** (To open the source analyzer the required folder in Navigator must be selected).

   Now the **Source Analyzer** window will open in workspace.
2. The source objects can be imported from the required Database "Northwind".
3. To import a source database object, select the menu item from main menu "***Sources → Import from Database***".
4. Now the **"import Table"** window opens.
5. Select the ODBC Data source name, Username, Owner name, Password for the Database tables, which are to be imported as source, Database objects and click on "Connect" button.

   e.g.: ODBC Data source name : nwdsn(SQL Server)
   Username : nwuser
   Owner name : nwuser
   Password: nwuser
6. After connecting, select the required tables from select tables list. And click on **"OK"**. For this example, select Employees table.
7. The selected table will be displayed in the Source Analyzer window of the Workspace along with the previous tables, which are used in CustomersDim and ProductDimension.

Warehouse Designer .

The warehouse designer is used to create the Target Database objects. To create the Target Database object, the steps are as follows:

1. From the main menu select **"Tools → Warehouse Designer"**, or use the icon .

   The Warehouse Designer window opens in the Workspace.
2. Explore the **"Sources"** folder, drag and drop the "Employees" table to the Warehouse Designer Workspace.

3. Double click this dragged table. **"Edit tables"** window opens. In the table tab, change the target table name to "EEMPLOYEEDIMENSION".
4. Add two new columns for the target table: they are 'Empno' and 'Flag'. The purpose of these columns is discussed in the next section.
5. Assign the primary key to 'Empno' column and remove the Primary key to 'Empid' column.
6. Go to Columns tab and remove the columns "Photo", "Notes", "PhotoPath" and "Last name".
7. The columns can be removed by clicking on the column number and clicking on "Cut" button shown below:
8. Rename "First Name" column as "Employeename" and set the size with 30. See Fig. 5.7.

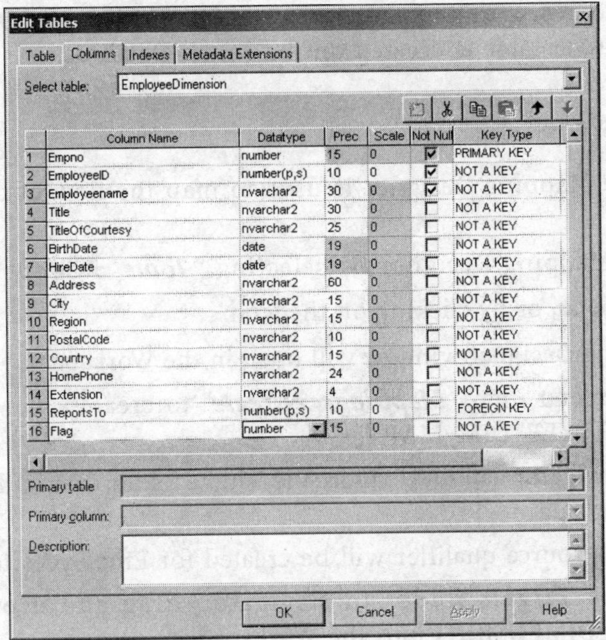

	Column Name	Datatype	Prec	Scale	Not Null	Key Type
1	Empno	number	15	0	☑	PRIMARY KEY
2	EmployeeID	number(p,s)	10	0	☑	NOT A KEY
3	Employeename	nvarchar2	30	0	☑	NOT A KEY
4	Title	nvarchar2	30	0	☐	NOT A KEY
5	TitleOfCourtesy	nvarchar2	25	0	☐	NOT A KEY
6	BirthDate	date	19	0	☐	NOT A KEY
7	HireDate	date	19	0	☐	NOT A KEY
8	Address	nvarchar2	60	0	☐	NOT A KEY
9	City	nvarchar2	15	0	☐	NOT A KEY
10	Region	nvarchar2	15	0	☐	NOT A KEY
11	PostalCode	nvarchar2	10	0	☐	NOT A KEY
12	Country	nvarchar2	15	0	☐	NOT A KEY
13	HomePhone	nvarchar2	24	0	☐	NOT A KEY
14	Extension	nvarchar2	4	0	☐	NOT A KEY
15	ReportsTo	number(p,s)	10	0	☐	FOREIGN KEY
16	Flag	number	15	0	☐	NOT A KEY

Fig. 5.7

Note.....

In some OLAP tools (e.g., Cognos and Business Objects), the datatype "nvarchar2" will not be accepted. In such a case, you need to convert the data type to "varchar2". Also, you may have to change the "nchar" to "char". If required, you can change the data type here itself, or you can change it at the time of using Cognos or Business Objects. The detailed procedure for making the changes is given in Section 7.2.

9. Now the template for the target table is designed. To create the Target table in the Target Database, select the menu item ***"Targets→Generate/Execute SQL"*** from the main menu.
10. Now the **"Database Object Generation"** window opens.
11. In "Generation objects" group, check "*Create table*" and "*Primary key*" check boxes and from "Generate From" group, select the radio button "Selected tables".
12. Now click on "*Generate and Execute*".
13. **"Connect to an ODBC Data source"** dialog opens. Enter ODBC data source, Username, Password and click on "Connect".

    e.g.: ODBC Data Source : scott (Oracle in ora home 90)
    Username : nwdwh
    Password : nwpwd
14. The following message box will pop up: "File MKTABLES.SQL already exists Do you want to overwrite the contents of this file?" Click on **"OK"**.
    Now the Target table is created on the Target Database.

Mapping Designer

Recall that the Mapping Designer is used to map the flow of data from Source to Target.

1. Open the Mapping Designer by selecting ***"Tools → Mapping Designer"*** from the main menu, or by clicking on the icon:
   The Mapping Designer window will open in the Workspace.
2. Select the menu item ***"Mappings→Create"*** to create a new mapping with the name EMPLOYEE_DIM_MAP.
3. From the Navigator window, explore the Source folder, drag and drop the Employees table to workspace.
4. By default, a source qualifier will be created for Employees table.
5. Explore the Targets folder in Navigator, drag and drop the target table (EMPLOYEEDIMENSION) into the Workspace.
6. Create a Transformation of type Expression and assign it the name "EXPRESSION". This transformation is used to concatenate the last name and first name of the employee and assign to Employee name column of Target table.
7. Drag and drop 'First Name' and 'Last Name' columns of Source Qualifier to EXPRESSION.
8. Go to *"Ports"* tab of **"Edit Transformations"** window and create new ports with

the Port Names "Employeename" and "Flag" as shown in Fig. 5.8. Write the expression as follows.

Employeename column expression is: CONCAT(FirstName,LastName)

Flag column expression is: 1

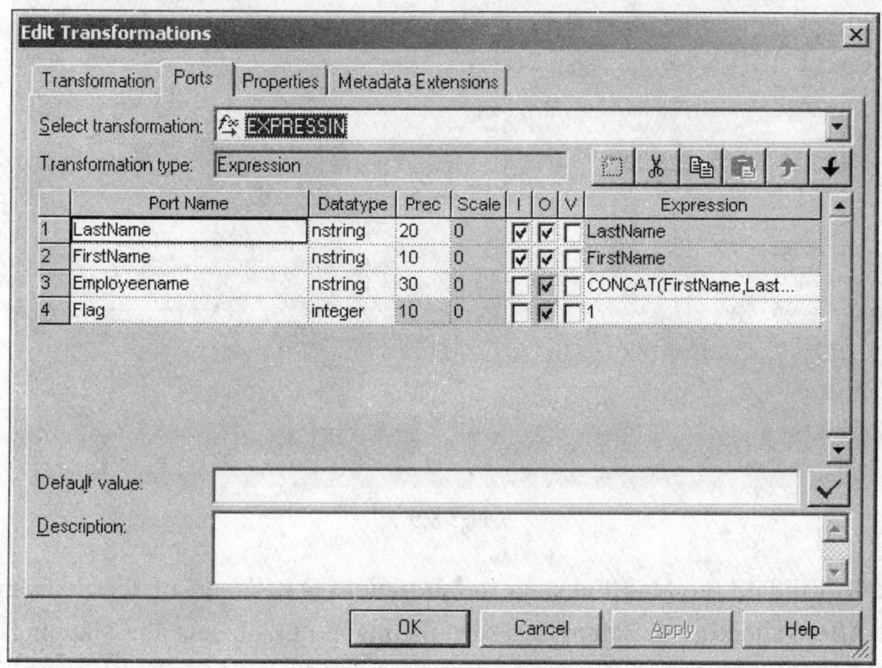

Fig. 5.8

9. Validate the expression and apply the settings.
10. Drag and drop the 'Employeename' and 'Flag' columns of 'EXPRESSION' to 'Employeename' and 'Flag' columns of Target table.
11. Drag and drop the required columns from Source Qualifier to Target table.
12. Create a Transformation, Sequence Generator with the name "SEQGENERATOR".
13. Drag and drop the 'NEXTVAL' column of SEQGENERATOR to Empno column of Target table.
14. Now the mapping will be as shown in Fig. 5.9.

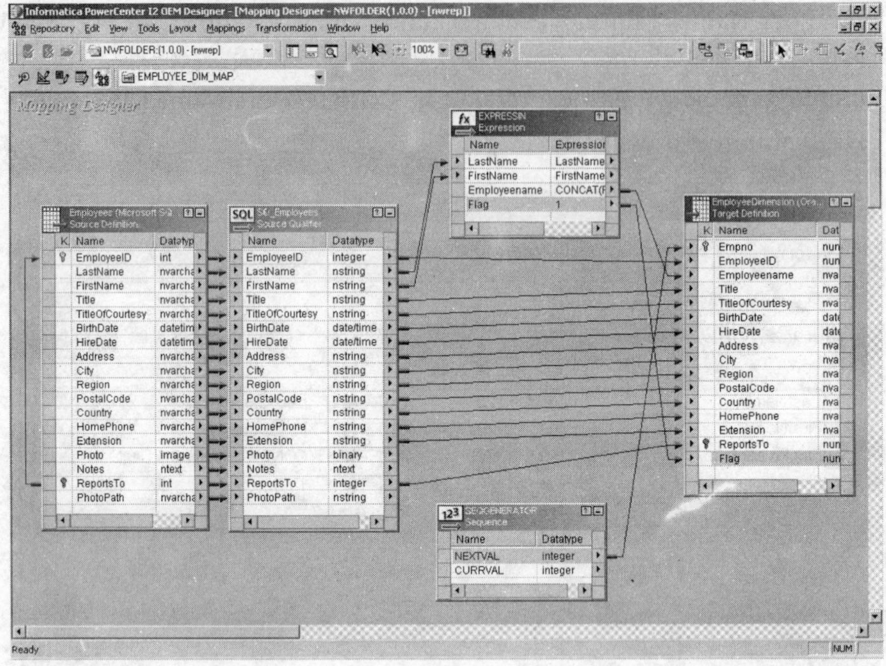

Fig. 5.9

15. To validate the Mappings, go to "*Mappings→ Validate*" of the main menu.
16. After validating the Mappings save the mappings. To save the Mappings go to "*Repository→ Save*".

Workflow Manager

We will create two relational connections, and configure and execute the server.

1. **Defining Tasks**
   i) To define the task, a session object must be created. Before creating a session, select the folder "NWFOLDER" and click on "*Tools → Task Developer*".
   ii) "Task Developer" window opens in the workspace.
   iii) To create a session object, select "*Tasks → Create*".
   iv) Now "Create Task" window opens. Enter the values "Select the task type to create" as "Session" and enter a user-defined name for the task, then click on "*Create*".

   e.g.: Select the task type to create : Session

   Enter a new name for this task : EMPLOYEEDIMSESS.

v) The **"Mappings"** window opens. Now we have to select the mapping, which was created in "Designer tool" (in this example, select EMPLOYEE_DIM_MAP).

vi) Click on **"OK"**, and on **"Done"** of "Create Task" dialog box.

vii) Double click on the created session (EMPLOYEEDIMSESS).

viii) "Edit Tasks" window opens, in it go to sources tab.

ix) In the "Value" column, click on the down arrow button.

x) "Relational Connection Browser" window opens. Select the Source relational connection. In our example select the "SOURCE" for all the four source tables and click on "OK".

xi) Go to *Targets* tab and again select the down arrow button of Values column.

xii) **"Relational Connection Browser"** window opens. Select the Target object (TARGET) and click on **"OK"**.

xiii) In the Target tab, select the *"Properties"* tab located at the bottom.

xiv) Change the value of the "Target Load Type" as "Normal".

xv) Click on **"Apply"**, and then on "OK".

xvi) Save the task by selecting "***Repository → Save***".

xvii) To validate the session, select the task, which is created and select the menu item "***Tasks→ Validate***".

2. **Creating a Workflow**

i) Select the menu item "***Tools→ Workflow Designer***". Or, select the icon

Now the Workflow Designer window opens in Workspace.

ii) Select the menu item "***Workflows → Create***" to create a workflow.

iii) In General tab, enter the name of workflow.

E.g.: Name: EMPLOYEEDIMWF.

iv) Click on "OK". Before clicking on **"OK"**, check whether the server name is there in the server edit box or not. If not, configure the server, and then start the server.

v) Explore the Sessions folder from the Navigator and select the created session (EMPLOYEEDIMSESS); drag and drop it into the Workflow Designer workspace.

vi) From the Tool bar, select the Link Tasks icon (shown below), and drag the link from Workflow to Task.

vii) Save the workflow by selecting "***Repository → Save***".

viii) To start workflow, select the menu item "***Workflow → Start Workflow***".

ix) "Workflow Monitor" icon will appear on the System Tray.

x) Open the "Workflow Monitor" by double clicking on it.

xi) You can see the status of our workflow. If the Workflow is successful, the "EMPLOYEEDIMSESS" and "EMPLOYEEDIMWF" are shown in the Succeeded part. To view how many Rows got transferred from source to target, double click on the "EMPLOYEEDIMSESS".

xii) "Properties of EMPLOYEEDIMSESS" window opens. In this window, you can see the status, if any errors occurred, the error messages are displayed in the First Error entry in this window.

xiii) For this example, the "Source Success Rows" entry will contain 9 and the "Target Success Rows" will also contain 9.

Thus we have successfully completed the workflow of transferring the sources rows from Employees table and moving the successful rows to the target table "nwdwh".

Checking the Output

To see whether the target rows have been dumped into the target table, connect to the target table in the target database using the following SQL statements.

SQL syntax: *connect <username>/<password>*

e.g. SQL> connect nwdwh/nwpwd;
Connected.

To see the rows of the target table, use the following SQL statement.

SQL syntax: select * from <table name>;

e.g. SQL> select count(*) from employeedimension; 9

5.2.9 Creation of Time Dimension Mapping

Source Analyzer

Now let us define the source Database object for Time Dimension.

1. From main menu, select "***Tools → Source Analyzer***". The Source Analyzer window will open in workspace.
2. To import a source database object, select the menu item from main menu "***Sources → Import from Database***". The **"Import Table"** window opens.
3. Select the ODBC Data Source name, Username, Owner name, Password for the Database tables, which are to be imported as source, Database objects and click on **"Connect"**.

e.g.:

ODBC Data source name	:	nwdsn (SQL Server)
User name	:	nwuser
Owner name	:	nwuser
Password	:	nwuser

4. After connecting, select the required tables from select tables list and click on "OK". For this example, select Orders table.
5. The selected table will be displayed in the Source Analyzer window of the workspace along with the previous tables, which are used in CUSTOMERSDIM, PRODUCTDIMENSION and EMPLOYEEDIMENSION.

Warehouse Designer

Using warehouse designer, create the target database. The procedure is as follows:

1. From the main menu select "*Tools → Warehouse Designer*" or click on the icon:

   The Warehouse Designer window opens in the Workspace.
2. Create the target table by selecting the menu item "*Targets→Create*" and assign the name "TIMEDIMENSION".
3. Now double click on the Target table. **"Edit tables"** window opens.
4. Go to Columns tab and add the columns, "Saledate", "Year", "Month", "Day", "Quarter" and "Weekday" as shown in Fig. 5.10.

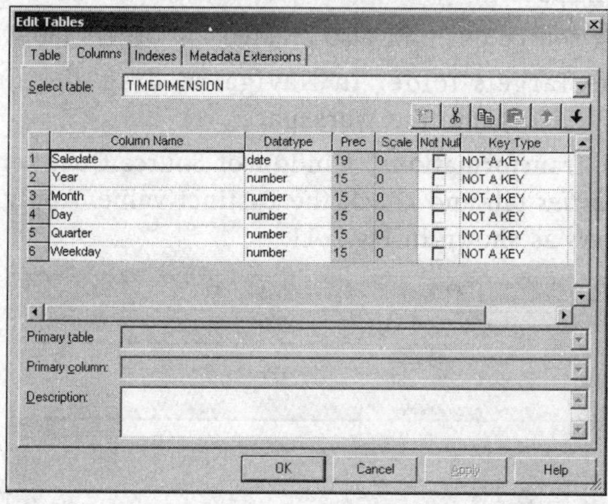

Fig. 5.10

5. Now, the template for the target table is designed. To create the Target table in the Target Database, select the menu item "*Targets→Generate/Execute SQL*" from the main menu.
6. The **"Database Object Generation"** window opens.
7. Select the radio button "Selected tables" and click on "*Generate and Execute*".
8. **"Connect to an ODBC Data source dialog opens"**. In this dialog, enter

ODBC Data Source, Username, Password and click on "Connect".

e.g.: ODBC Data Source : scott (Oracle in ora home 90)
Username : nwdwh
Password : nwpwd

9. A message box will be pop up with the message, "File MKTABLES.SQL already exists, do you want to overwrite the contents of this file?" Click on **"OK"**.

The Target table is now created in the Target Database.

Mapping Designer

1. Open the Mapping Designer by selecting "***Tools → Mapping Designer***" from the main menu; or by clicking the icon
The Mapping Designer window will open in the Workspace.
2. Select the menu item "***Mappings→Create***" to create a new mapping with the name TIME_DIM_MAP.
3. From the Navigator window, explore the Source folder, drag and drop the Orders table to workspace.
4. By default, a source qualifier also created for Orders table.
5. Explore the Targets folder in Navigator, drag and drop the target table (TIMEDIMENSION) into the Workspace.
6. Go to **"Edit Transformations"** window of Source Qualifier transformations and go to *Properties* tab and check the Distinct value. Apply the settings to avoid duplicate rows as shown in Fig. 5.11.

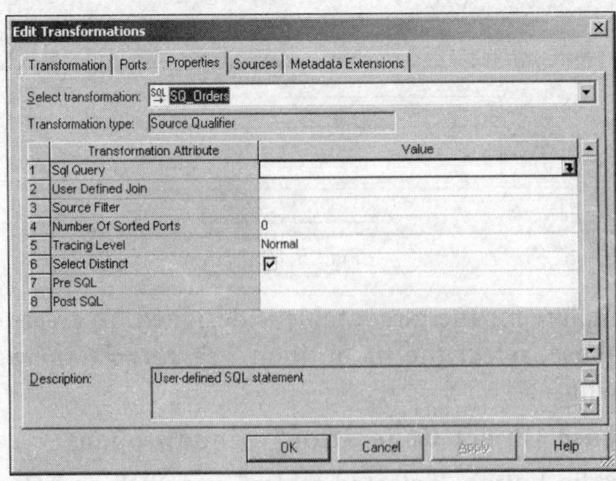

Fig. 5.11

7. Create a Transformation of type "Expression" and assign it the name "EXPRESSION".

This transformation is used to format the date.

8. Drag and drop ‘ShippedDate’ column of Source Qualifier to EXPRESSION.
9. Go to “Ports” tab of “Edit Transformations” window and create new ports with the Port Name “Year”, “Month”, “Day”, “Quarter” and “Weekday” and write the expressions as follows. See Fig. 5.12.

   Year port Expression is : GET_DATE_PART(ShippedDate,’YYYY’)

   Month port Expression is : GET_DATE_PART(ShippedDate,’MM’)

   Day port Expression is : GET_DATE_PART(ShippedDate,’DD’)

   Quarter port Expression is : IIF(GET_DATE_PART(ShippedDate,’MM’)<4,1,
   IIF(GET_DATE_PART(ShippedDate,’MM’)<7,2,
   IIF(GET_DATE_PART(ShippedDate,’MM’)<10, 3,
   IIF(GET_DATE_PART(ShippedDate,’MM’)<13, 4))))

   Weekday port Expression is: IIF(TO_CHAR(ShippedDate,’D’)=’1',1,
   IIF(TO_CHAR(ShippedDate, ‘D’)=’2',2,
   IIF(TO_CHAR(ShippedDate, ‘D’)=’3',3,
   IIF(TO_CHAR(ShippedDate, ‘D’)=’4',4,
   IIF(TO_CHAR(ShippedDate, ‘D’)=’5',5,
   IIF(TO_CHAR(ShippedDate, ‘D’)=’6',6,
   IIF(TO_CHAR(ShippedDate, ‘D’)=’7',7,NULL)))))))

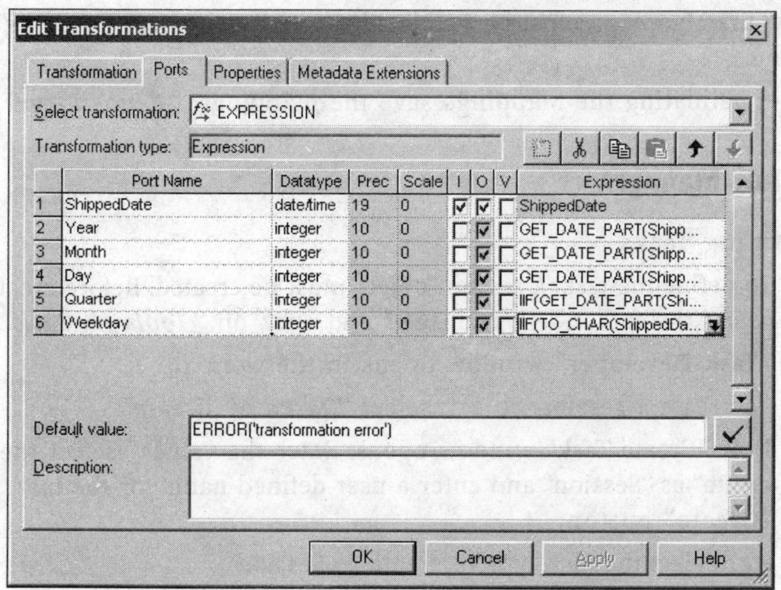

Fig. 5.12

10. Drag and drop the 'Year', 'Month', 'Day', 'Quarter', and 'Weekday' column of 'EXPRESSION' to respective columns of Target table and ShippedDate of EXPRESSION to the Saledate column of the Target table, then the mapping looks as in Fig. 5.13.

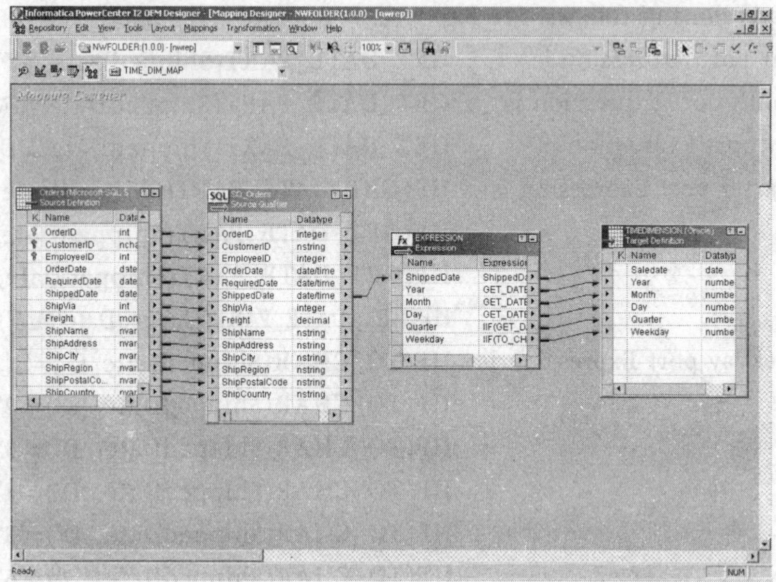

Fig. 5.13

11. Now the Mappings must be validated. Go to "*Mappings→Validate*" of the main menu.
12. After validating the Mappings save the mappings: "*Repository→Save*".

Workflow Manager

1. **Defining Tasks**
   i) To define the task, a session object must be created. Before creating a session select the folder "NWFOLDER" and click on "*Tools → Task Developer*".
   ii) **"Task Developer"** window opens in the workspace.
   iii) To create a session object, select "*Tasks → Create*".
   iv) Now **"Create Task"** window opens. Enter the values "Select the task type to create" as "Session" and enter a user-defined name for the task, then click on **"Create"** button.

      e.g.: Select the task type to create : Session

      Enter a new name for this task : TIMEDIMSESS.

v) The **"Mappings"** window opens. Now we have to select the mapping, which was created in "Designer" tool (in this example, select TIME_DIM_MAP).

vi) Click on **"OK"**, and on **"Done"** of "Create Task" dialog.

vii) Double click on the created session (TIMEDIMSESS).

viii) "Edit Tasks" window opens, go to sources tab.

ix) In the "Value" column, click on the down arrow button.

x) **"Relational Connection Browser"** window opens. Select the Source relational connection. In our example, select the "SOURCE" for all the four source tables and click on "OK".

xi) Go to *Targets* tab and again select the down arrow button of Values column.

xii) **"Relational Connection Browser"** window opens. In this window, select the Target object (TARGET) and click on **"OK"**.

xiii) In the Target tab, select the *"Properties"* tab located at the bottom.

xiv) Change the value of the "Target Load Type" as "Normal".

xv) Click on **"Apply"**, and on **"OK"**.

xvi) Save the task by selecting ***"Repository → Save"***.

xvii) To validate the session, select the task which is created and select the menu item ***"Tasks → Validate"***.

2. **Creating a Workflow**

i) Open the Workflow workspace either by selecting the menu item ***"Tools → Workflow Designer"***; or clicking on the icon Workflow Designer

ii) The Workflow Designer window opens in Workspace.

iii) Now select the menu item ***"Workflows → Create"*** to create a workflow.

iv) In General tab, enter the name of workflow.

e.g.: Name: TIMEDIMWF.

v) Click on **"OK"**. Before clicking on "OK", check whether the server name is there in the server edit box or not. If not, configure the server and then start the server.

vi) Explore the Sessions folder from the Navigator and select the created session (TIMEDIMSESS) and drag and drop it into the Workflow Designer workspace.

vii) From the Tool bar select, the Link Tasks icon (shown below), and drag the link from Workflow to Task.

viii) Save the workflow by selecting ***"Repository→Save"***.

ix) To start workflow select the menu item ***"Workflow → Start Workflow"***.

x) "Work flow Monitor" icon will appear on the System Tray.

xi) Open the "Workflow Monitor" by double clicking on it.

xii) Now you can see the status of the workflow. If the workflow is successful, "TIMEDIMSESS" and "TIMEDIMWF" are shown in the Succeeded part. To view how many Rows got transferred from source to target double click on the "TIMEDIMSESS".

xiii) "Properties of TIMEDIMSESS" window opens. In this window, you can see the status, if any errors occurred, the error messages are displayed in the First Error entry in this window.

xiv) For this example, the "Source Success Rows" entry will contain 388 and the "Target Success Rows" will also contain 388.

Thus we have successfully completed the workflow of transferring the source rows from Orders table and moving the successful rows to the target table "nwdwh".

Checking the Output

To see whether the target rows have been dumped into the target table, connect to the target table in the target database using the following SQL statements.

SQL syntax: connect <username>/<password>

e.g.: SQL> connect nwdwh/nwpwd;

Connected.

To see the rows of the target table, use the following SQL statement.

*SQL syntax: select * from <table name>;*

e.g.: SQL> select count(*) from timedimension; 388

5.2.10 Creation of Sales Fact Mapping

Source Analyzer

Now we have to define source Database objects for Sales Fact. To create the Sales Fact, we need Orders, Products, Customers, OrderDetails, which were imported previously and one more table from the target, which we have created, "EMPLOYEEDIMENSION".

To import the EMPLOYEEDIMENSION, the procedure is as follows:

1. From Designer tool main menu, select "*Tools → Source Analyzer*" (To open the source analyzer, the required folder in Navigator must be selected), then the Source Analyzer window opens in Workspace.
2. To import a source Database object, select the menu item from the main menu "*Sources → Import from Database*", then the "Import Table" window opens.

3. Select the ODBC Data Source name, Username, Owner name, Password for the Database tables, which are to be imported as source database objects and click on "Connect".

   e.g.: ODBC Data Source name : scott (Oracle in OraHome90)
   Username : nwdwh
   Owner name : nwdwh
   Password : nwpwd

4. After connecting, select the required table (EMPLOYEEDIMENSION) from select tables list and click on **"OK"**.
5. The selected table will be displayed in the Source Analyzer window of the Workspace along with the previously imported tables.

Warehouse Designer

The warehouse designer is used to create the Target Database objects. The procedure is as follows:

1. From the main menu, select "***Tools → Warehouse Designer***". Alternatively, click on the icon
2. The Warehouse Designer window opens in the Workspace.
3. Create a new target table (Sales Fact) with the columns as shown in Fig. 5.14.

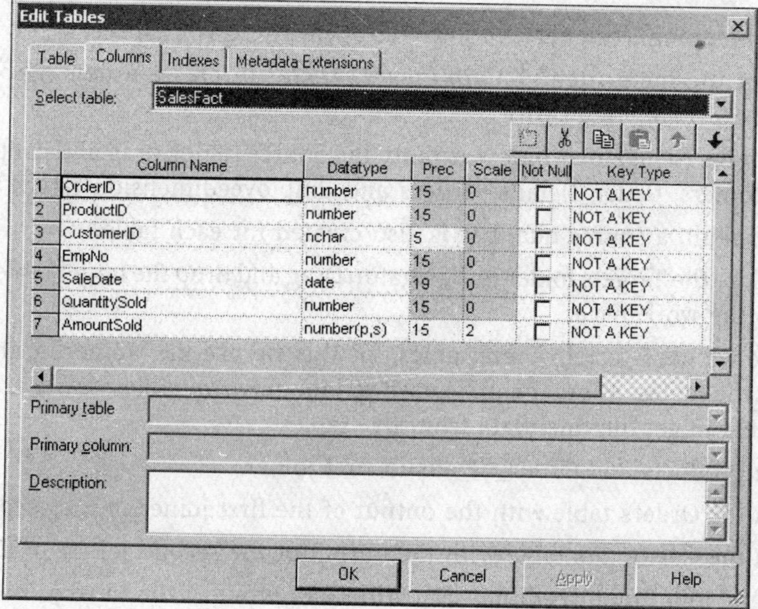

Fig. 5.14

4. The template for the target table is designed. To create the Target table in the Target Database, select the menu item "*Targets→Generate/Execute SQL*" from the main menu, then the "Database Object Generation" window opens.
5. Select the radio button "Selected tables".
6. Now, click on "*Generate and Execute*".
7. "Connect to an ODBC Data Source" dialog opens. Enter ODBC data source, Username, Password and click on "Connect".

   e.g.: ODBC Data Source : scott (Oracle in ora home 90)

   Username : nwdwh

   Password : nwpwd
8. A message box will be displayed with the message, "File MKTABLES.SQL already exists. Do you want to overwrite the contents of this file?" Click on "OK".
9. Now the Target table (SALESFACT) is created on the Target Database.

Mapping Designer

The Mapping Designer is used to map the flow of data from Source to Target. The procedure is as follows:

1. Open the Mapping Designer by selecting "*Tools → Mapping Designer*" from the main menu. Alternatively, click on the icon

   The Mapping Designer window will open in the Workspace.
2. Select the menu item, "*Mappings→Create*" to create a new mapping with the name SALES_FACT_MAP.
3. From the Navigator window, explore the Source folder, drag and drop the Products, Customers, Order_Details, Orders and Employeedimension tables to workspace.
4. By default, a source qualifier is also created for each table.
5. Explore the Targets folder in Navigator, Drag and drop the target table (SALESFACT) into the workspace.
6. Here we need to join these tables, for this we use the "Joiner" transformation to join the tables. A joiner can be used to join only two tables, so we are going to four joiners to get the final data from five tables.
7. Join Products and Order_details in first joiner.
8. Join the Orders table with the output of the first joiner in the second joiner
9. Join the Customers table with the output of the second joiner in the third joiner.
10. Finally join Employeedimension with the output of the third joiner in the fourth joiner.

11. Drag and drop respective columns of the fourth joiner to the target definition (SalesFact).

    The join conditions are as follows:

    JOINER1 condition: ProductID=ProductID1

    JOINER2 condition: OrderID=OrderID1.

    JOINER3 condition: CustomerID= CustomerID1.

    JOINER4 condition: EmployeeID=EmployeeID1.

12. Create a Transformation of type Expression and assign it the name "EXPRESSION". This transformation is used to calculate the Amount sold by using the Quantity sold, UnitPrice, Discount.
13. Drag and drop the columns 'Quantity', 'UnitPrice', 'Discount' from JOINER4 to EXPRESSION.
14. Create a new OUT port with the name "Amountsold" with an expression. (Quantity * UnitPrice1)-((Quantity * UnitPrice1) * Discount), as shown in Fig. 5.15.

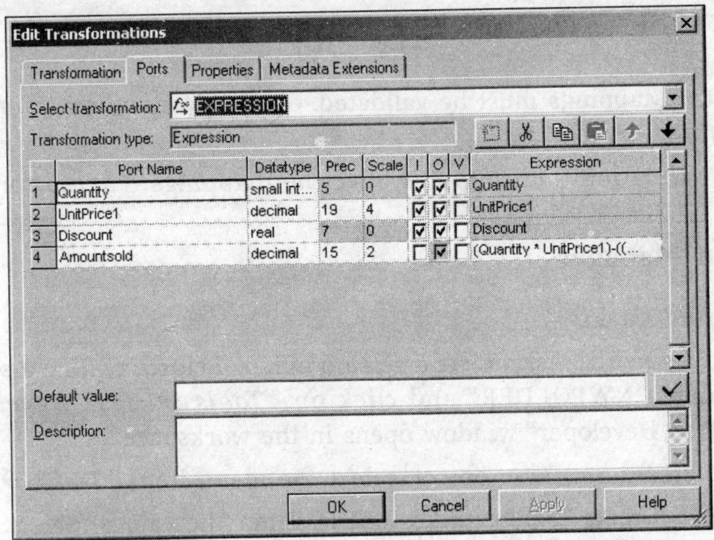

Fig. 5.15

15. Drag and drop 'Quantity' and 'Amountsold' columns of EXPRESSION transformation to the Target table, then the Mapping Designer looks as in Fig. 5.16.

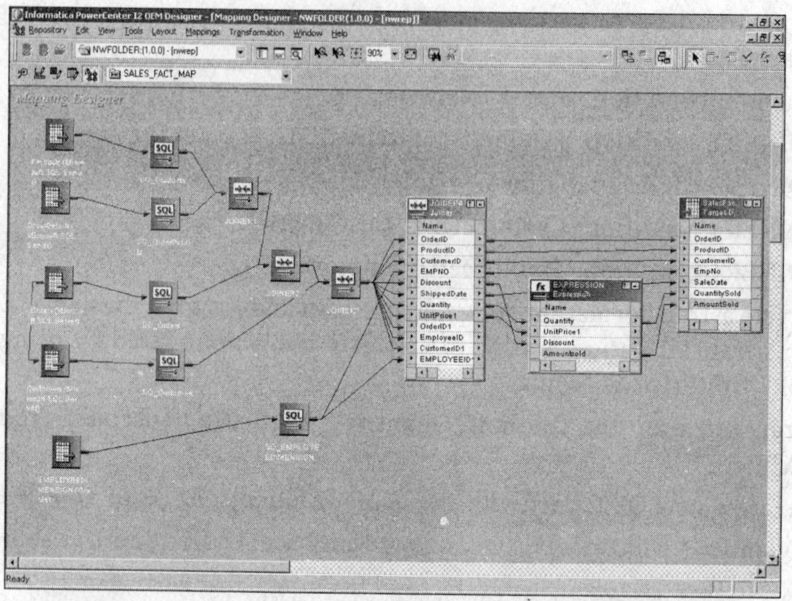

Fig. 5.16

16. Now the Mappings must be validated. Go to "*Mappings→Validate*" of the main menu.
17. After validating the Mappings, save the mappings: "***Repository→Save***".

Workflow Manager

1. **Defining Tasks**
   i) To define the task, create a session object. Before creating a session, select the folder "NWFOLDER" and click on "***Tools → Task Developer***", then the "Task Developer" window opens in the workspace.
   ii) To create a session object, select the menu item "***Tasks → Create***".
   iii) Now **"Create Task"** window opens. Enter the values "Select the task type to create" as "Session" and enter a user-defined name for the task, then click on "**Create**".

   e.g.: Select the task type to create : Session
   Enter a new name for this task : SALESFACTSESS.

   iv) The "Mappings" window opens. Now we have to select the mapping which was created in "Designer" tool (in this example, SALES_FACT_MAP).
   v) Click on **"OK"**, and on **"Done"** of "Create Task" dialog.
   vi) Double click on the created session (SALESFACTSESS).

vii) "Edit Tasks" window opens, go to sources tab.

viii) In the "Value" column, click on the down arrow button.

ix) **"Relational Connection Browser"** window opens. Select the Source relational connection. In our example, select the "SOURCE" for all the four source tables except EMPLOYEEDIMENSION table and for EMPLOYEEDIMENSION table, select the "TARGET", because we imported that table from ORACLE; and click on **"OK"**.

x) Go to Targets tab and again select the down arrow button of Values column.

xi) **"Relational Connection Browser"** window opens. In this window, select the Target object (TARGET) and click on **"OK"**.

xii) In the Target tab, select the *"Properties"* tab located at the bottom.

xiii) Change the value of the "Target Load Type" as "Normal".

xiv) Click on **"Apply"**, and on **"OK"**.

xv) Save the task: ***"Repository → Save"***.

xvi) To validate the session, select the task which is created and select the menu item ***"Tasks→ Validate"***.

2. **Creating a Workflow**

i) Select the menu item ***"Tools→ Workflow Designer"***. Or, click on the icon

ii) The Workflow Designer window opens in Workspace.

iii) To create a workflow, select the menu item, "*Workflows → Create*".

iv) In General tab, enter the name of workflow.

E.g.: Name: SALESFACTWF.

v) Click on **"OK"**. Before clicking on "OK", check whether the server name is there in the server edit box or not. If not, configure the server and then start the server.

vi) Explore the Sessions folder from the Navigator and select the created session (SALESFACTSESS) and drag and drop it into the Workflow Designer workspace.

vii) From the Tool bar, select the Link Tasks icon (shown below), and drag the link from Workflow to Task.

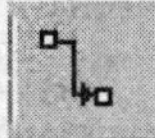

viii) Save the workflow by selecting ***"Repository→Save"***.

ix) To start workflow, select the menu item ***"Workflow → Start Workflow"***.

x) "Work flow Monitor" icon will appear on the System Tray.

xi) Open the "Workflow Monitor" by double clicking on it.

xii) Now, we can see the status of our workflow. If the Workflow is successful, then the "SALESFACTSESS" and "SALESFACTWF" are shown in the Succeeded part. To view how many Rows got transferred from source to target, double click on the "SALESFACTSESS".

xiii) **"Properties of SALESFACTSESS"** window opens. In this window, you can see the status, if any error occurs, the error messages are displayed in the First Error entry in this window.

xiv) For this example, the "Source Success Rows" entry will contain 2155 and the "Target Success Rows" will also contain 2155.

Checking the Output

To see whether the target rows have been dumped into the target table, connect to the target table in the target database:

SQL syntax: connect <username>/<password>

e.g. SQL> connect nwdwh/nwpwd;

Connected.

To see the rows of the target table:

SQL syntax: select * from <table name>;

e.g. SQL> select count(*) from salesfact;

2155

5.2.11 Applying Type 1 SCD on Product Dimension

In this section, we will demonstrate the **Type 1 slowly changing dimension** on Product Dimension. Suppose a product is discontinued and the information is updated in Products table of Northwind database (Source database). This information needs to be updated in the target database (data warehouse), without disturbing the remaining data. To demonstrate this scenario, we will apply Type 1 slowly changing dimension.

We will work on the tables which are used in the previous sections to create the dimensions. The tables required as sources are CATEGORIES, SUPPLIERS, PRODCUTS AND ORDER_DETAILS. The table required as target is PRODUCTDIMENSION. Since these tables already exist in the Source Analyzer and Warehouse Designer, there is no need to import or create the respective tables. Hence you can start directly from

Mapping Designer in Designer tool.

Mapping Designer

The Mapping Designer is used to map the flow of data from Source to Target. The procedure is as follows:

1. Open the Mapping Designer from Designer tool by selecting "*Tools → Mapping Designer*" from the main menu. Alternatively, click on the icon

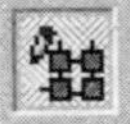

2. The Mapping Designer window will open in the Workspace.
3. Select the menu item "*Mappings→Create*" to create a new mapping with the name PRODUCT_DIM_MAP_TYPE1.
4. From the Navigator window explore the Source folder, drag and drop the Products, Suppliers, Categories, Order_Details tables to workspace.
5. By default, a source qualifier also created for each table.
6. Explore the Targets folder in Navigator, Drag and drop the target table (PRODUCTDIMENSION) into the Workspace.
7. In this example, we use the "Joiner" transformation to join tables. A joiner can be used to join only two tables, so we will use three joiners to get the final data from four tables.
8. Join Products and Order_details tables in first joiner.
9. Using second joiner, join the Suppliers table with the output of the first joiner.
10. Using third joiner, join Categories table with the output of the second joiner. The join conditions for each joiner are as follows:
    JOINER1 condition: ProductID=ProductID1
    JOINER2 condition: SupplierID=SupplierID1
    JOINER3 condition: CategoryID=CategoryID1.
11. Drag and drop respective columns of the joiner3 to the target definition (PRODUCTDIMENSION). The Mapping after using the three joiners will be as shown in Fig. 5.17.

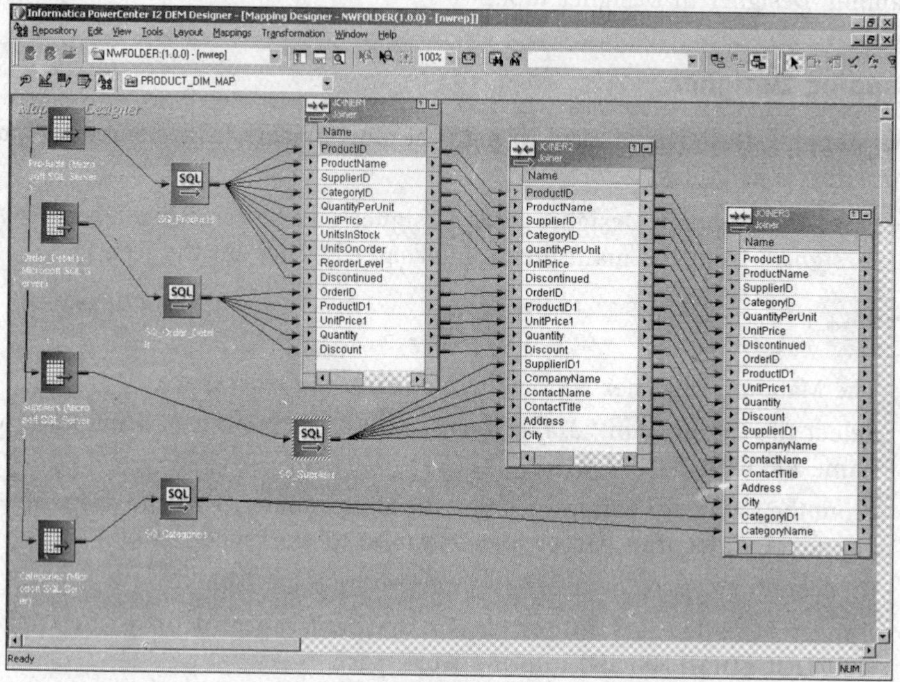

Fig. 5.17

Here, the data available in the target database and source database have to be retrieved and compared and so we will use LOOKUP transformation.

12. Select the Transformation of type "Lookup", by selecting the menu item "*Transformation → Create*" and name the Transformation as "LOOKUP".
13. After selecting the transformation as Lookup, "Select Lookup Table for Lookup Transformation" window opens. Select the Location of Lookup table as "TARGET" and Select the Lookup table you want this transformation to use as "ProductDimension" and click on "OK".
14. Click on "Done" of "Create Transformations" window.
15. Drag and drop the PRODUCTID column of JOINER3 to Lookup.
16. Double click on "LOOKUP" and go to "Conditions" tab to write the Lookup condition.
17. Select the "Add a new condition" icon and write the condition as shown in Fig. 5.18.

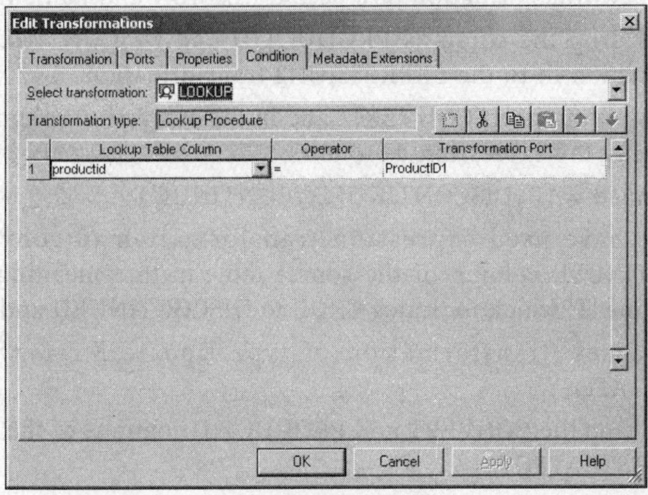

Fig. 5.18

18. Go to **"Properties"** tab. In "Properties" tab, go to "Value" column of "Location Information" and click on down arrow button. **"Select Database"** window opens. In that, select the Database connection as "TARGET" and click on **"OK"**.
19. Click on **"Apply"** and on **"OK"** of "Edit Transformations" window.
20. To create the new transformation of type "Expression", select the menu item "***Transformation → Create***" and name it as "EXPRESSION".
21. Now drag and drop the PRODUCTID and DISCONTINUED columns of the LOOKUP transformation in to the "EXPRESSION" transformation.
22. From JOINER3 transformation drag and drop the columns PRODUCTID and DISCONTINUED in to EXPRESSION transformation.
23. Create a new output port by name FORMAT in the EXPRESSION transformation.
24. In the "Expression" column of the FORMAT port, write the expression as shown below:

    IIF((productid=ProductID1) AND (Discontinued1 != IIF (discontinued=' DISCONTINUED','T','F')),1,0)
25. Create a new transformation of type "Filter" and name it as FILTER.
26. Drag and drop the columns PRODUCTID and DISCONTINUED from the JOINER3 in to the FILTER transformation.
27. Also drag and drop the FORMAT column of the EXPRESSION transformation in to the FILTER transformation.
28. Double click on "FILTER" to write the filter condition, just put the "FORMAT" column in the "Formula Editor" of "Expression Editor". Validate the condition and apply the settings.

29. Create a new transformation of type EXPRESSION and name it as EXPRESSION2.
30. Drag and drop the columns PRODUCTID and DISCONTINUED of the FILTER transformation in to the EXPRESSION2 transformation.
31. Add a new output port "CONVERT" and in the expression column of the CONVERT port, specify the expression as follows:

IIF(Discontinued = 'T','DISCONTINUED','CONTINUE')

32. Here we have used expression transformation to convert the values of DISCONTINUED column of the source table in to a meaningful value. We have changed the 'T' which indicates TRUE to DISCONTINUED and 'F' to CONTINUE.
33. Create a new transformation of type Update Strategy and name it as UPDTSTRATEGY.
34. Drag and drop the CONVERT and PRODUCTID columns of the EXPRESSION2 into the UPDTSTRATEGY.
35. Double click on UPDTSTRATEGY and in the "Formula Editor", enter the following text: DD_UPDATE.
36. Map the PRODUCTID and CONVERT columns of the UPDTSTRATEGY with the PRODUCTID AND FLAG columns of the target table.

    The final mappings will appear as shown in Fig. 5.19.

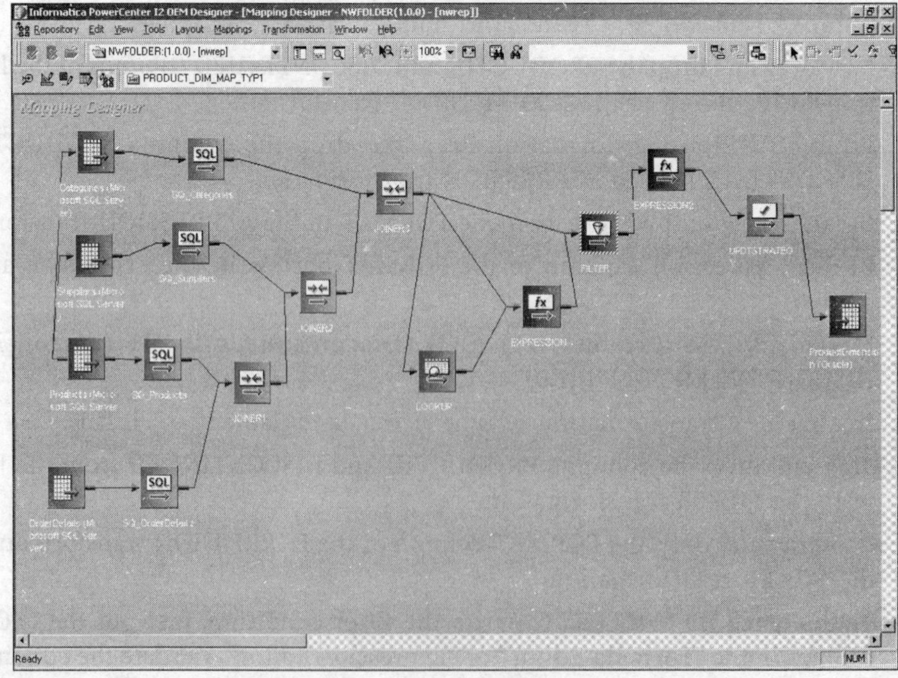

Fig. 5.19

37. To validate the Mappings go to "*Mappings→Validate*" of the main menu.
38. After validating the Mappings save the mappings: "*Repository→Save*".

Workflow Manager

1. **Defining Tasks:**
   i) To define the task, create a session object. Before creating a session, select the folder "NWFOLDER" and click on "*Tools → Task Developer*", then the **"Task Developer"** window opens in the workspace.
   ii) To create a session object, select "***Tasks → Create***".
   iii) Now **"Create Task"** window opens. Enter the values "Select the task type to create" as "Session" and enter a user-defined name for the task, then click on **"Create"**.

   e.g.: Select the task type to create: Session
   Enter a new name for this task: PRODUCTTYPE1SES.

   iv) The "Mappings" window opens. Select the mapping which was created in "Designer" tool (in this example, PRODUCT_DIM_MAP_TYPE1)
   v) Click on **"OK"**, and click on **"Done"** of "Create Task" dialog.
   vi) Double click on the created session (PRODUCTTYPE1SESS).
   vii) **"Edit Tasks"** window opens, go to sources tab.
   viii) In the "Value" column, click on the down arrow button.
   ix) **"Relational Connection Browser"** window opens. Select the Source relational connection. In this example, select the "SOURCE" for all the four source tables and click on **"OK"**.
   x) Go to Targets tab and again select the down arrow button of Values column.
   xi) **"Relational Connection Browser"** window opens. Select the Target object (TARGET) and click on **"OK"**.
   xii) In the Target tab, select the *"Properties"* tab located at the bottom.
   xiii) Change the value of the "Target Load Type" as "Normal".
   xiv) Click on **"Apply"**, and on **"OK"**.
   xv) Save the task: "***Repository → Save***".
   xvi) To validate the session, select the task which is created and select the menu item "***Tasks→ Validate***".
2. Creating a Work flow:
   i) Select the menu item "***Tools→ Workflow Designer***". Otherwise, click on the icon 

ii) Now the Workflow Designer window opens in Workspace.

iii) Select the menu item "*Workflows→Create*" to create a workflow.

iv) In General tab, enter the name of workflow.

e.g.: Name: PRODUCTDIMTYPE1WF.

v) Click on "OK". Before clicking on "OK", check whether the server name is there in the server edit box or not. If not, configure the server and then start the server.

vi) Explore the Sessions folder from the Navigator and select the created session (PRODUCTTYPE1SESS) and drag and drop it into the Workflow Designer workspace.

vii) From the Tool bar, select the Link Tasks icon (shown below), and drag the link from Workflow to Task.

viii) Save the workflow: "*Repository → Save*".

ix) Start workflow: "*Workflow → Start Workflow*".

x) "Workflow Monitor" icon will appear on the System Tray.

xi) Open the "Workflow Monitor" by double clicking on it.

xii) Now you can see the status of our workflow. If the Workflow is successful, then the "PRODUCTTYPE1SESS" and "PRODUCTDIMTYPE1WF" are shown in the Succeeded part. To view how many Rows got transferred from source to target, double click on the "PRODUCTTYPE1SESS".

xiii) "Properties of PRODUCTTYPE1SESS" window opens. In this window, you can see the status, if any errors occurred the error messages are displayed in the First Error entry in this window.

Checking the Output

To see the output of this mapping, first modify at least one record of the source table (Products). So modify the value of the DISCONTINUED column of the record with ProductID as 77 to 'T' and run the PRODUCTDIMTYPE1WF workflow.

To see whether the change made in the source table has been affected in the target database, use the following SQL statements.

SQL syntax: connect <username>/<password>

E.g. SQL> connect nwdwh/nwpwd;

Connected.

```
SQL> select productid, discontinued from Products where productid=77;
PRODUCTID                DISCONTINUED
77                       DISCONTINUED
1 rows selected.
```

Thus we have successfully updated the DISCONTINUED column of the PRODUCTDIMENSION successfully using Type 1 slowly changing dimension.

5.2.12 Applying Type2 SCD on Employee Dimension

In the previous examples, we have created EMPLOYEEDIMENSION in the data warehouse as target table and EMPNO and Flag columns were also added. We assigned the value of '1' to the Flag. We will use this column to maintain the past record of the employee. For example, if the title (i.e., designation) of the employee has been changed, then we will keep the past record as it is and add a new record with the new information by setting the Flag value to '1' and the previous records Flag value will be changed to '0'. By using the Flag column, we can identify the recent record.

Suppose a particular Employee with EMPLOYEEID of 9 has been promoted from "Sales Representative" to "Sales Manager", in the source data. This modification must be reflected in the target database, EMPLOYEEDIMENSION (data warehouse). To reflect this modification in the EMPLOYEEDIMENSION table, we will use Type 2 slowly changing dimension. At the end of this section, you are going to see the target table information about EMPLOYEEID = 9, is as follows:

EMPNO	EMPLOYEEID	TITLE	FLAG
9	9	Sales Representative	0
10	9	Sales Manager	1

Since source and target tables already exist in the Source Analyzer and Warehouse Designer, there is no need to import or create the respective tables. So, you can directly start from Mapping Designer in Designer tool.

Mapping Designer

1. Create a map with same source and same target as we used in EMPLOYEE_DIM_MAP.
2. Create new transformation of type Lookup and assign the name "LOOKUP" and click on **"Create"**.
3. **"Select Look Up Table for Lookup Transformation"** window opens. Select the Location of Lookup table as "TARGET" and Select the Lookup table you want in this transformation, "EMPLOYEEDIMENSION" and click on **"OK"**.

4. Click on "Done" of "Create Transformations" window.
5. Drag and drop "EmployeeId" column of Source Qualifier to LOOKUP.
6. Double click on "LOOKUP" and go to "Conditions" tab to write the Lookup condition.
7. Select the "Add a new condition" icon and write the condition as shown in Fig. 5.20.

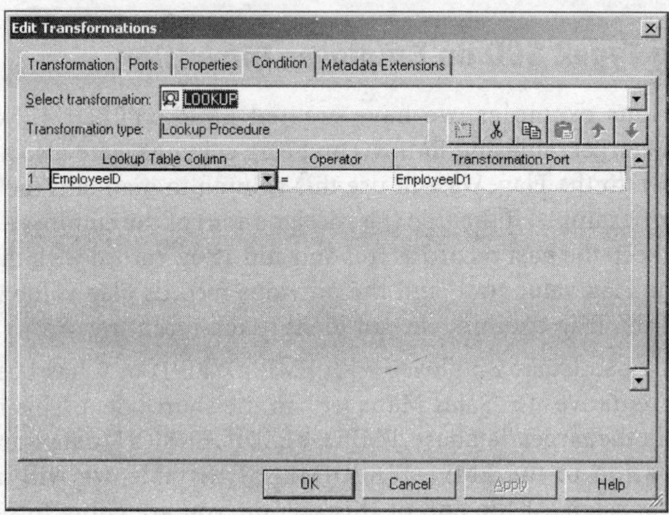

Fig. 5.20

8. Go to *"Properties"* tab. From the "Properties" tab, in "Value" column of "Location Information", click on down arrow button. **"Select Database"** window opens, select the Database connection as "TARGET" and click on **"OK"**.
9. Click on "Look Up SQL override".
10. "SQL Editor" window opens. Enter ODBC Data source, Username and Password.

    E.g.: ODBC Data Source : scott (Oracle in ORA Home90)

    User name : nwdwh

    Password : nwpwd
11. Click on "*Generate SQL*".
12. To the generated SQL statement, add the following condition at the end of statement: WHERE Employeedimension.Flag=1.
13. Validate the SQL statement and click on "OK".
14. Click on "Apply" and on "OK" of "Edit Transformations" window.
15. To create a new transformation, select the menu item "*Transformation → Create*".

16. In the "Create Transformation" window, select the type of Transformation as "Expression" and assign it the name as "EXPRESSION2" and click on "Create" and on "Done".
17. Drag and drop "Empno", "Employeeid" and "Title" from LOOKUP to EXPRESSION2.
18. Excluding "Photo", "Notes" and "PhotoPath", drag and drop the remaining columns of Source Qualifier to Expression.
19. Create four new OUT ports as shown in Fig. 5.21 and write the Expressions.

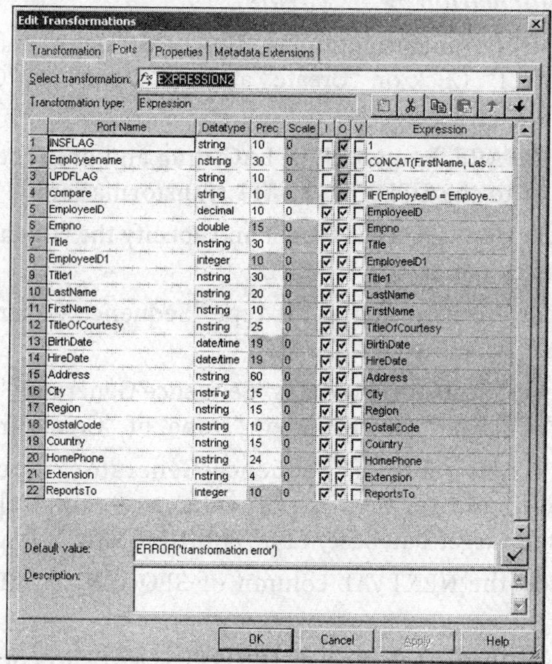

Fig. 5.21

INSFLAG condition is	:	1
UPDFLAG condition is	:	0
Employeename condition is	:	CONCAT(FirstName,LastName)
Compare condition is	:	IIF(EmployeeID = EmployeeID1 AND Title! = Title1,TRUE,FALSE)

20. After creating the OUT ports and specifying conditions for them as shown above, click **"OK"** of the **"Edit Transformations"** window.
21. To create the new transformation of type "Filter" by selecting the menu item "*Transformation → Create*".
22. Select the type of Transformation as "Filter" and assign it the name as "FILTER1". Click on **"Create"** and on **"Done"** of "Create Transformation" window.

23. Drag and drop all the columns of the EXPRESSION2, which are dragged into it from the Source Qualifier excluding FirstName and LastName.
24. Drag and drop INSFLAG, UPDFLAG, Employeename and Empno from EXPRESSION2 to FILTER1.
25. Write the FILTER1 condition
26. Condition is: COMPARE.
27. Create a new Transformation of type "Update Strategy" by selecting the menu item "***Transformation → Create***".
28. Select the type of Transformation as "Update Strategy" and assign it the name as "UPDATESTRAT1". Click on **"Create"** and on **"Done"** of "Create Transformation" window.
29. Excluding COMPARE, Empno, UPDFLAG, drag and drop the remaining columns of the FILTER1 in to the UPDATESTRAT1 transformation.
30. Now double click on UPDATESTRAT1 and specify the "Update Strategy Expression" of the Properties tab as DD_INSERT.
31. To create a new Transformation of type "Sequence Generator", select the menu item "***Transformation → Create***".
32. Select the type of Transformation as "Sequence Generator " and assign it the name as "SEQGEN". Click on "Create" and on "Done" of "Create Transformation" window.
33. To set the current value of "Sequence Generator", double click on SEQGEN transformation, and set the Current value as 9, since already nine employees (entries) in the target database, EPLOYEEDIMENSION (data warehouse).
34. Drag and drop the NEXTVAL column of SEQGEN to EMPNO column of target table.
35. Drag and drop all the columns of UPDATESTRAT1 to corresponding columns of first target table.
36. Create one more "Update Strategy" transformation by selecting the menu item "***Transformation → Create***".
37. Select the type of Transformation as "Update Strategy" and assign it the name as "UPDATESTRAT2". Click on "Create" and on "Done" of "Create Transformation" window.
38. Drag and drop Empno and UPDFLAG columns of FILTER1 to UPDATESTART2.
39. Now double click on UPDATESTRAT2 and specify the "Update Strategy Expression" of the Properties tab as DD_UPDATE.
40. Drag and drop UPDFLAG and Empno columns of UPDATESTRAT2 to second target table.
41. Now the mapping looks as in Fig. 5.22.

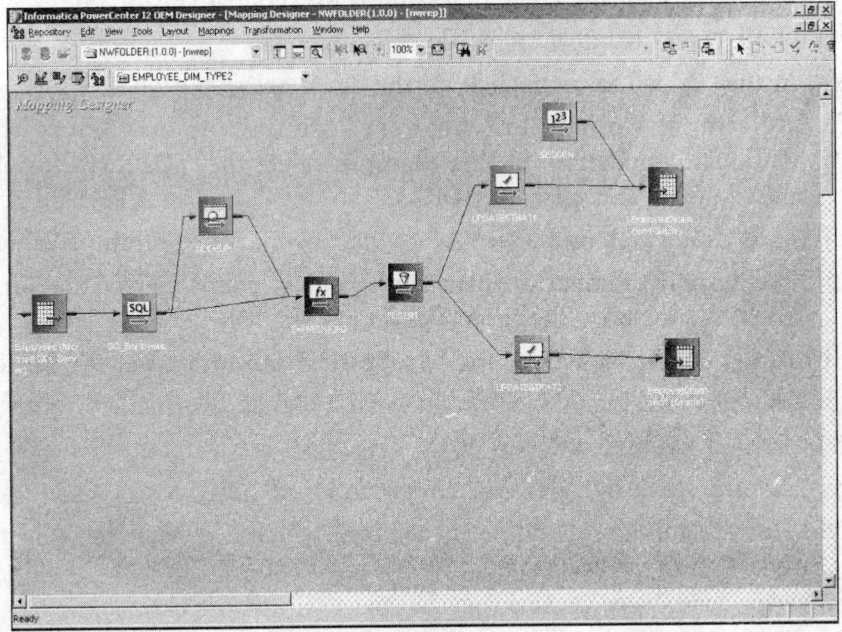

Fig. 5.22

42. Now the Mappings must be validated: Go to "*Mappings→Validate*" of the main menu.
43. After validating the Mappings save the mappings: "*Repository→Save*".

Workflow Manager

1. **Defining Tasks**
   i) To define the task, create a session object. Before creating a session, select the folder "NWFOLDER" and click on "*Tools → Task Developer*".
   ii) "Task Developer" window opens in the workspace.
   iii) To create a session object. Select "*Tasks → Create*".
   iv) Now "**Create Task**" window opens. Enter the values "Select the task type to create" as "Session" and enter a user-defined name for the task, then click on "**Create**" button.

      E.g.: Select the task type to create : Session

      Enter a new name for this task : EMPLOYEETYPE2SESS.
   v) The "**Mappings**" window opens. Select the mapping which was created in "Designer" tool (in this example, EMPLOYEE_DIM_TYPE2).
   vi) Click on "OK" and on "Done" of "**Create Task**" dialog box.

vii) Double click on the created session (EMPLOYEETYPE2SESS).

viii) "Edit Tasks" window opens, go to sources tab.

ix) In the "Value" column, click on the down arrow button.

x) **"Relational Connection Browser"** window opens. Select the Source relational connection. In this example, select the "SOURCE" for all the four source tables and click on **"OK"**.

xi) Go to Targets tab and again select the Down arrow button of Values column.

xii) **"Relational Connection Browser"** window opens. Select the Target object (TARGET) for both the targets and click on **"OK"**.

xiii) In the Target tab, select the **"Properties"** tab located at the bottom.

xiv) Change the value of the "Target Load Type" as "Normal" for both targets.

xv) Click on **"Apply"**, and on **"OK"**.

xvi) Save the task by selecting **"*Repository → Save*"**.

xvii) To validate the session, select the task, which is created and select the menu item **"*Tasks→ Validate*"**.

2. **Creating a Workflow**

i) Select the menu item, **"*Tools→ Workflow Designer*"**. Alternatively, click on the icon

Now the Workflow Designer window opens in Workspace.

ii) To create the Workflow, select the menu item **"*Workflows → Create*"**

iii) In General tab, enter the name of workflow.

e.g.: Name: EMPLOYEETYPE2WF.

iv) Click on **"OK"**. Before clicking on "OK", check whether the server name is there in the server edit box or not. If not, configure the server and then start the server.

v) Explore the Sessions folder from the Navigator and select the created session (EMPLOYEETYPE2SESS) and drag and drop it into the Workflow Designer workspace.

vi) From the Tool bar, select the Link Tasks icon (shown below) and drag the link from Workflow to Task.

i) Save the workflow: **"*Repository→ Save*"**.

ii) Start workflow: **"*Workflow → Start Workflow*"**.

iii) "Work flow Monitor" icon will appear on the System Tray.

iv) Open the "Workflow Monitor" by double clicking on it.

v) Now you can see the status of our workflow. If the Workflow is successful, "EMPLOYEETYPE2SESS " and " EMPLOYEETYPE2WF " are shown in the Succeeded part. To view how many Rows got transferred from source to target double click on the " EMPLOYEETYPE2SESS ".

vi) "Properties of EMPLOYEETYPE2SESS " window opens. In this window, you can see the status, if any errors occurred the error messages are displayed in the First Error entry in this window.

vii) For this example, the "Source Success Rows" entry will contain 9 and the "Target Success Rows" will contain 2.

Checking the Output

To see whether the target rows have been dumped into the target table, connect to the target table in the target database using the following SQL statements.

SQL syntax: *connect <username>/<password>*

e.g. SQL> connect nwdwh/nwpwd;

Connected.

To see the rows of the target table, use the following SQL statement.

SQL syntax: select * from <table name>;

e.g. SQL> select from employeedimension;

EMPNO	EMPLOYEEID	TITLE	FLAG
1	1	Sales Representative	1
2	2	Vice President, Sales	1
3	3	Sales Representative	1
4	4	Sales Representative	1
5	5	Sales Manager	1
6	6	Sales Representative	1
7	7	Sales Representative	1
8	8	Inside Sales Coordinator	1
9	9	Sales Representative	0
10	9	Sales Manager	1

10 rows selected.

Summary

- ETL Life cycle involves creation of a repository, creation of folders, designing transformations (or mappings) between source and target, creation of workflows and tasks, execution of tasks, and monitoring of the tasks.
- Before using the Informatica ETL tool, the administrator must create a Repository user in the database.
- Designer tool is used to select source and target databases.
- Source analyzer is used to define source database objects.
- Warehouse designer is used to create target database objects.
- Mapping designer is used to map the flow of data between the source and target
- The changes in the database fields can be stored in a data warehouse using slowly changing dimensions.

6 Cognos

Chapter Objectives

- Overview of Cognos
- Generation of business intelligence reports using Cognos Impromptu through case studies

Cognos is a very powerful suite for development of data warehouses. This suite is used extensively for development of data mines, data marts and data warehouses. In this chapter, we will demonstrate how to use Cognos Impromptu tools for report generation.

6.1 Overview of Cognos

Cognos development suite (www.cognos.com) is a rich set of tools for development of data mines, data marts and data warehouses. Some of the tools in this suite are:

Cognos DecisionStream: A tool for extraction, transformation of loading of data from the source databases to the target database.

Cognos Impromptu Web Reports: A tool for generation of business intelligence reports.

Cognos Scenario: A tool that is used to find the hidden trends and patterns in data.

Cognos Query: A tool for data navigation to process ad hoc queries.

Cognos PowerPlay: A tool for multi-dimensional on-line analysis of data.

In this chapter, we will study how to use Cognos Impromptu through case studies.

6.2 Development Environment

The case studies presented in this chapter have been tested in the following development environment:

- MS SQL Server (source database) running on Windows 2003 server.
- Oracle target database (developed using Informatica in the previous chapter) running on Windows 2003 server.
- Cognos tools running on Windows 2000 Professional and connected to the Windows 2003 server over a Local Area Network.

6.3 Case Study #1

In this case study, we will generate a report from PRODUCTDIMENSION table highlighting the lowest and highest price of products in each category with different colors. The final report looks as shown in Fig. 6.1.

Available Products Date: Saturday, August 06, 2005

Categoryname	Productname	Quantityperunit	Unitprice
Beverages	Côte de Blaye	12	$263.50
	Ipoh Coffee	16	$46.00
	Chang	24	$19.00
	Chartreuse verte	750	$18.00
	Chai	10	$18.00
	Lakkalikööri	500	$18.00
	Steeleye Stout	24	$18.00
	Outback Lager	24	$15.00
	Laughing Lumberjack Lager	24	$14.00
	Sasquatch Ale	24	$14.00
	Rhönbrau Klosterbier	24	[illegible]
Condiments	Vegie-spread	15	$43.90
	Northwoods Cranberry Sauce	12	$40.00
	Sirop d'érable	24	$28.50
	Grandma's Boysenberry Spread	12	$25.00
	Chef Anton's Cajun Seasoning	48	$22.00
	Louisiana Fiery Hot Pepper Sauce	32	$21.05
	Gula Malacca	20	$19.45
	Louisiana Hot Spiced Okra	24	$17.00
	Genen Shouyu	24	$15.50
	Aniseed Syrup	12	$10.00
Confections	Sir Rodney's Marmalade	30	$81.00
	Tarte au sucre	48	$49.30
	Schoggi Schokolade	100	$43.90
	Gumbär Gummibärchen	100	$31.23
	Maxilaku	24	$20.00

Highest Unit Price in Beverages

Lowest Unit Price in Beverages

Fig. 6.1

To generate this report, the procedure is as follows:

1. Open the "Cognos Impromptu Administrator" tool:

   "***Start→ Programs→ Cognos EP Series 7→ Cognos Impromptu Administrator***", then the "Impromptu" window, shown in Fig. 6.2, opens.

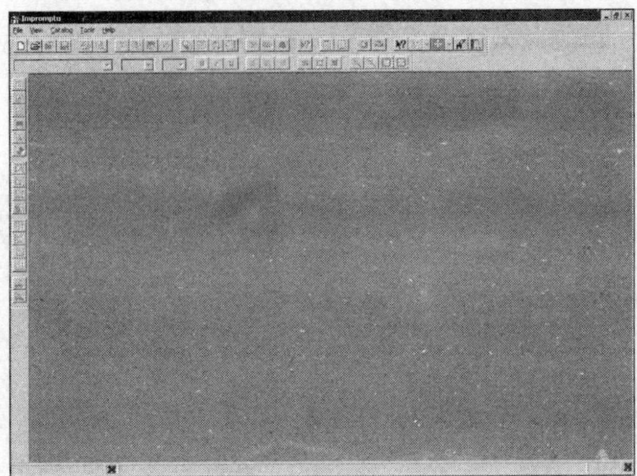

Fig. 6.2

6.3.1 Connecting to the Database

We must connect to Database to build reports. The procedure to connect to Database is as follows:

1. Select the menu item ***"Catalog→Databases"***.
2. "Database Definition Manager" window (Fig. 6.3) opens.

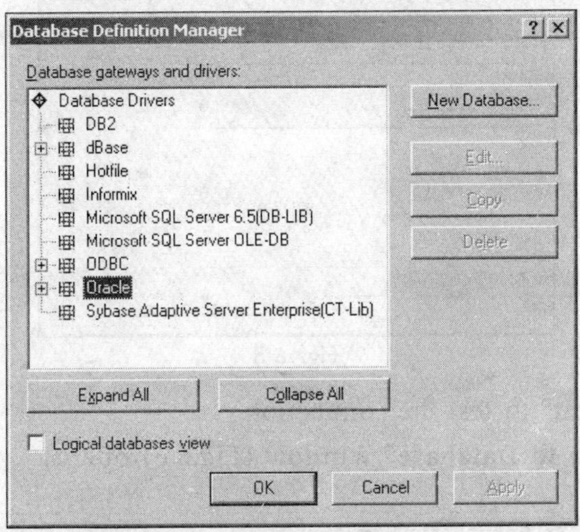

Fig. 6.3

3. Select **"Oracle"** from **"Database gateways and drivers"** list and click on **"New Database"** button.
4. **"Database Definition-Oracle"** window (Fig. 6.4) opens.

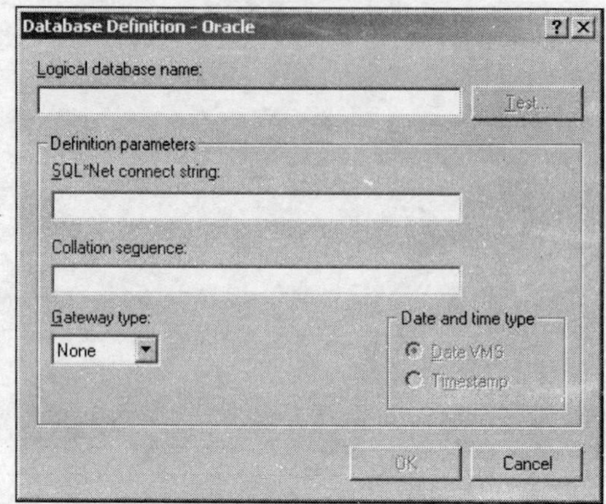

Fig. 6.4

5. Enter "Logical database name", "SQL *Net connect string".

   e.g.: Logical database name: nwdbconnection

   SQL *NET connect string: orcl

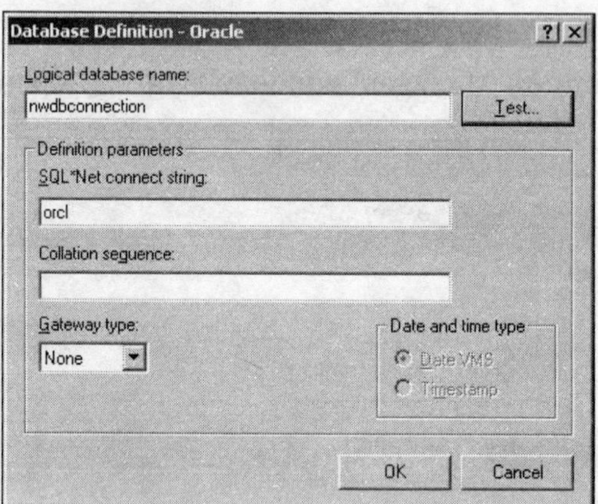

Fig. 6.5

6. Click on **"Test"** to test the connection.
7. **"Test Attach to Database"** window (Fig.6.6) opens.

Test Attach to Database

User ID: nwdim

Password: *****

OK

Cancel

Fig. 6.6

8. Enter the User ID and Password to test the connection with the database.
   e.g.: User ID : nwdim
   Password : nwpwd
9. Successful attachment message box will be displayed, click on **"OK"** button.
10. Click on **"OK"** of "Database Definition" window.
11. "Database Definition Manager" window, shown in Fig. 6.7, opens.

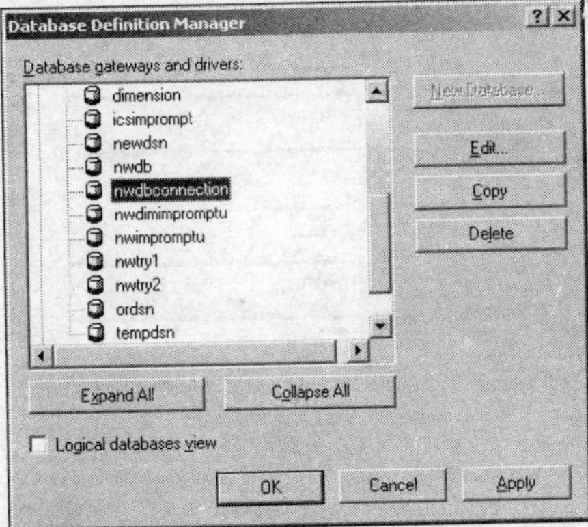

Fig. 6.7

12. Click on **"Apply"** and **"OK"**.

6.3.2 Creating Catalog

1. To create a new catalog, select the menu item ***"Catalog → New"***.
2. "New Catalog" window opens.
3. Enter catalog file name and select the database name, as shown in Fig. 6.8.
   e.g.: File name : nwcatalog
   Database Name : nwdbconnection.

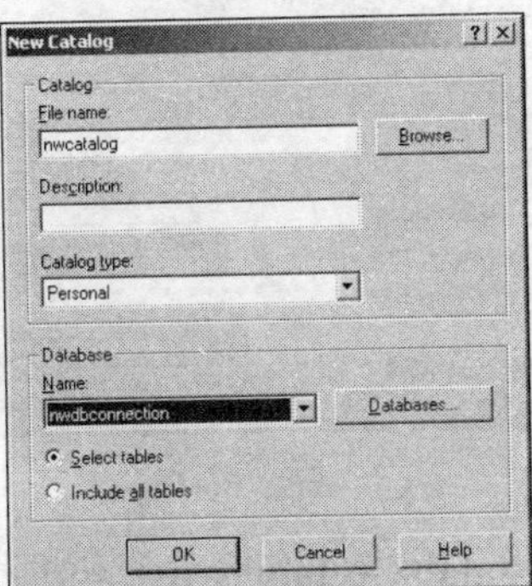

Fig. 6.8

4. Click on **"OK"**.
5. "Catalog Logon NWCATALOG.CAT" window opens. Enter database User ID and Password, as shown in Fig. 6.9.

   e.g.: User ID : nwdim

   Password : nwpwd

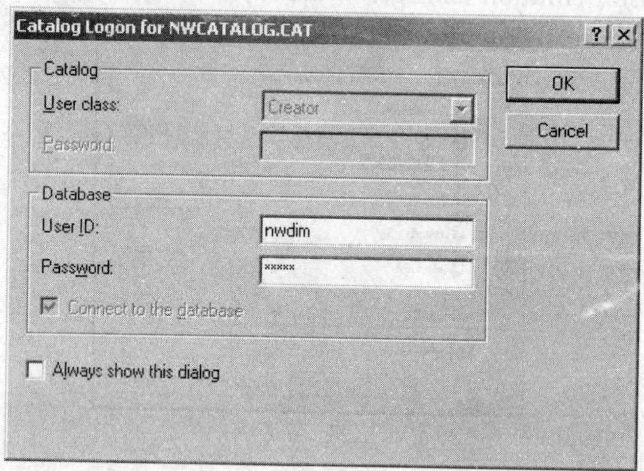

Fig. 6.9

6. Click on **"OK"**.
7. **"Tables"** window (Fig. 6.10) opens.

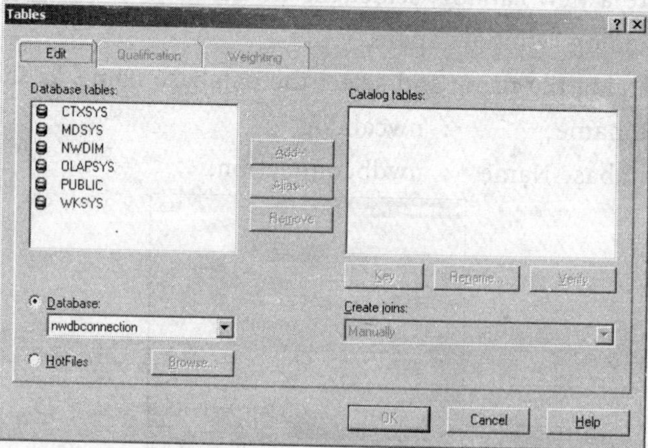

Fig. 6.10

8. Select NWDIM from database tables list and click on **"Add"** (Fig. 6.11).

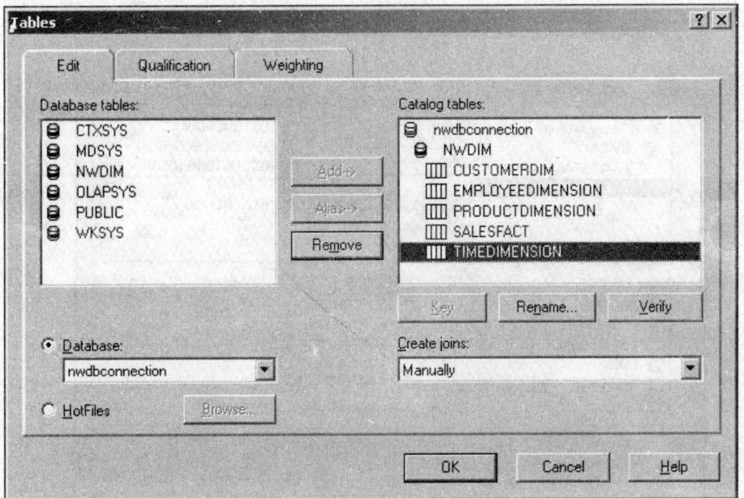

Fig. 6.11

9. Click on **"OK"**.
10. **"Joins"** window (Fig. 6.12) opens.

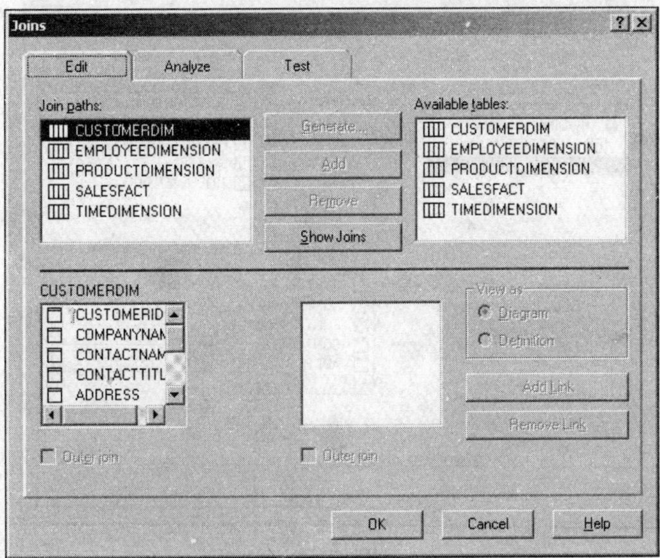

Fig. 6.12

11. Select SALESFACT table from "Join paths" list and select CUSTOMERDIM from "Available tables" list, click on **"Add"** (Fig. 6.13).

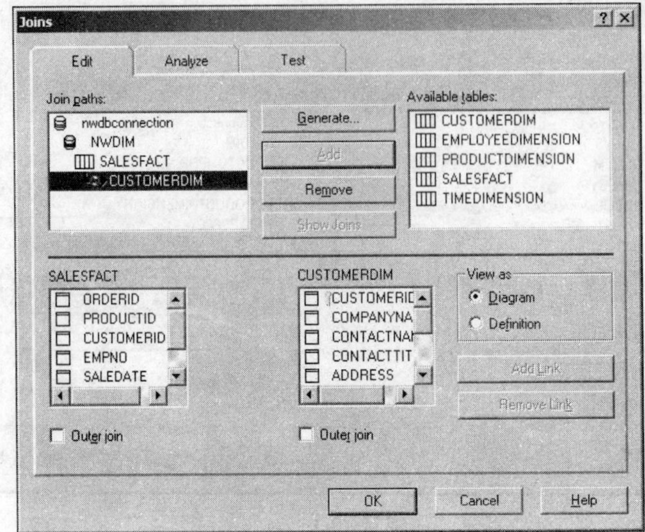

Fig. 6.13

12. Select CUSTOMERID from SALEFACT, select CUSTOMERID from CUSTOMERDIM and click on **"Add Link"** (Fig. 6.14)

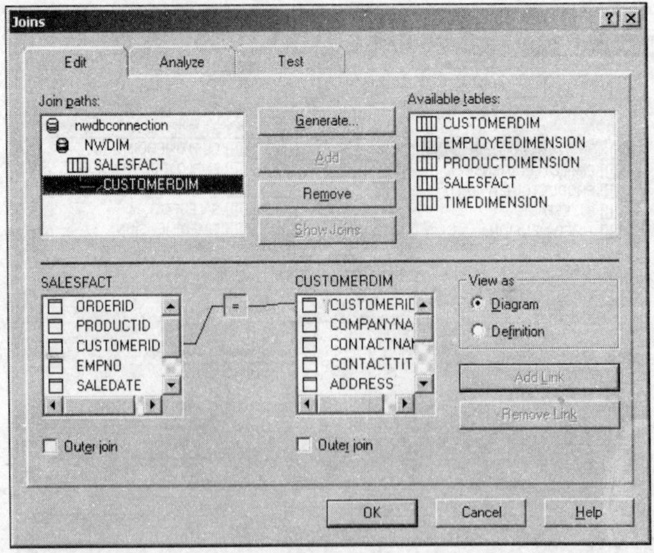

Fig. 6.14

13. Select SALESFACT from "Join paths" list, select EMPLOYEEDIMENSION from "Available tables" list and click on **"Add"**.

14. Select EMPNO from SALESFACT, select EMPNO from EMPLOYEEDIMENSION and click on **"Add Link"** (Fig. 6.15).

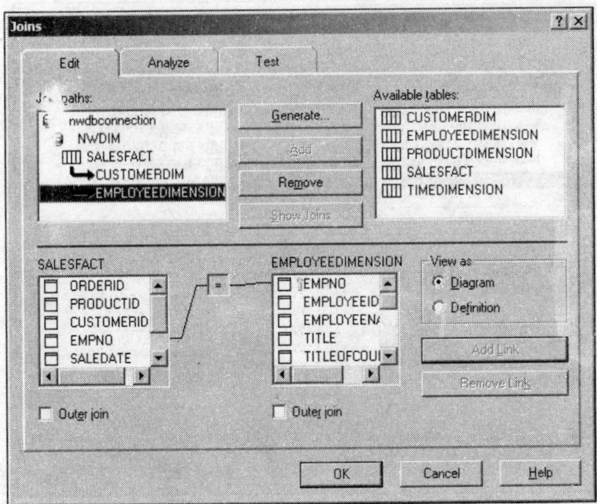

Fig. 6.15

15. Select SALESFACT from "Join paths" list, select PRODUCTDIMESION from "Available tables" list and click on **"Add"**.
16. Select PRODUCTID from SALESFACT, select PRODUCTID from PRODUCTDIMENSION and click on **"Add Link"** (Fig. 6.16).

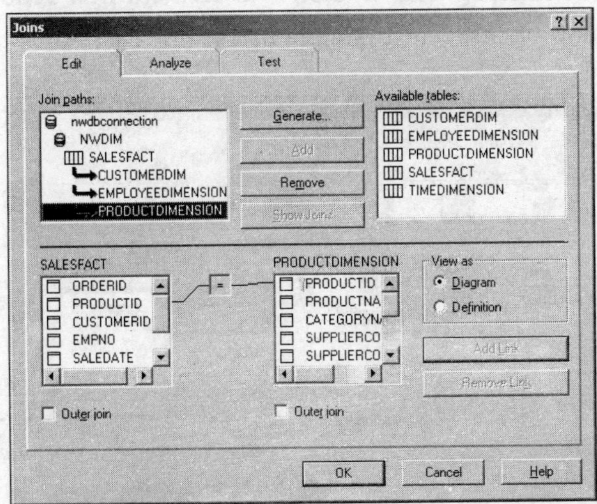

Fig. 6.16

17. Select SALESFACT from "Join paths" list, select TIMEDIMESION from "Available tables" list and click on **"Add"**.
18. Select SALEDATE from SALESFACT, select SALEDATE from TIMEDIMENSION and click on **"Add Link"** (Fig. 6.17).

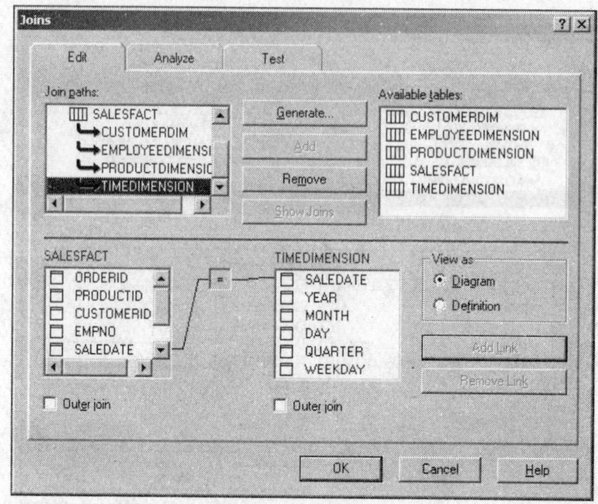

Fig. 6.17

19. Click on **"OK"** of "Joins" window.

6.3.3 Creating a Report

1. Select the menu item ***"File → New"*** to create a new report.
2. **"New"** window opens. Select "simple list" from "Fast Find" tab and click on **"OK"** (Fig. 6.18)

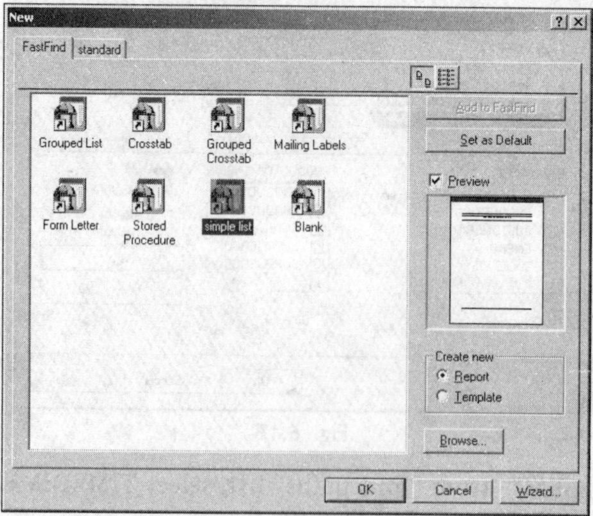

Fig. 6.18

3. "Query" window, shown in Fig. 6.19 opens. Click on **"Data"** tab.

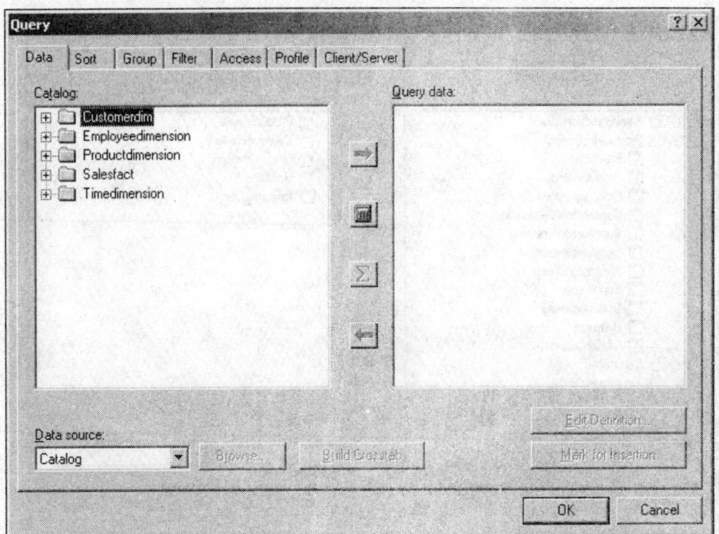

Fig. 6.19

4. Explore "Productdimension" from "Catalog" list and select Productname, Categoryname, Quantityperunit, Unitprice and Discontinued and click on "→" button (Fig. 6.20).

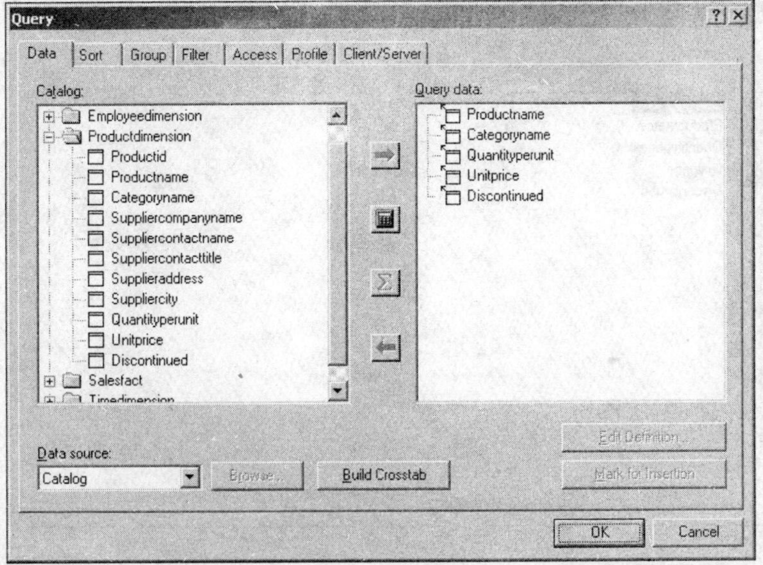

Fig. 6.20

5. Select Discontinued from "Query data" list and click on **"Mark for Insertion"** button, to make it (Discontinued column) invisible in the report (Fig. 6.21).

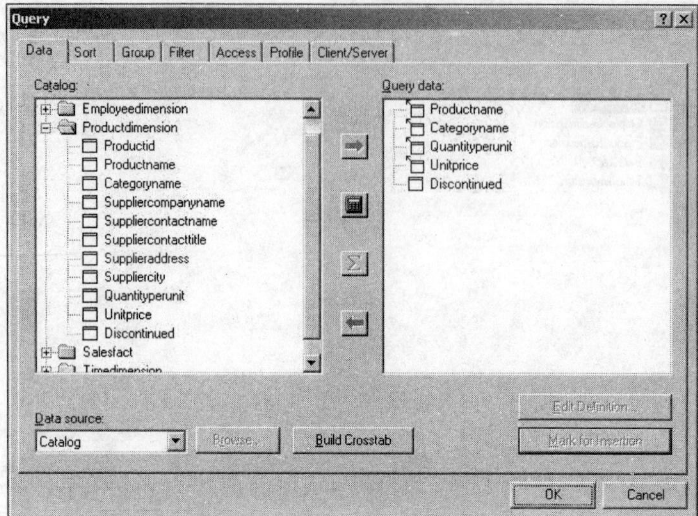

Fig. 6.21

6. Go to Sort tab. Select Category name from "Sort Order" list and click on **"Ascending"** button (Fig. 6.22).

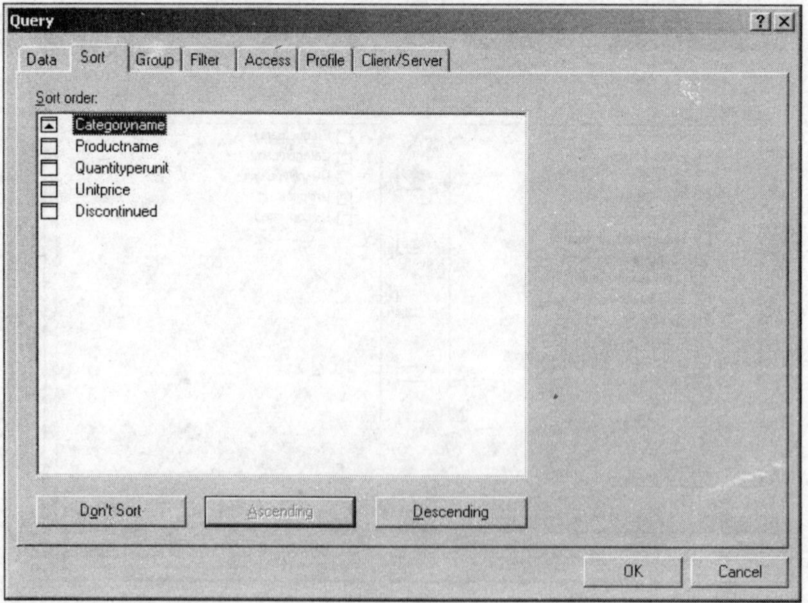

Fig. 6.22

7. Go to Group tab. Select Categoryname from "Group Order" list and click on **"Group"** (Fig. 6.23).

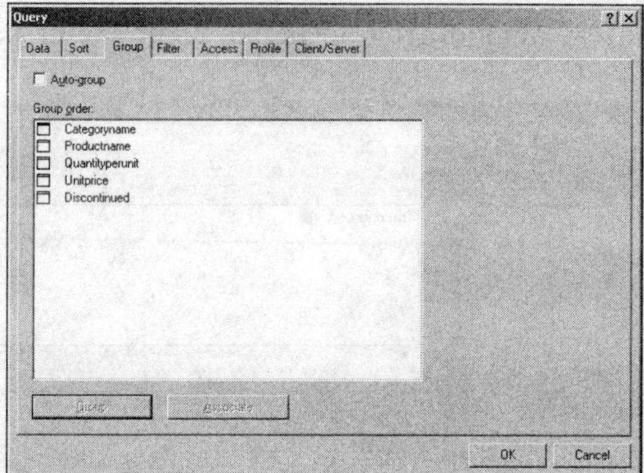

Fig. 6.23

8. Go to **Filter** tab (Fig. 6.24).

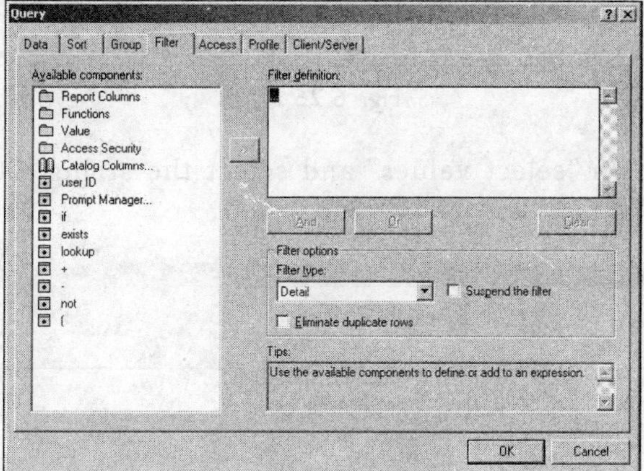

Fig. 6.24

9. Double click on **"Catalog Columns"** from "Available components" list.
10. "Catalog" window opens. Explore Productdimension folder and select Discontinued column and click on **"OK"** (Fig. 6.25).

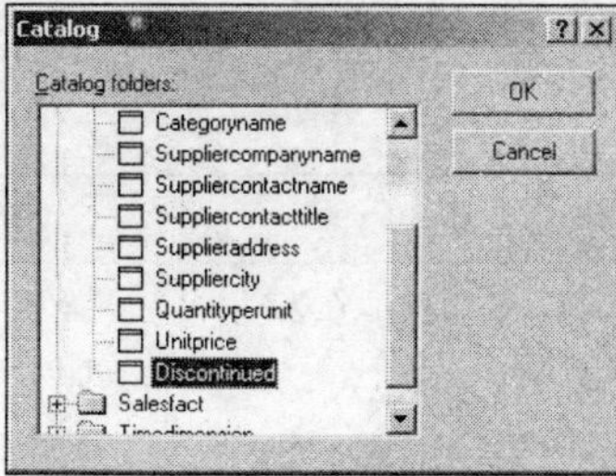

Fig. 6.25

11. Double click on **"="** symbol from available components list (Fig. 6.26).

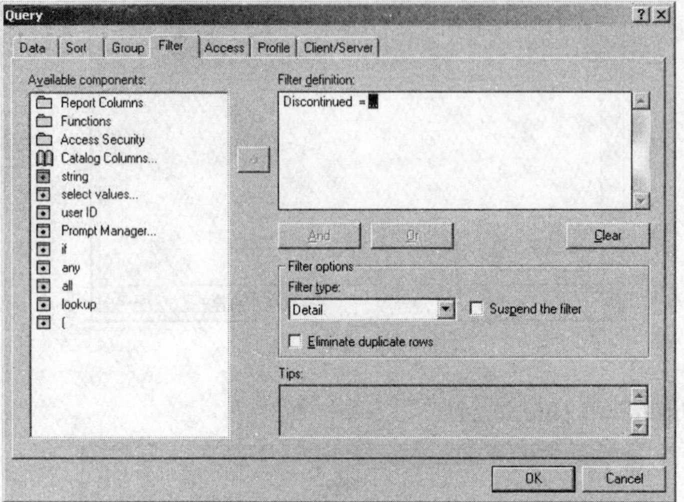

Fig. 6.26

12. Double click on "select values" and select the string 'CONTINUE' in "Filter definition" (Fig. 6.27).

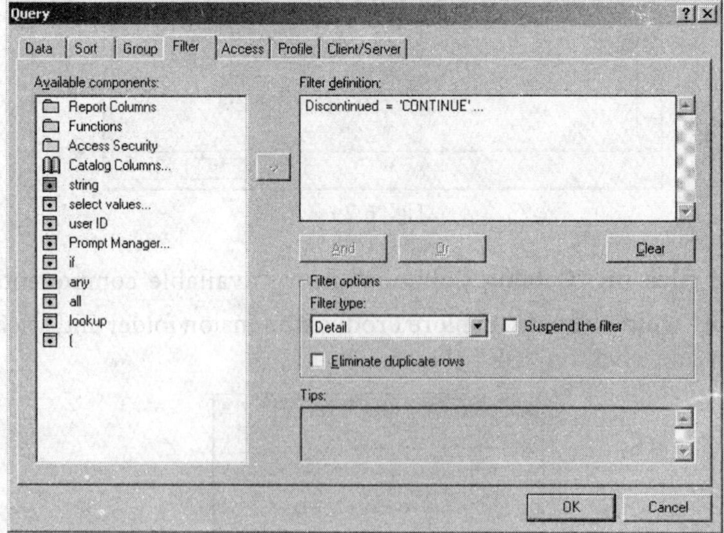

Fig. 6.27

13. Click on **"OK"** of "Query" window.
14. Now the simple report will be displayed for the specified columns, with the

specified grouping, with specified sorting and for the specified filter as shown in Fig. 6.28.

Date: 8/6/05

<Type here to customize title>

Productname	Categoryname	Quantityperunit	Unitprice
Chartreuse verte	Beverages	750	18.0000
Chai		10	18.0000
Chang		24	19.0000
Côte de Blaye		12	263.5000
Ipoh Coffee		16	46.0000
Outback Lager		24	15.0000
Lakkalikööri		500	18.0000
Rhönbräu Klosterbier		24	7.7500
Laughing Lumberjack Lager		24	14.0000
Steeleye Stout		24	18.0000
Sasquatch Ale		24	14.0000
Northwoods Cranberry Sauce	Condiments	12	40.0000
Louisiana Fiery Hot Pepper Sauce		32	21.0500
Louisiana Hot Spiced Okra		24	17.0000
Vegie-spread		15	43.9000
Chef Anton's Cajun Seasoning		48	22.0000
Grandma's Boysenberry Spread		12	25.0000
Aniseed Syrup		12	10.0000
Sirop d'érable		24	28.5000
Gula Malacca		20	19.4500
Genen Shouyu		24	15.5000
Sir Rodney's Scones	Confections	24	10.0000
Valkoinen suklaa		12	16.2500
Maxilaku		24	20.0000
Chocolade		10	12.7500
Zaanse koeken		10	9.5000
Gumbär Gummibärchen		100	31.2300

Fig. 6.28

15. Select the Category column by clicking on header of the column, then all the category names of that column will get selected.
16. Drag and drop the Category column before Productname column. Then the screen will look as in Fig. 6.29.

Date: 8/6/05

<Type here to customize title>

Categoryname	Productname	Quantityperunit	Unitprice
Beverages	Chartreuse verte	750	18.0000
	Chai	10	18.0000
	Chang	24	19.0000
	Côte de Blaye	12	263.5000
	Ipoh Coffee	16	46.0000
	Outback Lager	24	15.0000
	Lakkalikööri	500	18.0000
	Rhönbräu Klosterbier	24	7.7500
	Laughing Lumberjack Lager	24	14.0000
	Steeleye Stout	24	18.0000
	Sasquatch Ale	24	14.0000
Condiments	Northwoods Cranberry Sauce	12	40.0000
	Louisiana Fiery Hot Pepper Sauce	32	21.0500
	Louisiana Hot Spiced Okra	24	17.0000
	Vegie-spread	15	43.9000
	Chef Anton's Cajun Seasoning	48	22.0000
	Grandma's Boysenberry Spread	12	25.0000
	Aniseed Syrup	12	10.0000
	Sirop d'érable	24	28.5000
	Gula Malacca	20	19.4500
	Genen Shouyu	24	15.5000
Confections	Sir Rodney's Scones	24	10.0000
	Valkoinen suklaa	12	16.2500
	Maxilaku	24	20.0000
	Chocolade	10	12.7500
	Zaanse koeken	10	9.5000
	Gumbär Gummibärchen	100	31.2300

Fig. 6.29

17. To change the title of the report, select the title, "<Type here to customize title>", right click on it and select the menu item **"Edit"** from the pop up menu.
18. Enter the title of the report as "Available Products". To change the text color of the title, select the required font color from the tool bar of "Font Color" drop down list. After changing the title and the color of the font of the title, the report looks as shown in Fig. 6.30.

Date: 8/6/05

Available Products

Categoryname	Productname	Quantityperunit	Unitprice
Beverages	Chartreuse verte	750	18.0000
	Chai	10	18.0000
	Chang	24	19.0000
	Côte de Blaye	12	263.5000
	Ipoh Coffee	16	46.0000
	Outback Lager	24	15.0000
	Lakkalikööri	500	18.0000
	Rhönbräu Klosterbier	24	7.7500
	Laughing Lumberjack Lager	24	14.0000
	Steeleye Stout	24	18.0000
	Sasquatch Ale	24	14.0000
Condiments	Northwoods Cranberry Sauce	12	40.0000
	Louisiana Fiery Hot Pepper Sauce	32	21.0500
	Louisiana Hot Spiced Okra	24	17.0000
	Vegie-spread	15	43.9000
	Chef Anton's Cajun Seasoning	48	22.0000
	Grandma's Boysenberry Spread	12	25.0000
	Aniseed Syrup	12	10.0000
	Sirop d'érable	24	28.5000
	Gula Malacca	20	19.4500
	Genen Shouyu	24	15.5000
Confections	Sir Rodney's Scones	24	10.0000
	Valkoinen suklaa	12	16.2500
	Maxilaku	24	20.0000
	Chocolade	10	12.7500
	Zaanse koeken	10	9.5000
	Gumbär Gummibärchen	100	31.2300

Fig. 6.30

19. You can also change the date format which is displayed on the report. To change the date format of the date, select the date and right click on it.
20. From the pop up menu, select the menu item, "Format", then the "Format" window opens (Fig. 6.31).

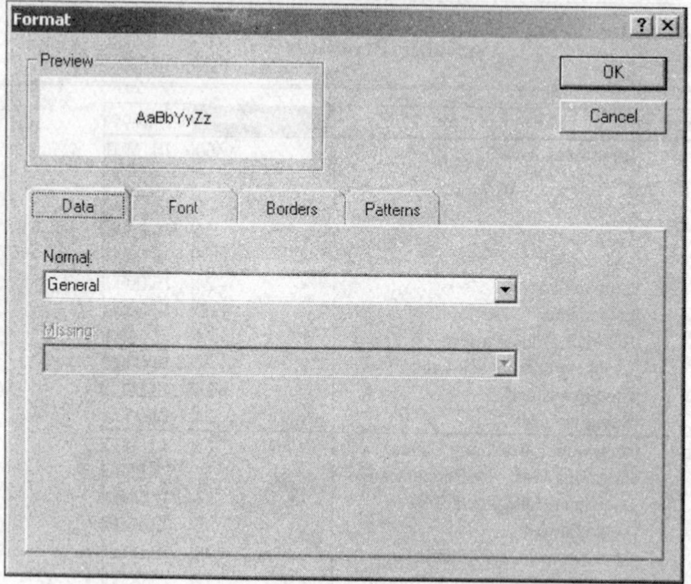

Fig. 6.31

21. To change the date format, go to Data tab. In that, select the drop down list box of Normal. From the list, select the required date format.

    e.g: dddd, mmmm dd, yyyy

22. In this window, we can also change font style, borders and patterns of the date displayed on the report.

23. Click on **"OK"** to close the Format window. Now, you can see that the format of the date on the report changes as required. After changing the date format, the date looks as shown below:

Date: Saturday, August 06, 2005

24. You can also change the font and color of the text that is displayed for the columns headers of the report. To change them, select all the column headers of the report by clicking at the starting of the first column header from left side. Notice that all the column headers get selected. Now, select the required color from the drop down list box of "Font Colors" from the tool bar. After changing the color of the headers of the columns, the report looks as shown in Fig. 6.32.

Categoryname	Productname	Quantityperunit	Unitprice
Beverages	Chartreuse verte	750	18.0000
	Chai	10	18.0000
	Chang	24	19.0000
	Côte de Blaye	12	263.5000
	Ipoh Coffee	16	46.0000
	Outback Lager	24	15.0000
	Lakkaliköori	500	18.0000
	Rhönbräu Klosterbier	24	7.7500
	Laughing Lumberjack Lager	24	14.0000
	Steeleye Stout	24	18.0000
	Sasquatch Ale	24	14.0000
Condiments	Northwoods Cranberry Sauce	12	40.0000
	Louisiana Fiery Hot Pepper Sauce	32	21.0500
	Louisiana Hot Spiced Okra	24	17.0000
	Vegie-spread	15	43.9000
	Chef Anton's Cajun Seasoning	48	22.0000
	Grandma's Boysenberry Spread	12	25.0000
	Aniseed Syrup	12	10.0000
	Sirop d'érable	24	28.5000
	Gula Malacca	20	19.4500
	Genen Shouyu	24	15.5000
Confections	Sir Rodney's Scones	24	10.0000
	Valkoinen suklaa	12	16.2500
	Maxilaku	24	20.0000
	Chocolade	10	12.7500
	Zaanse koeken	10	9.5000
	Gumbär Gummibärchen	100	31.2300

Fig. 6.32

To change the format of the Column Data and Unit price:

1. You can change the style of display of the data "UnitPrice" of the report. To change the style, select the whole column UnitPrice.
2. Right click on the selection, from the pop up menu, select menu item "Format".
3. The "Format" window opens. In the "Data" tab, select the option "Currency" from the drop down list "Positive".
4. Click on **"OK"** of the "Format" window. Now the report looks as shown in Fig. 6.33.

Date: Saturday, August 06, 2005

Available Products

Categoryname	Productname	Quantityperunit	Unitprice
Beverages	Chartreuse verte	750	$18.00
	Chai	10	$18.00
	Chang	24	$19.00
	Côte de Blaye	12	$263.50
	Ipoh Coffee	16	$46.00
	Outback Lager	24	$15.00
	Lakkalikööri	500	$18.00
	Rhönbräu Klosterbier	24	$7.75
	Laughing Lumberjack Lager	24	$14.00
	Steeleye Stout	24	$18.00
	Sasquatch Ale	24	$14.00
Condiments	Northwoods Cranberry Sauce	12	$40.00
	Louisiana Fiery Hot Pepper Sauce	32	$21.05
	Louisiana Hot Spiced Okra	24	$17.00
	Vegie-spread	15	$43.90
	Chef Anton's Cajun Seasoning	48	$22.00
	Grandma's Boysenberry Spread	12	$25.00
	Aniseed Syrup	12	$10.00
	Sirop d'érable	24	$28.50
	Gula Malacca	20	$19.45
	Genen Shouyu	24	$15.50
Confections	Sir Rodney's Scones	24	$10.00
	Valkoinen suklaa	12	$16.25
	Maxilaku	24	$20.00
	Chocolade	10	$12.75
	Zaanse koeken	10	$9.50

Fig. 6.33

Highlighting the lowest and highest priced products:

1. Select II, III & IV columns of the table and right click on the selection. From the pop menu, select the menu item "Conditional Formats", then "Conditional Formats" window (Fig. 6.34) opens.

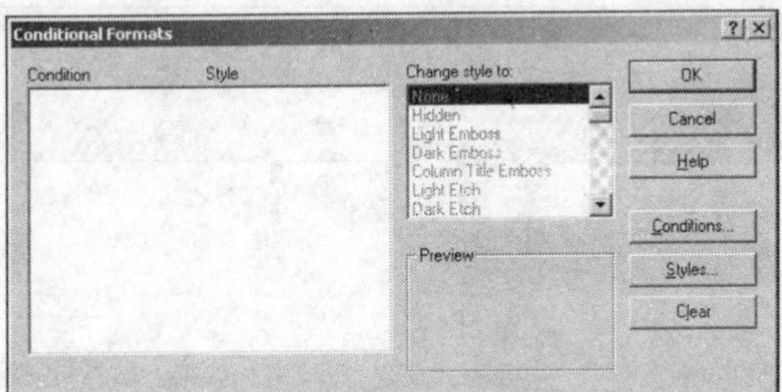

Fig. 6.34

2. Click on the **"Conditions"** to enter the conditions for formatting the data; then the "Conditions" window opens (Fig. 6.35).

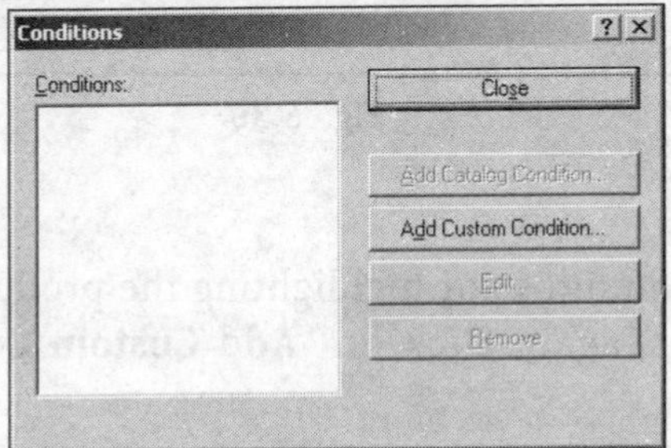

Fig. 6.35

3. Click on **"Add Custom Condition"** to add the required condition, then "Condition Definition" window opens.
4. Enter a name for the condition as "HighestProdPrice" in the edit box provided with caption as "Name".
5. Double click on "summaries" from the "Available Components" list.
6. Now, you can see in the "Available Components" list, all the functions available in the "summaries" list. From that select the "rank" by double clicking it.
7. The rank function will be added to the "Expression" edit box.
8. Double click on "Report Columns" of the "Available Components" list.
9. In the "Available Components" list, we can see all the columns that are present in the report.
10. Double click on "Unit Price" to add the column to the "Expression" edit box.
11. Double click on "=" symbol of the "Available Components" list.
12. Double click on "number" of the "Available Components" list.
13. Enter the number as "1".
14. Finally the expression in the "Expression" edit box must look as shown in Fig. 6.36.

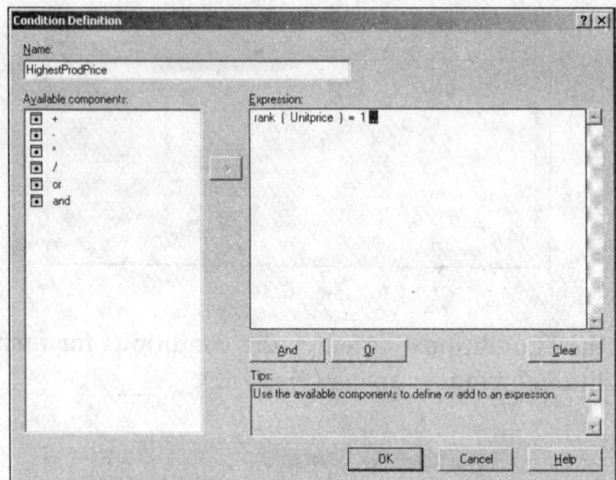

Fig. 6.36

15. Click on **"OK"**.
16. Add one more condition for highlighting the product, which is having lowest unit price. To do this, again click on **"Add Custom Condition"** of the "Conditions" window.
17. In the "Condition Definition" window, enter the condition name as "LowCostProd" and in the Expression edit box specify the condition as

    Rank (unitprice) = maximum (rank (unitprice)).

    Now the "Condition Definition" window looks as shown in Fig. 6.37.

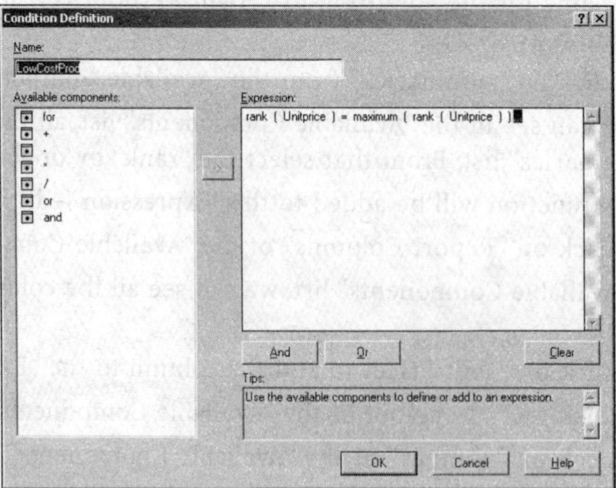

Fig. 6.37

18. Click the **"OK"** of the "Condition Definition" window.

19. Click **"Close"** of the "Conditions" window.
20. The created conditions will be added to the "Conditions Formats" window (Fig. 6.38).

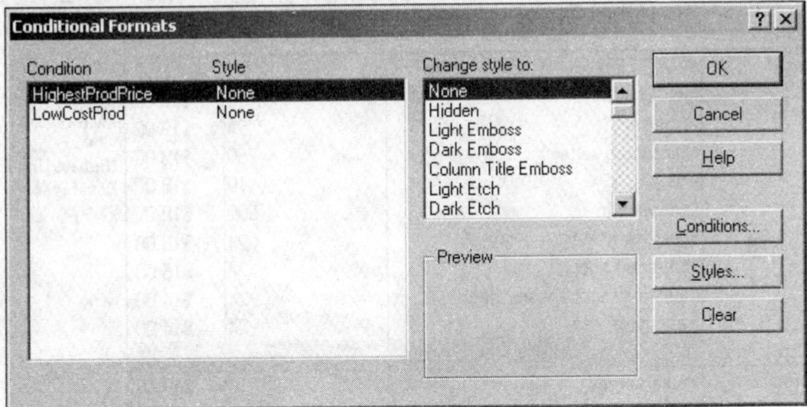

Fig. 6.38

21. You have to specify the style for each condition. To specify the style, select the condition and from the "Change style to:" list box, select the required style.
22. After selecting the required styles for each condition. The "Conditional Formats" window looks as shown in Fig. 6.39.

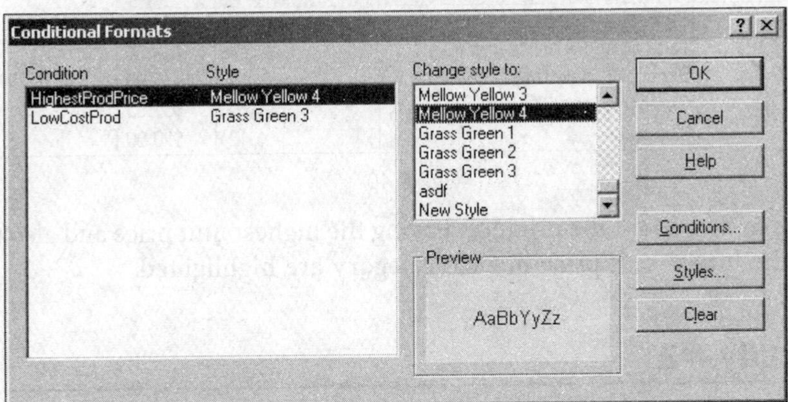

Fig. 6.39

23. Click **"OK"** of the "Conditional Formats" window.
24. After specifying the conditions for formatting the report, the final report looks as shown in Fig. 6.40.

Available Products Date: Saturday, August 06, 2005

Categoryname	Productname	Quantityperunit	Unitprice
Beverages	Côte de Blaye	12	$263.50
	Ipoh Coffee	16	$46.00
	Chang	24	$19.00
	Chartreuse verte	750	$18.00
	Chai	10	$18.00
	Lakkalikööri	500	$18.00
	Steeleye Stout	24	$18.00
	Outback Lager	24	$15.00
	Laughing Lumberjack Lager	24	$14.00
	Sasquatch Ale	24	$14.00
	Rhönbräu Klosterbier	24	$7.75
Condiments	Vegie-spread	15	$43.90
	Northwoods Cranberry Sauce	12	$40.00
	Sirop d'érable	24	$28.50
	Grandma's Boysenberry Spread	12	$25.00
	Chef Anton's Cajun Seasoning	48	$22.00
	Louisiana Fiery Hot Pepper Sauce	32	$21.05
	Gula Malacca	20	$19.45
	Louisiana Hot Spiced Okra	24	$17.00
	Genen Shouyu	24	$15.50
	Aniseed Syrup	12	$10.00
Confections	Sir Rodney's Marmalade	30	$81.00
	Tarte au sucre	48	$49.30
	Schoggi Schokolade	100	$43.90
	Gumbär Gummibärchen	100	$31.23
	Maxilaku	24	$20.00

Highest Unit Price in Beverages

Lowest Unit Price in Beverages

Fig. 6.40

Thus in the report, the products having the highest unit price and also the products having the lowest unit price in each category are highlighted.

6.4 Case Study #2

In this case study, we will generate a report that displays quantity sold and total amount sold for each product in the year 1996. To generate this report, we require PRODUCTDIMENSION and SALESFACT tables to get the Total Quantitysold and Total Amountsold for each Product category-wise in the year 1996. The report also shows the Total Quantitysold and Total Amountsold for each category and also for all Categories i.e., total sales in 1996 by quantity and amount. The final report looks as shown in Fig. 6.41.

Date: Saturday, August 06, 2005

Sales for 1996

Categoryname	Productname	Total Quantitysold	Total Amountsold
Beverages	Chai	125	$1,605.60
	Chang	201	$2,732.96
	Chartreuse verte	266	$3,558.24
	Côte de Blaye	140	$24,874.40
	Guaraná Fantásti	158	$556.74
	Ipoh Coffee	136	$4,931.20
	Lakkalikööri	111	$1,542.24
	Laughing Lumberj	5	$42.00
	Outback Lager	126	$1,449.00
	Rhönbräu Klosterl	120	$738.42
	Sasquatch Ale	90	$1,002.40
	Steeleye Stout	244	$3,304.80
	Beverages Total Sold:	**1722**	**$46,338.00**
Condiments	Aniseed Syrup	30	$240.00
	Chef Anton's Caju	107	$1,851.52
	Chef Anton's Gum	129	$1,931.20
	Genen Shouyu	25	$310.00
	Grandma's Boyse	36	$720.00
	Gula Malacca	138	$2,042.12
	Louisiana Fiery H	155	$2,473.80
	Louisiana Hot Spi	30	$408.00
	Northwoods Cranb	140	$3,920.00
	Original Frankfurte	49	$509.60
	Vegie-spread	109	$3,348.54
	Condiments Total Sold:	**948**	**$17,754.78**

Fig. 6.41

To generate this report, the procedure is as follows:

1. Open the "Cognos Impromptu Administrator" tool:
   "***Start→ Programs→ Cognos EP Series 7→ Cognos Impromptu Administrator***", then the "Impromptu" window opens.
2. Open the catalog, which was created in the previous example by selecting the menu item "***Catalog → Open***". "Open Catalog" window opens. Select the catalog "nwcatalog".
3. "Catalog Logon for NWCATALOG.CAT" window opens. Enter the database User ID and Password, and then the "Impromptu" window opens.

   e.g.: User ID : nwdim

   Password : nwpwd

6.4.1 Creating Report

1. Select the menu item, ***"File → New"*** to create a new report.
2. "New" window opens. Select "simple list" from "Fast Find" tab and click on **"OK"** (Fig. 6.42).

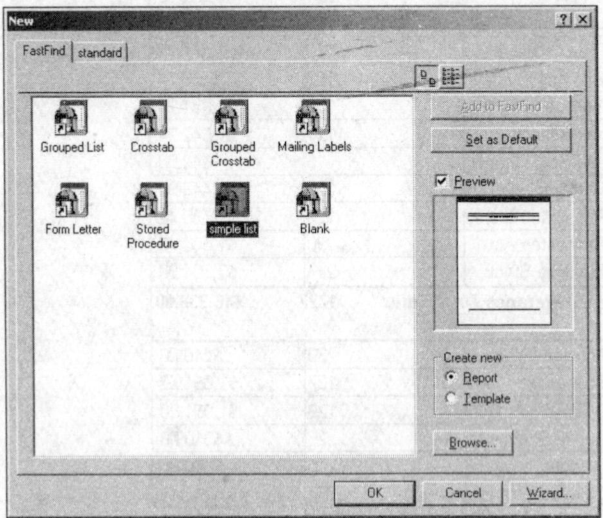

Fig. 6.42

3. "Query" window opens. Go to "Data" tab (Fig. 6.43).

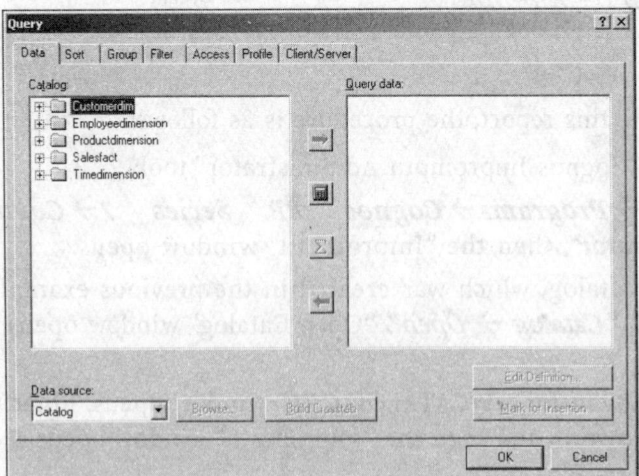

Fig. 6.43

4. Explore "Productdimension" from "Catalog" list and select Categoryname, Productname and click on **"→"** button.

5. Explore "Timedimension" from "Catalog" list and select Year and click on "→" button.
6. To make invisible the column, "Year" in final report, select "Year" column of "Query data" and click on **"Mark for Insertion"**.
7. Explore "Salesfact" from "Catalog" list and select **"QuantitySold"**. Now the click on the "Summation" button, the icon looks like as shown below; then the "Summary of QuantitySold" window opens. In it select the "Total" button and click on **"OK"** button. The "Total QuantitySold" is added to the "Query data" list box.

8. Similarly, from the "Salesfact" add the **"Total Amountsold"** to the "Query data" list. Now the "Query" window looks as shown in Fig. 6.44.

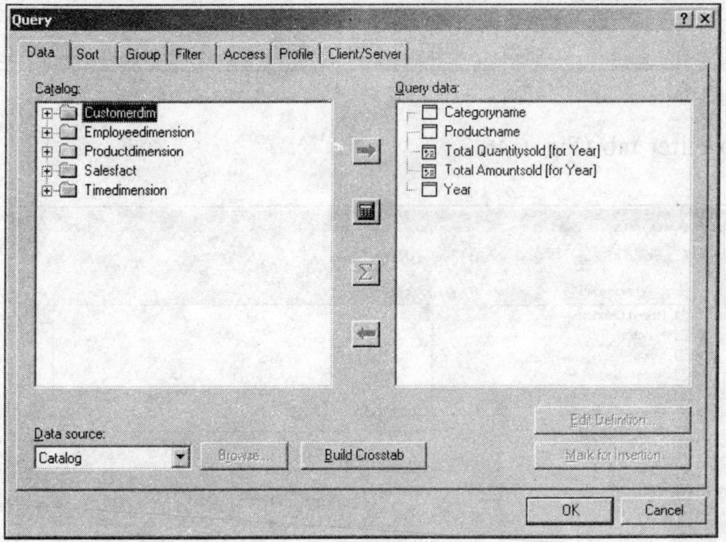

Fig. 6.44

9. Go to Sort tab and accept the default selected sorting columns of the report.
10. Go to Group tab, select Categoryname from "Group Order" list and click on "Group", also select Productname and click on "Group". Ensure that the Category name appears first in the "Group" list (Fig. 6.45).

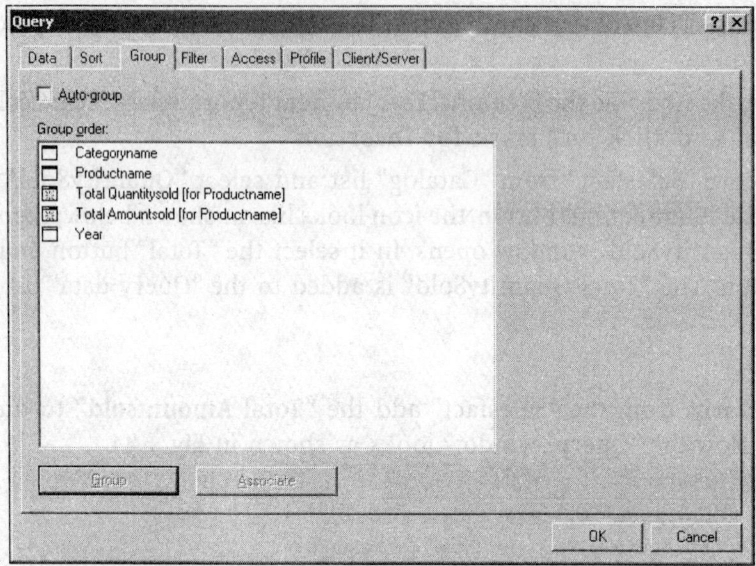

Fig. 6.45

11. Go to Filter tab (Fig. 6.46)

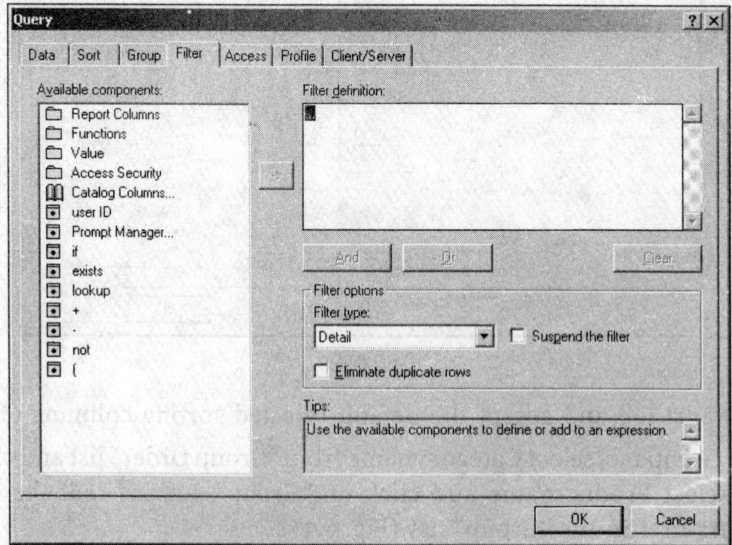

Fig. 6.46

12. Double click on "Catalog Columns" from "Available components" list.
13. "Catalog" window opens. Explore Timedimension folder and select Year column and click on **"OK"** (Fig. 6.47).

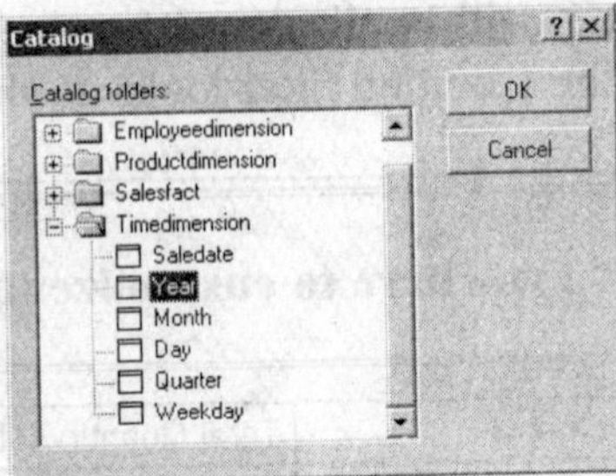

Fig. 6.47

14. Double click on **"="** symbol from available components list (Fig. 6.48).

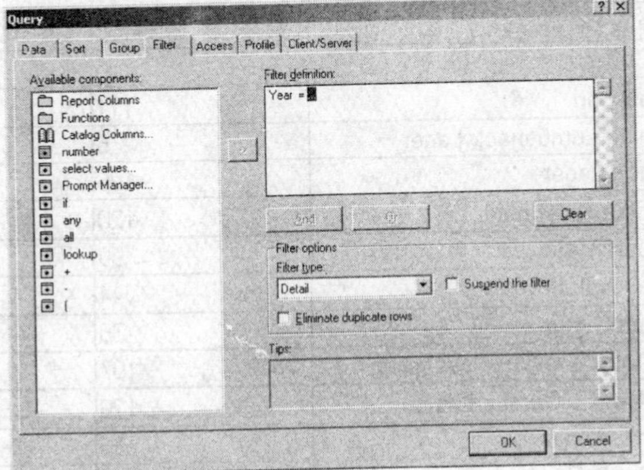

Fig. 6.48

15. Double click on "select values" and select the value 1996, then the "Filter definition" looks as shown in Fig. 6.49.

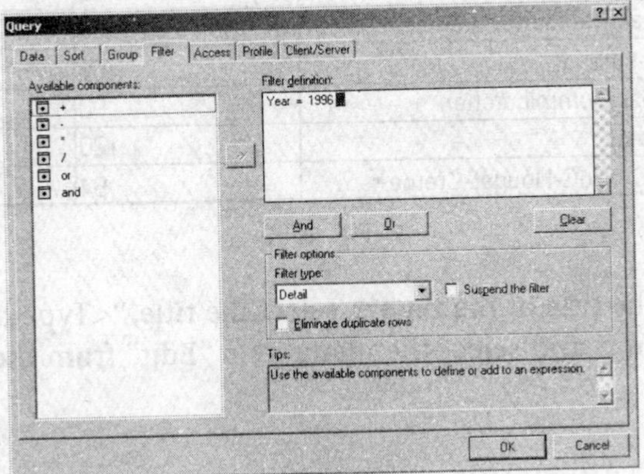

Fig. 6.49

16. Click on "OK" of "Query" window.

17. Now, the simple report will be displayed for the specified columns by grouping and sorting, and by the specified filter looks as shown in Fig. 6.50.

<Type here to customize title> Date: 8/6/05

Categoryname	Productname	Total Quantitysold	Total Amountsold
Beverages	Chai	125	1605.6
	Chang	201	2732.96
	Chartreuse verte	266	3558.24
	Côte de Blaye	140	24874.4
	Guaraná Fantástica	158	556.74
	Ipoh Coffee	136	4931.2
	Lakkalikööri	111	1542.24
	Laughing Lumberjack Lager	5	42
	Outback Lager	126	1449
	Rhönbräu Klosterbier	120	738.42
	Sasquatch Ale	90	1002.4
	Steeleye Stout	244	3304.8
Condiments	Aniseed Syrup	30	240
	Chef Anton's Cajun Seasoning	107	1851.52
	Chef Anton's Gumbo Mix	129	1931.2
	Genen Shouyu	25	310
	Grandma's Boysenberry Spread	36	720
	Gula Malacca	138	2042.12
	Louisiana Fiery Hot Pepper Sauce	155	2473.8
	Louisiana Hot Spiced Okra	30	408
	Northwoods Cranberry Sauce	140	3920
	Original Frankfurter grüne Soße	49	509.6
	Vegie-spread	109	3348.54
Confections	Gumbär Gummibärchen	90	2054.25
	Maxilaku	120	1920
	NuNuCa Nuß-Nougat-Creme	64	716.8

Fig. 6.50

18. To change the title of the report, select the title, "<Type here to customize title>", right click on it and select the menu item "Edit" from the pop up menu.

19. Enter the title of the report as "Sales for 1996". To change the text color of the title, select the required font color from the tool bar of "Font Color" drop down list. After changing the title and the color of the font of the title, the report looks as shown in Fig.6.51.

Date: 8/6/05

Sales for 1996

Categoryname	Productname	Total Quantitysold	Total Amountsold
Beverages	Chai	125	1605.6
	Chang	201	2732.96
	Chartreuse verte	266	3558.24
	Côte de Blaye	140	24874.4
	Guaraná Fantásti	158	556.74
	Ipoh Coffee	136	4931.2
	Lakkalikööri	111	1542.24
	Laughing Lumberj	5	42
	Outback Lager	126	1449
	Rhönbräu Klosterl	120	738.42
	Sasquatch Ale	90	1002.4
	Steeleye Stout	244	3304.8
Condiments	Aniseed Syrup	30	240
	Chef Anton's Caju	107	1851.52
	Chef Anton's Gum	129	1931.2
	Genen Shouyu	25	310
	Grandma's Boyse	36	720
	Gula Malacca	138	2042.12
	Louisiana Fiery H	155	2473.8
	Louisiana Hot Spi	30	408
	Northwoods Cranb	140	3920
	Original Frankfurte	49	509.6
	Vegie-spread	109	3348.54
Confections	Gumbär Gummibä	90	2054.25
	Maxilaku	120	1920
	NuNuCa Nuß-Nou	64	716.8

Fig. 6.51

20. You can change the date format, as explained in the previous section.
21. You can also change the font and color of the text that is displayed for the columns headers of the report. To change them, select all the column headers of the report, by clicking at the starting of the first column header from left side. Notice that all the column headers get selected. Now, select the required color from the drop down list box of "Font Colors" from the tool bar. After changing the color of the headers of the columns, the report looks as shown in Fig. 6.52.

Sales for 1996 Date: Saturday, August 06, 2005

Categoryname	Productname	Total Quantitysold	Total Amountsold
Beverages	Chai	125	1605.6
	Chang	201	2732.96
	Chartreuse verte	266	3558.24
	Côte de Blaye	140	24874.4
	Guaraná Fantásti	158	556.74
	Ipoh Coffee	136	4931.2
	Lakkalikööri	111	1542.24
	Laughing Lumberj	5	42
	Outback Lager	126	1449
	Rhönbräu Klosterl	120	738.42
	Sasquatch Ale	90	1002.4
	Steeleye Stout	244	3304.8
Condiments	Aniseed Syrup	30	240
	Chef Anton's Caju	107	1851.52
	Chef Anton's Gum	129	1931.2
	Genen Shouyu	25	310
	Grandma's Boyse	36	720
	Gula Malacca	138	2042.12
	Louisiana Fiery H	155	2473.8
	Louisiana Hot Spi	30	408
	Northwoods Cranl	140	3920
	Original Frankfurt	49	509.6
	Vegie-spread	109	3348.54
Confections	Gumbär Gummib	90	2054.25
	Maxilaku	120	1920
	NuNuCa Nuß-Nou	64	716.8

Fig. 6.52

To change the format of the column data "Total Amountsold":

1. You can change the style of display of the data, Total Amountsold of the report. To change the style, select the whole column, Total Amountsold.

2. Right click on the selection, from the pop up menu, select menu item "Format".
3. The "Format" window opens. In the "Data" tab, select the option "Currency" from the drop down list "Positive".
4. Click on "OK" of the "Format" window. Now the report looks as shown in Fig. 6.53.

Sales for 1996 Date: Saturday, August 06, 2005

Categoryname	Productname	Total Quantitysold	Total Amountsold
Beverages	Chai	125	$1,605.60
	Chang	201	$2,732.96
	Chartreuse verte	266	$3,558.24
	Côte de Blaye	140	$24,874.40
	Guaraná Fantásti	158	$556.74
	Ipoh Coffee	136	$4,931.20
	Lakkalikööri	111	$1,542.24
	Laughing Lumberj	5	$42.00
	Outback Lager	126	$1,449.00
	Rhönbräu Klosterl	120	$738.42
	Sasquatch Ale	90	$1,002.40
	Steeleye Stout	244	$3,304.80
Condiments	Aniseed Syrup	30	$240.00
	Chef Anton's Caju	107	$1,851.52
	Chef Anton's Gum	129	$1,931.20
	Genen Shouyu	25	$310.00
	Grandma's Boyse	36	$720.00
	Gula Malacca	138	$2,042.12
	Louisiana Fiery H	155	$2,473.80
	Louisiana Hot Spi	30	$408.00
	Northwoods Cranl	140	$3,920.00
	Original Frankfurte	49	$509.60
	Vegie-spread	109	$3,348.54
Confections	Gumbär Gummibä	90	$2,054.25
	Maxilaku	120	$1,920.00

Fig. 6.53

Calculating the subtotals category-wise, Total Quantity sold and Total Amount sold:

1. Select the Total Quantitysold column. Now the report looks like as shown in Fig. 6.54.

Sales for 1996 Date: Saturday, August 06, 2005

Categoryname	Productname	Total Quantitysold	Total Amountsold
Beverages	Chai	125	$1,605.60
	Chang	201	$2,732.96
	Chartreuse verte	266	$3,558.24
	Côte de Blaye	140	$24,874.40
	Guaraná Fantástic	158	$556.74
	Ipoh Coffee	136	$4,931.20
	Lakkalikööri	111	$1,542.24
	Laughing Lumberj	5	$42.00
	Outback Lager	126	$1,449.00
	Rhönbräu Klosterl	120	$738.42
	Sasquatch Ale	90	$1,002.40
	Steeleye Stout	244	$3,304.80
Condiments	Aniseed Syrup	30	$240.00
	Chef Anton's Caju	107	$1,851.52
	Chef Anton's Gum	129	$1,931.20
	Genen Shouyu	25	$310.00
	Grandma's Boyse	36	$720.00
	Gula Malacca	138	$2,042.12
	Louisiana Fiery H	155	$2,473.80
	Louisiana Hot Spi	30	$408.00
	Northwoods Cranb	140	$3,920.00
	Original Frankfurte	49	$509.60
	Vegie-spread	109	$3,348.54
Confections	Gumbär Gummibä	90	$2,054.25
	Maxilaku	120	$1,920.00
	NuNuCa Nuß-Nou	64	$716.80

Fig. 6.54

2. Click on the icon for summation to calculate the sum.

3. The report looks like as shown in Fig. 6.55.

Sales for 1996 Date: Saturday, August 06, 2005

Categoryname	Productname	Total Quantitysold	Total Amountsold
Beverages	Chai	125	$1,605.60
	Chang	201	$2,732.96
	Chartreuse verte	266	$3,558.24
	Côte de Blaye	140	$24,874.40
	Guaraná Fantásti	158	$556.74
	Ipoh Coffee	136	$4,931.20
	Lakkalikööri	111	$1,542.24
	Laughing Lumberj	5	$42.00
	Outback Lager	126	$1,449.00
	Rhönbräu Klosterl	120	$738.42
	Sasquatch Ale	90	$1,002.40
	Steeleye Stout	244	$3,304.80
		1722	
Condiments	Aniseed Syrup	30	$240.00
	Chef Anton's Caju	107	$1,851.52
	Chef Anton's Gum	129	$1,931.20
	Genen Shouyu	25	$310.00
	Grandma's Boyse	36	$720.00
	Gula Malacca	138	$2,042.12
	Louisiana Fiery H	155	$2,473.80
	Louisiana Hot Spi	30	$408.00
	Northwoods Cranb	140	$3,920.00
	Original Frankfurte	49	$509.60
	Vegie-spread	109	$3,348.54

Fig. 6.55

4. Select all the items of Total Amount sold column and click on sum button as explained above (Fig. 6.56).

Sales for 1996 Date: Saturday, August 06, 2005

Categoryname	Productname	Total Quantitysold	Total Amountsold
Beverages	Chai	125	$1,605.60
	Chang	201	$2,732.96
	Chartreuse verte	266	$3,558.24
	Côte de Blaye	140	$24,874.40
	Guaraná Fantásti	158	$556.74
	Ipoh Coffee	136	$4,931.20
	Lakkalikööri	111	$1,542.24
	Laughing Lumberj	5	$42.00
	Outback Lager	126	$1,449.00
	Rhönbräu Klosterl	120	$738.42
	Sasquatch Ale	90	$1,002.40
	Steeleye Stout	244	$3,304.80
		1722	
Condiments	Aniseed Syrup	30	$240.00
	Chef Anton's Caju	107	$1,851.52
	Chef Anton's Gum	129	$1,931.20
	Genen Shouyu	25	$310.00
	Grandma's Boyse	36	$720.00
	Gula Malacca	138	$2,042.12
	Louisiana Fiery H	155	$2,473.80
	Louisiana Hot Spi	30	$408.00
	Northwoods Cranl	140	$3,920.00
	Original Frankfurte	49	$509.60
	Vegie-spread	109	$3,348.54

Fig. 6.56

5. To add the Text Frame select the Text Frame icon.

6. Copy the Beverage by right clicking on the text and selecting "Copy" from pop up menu.
7. Select the place where you want text to appear.

8. Paste the copied text and enter "Total sold:" and change the color. Now the report looks like as shown in Fig. 6.57.

Sales for 1996 Date: Saturday, August 06, 2005

Categoryname	Productname	Total Quantitysold	Total Amountsold
Beverages	Chai	125	$1,605.60
	Chang	201	$2,732.96
	Chartreuse verte	266	$3,558.24
	Côte de Blaye	140	$24,874.40
	Guaraná Fantásti	158	$556.74
	Ipoh Coffee	136	$4,931.20
	Lakkalikööri	111	$1,542.24
	Laughing Lumberj	5	$42.00
	Outback Lager	126	$1,449.00
	Rhönbräu Klosterl	120	$738.42
	Sasquatch Ale	90	$1,002.40
	Steeleye Stout	244	$3,304.80
	Beverages Total sold:	**1722**	**$46,338.00**
Condiments	Aniseed Syrup	30	$240.00
	Chef Anton's Caju	107	$1,851.52
	Chef Anton's Gum	129	$1,931.20
	Genen Shouyu	25	$310.00
	Grandma's Boyse	36	$720.00
	Gula Malacca	138	$2,042.12
	Louisiana Fiery H	155	$2,473.80
	Louisiana Hot Spi	30	$408.00
	Northwoods Cranl	140	$3,920.00
	Original Frankfurte	49	$509.60
	Vegie-spread	109	$3,348.54

Fig. 6.57

9. Select the menu item "***File→Save***" to save the report. Enter the name of the report as "CATEGORYWISEREP1996".

6.5 Case Study #3

In this case study, we will generate a report showing total quantity sold and the total amount sold in each category for the year 1996, highlighting which category sold the highest. The final report will be as shown in Fig. 6.58.

Sales for 1996 Date: Monday, August 08, 2005

Categoryname	Total Quantitysold	Total Amountsold
Beverages	1722	$46,338.00
Condiments	948	$17,754.78
Confections	1200	$27,257.50
Dairy Products	1879	$36,711.37
Grains/Cereals	509	$9,219.92
Meat/Poultry	740	$24,617.86
Produce	489	$12,651.16
Seafood	1230	$18,765.96
	8717	$193,316.55

Fig. 6.58

To generate this report, the procedure is as follows:

1. Open the "Cognos Impromptu Administrator" tool: "***Start→ Programs→ Cognos EP Series 7→ Cognos Impromptu Administrator***", the "Impromptu" window opens.
2. Open the catalog which was created in the previous example by selecting the menu item "***Catalog → Open***", "Open Catalog" window opens. Select the catalog "nwcatalog".
3. "Catalog Logon for NWCATALOG.CAT" window opens. Enter the database User ID and Password, then the "Impromptu" window opens.

   e.g.: User ID : nwdim

   Password : nwpwd
4. Open the report of the previous example by selecting the menu item "***File → Open***". From the file open window box, select the report of the previous example.
5. "Catalog Logon for NWCATALOG.CAT" window opens. Enter the User ID and Password for the catalog and click on "**OK**".

   e.g: User ID : nwdim

   Password : nwpwd
6. The previous report shown in Fig. 6.59 opens. Select the menu item "***Report → Query***".

Sales for 1996			Date: Monday, August 08, 2005
Categoryname	Productname	Total Quantitysold	Total Amountsold
Beverages	Chai	125	$1,605.60
	Chang	201	$2,732.96
	Chartreuse verte	266	$3,558.24
	Côte de Blaye	140	$24,874.40
	Guaraná Fantásti	158	$556.74
	Ipoh Coffee	136	$4,931.20
	Lakkalikööri	111	$1,542.24
	Laughing Lumberj	5	$42.00
	Outback Lager	126	$1,449.00
	Rhönbräu Klosterl	120	$738.42
	Sasquatch Ale	90	$1,002.40
	Steeleye Stout	244	$3,304.80
	Beverages Total sold:	**1722**	**$46,338.00**
Condiments	Aniseed Syrup	30	$240.00
	Chef Anton's Caju	107	$1,851.52
	Chef Anton's Gum	129	$1,931.20
	Genen Shouyu	25	$310.00
	Grandma's Boyse	36	$720.00
	Gula Malacca	138	$2,042.12
	Louisiana Fiery H	155	$2,473.80
	Louisiana Hot Spi	30	$408.00
	Northwoods Cranl	140	$3,920.00
	Original Frankfurte	49	$509.60
	Vegie-spread	109	$3,348.54

Fig. 6.59

7. In the "Query" window, go to "Group" tab (Fig. 6.60).

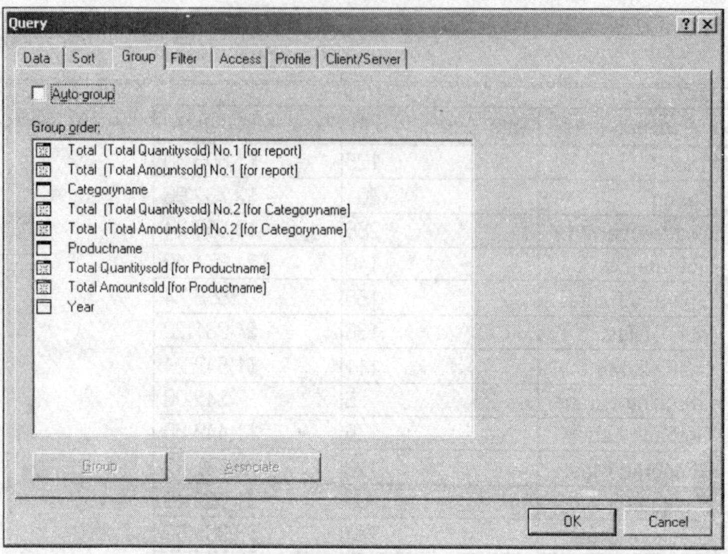

Fig. 6.60

8. Select the report column "Productname" and click on **"Ungroup"**; then the "Query" window looks as shown in Fig. 6.61.

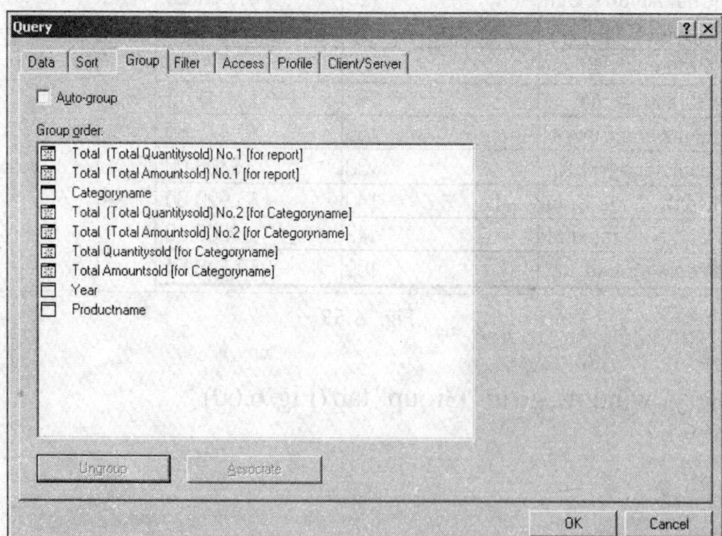

Fig. 6.61

9. Click on **"OK"** of the "Query" window, then the format of the report changes as shown in Fig. 6.62.

Sales for 1996 Date: Monday, August 08, 2005

Categoryname	Productname	Total Quantitysold	Total Amountsold
Beverages	Chai	1722	$46,338.00
	Chai		
	Chai		
	Chai		
	Chai		
	Chai		
	Chang		
	Chang		
	Chang		
	Chang		
	Chang		
	Chang		
	Chang		
	Chartreuse verte		
	Chartreuse verte		
	Chartreuse verte		
	Chartreuse verte		
	Chartreuse verte		
	Chartreuse verte		
	Chartreuse verte		
	Chartreuse verte		
	Côte de Blaye		
	Côte de Blaye		
	Côte de Blaye		
	Côte de Blaye		
	Côte de Blaye		
	Guaraná Fantásti		

Fig. 6.62

10. Select the column Productname by clicking on the header "Productname" (Fig. 6.63).

Sales for 1996 Date: Monday, August 08, 2005

Categoryname	Productname	Total Quantitysold	Total Amountsold
Beverages	Chai	1722	$46,338.00
	Chai		
	Chai		
	Chai		
	Chai		
	Chai		
	Chang		
	Chang		
	Chang		
	Chang		
	Chang		
	Chang		
	Chang		
	Chartreuse verte		
	Chartreuse verte		
	Chartreuse verte		
	Chartreuse verte		
	Chartreuse verte		
	Chartreuse verte		
	Chartreuse verte		
	Chartreuse verte		
	Côte de Blaye		
	Côte de Blaye		
	Côte de Blaye		
	Côte de Blaye		
	Côte de Blaye		
	Guaraná Fantásti		

Fig. 6.63

11. Right click on the selection, from the pop up menu, click on the menu item "Delete" and then the report looks as shown in Fig. 6.64.

Sales for 1996 Date: Monday, August 08, 2005

Categoryname	Total Quantitysold	Total Amountsold
Beverages	1722	$46,338.00
Beverages Total sold:	**1722**	**$46,338.00**
Condiments	948	$17,754.78
Condiments Total sold:	**948**	**$17,754.78**
Confections	1200	$27,257.50
Confections Total sold:	**1200**	**$27,257.50**
Dairy Products	1879	$36,711.37
Dairy Products Total sold:	**1879**	**$36,711.37**
Grains/Cereals	509	$9,219.92
Grains/Cereals Total sold:	**509**	**$9,219.92**
Meat/Poultry	740	$24,617.86
Meat/Poultry Total sold:	**740**	**$24,617.86**
Produce	489	$12,651.16
Produce Total sold:	**489**	**$12,651.16**
Seafood	1230	$18,765.96
Seafood Total sold:	**1230**	**$18,765.96**
	8717	$193,316.55

Fig. 6.64

12. Now select the row, that has the calculated totals, as shown in Fig. 6.65.

Sales for 1996 Date: Monday, August 08, 2005

Categoryname	Total Quantitysold	Total Amountsold
Beverages	1722	$46,338.00
Beverages Total sold:	1722	$46,338.00
Condiments	948	$17,754.78
Condiments Total sold:	**948**	**$17,754.78**
Confections	1200	$27,257.50
Confections Total sold:	**1200**	**$27,257.50**
Dairy Products	1879	$36,711.37
Dairy Products Total sold:	**1879**	**$36,711.37**
Grains/Cereals	509	$9,219.92
Grains/Cereals Total sold:	**509**	**$9,219.92**
Meat/Poultry	740	$24,617.86
Meat/Poultry Total sold:	**740**	**$24,617.86**
Produce	489	$12,651.16
Produce Total sold:	**489**	**$12,651.16**
Seafood	1230	$18,765.96
Seafood Total sold:	**1230**	**$18,765.96**
	8717	$193,316.55

Fig. 6.65

13. Right click on the selection, from the pop up menu, select the menu item "Delete", the report looks as shown in Fig. 6.66.

Sales for 1996 Date: Monday, August 08, 2005

Categoryname	Total Quantitysold	Total Amountsold
Beverages	1722	$46,338.00
Condiments	948	$17,754.78
Confections	1200	$27,257.50
Dairy Products	1879	$36,711.37
Grains/Cereals	509	$9,219.92
Meat/Poultry	740	$24,617.86
Produce	489	$12,651.16
Seafood	1230	$18,765.96
	8717	$193,316.55

Fig. 6.66

14. Select the Column "Total Amountsold" and click on **"Rank"** button from the toolbar, the icon looks as shown below:

Sales for 1996 Date: Monday, August 08, 2005

Categoryname	Total Quantitysold	Total Amountsold	Rank (Total Amountsold) No.2
Beverages	1722	$46,338.00	1
Condiments	948	$17,754.78	6
Confections	1200	$27,257.50	3
Dairy Products	1879	$36,711.37	2
Grains/Cereals	509	$9,219.92	8
Meat/Poultry	740	$24,617.86	4
Produce	489	$12,651.16	7
Seafood	1230	$18,765.96	5
	8717	$193,316.55	

Fig. 6.67

16. Select all the columns excluding Rank (Total Amount sold).
17. To write the conditional format, select all the items in the report and right click on the report and select the "Conditional Format" from the pop up menu. "Conditional Formats" window will be as shown in Fig. 6.68.

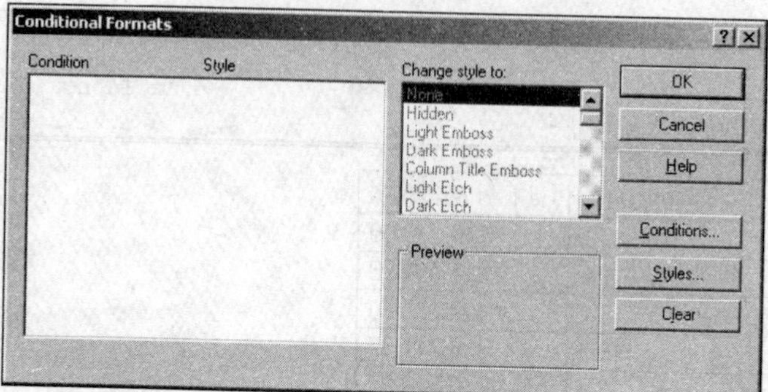

Fig. 6.68

18. Click on **"Conditions"** button in "Conditions" window opens (Fig. 6.69).

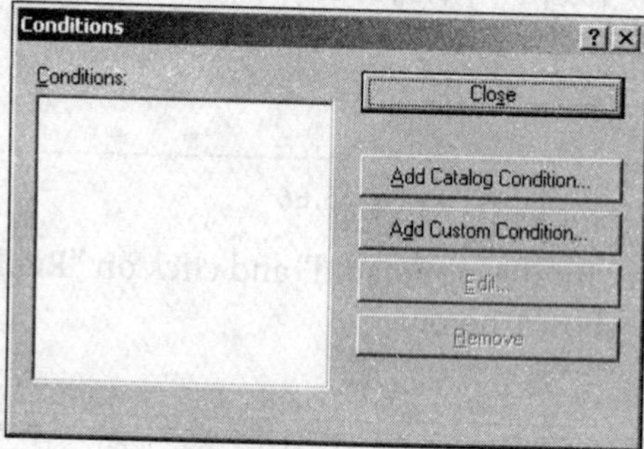

Fig. 6.69

19. Click on **"Add Custom Condition"**, then "Condition Definition" window (Fig. 6.70) opens.

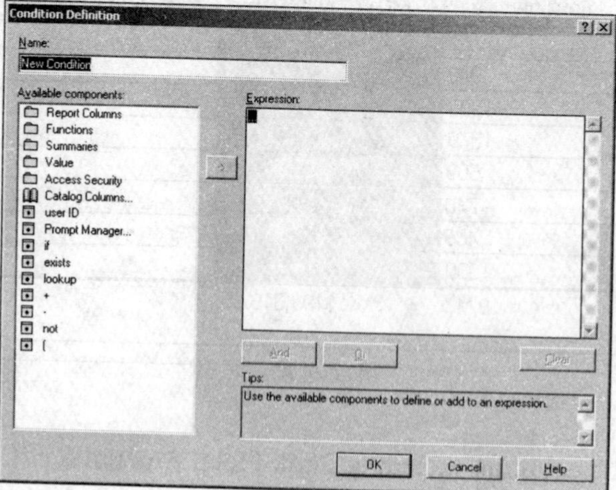

Fig. 6.70

20. Specify the condition as shown in Fig. 6.71.

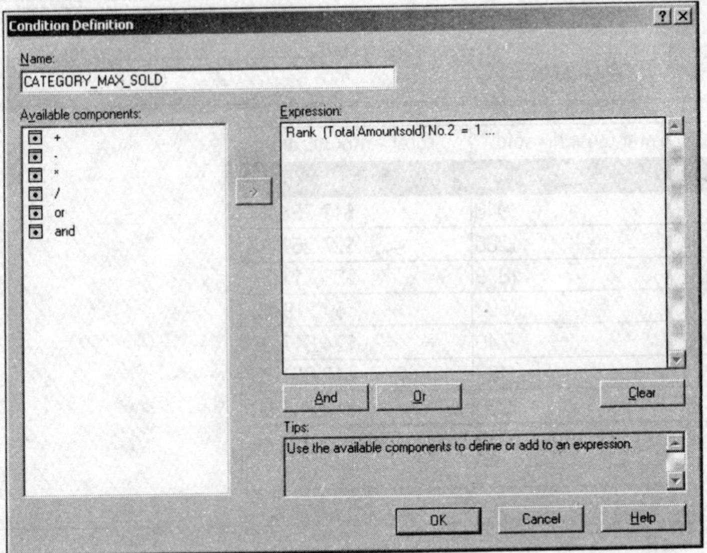

Fig. 6.71

21. Click on **"OK"**. Click on **"Close"** of "Conditions" window.
22. Select the item you want from the "Change style to:" and click on **"OK"**.
23. The report will be as shown in Fig. 6.72.

Sales for 1996 Date: Monday, August 08, 2005

Categoryname	Total Quantitysold	Total Amountsold	Rank (Total Amountsold) No.2
Beverages	1722	$46,338.00	1
Condiments	948	$17,754.78	6
Confections	1200	$27,257.50	3
Dairy Products	1879	$36,711.37	2
Grains/Cereals	509	$9,219.92	8
Meat/Poultry	740	$24,617.86	4
Produce	489	$12,651.16	7
Seafood	1230	$18,765.96	5
	8717	$193,316.55	

Fig. 6.72

24. Select the "Rank" column and delete the whole column, then the final report looks as shown in Fig. 6.73.

Sales for 1996 Date: Monday, August 08, 2005

Categoryname	Total Quantitysold	Total Amountsold
Beverages	1722	$46,338.00
Condiments	948	$17,754.78
Confections	1200	$27,257.50
Dairy Products	1879	$36,711.37
Grains/Cereals	509	$9,219.92
Meat/Poultry	740	$24,617.86
Produce	489	$12,651.16
Seafood	1230	$18,765.96
	8717	$193,316.55

Fig. 6.73

25. Select the menu item ***"File→Save"*** to save the report.

6.6 Case Study #4

In this case study, we will generate the annual sales report of all employees and display the information graphically using bar charts. The final report will be as shown in Fig. 6.74.

AndrewFuller

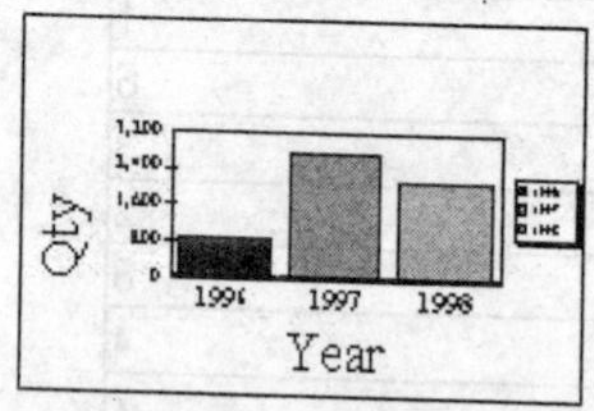

Year	Quantity	Amount
1996	885	$17,811.46
1997	2772	$71,168.14
1998	2181	$73,790.18

AnneDodsworth

Qty

1,200

800

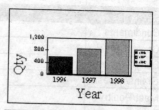

400

0

1997 1998

Year

Year	Quantity	Amount
1996	575	$9,894.51
1997	874	$24,412.89
1998	1193	$42,142.64

JanetLeverling

Fig. 6.74

To generate this report, the procedure is as follows:

1. Open the "Cognos Impromptu Administrator":
   "Start→ Programs→ Cognos EP Series 7→ Cognos Impromptu Administrator", "Impromptu" window opens.
2. Open the catalog which was created in the previous example by selecting the menu item ***"Catalog → Open",*** "Open Catalog" window opens. Select the catalog "nwcatalog".
3. "Catalog Logon for NWCATALOG.CAT" window opens. Enter the database User ID and Password, then the "Impromptu" window opens.

   e.g.: User ID : nwdim

   Password : nwpwd

6.6.1 Creating the Report

1. Select the menu item ***"File → New"*** to create a new report.
2. "New" window opens. Select "Grouped List" from "Fast Find" tab and click on **"OK"** (Fig. 6.75).

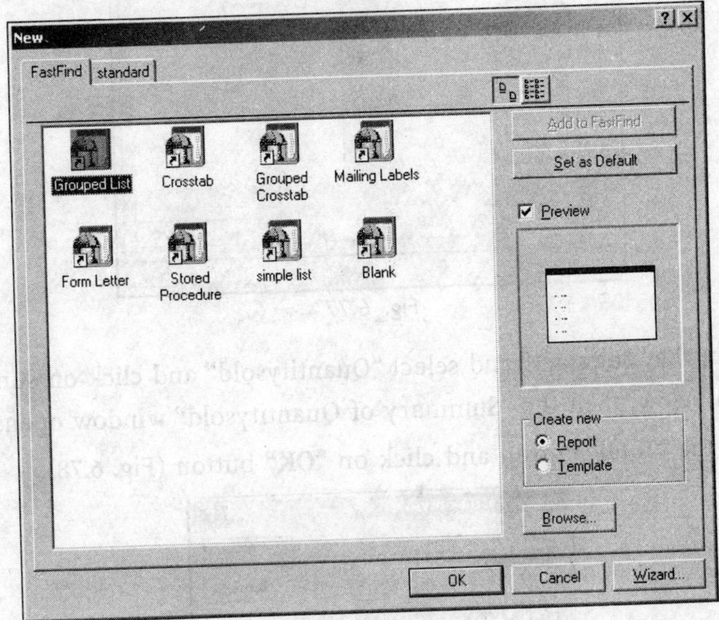

Fig. 6.75

3. **"Query"** window, shown in Fig. 6.76 opens. Select "Data" tab.

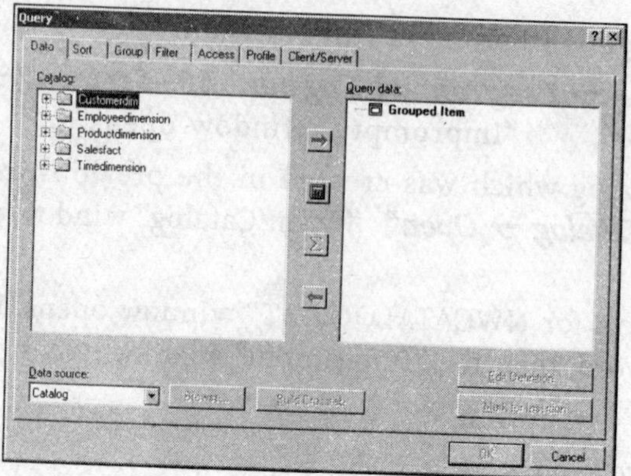

Fig. 6.76

4. Explore "Employeedimension" from "Catalog" list, select Employeename and click on "→" button; then the "Query" window looks as shown in Fig. 6.77.

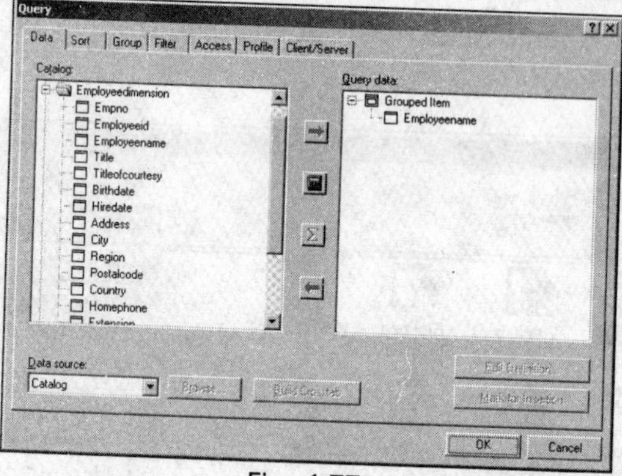

Fig. 6.77

5. Explore the "Salesfact" and select "Quantitysold" and click on summation button shown below; then the "Summary of Quantitysold" window opens. Σ
6. Select the "Total" button and click on **"OK"** button (Fig. 6.78).

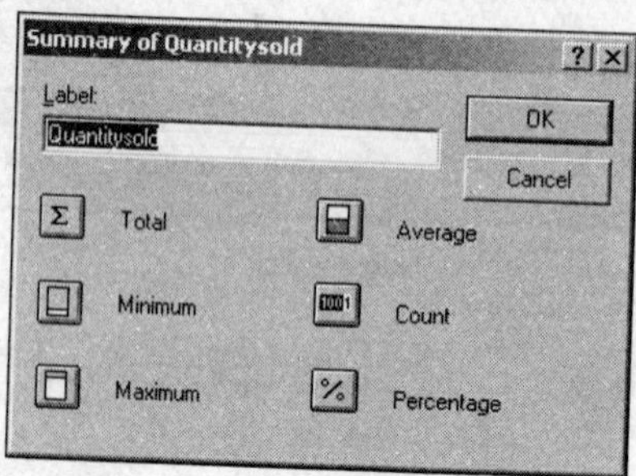

Fig. 6.78

7. In the same way, add the summation of "Amountsold" by exploring the "Salesfact," selecting the column Amountsold, click on the summation button and in the "Summary of Amountsold window, select the "Total" button to add the Total Amountsold to the "Query data" list, then the "Query" window looks as shown in Fig. 6.79.

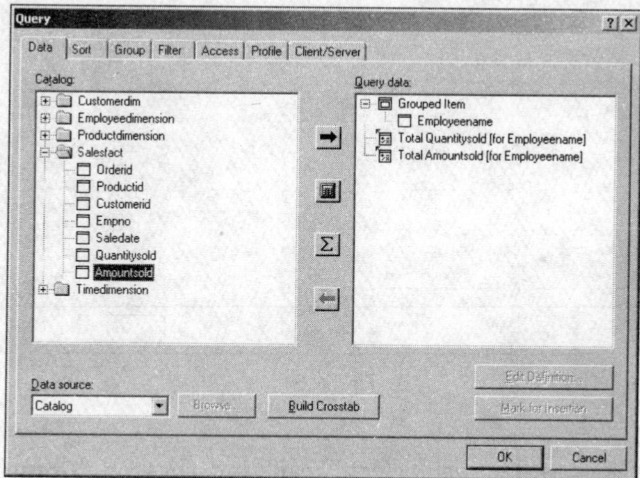

Fig. 6.79

8. Explore the Timedimension, select the column Year and click on "→" button. Now the "Query" window looks as shown in Fig. 6.80.

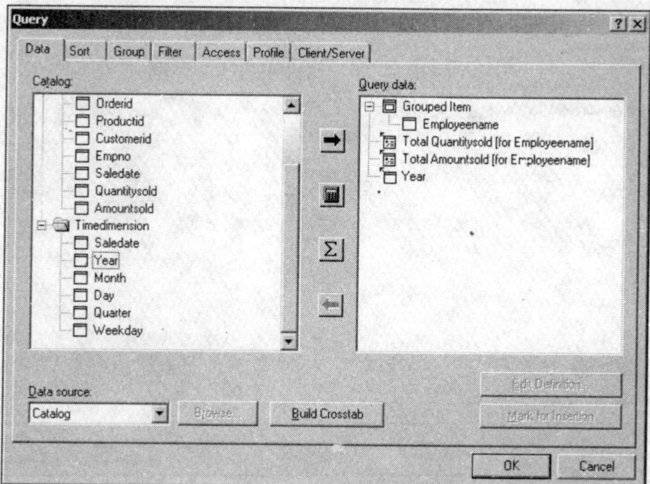

Fig. 6.80

9. In the "Sort" tab, accept the defaults and go to "Group" tab (Fig. 6.81).

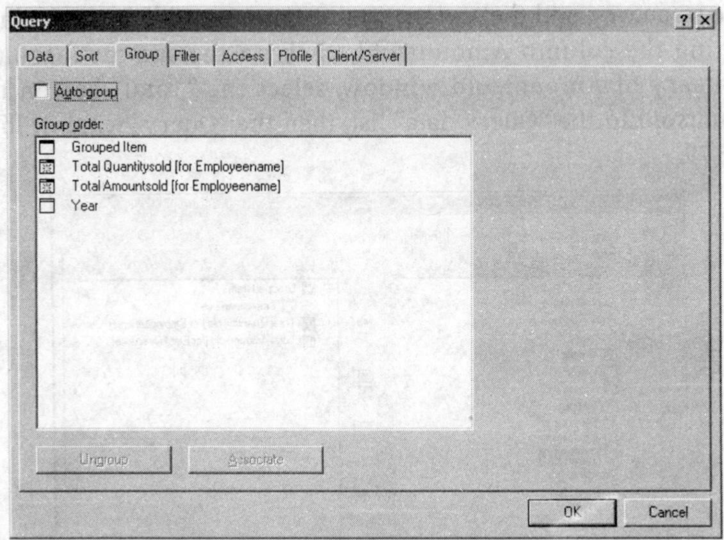

Fig. 6.81

10. In the "Group order" list, select "Year" and click on **"Group"**. Now the "Query" window looks as shown in Fig. 6.82.

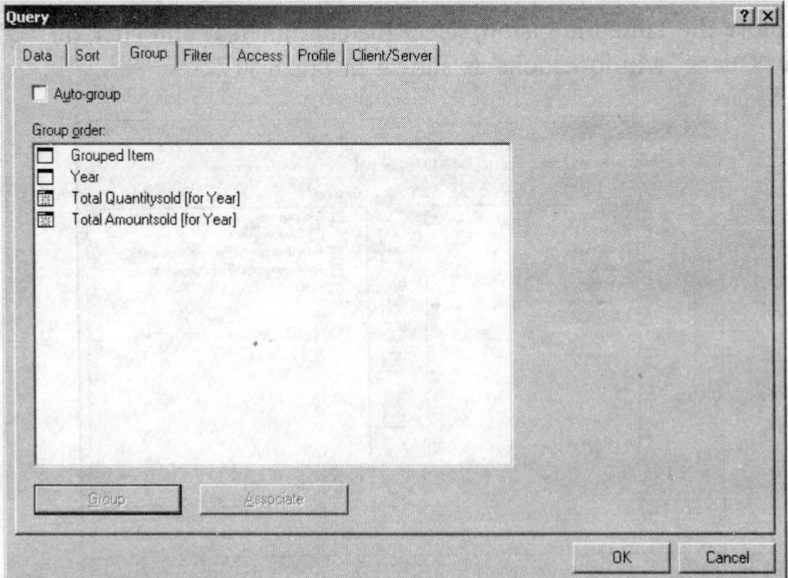

Fig. 6.82

11. Click on **"OK"** of "Query" window. Now the generated simple report looks as shown in Fig. 6.83.

Total Quantitysold	Total Amountsold	Year
AndrewFuller		
885	17811.46	1996
2772	71168.14	1997
2181	73790.18	1998
AnneDodsworth		
575	9894.51	1996
874	24412.89	1997
1193	42142.64	1998
JanetLeverling		
940	18223.96	1996
4247	103719.08	1997
2665	80869.8	1998
LauraCallahan		
710	19160.7	1996
2956	56954.03	1997

Fig. 6.83

12. Drag and drop the Year column of the report to the first column position. Now the report looks as shown in Fig. 6.84.

Year	Total Quantitysold	Total Amountsold

AndrewFuller

1996	885	17811.46
1997	2772	71168.14
1998	2181	73790.18

AnneDodsworth

1996	575	9894.51
1997	874	24412.89
1998	1193	42142.64

JanetLeverling

1996	940	18223.96
1997	4247	103719.08
1998	2665	80869.8

LauraCallahan

1996	710	19160.7
1997	2956	56954.03

Fig. 6.84

13 Change the text color of the Employeename, and color of the data of all rows as shown in Fig. 6.85.

Year	Total Quantitysold	Total Amountsold

AndrewFuller

1996	885	17811.46
1997	2772	71168.14
1998	2181	73790.18

AnneDodsworth

1996	575	9894.51
1997	874	24412.89
1998	1193	42142.64

JanetLeverling

1996	940	18223.96
1997	4247	103719.08
1998	2665	80869.8

LauraCallahan

1996	710	19160.7
1997	2956	56954.03

Fig. 6.85

14. To generate a bar chart for the data of each employee, select the menu item "***Insert → Chart Frame***".
15. After selecting the menu item, click on the report to select the point from where the chart must be inserted, then the "Chart Properties" window, shown in Fig. 6.86 opens.

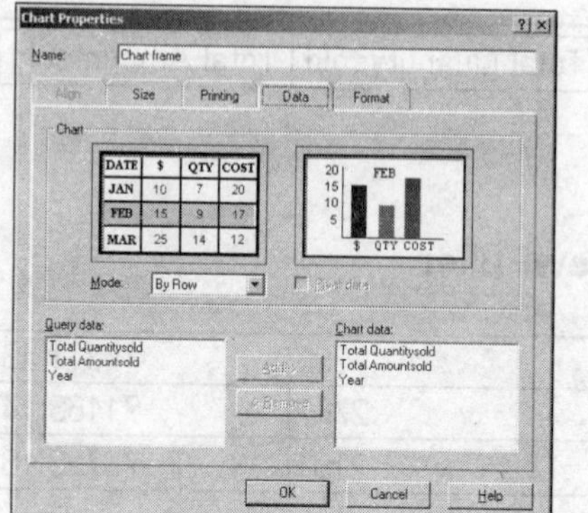

Fig. 6.86

16. From the "Chart data" list, remove the report columns "Total Amountsold and Year", by selecting the each column and click on **"Remove"** (Fig. 6.87)

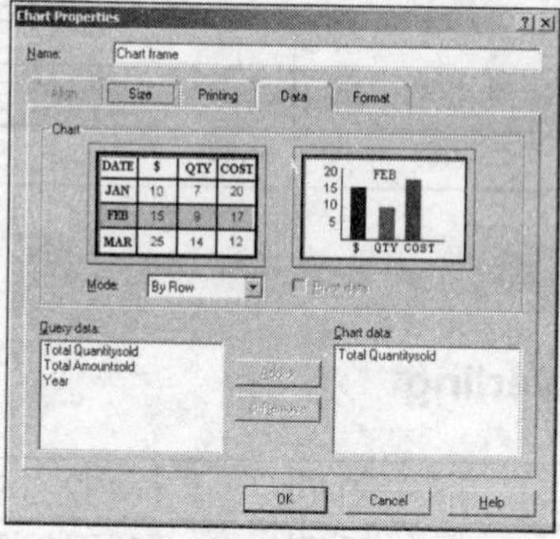

Fig. 6.87

17. From the "Mode" drop down list box provided, select the option "By Column". (Fig. 6.88).

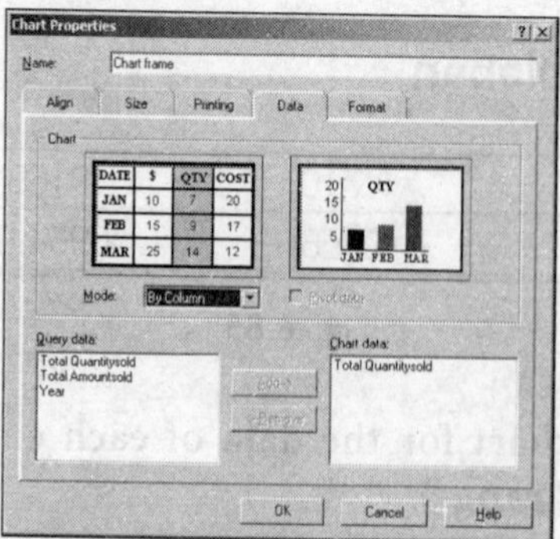

Fig. 6.88

18. Go to "Format" tab to select the style of the chart required, as shown in Fig. 6.89.

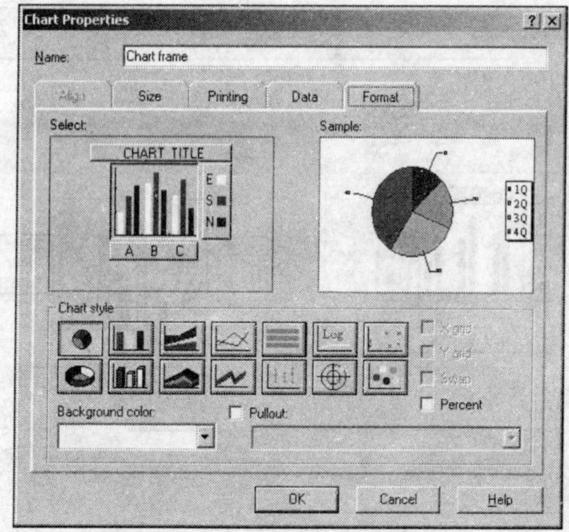

Fig. 6.89

19. To generate a bar chart, click on button of style (shown below) bar chart from the "Chart style" group box.

20. To change the chart title click on "CHART TITLE" from the "Select" group box and enter the chart title required in the edit box provided by caption "Chart title". If you do not require any chart title, just type one or more spaces. (Fig. 6.90).

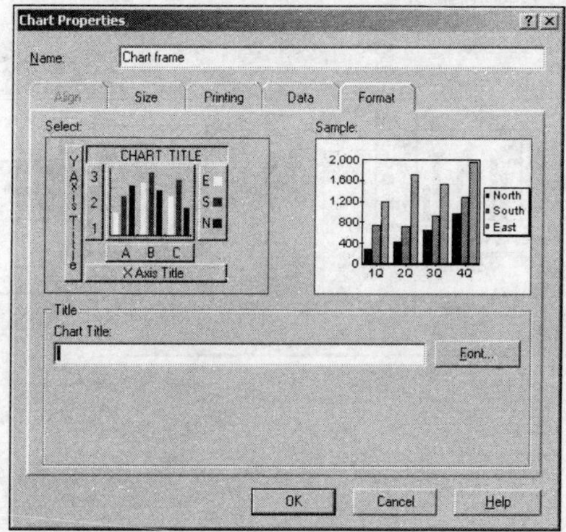

Fig. 6.90

21. To change the Y axis title, click on "Y Axis Title" button from the "Select" group box and the enter the "Y Axis Title" in the edit box provided. (Fig. 6.91).
e.g.: Y Axis Title: Qty

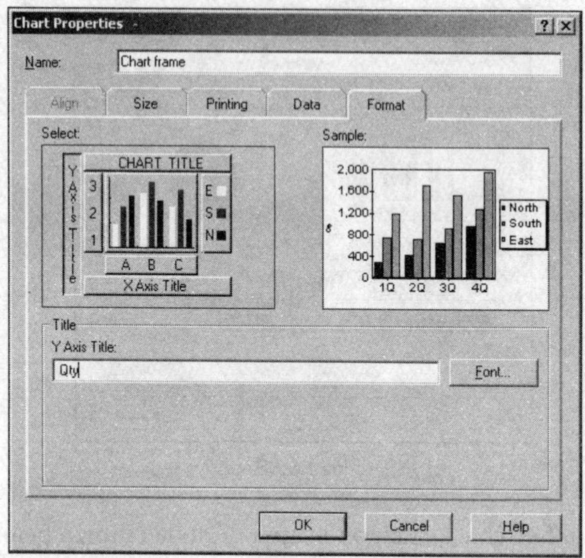

Fig. 6.91

22. To change the X axis title, click on "X Axis Title" from the "Select" group box and the enter the "X Axis Title" in the edit box provided, as in Fig. 6.92.

    e.g.: X Axis Title: Year

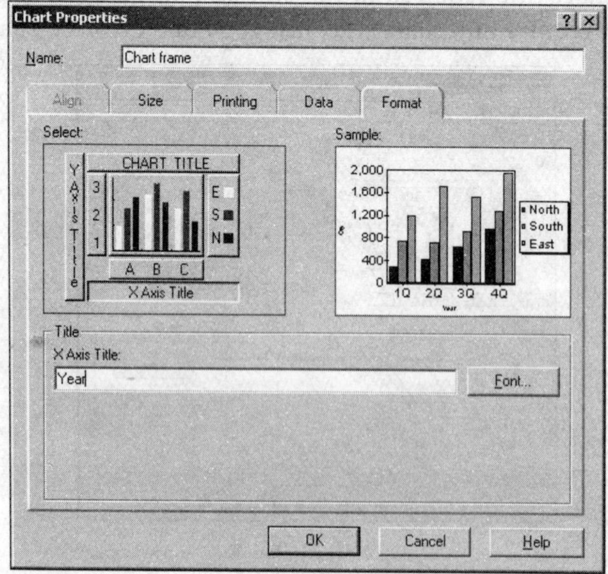

Fig. 6.92

23. Click on **"OK"** of "Chart Properties" window. After specifying all the chart properties, the chart is inserted in the Report, which looks as shown in Fig. 6.93.

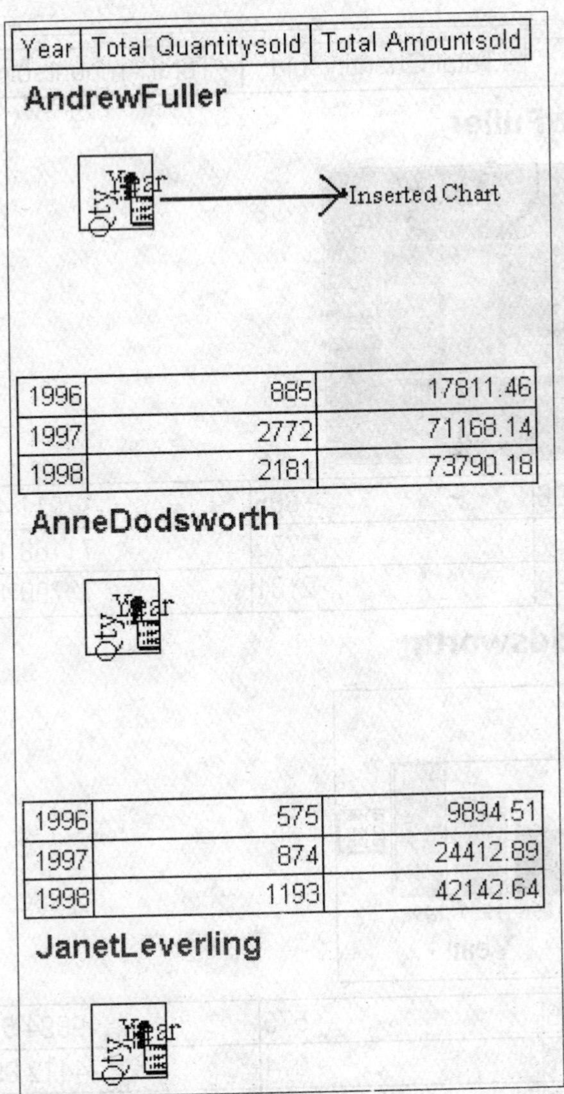

Fig. 6.93

24. Click on the inserted chart and by clicking on the selection points of the inserted chart, drag the chart to make the chart large in size, after making the chart little bit large in size, the report looks as shown in Fig. 6.94.

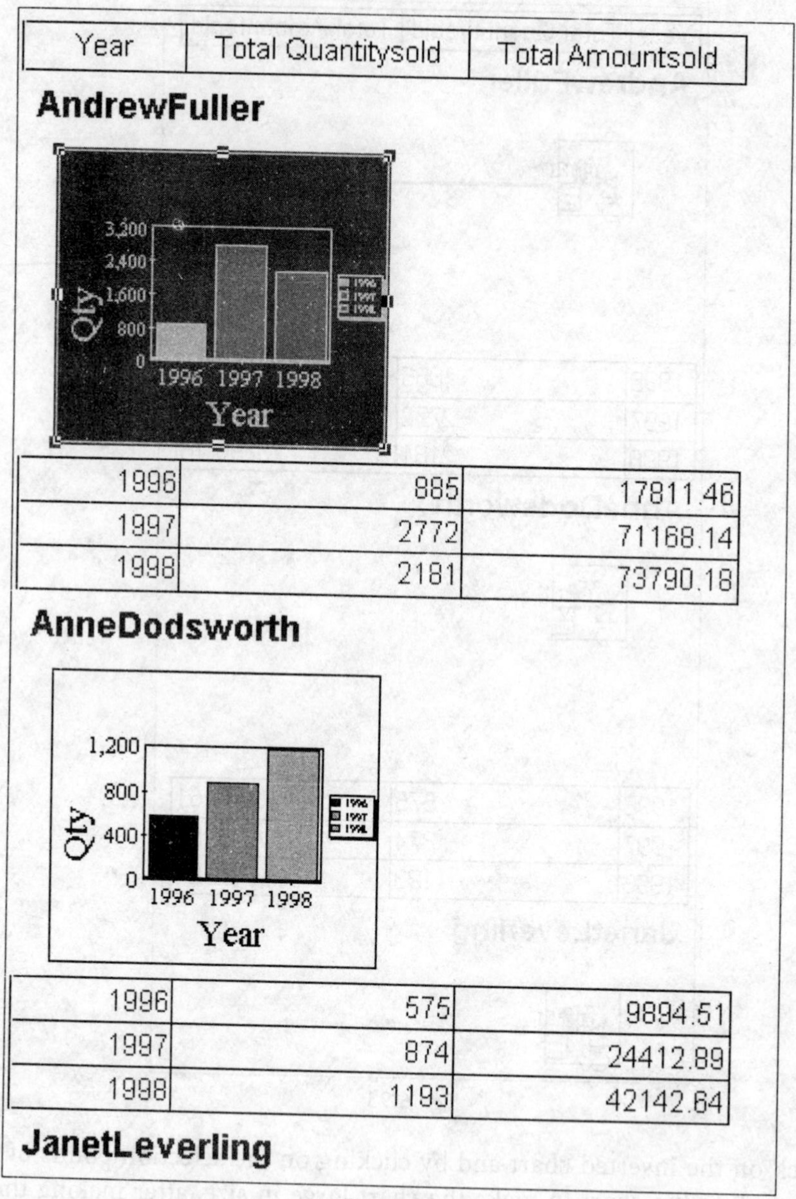

Year	Total Quantitysold	Total Amountsold

AndrewFuller

1996	885	17811.46
1997	2772	71168.14
1998	2181	73790.18

AnneDodsworth

1996	575	9894.51
1997	874	24412.89
1998	1193	42142.64

JanetLeverling

Fig. 6.94

25. Change the column header "Total Quantitysold" to "Quantity" and "Total Amountsold" to "Amount". After changing the column headers, the report looks as shown in Fig. 6.95.

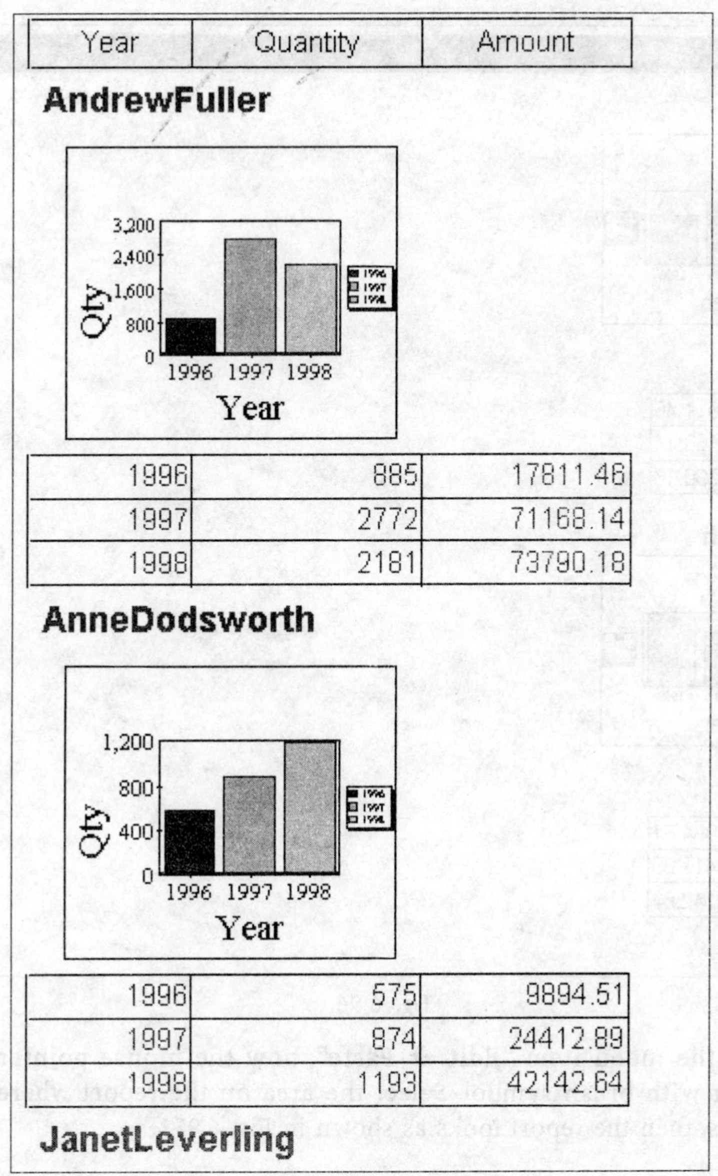

Year	Quantity	Amount

AndrewFuller

1996	885	17811.46
1997	2772	71168.14
1998	2181	73790.18

AnneDodsworth

1996	575	9894.51
1997	874	24412.89
1998	1193	42142.64

JanetLeverling

Fig. 6.95

26. Select the whole header row by clicking on the space available after the column Amount, right click on the selection, from the pop up menu, select the menu item "cut", to cut the row. Make sure that the selection appears as shown in Fig. 6.96.

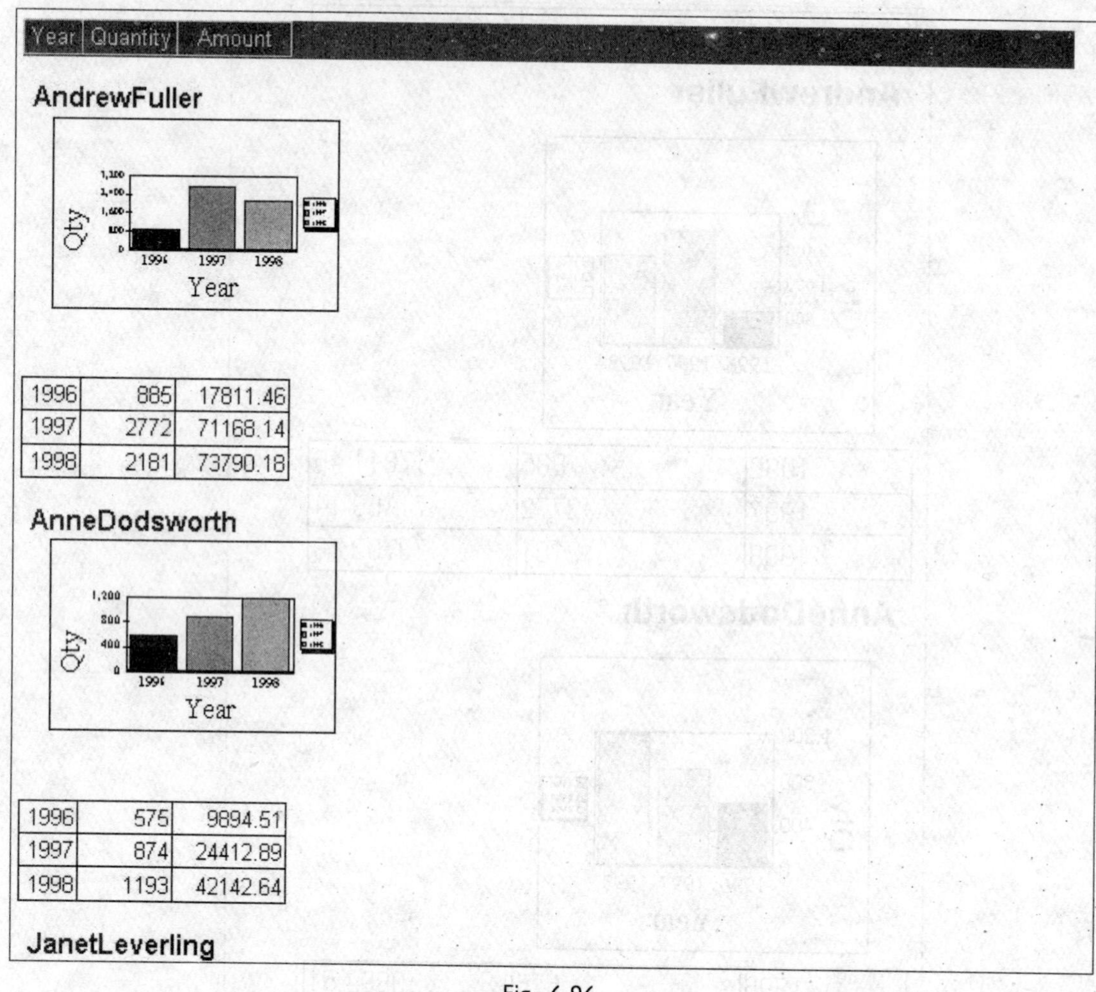

1996	885	17811.46
1997	2772	71168.14
1998	2181	73790.18

1996	575	9894.51
1997	874	24412.89
1998	1193	42142.64

Fig. 6.96

27. Select the menu item **"Edit → Paste"**, now the mouse pointer changes to a pointer with brush symbol. Select the area on the report where you want the headers, then the report looks as shown in Fig. 6.97.

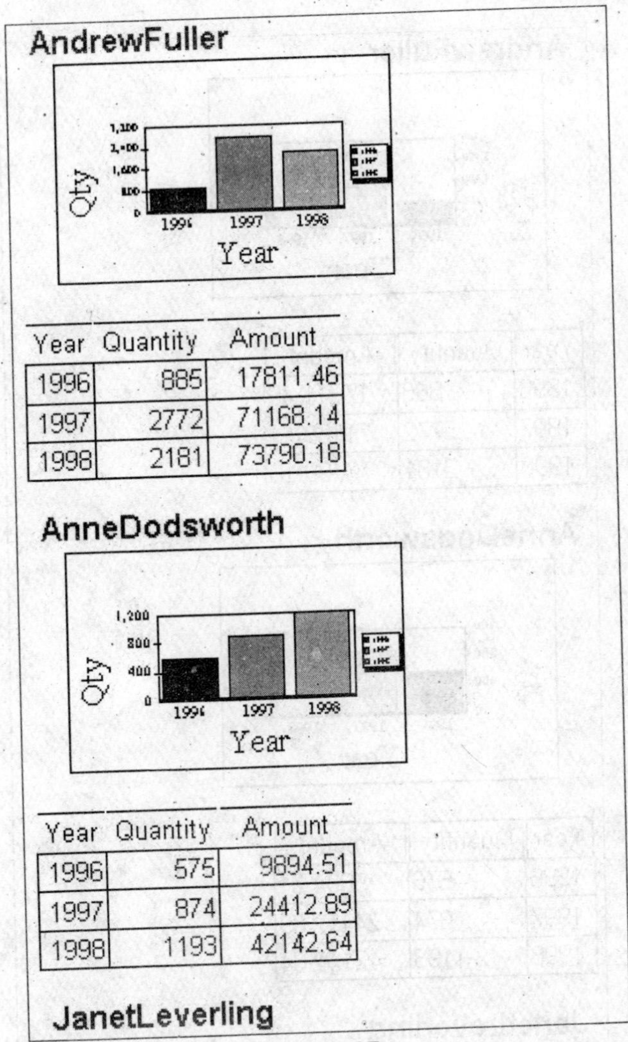

AndrewFuller

Year	Quantity	Amount
1996	885	17811.46
1997	2772	71168.14
1998	2181	73790.18

AnneDodsworth

Year	Quantity	Amount
1996	575	9894.51
1997	874	24412.89
1998	1193	42142.64

JanetLeverling

Fig. 6.97

28. Select the whole header and click on "Borders" from the tool bar (shown below), to display the borders for the headers.

29. Now the report looks as shown in Fig. 6.98.

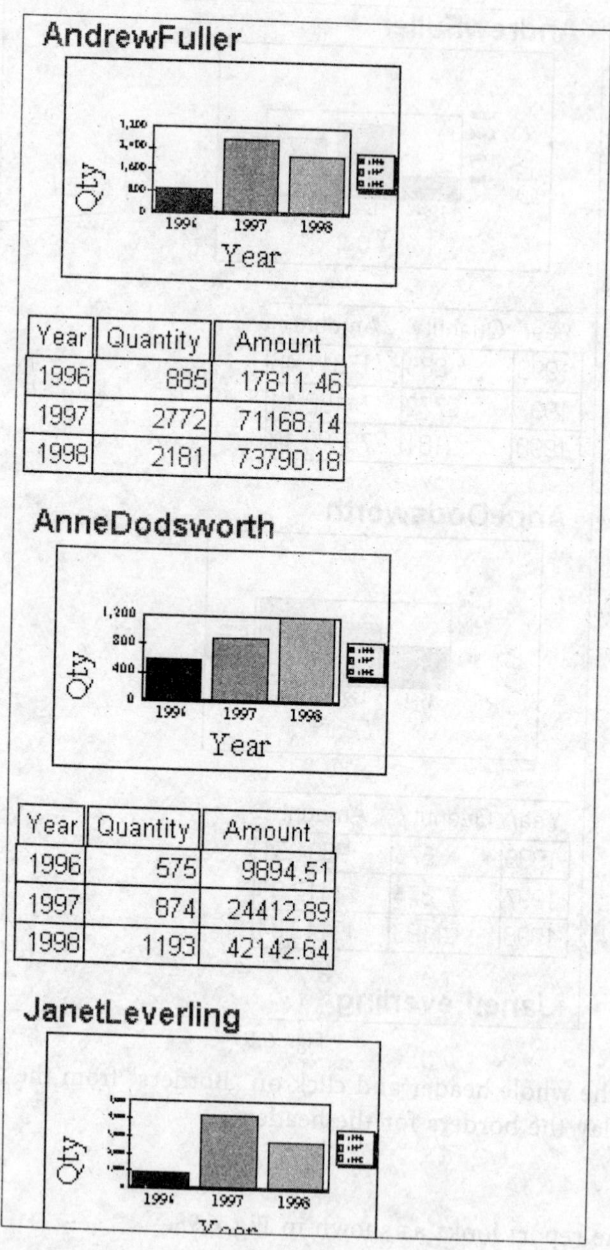

Year	Quantity	Amount
1996	885	17811.46
1997	2772	71168.14
1998	2181	73790.18

Year	Quantity	Amount
1996	575	9894.51
1997	874	24412.89
1998	1193	42142.64

Fig. 6.98

30. To change the data format of the Amount column of the report, select the Amount column.
31. Right click on the selected region and from the pop up menu, select the menu item

"Format". In the "Format" window, go to "Data" tab and change the value of the drop down list box "Positive" to "Currency", then the final report looks as shown in Fig. 6.99.

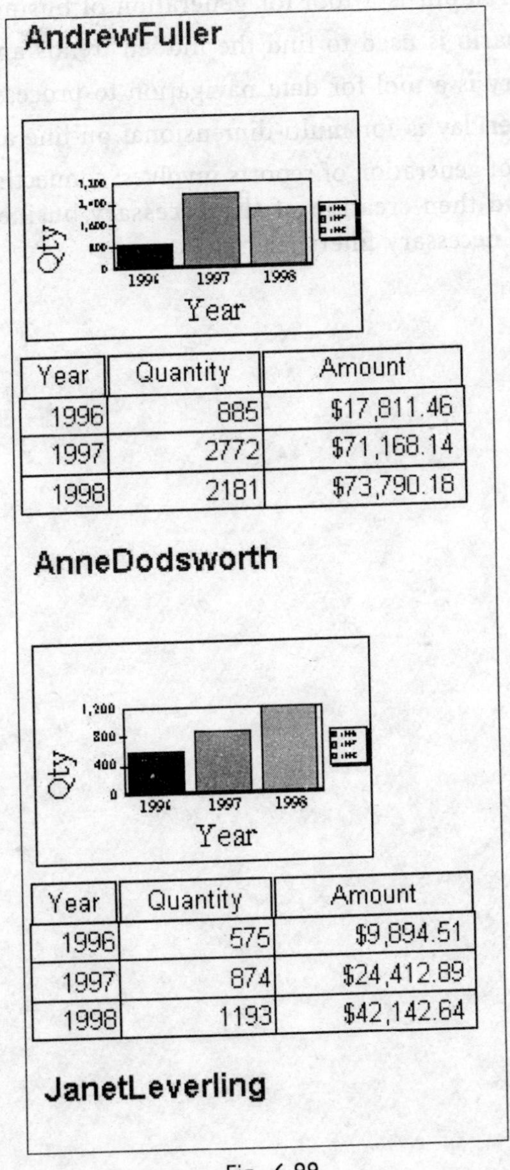

Fig. 6.99

32. Save the report by selecting the menu item **"File → Save"**.

Summary

- **Cognos DecisionStream** is a tool for extraction, transformation of loading of data from the source databases to the target database.
- **Cognos Impromptu** is a tool for generation of business intelligence reports.
- **Cognos Scenario** is used to find the hidden trends and patterns in data.
- **Cognos Query** is a tool for data navigation to process ad hoc queries.
- **Cognos PowerPlay** is for multi-dimensional on-line analysis of data.
- The process of generation of reports involves: connecting to the database, creating catalogue and then creation of the necessary business intelligence reports by applying the necessary filters, alerts, etc.

7 Business Objects

CHAPTER OBJECTIVES

- Overview of Business Objects
- Report generation using Business Objects using three case studies

Business Objects (BO) provides a complete suite of tools for data warehouse development. In this chapter, we will focus on its report generation tools. Using a number of case studies, we will describe the various features of BO and how to generate business intelligence reports.

7.1 Overview of Business Objects

Business Objects (www.businessobjects.com) provides a complete suite of tools for business intelligence. The various tools of this suite are:

Data Integration tools: These tools extract, transform and load the data from the source databases to the target database. There are two tools in this category: Data Integrator and Rapid Marts. Data Integrator is an ETL tool with a GUI. Rapid Marts is a packaged ETL with pre-built data models for reporting and query analysis that makes initial prototype development easy and fast for ERP applications. It provides pre-built reports also.

Data Integrator in turn has 4 components:

- Graphical designer: GUI to build and test ETL jobs for data cleansing, validation and auditing.
- Data integration server: To integrate data from different source databases.
- Metadata repository: To keep source and target metadata as well as transformation rules.
- Administrator: A web-based tool that can be used to start, stop, schedule and monitor ETL jobs. The ETL jobs can be in batch mode or real-time mode. As

multiple users can use the integrator, user management is also done by the administrator module.

The data integrator designer client runs on Windows platform. The Data Integrator server can be based on Windows, HP-UX, Solaris or Linux platform.

BI Platform: This platform provides a set of common services to deploy, use and manage the tools and applications. These services are: security, broadcasting, collaboration, metadata and developer services.

Reporting tools and Query & Analysis tools: These tools provide the facility for both standard reports generation, ad hoc queries and data analysis.

Performance management tools: These tools help in managing the performance of a business by analyzing and tracking key metrics and goals. Using dashboards, scorecards and alerting features, these tools are of immense use to the top management.

7.2 Development Environment

In this chapter, we will use the target database created in Chapter 5 using Informatica and use BO for report generation. For development, you can install the BO tools on the same machine as the target database. The case studies given in this chapter are tested in the following development environment:

- Source MS SQL database running on Windows 2003 server.
- Target Oracle database running on Windows 2003 server.
- Business Objects Reporting tools running on Windows 2003 server.

Note that during the development, you can use this type of setup. However, when the data warehouse is put to real use, the target database and the BO tools will be running on different machines.

7.3 Case Study #1

We will generate a report that gives the category-wise total quantity sold for each product. In each category, the highest sold product will be highlighted in red color. The final report will be as shown in Fig. 7.1.

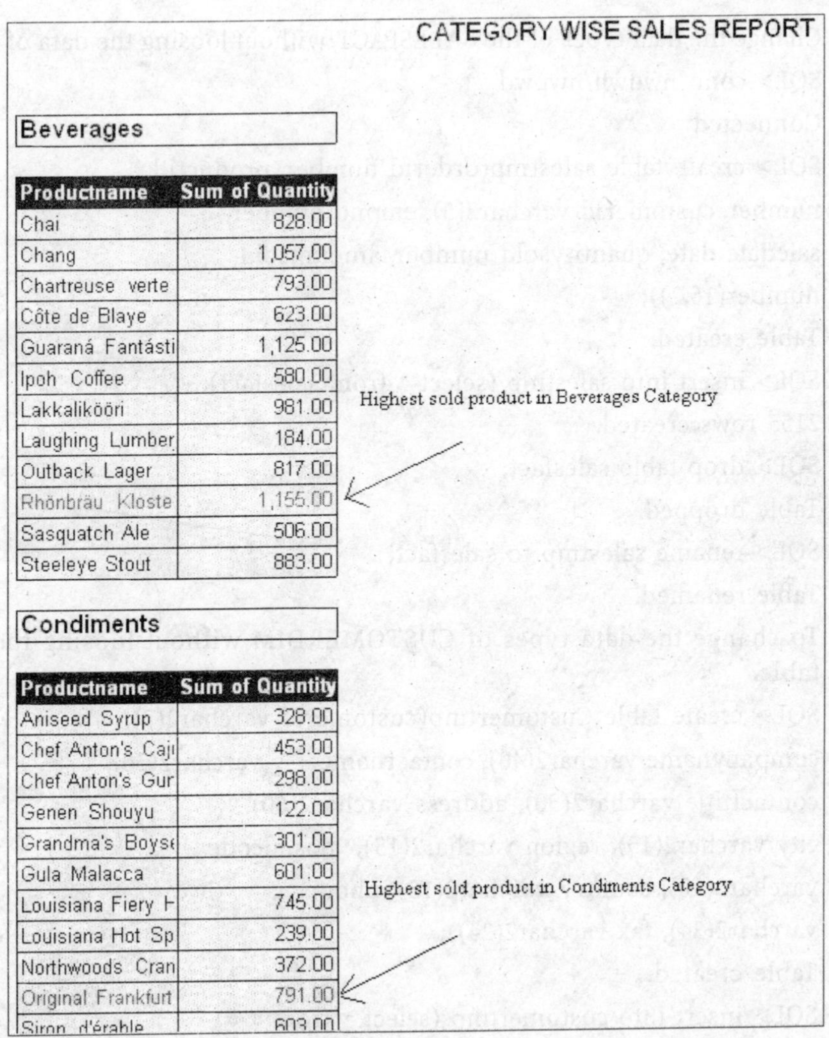

CATEGORY WISE SALES REPORT

Beverages

Productname	Sum of Quantity
Chai	828.00
Chang	1,057.00
Chartreuse verte	793.00
Côte de Blaye	623.00
Guaraná Fantásti	1,125.00
Ipoh Coffee	580.00
Lakkalikööri	981.00
Laughing Lumber	184.00
Outback Lager	817.00
Rhönbräu Kloste	1,155.00
Sasquatch Ale	506.00
Steeleye Stout	883.00

Condiments

Productname	Sum of Quantity
Aniseed Syrup	328.00
Chef Anton's Caj	453.00
Chef Anton's Gur	298.00
Genen Shouyu	122.00
Grandma's Boys	301.00
Gula Malacca	601.00
Louisiana Fiery H	745.00
Louisiana Hot Sp	239.00
Northwoods Cran	372.00
Original Frankfurt	791.00
Sirop d'érable	603.00

Fig. 7.1

Before starting the work on Business Objects, you need to change the data types of the columns for the tables SALESFACT, CUSTOMERDIM, and EMPLOYEEDIMENSION from nvarchar2 to varchar2 and nchar to char because BO (and also Cognos) does not support the data types nchar and nvarchar2. As we created some of the columns of the above tables with the data types nchar and nvarchar2, we have to change them to varchar2 now. In order to change the data types of the columns, the table must be empty. So, first copy all the data of a table to a temporary table with the required data types, then drop the original table and rename the temporary table with the original table name. You can change the data types through the following SQL statements in Oracle database.

1. Change the data types of the SALESFACT, without loosing the data of the table e.g.

```
SQL> conn nwdwh/nwpwd
Connected
SQL> create table salestmp(orderid number, productid
number, customerid varchar2(5), empno number,
saledate date, quantitysold number, amountsold
number(15,2));
Table created.
SQL> insert into salestmp (select * from salesfact);
2155 rows created.
SQL> drop table salesfact;
Table dropped.
SQL> rename salestmp to salesfact;
Table renamed.
```

2. To change the data types of CUSTOMERDIM without loosing the data of the table.

```
SQL> create table Customertmp(customerid varchar2(5),
companyname varchar2(40), contactname     varchar2(30),
contacttitle varchar2(30), address varchar2(60),
city varchar2(15), region varchar2(15),  postalcode
varchar2(10), country varchar2(15), phone
varchar2(24), fax varchar2(24));
Table created.
SQL> insert into customertmp (select * from
customerdim);
91 rows created.
SQL> drop table customerdim;
Table dropped.
SQL> rename customertmp to customerdim;
Table renamed.
```

3. To change the datatypes of EMPLOYEEDIMENSION without losing the data of the table.

```
SQL> create table Employeetmp(empno number, employeeid number(10),
employeename varchar2(30), titlevarchar2(30), titleofcourtesy varchar2(25),
```

birthdate date,hiredate date, address varchar2(60), city varchar2(15),region archar2(15), postalcode varchar2(10), country varchar2(15), homephone varchar2(24),extension varchar2(4),reportsto number(10), flag number);

Table created.

SQL> insert into Employeetmp (select * from

Employeedimension);

9 rows created.

SQL> drop table Employeedimension;

Table dropped.

SQL> rename Employeetmp to Employeedimension;

Table renamed.

To generate the report as shown in Fig. 7.1, the procedure is as follows:

1. Open the BO Designer:

   "Start → Programs → BusinessObjects5.1 → Designer".

   "Designer" window, shown in Fig. 7.2 opens.

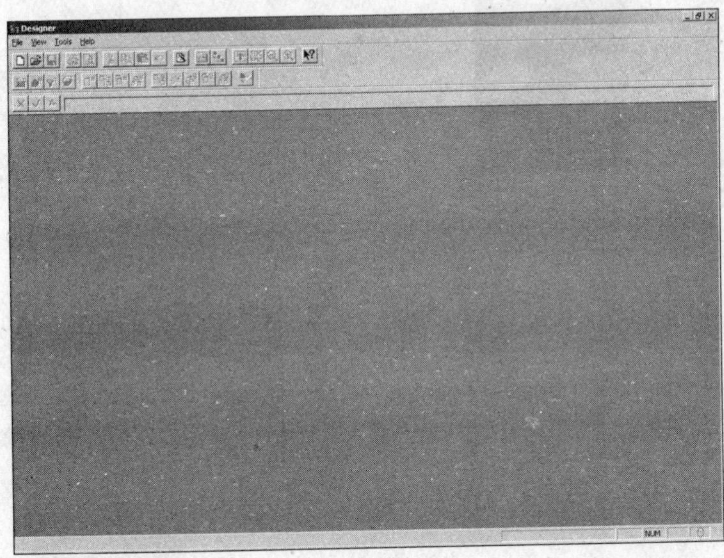

Fig. 7.2

2. Select the menu item ***"File → New".***
3. "Quick Design Wizard – Welcome Screen" window opens
4. "Quick Design Wizard – Step 1 of 4" window (Fig. 7.3) opens. Click on **"Begin"** button.

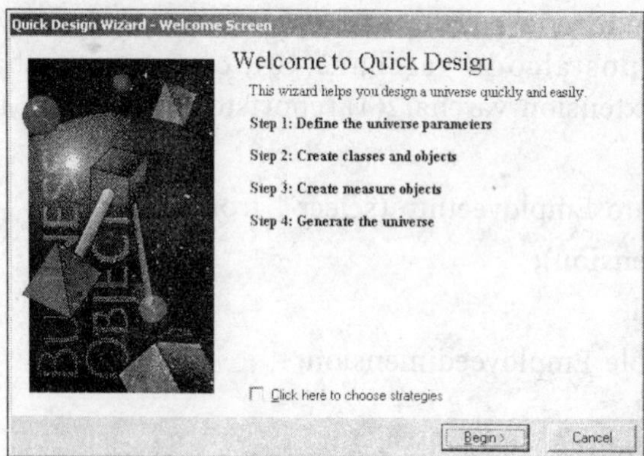

Fig. 7.3

The window shown in Fig. 7.4 appears. Enter the universe name. e.g.: nwuniverse

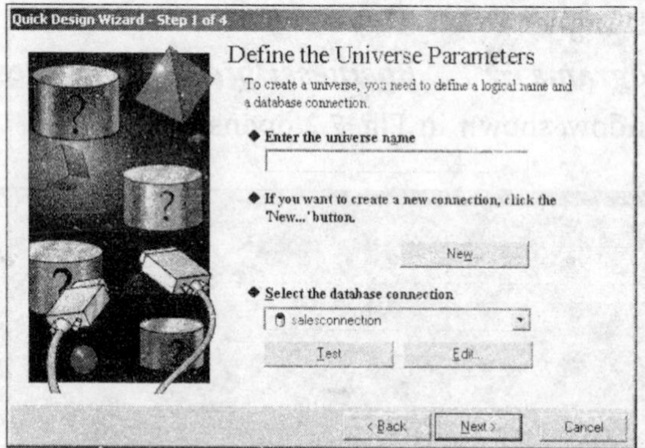

Fig. 7.4

5. To create a new connection, click on **"New"**, then "Add a connection" dialog opens.
6. From the "Add a connection" dialog, select "Oracle Client" (Fig.7.5) as our data warehouse database is in Oracle.

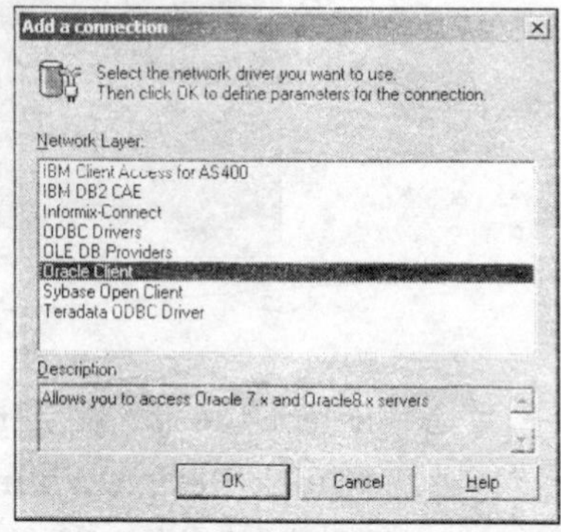

Fig. 7.5

7. Click on **"OK"**, then "Oracle Client" window opens as, shown in Fig. 7.6.

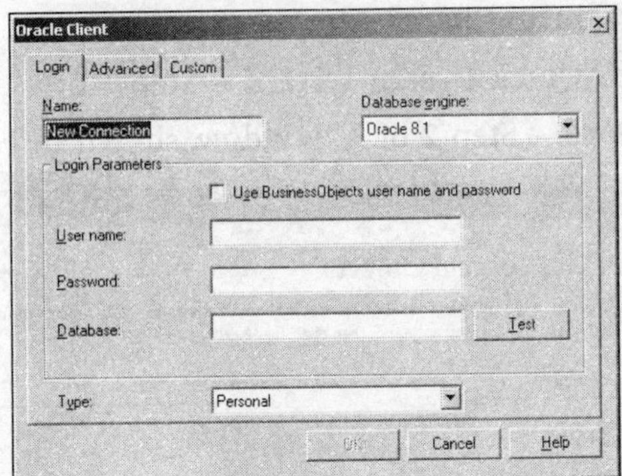

Fig. 7.6

8. Enter Name, User name, Password and ddatabase; select database engine and Type, as shown in Fig. 7.7.

   e.g.: Name : nwdbconnection
   User name : nwdwh
   Password : nwpwd
   Database : oemrep
   Database engine : Oracle 8.1
   Type : Personal

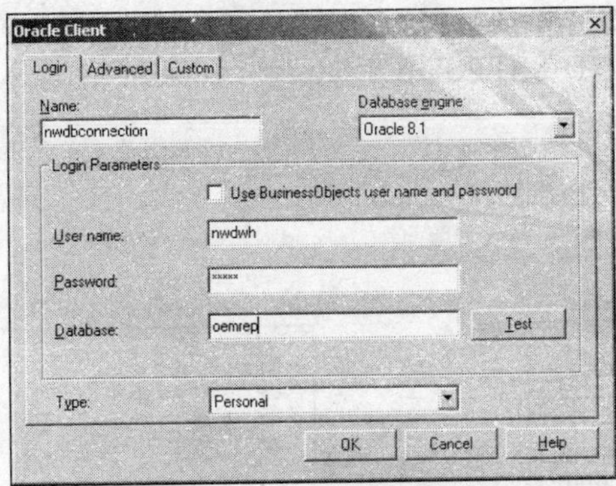

Fig. 7.7

9. To test the connection, click on **"Test"**.
10. "Test connection" information message box opens specifying that the server is responding. Click on **"OK"**. (Fig. 7.8).

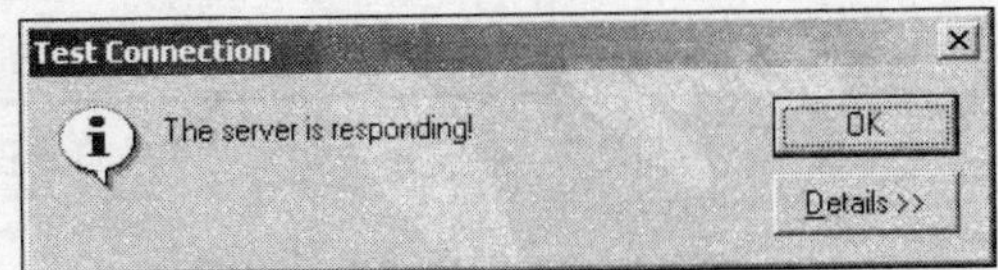

Fig. 7.8

11. Click on **"OK"** of "Oracle Client" window.
12. Click on **"Next"** of "Quick Design Wizard – Step 1 of 4".
13. "Quick Design Wizard – Step 2 of 4" window, shown in Fig. 7.9, opens.

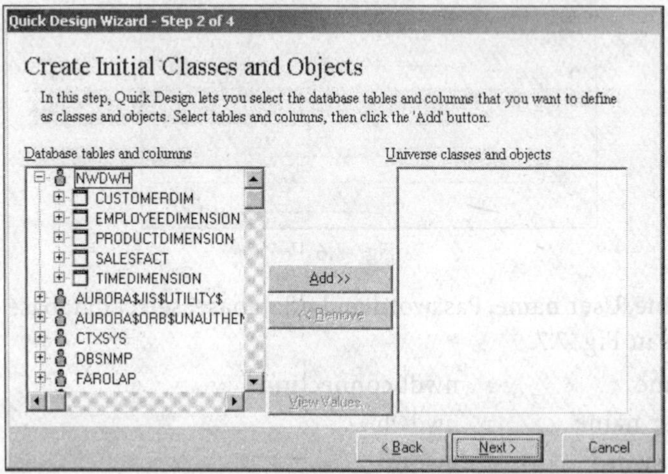

Fig. 7.9

14. On the left hand side, database tables and columns are displayed. On the right side, universe classes and objects are displayed, as in Fig. 7.10.
15. Select CUSTOMERDIM, EMPLOYEEDIMENSION, PRODUCTDIMENSTION, TIMEDIMENSION AND SALESFACT, click on **"Add"**.

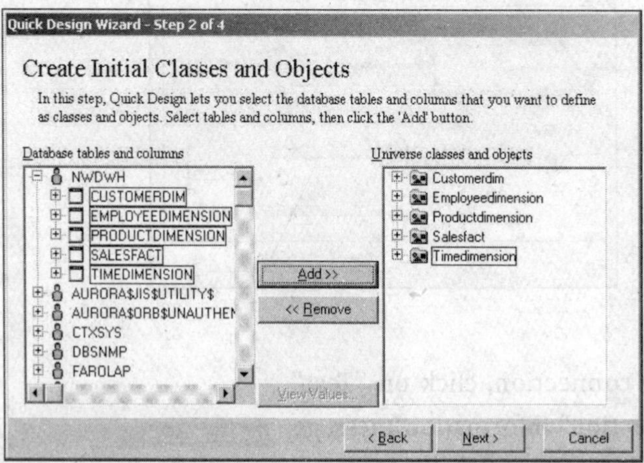

Fig. 7.10

16. Click on **"Next"**.
17. "Quick Design Wizard – Step 3 of 4" window, shown in Fig. 7.11, opens.

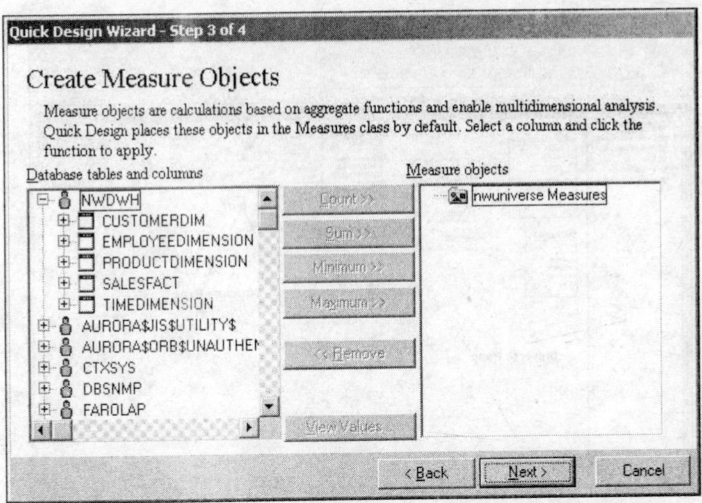

Fig. 7.11

18. Explore SALESFACT table from "Database tables and columns" list, select "QUANTITYSOLD" and click on **"Sum"**. Now the window looks as shown in Fig. 7.12.

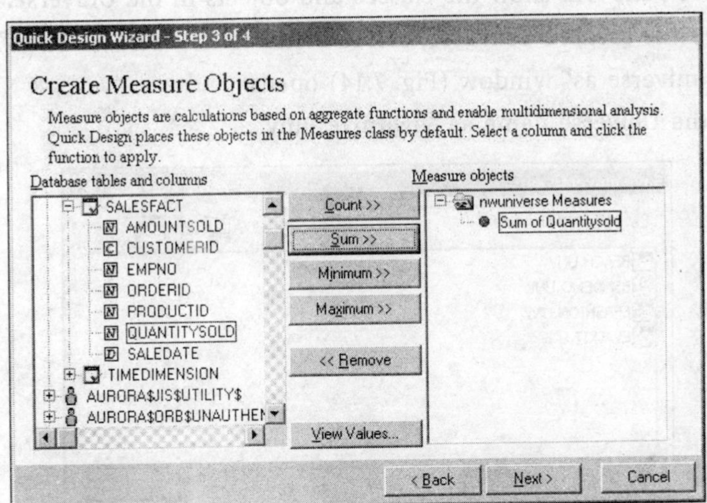

Fig. 7.12

19. Click on **"Next"**.
20. "Quick Design Wizard – Step 4of 4" window opens. Click on **"Finish"** button.
21. "Designer – nwuniver" window (Fig. 7.13) opens.

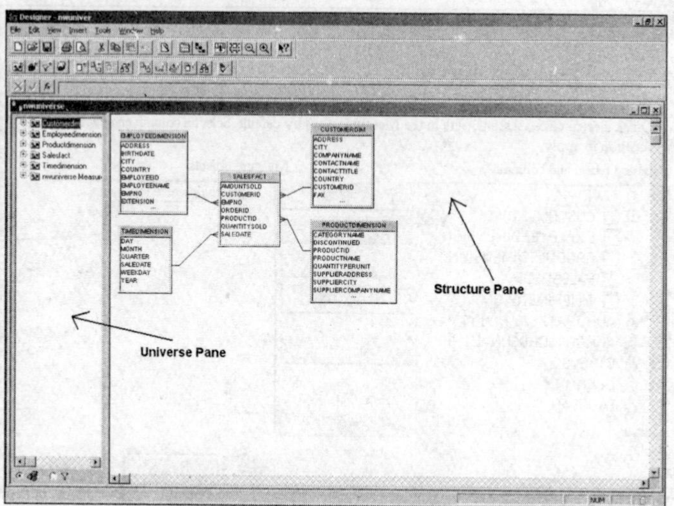

Fig. 7.13

22. The Structure Pane will show the joins on the tables which we used in Universe creation.
23. Universe Pane will show the classes and objects in the Universe.
24. To save the created Universe, select menu item ***"File → Save"***.
25. "Save universe as" window (Fig. 7.14) opens.
26. Enter the Universe name as "nwuniver.unv".

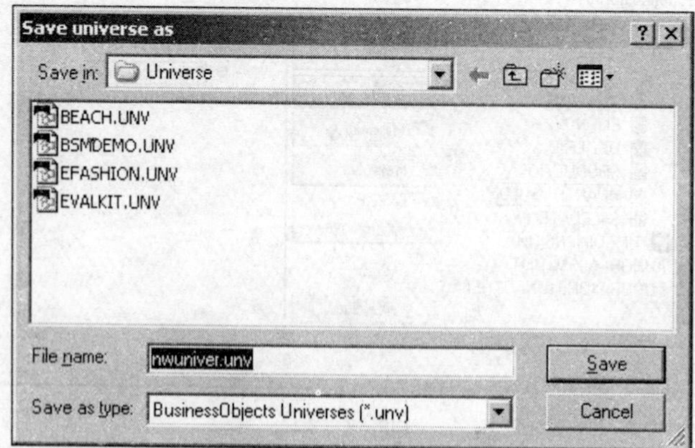

Fig. 7.14

27. Click on **"Save"**.
28. Select the menu item, ***"Tools → Run → BusinessObjects"***.
29. "New Report Wizard" window, shown in Fig. 7.15, opens.

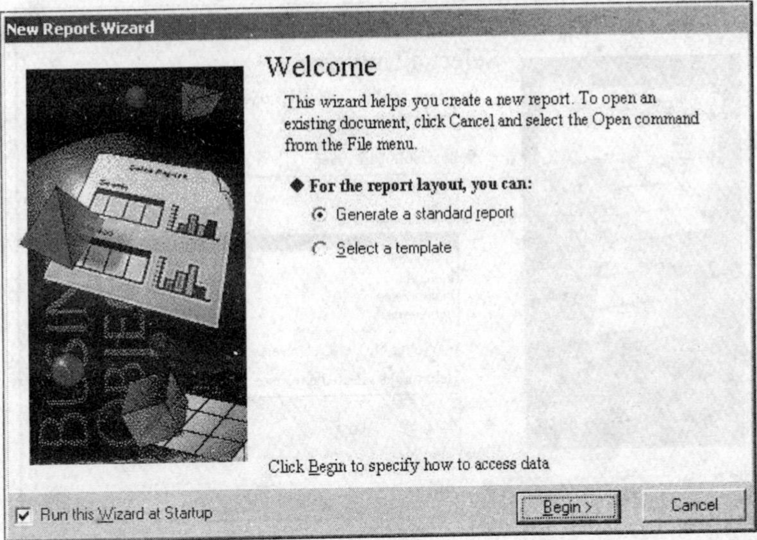

Fig. 7.15

30. Select "Generate a standard report" and click on **"Begin"**.
31. "Specify Data Access" page of "New Report Wizard" (Fig. 7.16) opens.

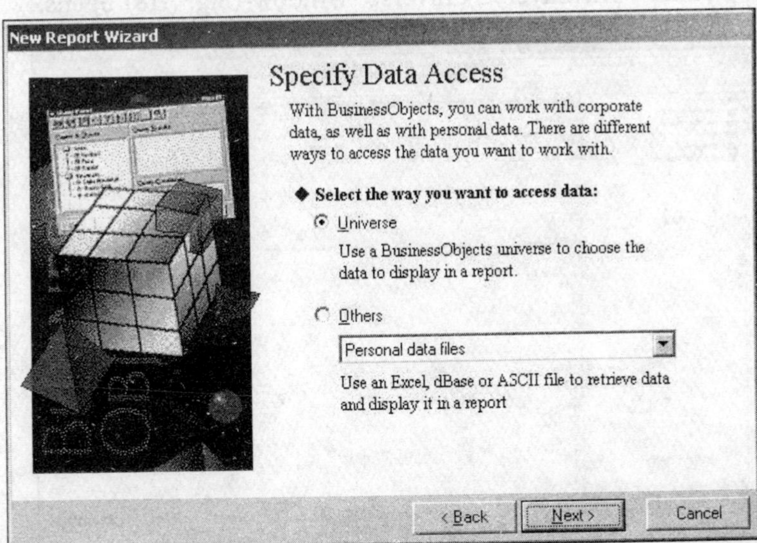

Fig. 7.16

32. Select "Universe" radio button and click on **"Next"**.
33. "New Report Wizard" dialog (Fig. 7.17) opens, select the universe from the list of "Available Universes".

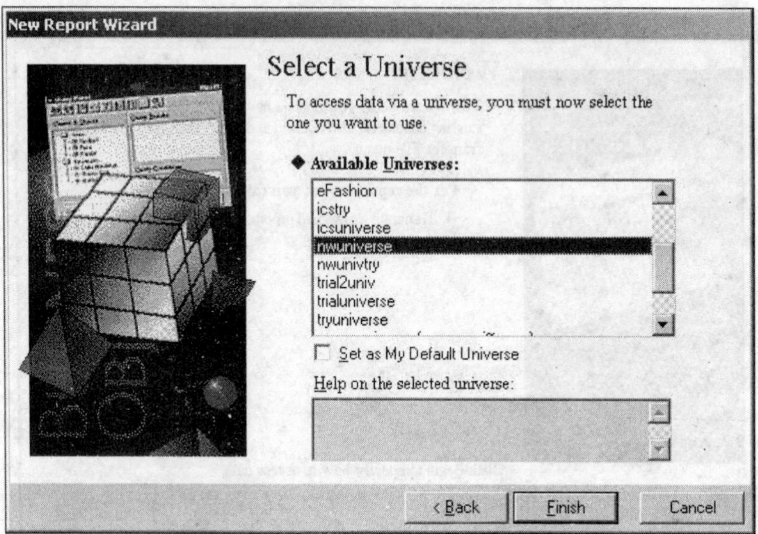

Fig. 7.17

Here, you need to select "nwuniverse" from "Available Universes" list and click on **"Finish"**.

34. "Query Panel – nwuniverse Universe" window (Fig. 7.18) opens.

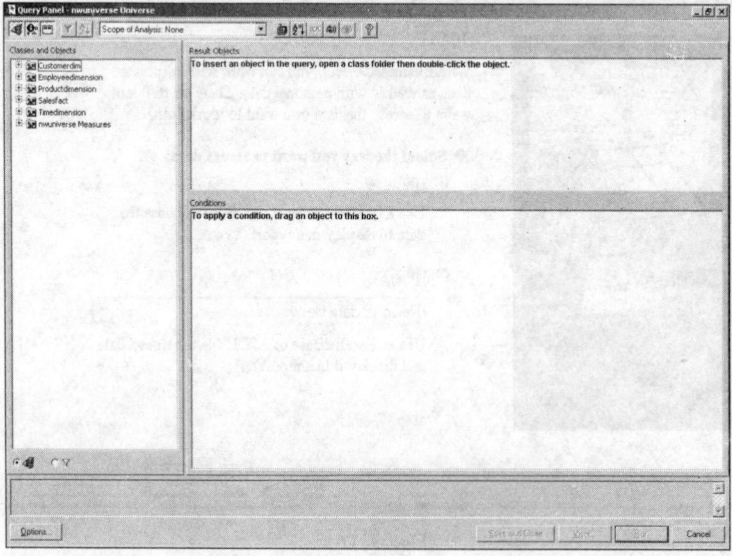

Fig. 7.18

35. Explore PRODUCTDIMENSION, NWUINVERSE MEASURES and SALESFACT from **"Classes and Objects"** list (Fig. 7.19).

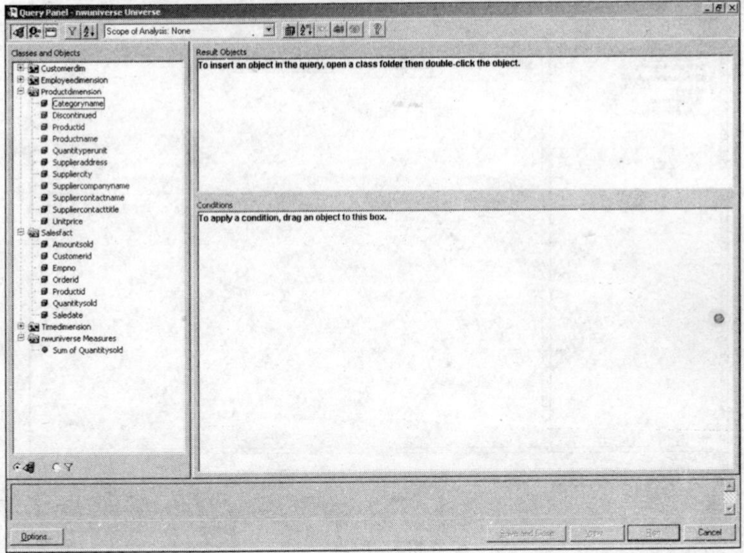

Fig. 7.19

36. Double click on PRODUCTNAME and CATEGORYNAME from PRODCUTDIMENSION.
37. After double clicking, you can see that the selected objects are added to Result objects pane, as in Fig. 7.20.

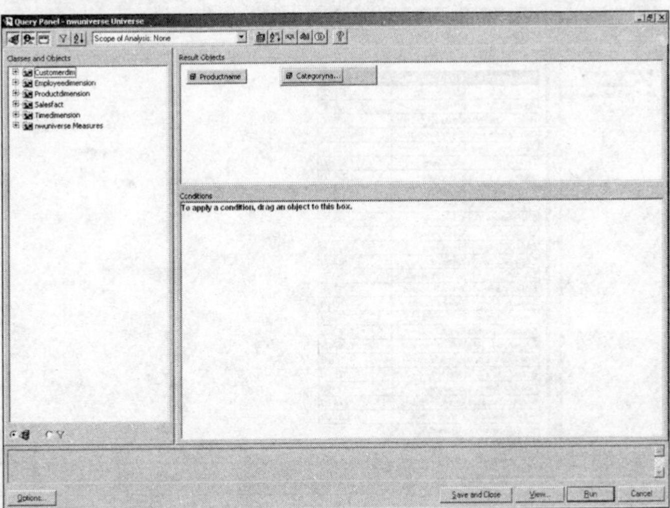

Fig. 7.20

38. Double click on "Sum of Quantity sold" object. Now the window looks as shown in Fig. 7.21.

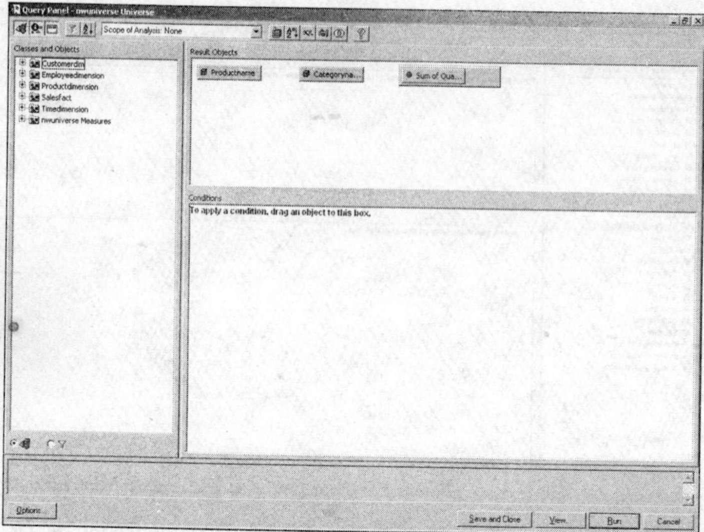

Fig. 7.21

39. Click on **"Run"**, located at right bottom corner of the screen, to generate the report.
40. "BusinessObjects – Document2" window, shown in Fig. 7.22, opens.

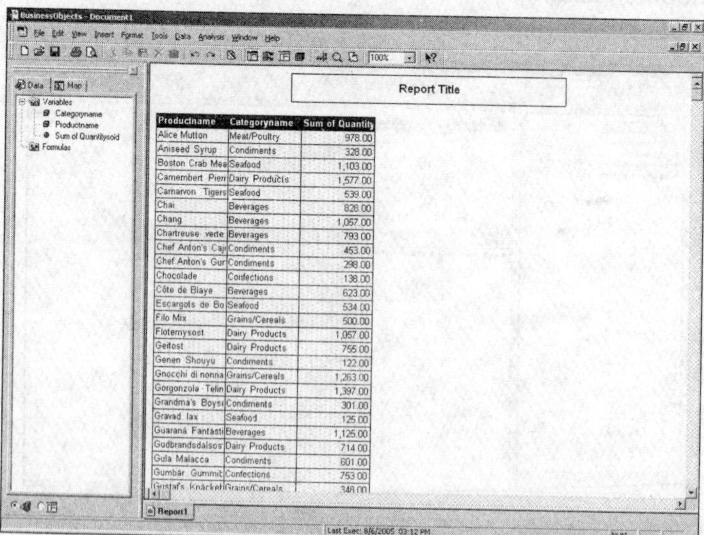

Productname	Categoryname	Sum of Quantity
Alice Mutton	Meat/Poultry	978.00
Aniseed Syrup	Condiments	328.00
Boston Crab Mea	Seafood	1,103.00
Camembert Pierr	Dairy Products	1,577.00
Carnarvon Tigers	Seafood	539.00
Chai	Beverages	828.00
Chang	Beverages	1,057.00
Chartreuse verte	Beverages	793.00
Chef Anton's Caj	Condiments	453.00
Chef Anton's Gur	Condiments	298.00
Chocolade	Confections	138.00
Côte de Blaye	Beverages	623.00
Escargots de Bo	Seafood	534.00
Filo Mix	Grains/Cereals	500.00
Flotemysost	Dairy Products	1,057.00
Geitost	Dairy Products	755.00
Genen Shouyu	Condiments	122.00
Gnocchi di nonna	Grains/Cereals	1,263.00
Gorgonzola Telin	Dairy Products	1,397.00
Grandma's Boysi	Condiments	301.00
Gravad lax	Seafood	125.00
Guaraná Fantásti	Beverages	1,125.00
Gudbrandsdalsos	Dairy Products	714.00
Gula Malacca	Condiments	601.00
Gumbär Gummib	Confections	753.00
Gustaf's Knäcke	Grains/Cereals	348.00

Fig. 7.22

41. Drag the first entry of Categoryname column to top of the report.
42. Now the report looks as shown in Fig. 7.23.

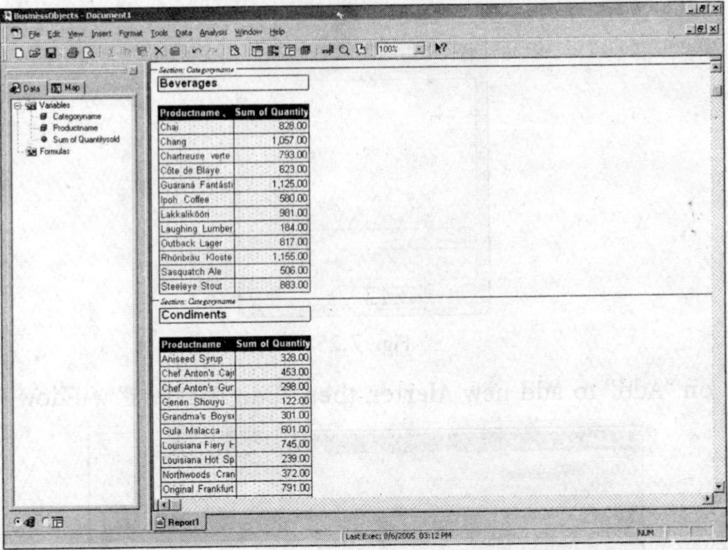

Fig. 7.23

43. To change the title of the report, click on "Report Title" and enter the title as "Category-wise Sales Report", as shown in Fig. 7.24.

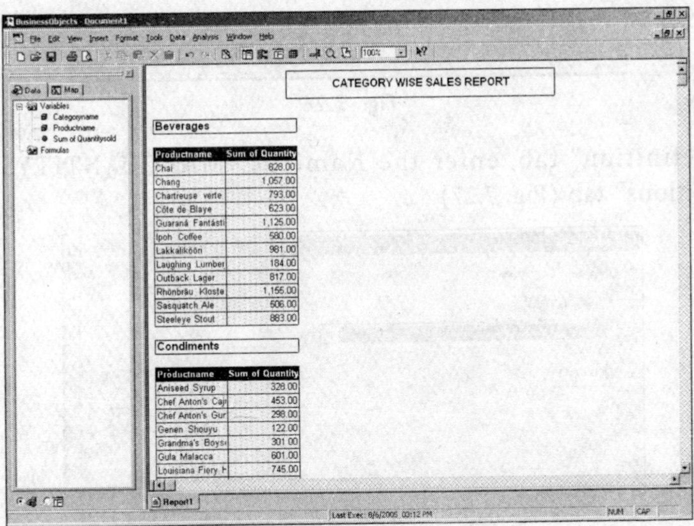

Fig. 7.24

44. Select all the columns by clicking on the column name holding the SHIFT key.
45. Select the menu item ***"Format → Alerters."***
46. "Alerters" window, shown in Fig. 7.25, opens.

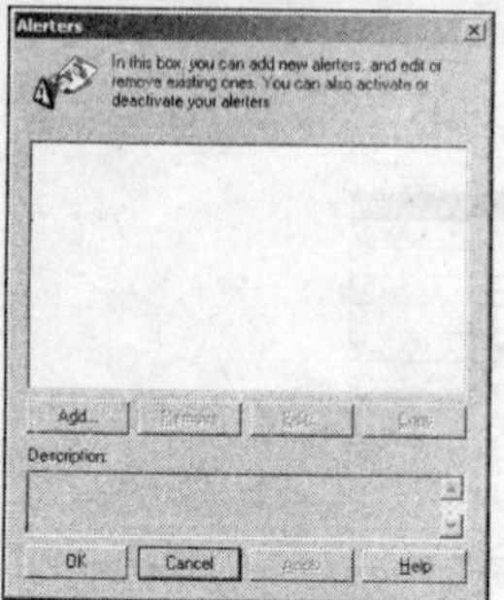

Fig. 7.25

47. Click on "Add" to add new Alerter, then "Edit Alerters" window (Fig. 7.26) opens.

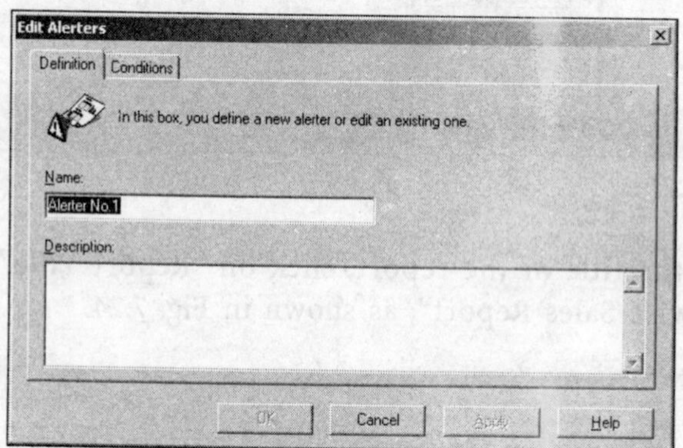

Fig. 7.26

48. In "Definition" tab, enter the Name as "MAXQUANTITYSOLD" and go to "Conditions" tab (Fig. 7.27).

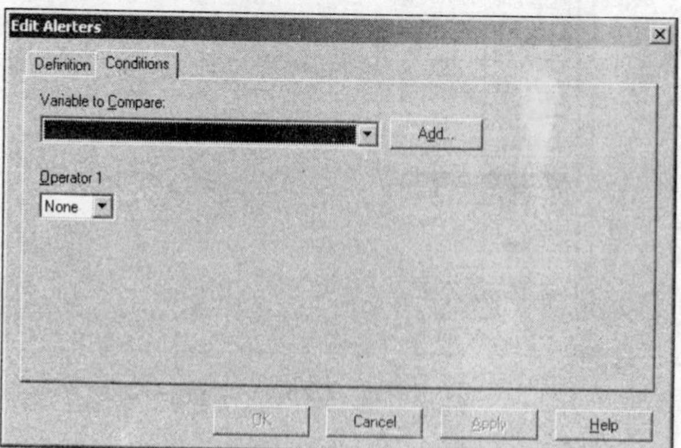

Fig. 7.27

49. Click on **"Add"** to add new condition, then "Variable Editor" window (Fig. 7.28) opens.

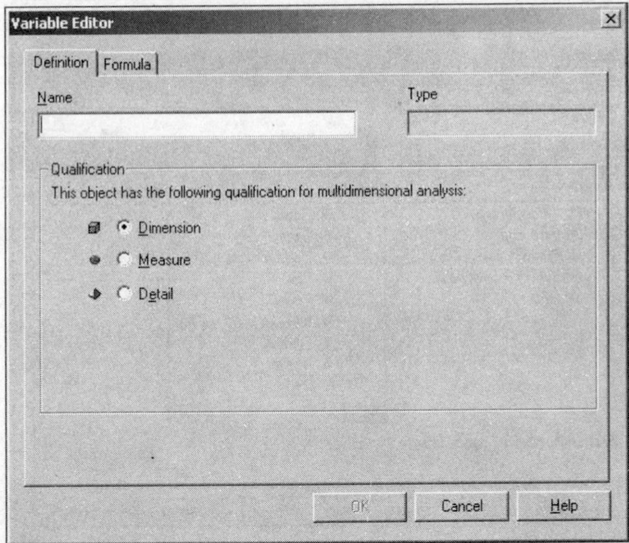

Fig. 7.28

50. Select the Measure radio button and enter the name as RNK_QTYSOLD.
51. Go to "Formula" tab (Fig.7.29).

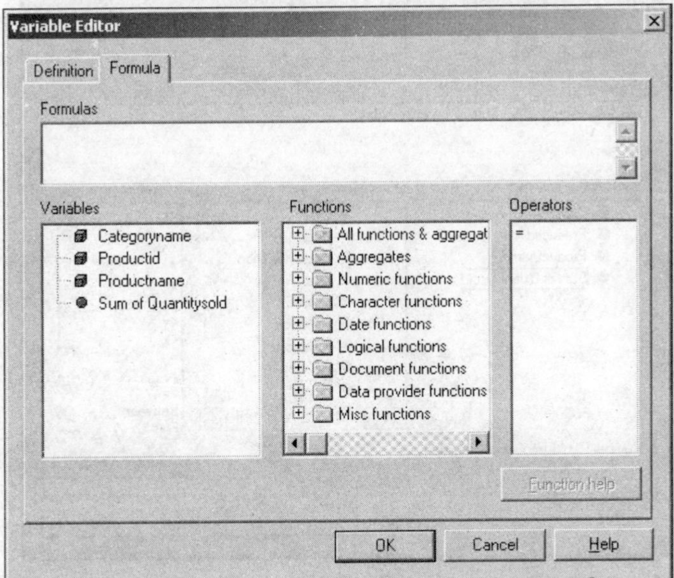

Fig. 7.29

52. Explore "All functions & Aggregates" item from the "Functions" list and double click on "Rank", as shown in Fig. 7.30.

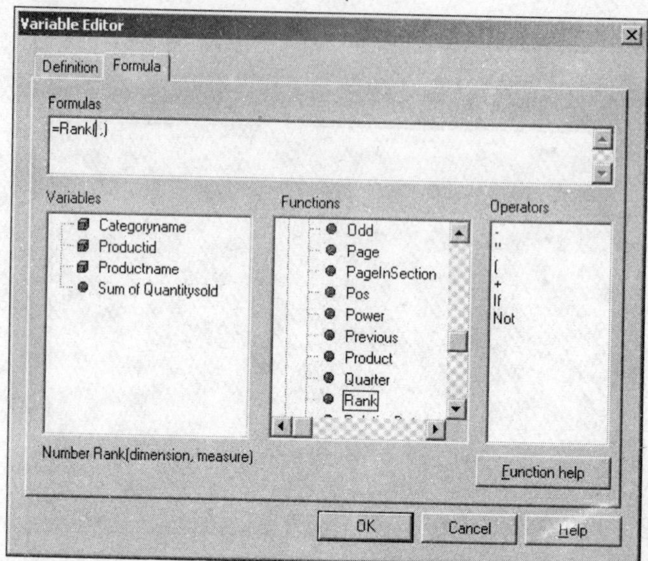

Fig. 7.30

53. Double click on "Productid" item and on "Sum of Quantitysold" item of "Variables" list. Now the screen will be as shown in Fig. 7.31.

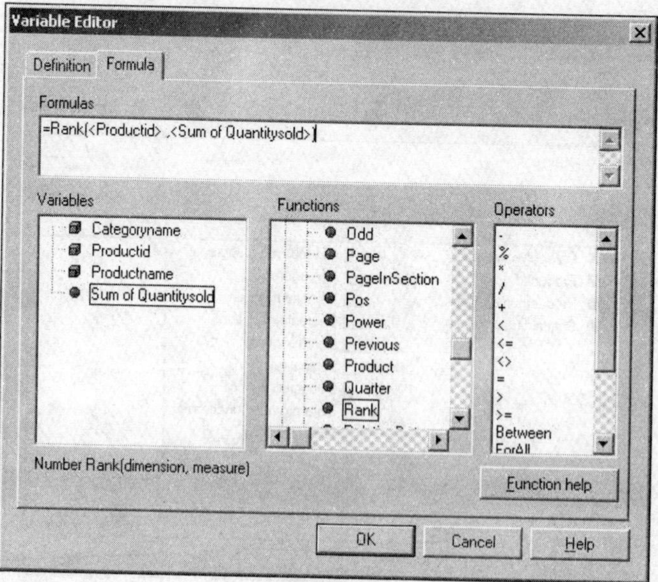

Fig. 7.31

54. Click on **"OK"**.

55. "Edit Alerters" window will be as shown in Fig. 7.32.

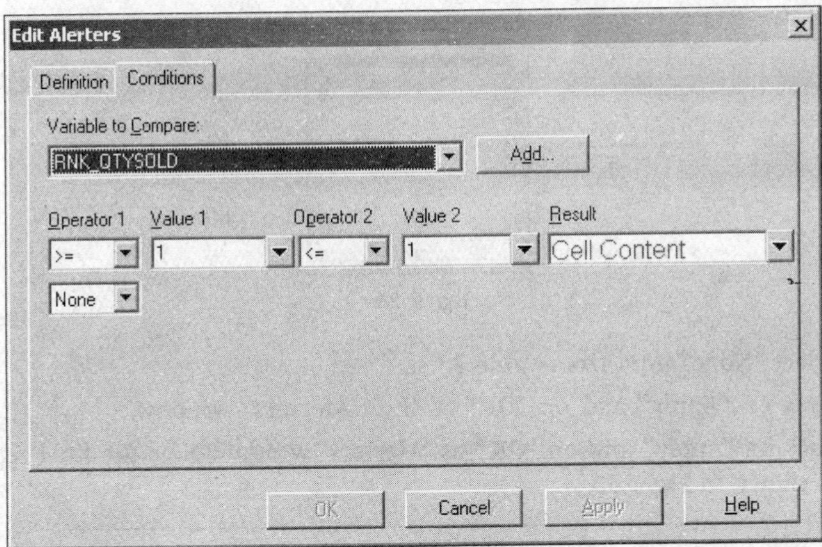

Fig. 7.32

56. Select **"="** as Operator 1 symbol and click on Value 1, then the small popup menu will pop (Fig.7.33).

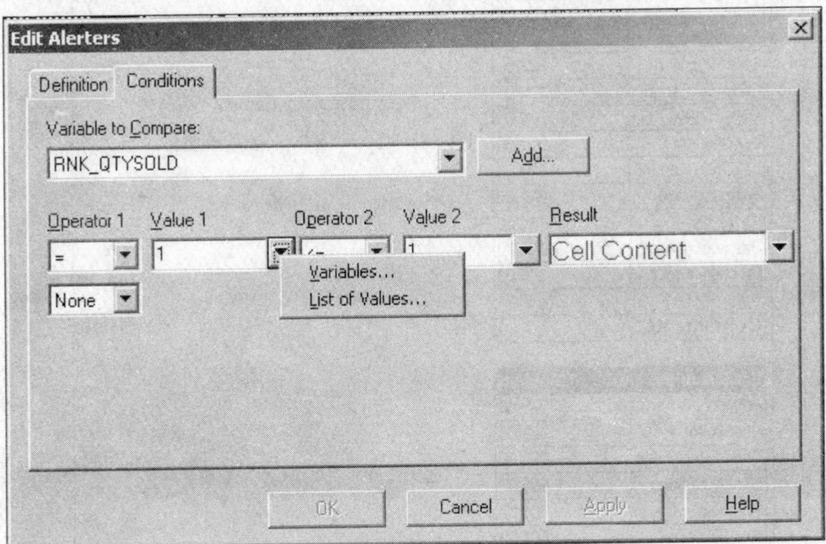

Fig. 7.33

57. Select "List of Values" from the popup menu.
58. "List of Values for <RNK_QTYSOLD>" window opens. Select "1", as shown in Fig. 7.34. Click on **"OK"**.

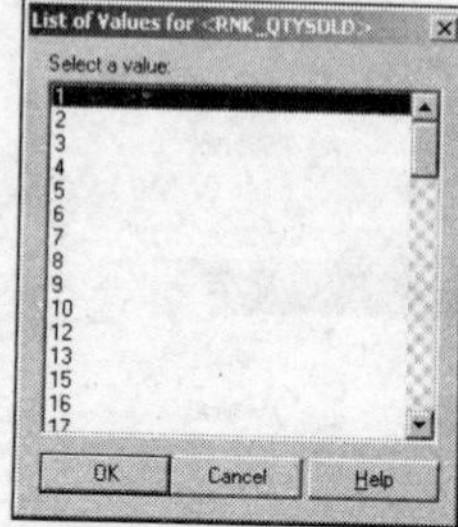

Fig. 7.34

59. Select "None" item from Value 2 list.
60. Click on **"Apply"** and on **"OK"** of "Edit Alerters" window.
61. Click on **"Apply"** and on **"OK"** of "Alerters" window. Now the final report will be as shown in Fig. 7.35.

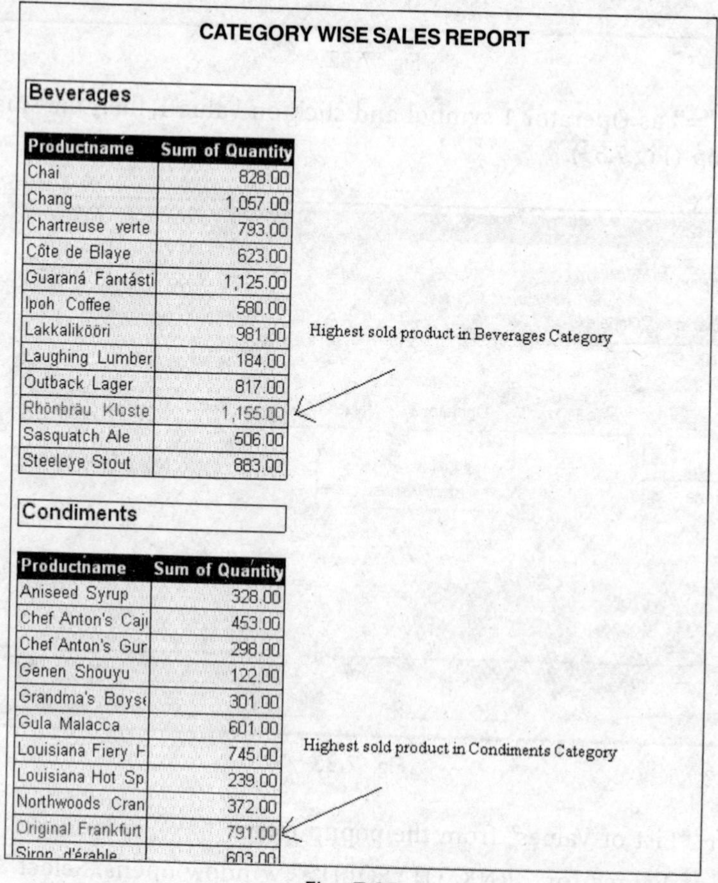

CATEGORY WISE SALES REPORT

Beverages

Productname	Sum of Quantity
Chai	828.00
Chang	1,057.00
Chartreuse verte	793.00
Côte de Blaye	623.00
Guaraná Fantásti	1,125.00
Ipoh Coffee	580.00
Lakkaliköōri	981.00
Laughing Lumber	184.00
Outback Lager	817.00
Rhönbräu Kloste	1,155.00
Sasquatch Ale	506.00
Steeleye Stout	883.00

Highest sold product in Beverages Category

Condiments

Productname	Sum of Quantity
Aniseed Syrup	328.00
Chef Anton's Caj	453.00
Chef Anton's Gur	298.00
Genen Shouyu	122.00
Grandma's Boyse	301.00
Gula Malacca	601.00
Louisiana Fiery H	745.00
Louisiana Hot Sp	239.00
Northwoods Cran	372.00
Original Frankfurt	791.00
Sirop d'érable	603.00

Highest sold product in Condiments Category

Fig. 7.35

62. Select the menu item ***"File→Save"*** to save the report.
63. "Save As" window opens.
64. Enter the "File Name" as MAXQUANTITYSOLD, and click on **"Save"**.

7.4 Case Study #2

In this case study, we will generate another report, employee-wise sales report. For each employee, the total quantity sold and amount sold will be displayed. The highest sales record will be highlighted (to give an award "Best Sales Rep of the Year" to that employee). The final report will be as in Fig. 7.36.

EMPLOYEE WISE SALES REPORT FOR 1998

Employeename	Sum of Quantity	Amount sold
AndrewFuller	2,181.00	73,790.18
AnneDodsworth	1,193.00	42,142.64
JanetLeverling	2,665.00	80,869.80
LauraCallahan	2,079.00	47,727.95
MargaretPeacock	2,181.00	51,163.02
MichaelSuyama	901.00	17,181.58
NancyDavolio	2,243.00	60,565.23
RobertKing	1,712.00	44,559.90
StevenBuchanan	787.00	19,691.89

Best Sales Representative for the year 1998

Fig. 7.36

1. Select ***"Start→ Programs→ BusinessObjects5.1→ Designer"***.
2. Select the menu item ***"File→Open"*** to open the universe.
3. "Open a Universe" window opens select the Universe which was created. e.g.: nwuniver.unv. Click on **"Open"**.
4. Explore "nwuniverse Measures" from the Universe Pane. (Fig. 7.37).

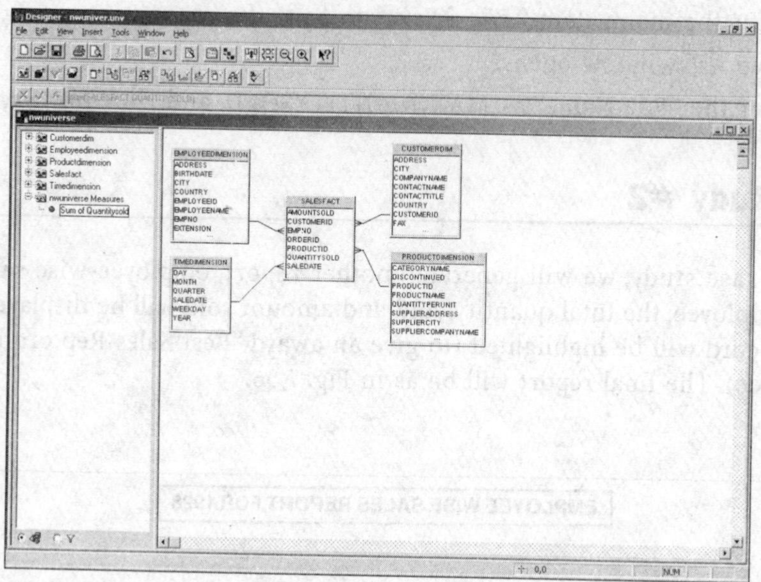

Fig. 7.37

5. Right click on the "nwuniverse Measures" and select the "Insert Object" item from the pop up menu.
6. "Edit Properties of Object1" window, shown in Fig. 7.38 opens.

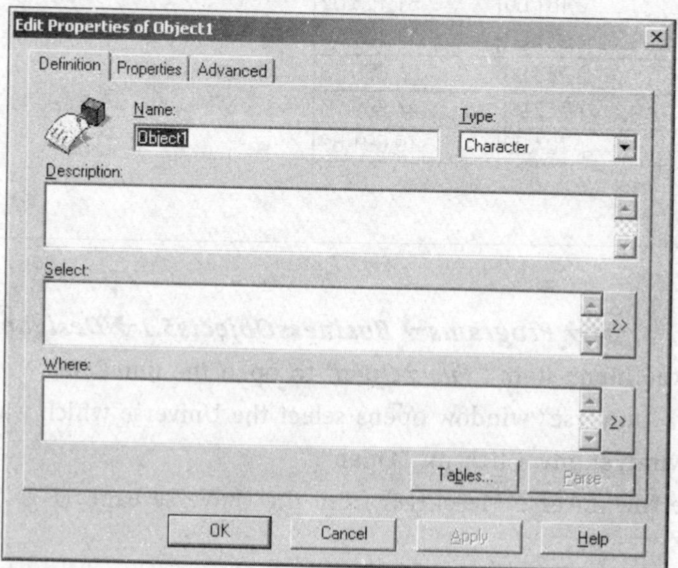

Fig. 7.38

7. Go to Properties tab. (Fig. 7.39).

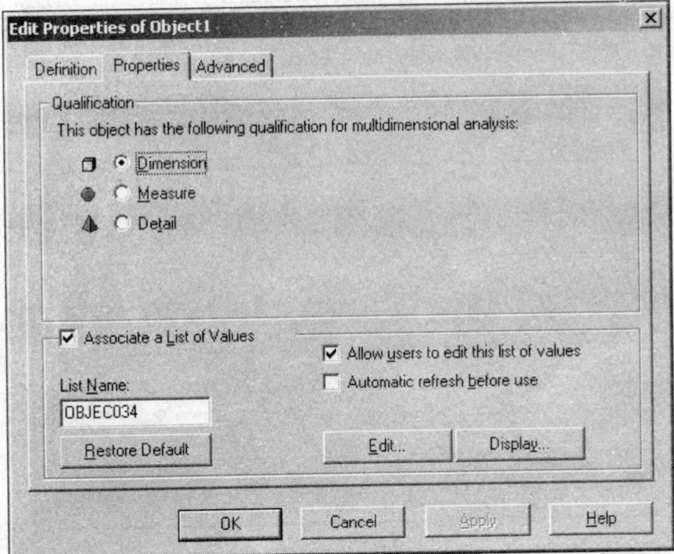

Fig. 7.39

8. Select the Qualification as "Measure", as shown in Fig. 7.40.

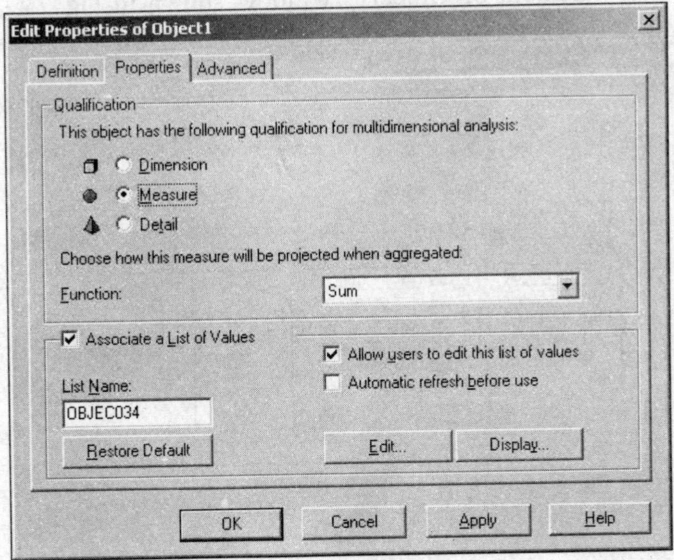

Fig. 7.40

9. Select the Function as "Sum".
10. Go to Definition tab, as shown in Fig. 7.41.

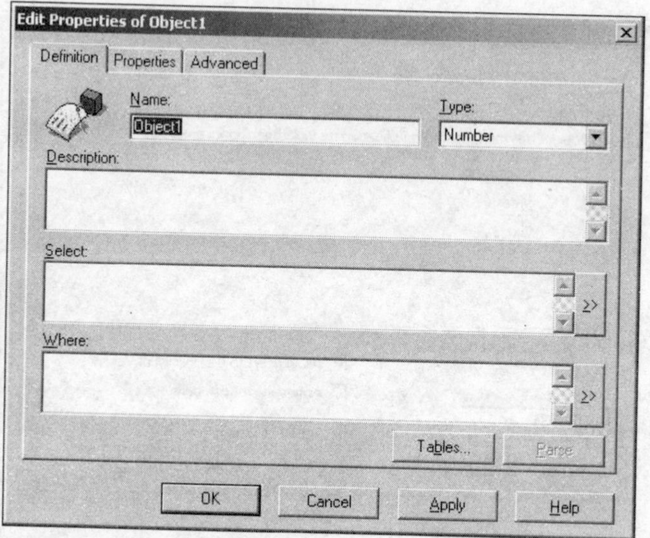

Fig. 7.41

11. Enter the Name as "Amount sold".
12. Click on the **">>"** arrow button on the right side of the Select.
13. "Edit Select Statement of 'Object1'" window, shown in Fig. 7.42, opens.

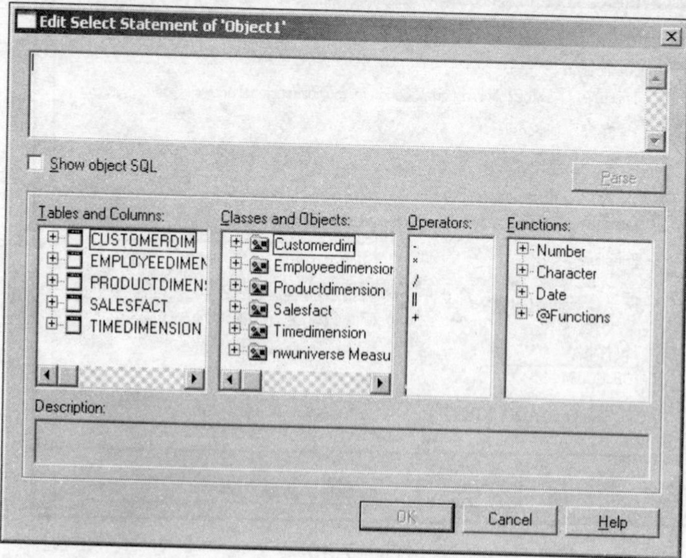

Fig. 7.42

14. Explore Number from the Functions list and double click on the "Sum()" function, as shown in Fig. 7.43.

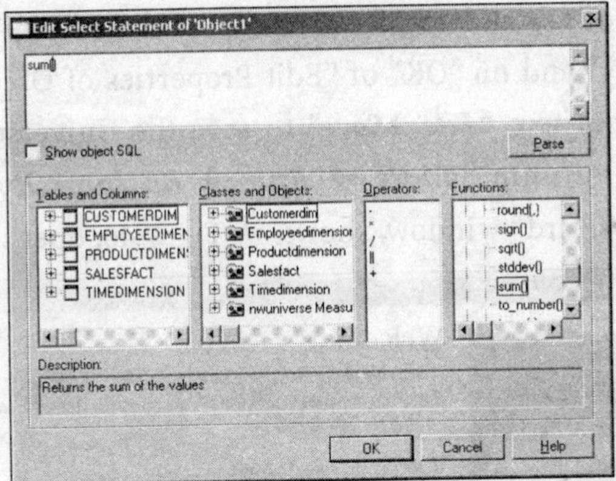

Fig. 7.43

15. Explore the SALESFACT table from the "Tables and Columns" list, as in Fig. 7.44.

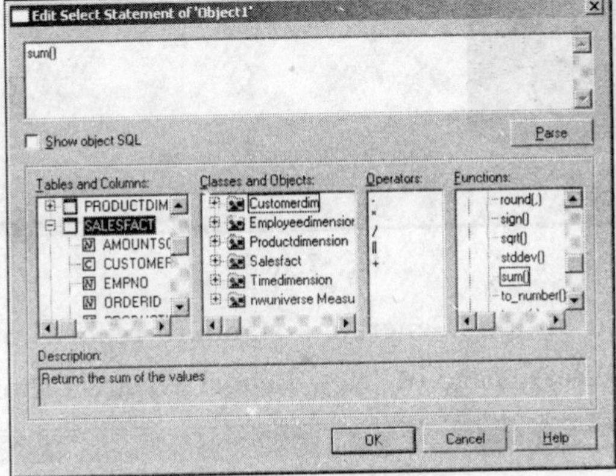

Fig. 7.44

16. Select the AMOUNTSOLD column and double click on it. (Fig. 7.45)

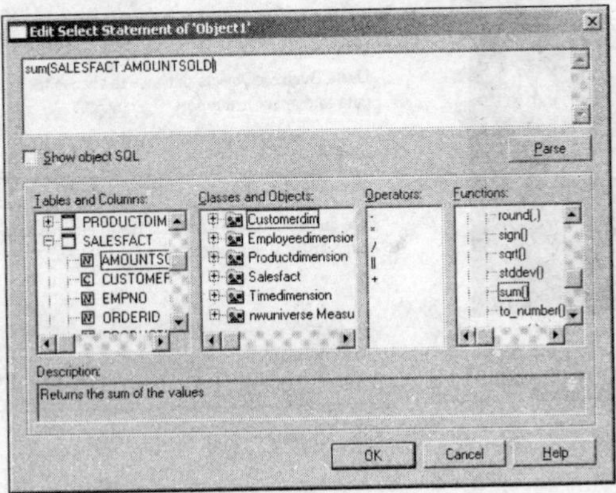

Fig. 7.45

17. Click on "Parse" to validate the statement and click on **"OK"**.
18. Click on "Apply" and on "OK" of "Edit Properties of Object1" window.
19. Select the menu item ***"File→Save"*** to save the Universe.
20. Select the menu item ***"Tools → Run → BusinessObjects"***.
21. "New Report Wizard" window, shown in Fig. 7.46, opens.

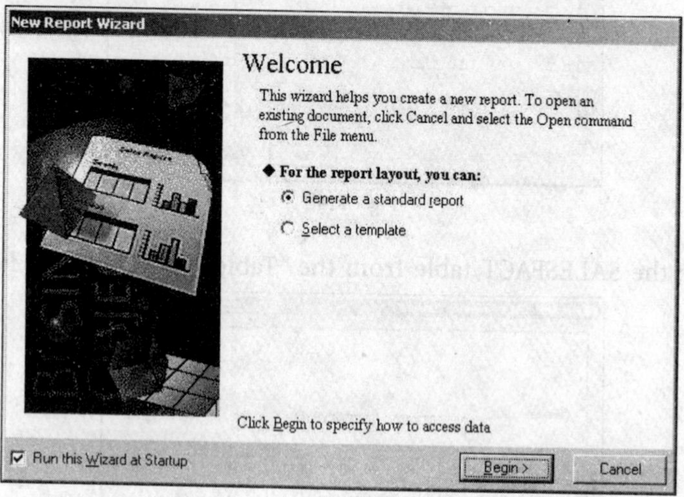

Fig. 7.46

22. Select the radio button "Generate a standard report" and click on **"Begin"**.
23. "Specify Data Access" page of "New Report Wizard", shown in Fig. 7.47, opens.

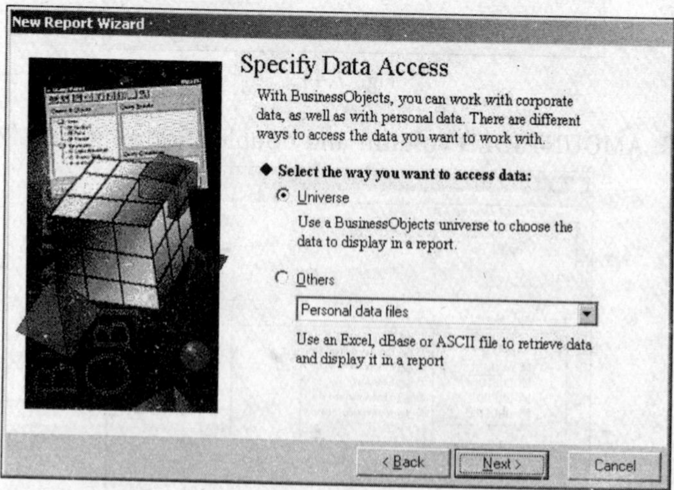

Fig. 7.47

24. Select "Universe" radio button and click on **"Next"**.

25. "Select a universe" screen of "New Report Wizard", shown in Fig. 7.48, opens.

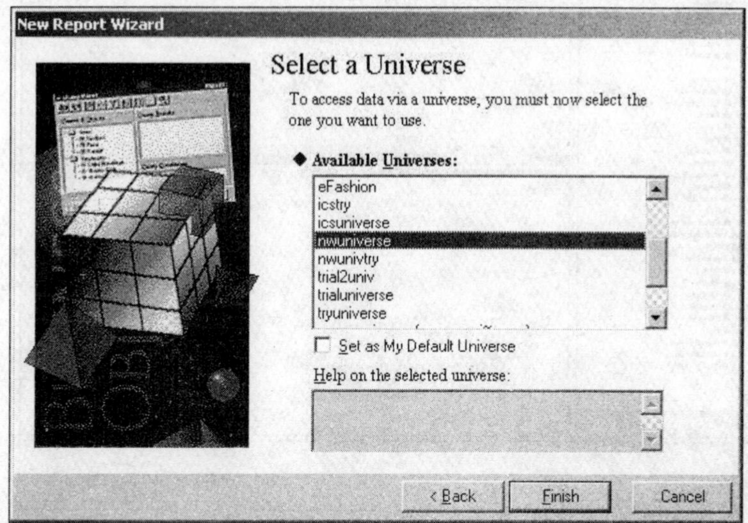

Fig. 7.48

26. Select "nwuniverse" from "Available Universes" list and click on **"Finish"**.
27. "Query Panel – nwuniverse Universe" window (Fig. 7.49) opens.

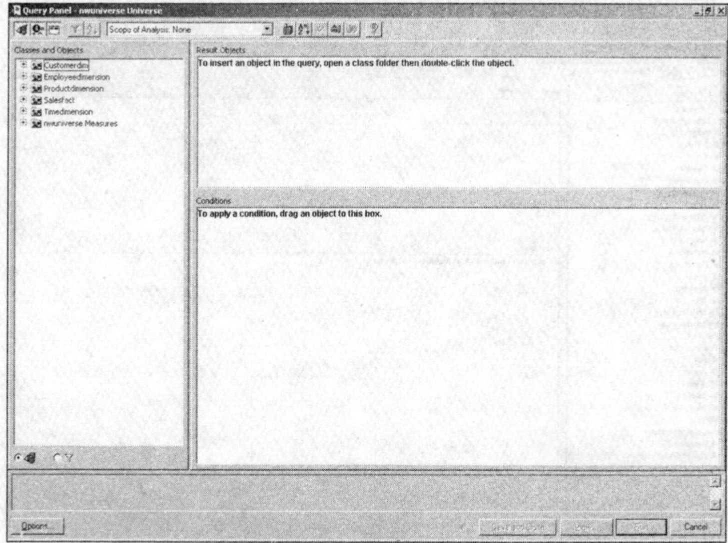

Fig. 7.49

28. Explore Employeedimension, Timedimension and Nwuniverse Measures from "Classes and Objects" list. (Fig. 7.50).

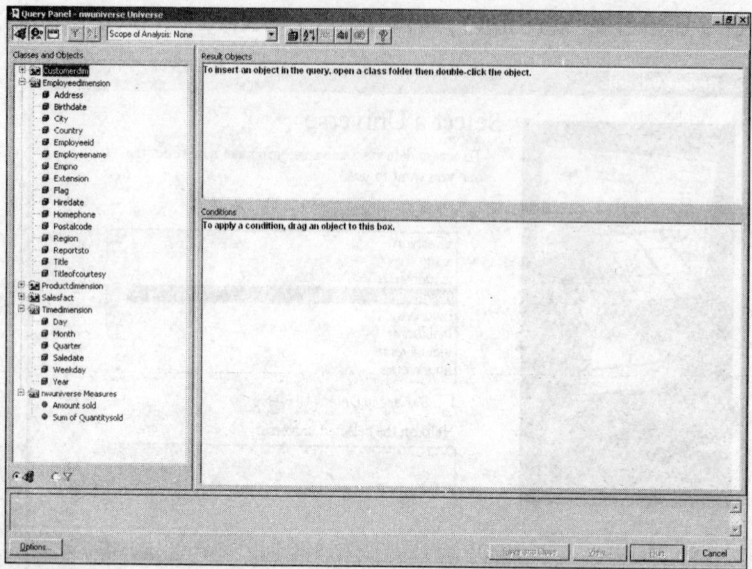

Fig. 7.50

29. Double click on Employeename from EMPLOYEEDIMENSION.
30. After double clicking, you can see that the selected object is added to Result objects pane, as shown in Fig. 7.51.

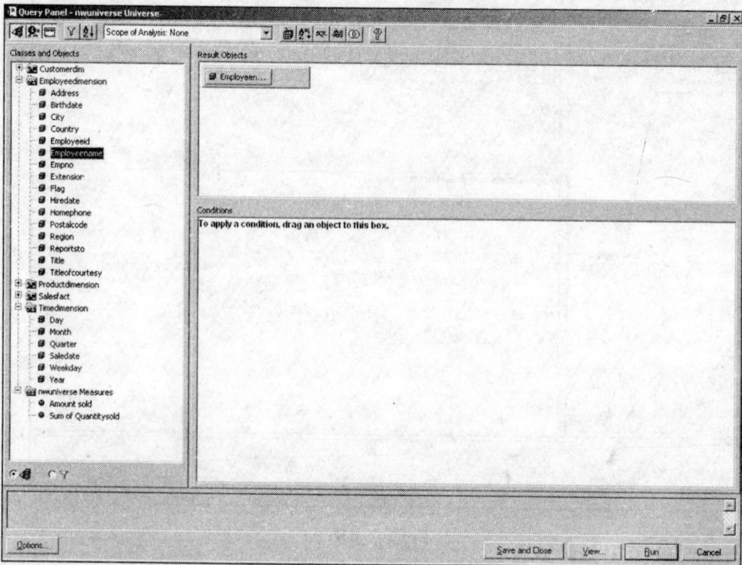

Fig. 7.51

31. Double click on "Year" from "Timedimension" as shown in Fig. 7.52.

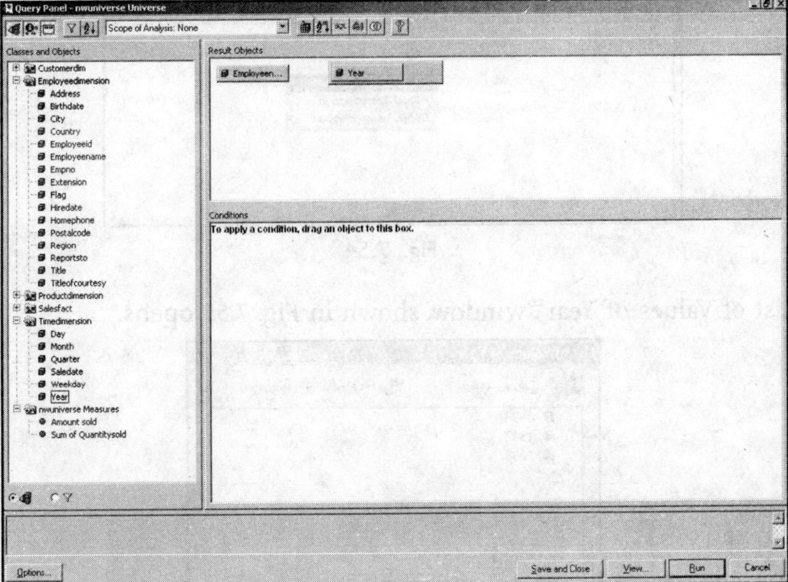

Fig. 7.52

32. Double click on "Sum of Quantity sold" and "Amount sold" objects. Now the window looks as shown in Fig. 7.53.

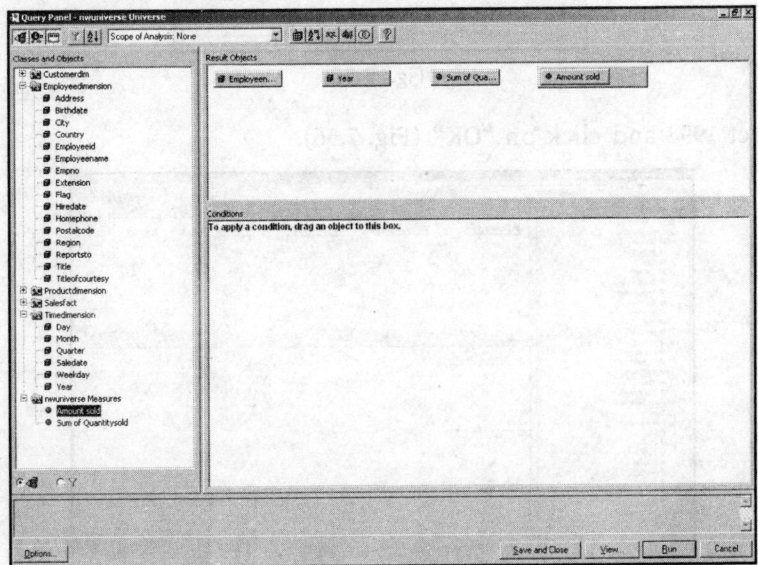

Fig. 7.53

33. Right click on "Year" of "Result Objects" and click on "Apply Simple Condition" from the pop up menu, as shown in Fig. 7.54.

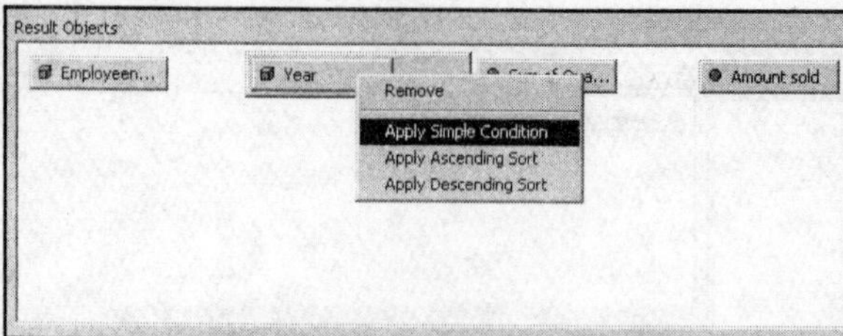

Fig. 7.54

34. "List of Values of Year" window, shown in Fig. 7.55 opens.

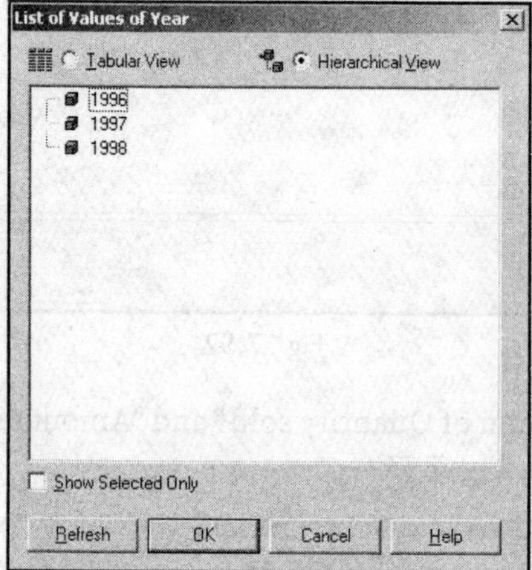

Fig. 7.55

35. Select 1998 and click on **"OK"** (Fig. 7.56).

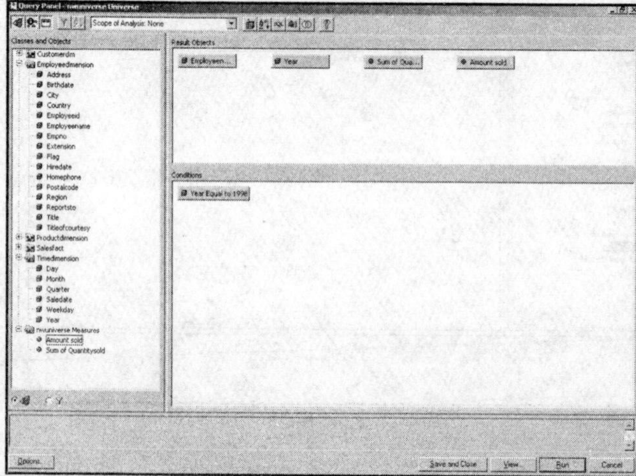

Fig. 7.56

36. Click on **"Run"** to generate the report.
37. "BusinessObjects – Document1" window, shown in Fig. 7.57, opens.

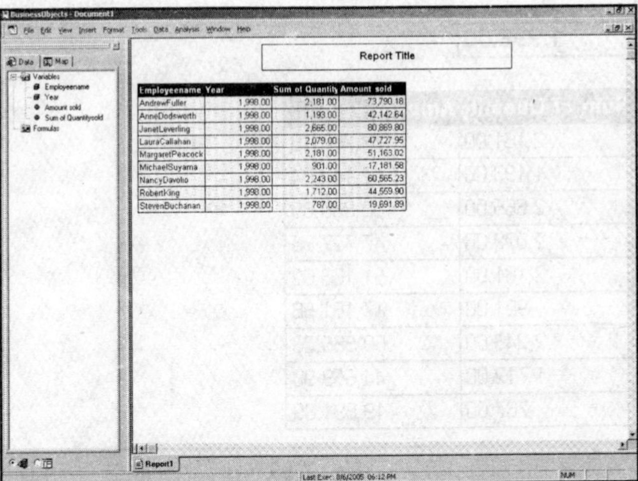

Employeename	Year	Sum of Quantity	Amount sold
AndrewFuller	1,998.00	2,181.00	73,790.18
AnneDodsworth	1,998.00	1,193.00	42,142.64
JanetLeverling	1,998.00	2,665.00	80,869.80
LauraCallahan	1,998.00	2,079.00	47,727.95
MargaretPeacock	1,998.00	2,181.00	51,163.02
MichaelSuyama	1,998.00	901.00	17,181.58
NancyDavolio	1,998.00	2,243.00	60,565.23
RobertKing	1,998.00	1,712.00	44,559.90
StevenBuchanan	1,998.00	787.00	19,691.89

Fig. 7.57

38. Drag the first entry of Year column to top of the report.
39. The report looks as shown in Fig. 7.58.

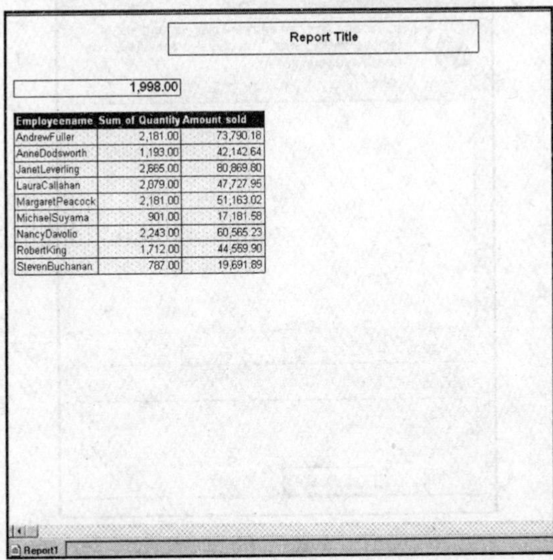

Employeename	Sum of Quantity	Amount sold
AndrewFuller	2,181.00	73,790.18
AnneDodsworth	1,193.00	42,142.64
JanetLeverling	2,665.00	80,869.80
LauraCallahan	2,079.00	47,727.95
MargaretPeacock	2,181.00	51,163.02
MichaelSuyama	901.00	17,181.58
NancyDavolio	2,243.00	60,565.23
RobertKing	1,712.00	44,559.90
StevenBuchanan	787.00	19,691.89

Fig. 7.58

40. To change the title of the report click on "Report Title" and enter the title as "Employee-wise Sales Report for 1998", as shown in Fig. 7.59.

EMPLOYEE WISE SALES REPORT FOR 1998

1,998.00

Employeename	Sum of Quantity	Amount sold
AndrewFuller	2,181.00	73,790.18
AnneDodsworth	1,193.00	42,142.64
JanetLeverling	2,665.00	80,869.80
LauraCallahan	2,079.00	47,727.95
MargaretPeacock	2,181.00	51,163.02
MichaelSuyama	901.00	17,181.58
NancyDavolio	2,243.00	60,565.23
RobertKing	1,712.00	44,559.90
StevenBuchanan	787.00	19,691.89

Fig. 7.59

41. Select all the columns by clicking on the column names holding the SHIFT key.
42. Select the menu item ***"Format → Alerters"***
43. "Alerters" window, shown in Fig. 7.60, opens.

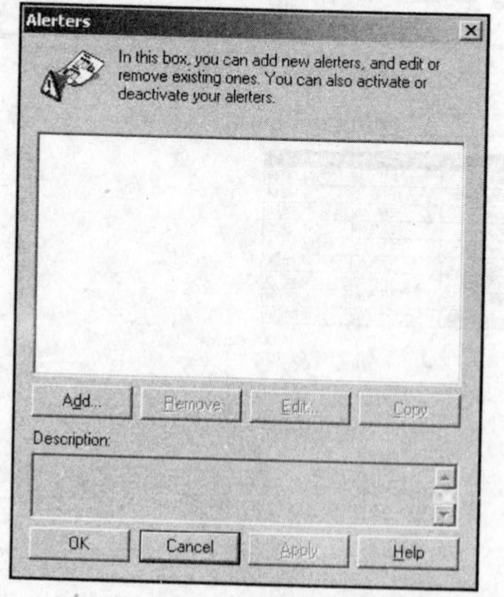

Fig. 7.60

44. Click on **"Add"** to add new Alerter.
45. "Edit Alerters" window, shown in Fig. 7.61, opens.

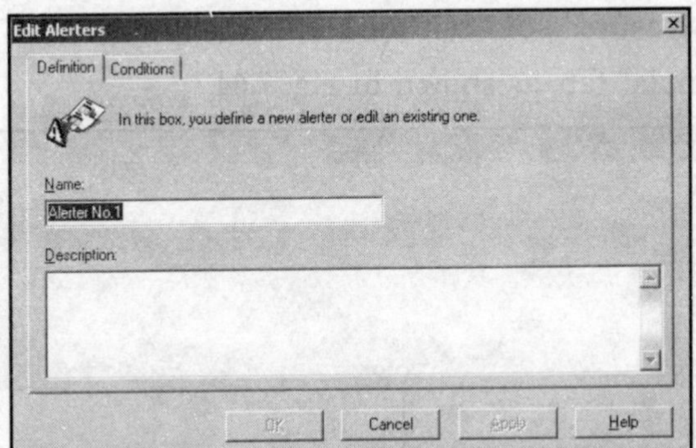

Fig. 7.61

46. In "Definition" tab, enter the Name as "MAXAMOUNTSOLD" and go to "Conditions" tab, as shown in Fig. 7.62.

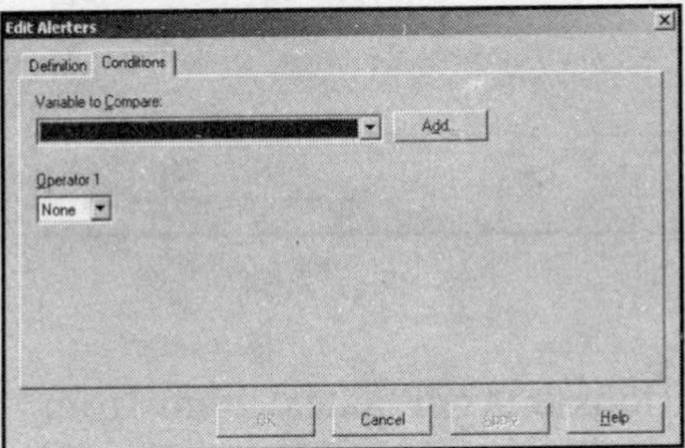

Fig. 7.62

47. Click on **"Add"** to add new condition.
48. "Variable Editor" window, shown in Fig. 7.63 opens.

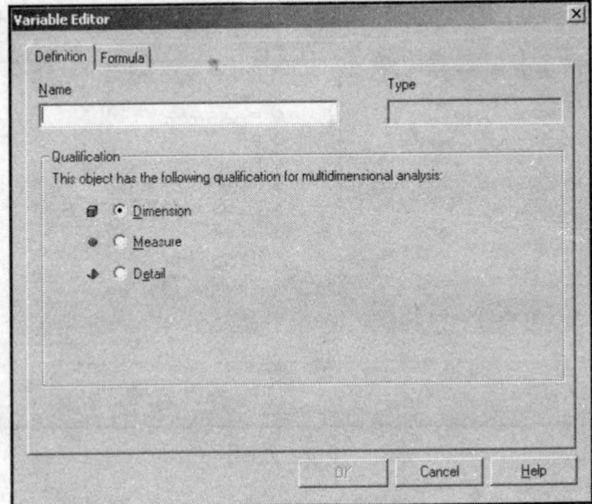

Fig. 7.63

49. Select the Measure radio button and enter the name as RNK_AMOUNT_SOLD.
50. Go to "Formula" tab, as shown in Fig. 7.64.

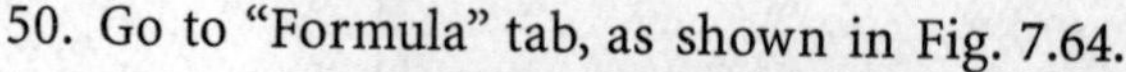

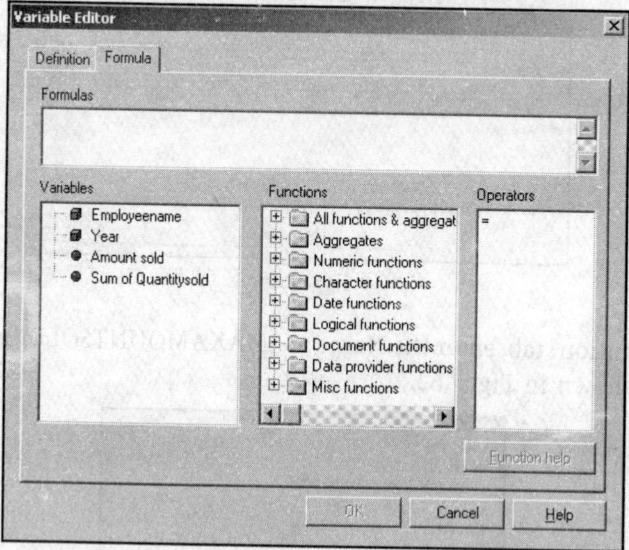

Fig. 7.64

51. Explore "All functions & Aggregates" item from the "Functions" list and double click on "Rank", as shown in Fig. 7.65.

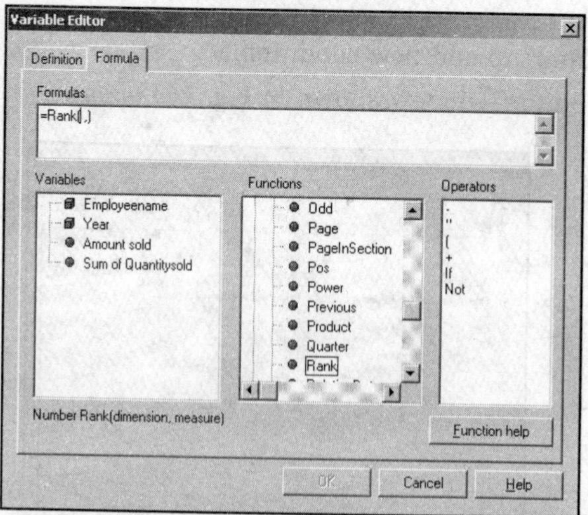

Fig. 7.65

52. Double click on "Employeename" item and on "Amount sold" item of "Variables" list. Then, the screen looks like as shown in Fig. 7.66.

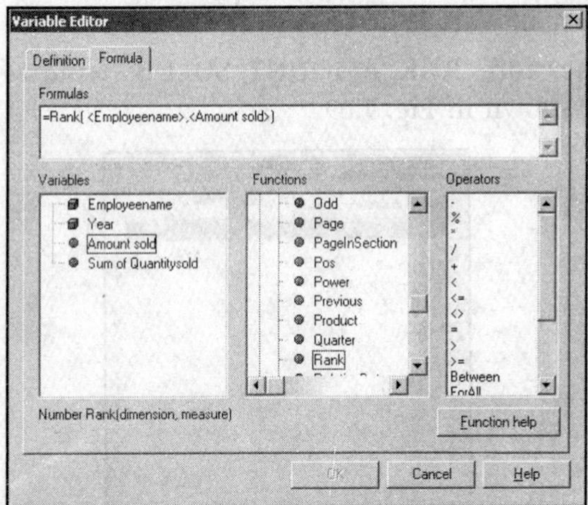

Fig. 7.66

53. Click on **"OK"**.
54. "Edit Alerters" window will be as shown in Fig. 7.67.

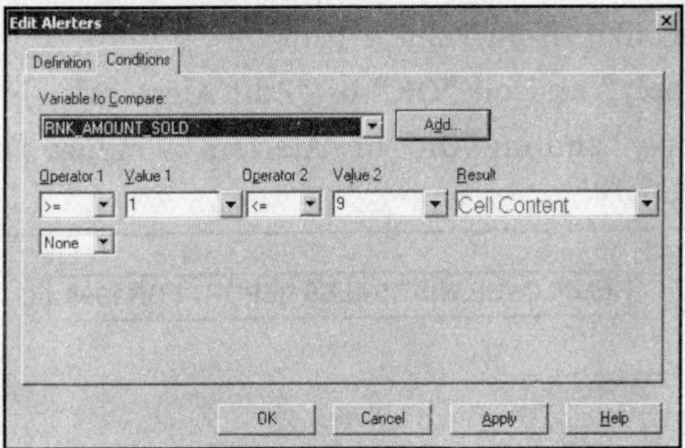

Fig. 7.67

55. Select **"="** as Operator 1 symbol and click on Value 1 then the small popup menu will pop, as shown in Fig. 7.68.

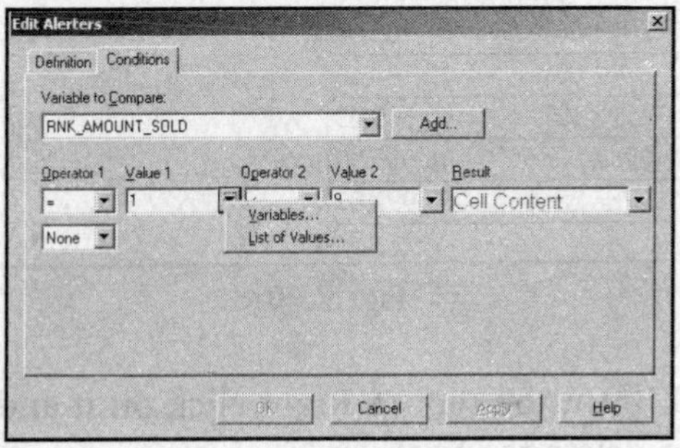

Fig. 7.68

56. Click on **"List of Values"**.
57. "List of Values for <RNK_AMOUNT_SOLD>" window opens. On that window, select "1", as shown in Fig. 7.69.

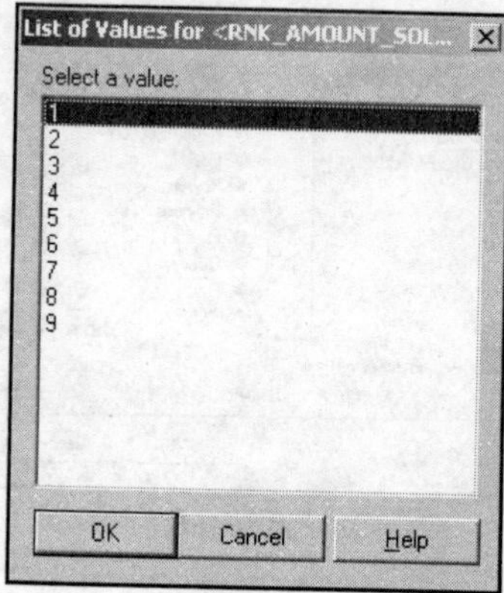

Fig. 7.69

58. Click on **"OK"**.
59. Select **"None"** item from Value 2 list.
60. Click on **"Apply"** and on **"OK"** of **"Edit Alerters"** window.
61. Click on "Apply" and on **"OK"** of **"Alerters"** window. Then the report will be as shown in Fig. 7.70.

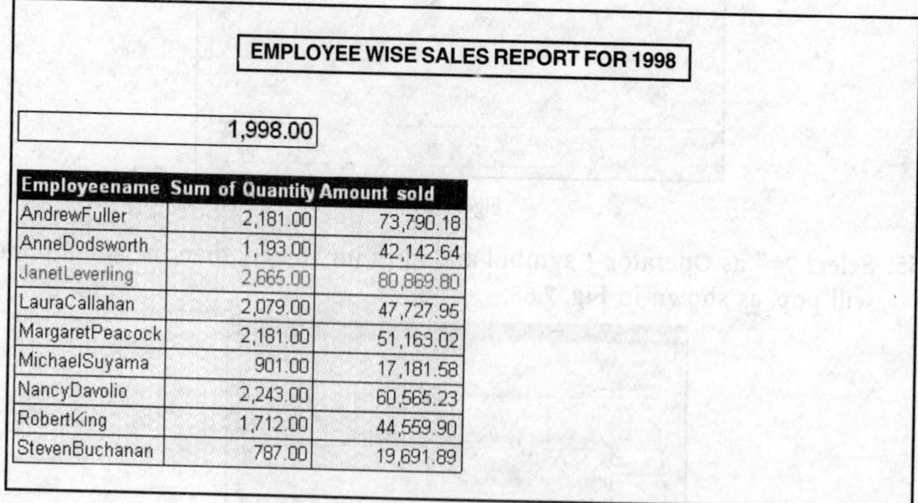

EMPLOYEE WISE SALES REPORT FOR 1998

1,998.00

Employeename	Sum of Quantity	Amount sold
AndrewFuller	2,181.00	73,790.18
AnneDodsworth	1,193.00	42,142.64
JanetLeverling	2,665.00	80,869.80
LauraCallahan	2,079.00	47,727.95
MargaretPeacock	2,181.00	51,163.02
MichaelSuyama	901.00	17,181.58
NancyDavolio	2,243.00	60,565.23
RobertKing	1,712.00	44,559.90
StevenBuchanan	787.00	19,691.89

Fig. 7.70

62. Select the "1998" from the report. Right click on it and click on **"Delete"** from the pop up menu to delete the year.

63. A message box will be displayed with the message, "Do you want to delete the section?" Click on **"OK"**.
64. Now, the final report looks like as shown in Fig. 7.71.

EMPLOYEE WISE SALES REPORT FOR 1998

Employeename	Sum of Quantity	Amount sold
AndrewFuller	2,181.00	73,790.18
AnneDodsworth	1,193.00	42,142.64
JanetLeverling	2,665.00	80,869.80
LauraCallahan	2,079.00	47,727.95
MargaretPeacock	2,181.00	51,163.02
MichaelSuyama	901.00	17,181.58
NancyDavolio	2,243.00	60,565.23
RobertKing	1,712.00	44,559.90
StevenBuchanan	787.00	19,691.89

Best Sales Representative for the year 1998

Fig. 7.71

65. Select the menu item **"*File→Save*"** to save the report.
66. "Save As" window opens.
67. Enter the "File Name" as MAXAMOUNTSOLD, and click on **"Save"**.

7.5 Case Study #3

In this case study, we will generate a report that shows the bar chart of quarterly sales of each category. The final report will be as shown in Fig. 7.72.

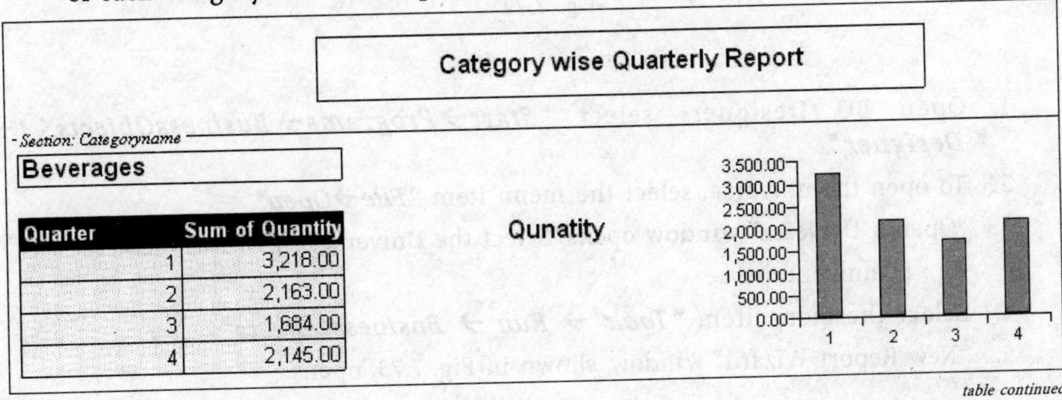

Category wise Quarterly Report

- Section: Categoryname

Beverages

Quarter	Sum of Quantity
1	3,218.00
2	2,163.00
3	1,684.00
4	2,145.00

table continued

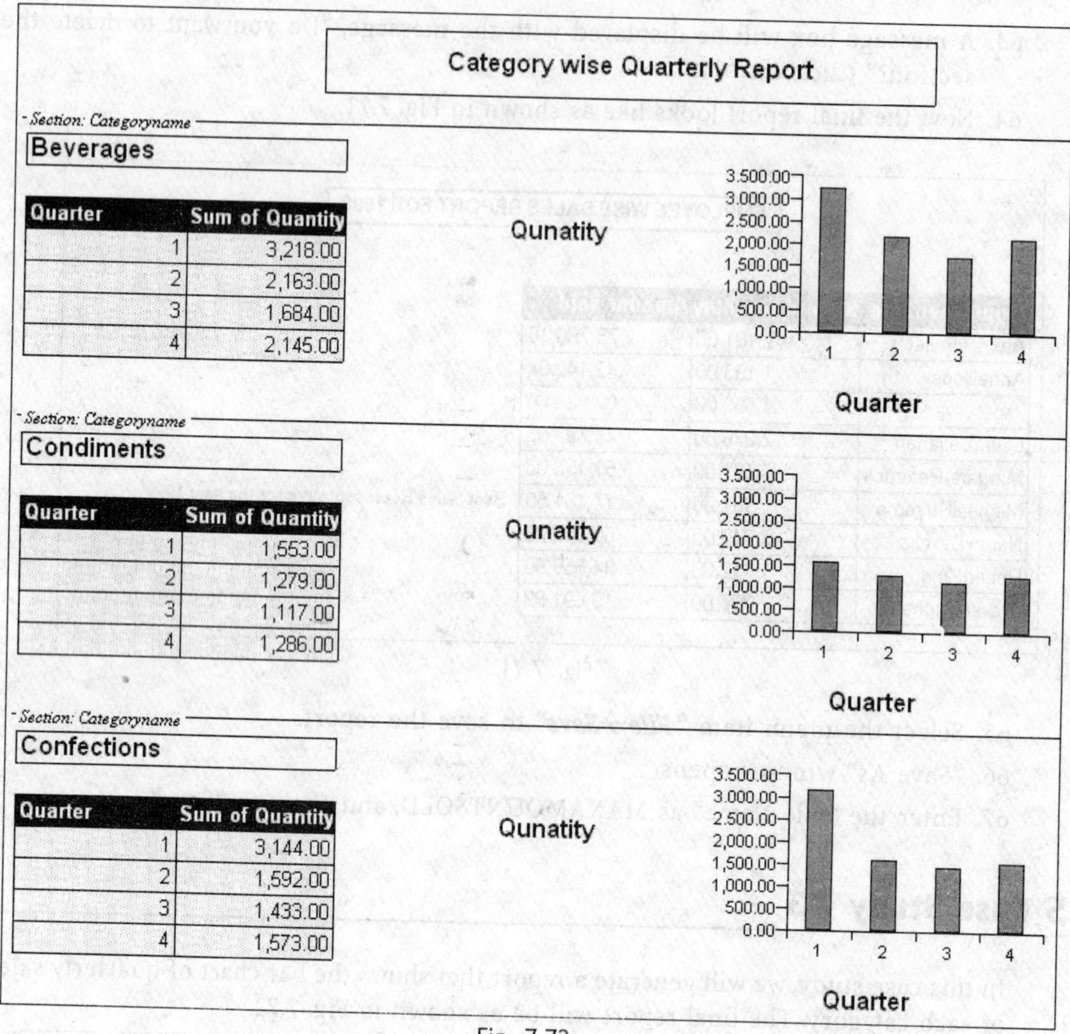

Category wise Quarterly Report

Section: Categoryname

Beverages

Quarter	Sum of Quantity
1	3,218.00
2	2,163.00
3	1,684.00
4	2,145.00

Section: Categoryname

Condiments

Quarter	Sum of Quantity
1	1,553.00
2	1,279.00
3	1,117.00
4	1,286.00

Section: Categoryname

Confections

Quarter	Sum of Quantity
1	3,144.00
2	1,592.00
3	1,433.00
4	1,573.00

Fig. 7.72

1. Open BO Designer: select ***"Start→ Programs→ BusinessObjects5.1→ Designer".***
2. To open the universe, select the menu item ***"File→Open"***.
3. "Open a Universe" window opens. Select the Universe which was created. e.g.: nwuniver.unv.
4. Select the menu item ***"Tools → Run → BusinessObjects".***
5. "New Report Wizard" window, shown in Fig. 7.73, opens.

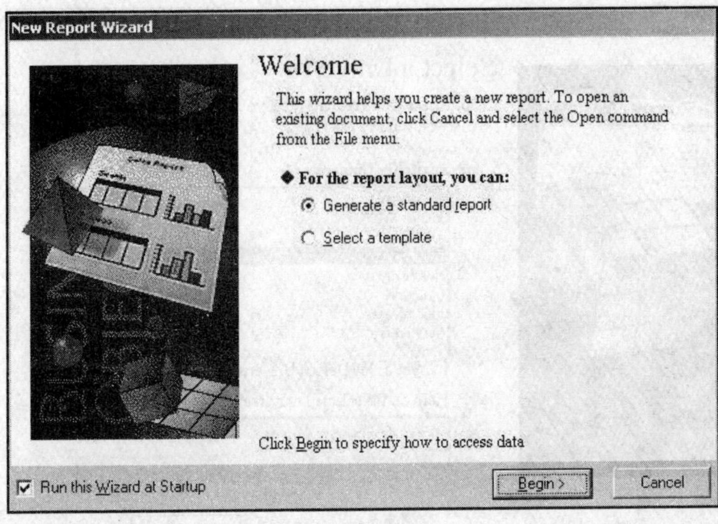

Fig. 7.73

6. Select the radio button "Generate a standard report" and click on **"Begin"**.
7. "Specify Data Access" page of **"New Report Wizard"**, shown in Fig. 7.74, opens.

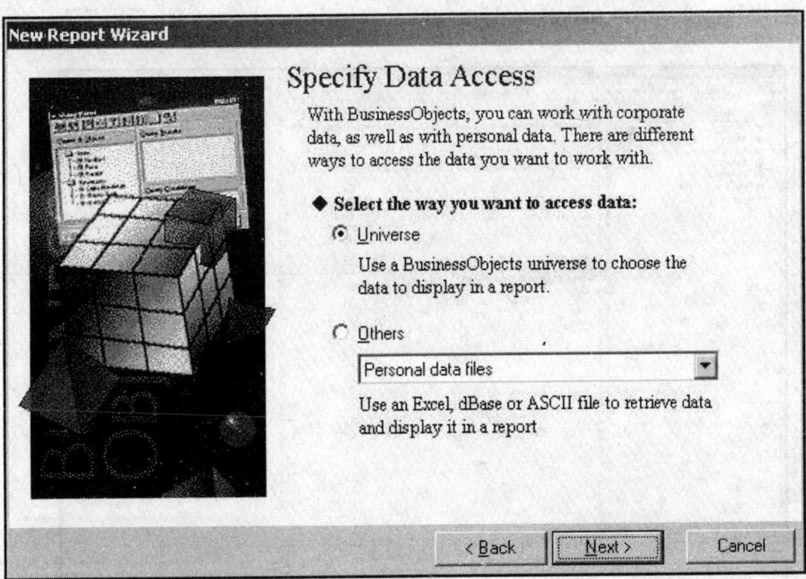

Fig. 7.74

8. Select "Universe" radio button and click on **"Next"**.
9. "Select a universe" screen of "New Report Wizard", shown in Fig. 7.75, opens.

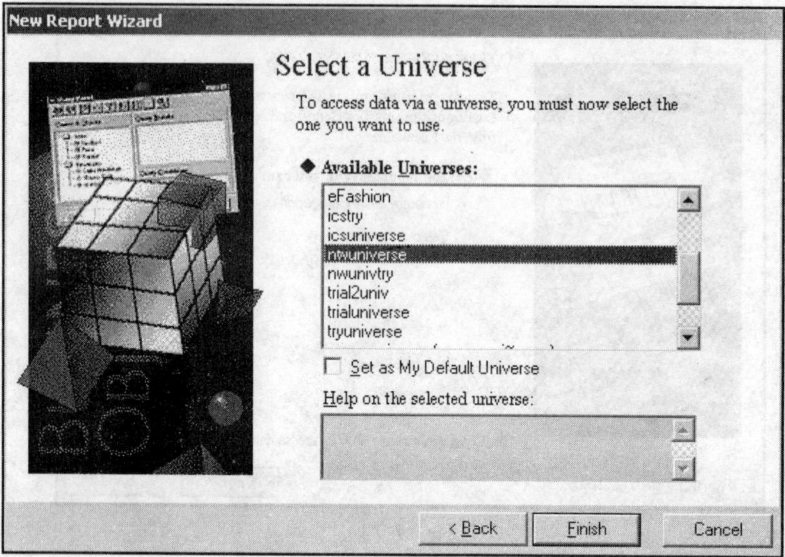

Fig. 7.75

10. Select "nwuniverse" from "Available Universes" list and click on **"Finish"**.
11. "Query Panel – nwuniverse Universe" window, shown in Fig. 7.76, opens.

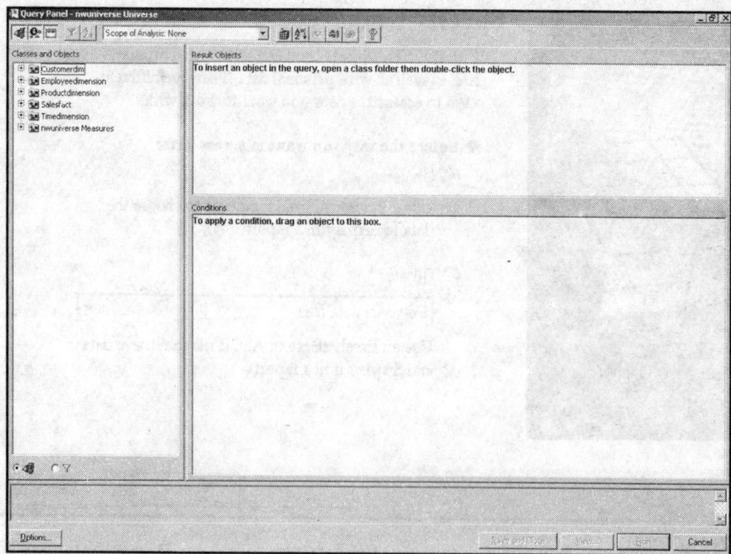

Fig. 7.76

12. Explore Productdimension, Timedimension and Nwuniverse Measures from "Classes and Objects" list (Fig. 7.77).

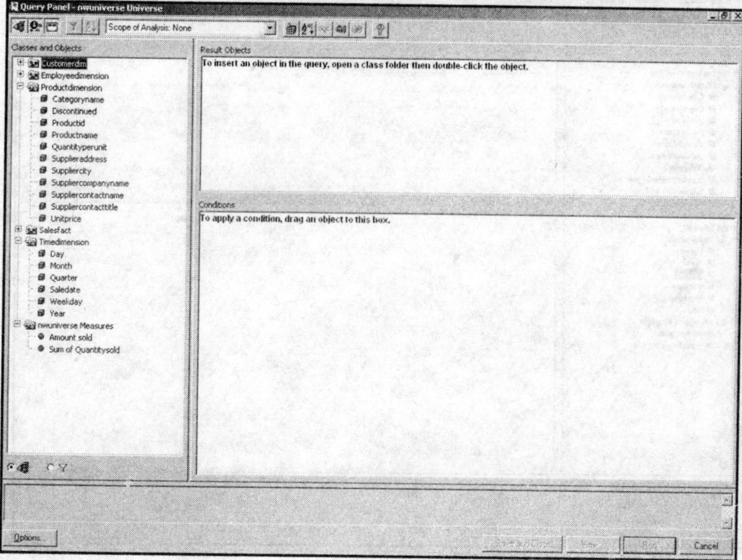

Fig. 7.77

13. Double click on "Categoryname" from "Productdimension."
14. After double clicking, you can see the selected objects are added to Result objects pane, as shown in Fig. 7.78.

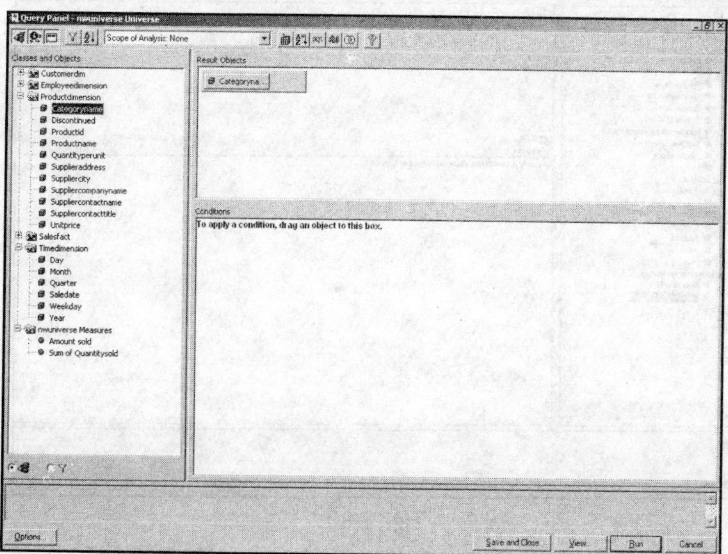

Fig. 7.78

15. Double click on "Quarter" from Timedimension, as shown in Fig. 7.79.

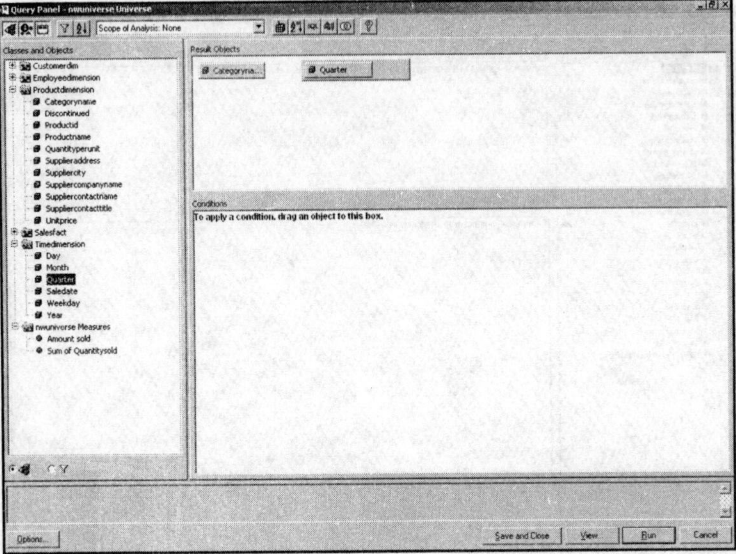

Fig. 7.79

16. Double click on "Sum of Quantity sold" object. Now the window looks as shown in Fig. 7.80.

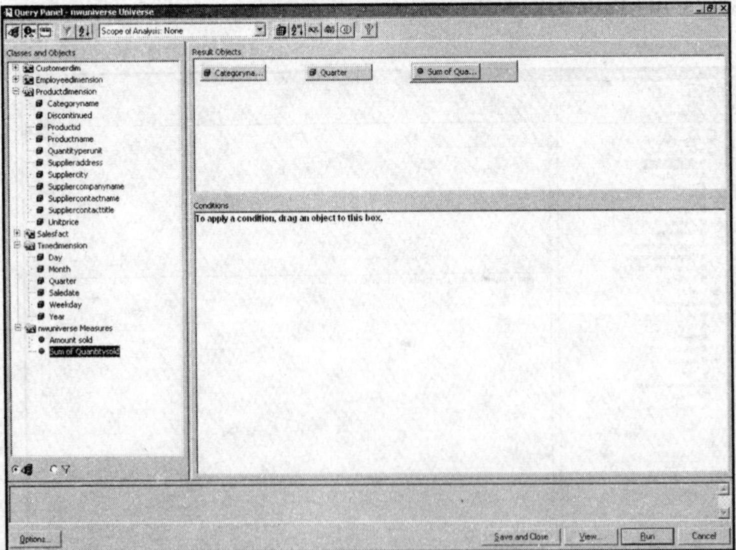

Fig. 7.80

17. Click on **"Run"** to generate the report.
18. "BusinessObjects – Document1" window, as shown in Fig. 7.81, opens.

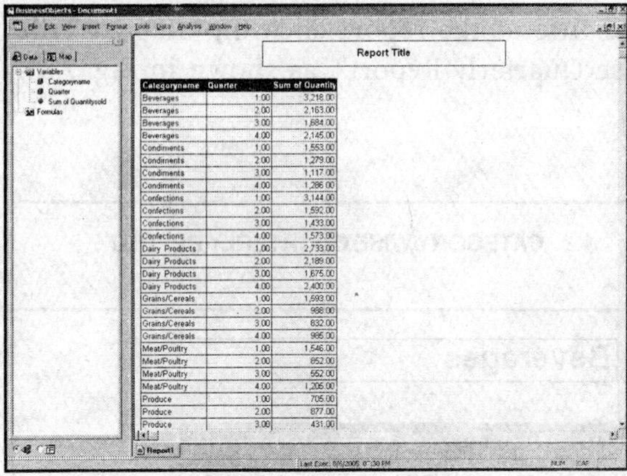

Categoryname	Quarter	Sum of Quantity
Beverages	1.00	3,218.00
Beverages	2.00	2,163.00
Beverages	3.00	1,684.00
Beverages	4.00	2,145.00
Condiments	1.00	1,553.00
Condiments	2.00	1,279.00
Condiments	3.00	1,117.00
Condiments	4.00	1,286.00
Confections	1.00	3,144.00
Confections	2.00	1,592.00
Confections	3.00	1,433.00
Confections	4.00	1,573.00
Dairy Products	1.00	2,733.00
Dairy Products	2.00	2,189.00
Dairy Products	3.00	1,675.00
Dairy Products	4.00	2,400.00
Grains/Cereals	1.00	1,593.00
Grains/Cereals	2.00	968.00
Grains/Cereals	3.00	832.00
Grains/Cereals	4.00	985.00
Meat/Poultry	1.00	1,546.00
Meat/Poultry	2.00	852.00
Meat/Poultry	3.00	552.00
Meat/Poultry	4.00	1,205.00
Produce	1.00	705.00
Produce	2.00	877.00
Produce	3.00	431.00

Fig. 7.81

19. Drag the first entry of Categoryname column to top of the report and then the report looks as shown in Fig. 7.82.

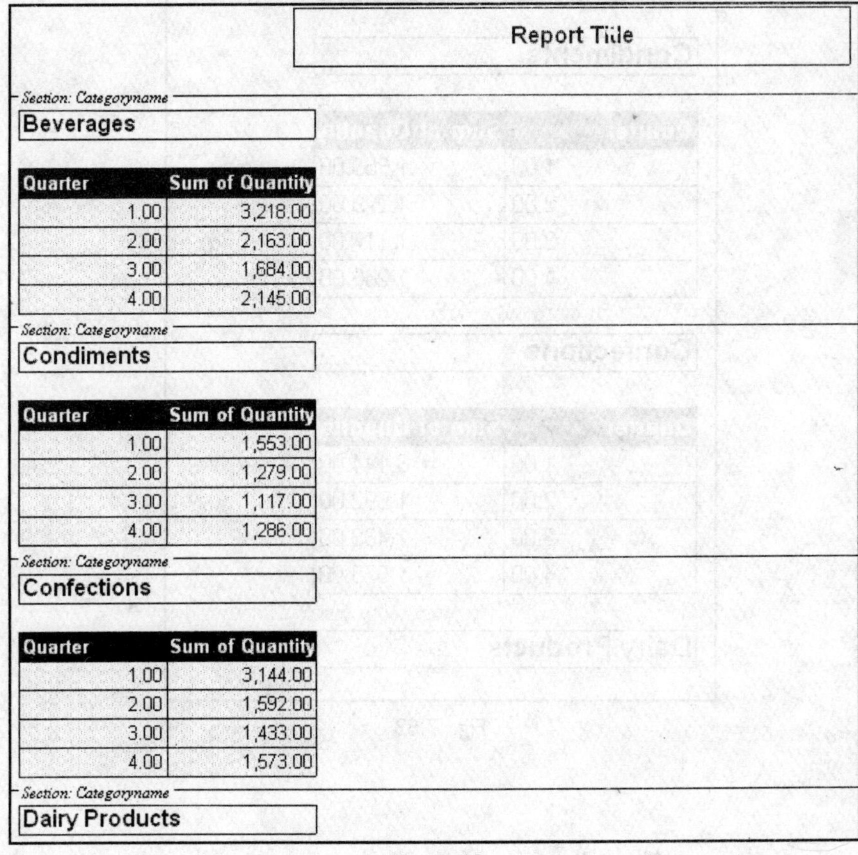

Report Title

Section: Categoryname

Beverages

Quarter	Sum of Quantity
1.00	3,218.00
2.00	2,163.00
3.00	1,684.00
4.00	2,145.00

Section: Categoryname

Condiments

Quarter	Sum of Quantity
1.00	1,553.00
2.00	1,279.00
3.00	1,117.00
4.00	1,286.00

Section: Categoryname

Confections

Quarter	Sum of Quantity
1.00	3,144.00
2.00	1,592.00
3.00	1,433.00
4.00	1,573.00

Section: Categoryname

Dairy Products

Fig. 7.82

20. To change the title of the report click on **"Report Title"** and enter the title as "Category-wise Quarterly Report", as shown in Fig. 7.83.

CATEGORY WISE QUARTERLY REPORT

Beverages

Quarter	Sum of Quantity
1.00	3,218.00
2.00	2,163.00
3.00	1,684.00
4.00	2,145.00

Condiments

Quarter	Sum of Quantity
1.00	1,553.00
2.00	1,279.00
3.00	1,117.00
4.00	1,286.00

Confections

Quarter	Sum of Quantity
1.00	3,144.00
2.00	1,592.00
3.00	1,433.00
4.00	1,573.00

Dairy Products

Fig. 7.83

21. Select all the quarter elements by clicking on the column name, as shown in Fig. 7.84.

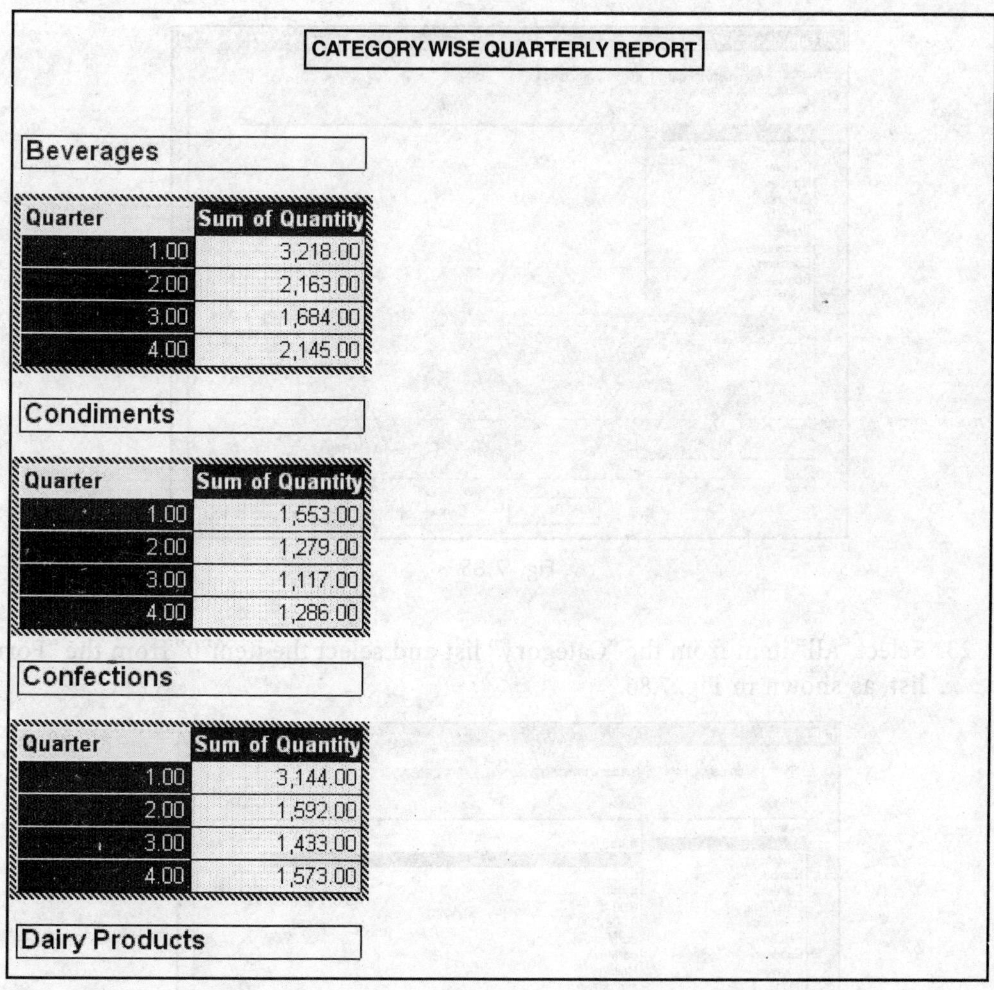

CATEGORY WISE QUARTERLY REPORT

Beverages

Quarter	Sum of Quantity
1.00	3,218.00
2.00	2,163.00
3.00	1,684.00
4.00	2,145.00

Condiments

Quarter	Sum of Quantity
1.00	1,553.00
2.00	1,279.00
3.00	1,117.00
4.00	1,286.00

Confections

Quarter	Sum of Quantity
1.00	3,144.00
2.00	1,592.00
3.00	1,433.00
4.00	1,573.00

Dairy Products

Fig. 7.84

22. Right click on the any of the entries of the Quarter column and select the "Format Cell" of the pop up menu then the "Cell Format" window (Fig. 7.85) opens.

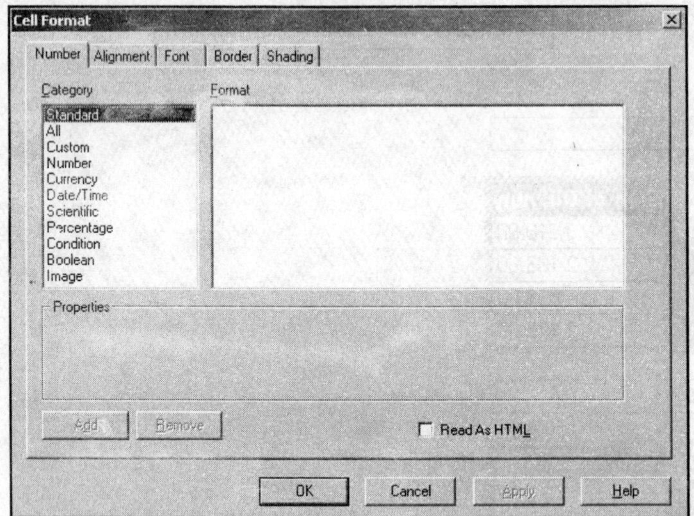

Fig. 7.85

23. Select "All" item from the "Category" list and select the item"0" from the "Format" list, as shown in Fig. 7.86.

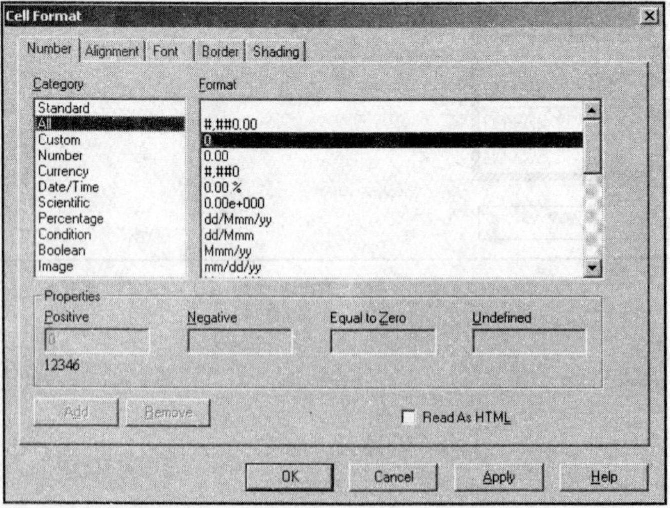

Fig. 7.86

24. Click on **"Apply"** and click on **"OK"** of the "Cell Format" window, and then the report will be as shown in Fig. 7.87.

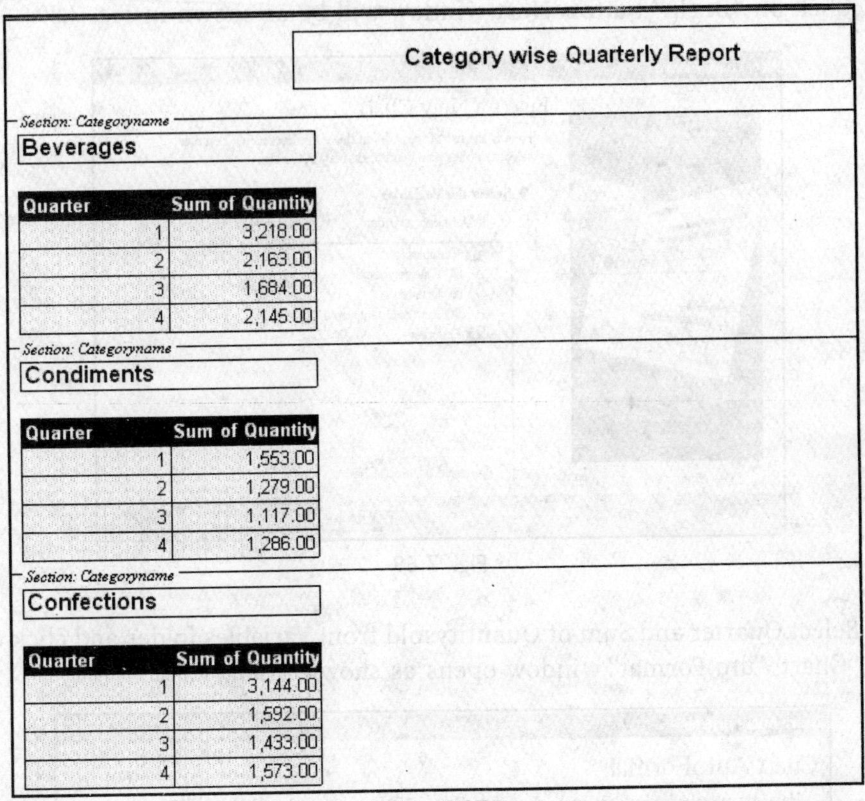

Category wise Quarterly Report

Section: Categoryname

Beverages

Quarter	Sum of Quantity
1	3,218.00
2	2,163.00
3	1,684.00
4	2,145.00

Section: Categoryname

Condiments

Quarter	Sum of Quantity
1	1,553.00
2	1,279.00
3	1,117.00
4	1,286.00

Section: Categoryname

Confections

Quarter	Sum of Quantity
1	3,144.00
2	1,592.00
3	1,433.00
4	1,573.00

Fig. 7.87

25. Select the menu item "***Insert→Chart***" to insert a chart. Now a cursor with bar chart icon will be displayed, click on the report where you want to place the chart. "New Chart" wizard with "Insert a new chart" (Fig. 7.88) will be displayed.

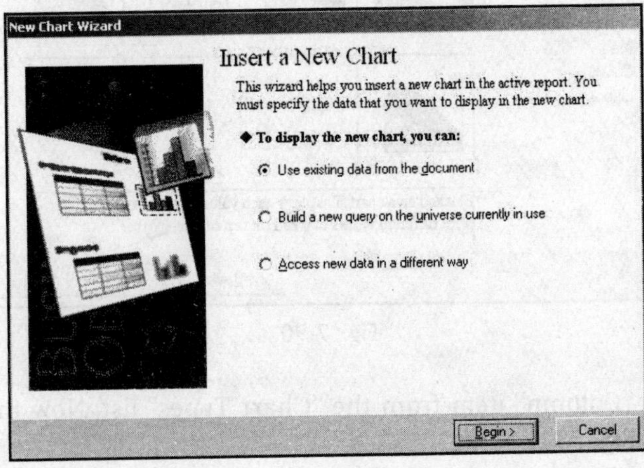

Fig. 7.88

26. Click on **"Begin"** button. Next window will be as shown in Fig. 7.89.

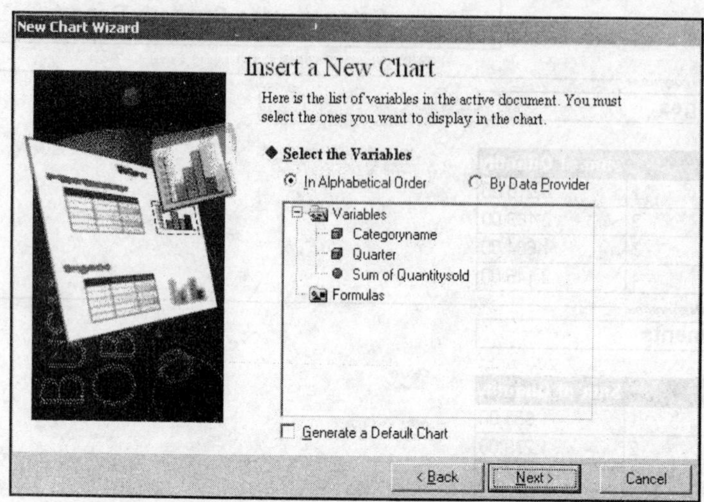

Fig. 7.89

27. Select Quarter and Sum of Quantitysold from Variables folder and click on **"Next"**. "Chart Auto Format" window opens as shown in Fig. 7.90.

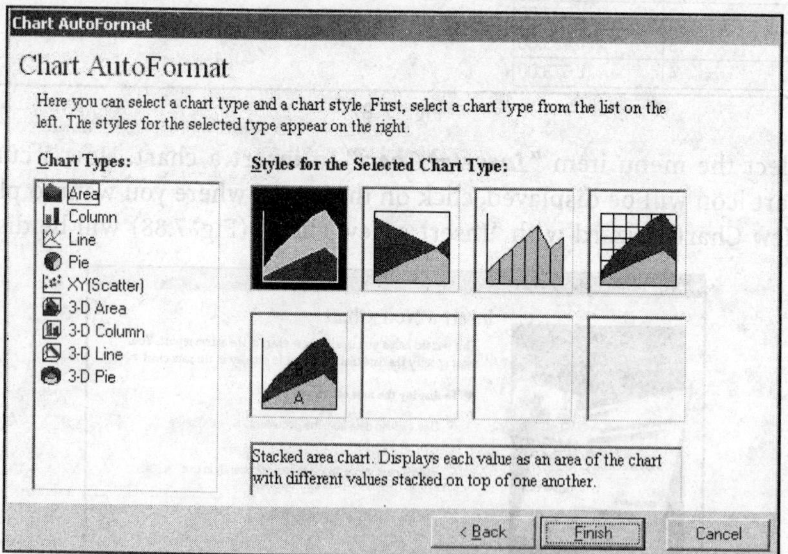

Fig. 7.90

28. Select the "Column" item from the "Chart Types" list. Now the screen appears as shown in Fig. 7.91.

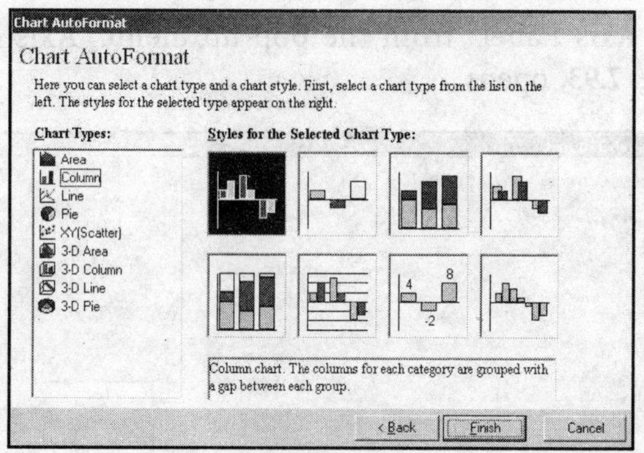

Fig. 7.91

29. Select the first style from the "Styles for the Selected Chart Type" and click on **"Finish"**, then the report will be as shown in Fig. 7.92.

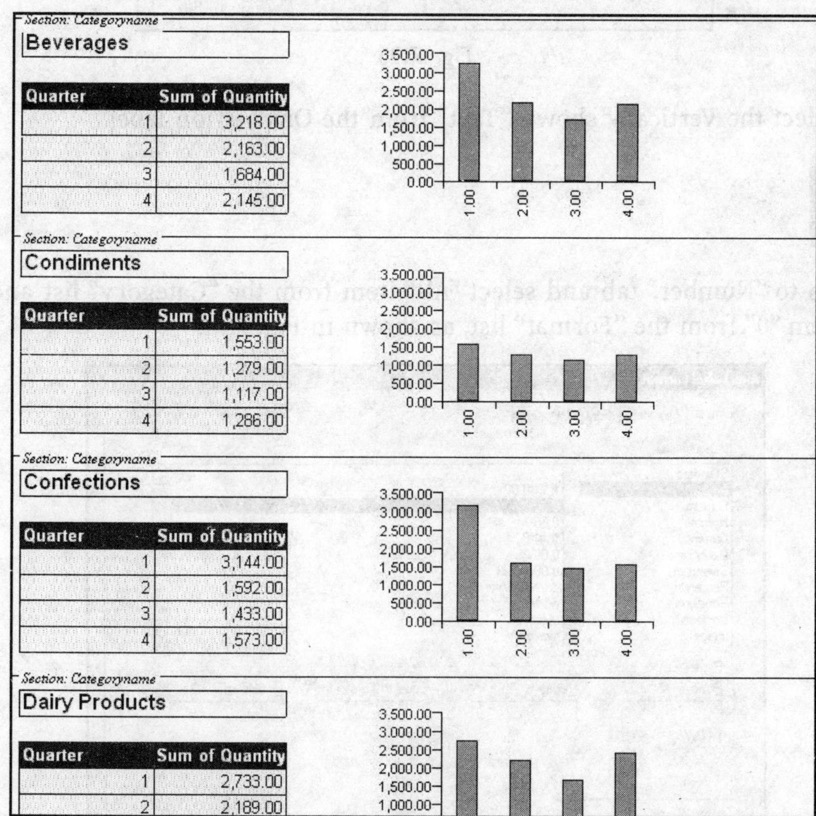

Section: Categoryname

Beverages

Quarter	Sum of Quantity
1	3,218.00
2	2,163.00
3	1,684.00
4	2,145.00

Section: Categoryname

Condiments

Quarter	Sum of Quantity
1	1,553.00
2	1,279.00
3	1,117.00
4	1,286.00

Section: Categoryname

Confections

Quarter	Sum of Quantity
1	3,144.00
2	1,592.00
3	1,433.00
4	1,573.00

Section: Categoryname

Dairy Products

Quarter	Sum of Quantity
1	2,733.00
2	2,189.00

Fig. 7.92

30. You can resize the chart.

31. Select the horizontally shown numbers and right click on the selected item, select

the "Format Axis Label" from the pop up menu. "Axis Label Format" window, shown in Fig. 7.93, opens.

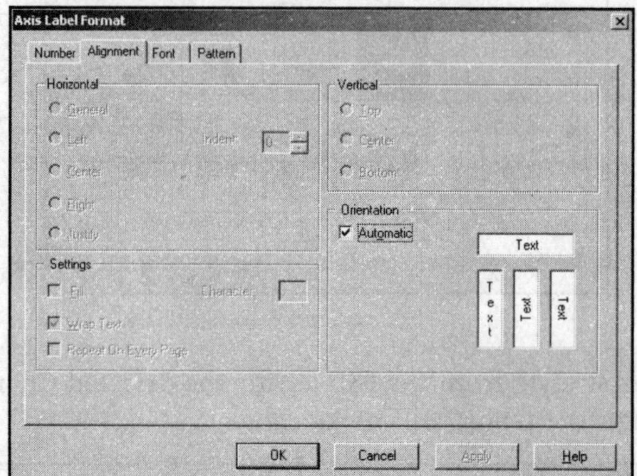

Fig. 7.93

32. Select the Vertically shown "Text" from the Orientation label.

33. Go to "Number" tab and select "All" item from the "Category" list and select the item "0" from the "Format" list, as shown in Fig. 7.94.

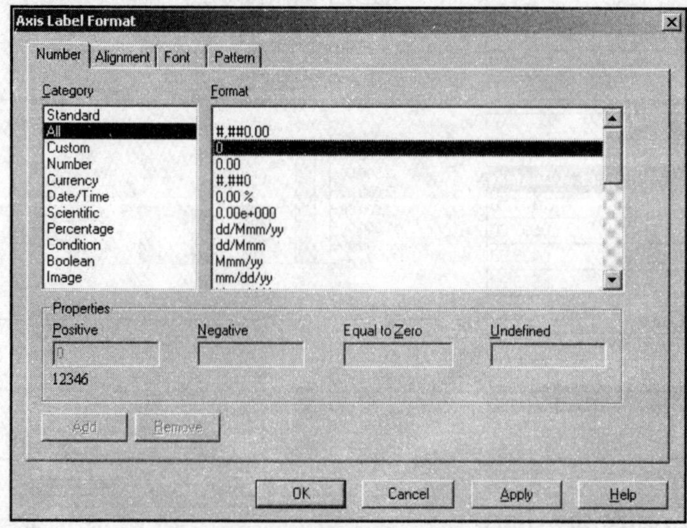

Fig. 7.94

34. Click on **"Apply"** and on **"OK"**. Now the report will be as shown in Fig. 7.95.

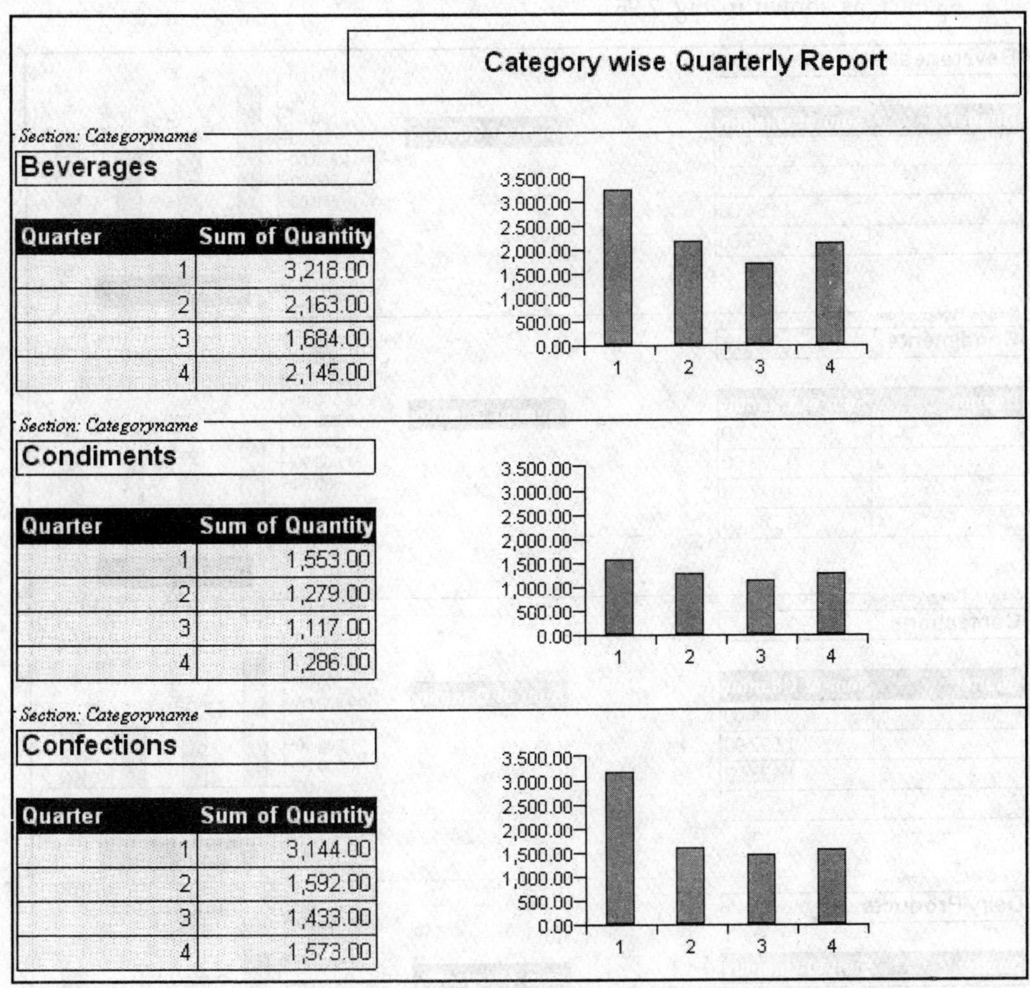

Category wise Quarterly Report

Section: Categoryname

Beverages

Quarter	Sum of Quantity
1	3,218.00
2	2,163.00
3	1,684.00
4	2,145.00

Section: Categoryname

Condiments

Quarter	Sum of Quantity
1	1,553.00
2	1,279.00
3	1,117.00
4	1,286.00

Section: Categoryname

Confections

Quarter	Sum of Quantity
1	3,144.00
2	1,592.00
3	1,433.00
4	1,573.00

Fig. 7.95

35. To add titles for X and Y axis of the report, copy the column names "Quarter" and "Sum of Quantity sold" and paste the column names in the required place in the chart, as shown in Fig. 7.96.

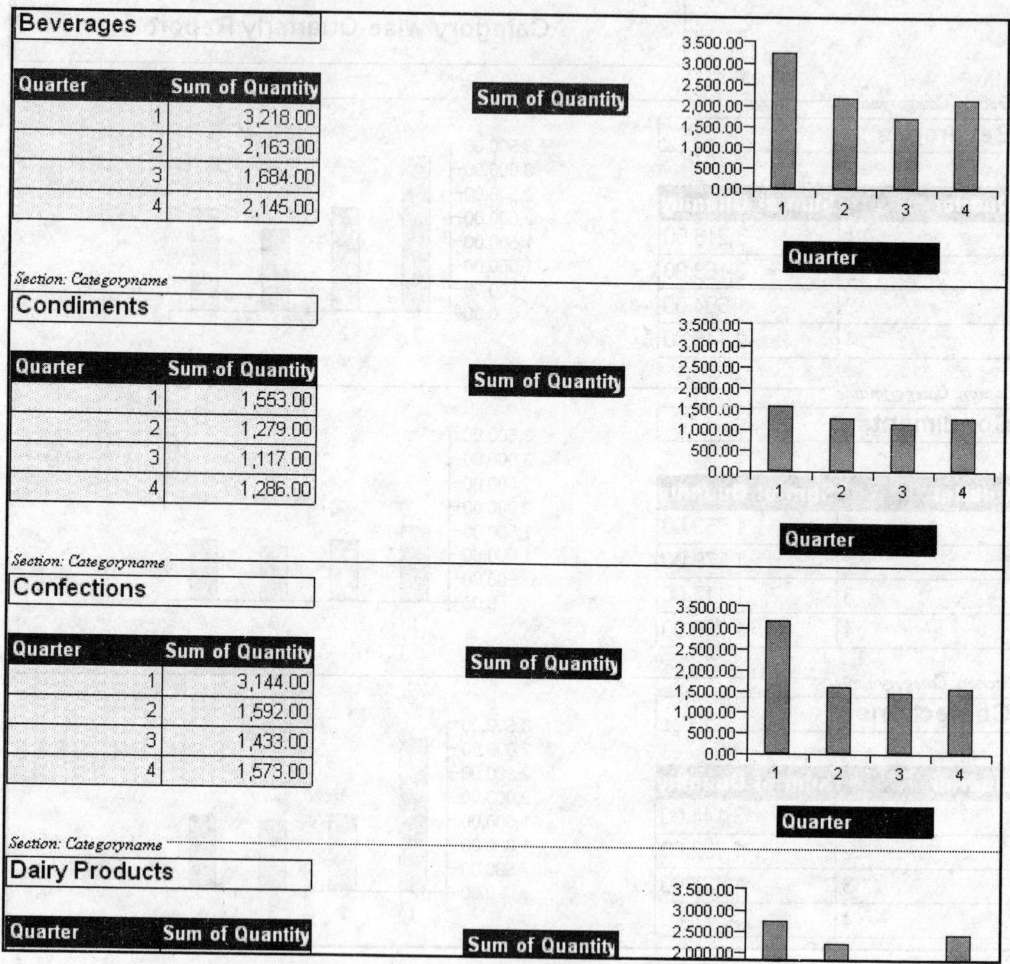

Fig. 7.96

36. Right click on the Quarter text and select the "Apply Standard style" from the pop up menu.
37. Right click on the Quartet text and select the "Format Cell" from the pop up menu. "Cell Format" window opens as shown in Fig. 7.97.

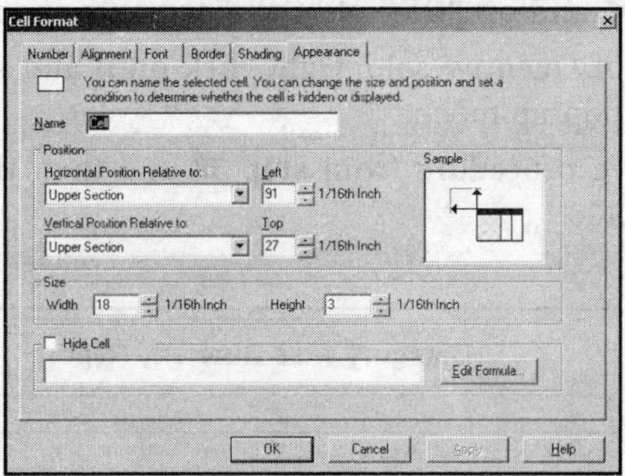

Fig. 7.97

38. Go to "Border" tab and select "None" from the "Presets" label, as shown in Fig. 7.98.

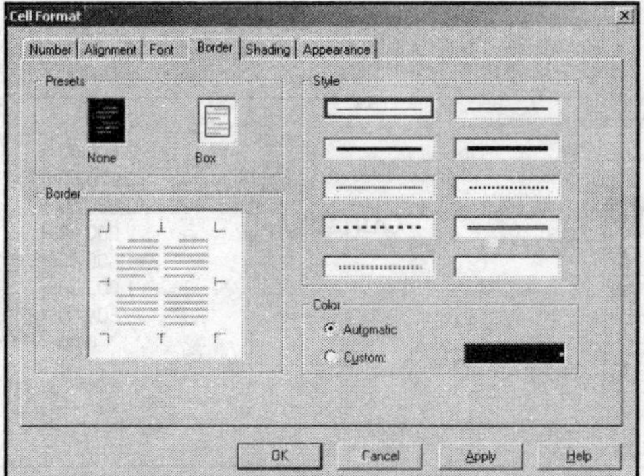

Fig. 7.98

39. Go to "Shading" tab and select Fore Ground Color as Black and Back Ground color as white, as shown in Fig. 7.99.

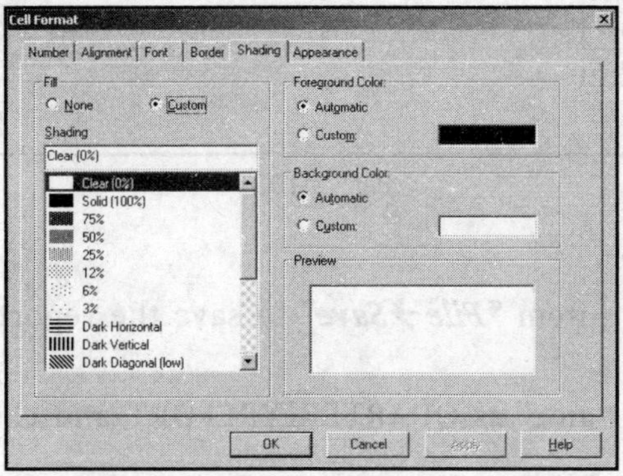

Fig. 7.99

40. Click on **"Apply"** and on **"OK"** of "Cell Format" window.
41. Select the Sum of Quantity sold, right click on it and select the "Apply Standard Style" from the pop up menu.
42. Repeat the above procedure from step 38 and then the final report will be as shown in Fig. 7.100.

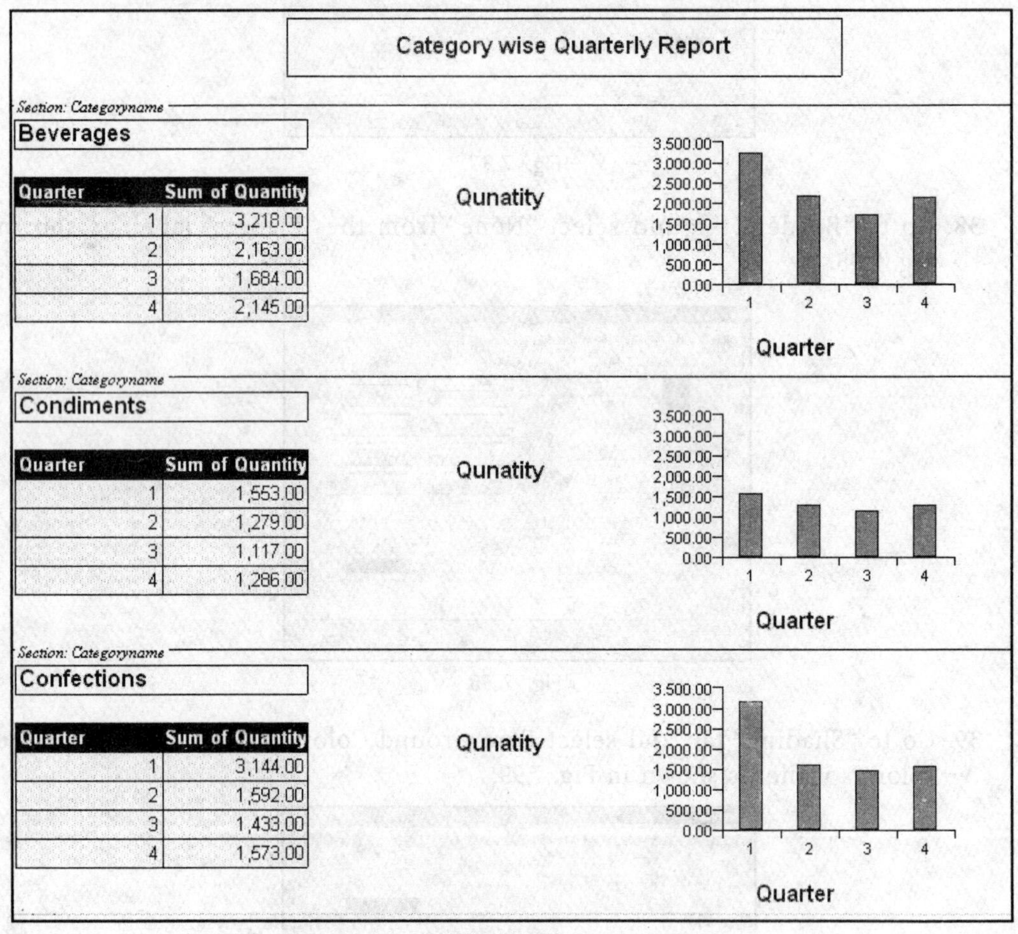

Category wise Quarterly Report

Section: Categoryname

Beverages

Quarter	Sum of Quantity
1	3,218.00
2	2,163.00
3	1,684.00
4	2,145.00

Section: Categoryname

Condiments

Quarter	Sum of Quantity
1	1,553.00
2	1,279.00
3	1,117.00
4	1,286.00

Section: Categoryname

Confections

Quarter	Sum of Quantity
1	3,144.00
2	1,592.00
3	1,433.00
4	1,573.00

Fig. 7.100

43. Select the menu item ***"File→Save"*** to save the report, then "Save As" window opens.
44. Enter the "File Name" as QUARTERLYREPORT, and click on **"Save"**.

Summary

- Business Objects provides a set of tools for building data warehouses very efficiently.
- Business Objects suite consists of data integration tools, business intelligence platform, report generation tools, query & analysis tools, and performance analysis tools.
- Data integration tools are used to extract data from existing databases, carry out the necessary transformations and load the data into the target database using a GUI.
- Data Integrator has four components: Graphical Designer is a GUI for the ETL process. Data integration server integrates the data from different sources. Metadata repository stores the source and target metadata. Administrator is used to administer the ETL jobs.
- BO is an excellent tool for generation of reports, carrying out detailed analysis, graphical presentation of the results and generation of alerts.

8 Data Stage

CHAPTER OBJECTIVES

- ETL process using DataStage
- Workflow monitoring using DataStage Director
- Various transformations using DataStage through case studies

In this chapter, we will focus on another popular tool DataStage for ETL process. DataStage can be used for carrying out the complex process of extraction, transformation and loading of data very efficiently through a GUI. We will explain this process using case studies.

.1 Overview of DataStage

DataStage provides a set of powerful tools for developing a data warehouse. It has a number of client and server components.

The server components consist of DataStage Repository, DataStage Server and DataStage Package Installer. The repository contains all the required data to build a data warehouse. DataStage Server runs the server jobs. DataStage Package installer provides the GUI to install packaged server jobs and plug-ins.

The process that connects to databases on other machines, extract data and load the data into the target database is called a "job". These jobs are compiled and run on the DataStage server. These are referred to as server jobs.

The DataStage client components (that can run on Windows 2000/XP/NT) consist of DataStage Manager, DataStage Designer, DataStage Director and DataStage Administrator.

DataStage Manager provides the user interface to view the contents of the data repository.

DataStage Designer is used to create the DataStage jobs. Using this tool, the data sources, transformations required and the destination database are specified. The jobs are compiled and executable files are created. These executable files can be scheduled by the DataStagae Director and run by the Server.

DataStage Director provides the user interface to schedule, run and monitor the server jobs.

DataStage Administrator is used to perform administration tasks such as administration of the users, creation of projects etc.

8.2 Development Environment

The case studies presented in this chapter have been tested in the following development environment:

- Oracle database running on Windows 2003 Server
- DataStage tools running on Windows 2003 Server

Scott database, the default database available with the Oracle installation is used for demonstration of various features of DataStage tools.

8.3 Working with DataStage ETL Tool

We will demonstrate the use of DataStage ETL tools through an example. In this example we will transfer the data from source database to destination database. The transformation that is done is to divide the employees department-wise. The target Tables are DEPT10, DEPT20 and DEPT30. The data for these tables is obtained from the EMP table.

8.3.1 Transformer Stage

To work with Transformer Stage, in DataStage Administrator, a job has to be designed and a project has to be created.

DataStage Administrator

1. To start DataStage Administrator, select "***Start→ Programs→ Ascential DataStage→ DataStage Administrator***".
2. "Attach To DataStage" dialog box, shown in Fig. 8.1, opens. Enter the "User Name" "Password" and click on **"OK"**.

   E.g.: User name : Administrator
   Password : password.

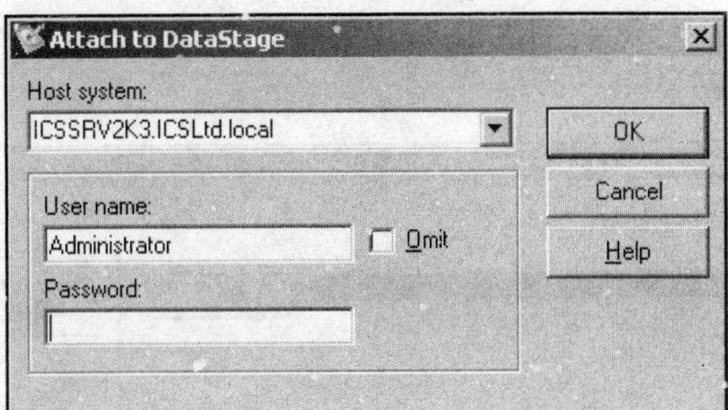

Fig. 8.1

3. "DataStage Administration" window, shown in Fig. 8.2, opens. Go to Projects tab, click on **"Add"** to add a new project.

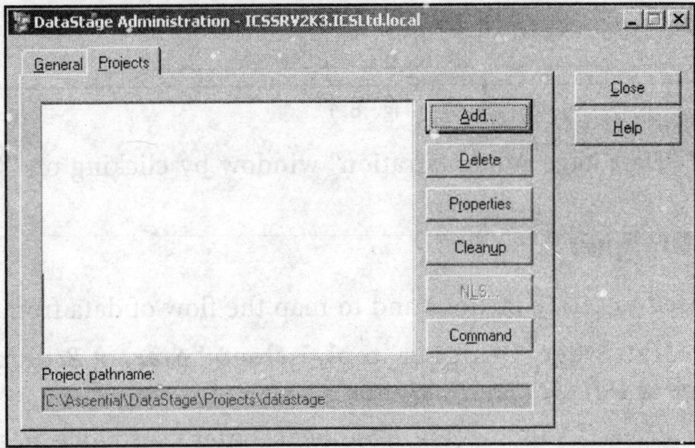

Fig. 8.2

4. **"Add Project"** window (Fig. 8.3) opens; enter the name of the project.
   E.g.: Name: Deptproject

Fig. 8.3

5. Click on **"OK"**.

6. The created project will be displayed in the Projects tab of "DataStage Administration" (Fig. 8.4).

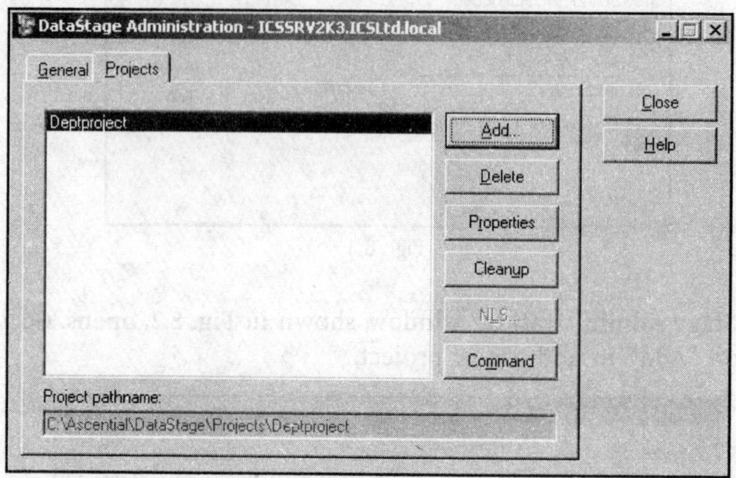

Fig. 8.4

7. Close the "DataStage Administration" window by clicking on **"Close"**.

DataStage Designer

This tool is used to create the jobs and to map the flow of data from source to target.

1. To start DataStage Designer tool, select ***"Start→ Programs→ Ascential DataStage→ DataStage Designer"***.
2. "Attach to Project" window (Fig. 8.5) opens. Enter user name, password and select the project.

   e.g.: User name : Administrator
   Password : password

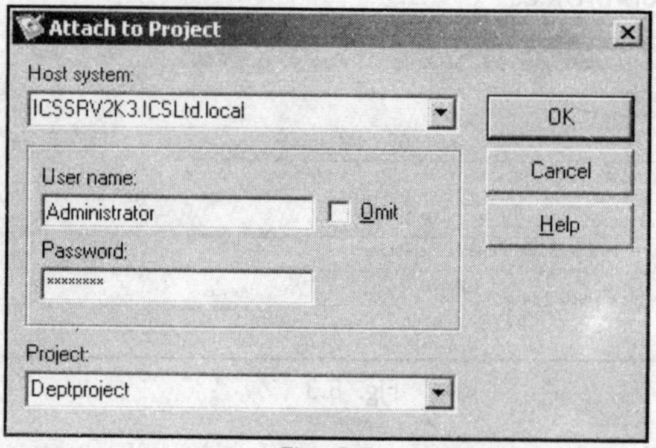

Fig. 8.5

3. Click on "OK".
4. **"DataStage Designer"** window opens. In that, "New" window opens. In "New" window, there are 3 tabs.
   i) New : To create a new job.
   ii) Existing : To open an existing job.
   iii) Recent : To view the recently opened jobs.
5. In "New" tab (Fig. 8.6) there are several types of job sequences, select "New Server Job".

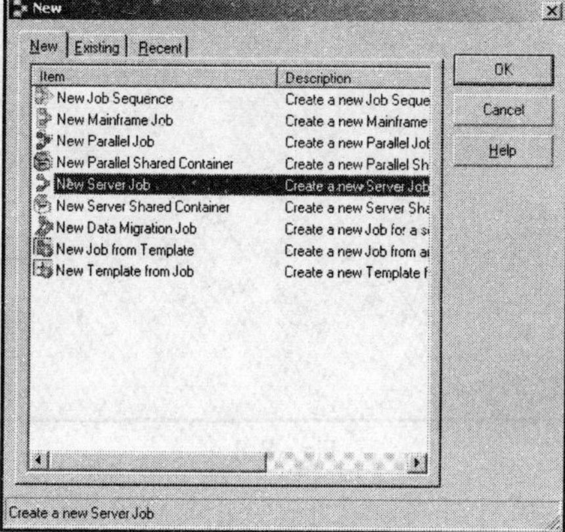

Fig. 8.6

6. Click on **"OK"**.
7. The actual Designer window opens (Fig. 8.7). From Palette window of Designer, click on "Database", select "Oracle", then it will show the different versions of Oracle database, from that select "Oracle OCI 9i".

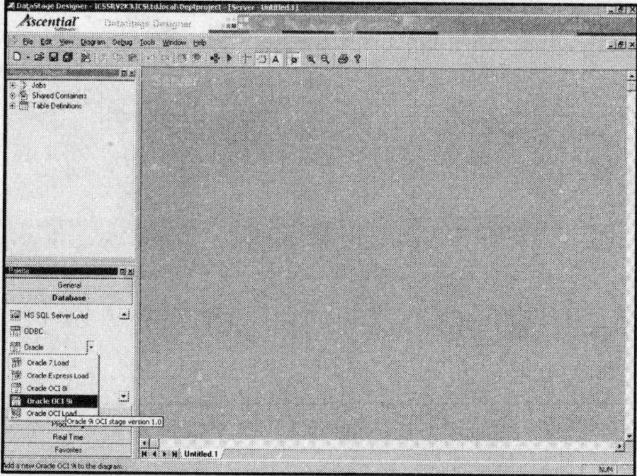

Fig. 8.7

8. Go to Workspace and click the mouse pointer in Workspace, the Oracle database icon will be created in Workspace, this will act as our source database and the Workspace looks as shown in Fig. 8.8.

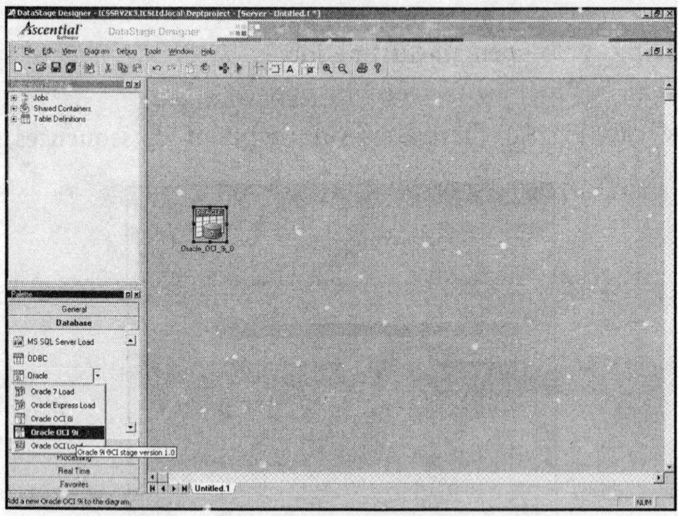

Fig. 8.8

9. Select the source database icon from the Workspace, right click on it, and select "Rename" from the popup menu, to rename it as "EmpSource", then the workspace looks as shown in Fig. 8.9.

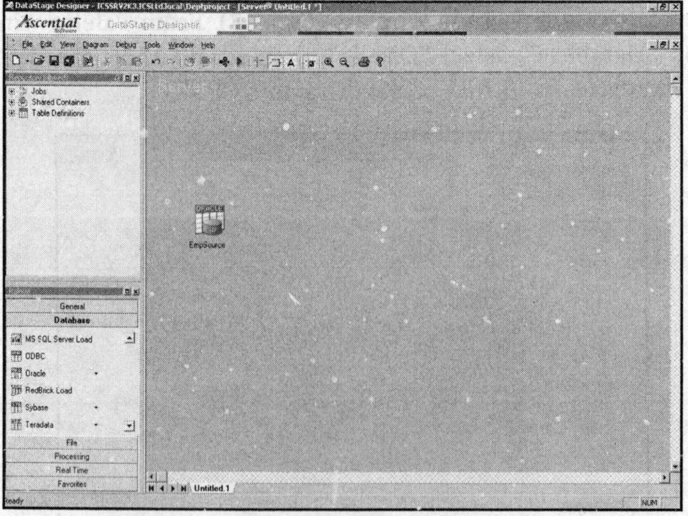

Fig. 8.9

10. From the ***"Palette"*** area, select the ***"Processing"*** and select ***"Transformer"***.

Drop the "Transformer" to the workspace and then the Workspace window looks as shown in Fig. 8.10.

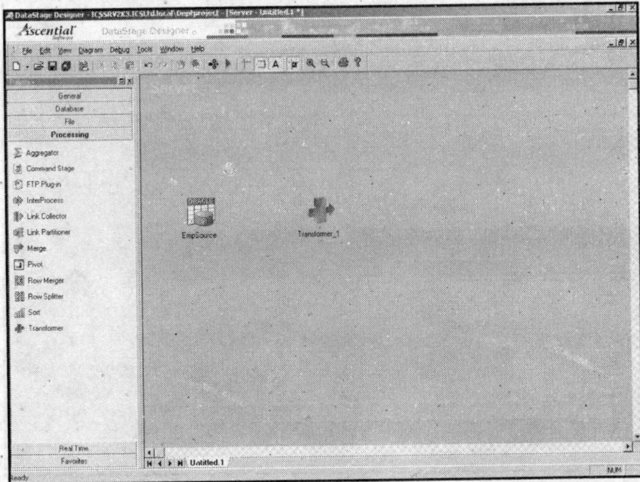

Fig. 8.10

11. Now, from "Palette" drag and drop three **"Oracle"** Databases, which will act as 3 targets for this job. Rename them as "Dept10", "Dept20" and "Dept30", then the Workspace looks as shown in Fig. 8.11.

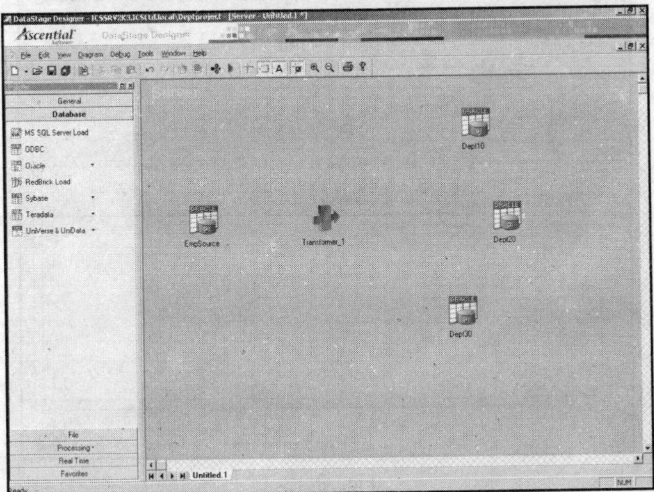

Fig. 8.11

12. From "***Palette→General***", select "Link", then in Workspace drag and drop the mouse pointer from source database object to Transformer, to connect the source and the transformer.

13. Similarly draw a "Link" from Transformer to each target, then the mappings from source to targets appear as shown in Fig. 8.12.

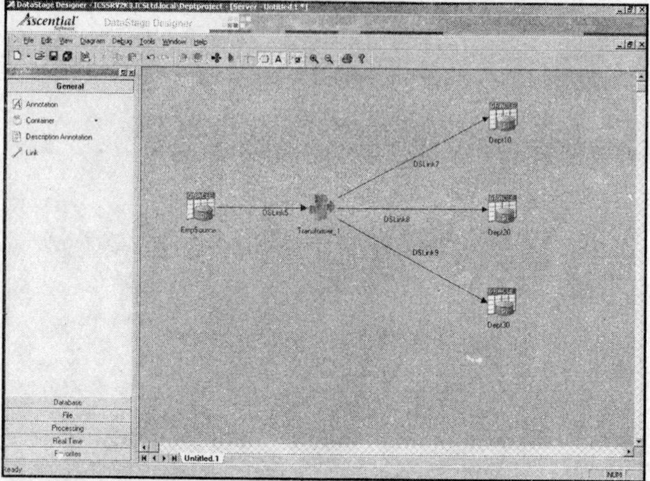

Fig. 8.12

14. Open the "Properties" window of EmpSource either by double clicking on it or by selecting "Properties" from the pop up menu by right clicking on EmpSource. (Fig. 8.13).

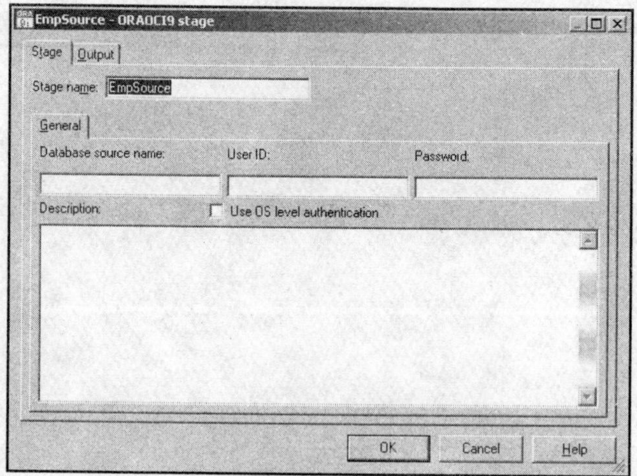

Fig. 8.13

15. In the "Properties" window of EmpSource in "Stage" tab, there is another sub-tab, "General". Enter the Database source name, User ID and Password, as shown in Fig. 8.14.

e.g.: Database source name : oemrep
User ID : scott
Password : tiger

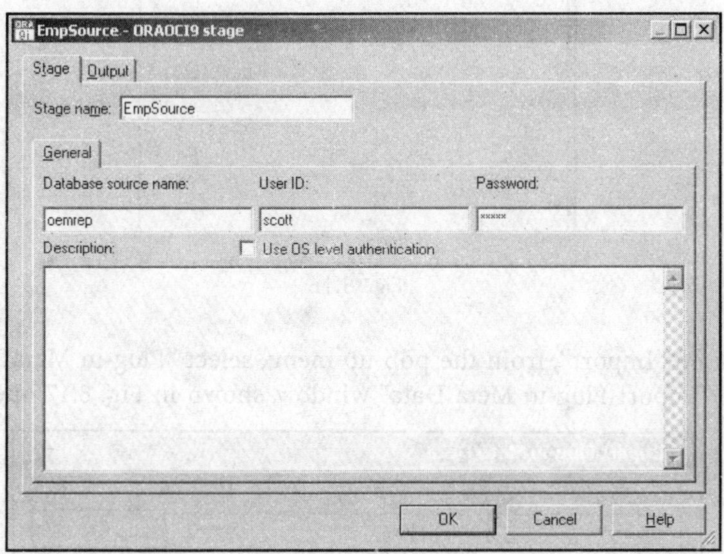

Fig. 8.14

16. Go to "Output" tab, from it select the sub tab "Columns", as shown in Fig. 8.15.

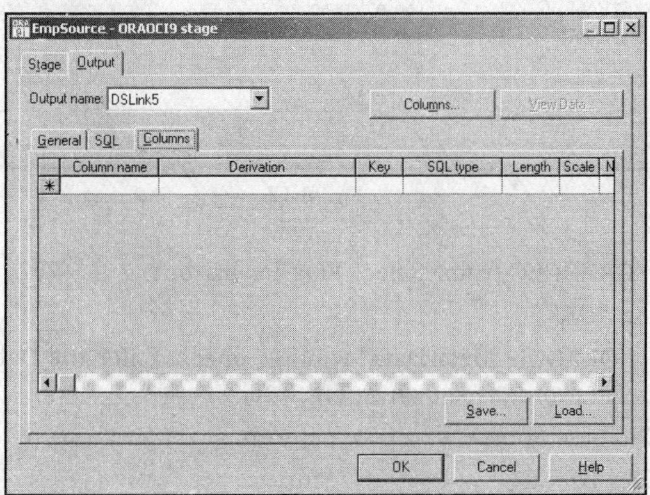

Fig. 8.15

17. In "Columns" tab, click on "Load" button, then "Table Definitions" window (Fig. 8.16) opens.

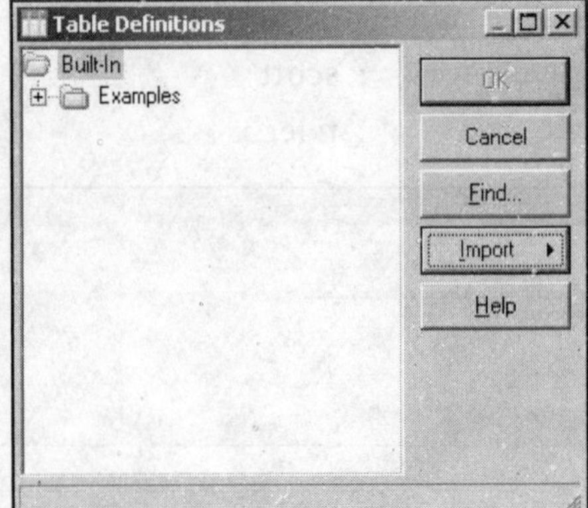

Fig. 8.16

18. Click on "Import", from the pop up menu, select "Plug-in MetaData Definitions", then "Import Plug-in Meta Data" window, shown in Fig. 8.17 opens.

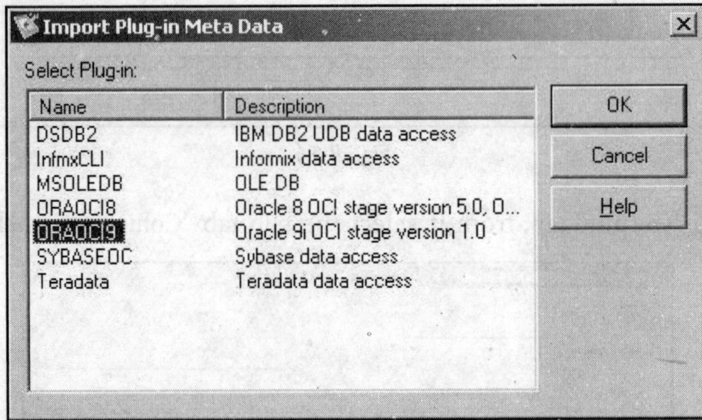

Fig. 8.17

19. Select "ORAOCI9" from "Select Plug-in" list box.
20. Click on **"OK"**.
21. "Import ORAOCI9 Meta Data" window opens. Enter the Database Source Name, User ID, Password, as shown in Fig. 8.18.

    E.g.: Database Source Name : oemrep

    User ID : scott

    Password : tiger

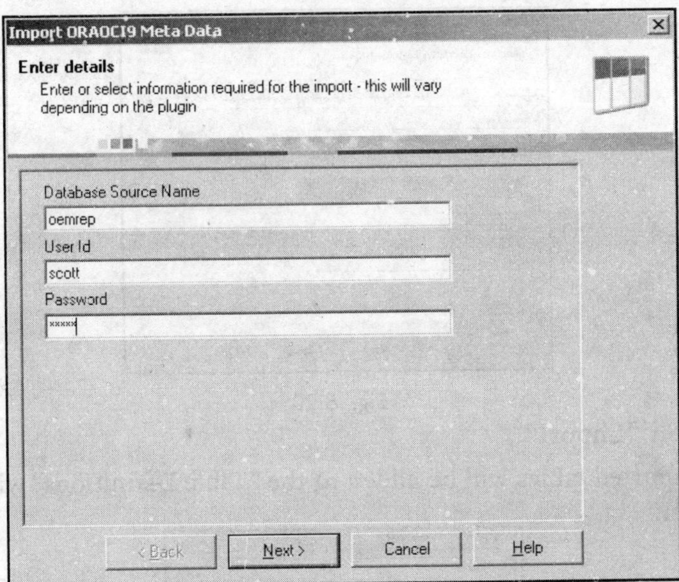

Fig. 8.18

22. Click on **"Next"**.
23. In the next page, accept all the default values and click on "Next" (Fig. 8.19).

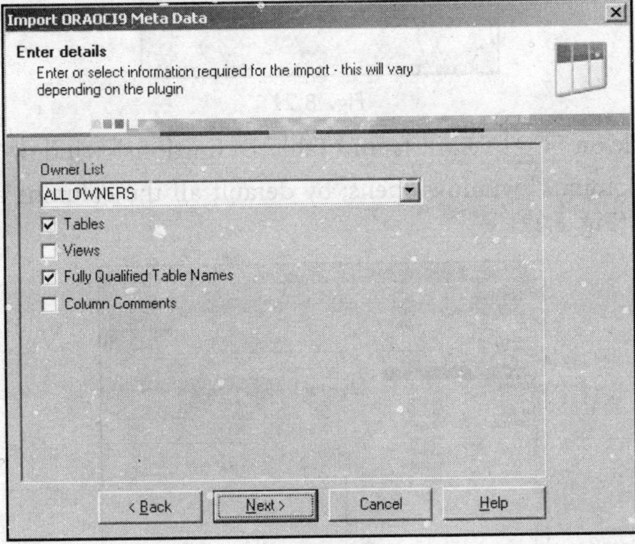

Fig. 8.19

24. From the "Select tables" list box, select the tables SCOTT.DEPT and SCOTT.EMP as shown in Fig. 8.20.

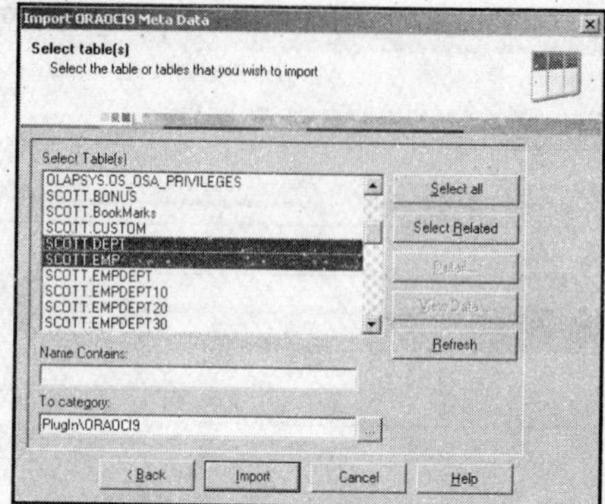

Fig. 8.20

25. Click on **"Import"**.
26. The imported tables will be added to the "Table Definitions" window as shown in Fig. 8.21.

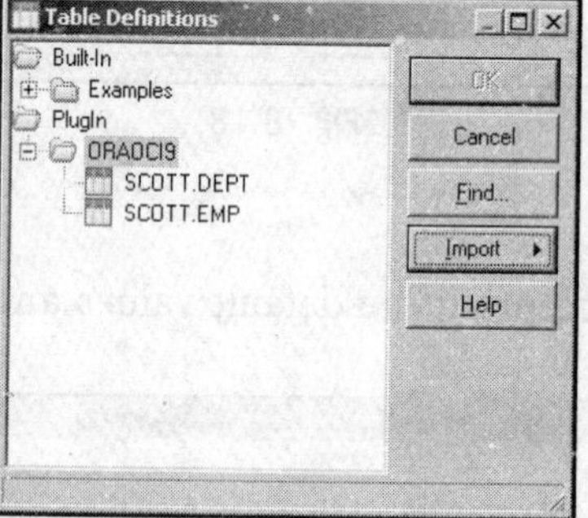

Fig. 8.21

27. Now, click on SCOTT.EMP from "Table Definitions" window and click on **"OK"**.
28. "Select Columns" window opens; by default all the columns are selected, so click on "OK" (Fig. 8.22).

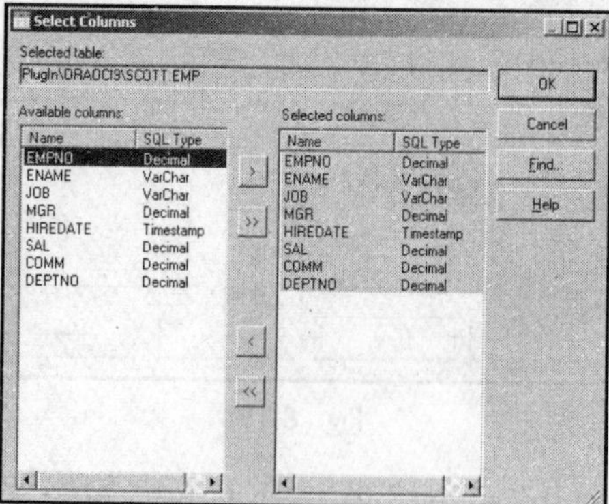

Fig. 8.22

29. All the selected columns will be added to the "Columns" sub-tab of the "Output" tab, as shown in Fig. 8.23.

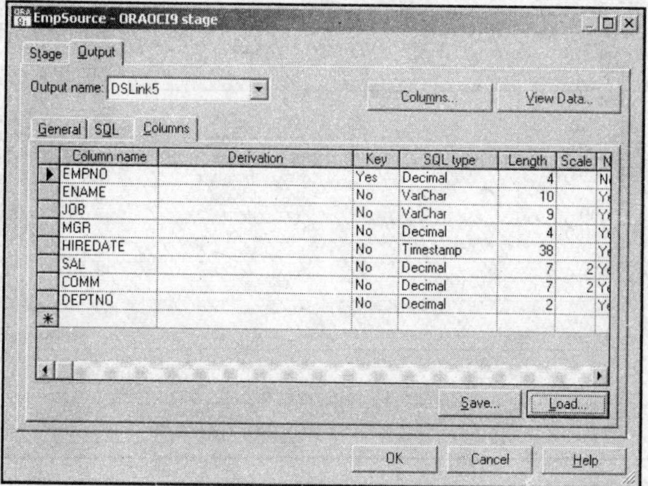

Fig. 8.23

30. Again click on "Load" button in the "Columns" tab. "Table Definitions" window opens. In it select "SCOTT.DEPT" and click on **"OK"**.

31. From "Select Columns" window, select DNAME and LOC columns of the DEPT table and click on "OK" (Fig. 8.24).

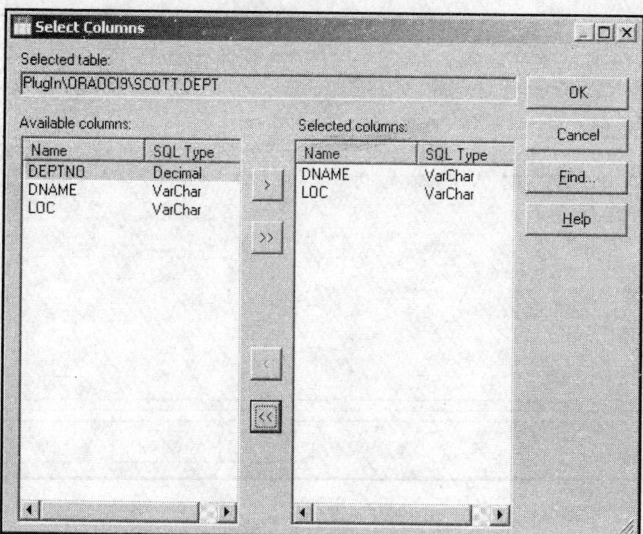

Fig. 8.24

32. The selected columns will be added to the "Columns" sub-tab of the "Output" tab, as shown in Fig. 8.25.

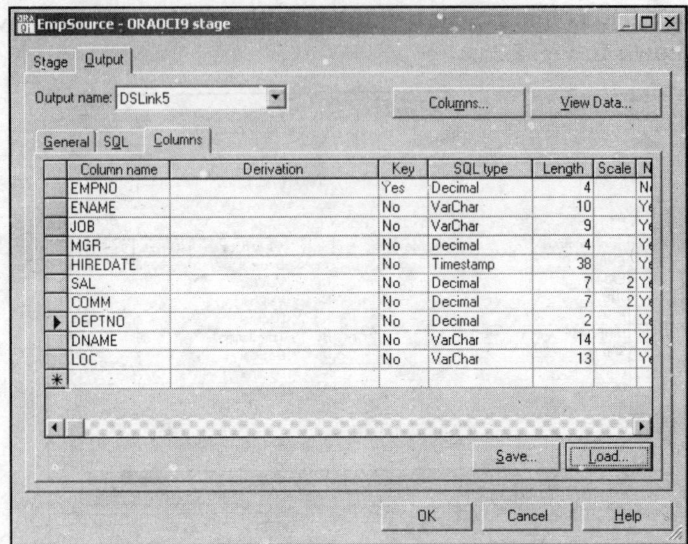

Fig. 8.25

33. Go to “SQL” sub-tab of the “Output” tab, as shown in Fig. 8.26.

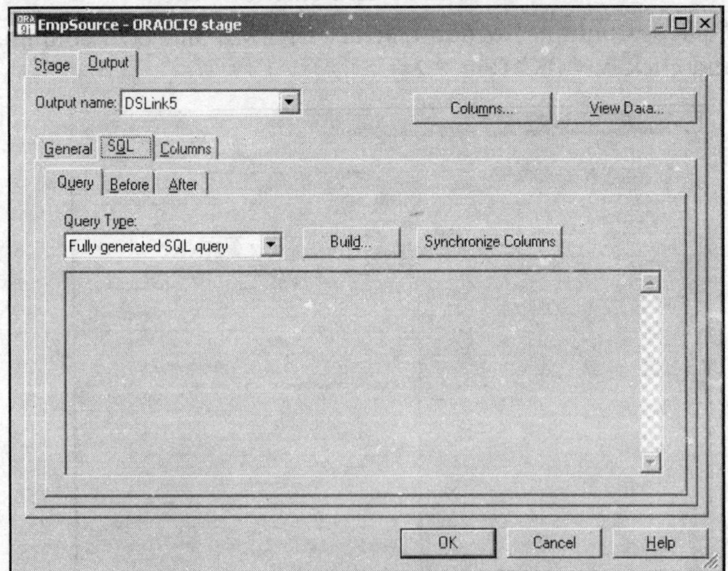

Fig. 8.26

34. Click on “Build” of the “Query” sub-tab of the “SQL” tab.
35. “Build Fully Generated Query” window (Fig. 8.27) opens.

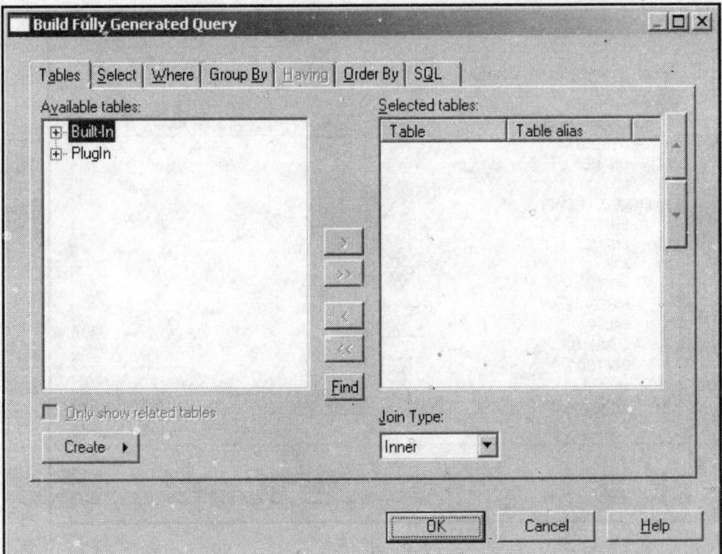

Fig. 8.27

36. Select the tables EMP and DEPT from the "PlugIn→ORAOCI9 " tree control. After selecting the tables, click on ">" button to add the selected tables to "Selected Tables" list as shown in Fig. 8.28.

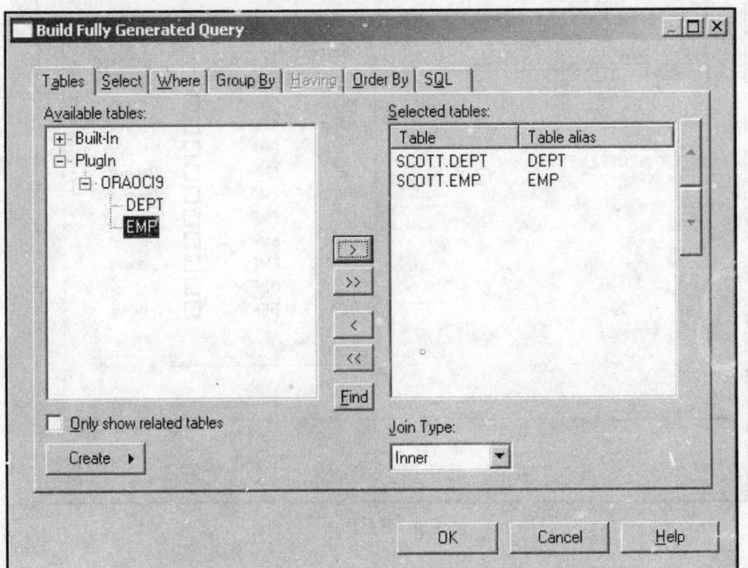

Fig. 8.28

37. Go to "Select" tab of "Build Fully Generated Query", as shown in Fig. 8.29.

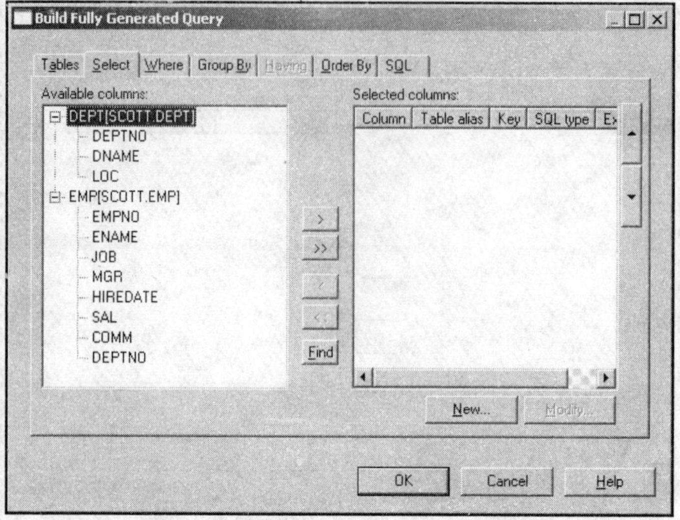

Fig. 8.29

38. Add all the columns of EMP table and DNAME, LOC columns of the DEPT table to the "Selected columns" list as shown in Fig. 8.30.

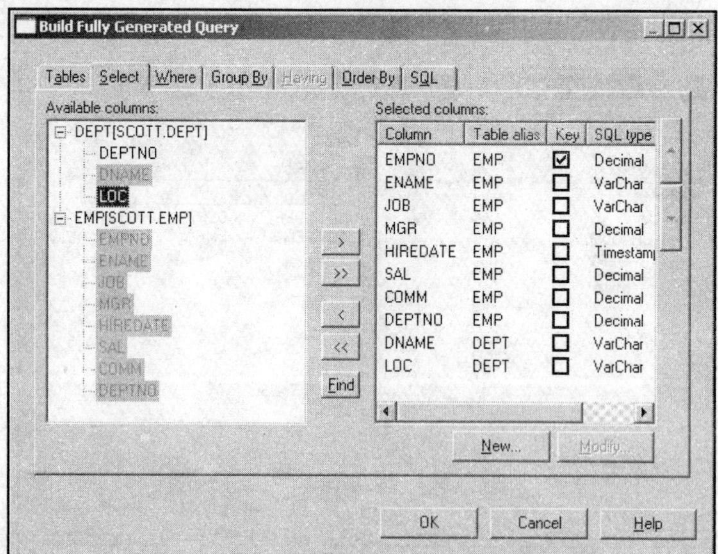

Fig. 8.30

39. Go to "Where" tab of the "Build Fully Generated Query" window. By default, the condition is selected as "DEPT.DEPTNO=EMP.DEPTNO". If it is not selected by default, enter that condition as shown in Fig. 8.31.

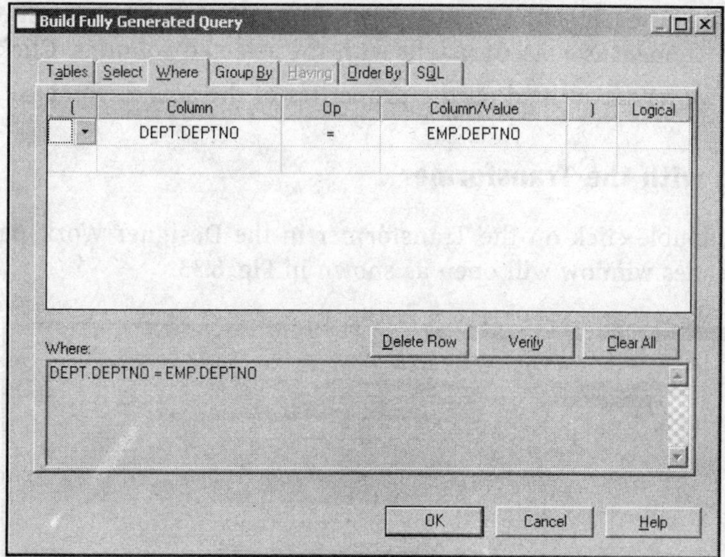

Fig. 8.31

40. Click on **"Verify"** to validate the condition.
41. The required SQL statement for the source is ready. To view the full SQL statement, go to **"SQL"** tab of this window. There, you can see the query as shown in Fig. 8.32.

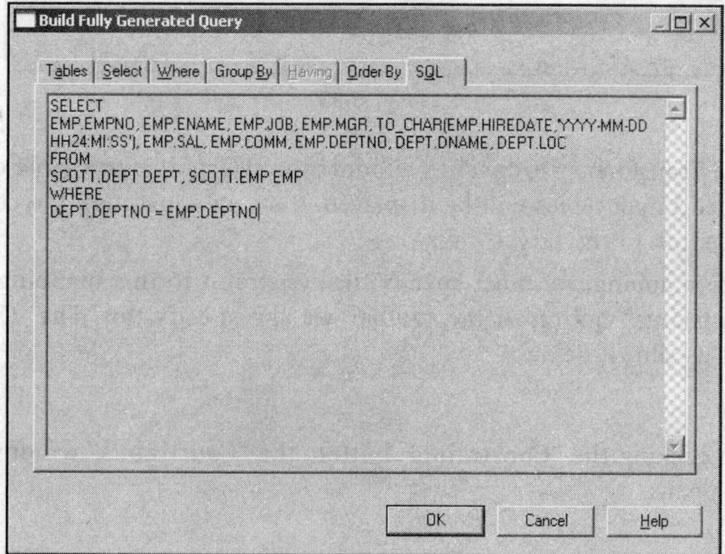

Fig. 8.32

42. Click on "OK". Then a message box will be displayed indicating that the selected SQL statement is not consistent with the selected columns. Click on **"OK"**.
43. Thus we have specified all the properties of the source database.

Working with the Transformer

1. Now, double click on the Transformer in the Designer Workspace, Transformer Properties window will open as shown in Fig. 8.33.

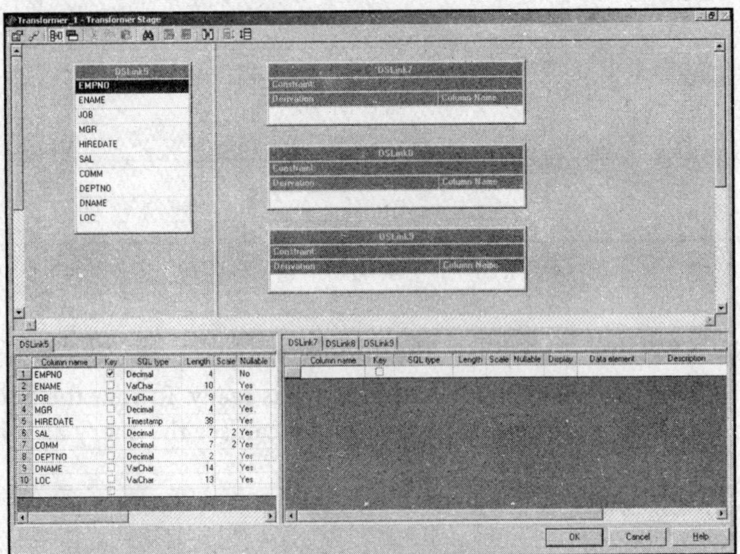

Fig. 8.33

2. In the Transformer Properties window, the selected source table columns and the selected target tables will be displayed. Here, we must map the columns from the source link to the target link.
3. Before mapping, we must specify the constraint to this mapping. By clicking on **"Constraints"** button of the toolbar, we can specify this. The "Constraints" icon looks as shown below.

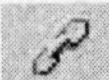

4. After clicking the "Constraints" button, the "Constraints" window, shown in Fig. 8.34, opens.

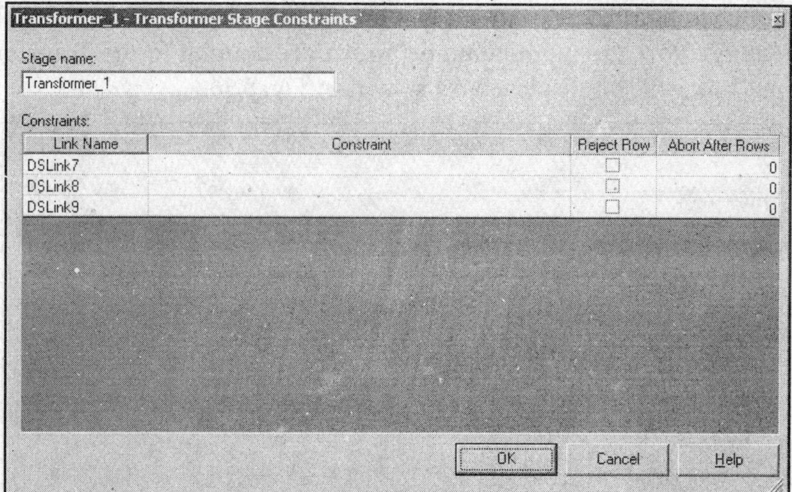

Fig. 8.34

5. In this window, double click on **"Constraint"** edit box provided in the row of the first target table (Dept10) link name. The "Constraint' edit box maximizes in size as shown in Fig. 8.35.

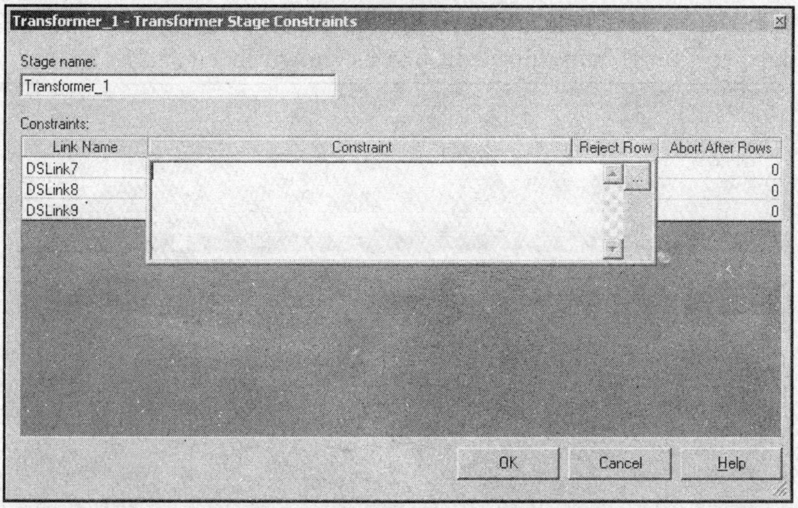

Fig. 8.35

6. Here, you can specify the constraint by clicking on the "Browse" button (shown below), which is located at the right of the constraint edit box.

7. After clicking browse button, a popup menu will open, from that select the "Input Column". Now, the input columns, which are coming to the Transformer from the input link, will be displayed, as shown in Fig. 8.36.

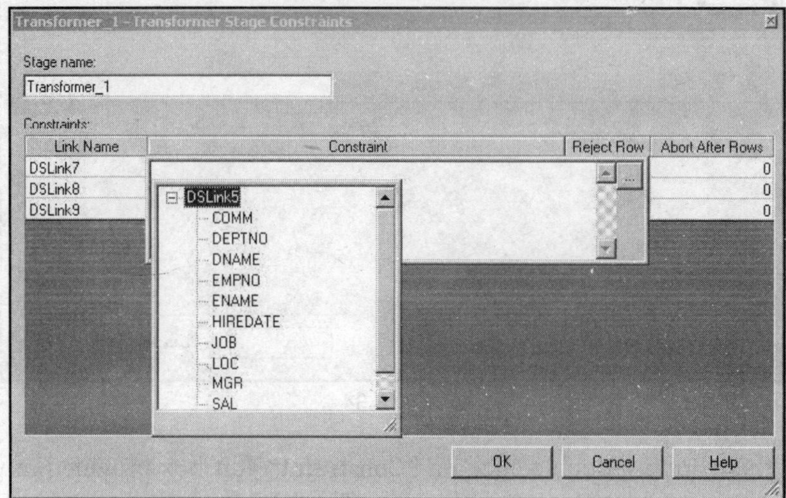

Fig. 8.36

8. From that, select DEPTNO by clicking on it. Thus the column DEPTNO will be added to the "Constraints" edit box as shown in Fig. 8.37.

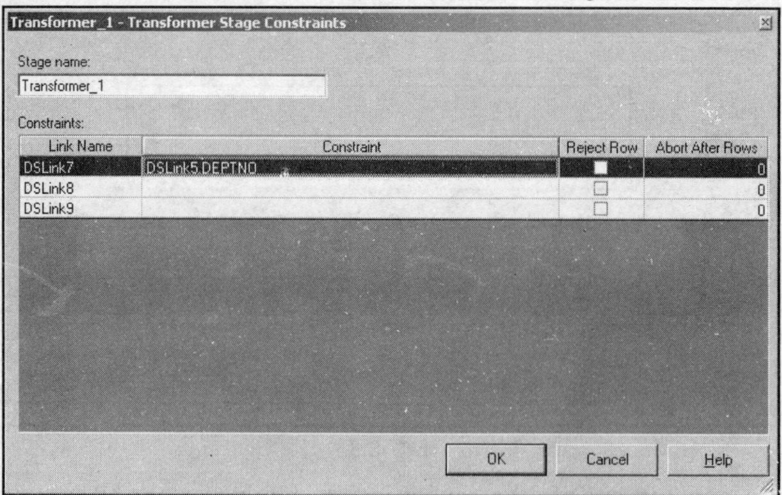

Fig. 8.37

9. Again double click on the "Constraint", then constraint edit box maximizes, in that click once and click on the browse button on the right side of the constraint edit box, then all the operations, which can be performed on that column will be displayed, from that select "=" operator, as shown in Fig. 8.38.

Transformer_1 - Transformer Stage Constraints
Stage name:
Transformer_1
Constraints:
Link Name
Constraint
Reject Row
Abort After Rows
DSLink7
DSLink8
DSLink9
DSLink5.DEPTNO
+
-
*
/
^
=
<>
<
<=
>
>=
Concatenate
Substring
Matches
And
Or
0
0
0
OK
Cancel
Help

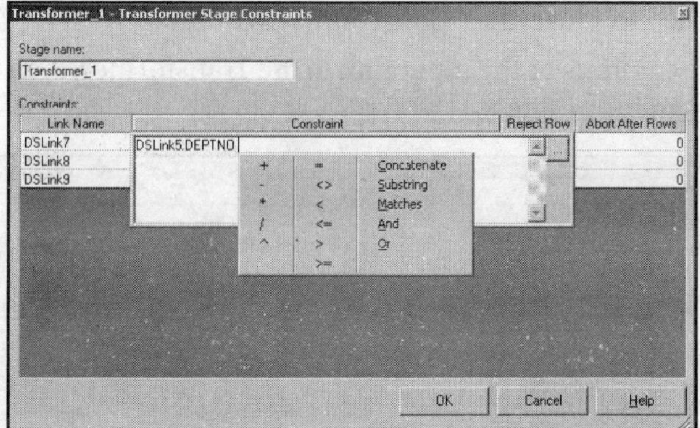

Fig. 8.38

10. Enter the value 10 after the "=" operator. Thus the final constraint will look as shown in Fig. 8.39.

Transformer_1 - Transformer Stage Constraints
Stage name:
Transformer_1
Constraints:
Link Name
Constraint
Reject Row
Abort After Rows
DSLink7
DSLink8
DSLink9
DSLink5.DEPTNO =10
0
0
0
OK
Cancel
Help

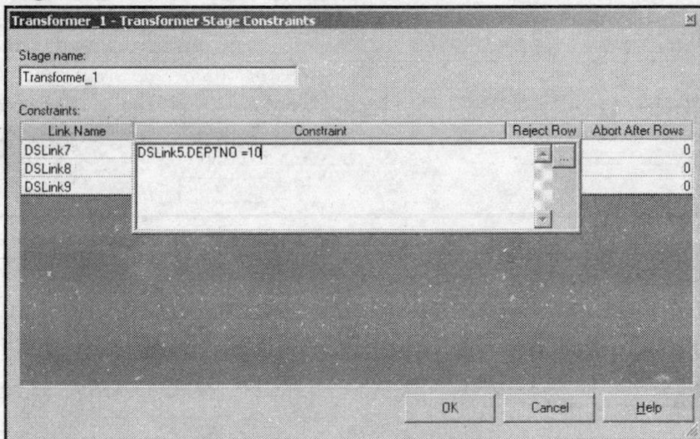

Fig. 8.39

11. In a similar manner, enter the constraint for the other two links as shown in Fig. 8.40.

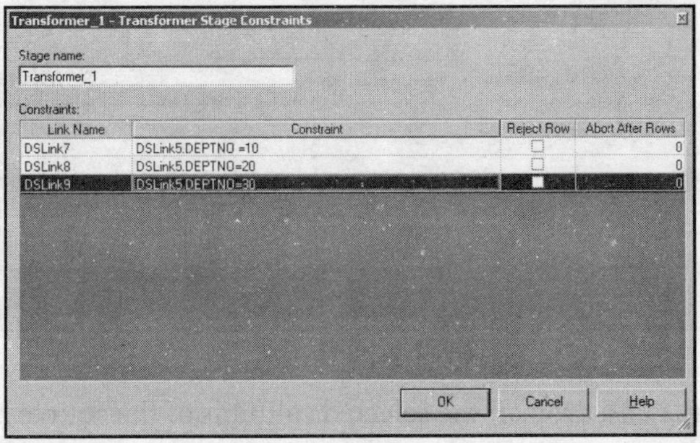

Transformer_1 - Transformer Stage Constraints
Stage name:
Transformer_1
Constraints:
Link Name
Constraint
Reject Row
Abort After Rows
DSLink7
DSLink5.DEPTNO =10
0
DSLink8
DSLink5.DEPTNO=20
0
DSLink9
DSLink5.DEPTNO=30
0
OK
Cancel
Help

Fig. 8.40

12. Click on **"OK"** to close the "Constraints" window.
13. Select all the columns of the input link to the Transformer, then transformer window appears as shown in Fig. 8.41.

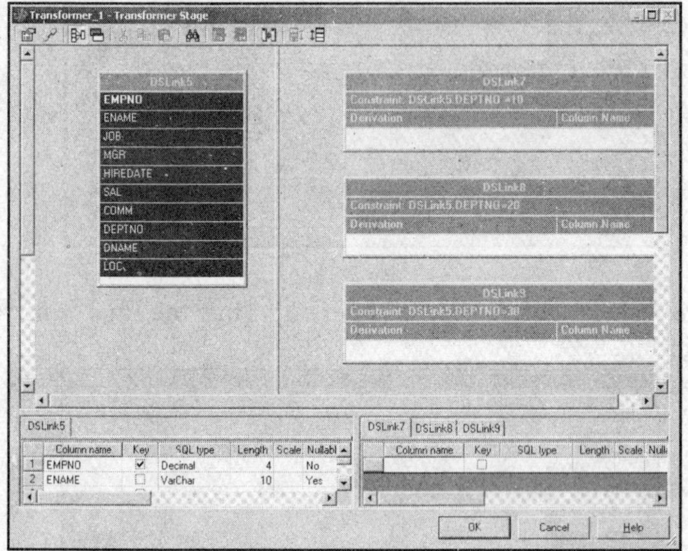

Fig. 8.41

14. Now, drag and drop all the selected columns from the source link to the first target (Dept10) link. Now the mapping will be as shown in Fig. 8.42.

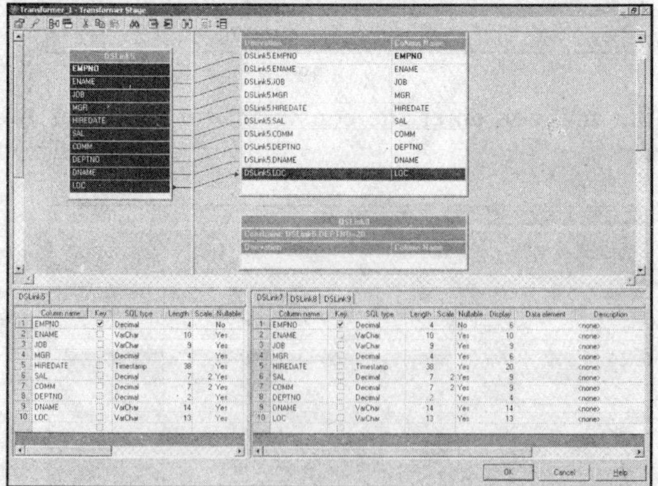

Fig. 8.42

15. Similarly, drag and drop all the selected columns of the source link to the remaining target links.

16. Thus, the final mapping looks as shown in Fig. 8.43.

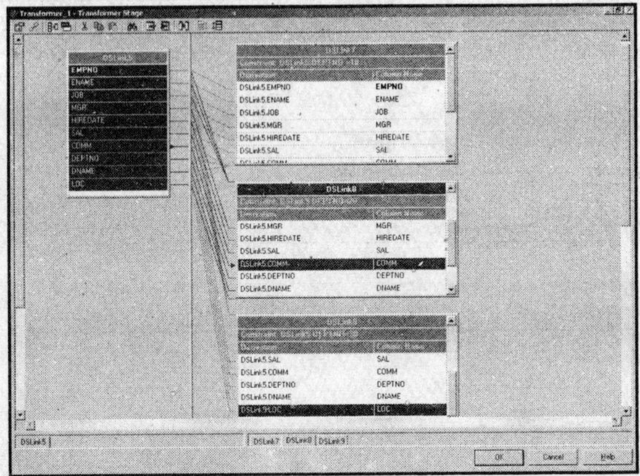

Fig. 8.43

17. Click on **"OK"** of the Transformer Properties window.

Target Database

1. To specify the Properties of the first target table i.e., Dept10, double click on it.
2. "Dept10" properties window opens. In "General" tab, enter the Database source name, user id and password, as in Fig. 8.44.

   e.g: Database Source Name : oemrep
   User ID : scott
   Password : tiger

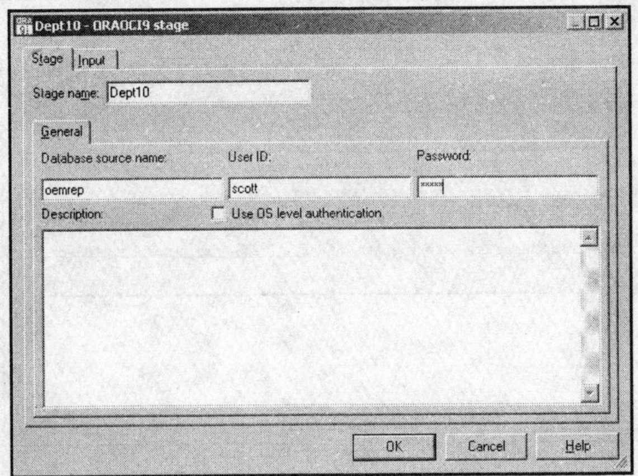

Fig. 8.44

3. Here, we are going to create the target database in the same database used as source database, that is in the database user, scott.

4. Go to “Input” tab of the “Dept10” properties window (Fig. 8.45).

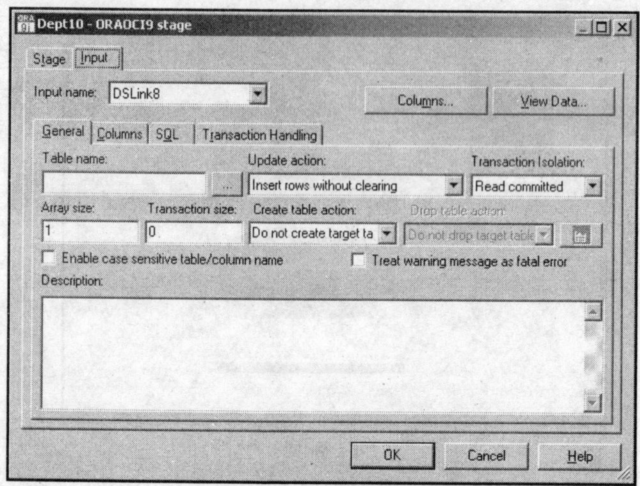

Fig. 8.45

5. From the “General” sub-tab of the “Input” tab enter the table name, which is to be created in the target database. Also select your required actions for “Update action”, “Create table action” and “Drop table action”, as in Fig. 8.46.

e.g.: Table name : Dept10
Update action : Insert rows without cleaning
Create table action : Generate DDL
Drop table action : Generate DDL

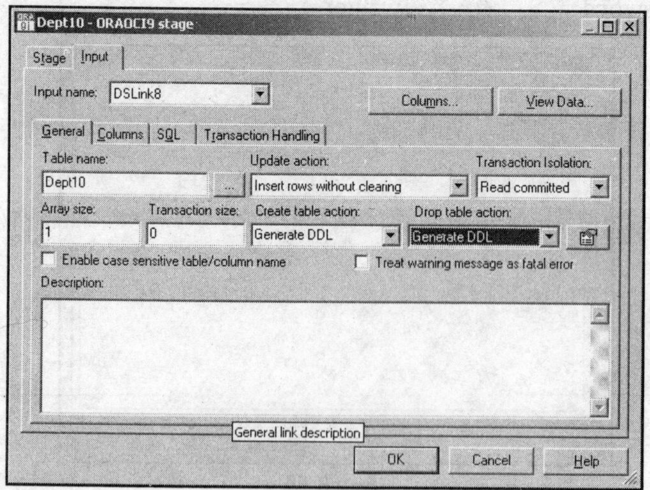

Fig. 8.46

6. Click on **“OK”** of the “Dept10” properties dialog box.

7. Repeat the Step 1 to 6 for Dept20 and Dept30.
8. Now, in the Properties dialog box, you can see the columns, which are going to be received by each of the target table by clicking on the "Columns" sub tab of the "Input" tab. For example, the "Columns" tab for the Dept30 table looks as shown in Fig. 8.47.

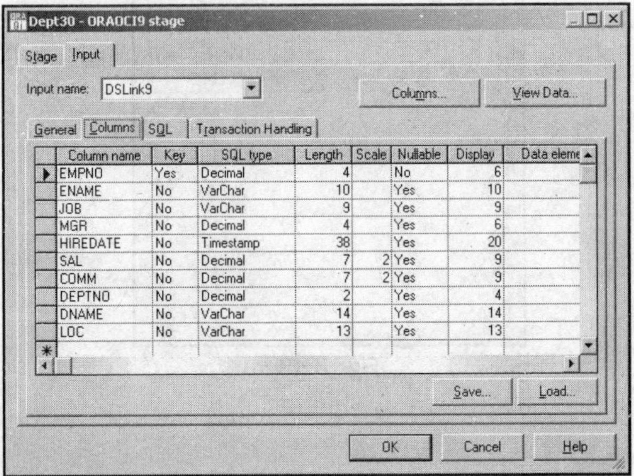

Column name	Key	SQL type	Length	Scale	Nullable	Display	Data eleme
EMPNO	Yes	Decimal	4		No	6	
ENAME	No	VarChar	10		Yes	10	
JOB	No	VarChar	9		Yes	9	
MGR	No	Decimal	4		Yes	6	
HIREDATE	No	Timestamp	38		Yes	20	
SAL	No	Decimal	7	2	Yes	9	
COMM	No	Decimal	7	2	Yes	9	
DEPTNO	No	Decimal	2		Yes	4	
DNAME	No	VarChar	14		Yes	14	
LOC	No	VarChar	13		Yes	13	

Fig. 8.47

9. Similarly, the generated SQL query for the target database table can be seen by going to the "SQL" sub tab of the "Input' tab of the target database table. For example, the SQL statement generated for the target database table Dept30 looks as shown in Fig. 8.48.

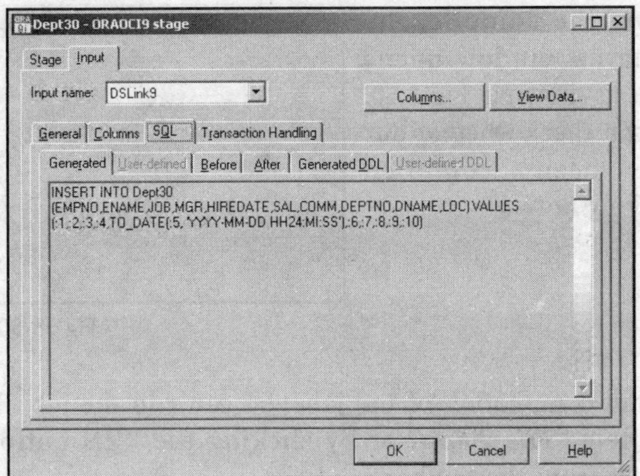

Fig. 8.48

10. Thus we have specified all the properties of our mappings. To save the mappings of the Designer, select ***"File→Save"***.

11. Now, **"Create New Job"** window opens. Specify the job name and click on **"OK"**, as shown in Fig. 8.49.

    e.g.: Job name: EmpDeptJob

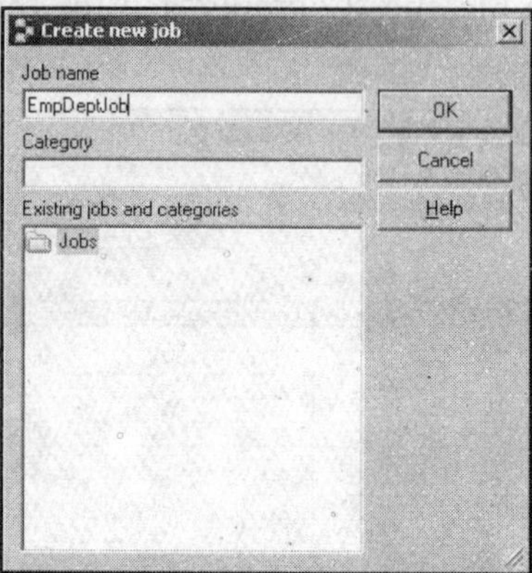

Fig. 8.49

Running the Job

1. After saving the job, we must compile the job. To compile the job, select "***File→Compile***" or just click on "Compile" of the toolbar, which looks as shown below.

2. By pressing the compile, the compile status window opens which looks as shown in Fig. 8.50. Here, you can check whether our job has been compiled successfully or not.

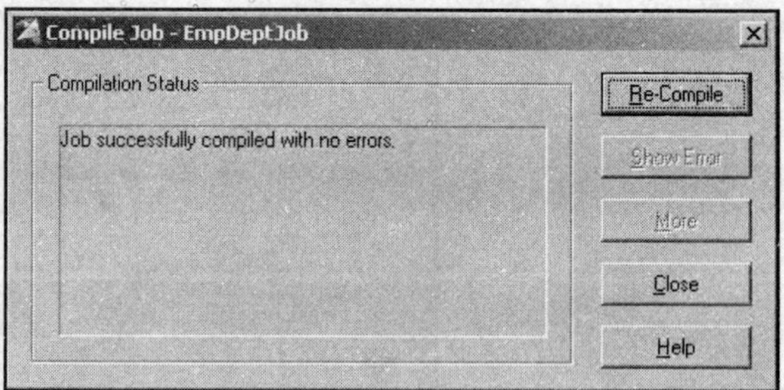

Fig. 8.50

3. On successful compilation of the job, you can run the job. To run the job, select the menu item "***File→Run***" or by clicking the RUN button, which is an icon shown below, from the toolbar.

4. By clicking on the run button, **"Job Run Options"** window opens. Click on **"Run"**, as shown in Fig. 8.51.

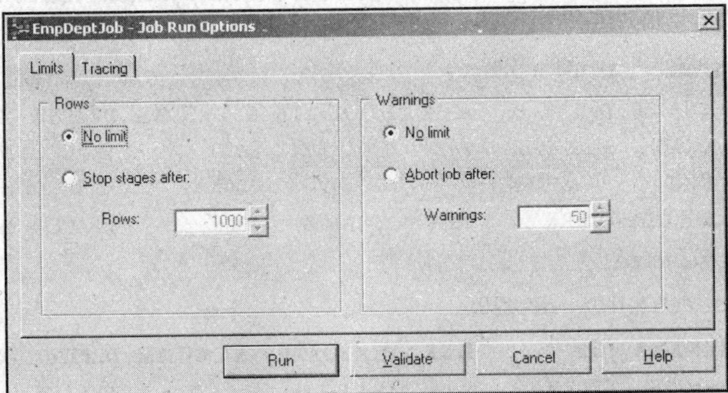

Fig. 8.51

5. Then the "Job Run Options" window closes and the Designer Window opens.
6. If your job is completed successfully, the mappings (links) of the workflow from source to the target are changed to green in color. If your job fails, then the mappings (links) are changed to red in color.
7. Now, you can see how many records are transferred from source to target on each link as shown in Fig. 8.52.

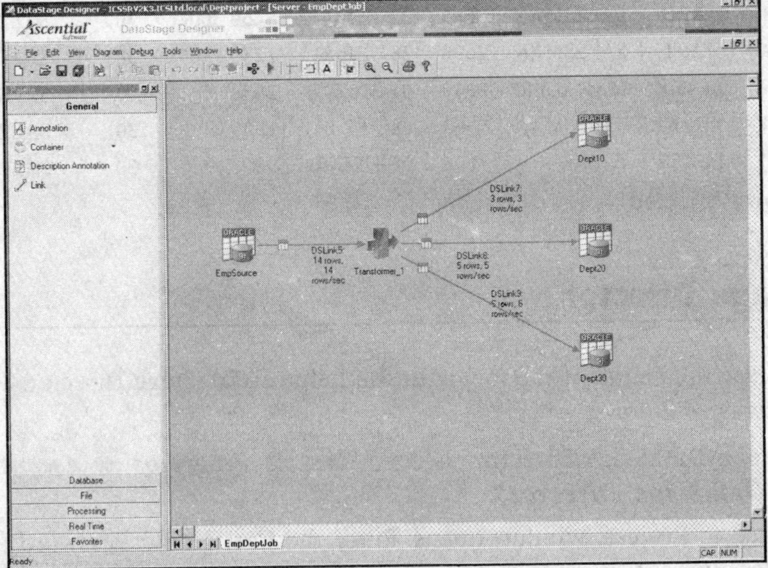

Fig. 8.52

Checking the Output

To see whether the source rows have been successfully transferred to the target tables DEPT10, DEPT20, DEPT30, execute the following SQL statements:

SQL> select * from dept10;

EMPNO	ENAME	JOB	MGR	HIREDATE	SAL	COMM	DEPTNO	DNAME	LOC
7782	CLARK	MANAGER	7839	09-JUN-81	2450		10	ACCOUNTING	NEWYORK
7839	KING	PRESIDENT		17-NOV-81	5000		10	ACCOUNTING	NEWYORK
7934	MILLER	CLERK	7782	23-JAN-82	1300		10	ACCOUNTING	NEWYORK

3 rows selected.

SQL> select * from dept20;

EMPNO	ENAME	JOB	MGR	HIREDATE	SAL	COMM	DEPTNO	DNAME	LOC
7369	SMITH	CLERK	7902	17-DEC-80	800		20	RESEARCH	DALLAS
7566	JONES	MANAGER	7839	02-APR-81	2975		20	RESEARCH	DALLAS
7788	SCOTT	ANALYST	7566	19-APR-87	3000		20	RESEARCH	DALLAS
7876	ADAMS	CLERK	7788	23-MAY-87	1100		20	RESEARCH	DALLAS
7902	FORD	ANALYST	7566	03-DEC-81	3000		20	RESEARCH	DALLAS

5 rows selected.

SQL> select * from dept30;

EMPNO	ENAME	JOB	MGR	HIREDATE	SAL	COMM	DEPTNO	DNAME	LOC
7499	ALLEN	SALESMAN	7698	20-FEB-81	1600	300	30	SALES	CHICAGO
7521	WARD	SALESMAN	7698	22-FEB-81	1250	500	30	SALES	CHICAGO
7654	MARTIN	SALESMAN	7698	28-SEP-81	1250	1400	30	SALES	CHICAGO
7698	BLAKE	MANAGER	7839	01-MAY-81	2850		30	SALES	CHICAGO
7844	TURNER	SALESMAN	7698	08-SEP-81	1500	0	30	SALES	CHICAGO
7900	JAMES	CLERK	7698	03-DEC-81	950		30	SALES	CHICAGO

6 rows selected

8.4 DataStage Director

You can see the status of the job, with the help of DataStage Director. The procedure to do this is as follows:

1. To open DataStage Director, select ***"Start → Programs → Ascential DataStage → DataStage Director".***
2. "Attach to Project" window opens. Enter the User Name, Password and select the project, whose project status we need observe and click on **"OK"**, then the "DataStage Director" window for the selected project opens.

e.g.: User name : Administrator
Password : password
Project : Deptproject

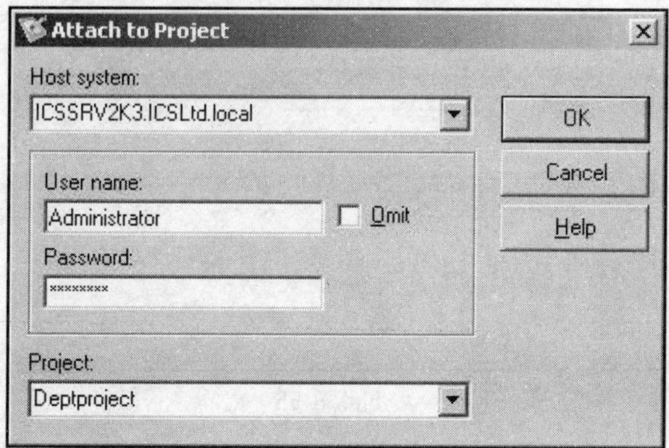

Fig. 8.53

3. In the Director window, you can see all the jobs, which exist in the opened project. The "DataStage Director" is the client component that validates, schedules, runs, and monitors jobs run by the DataStage Server. These tasks are carried out from the DataStage Director Window.

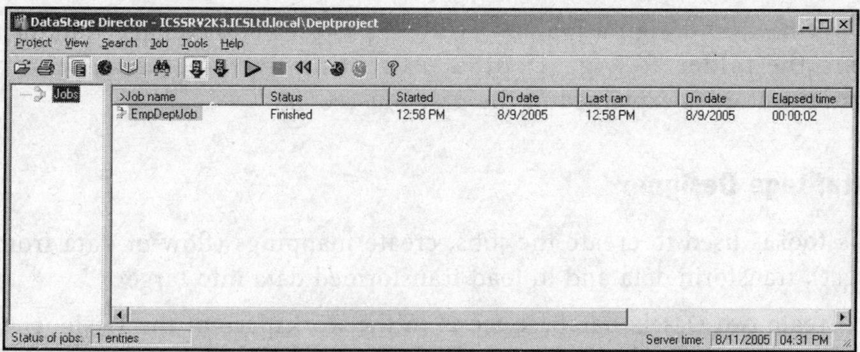

Fig. 8.54

4. Select the job, "SortSeqGen" and select the menu item ***"View → Log"*** to see the detailed log, as shown in Fig. 8.55.

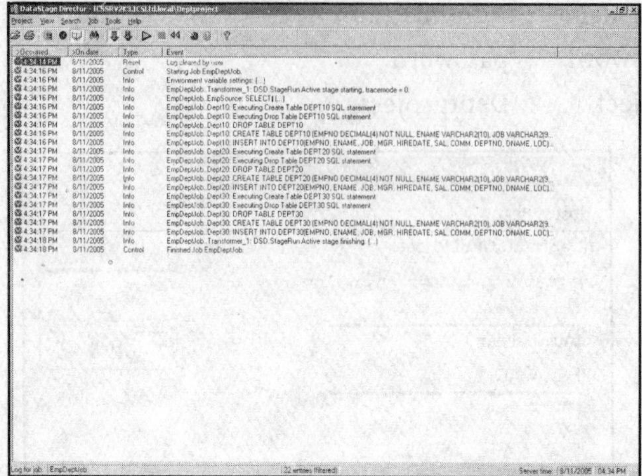

Fig. 8.55

8.5 Aggregator Stage

In this section, we will demonstrate the aggregator stage. As an example, we will calculate the monthly expenditure to the company per department from SCOTT.EMP table by adding the salaries of the employees in each department.

We need to design a job and create a project in "DataStage Administrator" and name the folder as "Agg_DeptSal". Creating a project using the "DataStage Administrator" is explained in the previous section.

DataStage Designer

This tool is used to create the jobs, create mappings (flow of data from source to target), transform data and to load transformed data into target.

1. Create two Oracle database icons in the workspace of the Designer (creation of the databases in the workspace is explained in the previous section). One will act as Source Database and one will act as Target Database; rename the icons in the Workspace as "Scott_Emp" and "Scott_SumSal".
2. Select the **"Aggregator"** from the **"Palette"** and click in the workspace to insert an "Aggregator" stage in the Workspace, rename it as Agg_SumSal.
3. Create a link from Scott_Emp to Aggregator and also create a link from Aggregator to Scott_SumSal. We can rename the links, which are created in the workspace, rename the links of the Aggregator source to Agg_Source and target of Aggregator to Agg_Target, which appear as shown in Fig. 8.56.

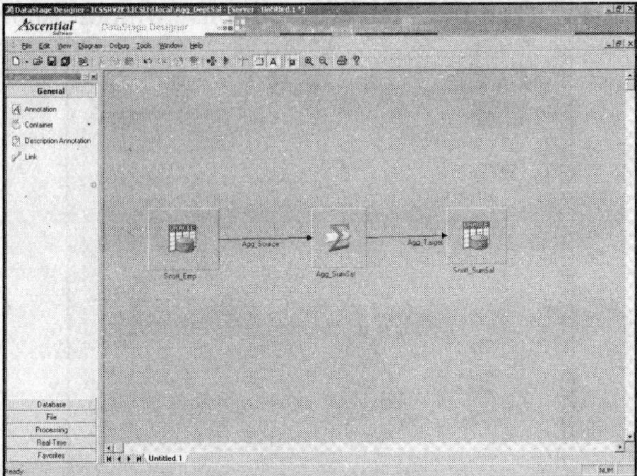

Fig. 8.56

4. Specify the properties of the source database (Scott_Emp), by double clicking on it and data extraction from the EMP of default user, "scott" from Oracle database.
5. Similarly, specify the properties for the target database (Scott_SumSal) and attach it to a new target table, "DeptSumSal" in the Oracle Database of default user "scott" (creation of target database table was explained in the previous section). Also select the values for "Create table action" and "Drop table action" as explained in the previous section.
6. To specify the properties of the Agg_SumSal, double click on it or by right clicking on it and selecting "Properties" from the pop up menu.
7. Go to "Output" tab, in the "Output" tab go to sub tab "Columns". See Fig. 8.57.

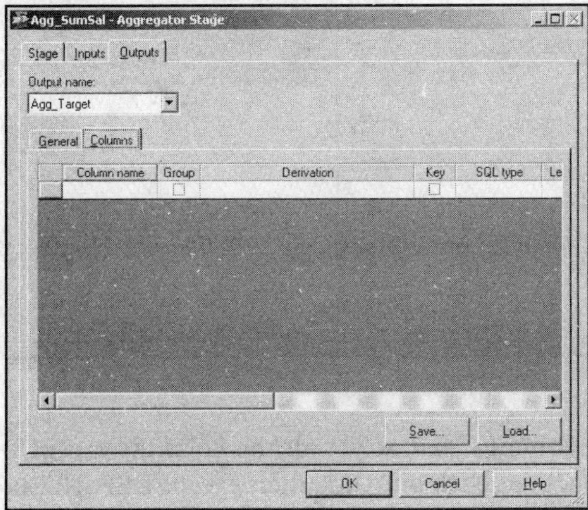

Fig. 8.57

8. Click on **"Load"**, then the **"Table Definitions"** window, shown in Fig. 8.58, opens.

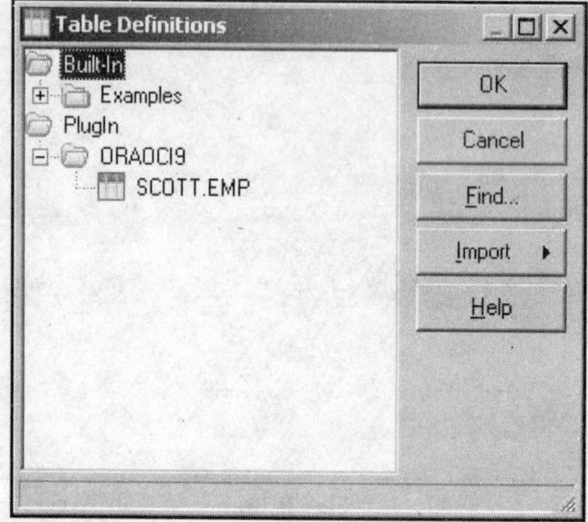

Fig. 8.58

9. Select "SCOTT.EMP" and click on **"OK"**, then "Select Columns" window (Fig. 8.59) opens.

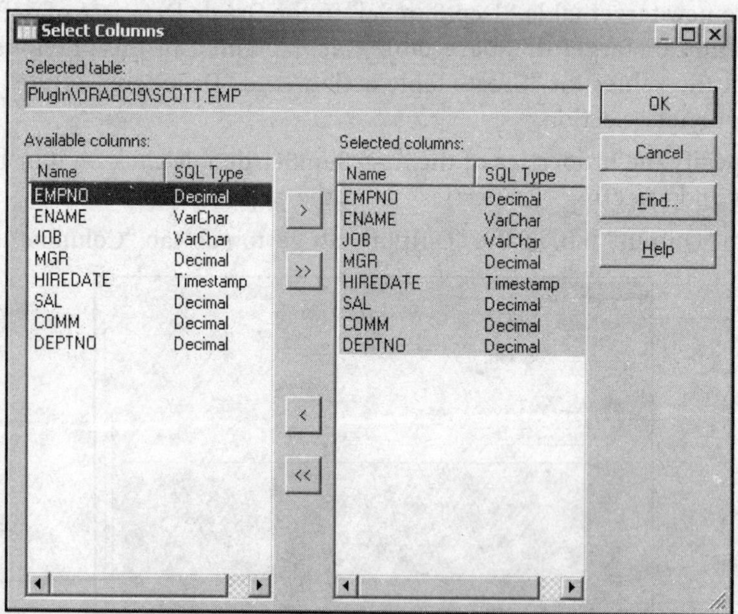

Fig. 8.59

10. In "Selected Columns" list, select all the columns except DEPTNO and SAL, click on "<" button, then click on "OK", then except DEPTNO and SAL, other items will be removed from the "Selected Columns" list, as shown in Fig. 8.60.

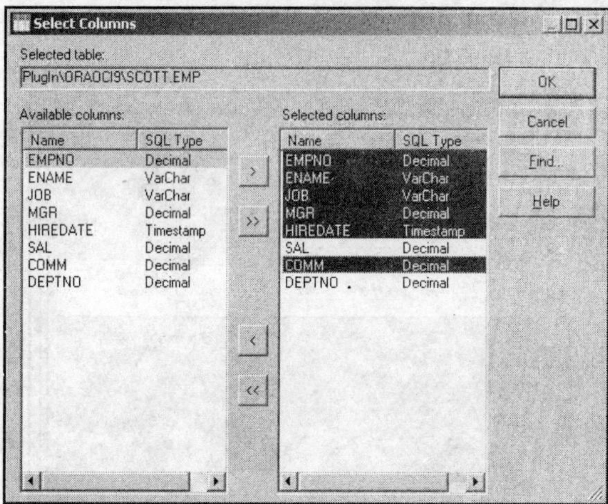

Fig. 8.60

11. Select column name DEPTNO in the "Columns" sub tab of "Outputs" tab and right click on it, from the pop up menu, select "Edit Cell" to edit the "Derivation of DEPTNO column, then the "Derivation" window (Fig. 8.61) opens.
12. Select "Source Column" value as "Agg_Source.DEPTNO" and check the "Group by this column", option and click on **"OK"**.

Fig. 8.61

13. Select the column "SAL" in the "Columns" sub tab of "Outputs" tab and right click on it, from the pop up menu, select the menu item "Edit Cell" to edit the derivation of "SAL" column.
14. From the "Derivation" window, select "Agg_Source.SAL" from the "Source column" drop down list box and SUM from "Aggregate function" drop-down list box, make sure to uncheck the option "Group by this column" and click on "OK", then the "Derivation" window will be as shown in Fig. 8.62.

Fig. 8.62

15. Finally, the output tab of the "Agg_SumSal – Aggregator Stage" window, aggregator looks as shown in Fig. 8.63.

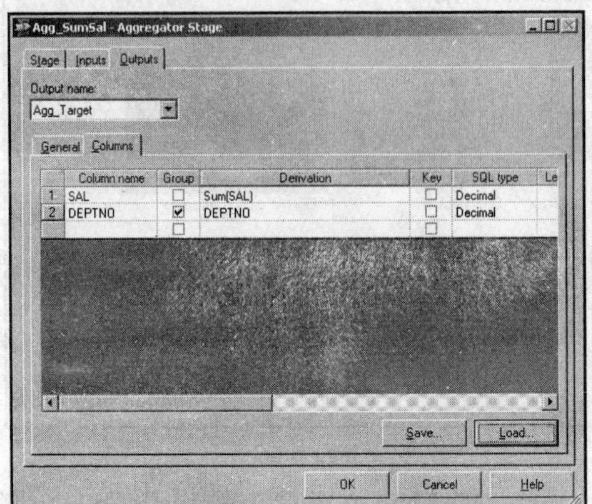

Fig. 8.63

16. Click on **"OK"** of "Agg_SumSal", Aggregator properties window.
17. Save the job with the name "DEPTSUMSAL", by selecting menu item ***"File → Save"***.
18. Compile the job by clicking on **"Compile"** button from the tool bar.

Running the Job

1. To run the job, select "Run" button from the toolbar or select menu item ***"File → Run"***, then the **"Run Job Options"** window opens, from that click on **"Run"**.
2. If your job is completed successfully, the mappings (links) of the workflow from source to the target are changed to green in color. If your job fails, then the mappings (links) are changed to red in color.
3. The number of rows transferred from the source database to the Agg_SumSal Aggregator, shown on the link, "Agg_Source" (in this example "14 rows") and from Agg_SumSal to Scott_SumSal on the link, "Agg_Target"(in this example "3 rows"), which appears as shown in Fig. 8.64.

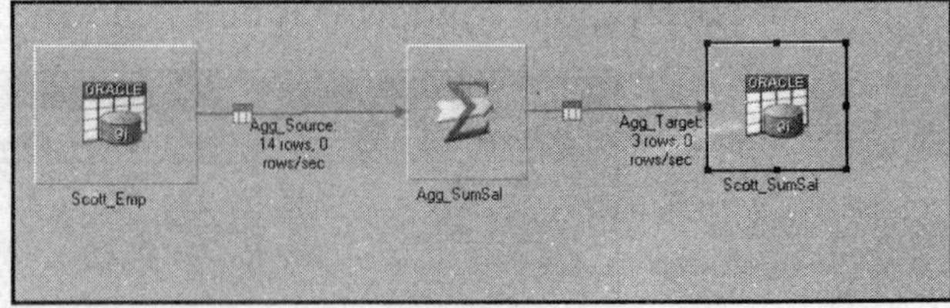

Fig. 8.64

Checking the Output

In the previous section, we have demonstrated how to verify the data in the target database. In this section, we will show another way of checking the output.

1. Open the properties dialog of the "Scott_SumSal" (target database) by double clicking on it.
2. In the properties window, go to "Input" tab and click on **"View Data"**, to see the data of the target table, which looks as shown in Fig. 8.65.

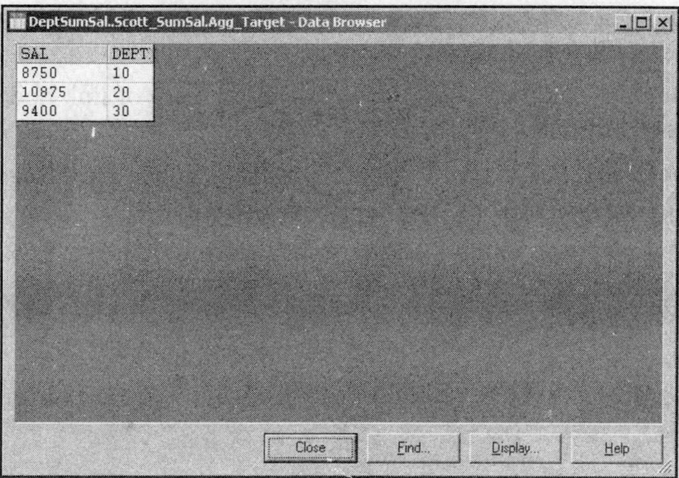

Fig. 8.65

8.6 Case Study: Sorting Transformation

In this case study, we will demonstrate sorting transformation—sorting of all employee details based on salaries in ascending order from EMP table and adding a new column, SLNO to maintain the sequence number.

Create a New Project

We need to design a new job and create a new project for the job in "DataStage Administrator" and name the folder as "SortSeqGen". Creating projects using the DataStage Administrator was explained in the previous section; refer to that section to create the folder also.

DataStage Designer

This tool is used to create the jobs and to map the flow of data from source to target.

1. Create two Oracle database icons in the workspace of the Designer, as explained in the previous section. One will act as Source Database and another one will act as Target Database. Rename the icons in the workspace as "Scott_EmpSource" and "Scott_SeqSortTarget" for source and target databases respectively.
2. Select **"Sort"** stage from the **"Palette"** and click in the workspace to insert a sort stage in the Workspace, rename it as "Sort_Sal".
3. Select a "Transformer" from the "Palette" and click in the workspace to insert a "Transformer" stage in the Workspace, rename it to "Trans_SeqGen".
4. Join the source table, "Scott_EmpSource" and Sort_Sal with the help of link and rename the link as Lnk_Emp_Source.
5. Join the Sort_Sal and Trans_SeqGen with the help of link and rename the link as Lnk_Sort_Source.
6. Join the Trans_SeqGen and target database, "ScottSeqSortTraget" with the help of link and rename the link as Lnk_Trans_Source.
7. The final mapping in the Designer looks as shown in Fig. 8.66.

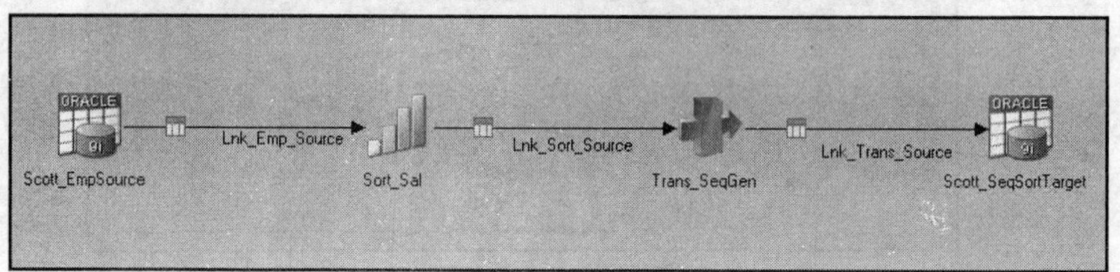

Fig. 8.66

8. Specify the properties of the source database by double clicking on it, now the Scott_EmpSource database in the Workspace refers to EMP table of the Oracle database belonging to the database user "Scott".
9. Similarly specify the properties for Scott_SeqSortTarget (target) and attach it to a new target table "SORTSEQUENCETARGET" in the Oracle Database of user "Scott", as explained in the previous section. Also select the value as "Generate DDL" for "Create table action" and "Drop table action".
10. To specify the properties of the Sort_Sal, double click on it or right click on it and select **"Properties"** menu item from the pop up.
11. In **"Properties"** dialog box, go to **"Output"** tab and go to sub tab "Columns". See Fig. 8.67.

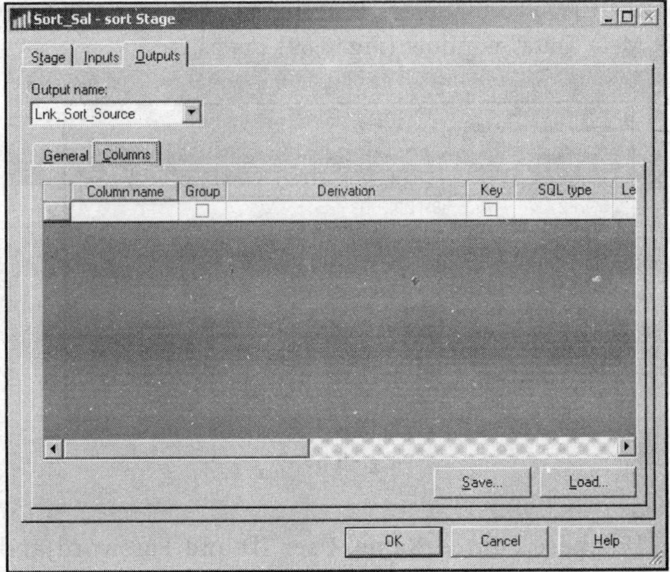

Fig. 8.67

12. Click on **"Load"**, then the **"Table Definitions"** window opens.
13. Click on "Import", select the menu item, "Plug-in Metadata Definitions", then **"Import Plug-in Metadata"** window (Fig. 8.68) opens.

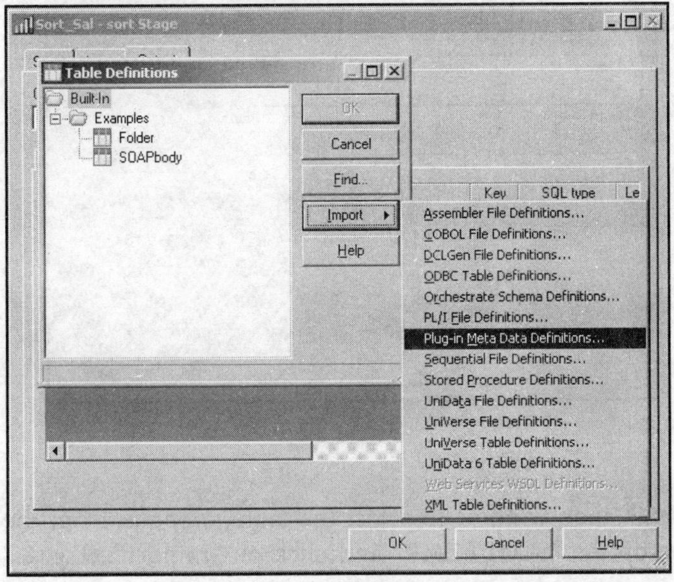

Fig. 8.68

14. Select "ORAOCI9" from "Select Plug-in" list box and click "OK", then "Import ORAOCI9 Meta Data" window (Fig. 8.69) opens.

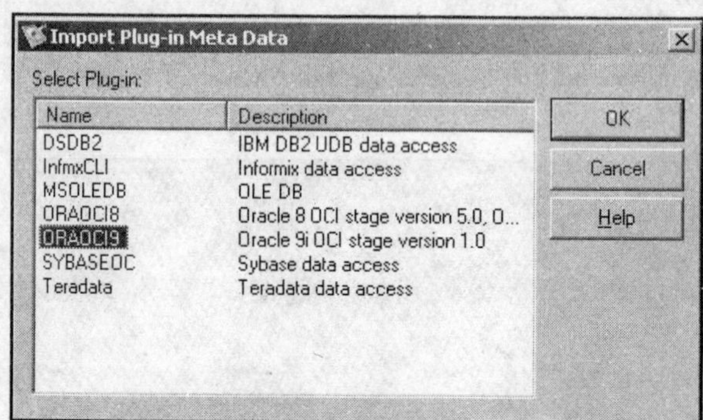

Fig. 8.69

15. Enter the Database Source Name, User ID and Password and click on "Next". See Fig. 8.70.

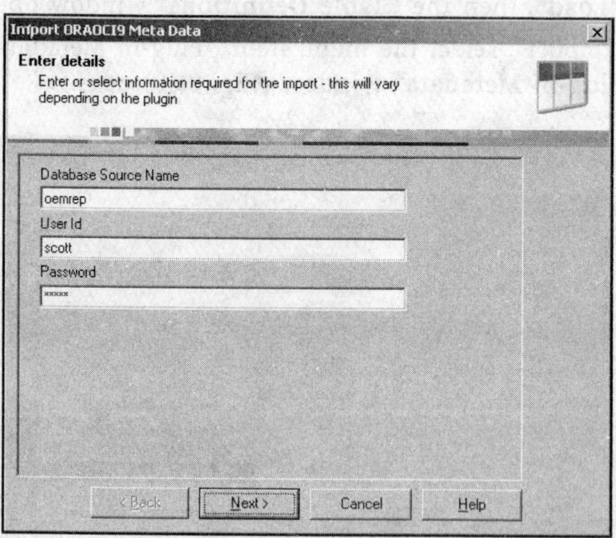

Fig. 8.70

16. Click **"Next"**, then window to select the table(s) opens, from the Select Tables list, select the option "SCOTT.EMP" and click on "Import". (Fig. 8.71)

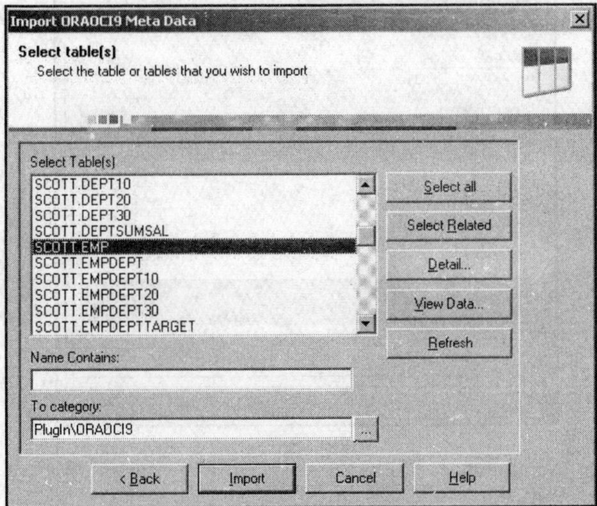

Fig. 8.71

17. The imported table will be added to the "Table Definitions" window, as shown in Fig. 8.72.

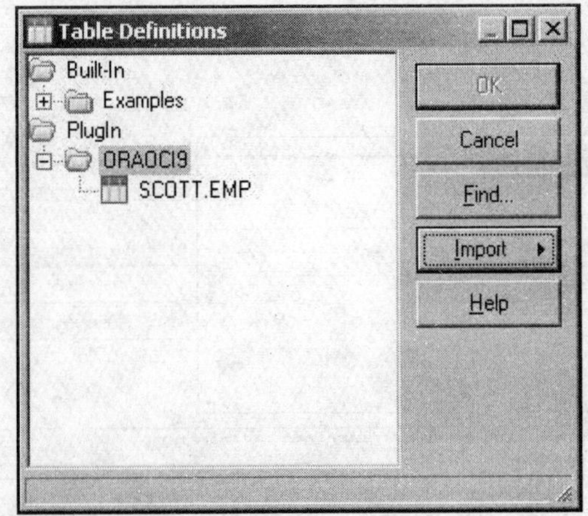

Fig. 8.72

18. Select "SCOTT.EMP" and click on **"OK"**, then **"Select Columns"** window opens.
19. In "Selected Columns" list, since we require all the columns that are selected, click on **"OK"**. All the selected columns will be added to output columns list of Sort_Sal as shown in Fig. 8.73.

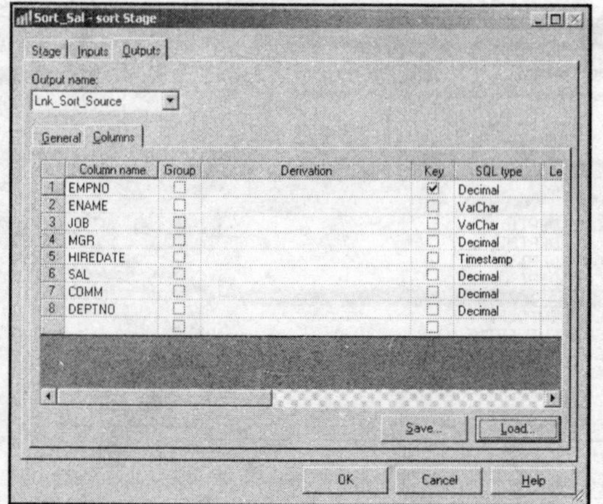

Fig. 8.73

20. Go to Stage tab, in it go to **"Properties"** sub-tab. Enter the value for "Sort Specification" as SAL ASC (ascending order by SAL (salary) column), as shown in Fig. 8.74.

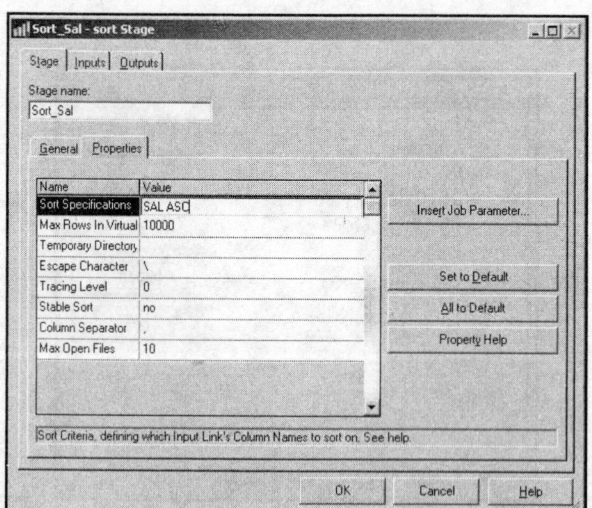

Fig. 8.74

21. Click on **"OK"** of "Sort_Sal – sort Stage" dialog box.
22. Select the Transformer "Trans_SeqGen", right click on it and from the pop up menu, select the menu item, **"Properties"**. See Fig. 8.75.

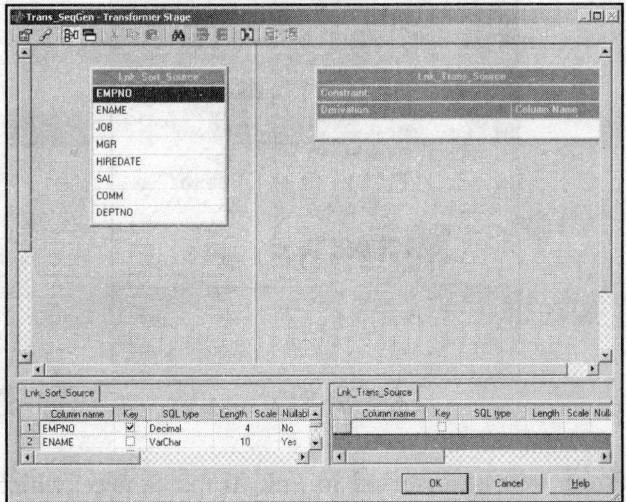

Fig. 8.75

23. Select all the columns of the “Lnk_Sort_Source”, drag and drop them in to “Lnk_Trans_Source”, as shown in Fig. 8.76.

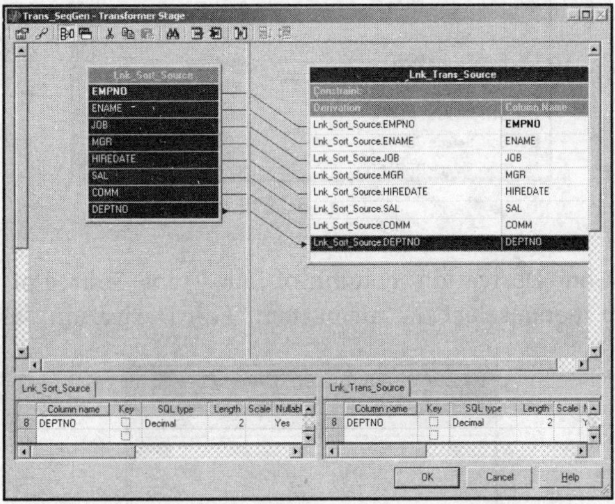

Fig. 8.76

24. Select any column of Lnk_Trans_Source and right click on it, from the pop up menu, select the menu item “Insert New Column”, as shown in Fig. 8.77.

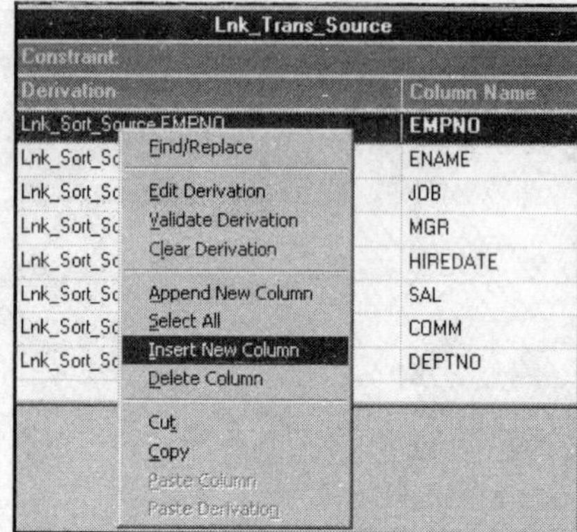

Fig. 8.77

25. A new column will be inserted in Lnk_Trans_Source, which looks as shown in Fig. 8.78.

Lnk_Trans_Source

Constraint:

Derivation	Column Name
	New
Lnk_Sort_Source.EMPNO	**EMPNO**
Lnk_Sort_Source.ENAME	ENAME
Lnk_Sort_Source.JOB	JOB
Lnk_Sort_Source.MGR	MGR
Lnk_Sort_Source.HIREDATE	HIREDATE
Lnk_Sort_Source.SAL	SAL
Lnk_Sort_Source.COMM	COMM
Lnk_Sort_Source.DEPTNO	DEPTNO

Fig. 8.78

26. Right click on "Derivation" column of Lnk_Trans_Source of "New" column, from the pop up menu, select the menu item "Edit Derivation", as shown in Fig. 8.79.

Lnk_Trans_Source

Constraint:

Derivation	Column Name
Lnk_Sort_Source.MGR	MGR
Lnk_Sort_Source.HIREDATE	HIREDATE
Lnk_Sort_Source.SAL	SAL
Lnk_Sort_Source.COMM	COMM
Lnk_Sort_Source.DEPTNO	DEPTNO

Fig. 8.79

27. Click on browse button; select the "DS Transform" from the pop up menu, as shown in Fig.8.80. .

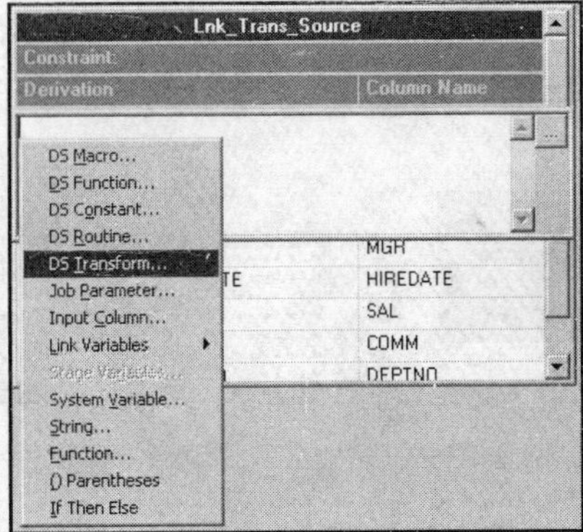

Fig. 8.80

28. From the pop up window (shown in Fig. 8.81) explore "sdk" folder, double click on the folder "Key Mgt", and click on "Key Mgt Get Next Value Concurrent (% Sequence Name%)".

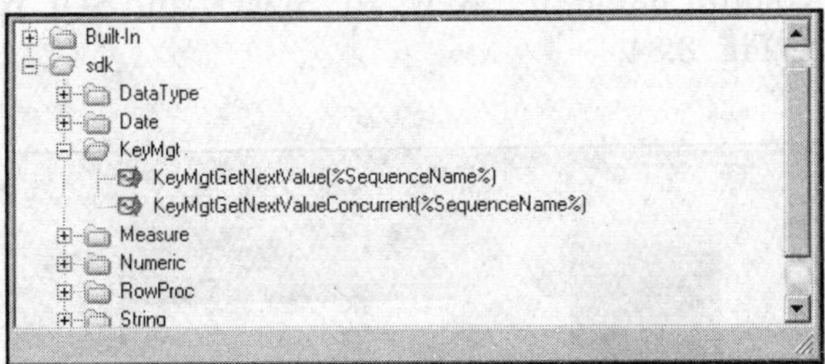

Fig. 8.81

29 Thus the select Key Management function will be added to the Derivation edit box of New column, as shown in Fig. 8.82.

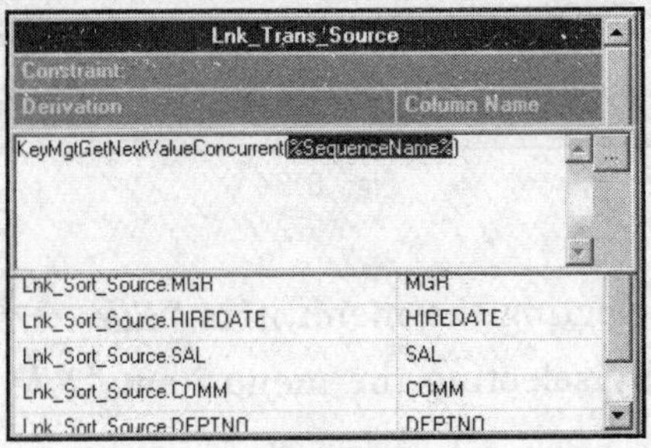

Lnk_Trans_Source
Constraint:
Derivation | Column Name
KeyMgtGetNextValueConcurrent(%SequenceName%)
Lnk_Sort_Source.MGR | MGR
Lnk_Sort_Source.HIREDATE | HIREDATE
Lnk_Sort_Source.SAL | SAL
Lnk_Sort_Source.COMM | COMM
Lnk_Sort_Source.DEPTNO | DEPTNO

Fig. 8.82

30. Delete the value "%SequenceName%" and enter value "0" as parameter for KeyMgtGetNextValueConcurrent function, double click on New column name of Lnk_Trans_Source tab located at the bottom, to change the column name, as shown in Fig. 8.83.

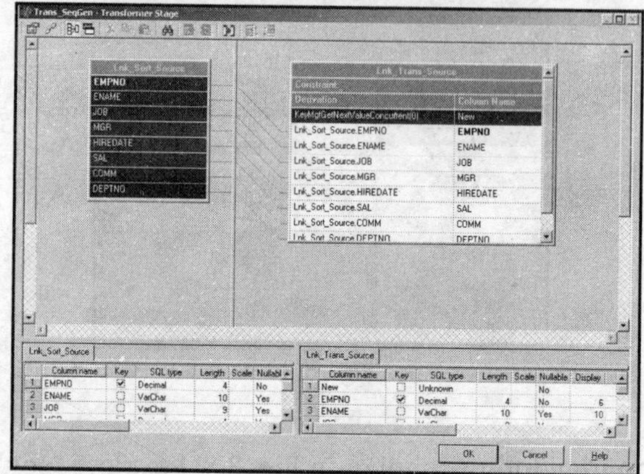

Fig. 8.83

31. Change the column name of "New" to "SLNO" and SQL type as Integer and click on **"OK"**. See Fig. 8.84.

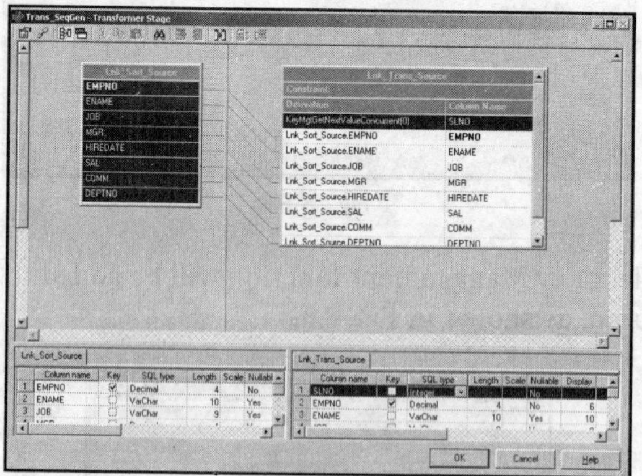

Fig. 8.84

32. Save the job by selecting the menu item ***"File → Save"***.
33. Compile the job by selecting the menu item ***"File → Compile"***.

Running the Job

1. To run the job, select "Run" button from the toolbar or select menu item ***"File → Run"***. "Run Job Options" window opens, click on **"Run"**.
2. If your job is completed successfully, the mappings (links) of the workflow from source to the target are changed to green color. If your job fails, then the mappings (links) are changed to red color.
3. The number of rows transferred from the source database to the Sort_Sal, shown on the link "Lnk_Emp_Source" (in this example "14 rows") and from Sort_Sal to Trans_SeqGen on the link Lnk_Sort_Source (in this example "14 rows") and from Trans_SeqGen to Scott_SeqSortTraget on the link, Lnk_Trans_Source (in this example "14 rows"), which appear as shown in Fig. 8.85.

Fig. 8.85

Checking the Output

1. Go to properties of the "Scott_SeqSortTarget" (target database) by double clicking on it.
2. From the "Properties" window go to "Input" tab and click on "View Data", to see the data of the target table, which appears as shown in Fig. 8.86.

SortSegGen..Scott_SeqSortTarget.Lnk_Trans_Source - Data Browser

SLNO	EMPNO	ENAME	JOB	MGR	HIREDATE	SAL	COMM	DEPT
1	7369	SMITH	CLERK	7902	1980-12-17 00:00:00	800		20
2	7900	JAMES	CLERK	7698	1981-12-03 00:00:00	950		30
3	7876	ADAMS	CLERK	7788	1987-05-23 00:00:00	1100		20
4	7654	MARTIN	SALESMAN	7698	1981-09-28 00:00:00	1250	1400	30
5	7521	WARD	SALESMAN	7698	1981-02-22 00:00:00	1250	500	30
6	7934	MILLER	CLERK	7782	1982-01-23 00:00:00	1300		10
7	7844	TURNER	SALESMAN	7698	1981-09-08 00:00:00	1500	0	30
8	7499	ALLEN	SALESMAN	7698	1981-02-20 00:00:00	1600	300	30
9	7782	CLARK	MANAGER	7839	1981-06-09 00:00:00	2450		10
10	7698	BLAKE	MANAGER	7839	1981-05-01 00:00:00	2850		30
11	7566	JONES	MANAGER	7839	1981-04-02 00:00:00	2975		20
12	7902	FORD	ANALYST	7566	1981-12-03 00:00:00	3000		20
13	7788	SCOTT	ANALYST	7566	1987-04-19 00:00:00	3000		20
14	7839	KING	PRESIDENT		1981-11-17 00:00:00	5000		10

Close | Find... | Display... | Help

Fig. 8.86

Checking the Detailed log with DataStage Director

We can see the status of the job running with the help of DataStage Director.

1. To open DataStage Director, select ***"Start → Programs → Ascential DataStage → DataStage Director".***
2. **"Attach to Project"** window opens (Fig. 8.87). Enter the User Name, Password and select the project and click on **"OK"**. **"DataStage Director"** window for the selected project opens. .

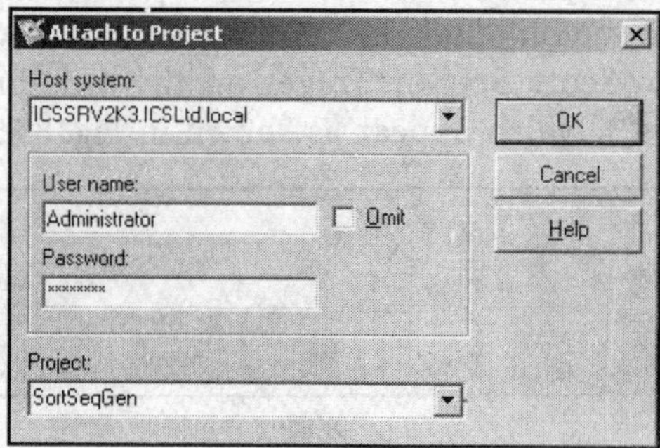

Fig. 8.87

5. In the Director window, you can see all the jobs, which exist in the selected project, as shown in Fig. 8.88.

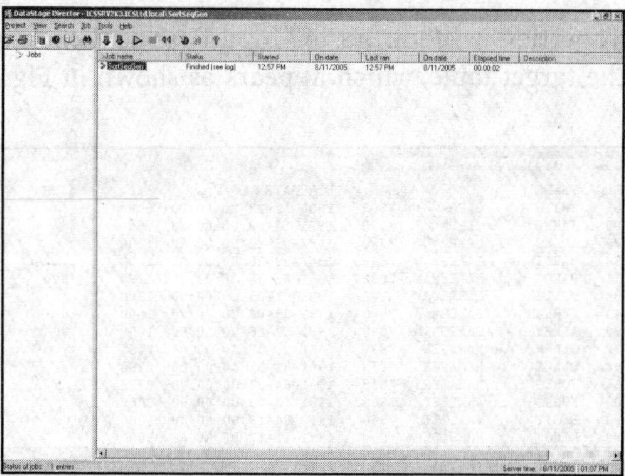

Fig. 8.88

6. Select the job, "SortSeqGen" and go to menu item ***" View → Log"*** to view log, shown in Fig. 8.89.

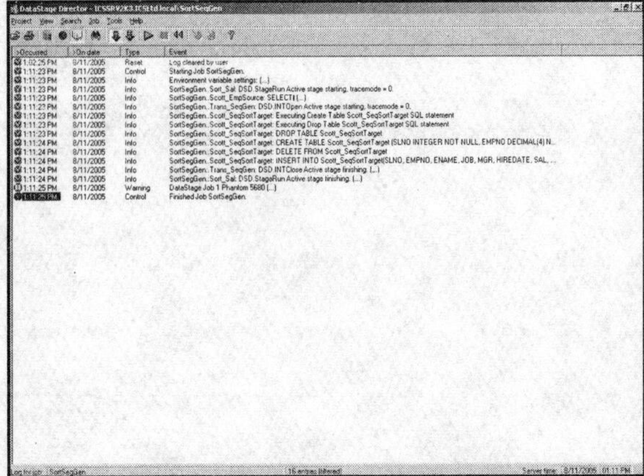

Fig. 8.89

Summary

- **DataStage** provides a set of powerful tools for developing a data warehouse. It has a number of client and server components.
- The **server components** consist of DataStage Repository, DataStage Server and DataStage Package Installer. The repository contains all the required data to build a data warehouse. DataStage Server runs the server jobs. DataStage Package installer provides the GUI to install packaged server jobs and plug-ins.
- The process that connects to databases on other machines, extract data and load the data into the target database is called a "job". These jobs are compiled and run on the DataStage server. These are referred to as server jobs.
- **DataStage client components** (that can run on Windows 2000/XP/NT) consist of DataStage Manager, DataStage Designer, DataStage Director and DataStage Administrator.
- **DataStage Manager** provides the user interface to view and contents of the data repository.
- **DataStage Designer** is used to create the DataStage jobs. Using this, the data sources, transformations required and the destination database are specified. These jobs are compiled and executable files are created. These executable files can be scheduled by the DataStage Director and run by the Server.
- DataStage Director provides the user interface to schedule, run and monitor the server jobs.
- DataStage Administrator is used to perform administration tasks such as administration of the users, creation of projects etc.

Appendix A

Acronyms and Abbreviations

API	Application Programming Interface
ASCII	American Standard Code for Information Interchange
ATM	Automated Teller Machine/Any Time Money
ATP	Acceptance Test Plan
ATR	Acceptance Test Report
BI	Business Intelligence
BO	Business Objects
BPO	Business Process Outsourcing
BPM	Business Process Modeling
CEO	Chief Executive Officer
CFO	Chief Financial Officer
CTO	Chief Technology Officer
CRM	Customer Relations Management
C/S	Client/Server
DBA	Data Base Administrator
DBMS	Data Base Management System
DDL	Data Definition Language
DM	Data Modeling
DOLAP	Desktop On Line Analytical Processing
DSN	Data Source Name
DSS	Decision Support System
DW	Data Warehouse
DWT	Data Warehousing Tools
EIS	Enterprise Information System
ERD	Entity Relationship Diagram
ERP	Enterprise Resource Planning
ETL	Extraction, Transformation and Loading

ETM	Extract, Transform and Move
ETT	Extraction, Transformation and Transportation
GB	Giga Bytes
GUI	Graphical User Interface
HOLAP	Hybrid On Line Analytical Processing
HTML	Hyper Text Markup Language
IS	Information System
JDBC	Java Database Connectivity
KPI	Key Performance Indicator
LAN	Local Area Network
MB	Mega Bytes
MDBMS	Multi-dimensional Database Management System
MDDB	Multi-Dimensional Data Base
MDX	Multi-Dimensional Expressions
MOLAP	Multi-dimensional On Line Analytical Processing
ODBC	Open Data Base Connectivity
ODS	Operational Data Store
OLAP	On Line Analytical Processing
OLTP	On Line Transaction Processing
OS	Operating System
QA	Quality Assurance
RAID	Redundant Array of Inexpensive Disks
RDBMS	Relational Data Base Management System
ROLAP	Relational On Line Analytical Processing
SCD	Slowly Changing Dimension
SCM	Supply Chain Management
SQA	Software Quality Assurance
SQL	Structured Query Language
SOA	Service Oriented Architecture
TB	Tera Bytes
TCP/IP	Transmission Control Protocol/Internet Protocol
VPN	Virtual Private Network
WAN	Wide Area Network
XML	eXtensible Markup Language

Appendix B

Glossary

Acceptance Testing: Testing carried out by the client/customer before accepting the software for operational use.

Aggregate: Data stored in a summarized form. Aggregates improve the performance of the BI tools and reduce the storage space requirement.

Alert: An automatic indication (audible or visible) given by a computer to inform about a specific important event. Alerts are set to draw the attention of the user to the occurrence of an event.

API: Function calls of a software package/library that facilitate application development by the end users.

Attributes: The data that describe an entity. For example, if person is an entity, his/her name, address etc. are the attributes that describe that person.

Business Intelligence: Knowledge extracted from business data that aids in the management to take strategic business decisions.

Business Process: The step-by-step procedure to carry out a particular activity in business such as production, marketing, sales, finance, etc.

Changing Dimension: If the attributes of the dimension table change over a period of time, the dimension is called the changing dimension. For example, in the location dimension, the address fields may change over a period of time if the person changes his address. Some attributes do not change at all, for example, date of birth in time dimension.

Click Stream Data: Data collected by web servers when the users browse a site. The click stream data is used to find out the user profile, his/her preferences etc. for business activities such as sales promotion campaigns.

Coding Standards: Guidelines formulated by an organization to be followed by all programmers while doing the coding. The coding standards for different programming languages, databases, etc. will be developed by the SQA department.

Configuration Management: The management of different versions and releases of documents and software source code. Whenever any change is made to any of the work products such as software requirements specification document, design, document, test plans, source code etc., a well-defined procedure has to be followed. This procedure or process is known as configuration management.

Conformed Dimension: A dimension that has the same meaning for all fact tables in a data mart/data warehouse. The advantage of conformed dimensions is that such fact tables can be joined.

Conformed Fact: Metrics or measures or facts of a business process that have the same meaning in different data marts so that the data marts can be easily combined into a data warehouse.

Cube: The structure that represents multi-dimensional data. A cube contains dimensions, hierarchies, levels and facts (measures). The dimensional model can be viewed as a cube, each side corresponding to a dimension.

Data: Collection of facts obtained from a business process.

Database: Repository of data.

Data Cleansing: The process of ensuring that the data is clean by removing inaccuracies, removing vagueness, ensuring that the format is uniform, etc.

Data Mart: A scaled-down version of data warehouse for a particular region or for a particular department. A collection of data marts is called a data warehouse.

Data Migration: Moving data from one platform to another platform or from one environment to another environment. It can be simply moving the data from one OS to another OS or a RDBMS data from one database to another.

Data Mining: Storing the data after finding out the hidden patterns and relationships amongst the various attributes using statistical analysis, clustering techniques, etc.

Data Modeling: Converting the raw data into a well-defined structure. E-R model is used for RDBMS and dimensional model is used for data warehouses.

Data Quality Assurance: Ensuring that the data is as per the required/specified standards to maintain data accuracy, integrity and consistency. See Data cleansing.

Data Scrubbing: See data cleansing.

Data Staging: Data staging is a process that involves extraction, transformation and loading of data and quality assurance of the data before the data warehouse is made operational.

Data Transformation: Converting the data into a form suitable for development of a data warehouse is called Data Transformation. The transformation operations include: cleansing, normalization, modifying the field names and data types, making the data more readable, conversion to multidimensional model, getting aggregates, sorting, etc.

Data Warehouse: A system that provides business intelligence.

Degenerate Dimension: A dimension without any attributes.

Development Life Cycle Models: The models used to develop software by dividing the entire life cycle into different stages or phases. See waterfall model and prototyping model.

Dimensional Model: The data model which organizes the data in such a way that the data can be viewed in different dimensions for obtaining business intelligence.

Dimension Table: Table in multi-dimensional model. Dimension table has a primary key to connect to the fact table and a number of attributes that describe the dimension. For example, product dimension table has attributes such as product code, product type, description, weight, volume etc.

DOLAP: Desktop On Line Analytical Processing tools are desktop/client based low cost tools for OLAP.

Drill Down: Viewing the data with a greater detail. In other words, breaking down the answer to a greater detail.

Drill Up: Viewing the data in a summarized form or as aggregates is called Drillup. In other words, analyzing the data in less detail.

Entity: A person, place or an item about which data is stored in a database.

ERP: Enterprise Resource Planning software facilitates management of organization's resources efficiently. The ERP packages are capable of handling different divisional activities such as human resources, finance, inventory, purchase, sales, customer support, bank transactions etc.

ETL: Extraction, Transformation and Loading. These are the three important processes to move the desired data from multiple data sources to the target database of the data warehouse. The data sources can be legacy systems, flat files, RDBMS or ERP systems making ETL an extremely challenging and time consuming job.

ETM: Extract, Transform and Move. Another acronym used in place of ETL.

ETT: Extract, Transform and Transfer. Another acronym used in place of ETL.

Evolutionary Development: A software development life cycle model wherein development is carried out in an evolutionary manner. Initially, only a small subset of the requirements is implemented and then some more features are added and so on. Also known as incremental building. A good model to be followed for some complex data warehouses.

Fact Table: It regers to the central table in a data warehouse dimensional model. The fact table contains the measures of metrics (facts) of the business process. For example, in sales fact table, the facts are monthly sales or quarterly sales. The fact table contains two types of fields—business facts and foreign keys of dimension tables.

Gantt (bar) Chart: The chart used by managers to review the various activities of a project. Gantt chart shows each activity's start time and target completion time.

HOLAP: Hybrid OLAP has the capabilities of both ROLAP and MOLAP.

Information: Processed data that can be of use to human beings.

Knowledge: Analyzed information useful for decision-making.

Legacy system: An 'old' system. A legacy database is a database that uses an old database engine such as dBase III.

Measure: See Metric.

Metadata: Data about data. In other words, data that describes data.

Metric: Measure of a particular business process/activity. For example, employee productivity is a metric used to measure the average productivity of an employee in an organization. This metric can be obtained by dividing the total profit with the number of employees.

Primary Key: The attribute (or a combination of attributes) that uniquely identifies an entity in a table.

Process: Step-by-step procedure to convert raw material into finished product.

Prototype: A scaled-down version of the proposed software to be developed. A prototype will give a good idea to the end users about the software that is going to be developed. A prototype has to be developed very fast and hence generally, scripting languages and sophisticated tools are used.

Relation: The association between two entities in E-R model. The relation can be one-to-one or one-to-many or many-to-one or many-to-many.

Requirements Engineering: The first stage in software development. In this stage, the development team members obtain the requirements from the users, prepare an SRS document and get the document validated by the users.

Software Development Process: The step-by-step procedure to covert a problem definition into a working software product.

Software Engineering: The discipline (or the subject) that deals with systematic development of software.

SRS: Software Requirements Specifications. The document that captures the complete specifications of the proposed software. The SRS document contains both functional requirements as well as non-functional requirements such as security requirements, legal requirements, performance requirements, etc.

Stress Testing: Testing carried out on a software product to check its performance at its peak use. For example, if a DBMS has to give a response time of 15 seconds for a particular query when 10 users are accessing the database simultaneously, testing the software for its response time when more than 10 users access the database simultaneously.

Test Cases: A set of inputs given to a software to test its functionality, choosing the test cases is the most important step in testing because the test cases can reveal the bugs in coding.

Test Plan: A document prepared to carry out the testing of a system systematically. Test plan covers the hardware and software environment in which the software has to be tested, the testing team, the documents to be generated during the testing phase, the time frame for testing, the various types of testing to be carried out and the test cases for which the system has to be tested.

Time-variant Data: Data that varies with time.

Waterfall Model: The most widely used model for commercial software development. In this model, software development is divided into five stages—requirements engineering, design, implementation and unit testing, integration and system testing, and operation and maintenance.

Work Products: Various documents generated during the development of software are called work products. SRS, design document, test plan, test report, source code, user manual, configuration management plan are some important work products.

Appendix C

References and Internet Resources

www.ascential.com	DataStage
www.ca.com	Computer Associates (ERWin Data modeler)
www.businessobjects.com	Business Objects
www.cognos.com	Cognos Inc.
www.DMreivew.com	DM Review and Source Media Inc.
www.elearn.cdacindia.com	E-learning portal of CDAC
www.freedatawarehouse.com	Portal for learning data warehouse concepts
www.informatica.com	Informatica Corporation
www.learndatamodeling.com	Portal for learning data warehouse concepts
www.microsoft.com	Microsoft Corporation
www.microstrategy.com	MicroStrategy Inc.
www.oracle.com	Oracle Corporation
www.rational.com	IBM Rational Suite
www.sap.com	SAP
www.sas.com	SAS Institute Inc.

Reference Books

Ian Sommerville, Software Engineering, Addison-Wesley Publishing Co., 1996.

K.V.K.K. Prasad, Software Testing Tools, Dreamtech Press, 2005.

Ralph Kimball, Margy Ross and Warren Thornthwaite, The Data Warehouse Lifecycle Toolkit, John Wiley & Sons, 2005.

Ralph Kimball and Joe Caserta, The Data Warehouse ETL Toolkit, Wiley Dreamtech India Pvt. Ltd., 2005.

Roger Pressman, Software Engineering: A Practitioner's Approach, McGraw Hill Inc., 1997.

W.H. Inmon, Building the Data Warehouse, Wiley Dreamtech India Pvt. Ltd., 2005.